Barbara Reed
SP 08

PSYCHOLOGICAL TESTING

A Practical Introduction

Thomas P. Hogan
University of Scranton

Second Edition

JOHN WILEY & SONS, INC.

THE WILEY BICENTENNIAL–KNOWLEDGE FOR GENERATIONS

*E*ach generation has its unique needs and aspirations. When Charles Wiley first opened his small printing shop in lower Manhattan in 1807, it was a generation of boundless potential searching for an identity. And we were there, helping to define a new American literary tradition. Over half a century later, in the midst of the Second Industrial Revolution, it was a generation focused on building the future. Once again, we were there, supplying the critical scientific, technical, and engineering knowledge that helped frame the world. Throughout the 20th Century, and into the new millennium, nations began to reach out beyond their own borders and a new international community was born. Wiley was there, expanding its operations around the world to enable a global exchange of ideas, opinions, and know-how.

For 200 years, Wiley has been an integral part of each generation's journey, enabling the flow of information and understanding necessary to meet their needs and fulfill their aspirations. Today, bold new technologies are changing the way we live and learn. Wiley will be there, providing you the must-have knowledge you need to imagine new worlds, new possibilities, and new opportunities.

Generations come and go, but you can always count on Wiley to provide you the knowledge you need, when and where you need it!

WILLIAM J. PESCE
PRESIDENT AND CHIEF EXECUTIVE OFFICER

PETER BOOTH WILEY
CHAIRMAN OF THE BOARD

ASSOCIATE PUBLISHER	Jay O'Callaghan
ACQUISITIONS EDITOR	Christopher Johnson
PRODUCTION ASSISTANT	Andrea Juda
EXECUTIVE MARKETING MANAGER	Jeffrey Rucker
MEDIA EDITOR	Lynn Pearlman
ASSOCIATE EDITOR	Maureen Clendenny
EDITORIAL ASSISTANT	Katie Melega
PHOTO EDITOR	Hilary Newman
DESIGNER	Kevin Murphy
COVER DESIGN	David Levy
COVER PHOTO	PhotoDisc/Getty Images, Inc.

This book was set in Bembo by Thomson Digital and printed and bound by RR Donnelley. The cover was printed by Phoenix.

This book is printed on acid free paper.

To order books or for customer service please, call 1-800-CALL WILEY (225-5945).

ISBN-13 978- 0-471-73807-7
ISBN-10 0-471-73807-7

Printed in the United States of America

10 9 8 7 6 5 4 3 2 1

For Peg and the kids

Preface

Purpose and Emphases

This book provides an introduction to the field of psychological testing. It is intended for the student of psychology and allied disciplines. The book attempts to offer a practical approach, with an emphasis on active learning strategies. Practicality is attained by treating tests in their real-life, contemporary application in psychology. Active learning strategies are emphasized by supplying the student with TRY IT exercises sprinkled throughout the text that require application of the concepts and procedures treated in the text. Too many textbooks on psychological testing are written as reference works, almost like encyclopedias, rather than as textbooks. A textbook should be primarily a learning device. Reference works are useful, but not as textbooks, except perhaps for very advanced students. Research on student learning has amply demonstrated that active engagement with the material maximizes learning. Liberal use is made of Internet resources. Much information formerly inaccessible to students of psychological testing, short of Herculean efforts on the instructor's part, is now readily available on the Internet. The text encourages utilization of these resources. In addition to the exercises incorporated directly into the text, each chapter begins with a list of learning objectives and concludes with a summary of major points, a list of key terms, and additional exercises. Key Point Summaries accompany major chunks of material within chapters. These intermediate summaries should help students stay organized. All these features should aid student learning.

The list of objectives at the beginning of each chapter should serve as "advance organizers" to help focus students' attention. The summary at the end of each chapter will aid in bringing closure, sometimes after a difficult journey through the material. The list of key terms should supplement the summary points. An ample supply of exercises is given at the end of each chapter. Their character varies. Some emphasize technical matters, others are "thought" questions, and still others call on students to find information through Internet resources. No one is expected to complete all these exercises. However, the instructor can make a judicious selection to be performed by individuals or small groups of students. The end-of-chapter exercises are more challenging than the TRY IT examples embedded in the main text, but I have tried to design most of these exercises so that each can be completed in 10 to 20 minutes, some in as little as 2 to 3 minutes. Students should find that completing at least a few of these exercises helps understanding and retention of the material.

The book's emphasis on practicality does not imply a lack of rigor or avoidance of difficult topics. On the contrary, the text meets hard material head-on. Psychological testing is not an easy subject. The text does not attempt to "dumb down" this material. It does, however, attempt to show the actual practice of psychological testing and give examples of the concepts and procedures of testing in contemporary applications.

Student Background

When preparing the text, I assumed that students had completed a course in elementary statistics, including the following topics: methods for tabular and graphic summaries of raw data, including shapes of distributions; measures of central tendency, variability, and (zero-order) correlation and regression; the elements of sampling theory, interval estimation, and hypothesis testing, including t-tests, one-way and two-way analysis of variance. I have also assumed that the students have forgotten a substantial amount of this material. Hence the text provides "refreshers" on various topics from elementary statistics throughout the first several chapters. Because of students' predisposition to avoid anything appearing in an appendix, I have incorporated these statistics refreshers into the main text. The unusual student who actually remembers most of what was covered in elementary statistics can skip the refreshers. Instructors will need to use their own judgment regarding how much time to spend on these refreshers. In addition, the text covers certain topics from multivariate statistics, especially multiple correlation and factor analysis. A few students may have had exposure to these topics in a statistics or research methods course before taking the course in psychological testing. However, most students would not have had such exposure, and no prior knowledge of these topics is assumed.

Organization

The book divides naturally into two major sections. Part I covers the basic concepts of psychological testing. Chapter 1 presents an overview of the field, including the typical uses of psychological tests. Chapter 2 provides a much more complete treatment of sources of information about tests than is available elsewhere. I have done this for two reasons. First, students, as well as others, frequently ask the question: "Is there a test that measures _____?" I want students using this text to know how to answer that common question. Second, in later chapters, students are asked to use the sources of information covered in Chapter 2 to find real-life examples of concepts, procedures, and examples of tests. In an earlier version of the manuscript, Appendix A on test reviewing and test selection was part of Chapter 2. However, I have obviously relegated these topics to an appendix since they are not really sources of information about tests, yet they are natural outgrowths of the use of these sources. I urge instructors to have their students complete a test review and a test selection exercise as course projects. These are exceptionally valuable learning exercises. The Instructor's Manual (see Term Projects) gives further suggestions on these topics.

Chapters 3–6 cover the foundational topics of norms, reliability, validity, and test development. In each of these chapters, most of the material should be covered with all students. The remaining material is somewhat more advanced or more technical. Instructors may include all of this more advanced material, some of it, or none of it, depending on their areas of interest and on the special needs of their students. Chapter 6 on test development is complemented by Appendix B on steps in building a simple test. Some instructors require students to build a simple test as a class exercise, and Appendix B should be helpful in these cases. The small data sets in

Appendix D may be used with standard statistical packages for practical exercises related to the concepts in Chapters 3–6. Selected end-of-chapter exercises call for use of these data sets. Some instructors will want to use their own data sets instead.

The balance to be struck between classical test theory (CTT) and item response theory (IRT) in Chapters 3–6 has presented a particular challenge. CTT is hard enough for novices to swallow; IRT often evokes a choking response. In current practice, IRT procedures are now applied routinely. Students will encounter IRT procedures, as well as CTT procedures, in nearly all recently developed tests. Even the beginning student needs familiarity with the concepts and language of IRT. Therefore, in accordance with my intent to be practical, Chapters 3–6 provide a good dosage of IRT, as well as CTT, procedures. Of course, instructors will need to strike the right balance for the needs of their own students.

Part II provides an introduction to the major categories of psychological tests. For each category, a chapter outlines the major conceptual and procedural approaches and gives a *few* examples of tests in the category. I have tried to resist the temptation to list test after test with brief descriptions of each because I do not believe that students learn anything useful from such cataloging. In fact, they probably learn nothing at all from such lists. Ordinarily, when a test is introduced in Part II, I have tried to describe it in enough detail and in such a way that the introductory student can learn something from it. I have made just a few exceptions to this rule for extraordinary cases. Selection of examples for the chapters in Part II has been guided *primarily* by frequency of actual test usage—this in accordance with the intention to be practical—and secondarily by the desire to illustrate some variety in approaches to testing within a category. While covering the chapters in Part II, I hope instructors will have a supply of specimen sets to show their students. It would be convenient to have specimen sets for all the major examples used in the text. However, if these are not available, but specimen sets for alternative tests are, it is probably preferable to use these alternatives as examples rather than the examples given in the text. Particularly for novices in the field, it is not a very meaningful experience to read about a test without seeing it and literally feeling it. Chapters 7–15 cover the major applications of psychological tests.

Part II concludes with a chapter on ethical and legal issues. The chapter does not fit thematically with the other chapters in Part II. However, the chapter is clearly necessary. I did not think students could appreciate some of the issues treated in this chapter until they had completed all other chapters. Not wanting a Part III with only one chapter, rather like the forbidden one-sentence paragraph, I simply included the chapter on ethical and legal issues at the end of Part II.

New to the Second Edition

The second edition preserves the major features of the first edition, while introducing two major structural changes, numerous updates especially for new editions of the tests used as examples, and a few minor adaptations. In deciding on these revisions, I depended heavily on the very helpful comments from users of the first edition.

The first major structural change was the elimination of Chapter 15, Special Applications. Users found the topics covered therein to be interesting but lower in priority than any of the other chapters. The section on Behavioral Assessment was preserved by transfering it to the new Chapter 13, described next.

The second structural change involved Chapter 12. This chapter, the longest chapter in Part II of the first edition, was split into two separate chapters. The new Chapter 12 preserved treatment of the general nature of self-report inventories, the problem of response sets, and methods of developing self-report inventories. It also retained coverage of the EPPS, NEO-PI, and Piers-Harris, although the new edition of Piers-Harris was introduced. The chapter concludes with a new section on measures related to positive psychology. The new Chapter 13, Clinical Instruments and Methods, includes the MMPI, MCMI, BDI, EDI (3rd ed.), and STAI from the previous Chapter 12. The new Chapter 13 also covers the clinical interview, including SCID; the SCL-90-R; and an entirely new section on behavior rating scales.

Among the more modest changes, a few sections have been eliminated as nonessential or reduced in size to provide more focused coverage. Many of the tests covered in the first edition have appeared in new editions—just in the short space of four years. I have tried to catch all the new editions. The more modest changes and updates include the following.

Chapter 1 provides a more compact treatment of the history of testing and describes the most recent computer-related developments. Chapter 2 updates all of the sources of information. Chapter 3 remains largely intact but eliminates description of ipsative scores and reduces treatment of the correction for guessing. In Chapter 4, treatment of reliability of criterion-referenced tests is truncated, and reliability of physical fitness measures is dropped. Chapter 5 introduces the language of the "jingle" and "jangle" fallacies and reduces coverage of expectancy tables, used less every year due to conversion to regression-generated predictions. Chapter 6 includes a more recent Haladyna table on recommendations for multiple-choice questions; and the "Top 10" list at the end of the chapter has been moved to Appendix B in order to make an already difficult chapter more manageable for students.

Chapter 7 has new sections on the meaning of intelligence and practical correlates of intelligence; and it updates findings and references on the rapidly expanding field of genetics. Chapter 8 covers these new editions: WISC-IV, SB5, Vineland-II; and it includes AAMR's revised definition of mental retardation. Chapter 9 covers these new editions: OLSAT8, SAT, ACT, GRE, especially the writing portions of these last three tests. Chapter 10 reduces coverage of the history of neuropsychological assessment, and it updates to newer editions of tests. Part of the treatment of laws related to this type of assessment is reserved for Chapter 16. Chapter 11 includes the new edition of the Stanford Achievement Test (SAT10), eliminates description of one state testing program, but expands coverage of statement assessment programs in general, especially in the context of the No Child Left Behind Act. Revisions in Chapters 12 and 13 have already been described. Chapter 14 (Projective Techniques, the former Chapter 13) updates Exner's most recent work on the Rorschach but otherwise remains much the same. Chapter 16 contains significant additions on the most recent version of IDEA and updates the effects of NCLB; the chapter compacts the treatment of several court cases and adds the recent Karraker case.

Appendix C includes updated contact information for major test publishers. Finally, in the many TRY IT and end-of-chapter exercises, references to the now defunct ERIC Test Locator have been deleted and references to the ETS Test Collection URL have been updated.

A new Appendix E provides answers to some of the TRY IT exercises embedded within chapters and to some end-of-chapter exercises.

The Instructor's Manual and Test Bank have been thoroughly updated to reflect the changes from first to second edition.

To the Student

I hope that this text will provide all students with an appreciation for the basic issues in psychological testing. For those students who go on to advanced training, I hope the text provides a solid foundation for this additional work. Finally, I hope the text will motivate some students to ultimately make significant contributions to this field.

Thomas P. Hogan
February 2006
Scranton, Pennsylvania

Acknowledgments

Accounting for the myriad contributions to preparation of this book is a daunting and humbling task. So many people have done so much to assist me. I am very grateful, especially to the following. To all my students over many years, for their willingness to suggest ways to present concepts about testing in effective ways, with special thanks to Kimberly Evalenko and Allison Smith for assistance with research and manuscript preparation. Also at my home institution, the University of Scranton, to the library staff for their unique combination of competence and caring. To the many publishers who granted permission for reproductions and to their staff who gave helpful advice about their test products. I am especially grateful to the following individuals who provided feedback on their actual use of the first edition as well as comments on the plan for revision: Ira H. Bernstein, University of Texas—Arlington; Jeffrey B. Brookings, Wittenberg University; Douglas Maynard, SUNY—New Paltz; Robert Resnick, Randolph Macon College; and Marie D. Thomas, California State University—San Marcos. In addition, my thanks to John Suler, Rider University; Stefan Schulenberg, University of Mississippi; and David Trumpower, Marshall University, who provided useful comments and suggestions on revised chapters. All of the above individuals helped to create an improved textbook.

To my academic mentor, the renowned Anne Anastasi; to Dorothea McCarthy, who arranged for my first job in the field of testing; and to Joseph Kubis for his pedagogical flair. To my professional mentors, Dena Wadell and Roger Lennon, who showed me the interface of theory and practice. To my professional colleagues, beginning with William Tsushima, whose early help was more important than he can possibly imagine. Very special thanks to my University of Scranton colleague

John Norcross who encouraged me to undertake this project and who served as a sounding board on a host of issues. And, of course, to Brooke Cannon for her excellent contribution in the form of the chapter on neuropsychological assessment. With all that help, you'd think the book would be perfect. Alas, that is probably not the case. I must take responsibility for any imperfections that might have crept into the work. Finally, I want to thank my wife, Peg, and our children for moral support (and some really helpful suggestions) throughout the endeavor.

Brief Contents

Contents

PART TWO   253

Chapter 7: Intelligence: Theories and Issues   255

Chapter 8: Individual Tests of Intelligence   289

PART I

Part I of this book provides an overview of the field of psychological testing, then concentrates on fundamental principles and procedures applicable to all types of tests. Chapter 1 introduces the student to the field as it exists today. This chapter also sketches how the field came to be this way. Chapter 2 reviews sources of information that students may use to help find out more about tests. These sources are used frequently in later chapters to identify tests employed for particular purposes. Hence, it is important for the student to learn the use of these sources.

Chapters 3–6 present the fundamental principles used to judge all types of tests. These chapters cover norms (3), reliability (4), validity (5), and test development (6). This is not easy material. However, it is essential that the student learn these basic concepts. They provide the basis for treatment of specific tests in Part II of the book. The student should complete the little TRY IT exercises sprinkled throughout the text to help the material "sink in." Although Chapters 1 and 2 may be read in a leisurely manner, Chapters 3–6 require intense concentration and much review. Studying these chapters properly will pay big dividends when the later chapters arrive.

CHAPTER 1

The World of Psychological Testing

Objectives

1. List the major categories of tests, giving at least one example for each category.

2. Identify the major uses and users of tests.

3. Summarize major assumptions and fundamental questions involved in testing.

4. Outline significant features of the major periods in the history of testing.

5. Identify the six major forces influencing the development of testing.

6. Give a definition of a "test."

Introduction

This chapter provides an overview of the world of testing. Of course, everyone knows, at least roughly, what we mean by a "test" or "testing." Everyone has at least some familiarity with a variety of tests, for example, college admission tests, final examinations in courses, vocational interest inventories, and perhaps some personality measures. However, as we begin formal study of this world, it is important that we develop both a more comprehensive and a more precise understanding of the field. More comprehensive so that we consider all types of tests and all relevant issues: We do not want to miss anything important. More precise so that we begin to acquire the technical expertise needed by professionals within the broader fields of psychology and allied disciplines: We will not be satisfied with just a passing acquaintance with these topics.

This is an ambitious agenda for one chapter. However, this opening chapter seeks only to provide an overview of these matters. The remaining chapters supply the details. There are a variety of ways to accomplish our goal of providing an overview and orientation to the field. No single way is best. We will use five perspectives or approaches to introduce the field, viewing it, as it were, from different angles or through different lenses. First, we outline the major categories of tests. Most of these categories correspond to chapters in the latter half of this book. In the process of describing these major categories, we mention examples of some of the more widely used tests. Second, we identify the major uses and users of tests. Who actually uses these tests and for what purposes? Third, we outline the primary issues that we worry about in testing. Notice that this outline—the list of principal worries—corresponds to the chapters in the first half of the book. Fourth, we trace the historical roots of contemporary testing. We mark off major periods in this history and identify some major forces that have shaped the field. Fifth, we examine some of the attempts to define *test*, *testing*, and some related terms. When we finish viewing the field through these five perspectives, we should have a good overview of the field of testing.

Key Points Summary 1.1

Five Ways to Introduce the Field

1. Categories of Tests
2. Uses and Users of Tests
3. Issues: Assumptions and Questions
4. Historical Periods and Forces
5. By Definition

Major Categories of Tests (with Some Examples)

We begin our exploration of the world of testing by identifying the major categories of tests. Any such classification is necessarily fuzzy around the edges. Categories often blend into one another rather than being sharply different. Nevertheless, some organizational scheme helps us to comprehend the breadth of the field. Key Points Summary 1.2 provides a classification scheme we use throughout the book. In fact, Chapters 8–13 follow this organization. This introductory chapter just touches on the major categories. Each category receives in-depth treatment later.

The first major division encompasses **mental ability tests.** In the world of psychological testing, the term *mental ability* includes a wide variety of cognitive functions, such as memory, spatial visualization, and creative thinking. Historically, the area has centered on intelligence, broadly defined. This category subdivides into individually administered intelligence tests, group-administered intelligence tests, and a variety of other ability tests, that is, other than intelligence tests. An example of an individually administered intelligence test is the *Wechsler Adult Intelligence Scale,*[1] abbreviated WAIS. Another classic example in this category is the *Stanford-Binet Intelligence Scale*. These tests are administered to individual examinees, one-on-one, by trained psychologists to provide an index of the overall mental ability of individuals. An example of a group-administered intelligence test is the *Otis-Lennon School Ability Test* (OLSAT). This test is administered to groups of students, usually in classroom settings, to gauge mental ability to succeed in typical school subjects. Another example of tests in this category is the SAT[2] used to predict success in college.

TRY IT! ....

To see how we cover a category in more depth later, flip to page 290. Quickly scan pages 290–296.

You will see how subsequent chapters give details about tests mentioned in this opening chapter.

....

There are many other types of mental ability tests—nearly an infinite variety—including tests of memory, quantitative reasoning, creative thinking, vocabulary, and spatial ability. Sometimes these mental functions are included in the tests of general mental ability, but sometimes they are tested separately.

---

[1] In this opening chapter, we refer only to the first editions of tests. In subsequent chapters, we refer to the more recent editions and their corresponding initials, for example, WAIS-III, MMPI-2, and so on.

[2] For many years, this test was titled the *Scholastic Aptitude Test*. The title was officially changed to the *Scholastic Assessment Test* in 1992 and later simply to the initials SAT. The old titles still appear in many publications. The reference here is specifically to the SAT I: Reasoning Test. The SAT II: Subject Tests is a series of tests in specific fields such as literature, French, and chemistry.

Key Points Summary 1.2
Major Categories of Tests

Mental Ability Tests
    Individually Administered
    Group Administered
    Other Abilities
Achievement Tests
    Batteries
    Single Subject
    Certification, Licensing
    Government-sponsored Programs
    Individual Achievement Tests
Personality Tests
    Objective Tests
    Projective Techniques
    Other Approaches
Interests and Attitudes
    Vocational Interests
    Attitude Scales
Neuropsychological Tests

The next major category includes **achievement tests.** These tests attempt to assess a person's level of knowledge or skill in a particular domain. We cover here only professionally developed, standardized tests. We exclude the vast array of teacher-made tests used daily in the educational enterprise. Even excluding teacher-made tests, achievement tests are easily the most widely used of all types of tests. The first subdivision in this area includes achievement batteries used in elementary and secondary schools. Nearly everyone reading this book would have taken one or more of these achievement batteries. Examples include the *Stanford Achievement Test,* the *Metropolitan Achievement Tests,* and the *Iowa Tests of Basic Skills.* All these batteries consist of a series of tests in such areas as reading, mathematics, language, science, and social studies. The second subdivision includes single-subject tests that cover only one area, such as psychology, French, or geometry. An example of such a test—one that many readers of this book have taken or will take—is the *Graduate Record Examinations* (GRE): Subject Test in Psychology.

The third subdivision includes an incredible variety of tests used for purposes of certification and licensing in such fields as nursing, teaching, physical therapy, airline piloting, and so on. None of the tests in this category is a household name. But they have important consequences for people in specific vocational fields. Fourth, various government agencies sponsor certain achievement testing programs. Most prominent among these are statewide achievement testing programs in such basic subjects as reading, writing, and mathematics. In fact, such state assessment programs have assumed enormous importance in recent years as a result of new federal laws. In some states, high school graduation depends partly on performance on these tests. Other government-sponsored programs provide information about nationwide performance in a variety of areas. The most well known of these efforts are the National Assessment of Educational Progress (NAEP) and the Trends in International Mathematics and Science Study (TIMSS), both of which are the subject of frequent reports in the public media.

Finally, there are individually administered achievement tests. The first four types of achievement tests are typically group administered. However, some achievement tests are individually administered in much the same way as individually administered mental ability tests are. The individually administered achievement tests aid in the diagnosis of such conditions as learning disabilities.

The next major category includes the variety of tests designed to yield information about the human personality. The first subdivision includes what we call **objective personality tests.** In testing parlance, objective simply means the tests are objectively scored, based on items answered in a true-false or similar format. Examples of these objective personality tests are the *Minnesota Multiphasic Personality Inventory,* abbreviated MMPI, the *Beck Depression Inventory* (BDI), and the *Eating Disorder Inventory* (EDI). The MMPI provides a profile showing how similar the examinee's responses are to the responses of several clinical groups. The BDI-II and EDI, as suggested by their titles, try to measure depression and eating disorders, respectively. For both convenience and conceptual clarity, in subsequent chapters we divide these objective tests into those designed to measure personality traits within the normal range and those designed as clinical instruments to measure pathological or disabling conditions.

TRY IT!

Part of becoming a professional in this field involves learning the initials for tests. The initials are used routinely in psychological reports and journal articles, often without reference to the full name of the test. Become accustomed to it! Without referring to the text, see if you can give the full test title for each of these sets of initials:

SAT _____   WAIS _____

GRE _____   MMPI _____

The second major subdivision of personality tests includes **projective techniques.** With all these techniques, the examinee encounters a relatively simple but unstructured task. We hope that the examinee's responses will reveal something about his or her personality. The most famous of these techniques is the *Rorschach Inkblot Test*—sometimes just called the Rorschach, other times called the inkblot test. Other examples are human figure drawings, sentence completion techniques, and reactions to pictures. We include under personality measures a third category, simply labeled "other approaches," to cover the myriad of other ways psychologists have devised to satisfy our limitless fascination with the human personality.

The next major category of tests encompasses measures of interests and attitudes. The most prominent subdivision in this category includes **vocational interest measures.** These tests are widely used in high schools and colleges to help individuals explore jobs relevant to their interests. Examples of such tests are the *Strong Interest Inventory* (SII) and the *Kuder Career Search* (KCS). In fact, there are several versions of both the "Strong" and "Kuder" tests. This category also includes numerous measures of attitudes toward topics, groups, and practices. For example, there are measures for attitude toward capital punishment, attitude toward the elderly, and so on.

Our final category includes **neuropsychological tests.** These are tests designed to yield information about the functioning of the central nervous system, especially the brain. From some perspectives, this should not be a separate category because many of the tests used for neuropsychological testing simply come from the other categories. Much neuropsychological testing employs ability tests and often uses personality tests, too. However, we use a separate category to capture tests used specifically to assess brain functions. Of special interest are tests of memory for verbal and figural material, psychomotor coordination, and abstract thinking.

TRY IT!

Here is a simple test used by neuropsychologists. It is called a Greek cross. Look at the figure for a moment. Then put it aside and try to draw it from memory. What behaviors and mental processes do you think are involved in this test?

Some Additional Ways to Categorize Tests

Thus far, we have categorized tests according to their predominant type of content. In fact, this is the most common and, from most perspectives, the most useful way to classify tests. However, there are a number of other ways to classify tests. We will list them briefly. See Key Points Box 1.3.

Paper-and-Pencil versus Performance Tests

In a **performance test** the examinee completes some action such as assembling a product, delivering a speech, conducting an experiment, or leading a group. In a

---

Key Points Summary 1.3

Some Additional Ways to Categorize Tests

- Paper-and-pencil versus Performance
- Speed versus Power
- Individual versus Group
- Maximum versus Typical Performance
- Norm-referenced versus Criterion-referenced

---

paper-and-pencil test, the examinee responds to a set of questions usually, as implied by the title, using paper and pencil. Many paper-and-pencil tests use multiple-choice, true-false, or similar item types. With the increasing use of tests delivered via computer, as we describe more fully later, some of the distinction between paper-and-pencil and performance tests becomes blurred.

Speed versus Power Tests

The essential purpose of a **speed (or speeded) test** is to see how fast the examinee performs. The task is usually quite simple. The person's score is how many items or tasks can be completed in a fixed time or how much time (e.g., in minutes or seconds) is required to complete the task. For example, how quickly can you cross out all the "e's" on this page? How quickly can you complete 50 simple arithmetic problems such as $42 + 19$, 24×8, and so on? A **power test,** on the other hand, usually involves challenging material, administered with no time limit or a very generous limit. The essential point of the power test is to test the limits of a person's knowledge or ability (other than speed). The distinction is not necessarily all-or-none: pure speed versus pure power. Some power tests may have an element of speed. You can't take forever to complete the SAT. However, mental prowess and knowledge rather than speed are the primary determinants of performance on a power test. Some speed tests may have an element of power. You have to do some thinking and perhaps even have a plan to cross out all the "e's" on the page. However, crossing out "e's" is primarily a matter of speed, not rocket science.

Individual versus Group Tests

This distinction refers simply to the mode of test administration. An **individual test** can be administered to only one individual at a time. The classic examples are individually administered intelligence tests. An examiner presents each question or task to the individual and records the person's response. A **group test** can be administered to many individuals at the same time, that is, to a group. Of course, individuals receive their own scores from a group-administered test. In general, any group-administered test can be administered to one individual at a time, when circumstances warrant, but individually administered tests cannot be given to an entire group at once.

Maximum versus Typical Performance

Here is another useful distinction between types of tests. Some tests look for **maximum performance.** How well can examinees perform when at their best? This is usually the case with achievement and ability tests. On the other hand, we sometimes want to see a person's **typical performance.** This is usually the case with personality, interest, and attitude tests. For example, on a personality test we want to know how extroverted a person typically is, not how extroverted the person can be if he is trying real hard to appear extroverted.

Norm-referenced versus Criterion-referenced

Many tests have norms based on performance of cases in a standardization program. For example, you may know that your score on the SAT or ACT is at the 84th percentile, meaning that you scored better than 84% of persons in the national norm group. This constitutes a **norm-referenced interpretation** of your performance on the test. In contrast, some test interpretation depends on reference to some clearly defined criterion rather than on reference to a set of norms. For example, an instructor may say: I want you to know all the key terms at the end of the chapter. On the instructor's test, you correctly define only 60% of the key terms, and this is considered inadequate—regardless of how well other people did on the test. This is **criterion-referenced interpretation.** Actually, it is the method of interpretation rather than the test itself that is either norm-referenced or criterion-referenced. We explore this distinction more fully in Chapter 3.

Uses and Users of Tests

A second way to introduce the world of testing is to identify the typical uses and users of tests. For the various categories of tests listed in the previous section, who actually uses these tests? What are the settings in which these tests are used? Consider these examples.

- John is a clinical psychologist in private practice. He sees a lot of clients suffering from anxiety and depression. Some cases may be mild, susceptible to short-term behavioral and cognitive-behavioral therapy. Others may be much more chronic where the presenting symptoms overlay a potentially schizophrenic condition. Early in his assessment of the clients, John routinely uses the MMPI and, for particularly perplexing cases, the Rorschach Inkblot Test.

- Kristen is a school psychologist. For students referred to her by teachers, she regularly reviews the school records containing scores from the *Otis-Lennon School Ability Test* and *Stanford Achievement Test.* In addition, she will administer the *Wechsler Intelligence Scale for Children* (WISC) and apply a behavior rating scale.

- Frank is a high school counselor. He supervises the school's annual administration of the *Strong Interest Inventory* (SII). Results of the test are distributed in homerooms. Frank cannot meet with every student about the SII results, but he prepares materials for homeroom teachers to help students interpret their reports.

- Carole is a developmental psychologist. She is interested in the stresses children undergo as they move from prepuberty to adolescence. In her longitudinal study, she uses a measure of self-concept (the *Piers-Harris Children's Self-concept Scale*) to track changes in how participants feel about themselves. She also has intelligence test scores for the participants, taken from school records, simply to help describe the nature of her sample.

- Brooke is a neuropsychologist. In a product liability suit brought against an automobile manufacturer by an individual claiming to have sustained brain injury in an accident, Brooke, on behalf of the manufacturer, presents evidence garnered from a variety of tests that no brain injury occurred.

- Bill is assistant director of human resources for MicroHard, a company that hires nearly 100 new secretaries each year at its four different locations. Bill oversees the testing of 500 secretarial candidates per year. He tries to ensure that they have the skills, both technical and interpersonal, that will make them productive members of the "MicroHard team."

- Joe works for the State Department of Education. The legislature just adopted a bill requiring that all students pass tests in reading, mathematics, and writing to receive a high school diploma. Joe— lucky fellow—must organize preparation of these tests.

These are all examples of the typical uses and users of tests. Let us provide a more systematic catalog of the major uses and users of tests. As listed in Key Points Box 1.4, we identify four major groups of users. There is considerable diversity within each group, but each group is relatively distinct in the way it uses tests. We also note that each group uses nearly all kinds of tests, as defined in the previous section, although certain types of tests predominate within each group.

Key Points Summary 1.4
Major Contexts for Use of Tests

1. Clinical
2. Educational
3. Personnel
4. Research

The *first* category includes the fields of clinical psychology, counseling, school psychology, and neuropsychology. We will label all these applications as *clinical use*. In these professional applications, the psychologist is trying to help an individual who has (or may have) some type of problem. The problem may be severe (e.g., schizophrenia) or mild (e.g., choosing a college major). Testing helps to identify the nature and severity of the problem and, perhaps, provides some suggestions about how to deal with the problem. Testing may also help to measure progress in dealing with the problem.

A host of surveys have documented the extent of clinical test usage. We provide here highlights from a sampling of these surveys. In later chapters, we will describe uses of particular tests.

- Psychologists practicing in mental health settings and state hospitals spend 15 to 18% of their time in assessment activities (Corrigan, Hess, & Garman, 1998; Frauenhoffer, Ross, Gfeller, Searight, & Piotrowski, 1998).
- Over 80% of neuropsychologists spend 5 or more hours per week on assessment and one-third of them spend more than 20 hours per week on assessment (Camara, Nathan, & Puente, 2000).
- School psychologists spend about one-half of their professional time on assessment activities (Hutton, Dubes, & Muir, 1992; Reschly, 2000).
- A sample of 100 forensic neuropsychological reports prepared for certain personal injury cases incorporated an average of 12 different tests per report, with as many as 32 tests in one report (Lees-Haley et al., 1995).
- In a study of counseling psychologists, two-thirds reported using objective tests, and just less than one-third reported using projective tests (Watkins, Campbell, & McGregor, 1988).

All these groups utilize intelligence tests (primarily individually administered tests), objective personality tests, and projective techniques. Most of the groups also employ neuropsychological tests. Counseling psychologists often use vocational interest measures.

An overview of the surveys shows that tests play a prominent role in the professional practice of psychology. We should add that for all these fields advanced training in the administration and interpretation of tests is required. Doctoral-level work in fields such as clinical, counseling, and school psychology typically entails several full courses in testing beyond the introductory work covered in this book.

A *second* major use of tests is in *educational settings,* apart from the clinical use that occupies the school psychologist or counselor. We refer here primarily to use of group-administered tests of ability and achievement. The actual users of the test information include teachers, educational administrators, parents, and the general public, especially as represented by such officials as legislators and school boards. Use of standardized testing in educational settings resolves into two major subdivisions. First, there are achievement tests used for determining levels of student learning. Limiting our counts to standardized achievement tests (i.e., excluding the vast array of teacher-made tests), there are tens of millions of these tests administered annually. As described more fully in Chapter 11, schools administer series of standardized achievement tests throughout the grades. Achievement tests are also used to document competence for certification or licensing in a wide variety of professions.

The second primary use of tests in educational settings is to predict success in academic work. Prime examples in this category are tests for college and professional school admissions. For example, close to 2 million students take the SAT-I each year, while nearly 1 million students take the *American College Testing* (ACT) Program. Approximately 300,000 *Graduate Record Examination* (GRE): General tests are administered annually, as are about 100,000 *Law School Admission Tests* (LSAT). Even larger numbers of elementary and secondary school students take group-administered mental ability tests as part of regular school testing programs.

The *third* major category of test usage involves *personnel or employment* testing. Primary users in this category are businesses and the military. There are two essential tasks. The first task is to select individuals most qualified to fill a position. "Most qualified" usually means "most likely to be successful." For example, we may want to select from a pool of applicants the individuals who are most likely to be successful salespersons, managers, secretaries, or telemarketers. Tests may be useful in this selection process, as suggested in Figure 1.1. The tests may include measures of general mental ability, specific job-related skills, and personality characteristics. Of

FIGURE 1.1 Having good measures of a person's abilities and interests can be helpful.

Source: Reprinted with permission of offthemark.com. Atlantic Feature Syndicate.

course, nontest information will also be used. For example, letters of recommendation and records of previous employment are typical nontest sources of information.

The second task in the employment area has a different opening scenario. In the first case, we had a pool of applicants, and we selected from that pool. In the second case, we have a group of individuals who will be employed, and we need to assign them to different tasks to optimize the organization's overall efficiency. This is a common objective in the military where a large number of individuals are to be deployed. Once inducted, none of them will be de-selected—all will be used in one way or another. Tests may provide useful information about the optimum allocation of the human resources in this scenario. The *Armed Services Vocational Aptitude Battery* (ASVAB) was designed for this use. Among 1,000 new recruits, some may be particularly adept at mechanical activities, others at clerical activities, and still others at highly verbal communication tasks. To some extent, individuals' preferences may also influence the allocation of personnel. And, of course, previous specialized training will be important.

The *fourth* major category of test usage is *research*. This is clearly the most diverse category. Tests are used in every conceivable area of research in psychology, education, and other social/behavioral sciences. For convenience, we can identify three subcategories of research usage. First, tests often serve as the dependent variable in a research study. More specifically, the test serves as the *operational definition of the dependent variable.* For example, in a study of the effects of caffeine on short-term memory, the *Wechsler Memory Scale* may be the operational definition of "memory." In a study of gender differences in self-concept, the *Piers-Harris Children's Self-concept Scale* may provide the definition of self-concept. In a longitudinal study of the effects of an improved nutrition program on school performance, the *Stanford Achievement Test,* administered in each of grades 2–6, may serve as the measure of performance. There are several major advantages to using an existing test as the operational definition of a dependent variable in such studies. First, the researcher need not worry about developing a new measure. Second, the existing test should have known properties such as normative and reliability information. Third and most important, use of an existing test helps replicability by other researchers.

The second major category of research usage is for purposes of *describing samples.* Important characteristics of the samples used in a research study should be delineated. The Method section of a research article often provides information about age and gender of participants. Some characteristics are described by test information—for example, means and standard deviations on an intelligence, achievement, or personality test. In a study of college students, it may be helpful to know the average SAT or ACT scores for the students. In a study of elderly patients in a state hospital, it may be helpful to know the patients' scores on the MMPI. Note that in these instances the test scores are not used as dependent variables but only to describe the research samples.

The third major category of research usage involves *research on the tests themselves.* As we will see in the next chapter, entire journals are devoted to this type of research. Furthermore, the development of new tests is itself a major research enterprise. Because tests play a prominent role in the social/behavioral sciences, continuous research on the tests is an important professional contribution.

Major Issues: Assumptions and Questions

A third important way to introduce the field of testing is to examine the fundamental issues, assumptions, and questions in the field. When psychologists think carefully about tests, regardless of the type of test, what issues do they worry about and what assumptions are they making? Describing these basic issues and assumptions helps us understand what the field is all about.

Basic Assumptions

Let us begin this way of exploring the field by identifying the assumptions we seem to make. There are probably four partly overlapping but reasonably distinct assumptions. First, we assume that human beings have recognizable *traits or characteristics.* Examples of traits are verbal ability, memory, extroversion, friendliness, quantitative reasoning ability, self-esteem, knowledge of Irish history, and depression. Furthermore, we assume that these traits or characteristics describe *potentially important* aspects of persons. More specifically, we assume that *differences* between individuals are potentially important. There are many ways in which people are the same. We all need oxygen. Without it, we quickly expire. We do not differ much from one another in that regard. Nearly everyone uses language to some extent, a distinctively human characteristic. However, we also differ from one another in certain ways. Some people are much taller than other people. Some people are more depressed than others. Some people are more intelligent. We assume that such differences among people in the traits we test are important rather than trivial.

TRY IT! ....

We have just named a variety of human traits (verbal ability, depression, etc.). Try to name several more traits, some in the ability domain, some in the personality domain.

    Ability traits: _____

    Personality traits: _____

Key Points Summary 1.5

Four Crucial Assumptions

1. People differ in important traits.
2. We can quantify these traits.
3. The traits are reasonably stable.
4. Measures of the traits relate to actual behavior.

Less   More

FIGURE 1.2   The continuum assumed for a trait.

Second, we assume that we can *quantify* these traits. Quantification means arranging objects (in this case people) along a continuum. Think of a continuum as going from low to high or less to more. The continuum corresponds to the trait we are studying. At its most primitive level, quantification involves distinguishing among the objects on the continuum. The distinction may simply be into two categories, labeled 0 and 1. At the next level of sophistication, we use the concept of "more or less" along the continuum, as shown in Figure 1.2. People are arrayed along the continuum for a trait. We examine these concepts of quantification in more detail in Chapter 3. For now, we simply note our assumption that such quantification of a trait is a fundamental notion in our work. It is this "quantification" assumption that gives rise to use of the term *measure* in the field of testing. In fact, in many contexts, "measure" is used as a synonym for "test." For example, the question "How did you measure the child's intelligence?" means the same as "How did you test the child's intelligence?"

Third, we assume that the traits have some degree of *stability or permanence*. They need not be perfectly stable, but they cannot fluctuate wildly from moment to moment. If the trait itself is insufficiently stable, then, no matter how refined our test, we will not be able to do much with it.

Fourth, we assume that the reasonably stable traits that we quantify with our tests have important *relationships to actual behavior* in real-life situations. From a theoretical perspective, this fourth assumption is the least important of our assumptions. That is, as theorists, we might be content to show that we can quantify a particular psychological trait regardless of whether it relates to anything else. However, from a practical perspective, this fourth assumption is crucial. As pragmatists, we might say that no matter how elegantly a test quantifies a psychological trait, if the test does not relate to anything else, we are not very interested in it.

Fundamental Questions

We now consider the fundamental questions about tests. In many ways, these questions are related to or are outgrowths of the assumptions previously listed. By way of anticipation, we note that these fundamental questions are precisely the topics covered in Chapters 3, 4, and 5. In those chapters we learn how psychologists try to answer these fundamental questions.

First, we ask about the **reliability** of the test. Reliability refers to the stability of test scores. For example, if I take the test today and again tomorrow, will I get approximately the same score? We examine this topic in considerable detail in Chapter 4. Notice that this question is not exactly the same as that treated in our third assumption. That assumption dealt with the stability of the trait itself. The question of reliability deals with the stability of our measurement of that trait.

Second, we ask about the **validity** of the test. Validity refers to what the test is actually measuring. If a test purports to measure intelligence, how do we know whether the test is, in fact, measuring intelligence? If a test purports to measure depression, how do we know that it is measuring depression? Included within the area of validity is the concept of *fairness.* Fairness, which is the flip side of bias, deals with the question of whether the test measures in an equitable manner across various groups, for example, across genders, ages, ethnic/racial groups, and different geographic areas. Such a question is, at root, a matter of the test's validity. We treat validity in detail in Chapter 5.

Third, we ask how to interpret the scores from a test. Sheri got a score of 13 right out of 20 items on the arithmetic test. Is that good or bad? Pat answered "True" to 45 of the 60 items on the depression scale. Does that mean he is depressed or positively euphoric? Interpretation of test scores usually depends on the use of **norms.** Norms are based on the test scores of large groups of individuals who have taken the test in the past. In Chapter 3 we describe the types of norms used with tests and how these norms are developed.

Questions related to reliability, validity, and norms are the most basic questions we ask about tests. Attempts to answer these questions form the core of test theory. These are the topics we worry about for all types of tests. However, we should add two additional types of questions to our catalog of fundamental questions. Knowing how a test was developed often enhances our understanding of reliability, validity, and norms. Hence, test development becomes another crucial topic. In addition, we need to consider a host of practical issues. How much does the test cost? How long does it take? Is it easily obtained? Is it available in languages other than English? All of these practical questions are important, although they are not part of test theory.

Key Points Summary 1.6

Fundamental Questions about Tests

- Reliability
- Validity
- Norms
- Test Development
- Practical Issues

The Differential Perspective

As a final note in the consideration of fundamental assumptions and questions, we call attention to what we will label the differential perspective. In many areas of the social and behavioral sciences, we attempt to formulate laws or generalizations that apply, more or less, to everyone. For example, what is the most effective Skinnerian schedule of reinforcement for learning a skill? What is the optimum level of stress for performing a certain task? Does psychoanalysis cure phobias? The formulation of such questions suggests that there is an answer that will generally hold true for people. In contrast, the **differential perspective** assumes that the answer may differ for different people. We are more interested in how people are different than in how they are the same. This differential perspective pervades the world of testing. Being aware of this perspective will help you think about issues in testing.

The Historical Perspective

A fourth way to introduce the world of testing is by examining its historical origins. How did the field get where it is today? Knowing how we got here is often crucial for understanding today's issues. We provide this historical perspective in two ways. First, we outline major periods and events in the history of testing. Second, we sketch some of the major forces that have influenced the development of testing. In constructing this history, we have drawn on a number of sources, many of which recount the same details but from somewhat different perspectives. For the earlier periods, see Boring (1950), DuBois (1970), Hilgard (1987), Misiak (1961), and Murphy (1949).

The history of testing can be conveniently divided into *seven major periods* (see Key Points Box 1.7). Most of the periods have a dominant theme. The themes help to organize our understanding of the flow of events. We put chronological boundaries on the periods, with some rounding at the edges for pedagogical simplicity. We occasionally overstep the self-imposed boundaries to maintain continuity. In sketching the chronological development of the field, we avoid a mind-numbing recitation of dates, preferring to capture the spirit of different periods and transitions between these periods. We introduce a judicious selection of dates to highlight events that are particularly representative of a period. The reader will find it more useful to concentrate on the themes than on exact dates, although it is useful to commit a few dates to memory.

Remote Background: Up to 1840

The first period is rather artificial. It is so long as to nearly defy any meaningful summary. But we do need to start somewhere. Let us identify three noteworthy items in this broad expanse of time. First, we observe that the remote roots of psychology, as well as most fields, are in philosophy. Among the classical thinkers of

Key Points Summary 1.7

Major Periods in the History of Testing

1. Remote Background	Up to 1840	
2. Setting the Stage	1840–1880	40 years
3. The Roots	1880–1915	35 years
4. Flowering	1915–1940	25 years
5. Consolidation	1940–1965	25 years
6. Just Yesterday	1965–2000	35 years
7. And Now	2000–present	

ancient, medieval, and more modern times, there was a distinct lack of interest in the topic of individual differences or any notion of measuring traits. If we use the modern method of "citation frequency" to define authors' influence of the past 2,500 years, no doubt Aristotle, Plato, and Aquinas would emerge as the top three (beyond the sacred scriptures). Examination of the writings of these three giants, as well as their colleagues, reveals a dominant interest in defining what is common to human beings, what is generally true, rather than what is different about them. Consider, for example, Aristotle's *Peri Psyche* (also known by its Latin name *De Anima,* translated into English as *On the Soul*). Written about 350 B.C., the work is often cited as the first textbook on psychology, indeed essentially giving the name to the field. In the opening book of his treatise, Aristotle (1935) says, "We seek to examine and investigate first the nature and essence of the soul, and then its [essential] attributes" (p. 9). This is not the stuff of the differential perspective.

Plato, the other great luminary of the ancient world, whose influence also continues unabated, similarly concentrated on the general and, even more so than Aristotle, on the abstract. The most influential writer of the medieval period was Thomas Aquinas. With respect to psychological matters, he recapitulated much of Aristotle's work. Indeed, he saw his principal task as that of reconciling Christian theology with the Aristotelian synthesis. Hence, Aquinas adopts Aristotle's concepts of human abilities and manifests the same disinterest in human differences, preferring to concentrate on general characteristics of human nature. Of course, these philosophers were not fools. They were, in fact, keen observers of the human condition. They have occasional—often fascinating—comments on matters of individual differences, but such comments are strictly sidelights, not a focus of attention.

Following the medieval period, the Renaissance witnessed a true awakening to the individual. But this interest was reflected primarily in artistic productions, the glorious profusion of paintings, sculptures, and buildings that still leaves us breathless. Dominant thinkers of the late Renaissance and early modern period continued to concern themselves with how the human mind works. For example, Descartes,

Locke, Hume, and Kant framed questions—and gave answers—that formed part of the remote background for psychology's roots. Emphasis continued to be placed on what was common. Furthermore, there was virtually no reference to the human personality. For concise descriptions of the relevance of these individuals to psychology, see Misiak (1961).

Regarding the mode of examinations in our period of the remote past, DuBois (1970) observes that written examinations were not common in the Western educational tradition. The more common practice in the schools throughout ancient, medieval, and, indeed, up until the mid-1800s was oral examination. The vestiges of this practice remain today in the oral defense of an honors, master's, or doctoral thesis, popularly known as "taking your orals," as if it were some kind of distasteful pill (actually, it is much worse than any pill). DuBois notes that written examinations emerged in the remarkable string of Jesuit schools in the late 1500s, the predecessors of today's network of Jesuit secondary schools, colleges, and universities throughout the world. The Jesuit *Ratio Studiorum,* a kind of early curriculum guide, laid down strict rules (standardization!) for conducting written examinations.

Finally, some textbooks report the equivalent of civil service examinations being used routinely in China as early as 2000 B.C. However, Bowman (1989) argues convincingly that these reports are based on inadequate (we might say near apocryphal) historical sources and that the earliest such testing probably occurred around 200 B.C. Nevertheless, whether 200 or 2200 B.C., this is an interesting historical development. The system continued until the early twentieth century and may have had some influence on civil service testing in Western countries.

Setting the Stage: 1840–1880

Events in the years 1840–1880 set the stage for the stars who were to be the main characters in the drama that unfolded next. This stage-setting was a largely disconnected set of events. However, in retrospect, we can see the strands coming together. There were four such strands.

First, throughout this period, both scientific interest and public consciousness of mental illness increased enormously. From the early prodding of Phillipe Pinel in France, Samuel Tuke in England, and Benjamin Rush in the United States, a host of efforts to improve the diagnosis and treatment of the mentally ill arose. Dorothea Dix (Figure 1.3) epitomized the humanitarian side of the effort. Beginning around 1840, she conducted a virtually worldwide crusade, resulting in improvements in prison and hospital conditions. On the scientific side, methods for the diagnosis of mental illness, including mental retardation, began to emerge. For example, simple methods of assessing mental ability, such as the Seguin form board (see Figure 1.4), appeared. These early measures had no norms, no reliability data. But they foreshadowed at least elements of measures that would develop later.

A second significant development of this period was the adoption of formal written examinations by the Boston School Committee—essentially the city's school board—under the direction of Horace Mann, probably the most influential educator of the day. Mann advocated, not only in Boston but nationwide, for drastic improvement in the way schools evaluated their students.

FIGURE 1.3 Dorothea Dix: crusader for improvement in hospital conditions.

Source: Science Photo Library/Photo Researchers.

Third, the age of Darwin dawned. The world-shattering *On the Origin of Species by Means of Natural Selection* appeared in 1859. Perhaps more important for the incipient field of psychology were Darwin's subsequent books: *The Descent of Man, and Selection in Relation to Sex* in 1871 and *The Expression of the Emotions in Man and Animals* in 1872. Of course, all these turned the world on its ear. But why were these works important for psychology? Because they got people thinking about differences: first differences between species, then differences between individuals. Most specifically, the works got Francis Galton thinking about individual differences. More on Galton in a moment.

Fourth, experimental psychology emerged. The traditional birthdate for the field is 1879, the year Wilhelm Wundt opened his laboratory at the University in Leipzig, now a city of one-half million people located 75 miles south of Berlin, Germany. Experimental psychology was an outgrowth of physiology. The connecting link was

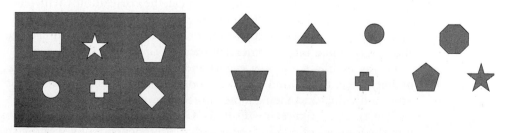

FIGURE 1.4 A Seguin-like form board.

Source: Archives of the History of American Psychology

Key Points Summary 1.8

Strands in Setting the Stage

- Increased interest in mental illness
- Adoption of written examinations
- Dawning of the age of Darwin
- Emergence of experimental psychology

---

psychophysics. Early experimental psychology was essentially synonymous with psychophysics. Its ultimate contribution to the world of testing, for good or ill, was twofold. First, like any good laboratory science, it concentrated on standardization of conditions and precision of measurement. Second, it concentrated on elemental processes: sensation, thresholds, perception, simple motor reactions, and so on. Wundt's laboratory was the training ground of choice for many early psychologists. Hence, Wundt's interests and methods exercised great influence on the fledgling field of psychology.

Thus, we come to about 1880. Experimental psychology is a new science. The world is abuzz about evolution. There is widespread interest in the mentally ill, including the mentally retarded. And some pioneers are trying to bring education into the scientific fold.

The Roots: 1880–1915

The roots of testing, as the enterprise exists today, were set in the 35-year period 1880–1915. The earliest measures that had lasting influence emerged in this period. Many of the basic issues and methodologies surfaced in more or less explicit form. At the beginning of the period, there were few—very few—examples one could point to and say: That's a test. By the end of the period, there was a panoply of instruments. Some of these, minus a few archaic words, are indistinguishable from today's tests. At the beginning of the period, the correlation coefficient and the concept of reliability had not been invented. By the end of the period, these methodological cornerstones of testing had not only been invented but had been elaborated and incorporated into an emergent theory of mental tests.

Let us highlight the key events and personalities of this exciting period. The highlights center around four key individuals. In addition, we will mention one other individual and then a loose confederation of other contributors.

The first key figure was **Francis Galton** (Figure 1.5). Many people consider him the founder of psychological testing. An independently wealthy British gentleman, he never had a real job, not even as a university professor. He dabbled. But when he did so, he did it in grand style, with astonishing creativity and versatility.

FIGURE 1.5 Francis Galton: dabbler extraordinaire and pipeline for evolutionary theory into psychology.

Source: Topham/The Image Works.

Fittingly, as a second cousin of Charles Darwin, Galton was the primary pipeline for transmitting evolution into the emerging field of psychology. Galton's interest lay in heredity, especially the inheritance of high levels of ability. He called it "genius" and studied it in a wide array of fields, including music, military and political leadership, and literature.

In trying to examine the relationships among the many variables he studied, Galton invented the bivariate distribution chart. As a follow-up, he induced Karl Pearson, a contemporary British mathematician, to invent the correlation coefficient. Galton had the time, resources, and personality to accomplish much. In addition, he was a proselytizer. He spread the word about methods of mental measurement. Despite the fact that he did not hold any prestigious position, it seemed that by 1910 everyone knew about Galton's work.

The key American contributor to the development of testing was **James McKeen Cattell.** After a brief stint at the University of Pennsylvania, he spent most of his professional career at Columbia University in New York City. Cattell's preparation was ideal for merging two methodological streams. He completed graduate work first with Wundt at Leipzig, honing his skills in rigorous laboratory studies of the psychophysical tradition. He then studied with Galton, apparently absorbing Galton's fascination with collecting data about individual differences in human traits. Consistent with the prevailing notion at the time, Cattell believed that the key to mental functioning was elemental processes. He created a battery of 50 tests, 10 of which were considered mainstays (see Table 1.1), covering such areas as sensory acuity, reaction time, visual bisection of a line, and judgments of short intervals of time. He administered these to groups of college students in hopes of predicting academic success—the conceptual grandparent of today's SATs and ACTs. He persuaded other psychologists to undertake similar projects. For reasons we will explore in Chapter 7, Cattell's tests were a colossal flop as predictors. Nevertheless, the work was highly influential. In a famous article of 1890, he coined the term *mental test* (Cattell, 1890), a term used

TABLE 1.1   *An Abbreviated List of Cattell's Ten Key Tests*

1. Dynamometer Pressure [grip-strength]
2. Rate of Movement
3. Sensation-areas
4. Pressure causing Pain
5. Least noticeable difference in Weight
6. Reaction-time for Sound
7. Time for naming Colours
8. Bi-section of a 50 cm. Line
9. Judgment of 10 seconds time
10. Number of letters remembered on once Hearing

to characterize the field for the next 50 years. Appropriately, a commentary by Galton followed the article.

TRY IT!

Which of the tests listed in Table 1.1 do you think might be the best predictors of academic success?

The third influential figure of this period was the Frenchman **Alfred Binet** (pronounced Bă-nay´). In his section on Mental Tests, Boring (1950) summarizes the matter succinctly: "The 1880s were Galton's decade in this field, the 1890s Cattell's, and the 1900s Binet's" (p. 573). Binet is truly the father of intelligence testing. Oddly, his original training was in the law, although he subsequently completed advanced training in medicine and natural sciences. Throughout most of his career, Binet concentrated on investigation of mental functions. In contrast to Galton,

Key Points Summary 1.9

Important Persons in Establishing the Roots

- Francis Galton
- James McKeen Cattell
- Alfred Binet
- Charles Spearman
- Developers of "New Tests"

Binet aimed at more holistic mental activities: using words, finding connections, getting the meaning, and so on. The Parisian schools at that time wanted to identify students more likely to profit from special schools than from regular classroom instruction. A committee, including Binet and Theodore Simon, set out to devise a method to identify these students. The result was the Binet-Simon Scale,[3] first published in 1905. It appeared in revised form, including the first use of "mental ages" in 1908 and again in 1911. In Chapter 8, we examine the grandchild of Binet's scale, the modern-day *Stanford-Binet Intelligence Scale.*

Fourth, there was the work of **Charles Spearman,** another Englishman. His contributions were of a distinctly different character than those of the first three individuals. Spearman did not invent any new types of tests or test items. He did not undertake any novel data collection projects. Spearman was a grand theorist and a number cruncher. In 1904, he published a paper announcing the "two-factor" theory of intelligence. Oddly, it appeared in the *American Journal of Psychology* rather than in a British outlet. Spearman undergirded his theory with the method of tetrad differences, the earliest form of the statistical technique eventually known as factor analysis. We describe details of this theory in Chapter 7. The important point here is that this was the first attempt to provide an empirically based theory of human intelligence, and it was an outcropping of the new methods of mental measurement. Previous theories were essentially philosophical. Here, based on test results (mostly from Galton-type tests), was a new kind of theory, accompanied by an entirely new mathematical methodology. This, indeed, was the stuff of a new science.

The final element in establishing the roots of testing is not so neatly identified. It was not just one person. Rather, it was a whole gaggle of persons, all pursuing the same goal in much the same way. This was the group of people feverishly building the earliest versions of educational achievement tests. They responded to much the same impulse as Horace Mann's: the need to bring education into the scientific world. If education was to be conducted in a scientific manner, then it needed precise, reliable measures. This was a different interest than Cattell's interest in prediction. These investigators wanted measures of the outcomes of education.

With near evangelistic zeal, a bevy of test authors created what they called "new-type" achievement tests. The principal concern was with the unreliability of essay and oral exams. The new-type tests were as objective as possible. In practice, this meant multiple-choice, true-false, and fill-in-the-blank test items. These items could be objectively scored, and they were more reliable than the "old-type" tests. The literature of the day is replete with references to the inadequacies of old-type tests. In today's parlance, the problem was inter-scorer reliability. Many people suppose that multiple-choice and similar types of items were invented to accommodate mass processing of tests by computers. Nothing could be more absurd. Computers did not even exist when the new-type tests emerged. Nor did answer-sheet scanners exist. Authors laboring in the achievement test field at this time were not concerned with scoring efficiency. Scoring reliability was their passion.

---

[3] We follow the modern practice of referring to this as the Binet-Simon Scale. In his own work, Binet did not use an official name for it. He simply referred to it as the "test" or the "scale."

The Flowering: 1915–1940

From its humble and rather disjointed roots of 1880–1915, testing entered a period of spectacular growth. At the beginning of this period, there were tests but few were standardized in the manner we think of such instruments today. By the end of the period, in a mere 35 years, thousands of such tests were available. The first editions of the great majority of tests that are widely used today sprang up during this period. This happened in every sphere of testing: mental ability, achievement, personality, interests, and so on. The extent of activity was simply breathtaking. Let us examine some of these developments.

The clear demarcation point between the period of roots and the period of flowering comes with Binet's scales crossing the Atlantic Ocean from France to the United States. We might date this anywhere between 1910 and 1916. Whatever the specific date chosen, the important point is the transatlantic crossing. Binet's work received almost immediate attention in the United States. Some of the new American versions were mainly translations, perhaps the earliest being Goddard's in 1910 (DuBois, 1970; Murphy, 1949). There were other translations and adaptations, too. However, the definitive event was publication of the Stanford Revision of the Binet Scales in 1916, popularly referred to as the Stanford-Binet. Engineered by Lewis Terman of Stanford University, the Stanford Revision involved new items (nearly doubling the original number), new tryout research, an ambitious national norming program, and the first widespread use of the ratio IQ—altogether a blockbuster. A researcher looking back on it today would scoff. At the time, it was like the first jet-powered aircraft, the first man on the moon, the first CD. Within a relatively short time, the Stanford-Binet became the benchmark definition of human intelligence, a mainstay of clinical practice, and perhaps the most distinctive symbol of psychology's contribution to the modern world. Thus began the period of flowering.

One of the most profoundly influential events in the history of testing was development of the first widely used group-administered intelligence test. This occurred in the context of psychologists' efforts to aid in processing the tidal wave of military recruits as the United States entered World War I in 1917. Arthur Otis, as part of his doctoral work under Lewis Terman (of Stanford-Binet fame), undertook creation of a group-administered form of the Stanford-Binet. Otis's work eventuated in the Army Alpha and Beta, verbal and nonverbal versions, respectively, administered to nearly 2 million military personnel. In 1918, the tests were made available for general use as the *Otis Group Intelligence Scale.* We will examine the lineal descendant of this test, the *Otis-Lennon School Ability Test,* in Chapter 9.

The Stanford-Binet and Otis tests established the use of a single score to represent intelligence. The major challenge to this practice arose in the work of L.L. Thurstone (1938), who maintained that there were seven (more or less) different dimensions of human intelligence. Thurstone's work spawned a host of multi-score intelligence tests in this period.

A flurry of publications in the relatively brief span of ten years, 1921–1930, established the preference for the "new-type" achievement test (McCall, 1922; Odell, 1928; Ruch, 1924, 1929; Ruch & Rice, 1930; Ruch & Stoddard, 1927; Toops, 1921; Wood, 1923). Although the previous era witnessed the earliest development of a host of "new-type" achievement tests, none gained widespread usage. The first truly national standardized achievement test was the *Stanford Achievement Test,* which appeared in 1923. Interestingly, one of its co-authors was Lewis Terman, principal architect of the Stanford revision of the Binet. The 1930s also witnessed the origin of several other well-recognized achievement batteries (e.g., Metropolitan, Iowa, and California series), as well as a host of single-subject tests in every conceivable area.

Personality testing, both objective and projective, also flourished during this period. The prototype of today's objective personality inventories, the *Woodworth Personal Data Sheet,* was devised to help process military recruits for World War I. It was essentially a paper-and-pencil interview, 116 items in all, each answered "Yes" or "No," to help detect individuals needing more thorough psychological examination. A host of similar instruments sprouted after World War I. Illustrating the profusion of new publications during this period are the following.

- Rorschach's inkblots appeared in 1921. By 1940, there were several different scoring systems for the inkblots.
- Strong and Kuder launched their pioneering work on vocational interest inventories (see Donnay, 1997; Zytowski, 1992); we describe the current versions of those tests in Chapter 15.
- The MMPI (see Chapter 13), though not appearing until just beyond the boundary of the period, was conceptualized during this time.
- Thurstone and Likert first attempted systematic measurement of attitudes; we describe their methods, still used today, in Chapter 15.

Earlier we recounted the benchmark event at the onset of this period of flowering: publication of the *Stanford-Binet Intelligence Scale* in 1916. Perhaps fittingly, the end of this period witnessed the arrival of the first major revision of this test in 1937. Almost coincidentally, in 1939, the *Wechsler-Bellevue Intelligence Scale* appeared. David Wechsler, a clinical psychologist working at New York City's Bellevue Hospital, was unhappy about using the Stanford-Binet—a test designed for children—with his adult clients. He created his test to be more suitable for adults.

First editions of three publications served like triple exclamation points near the conclusion of this remarkably fecund period in the history of testing. First was the publication of the highly theoretical journal *Psychometrika* in 1936; second was publication of the more pragmatically oriented *Educational and Psychological Measurement* in 1941; third was the first edition of Oscar K. Buros's *Mental Measurements Yearbook* in 1938, a work whose current edition we describe in detail in Chapter 2.

Consolidation: 1940–1965

Following the burst of activity on a multitude of fronts from 1915 to 1940, testing entered a period that might best be characterized as consolidation or maturity. This period lasted roughly from 1940 to 1965, another span of 25 years. Activity did not diminish—indeed, it continued to flourish. New, revised editions of many of the tests first developed in the previous period now appeared. Entirely new tests were also developed. Testing expanded in clinical practice, in the schools, in business, and in the military. But testing was no longer a new kid on the block. It was accepted professional practice. It was assumed that tests would play a prominent role in a variety of venues. A number of events signaled this newfound maturity.

Early in this period, of course, World War II (1939–1945) preoccupied everyone's attention. Tests, rather than being created anew as in World War I, were used widely and routinely for processing military personnel. Prominent psychologists, now trained in the testing methods developed in the previous period, guided these applications. In addition, clinical psychologists plied their trade in the treatment of war-related psychological casualties, in part using the tests now available.

The appearance of books or other written documents often defines an historical period. Thus, the Declaration of Independence signified the emergence of a new nation—although many other events could easily be taken as more important developments. Perhaps the best evidence of the consolidation of the field of testing during the period 1940–1964 was the appearance of a number of books summarizing the status of testing. These became classics in the field precisely because they could provide summaries of mature thinking about the major issues in the field. Twenty years earlier, say in 1930, it would not have been possible to write these books because thinking had not matured regarding the major issues.

Embedded within this period of consolidation was a particularly remarkable six-year span, 1949–1954, when a half-dozen soon-to-be classics appeared. Among these works were the earliest versions (in 1954 and 1955) of what would become the *Standards for Educational and Psychological Tests*, a sort of bible of the best thinking on technical matters related to tests. We cite excerpts from these *Standards* throughout later chapters.

In 1950, Harold Gulliksen's *Theory of Mental Tests,* the then-definitive work on psychometric theory, appeared. At about the same time, the first editions of two seminal textbooks on testing emerged: Lee Cronbach's *Essentials of Psychological Testing* in 1949 and Anne Anastasi's *Psychological Testing* in 1954. (See Figure 1.6.) Both books subsequently appeared in a number of revised editions, but these first editions helped to define a mature field of study. Thus, testing entered the 1960s with a wide array of instruments, established patterns of usage, a well-defined theoretical base, and benchmark publications summarizing all of this.

FIGURE 1.6   Authors of early textbooks on testing: Lee Cronbach and Anne Anastasi.
Source: (left): Stanford University News Service.
(right): Courtesy Jonathan Galente.

Just Yesterday: 1965–2000

Someone reading this book 50 years hence—if anyone does—will, no doubt, chuckle over a period labeled "just yesterday." Nevertheless, at this writing, the 35-year period 1965–2000 is "just yesterday." Much of the period occurred during the lifetime of today's reader. So, it all seems like it just happened. In fact, all of it is still unfolding, before our very eyes. The period merges imperceptibly into the present. Four significant topics appear to characterize the period 1965–2000.

First, test theory has changed dramatically. The period of consolidation essentially summarized what we now call **classical test theory.** The mid-1960s saw the emergence of **item response theory** or "modern test theory," a new set of methods for examining a whole range of issues related to the reliability, scaling, and construction of tests. The onset of the new theoretical approach is perhaps best signaled by the publication of *Statistical Theories of Mental Test Scores* by Frederic Lord and Melvin Novick (1968), that is, just at the beginning of the current period. This book, billed as the successor to Gulliksen's *Theory of Mental Tests,* ushered in a new era in test theory. Throughout the 1970s and continuing to the present, journals and textbooks devoted to testing exploded with applications of item response theory. We will refer to these developments in more detail in subsequent chapters.

Second, the mid-1960s witnessed the origins of both legislative and judicial activism regarding tests, emanating principally but not exclusively from the federal government. Heretofore, testing was not legislated—either for or against. Now, some types of tests were being required by law, while other types of tests, or certain uses of tests, were being prohibited. Uses of tests were challenged in the courts on a host of fronts: for placing students, for employment, for graduation, and in other ways. To say the least, this period of legislative and judicial activism presented a unique set of challenges. We examine specific cases arising within this milieu in Chapter 16.

Third, testing became the subject of widespread public criticism during this period. The criticisms were directed primarily at standardized tests of ability and achievement. Tests of interests, attitudes, and personality were mostly unscathed. During the 50 years before this period, testing was largely viewed as a new, valuable scientific tool. To be sure, there were debates, but they were mostly squabbles within the family, confined to the academic journals in psychology and education.

Key Points Summary 1.10

Significant Features: Just Yesterday

- Emergence of item response theory
- Legislative and judicial activism
- Public criticism of testing
- Influence of computers

Beginning in the mid-1960s, however, criticisms originated outside the field. They also intensified within the field, going much beyond the squabble stage. The barrage of criticism came in three main forms. First, several popular works with catchy titles appeared. Representative of this genre were such books as *The Brain Watchers* (Gross, 1962) and *The Tyranny of Testing* (Hoffman, 1962). Some of these critiques amounted to petty nitpicking. Gallons of ink were spilled over the 46 different ways one could interpret a given multiple-choice item. This made for great reading, and it was a constant irritant to test authors and publishers. These works had little practical effect on the development or use of tests. However, they did begin to raise questions in the public consciousness about the validity of tests. The second type of criticism was related to racial/ethnic differences in test scores. This was part of the same cloth as the legal and judicial issues mentioned earlier. This type of criticism stimulated an enormous amount of research on test bias, a topic we take up in detail in Chapters 6 and 16. The third type of criticism was the most sweeping. It essentially said that tests were getting at the wrong kinds of things. Multiple-choice achievement tests were missing important dimensions of student development. Even worse, it was claimed, the use of such tests encouraged the wrong kinds of teaching and learning habits. Intelligence tests, in addition to being biased, were not really measuring important mental abilities or, at least, were overlooking many of these abilities. If you like controversy, testing is a good field to be in today! Subsequent chapters will help us sort through all of these criticisms and examine how to analyze them.

Fourth, computers have pervasively influenced contemporary testing. It may come as a surprise to today's reader, but this influence is very recent. The roots of testing, its flowering, and its period of consolidation all preceded the computer age. However, in the last 30 to 40 years much about the current practice of testing has changed as a result of computers. We reserve the telling of this tale to our discussion of major forces influencing testing in the next section.

And Now: 2000–Present

To say that we are writing a history of the present is an oxymoron. It is also a very dangerous one. Mistaking a temporary blip for a major trend, or having a blindspot for the emergence of a truly significant trend can make one look foolish. Nevertheless, we conclude this sketch of the history of testing by identifying what appear to be notable developments in the current scene. We identify three such developments, prefacing the discussion by noting that the four trends from the previous period are still very much alive, and noting that what we label as current developments are outcroppings from the previous period.

First, there is the *explosive increase* in the number and diversity of tests. Every day brings the announcement of new instruments or revisions in existing editions. This growth phenomenon seems to be affecting all areas of psychological and educational testing. A notable subdivision of the activity occurs in statewide assessment programs, driven primarily by the recent *No Child Left Behind Act* (NCLB), implemented in 2002. As a result, in effect every state is now a test developer/publisher. But we are also witnessing a profusion of new tests of personality, various disorders, and mental abilities. Even cataloging all of the new entries has become a nearly impossible task, and evaluating them in a timely fashion presents a daunting challenge.

This meteoric growth emphasizes the need for proficiency in using sources of information about tests—precisely the topic of our next chapter. It also underscores the need to be competent in evaluating the plethora of new tests, competence we aspire to develop in Chapters 3–6.

Second is the pervasive influence of *managed care*. Of course, managed care did not start in 2000, but it was unheard of until the latter part of the previous period. It is now one of the most influential forces in clinical practice. Managed care exerts pressure on testing in several ways. It calls for more focused testing: Don't use a two-hour, omnibus battery if you can get by with a 15-minute more focused test. Managed care also demands careful links between diagnosis and treatment, on the one hand, and between treatment and outcomes, on the other hand. Therefore, the test results should point to treatment; and treatment outcomes should be documented. In practice, that means repeated use of a test to show improvement: defined as change in test score. Managed care has numerous other impacts, but we mention only those that are most relevant for testing.

The third and fourth areas of development both relate to computers but in very different ways. The next section (Major Forces) traces the long-term influence of computers on testing. We outline these latest developments there, noting here only that they relate to the great increase in *online administration and reporting* of tests and to the development of *computer programs that simulate human judgment* in the analysis of test responses. Both of these recent developments are revolutionizing certain aspects of the testing enterprise.

Major Forces

There is an alternative to chronology for viewing the history of testing. We can examine the major forces, trends, or recurring themes that helped create the field and brought it to the present. This is a riskier approach than the chronological one because we may overlook a significant trend or misjudge the influence of a force, hence offering easy prey to the critic. It is difficult to overlook a chronological period. However, for providing the new student with insights, this second approach may be more fruitful. Hence, we will take the risk. We identify here *six major forces* that have shaped the field of testing as we know it today.

The Scientific Impulse

The first major force influencing the development of testing is the scientific impulse. This force has prevailed throughout the history of testing. The writings of Galton, E. L. Thorndike, Cattell, Binet, and the other founders are replete with references to the need to measure scientifically. Educators, too, hoped that the development and application of "new-type" tests would make the educational enterprise scientific. The subtitle of Binet and Simon's 1905 article refers to "the necessity of establishing a scientific diagnosis." The opening sentence of Thorndike's (1904) introduction to the theory of mental measurement states that "experience

> **Key Points Summary 1.11**
> *Major Forces in the History of Testing*
>
> - The Scientific Impulse
> - Concern for the Individual
> - Practical Applications
> - Statistical Methodology
> - The Rise of Clinical Psychology
> - Computers

has sufficiently shown that the facts of human nature can be made the material for quantitative science" (p. v). This concern for being scientific, along with the concern for scorer reliability, motivated development of early achievement tests. Finally, the field of clinical psychology, which we will treat more fully and which has been one of the primary fields of application for testing, has resolutely proclaimed its allegiance to a scientific approach. Many other professions—for example, medicine, law, and social work—have emphasized practice. Clinical psychology, however, has always maintained that it was part science and part practice, utilizing what the field calls the *scientist-practitioner model* (see Baker & Benjamin, 2000).

Concern for the Individual

Testing has grown around an intense interest in the individual. This orientation is perhaps inevitable since testing deals with individual differences. This is part of the "differential perspective" we referenced earlier. Recall that one strand in the immediate background for establishing the roots of testing was the upsurge in concern for the welfare of the mentally ill. Many, though not all, of the practical applications mentioned later related to concern for individuals. Binet's work aimed to identify individuals who could profit more from special schools than from regular schools. Wechsler's first test aimed to give a fairer measure of intelligence for adults. The original SATs were intended to eliminate or minimize any disadvantage students from less affluent secondary schools might have in entering college. Vocational interest measures aimed to help individualize job selection. Of course, there were exceptions to this pattern. Furthermore, in retrospect, one might question whether certain applications actually did help the individual. However, in reading a fair selection of test manuals and the professional literature of testing throughout its history, one is struck by the frequent references to improving the lot of individuals.

Practical Applications

Virtually every major development in testing resulted from work on a practical problem. Binet tried to solve a practical problem for the Parisian schools. Wechsler wanted a better test for his adult clinical patients. The MMPI aimed to help in the diagnosis of patients at one hospital. The SAT emerged as a cooperative venture among colleges to select students from diverse secondary school experiences. Prototypes of the first group-administered intelligence tests and personality inventories developed around the need to process large numbers of military personnel in World War I. To be sure, we can find exceptions to the pattern. In some instances, notable developments resulted from theoretical considerations. However, the overall pattern seems quite clear: Testing has developed in response to practical needs. If you like the applied side of psychology, you should like the field of testing. Although our Chapters 3–6 may seem abstract, the issues treated there all arise from practical needs.

Statistical Methodology

The development of testing has an intriguing, interactive relationship with the development of statistical methodology. One ordinarily thinks of this as a one-way street: Testing borrows methods from statistics. However, a number of statistical methods were invented specifically in response to developments in testing. The methods were then widely adopted in other fields. The first example was the display of bivariate data, invented by Galton. To further this work, Galton induced the English mathematician Karl Pearson to create the correlation coefficient. Spearman then spun off his rank-order version of the correlation. More important, in crafting his theory of intelligence, Spearman worked out the method of tetrad difference, the conceptual grandparent of modern factor analysis. The great leap forward in factor analysis came with Thurstone's work on primary mental abilities. Many of the further elaborations of factor analysis resulted from the continuing Spearman-Thurstone war of words and data over the fundamental nature of intelligence, an active battlefield to this day. Thus, the history of testing has gone hand-in-glove with the history of at least certain statistical methods.

The Rise of Clinical Psychology

Clinical psychology constitutes one of the major areas of application for testing. In turn, clinical psychology is one of the major areas of the application of psychology. This is particularly true if we construe the term *clinical* broadly to include counseling psychology, school psychology, and the applied side of neuropsychology. On the one hand, persons in clinical practice have needed, pressed for, and helped to create a plethora of tests. On the other hand, as new tests have arisen, those in clinical practice have utilized them. For brief histories of clinical psychology, see Phares and Trull (1997), Nietzel, Bernstein, and Milich (1998), Todd and Bohart (1994) or almost any other introduction to the field. For a more in-depth study, although it is limited to the years before 1970, see Reisman (1976).

The founding of clinical psychology is generally credited to Lightner Witmer. As was true for so many of the early psychologists, Witmer received his advanced training from Wundt. Hence, he was steeped in the methodology of psychophysics. By agreeing to treat the famous "case of a chronic bad speller"—what, no doubt, we would today call a learning disability—he turned the methods of the psychology laboratory toward the treatment of a specific case. This occurred in 1896. Witmer went on to open the first psychological clinic, give the first course in clinical psychology (both at the University of Pennsylvania), and establish a journal devoted to clinical psychology. Whatever tests were available at the time, no matter how crude, guided diagnosis and treatment.

The early history of clinical psychology reads much like the early history of testing: the Binet, the Rorschach, and so on. As new tests came along, clinicians used them. In many instances, it was clinicians who developed the tests. Clinical psychologists participated actively in the military during World War I and World War II. Following World War II, the federal government invested heavily in the training of clinical psychologists. This led to explosive growth of the profession. With that growth came growth in the use of tests and the need for newer tests. This reciprocal relationship continues today. In terms of absolute numbers of tests used, the field of education leads the world of testing. In terms of the dizzying array of various types of tests available today, the clinical field (broadly conceived) has been most influential.

Computers

Computers have profoundly influenced the development of testing. As previously noted, this is a very recent phenomenon. The electronic computer was invented in 1946 and became commercially available in 1951. However, mainframe computers were not in widespread use until the 1960s. Desktop models first appeared around 1980 and proliferated beginning in the mid-1980s. Thus, virtually all of the applications of computer technology to testing occurred only in the most recent historical stage we sketched earlier.

To tell the story of computers' effect on testing, we need first to distinguish between scanners and computers. There is much confusion on this point. A **scanner** is an electrical or electronic device that counts marks on a test answer sheet. The machine is sometimes called a mark-sense scanner or reader. Despite popular reference to "computer answer sheets," answer sheets are not put into a computer. They are put into a scanner. The output from the scanner may (or may not) be input to a computer.

The earliest widely used scanner was the IBM 805 machine, which appeared in 1937 (see Figure 1.7). It was a bulky affair, about the size of an office desk. A clerk inserted answer sheets one-by-one into a slot in the machine. The machine worked by counting completed electrical circuits. Answer sheets had to be marked with graphite pencils because graphite was a good electrical conductor. An answer key told the machine where to look for correct answers. A graphite mark in the correct (keyed) spot on the answer sheet completed the circuit and tallied a count for the test score. The output was a simple number—the count of completed circuits—for the answer sheet. No computer was used; in fact, computers had not yet been

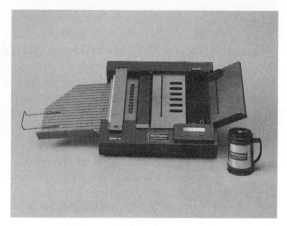

FIGURE 1.7 Pictures of IBM 805 and a modern, small-scale scanner, NCS Pearson OpScan® optical mark read (OMR) scanner.

Source: (left): Courtesy of IBM Archives. (right): Courtesy NCS Pearson.

invented. The IBM 805 was substantially more efficient and accurate than hand-scoring a test record. By today's standards, it truly was a dinosaur.

Today's typical scanner works by counting beams of light, either transmitted or reflected. The scanner shoots beams of light at the bubble targets on the answer sheet. A key tells the scanner where to look for marks. Any dark mark—pencil, ballpoint pen, and so on—will work. The scanner counts light beams either passing through the sheet or bouncing off the dark marks. Scanners of this type came into use in the 1950s and were being used routinely in the 1960s. See Baker (1971, 1993) for historical details.

Small models of scanners are now available at most colleges and schools, in clinics, businesses, and other agencies. High-powered versions used by test publishers, government agencies, and corporations specializing in scanning can process 150 answer sheets per minute (9,000/hr). Along with increases in speed came increases in the diversity of documents handled by scanners. Now, entire test booklets, not just stand-alone answer sheets, can be processed, although the stand-alone answer sheet is the norm. It is still the case that the basic output from the scanner is a count or record of marks. In some cases, the count is simply printed on the answer document. In other cases, the count, as well as the placement of each mark, is converted to some electronic medium such as magnetic tape or disk. This electronic record can be input to a computer.

Will answer sheets and scanners become tomorrow's dinosaurs? Quite possibly. We are already seeing examinees input answers directly to a computer from a keyboard. This is being done in classrooms, clinics, human resource offices, and even in centers located in malls. Furthermore, with improvements in voice recognition, answers to test questions (delivered, for example, over phone lines) can now be spoken. The spoken words are decoded and scored by comparison with acceptable answer templates. No doubt, additional technological wonders lie just ahead.

Key Points Summary 1.12
The Computer-Testing Relationship

- Statistical Processing
- Score Reporting
- Test Administration

Now we move on to computers. There are three major aspects to the relationship between computers and testing. There is an historical sequence to these aspects, but they differ more in character than in temporal order. Moreover, although there is an historical sequence, it is cumulative. That is, once a phase was entered, it stayed with the field. A new phase added to rather than replaced the earlier phase.

In the *first* phase, computers simply aided in *statistical processing* for test research. This phase began almost as soon as computers became commercially available. This was a tremendous boon to testing. It allowed for much larger research programs and routine use of sophisticated methodology. This type of development continues apace today. Desktop computers permit nearly every researcher to perform analyses in mere seconds, which in the past would have required entire teams of researchers months to perform. In later exercises in this book you will easily perform computer analyses that would have been considered a master's thesis 40 years ago.

In the *second* phase of the computer–testing relationship, computers prepared *reports of test scores*. This began with very simple reports. These simple reports were particularly useful for large-scale testing programs. A computer program would determine raw scores (e.g., number of right answers) using input from a scanner, convert raw scores into normed scores, and print out lists of examinee names and scores. Previously, all these operations had to be performed by hand. Computer printed reports of this type came into widespread use in the early 1960s. By today's standards, such reports were primitive: they featured all capital letters, all the same size type, carbon paper copies, and so on. At the time, they were wonders.

The later stages of this phase evolved naturally from the earlier, simple reports. Test developers gained expertise in programming skill. They also saw the creative possibilities of computer-based reports. By the early 1970s, we began to see a profusion of ever more elaborate computer-generated reports. Printer capabilities also exploded. Graphic displays and variations in type style now accompanied numerical information, the staple of earlier reports.

A major development in this phase was preparation of **narrative reports.** Reports of test performance were no longer confined to numbers. Performance might now be described with simple words or even continuous narrative, as if written by a professional psychologist. We explain how such reports are prepared in Chapter 3, and we sprinkle examples of actual reports throughout later chapters.

Developments along these lines continue today. Some readers of this text will likely contribute to new and improved reports of this sort.

The *third* phase of the computer–testing relationship deals with *test administration* by computer. From the test developer's perspective, there are two distinctly different types of test administration by computer. The examinee may not be aware of the difference. The first type, computer-based test administration, simply presents on a computer screen (the video monitor) the test questions very much as they appear in a printed booklet. Just put the test questions in a text file and have them pop up on the screen. The examinee inputs an answer on the keyboard. Nothing very exciting here, but it is paperless.

The second type, **computer-adaptive testing,** is revolutionary. Here the computer not only presents the items but also selects the next item based on the examinee's previous responses. We can illustrate simply with an arithmetic test. The screen presents you with an item, say, 26×179. If you answer correctly, the computer selects a harder item from its "bank" of test items, say, $1,372 \div 86$. Get that right and it moves to a still harder item. If you got the first item wrong, the computer moves you to an easier item, say, $38 + 109$. You get moved back and forth until the computer "decides" that it has a pretty accurate fix on your level of arithmetic ability. Hence, computer-adaptive testing is also called tailored-testing. The selection of items is tailored, like a suit, to the individual examinee. As you can imagine, much research must go into development of such computer adaptive testing for it to work properly. The research depends heavily on the item response theory mentioned earlier. This is one of the most rapidly growing areas of testing today. In subsequent chapters, we will explore some of the theories and methods underlying computer-adaptive testing.

This third phase of computer applications is now entering a new arena. In the recent past, the completion of tests online has become common. In one field, vocational interest assessment, online completion of inventories and reporting of scores are becoming standard. Other areas of application are not far behind. The main issue here is not so much the completion of the test but the delivery of test information (reports—many quite elaborate) to individuals without any training in interpreting that information and possibly without ready access to professional advice. As we will see in later chapters, interpretation of test information is not always a simple matter. Psychology has always emphasized the need for appropriate training in the interpretation of test information. Online reporting, quite apart from administration, creates a whole new scenario. For a useful overview of these emerging issues, see Naglieri et al. (2004).

Finally, there is the emerging application of what is called automated scoring. This means a computer program has been developed to simulate human judgment in the scoring of such products as essays, architectural plans, and medical diagnoses. Take, for example, an essay written by a college student. Typically, it would be scored (graded) by a faculty member. In very important cases, two or three faculty members might grade it, with the grades being averaged. With automated scoring, a computer program grades the essay! Such programs, introduced just within the past few years, are now being used in place of "human raters" for scoring of essays and other such products in large-scale testing programs. We describe these developments in more detail in Chapter 6. We simply note here that this is a "new ball game"— one likely to see substantial growth within the next decade with ever-wider areas of application. How about, for example, the computer scoring of responses to the Rorschach inkblot test?

TRY IT! ....

To try a simple computer-adaptive test, go to this website: http://edres.org/scripts/cat

> Click "Let's Get Started," then follow the directions. You do not need to complete the entire test. Just do a few test items and you will get the idea.

> Bookmark this website. You will use it again later.

....

A Final Word on Forces

In this section we have included only forces that affected most, if not all, types of tests. There have been other forces and trends largely restricted to one or a few types of tests. For example, cognitive psychology has affected intelligence testing. The accountability movement has affected achievement tests. We reserve treatment of these more restricted influences to the chapters on specific types of tests, for example, cognitive psychology in Chapter 7 and accountability in Chapter 11.

By Way of Definition

The final method for introducing the world of testing is by way of definition. What exactly do we mean by the term *test* or *testing*? From a strictly academic perspective, this would ordinarily be the first way to introduce a field. However, it is also a very dry, boring way to start. Thus, we preferred to begin with some other avenues of entry. Perhaps more important, having considered the other issues treated so far, we are now in a better position to reflect on some alternative definitions and to appreciate the differences in various sources.

According to the *Oxford English Dictionary* (*OED;* Simpson & Weiner, 1989), the word "test" comes from an Old French word, with the earliest recorded use in English being by Chaucer in 1368. In its origin, it meant a cup used for smelting gold or silver ore, perhaps an apropos reference for some high-stakes testing today. More to the point, the *OED* gives as one definition of test "the process or an instance of testing the academic, mental, physiological, or other qualities and conditions of a human subject" (Vol. 17, p. 826). This is not very helpful because it says, essentially, that a test is what you use when testing.

The glossary of the authoritative *Standards for Educational and Psychological Tests* (AERA et al., 1999) gives the following rather unwieldy definition for a test: "An evaluative device or procedure in which a sample of an examinee's behavior in a specified domain is obtained and subsequently evaluated and scored using a standardized process" (p. 183). Similar to the circularity of the *OED,* the same source defines psychological testing as "any procedure that involves the use of tests or inventories to assess particular psychological characteristics of an individual" (p. 180).

We referred earlier to the classic textbooks by Anastasi and Cronbach, both of which helped to define the field of testing in its period of consolidation. It is useful to examine their definitions of a test. Anastasi defined a test as "an objective and standardized measure of a sample of behavior" (Anastasi, 1954, p. 22). Cronbach wisely and candidly noted that "there is no fully satisfactory definition." He then goes on to say, "Perhaps the following definition is broad enough to cover the procedures with which this book is concerned: A test is a systematic procedure for observing behavior and describing it with the aid of numerical scales or fixed categories" (Cronbach, 1990, p. 32).

Can we abstract from all of this some common elements? There seem to be six common elements in what we mean by a "test" in the context of the behavioral sciences. First, a test is some type of *procedure or device*. All agree on that point. It may be helpful for us to add that a test is a procedure or device that yields information. Perhaps that is too obvious to state, but stating it will help later discussions. Hence, we add this item as a second point: a test yields *information*. Third, the procedure or device yields information about *behavior*. This aspect of the definition is what sets a test apart from, say, physical measurements such as height and weight or medical tests such as those used to detect a viral condition.

The contemporary reader pauses at this reference to "behavior." At least in ordinary language, behavior refers to some externally observable action, such as throwing a ball, punching someone, or delivering a speech. However, it is obvious that many tests are simply asking questions. Here are sample test questions: "Do you like people?" "What do you see in this inkblot?" "What is the capitol of Nebraska?" In what sense do the answers to these questions constitute behavior? Of course, we could construe "behavior" to mean anything a person does, including what the person thinks or knows. But that does seem to be stretching use of the word "behavior." The explanation for this usage probably goes back to the reign of behaviorism when it was unfashionable to talk about cognitive processes or anything "mental." In fact, most of the definitions we have presented here were originally formulated at that time and have been carried forward. However, we are much more comfortable with cognitive processes and mental functions today. We do not feel compelled to subsume them under the term behavior. Hence, for our purposes, we will expand the object of testing to include *behavior and cognitive processes.*

Fourth, many definitions emphasize that the test yields information only about a *sample* of behavior. When testing, we do not ordinarily take an exhaustive census of all of a person's behavior or cognitive processes. Rather, we examine a sample of the behavior or cognitive processes, often a rather small sample. This notion will become crucial in our consideration of reliability and validity. Fifth, a test is a *systematic, standardized* procedure. This is one of the most distinctive characteristics of a test. This characteristic differentiates a test from such sources of information as an informal interview or anecdotal observations—both of which may be useful sources of information, but they are not tests.

We need to digress at this point to clarify a potentially confusing matter of terminology. There are *three* uses of the term **standardized** in the world of testing. First, when that term is used in the definition of testing, it refers to uniform procedures for administering and scoring. There are definite, clearly specified methods for administering the test, and there are rules for scoring the test. It is essential that the test be

> ### Key Points Summary 1.13
> ### *Elements in the Definition of "Test"*
>
> - Process or Device
> - Yields Information
> - Behavior or Cognitive Processes
> - Sample of. . .
> - Standardized
> - Quantified

administered and scored according to these procedures. Second, in other contexts, standardized means that the test has norms—for example, national norms based on thousands of cases. In fact, the process of collecting these normative data is often referred to as the standardization program for the test. Clearly, this is a different meaning of the term *standardized* than the first meaning. One can have a test with fixed directions and scoring procedures without having any type of norms for the test. A third meaning, encountered especially in media reporting and public discussions, equates standardized testing with group-administered, machine-scored, multiple-choice tests of ability and achievement. For example, a newspaper headline may report "Local students improve on standardized tests" or "Cheating on standardized tests alleged." Or a friend may say, referring to performance on the SAT or ACT college admissions test, "I don't do very well on standardized tests." This third meaning is obviously much more restrictive than either of the first two. It is important for the student of psychological testing to distinguish among these three meanings of the term *standardized*.

A sixth and final element in the various definitions is some reference to *quantification or measurement*. That is, we finally put the information in numerical form. This element is quite explicit in some sources and seems to be implied in the others. The quantification may occur in a very crude form or in a highly sophisticated manner. For example, a crude quantification may involve forming two groups (depressed and nondepressed or competent and not competent). A more sophisticated kind of measurement may involve a careful scaling akin to measurement of height or weight.

Various sources differ on one matter of the definition of "test." This is the issue of the extent to which testing is evaluative. Some of the definitions stop with the information; other definitions include reference to an evaluative dimension, an inference or conclusion drawn from the information. Some books handle this point by distinguishing among the terms *test*, *assessment*, and *evaluation*. For example, some authors imply differences among these three statements: Abigail was tested with the Stanford-Binet. Abigail was assessed with the Stanford-Binet. Abigail was evaluated with the Stanford-Binet. In many sources, the three terms are used interchangeably. For example, the *Standards* (AERA et al., 1999) seem to merge the terms, defining a "test" as "an evaluative device" (p. 183) and "psychological testing" as "any procedure . . . to assess" (p. 180). We do not take a hard-and-fast position on this matter. We simply note that various sources handle the matter differently.

From the foregoing discussion, we formulate the following definition: **A test is a standardized process or device that yields information about a sample of behavior or cognitive processes in a quantified manner.**

Summary

1. We classify tests into five major categories: mental ability, achievement, personality, interests, and neuropsychological tests, with several subdivisions within some of the major categories. Use the acronym MAPIN to remember these categories.

2. Tests may also be characterized according to whether they are (a) paper-and-pencil or performance, (b) speed or power, (c) individually or group administered, (d) dependent on maximum or typical performance, and (e) norm-referenced or criterion-referenced in their interpretation.

3. The principal uses of tests include clinical, educational, personnel, and research.

4. Four important assumptions undergird the testing enterprise:
    *   That people have traits and that differences between people in these traits are important.
    *   That we can quantify these traits.
    *   That the traits have some reasonable degree of stability.
    *   That our quantification of the traits bears some relationship to actual behavior.

5. The three fundamental questions in testing relate to:
    *   Reliability—the stability of a measure.
    *   Validity—what a test really measures.
    *   Norms—the framework for interpreting test scores.

    We study these topics in depth in Chapters 3, 4, and 5. How tests are developed, covered in Chapter 6, and practical concerns such as time and cost are also important considerations.

6. We identified seven major periods in the history of testing. Understanding the dominant themes of these periods provides perspective on current issues in testing. The periods and the titles we gave them are:
    *   Up to 1840   Remote Background
    *   1840–1880   Setting the Stage
    *   1880–1915   The Roots
    *   1915–1940   Flowering
    *   1940–1965   Consolidation
    *   1965–2000   Just Yesterday
    *   2000–present   And Now

7. We identified six major forces influencing the development of testing as the field currently exists: the scientific impulse, concern for the individual, practical applications, statistical methodology, the rise of clinical psychology, and computers.

8. We developed the following six-element definition of a test: *A test is a standardized process or device that yields information about a sample of behavior or cognitive processes in a quantified manner.*

Key Terms

achievement tests
Binet, Alfred
Cattell, James McKeen
classical test theory
computer-adaptive
   testing
criterion-referenced
   interpretation
differential perspective
Galton, Francis
group test
individual test

item response theory
maximum performance
mental ability tests
narrative reports
neuropsychological tests
norm-referenced
   interpretation
norms
objective personality
   tests
paper-and-pencil test
performance test

power test
projective techniques
reliability
scanner
Spearman, Charles
speed (or speeded) test
standardized test
typical performance
validity
vocational interest
   measures

Exercises

1. Many university libraries will have Cattell's 1890 article in hard copy (see p. 24). Or you can access the article at http://psychclassics.yorku.ca. Find the article and check the list of tests described therein. What do you think of these tests as predictors of college success?

2. If you happen to be taking a history course at the same time as you are using this text, try to relate something in your history course to the periods of development in the history of testing. Do you observe any trends or forces in your history course that might have influenced developments in testing?

3. Most universities and even many departments within larger universities have their own scanners for processing test answer sheets. See if you can locate a scanner and watch it in operation. What is the "output" from the scanner?

4. Think of tests you have taken other than classroom tests. Categorize each test according to these distinctions: (a) paper-and-pencil versus performance, (b)

speed versus power, (c) individually or group administered, (d) dependent on maximum or typical performance, and (e) norm-referenced or criterion-referenced in interpretation.

5. Use the website http://psychclassics.yorku.ca/ to access Alfred Binet's classic work *New Methods for the Diagnosis of the Intellectual Level of Subnormals,* written in 1905. (Notice the use of terms such as imbecile and idiot. These would be considered derogatory terms today but were standard, clinical descriptors at that time.) From reading just the first few paragraphs of Binet's work, what do you think he was trying to do?

6. Access this website: http://www.nces.ed.gov/nationsreportcard for results of the National Assessment of Educational Progress (NAEP). How many grades are tested by NAEP? Reports are available for how many school subjects? Access the report for one subject of interest to you. What are some of the major findings for that subject?

7. Here are three traits: height, intelligence, friendliness. In which of these traits do you think people differ the most?

8. Recall our observation that many tests are known mainly by their initials. See if you can remember the full names for each of these sets of initials. (Page numbers tell where to find the full names.)

     GRE (p. 7) _____

     EDI (p. 7) _____

     SII (p. 8) _____

     LSAT (p. 365) _____

     BDI-II (p. 7) _____

9. Many of the classical documents in the history of testing (e.g., those of Darwin, Galton, Cattell, and Binet) can be viewed at this website: http://www.psychclassics.yorku.ca/. Check it out. Skim some of the documents to get a flavor for how the authors approached their topics.

10. To see an interesting graphical presentation of the relationships among people working on early intelligence tests, check this website: http://www.indiana.edu/~intell. Click on Interactive Map. How does Piaget fit in the map? How about Anastasi? You can access brief biographies of most of the people mentioned in our description of the history of testing by clicking on a name in the interactive map.

CHAPTER 2

Sources of Information about Tests

Objectives

1. Identify the nine major sources of information about tests.

2. Evaluate the strengths and weaknesses of each source.

3. Determine where you can find hard copy of sources in a local library.

4. Become proficient in accessing electronic versions of the sources.

Two Common Problems Requiring Information about Tests

One of the most common practical problems in the world of psychological testing is finding information about a particular test. The problem arises in two contexts. First, one hears about a test, knows little about it, and needs information about its characteristics. The following are examples of this first type of problem.

- A journal article refers to the ABC Personality Inventory. You are not familiar with this test, but you want to know what validity information is available for it.
- You are a school psychologist. You receive a report from another school about a student who has transferred to your school. The report includes scores from the Pennsylvania Nonverbal Intelligence test. You need to know about the norms for this test.
- You see an advertisement in a professional journal for the Hanson Index of Life Stress. You wonder if this test has been reviewed anywhere.

The second type of problem requiring test information is quite different. One sometimes needs to determine what tests might be available to serve a particular purpose. The following are examples of this type of problem.

- You are working in the Human Resources Department of a major corporation. You need a test of manual dexterity for selecting certain types of employees. Are there tests already developed for this purpose?
- You are a high school counselor serving on a school's Test Committee. The committee is looking for a diagnostic reading test. What tests should the committee review to reach a decision?
- Your research in children's mathematical development leads you to think that quantitative ability may be related to creative thinking ability. What tests of creative thinking should you consider using in your research project?

Both types of problems—finding information about a single test and obtaining a list of tests that might be used for some purpose—are very common. Furthermore psychologists encounter the problems with increasing frequency as the number of tests proliferates. In an earlier era, one could be reasonably familiar with a good fraction of the available tests. That is no longer true. Dozens of new or revised tests appear every year. Some of the databases we examine in this chapter contain over 10,000 tests. Hence, there is great need to be able to get information about tests. A recent report from the American Psychological Association (Turner, DeMers, Fox, & Reed, 2001) emphasized the professional responsibility to be competent in test selection. In fact, this report on test user qualifications lists "selection of appropriate tests" immediately after consideration of reliability, validity, and norms among the knowledge and skills test users should possess. Skill in selection and evaluation of tests has

---

Key Points Summary 2.1

Two Common Questions about Tests

1. How do I get information about a particular test?
2. What tests are available for a particular purpose?

become more important as the number of new and revised tests has proliferated in recent years. Fortunately, there are excellent sources of information to help answer these types of questions. This chapter describes these sources of information and examines their strengths and shortcomings.

Once you have identified a specific test, you will want to examine the test itself and its manuals. Initial inspection is usually based on what is called a **specimen set** or **examination kit** that contains one copy of the most basic materials for the test. These materials usually include the test booklet or other test stimuli, the directions for administering, documents for recording answers, and a technical manual. The sources of information covered in this chapter give information about tests from some source outside the test itself. Appendix A gives suggestions for conducting a review of the actual test materials.

All the remaining chapters in this book utilize the sources presented in this chapter. Specifically, you are often directed to these sources to find examples of topics treated in the other chapters. For example, as we discuss norms in the next chapter, you will be asked to find examples of norms. As we discuss intelligence tests in Chapter 8, you will be asked to find information about these tests in the sources introduced here. Hence, it is important to become proficient in using these sources now.

We identify nine major sources of information about tests: comprehensive lists of tests, systematic reviews of published tests, electronic listings, special purpose collections, books about single tests, textbooks on testing, professional journals, publishers' catalogs, and other users of tests. In the following sections we describe each of these sources of information. Then we compare their strengths and weaknesses, especially in relation to the two common problems identified above.

Special Note: Before reading the following two sections, you may wish to take a peek at the third section on Electronic Listings (p. 52). Much of what is covered in the next two sections can be accessed through the Internet. We present the *hard copy*

Key Points Summary 2.2

Nine Major Sources of Information about Tests

1. Comprehensive Lists of Tests
2. Systematic Reviews of Published Tests
3. Electronic Listings
4. Special Purpose Collections
5. Books about Single Tests
6. Textbooks on Testing
7. Professional Journals
8. Publishers' Catalogs
9. Other Users of Tests

treatment first because the hard copies preceded the electronic versions historically and establish the basic format for the electronic versions.

Comprehensive Lists of Tests

There are three comprehensive lists of tests. All three sources are designed to provide basic, descriptive information about tests. For example, the sources identify a test's purpose, whether it has subtests, the administration time, the publisher, and so on. These sources do *not* evaluate the quality of the test.

Two of these comprehensive lists include only published tests: *Tests in Print* and *Tests*. One of the sources includes only unpublished tests: *The Directory of Unpublished Mental Measures.*

Tests in Print VI (Murphy, Plake, Impara, & Spies, 2002), popularly known as **TIP,** attempts to list all tests that are commercially published in English. TIP contains entries for approximately 3,000 tests. Now in its sixth edition, TIP was first published in 1961. That first edition was prepared by Oscar Krisen (O. K.) Buros, who might be called the patron saint of information about tests. He also originated the *Mental Measurements Yearbook* (MMY) treated in the next section. Figure 2.1 provides a sample entry from TIP. Examine the figure to determine the type of information supplied. TIP also indexes all of the reviews appearing in the MMYs, which are described later. However, not every test appearing in TIP has been reviewed in one of the MMYs.

The second comprehensive list of tests is *Tests: A Comprehensive Reference for Assessments in Psychology, Education and Business,* 5th edition (Maddox, 2003). This publication is usually referred to simply as *Tests*. Its earlier editions, edited by D.J. Keyser and R.C. Sweetland, appeared in 1983, 1986, and 1991. Like TIP, *Tests* includes only measures that are published and in English. Figure 2.2 offers a sample entry from *Tests*. Examine the figure to see what information it provides.

The third comprehensive list of tests is the *Directory of Unpublished Experimental Mental Measures* (Goldman & Mitchell, 2003). As suggested by its title, this source, in contrast to TIP and Tests, focuses on unpublished measures; it does not include tests available from commercial publishers. Published by the American Psychological Association, the most recent Directory, Volume 8, contains 2,768 entries. It also contains a cumulative listing of tests included in the previous volumes. Entries for Volume 8 were obtained by scanning 36 journals for the period 1996–2000. Figure 2.3 provides a sample entry.

TRY IT! ....

Check your local library to see which of the comprehensive listings of tests are available. Make a record of access information for use in later exercises.

Source	*Location*
TIP	_____
Tests	_____
Directory of Unpublished…	_____

---

[200]
Assessment of Career Decision Making.
Purpose: Designed to "assess a student's career decision-making style and progress on three career decision-making tasks."
Population: Adolescents and adults.
Publication Date: 1985.
Acronym: ACDM.
Scores: 6 scales: Decision-Making Styles (Rational, Intuitive, Dependent), Decision-Making Tasks (School Adjustment, Occupation, Major).
Administration: Group.
Price Data, 1999: $65 per test kit including 4 test report prepaid mail-in answer sheets and manual (87 pages): $9.50 per test report mail-in answer sheet and scoring service; $35 per manual.
Time: (40) minutes.
Authors: Jacqueline N. Buck and M. Harry Daniels.
Publisher: Western Psychological Services.
Cross References: For reviews by Bruce J. Eberhardt and Nicholas A. Vacc, see 10:16 (8 references).

TEST REFERENCES

1. Blustein, D. L. (1987). Decision-making styles and vocational maturity: An alternative perspective *Journal of Vocational Behavior. 30,* 61–71.
2. Read, N. O., Ellott, M. R., Escobar, M. D., & Slaney, R. B. (1988). The effects of marital status and motherhood on the career concerns of reentry women *Career Development Quarterly 37,* 46–55.
3. Blustein, D. L., Ellis, M.V., & Dovens, L. E. (1989). The development and validation of a two-dimensional model of the commitment to career choice process. *Journal of Vocational Behavior 35,* 342–378.
4. Marin, P. A. & Spiete, H (1991). A comparison of the effect of two computer-based counseling interventions on the career decidedness of adults. *Career Development Quarterly 39,* 360–371.
5. Reynolds, J. & Gerstan, M. (1991). Learning style characterstics of adult dependent decision makers. Counseling and instructional implication. *Career Development Quarterly 40,*. 145–154.

FIGURE 2.1   Sample entry in *Tests in Print*.
Source: From: Murphy, L. L., Impara, J. C., & Plake, B. S. Tests in Print V. p. 58. Copyright © 1999. With permission of the publisher, Buros Institute of Mental Measurements.

Systematic Reviews

The second major source of information consists of two continuing series that provide systematic reviews of published tests. The reviews contain judgments about the measurement qualities of the tests, as well as expanded descriptions of their purposes and materials. "Measurement qualities" include such features as reliability, validity, norms, and test development procedures: precisely the topics of the next four chapters of this book.

The first and most well known of the systematic reviews is the *Mental Measurements Yearbook.* The most recent edition in this series is the *Sixteenth Mental Measurements Yearbook* (Spies & Plake, 2005). The first edition appeared in 1938. It was a mere 83 pages in comparison with the over 1,000 pages in the current edition. O. K. Buros originated the series. Hence, the publication, in whatever edition, is often referred to simply as "**Buros**" or "Buros's **MMY.**" Buros supervised preparation of the first eight editions in the series. After his death in 1978, the work was carried on by the

---

Attention-Deficit/Hyperactivity Disorder Test (ADHDT)

James E. Gilliam

Copyright: 1995 PRO-ED, Inc.

Population: Ages 3 through 23

Purpose: Identification and evaluation of attention deficit disorders

Description: Multiple-item checklist that is completed by teachers, parents, or others who are knowledgeable about a referred individual. Based on the diagnostic criteria for attention-deficit/hyperactivity disorder of the DSM-IV, the instrument contains, 36 items that describe characteristic behaviors of persons with ADHD. These items comprise three subtests representing the core symptoms necessary for the diagnosis of ADHD: hyperactivity, impulsivity, and inattention. Results are reported in standard scores and percentiles that are interpreted related to degree of severity and probability for males and females.

Format: Rating scale, untimed: 10 minutes

Scoring: Examiner evaluated

Cost: Complete kit (manual, protocols, and storage box) $86.00

FIGURE 2.2   Sample entry from *Tests.*

Source: From: Maddox, T. Tests: A comprehensive reference for assessments in psychology, education, and business (5th ed.). p. 2. Copyright © 2003. With permission of the publisher, Pro-Ed, Inc.

Buros Institute of Mental Measurements at the University of Nebraska–Lincoln. A new edition of MMY is published every three or four years. Actually, the reviewing process is continuous. As reviews are completed, they are made available online even before the next volume of MMY is formally published. The typical review in MMY is prepared by an author who is an expert in the content area treated by the test or by a testing expert. For example, a reading test may be reviewed by a reading specialist, a vocational interest test may be reviewed by a college counselor, or a professor of educational and psychological measurement may review either test.

An MMY review does not follow a rigid format but will typically cover the following topics. First the test's purpose is identified. Next a description of the test materials is given, covering the number and types of items, time limit, mode of administration, number of levels and forms, types of scoring, and manuals available for the test. The review then describes information about the test's validity, reliability, and norms. In these discussions, the test reviewer provides critical comments about the adequacy of these technical characteristics. The review often concludes with a recommendation about possible uses of the test—or a recommendation that the test not be used. More widely used tests may have several reviews provided by different authors.

■ ■ ■

5471

Test Name: BRIEF REASONS FOR LIVING INVENTORY

Purpose: To distinguish suicidal from nonsuicidal prison inmates.

Number of Items: 12

Format: All items are presented.

Reliability: Alpha was .86.

Validity: Correlations with the long version of the scale ranged from .58 to .94 across subscales. Correlations with suicide ideation were significant after control variables were introduced.

Authors: Ivanoff, A., et al.

Article: Fewer reasons for staying alive when you are thinking of killing yourself: The Brief Reasons for Living Inventory.

Journal: *Journal of Psychopathology and Behavioral Assessment,* March 1994, *16*(1), 1–13.

Related Research: Linehan, M. M., et al. (1983). Reasons for staying alive when you are thinking of killing yourself: The Reasons for Living Inventory. *Journal of Consulting and Clinical Psychology, 51,* 276–286.

FIGURE 2.3 Sample entry from *Directory of Unpublished Experimental Mental Measures.*
Source: From: Goldman, B. A., Mitchell, D. F., & Egelson, P. E. Directory of unpublished experimental mental measures (Vol. 7, p. 23). Copyright © 1997 by the American Psychological Association. Reprinted with permission.

Each of the recent MMYs has six useful indexes. The Index of Test Titles is an alphabetic listing of official test titles. The Index of Acronyms provides a list of common abbreviations for tests (e.g., GRE for Graduate Record Examination). The Classified Subject Index lists tests within very broad topical categories, for example, Reading or Fine Arts. A Publisher's Directory and Index includes names and addresses of all publishers whose tests are reviewed. The Index of Names lists all individuals who are test authors or reviewers, or who are in references included in the volume. Finally, the Score Index provides a list of all scores generated by the tests reviewed in the volume.

The second source of test reviews is **Test Critiques.** The most recent volume in this series is *Test Critiques,* Volume XI (Keyser, 2004). Originated by Keyser and Sweetland in 1984, *Test Critiques* is published by Pro-Ed, the same organization that publishes *Tests,* described earlier. The reviews in *Test Critiques* are much the same in scope and character as those in MMY. However, *Test Critiques* does not cover as many tests as MMY. Like MMY, *Test Critiques* provides several useful indexes, including an Index of Test Titles and an Index of Publishers, plus a cumulative index of reviews in all volumes in the series.

> **Key Points Summary 2.3**
>
> *Two Main Sources for Reviews of Tests*
>
> 1. Buros's *Mental Measurements Yearbook* (MMY)
> 2. *Test Critiques*

Electronic Listings

There are three major electronic sources of information about tests. Use of these sources can greatly increase the efficiency of searching for information.

ETS Test Collection on the Web

For many years, the Educational Testing Service has maintained an inventory of tests that has been available in a variety of forms, including special book collections and microfiche. Currently, the most usable form of the collection is Internet accessible on the Web. The current URL is http://sydneyplus.ets.org. If that URL changes, the collection can be accessed with an Internet search for **ETS Test Collection**.

Tests in the ETS Test Collection database can be searched by test title, author, commonly used initials (acronyms), or key word descriptor (i.e., names of variables or topics such as anxiety or creativity), as well as by several other means. Entries in the Test Collection are much like those in TIP and *Tests*, that is, they provide basic descriptive information about a test. Perhaps the most common use of the Test Collection is to identify tests available for a certain variable. Searching on a "descriptor" such as depression will likely yield a list of 20 to 30 tests for this variable. It is also especially helpful when one has only the name of a test (or even just initials for the test) and one needs to know the publisher or author.

Buros Reviews Available Electronically

Reviews in Buros's *Mental Measurements Yearbook*, from the tenth to the current edition, are available electronically in two ways. First, many academic libraries subscribe to a product offered by Ovid Technologies that contains full copies of the reviews. The product allows searches much like those in databases such as PsycInfo. That is, the name of a test is entered, and, if it has been reviewed, the reviews will appear. If a library subscribes to this product, a Buros review can be accessed for no charge.

The Buros Institute of Mental Measurements (BIMM; http://www.unl.edu/buros) also allows for online accession of Buros test reviews but imposes a fee for use of this service (currently $15 per review). An interesting incidental benefit of the BIMM site is that it allows for keyword searching of tests in the inventory of reviews. For example, you can keyword search on "creativity" and get a list of tests related to this construct, along with an indication of whether a Buros review exists for each test.

Key Points Summary 2.4

Two Important Websites to Search for Tests

To access the Buros Institute of Mental Measurements: http://www.unl.edu/buros/

To access the ETS Test Collection: http://sydneyplus.ets.org

TRY IT! ....

Access each of the websites given in this section. If possible, bookmark each of them for easy accession in future exercises. Also, see if your library has the MMY reviews on Ovid. Ask a reference librarian or see the library's listing of electronic databases.

....

Health and Psychosocial Instruments (HaPI)

Health and Psychosocial Instruments, abbreviated HaPI, is a database of descriptions for over 15,000 tests, rating scales, questionnaires, and so on, drawn principally from journal articles in health sciences and psychosocial sciences. The database is prepared by Behavioral Measurements Database Services (BMDS). It is available on CD-ROM from BMDS or online from Ovid Technologies. The HaPI database does not have a hard copy version.

Special Purpose Collections

Special purpose collections provide information about tests within a narrow range of topics. Information in such collections is typically like that in the comprehensive listings described earlier—that is, the special purpose collections provide basic descriptive information. However, in some instances these sources include both the entire test and brief evaluative comments. The special purpose collections often include both published and unpublished instruments. Most typically, they also include an overview of theoretical issues relevant to the area treated by the measures in the collection.

As the quantity and variety of tests have increased, these special purpose collections have provided a valuable adjunct to the more comprehensive but more cumbersome listings previously described. New special purpose collections are appearing all the time. Following is a representative but not exhaustive list of these special purpose collections.

Measuring Self-concept Across the Life Span (Byrne, 1996) is an excellent collection of tests of self-concept organized by age level. Each chapter reviews several tests that the author considers to be among the best measures of self-concept for that age level. The author's reviews are similar in character to those that might appear in MMY or *Test Critiques.*

Measures for Clinical Practice: A Sourcebook (Fischer & Corcoran, 2000) is a two-volume collection of simple paper-and-pencil measures of clinically relevant constructs. The first volume features measures for families, children, and couples. The second volume features measures for other adults.

Measures of Personality and Social Psychological Attitudes (Robinson, Shaver, & Wrightsman, 1991) is a widely cited collection of over 100 measures for such areas as self-concept, locus of control, and alienation. Both published and unpublished measures are included. This volume supersedes Robinson and Shaver (1973). *Scales for the Measurement of Attitudes* (Shaw & Wright, 1967) is also an excellent, though now somewhat dated, collection of scales to measure attitude. Measures for a mind-boggling array of attitudes are treated. The full scales are included, along with brief summaries of reliability, validity, and norms for each scale.

The *Sourcebook of Adult Assessment Strategies* (Schutte & Malouff, 1996) provides a collection of 67 scales organized according to major categories in the *Diagnostic and Statistical Manual of Mental Disorders* (DSM-IV; American Psychiatric Association, 1994). Like the two previously listed collections, this sourcebook includes the entire scale and brief evaluative comments for each scale covered.

Somewhat different than the other sources treated in this section is Newmark's (1996) *Major Psychological Assessment Instruments.* Rather than covering numerous tests, this book includes just ten of the most widely used clinical instruments. Each chapter provides in-depth treatment of one instrument.

Kapes and Whitfield's (2004) *A Counselor's Guide to Career Assessment Instruments,* now in its fourth edition, provides excellent, up-to-date coverage of a host of instruments relevant to the career counseling process. Hersen's (2004) edited volume *Psychological Assessment in Clinical Practice: A Pragmatic Guide* devotes chapters to such areas as substance abuse, eating disorders, and marital dysfunction; each chapter identifies and comments on the widely used instruments within that area. Finally, we mention Lopez and Snyder's (2003) *Positive Psychological Assessment: A Handbook of Models and Measures,* which considers various measures for a host of positive psychological constructs, including, for example, gratitude, empathy, and sense of humor, thus providing a measurement base for the burgeoning area of positive psychology. All of these books illustrate psychologists' attempts to catalog and evaluate measurement instruments in selected areas. They are invaluable sources for both the practitioner and the researcher.

Books about Single Tests

A few tests, very few, are so widely used that they are the subjects of entire books. The books typically present case studies based on the tests, describe test score profiles for certain types of cases, or explore special ways of scoring the tests. Examples are books about the Wechsler intelligence scales (see Chapter 8), the *Minnesota Multiphasic Personality Inventory* (MMPI; see Chapter 13) and the Rorschach Inkblot Test (see Chapter 14). The Wechsler scales have been featured in a number of books. A good example is the book edited by Prifitera, Saklofske, and Weiss (2005) containing advice from a host of experts on the interpretation of WISC-IV.

Dahlstrom, Welsh, and Dahlstrom's (1960, 1972) two-volume work on the MMPI helped establish the standard for book-length treatments about a single test. The work provides numerous case studies for various MMPI profiles. A host of more recent books treats the MMPI-2 (see, e.g., Butcher, 1999; Friedman, Lewak, Nichols, & Webb, 2001). Graham (2000) provides a comprehensive summary of research on the MMPI-2. The Rorschach has been the subject of many books giving detailed case studies and suggestions for coding responses. Lerner (1975) is an excellent example of these types of books. Other examples are Burstein and Loucks (1989) and Gacono and Meloy (1994). Provost (1993) is an example of a book devoted entirely to use of the *Myers-Briggs Type Indicator* (MBTI) in counseling. The book includes numerous case studies with MBTI profiles. Clinical use of the *Thematic Apperception Test* (TAT) and its derivatives is treated in detail in Bellak and Abrams (1997), a book now in its sixth edition. Finally, we note a series of books with titles beginning "Essentials of…" published in recent years by John Wiley & Sons for the most popular tests. Each specific title provides detailed treatment of one test or a group of similar tests, for example, the WAIS-III, MMPI-2, the Millon inventories, and the Rorschach.

Such books can be a rich source of information for individuals who use these tests extensively. The case studies can be fascinating. However, the books generally assume that the reader already has considerable training in test theory and use. These books are not designed for novices. Perhaps more important, there are very few tests for which such extensive treatment is available.

Textbooks on Testing

Textbooks on testing, such as this one, are not intended to be major sources of information about particular tests. The textbooks aid in teaching fundamental concepts about testing (reliability, validity, etc.) and illustrate the types of tests available in various domains. However, in accomplishing the latter step, textbooks about testing become a potentially useful source of information about tests. Nearly all textbooks about testing will include a few examples of intelligence tests, achievement tests, objective personality inventories, projective techniques, and so on. The examples will often, though not always, be chosen because of their frequency of use; occasionally a textbook will include a little-used test because it illustrates an unusual approach. The textbook authors will sometimes include critical commentary about the tests that are used as examples.

Journals

Many journals in the social and behavioral sciences include articles that depend on the use of tests. However, certain journals frequently include articles featuring particular tests or treating the technical aspects of testing. These journals can be important sources of information. Most articles in these journals are not about particular tests but about technical characteristics such as reliability and item analysis. These articles are like advanced topics from the next four chapters in this book. However, these journals sometimes contain test reviews. These journals also contain articles about technical qualities of specific tests, especially when used with a particular population.

The following journals concentrate almost exclusively on testing and measurement:

1. *Psychological Assessment.* One of the official journals of the American Psychological Association, this quarterly publication includes articles on a wide variety of testing issues, especially in the domains of personality and intelligence.

2. *Journal of Personality Assessment.* This bimonthly publication is the official journal of the Society for Personality Assessement. As suggested by the journal's title, it concentrates on tests related to personality.

3. *Educational and Psychological Measurement.* This classic journal covers a wide variety of topics related to testing. The Validity Section in each issue is devoted entirely to studies of the validity of particular tests.

4. *Journal of Educational Measurement.* A quarterly publication of the National Council on Measurement in Education (NCME), this journal concentrates on technical issues related to educational measurement. It sometimes includes test reviews.

5. *Measurement and Evaluation in Counseling and Development.* This journal deals with the use of tests of particular relevance to counselors. It often includes reviews of specific tests.

6. *Applied Measurement in Education.* A quarterly publication, this journal includes articles very similar in character to those in JEM (#4).

7. *Psychometrika.* This is the classic journal for advanced statistical topics related to measurement theory and practice. It is not for the novice in the field.

8. *Educational Measurement: Issues and Practices.* Another quarterly publication of NCME (see #4), this journal presents articles that emphasize practical matters of educational measurement.

9. *Applied Psychological Measurement.* Like *Psychometrika,* this journal treats advanced statistical and methodological issues related to testing. The journal includes special sections called the Computer Program Exchange and Computer Software Reviews.

The following journals concentrate on substantive areas in psychology but often include articles that feature specific tests or general concepts related to testing:

10. *Journal of Applied Psychology.* This bimonthly publication of the American Psychological Association concentrates on applications in human resources and industrial/organization psychology such as personnel selection, performance measurement, training, and work motivation.

11. *Personnel Psychology.* A quarterly publication covering areas similar to those in the *Journal of Applied Psychology.*

12. *Journal of Consulting and Clinical Psychology.* Published bimonthly, this official journal of the American Psychological Association obviously deals with clinical matters, many of which involve the use of tests.

13. *Journal of Counseling and Development.* A quarterly publication of the American Counseling Association, this journal includes many articles on the use of tests in counseling situations.

14. *Journal of Clinical and Experimental Neuropsychology.* This journal deals with research on brain disease, disorders, and dysfunction, often focusing on the place of tests in such research.

15. *Intelligence.* This journal provides many examples of the use of tests to measure intelligence, broadly conceived.

Publishers' Catalogs and Personnel

A key source of information about certain aspects of a test is the publisher's catalog. Obviously, this source is useful only for commercially published tests. The catalog is readily available on request from the publisher and is almost always available online (see Appendix C for publishers' websites). Figure 2.4 contains a catalog entry for a fairly simple test. For some of the more complex tests, a catalog may contain ten pages of material. The test publisher's catalog is the primary source of information about such matters as the current cost of the test, the variety of answer sheets and scoring services available, the most recent edition of the test, and other practical matters.

Major test publishers also have staff members in their home offices and field representatives covering different geographic regions. These individuals can be excellent sources of information about a variety of practical matters relating to a test. They can be contacted by using the publisher indexes in any of the comprehensive lists of tests presented earlier in this chapter. Publishers' websites also facilitate contacting appropriate representatives.

TRY IT!

Check the website for a test publisher listed in Appendix C. Access the site and determine if the publisher's full catalog is available. Also, check with your academic department to see if any test catalogs are available in hard copy. See if you can determine from the website or catalog a person you might contact for information about one of the publisher's tests.

Other Users

Other users of tests may be a helpful source of information. They will obviously know what tests they are currently using. They will often know about similar tests. For example, a school psychologist will know what tests are widely used for diagnosing learning disabilities. College admissions counselors will know what tests are

Be prepared to help the college students you work with...

College Adjustment Scales (CAS)

William D. Anton, PhD, and James R. Reed, PhD

College is a unique experience. Many people consider college an extension of high school and fail to realize that college students can experience psychological problems as well as adjustment problems. The College Adjustment Scales (CAS) is intended primarily for use in college counseling and guidance centers.

- 108 items screen for problems frequently experienced by college students.
- 4-point rating scale.
- Useful in clinical settings with college students as clients.
- Assesses 9 scales: anxiety, depression, suicidal ideation, substance abuse, self-esteem problems, interpersonal problems, family problems, academic problems, and career problems.
- Self-scoring carbonless answer sheet with a profiling area.
- Normative data were collected from 1,146 students enrolled in colleges and universities throughout the United States, and reflect U.S. college enrollment proportions for gender and ethnic groups.

PURPOSE:	Identify psychological and adjustment problems experienced by college students
FOR:	Students ages 17–30 years
ADMIN.:	Individual or group
TIME:	15–20 minutes

Reliability and Validity:

- Internal consistency reliability coefficients range from .80–.92.
- Supporting validity research.

Qualification Level: B

2A-1830-KT	CAS Introductory Kit (includes CAS Manual, 25 Reusable Item Booklets, and 25 Answer Sheets)
	Kit Value: $113.00 Kit Price $105.00
2A-1831-TM	CAS Professional Manual..................................35.00
2A-1832-TB	CAS Reusable Item Booklets (pkg/25) 39.00
2A-1833-AS	CAS Answer Sheets (pkg/25).........................39.00

FIGURE 2.4   Sample entry from a test publisher's catalog.

Source: From: Psychological Assessment Resources, January 2002 Catalog, p. 54. With permission of the publisher.

used for admission to college. Current users of tests in a particular domain can be helpful in quickly developing a list of possible candidates for a particular testing purpose. Of course, test selection is not a simple popularity contest. One needs to apply critical analysis in selecting a test. However, the initial task is often assembling a list of tests to which critical analysis is then applied.

Current users of tests can also be a valuable source of information about peculiar features of a test, peculiarities that are not revealed by even the most meticulous technical scrutiny but only by actual use of the test. For example, the time limit for one subtest in a multi-test battery may be exceptionally stringent or overly generous. Examinees may tend to misunderstand or overlook the directions for one part of a test. Or the norms for a test may be seriously askew. All of these practical matters may become apparent only to the regular user of a test.

Strengths and Shortcomings of the Sources

Each of the sources of information about tests described earlier has strengths and shortcomings. Intelligent and proficient use of these sources requires recognition of these plusses and minuses, described as follows.

The *comprehensive listings* of tests are most effective for casting a broad net to see what tests might be available for a particular purpose or to provide initial information about a particular test—for example, the intended age range for the test, the test's publisher, and so on. These listings do not provide any critical evaluation about the quality of a test. A test with extensive validity information and excellent national norms receives the same type of listing as a test with virtually no validity information and no norms at all.

The *systematic reviews* of tests are an excellent source for critical evaluations of tests. They provide an outstanding professional service. However, they are not perfect. First, reviews are simply not available for many tests. Second, the nature of the reviewing process is such that reviews are often not available for the most recent edition of widely used, frequently revised tests. There is always a lag time between publication of a test and appearance of reviews of it. Often the lag time is very substantial. In the meantime, the potential user needs to make a decision about whether to use the test. Third, a reviewer's opinion is just that—an opinion. The potential test user should take that opinion into account, but it is not the final word about the test's value.

The electronic listings, such as the ETS Test Collection, provide an enormous improvement in the accessibility of information about tests. What might take several hours of searching in hard copy sources can be accomplished in minutes with these websites. Obviously, one does need to have online access to utilize these services. However, such access is now quite routine. The more important limitation is the same as the limitation of the comprehensive listings. Some of the electronic listings provide only basic descriptive information about tests. A more important limitation is that entries can be quite dated: Once they get into the database, they stay forever. Thus, the user needs to watch out for the datedness and possible unavailability of an entry.

Special purpose collections are very useful for covering the tests available in a certain area. At the time they are published, such collections are typically up-to-date. However, such collections are not ordinarily updated on a regular basis. Within a few years, they may be seriously outdated as new tests or new editions of tests are published.

Books about single tests are usually a rich source of information about those tests. The books often contain interesting case studies, research beyond what is in the test manual, and an extended rationale for test interpretation. This source of information has two main drawbacks. First, such books are available for only a small number of tests. Typically, these are the most widely used tests. It is rare to find an entire book about less widely used tests. Second, the books tend to be written by persons who have a very positive feeling about the test. This is understandable, but it sometimes leads to an overly optimistic evaluation of the test.

Textbooks about testing provide one index of the popularity of a test. By consulting several textbooks on testing, one can get some idea of what tests might be widely used for a particular purpose. However, the fact that a test is included in a textbook should not be taken as an endorsement of the test or even as a valid indicator of the frequency of the test's use. A test may be included in a textbook because the test illustrates a particular approach to test construction, not because it is an especially good test. Many textbooks also have a habit of including tests that are seriously out-of-date.

The *journals* listed earlier are very important sources of information for the latest research about tests. However, they tend to concentrate more on developments in testing methodology than on tests themselves. When particular tests are treated in journal articles, the topic is most frequently about some special use of the test rather than the most typical use. For example, an article may investigate the use of a subtest within the *Wechsler Adult Intelligence Scale* with hearing-impaired persons over age 70. Another article may investigate whether scores on a test are affected by a change in time limits. Such research adds to the fund of knowledge about a test, but it may not be helpful for considering the ordinary use of a test.

Publishers' catalogs are the best source of information about such practical matters as the cost of the test, the array of materials available for it, scoring services, and so on. The publisher's catalog is not a useful source of information about the quality of a test. Catalogs abound with statements such as "a reliable test of…", "validated measure of…", "accurate national norms," and so on. These statements are not to be taken at face value. The publisher is, after all, in the business of selling the tests. The same can be said for publisher's representatives. They can be essential sources of information about some matters. But on other matters their statements must be taken with a grain of salt.

Other users of tests can be very helpful in identifying what tests are typically used for a given purpose. They are also important sources of information about the peculiarities of a test. However, some users are not up-to-date about the latest developments in a field. Their test usage may be determined more by inertia than by critical judgment and contemporary knowledge.

All the sources of information can be useful for some purposes and not for others. Ultimately, the test user must be able to combine all these sources with his or her own expertise in making a judgment about the suitability of a particular test for a particular purpose.

Summary

1. There are two common problems that require use of various sources of information about tests.
2. There are three comprehensive lists of tests that provide nonevaluative snapshots of large numbers of tests.
3. There are two major sources of systematic, evaluative reviews of tests: Buros's MMY and Test Critiques.
4. Several websites provide electronic access to the comprehensive listings and systematic reviews.
5. Special purpose collections offer lists of tests, often with evaluative comments, for tests in a restricted domain.

6. For a few widely used tests, book-length treatments give details regarding test characteristics and interpretation.
7. Textbooks on testing often give useful lists of some widely used tests.
8. A variety of professional journals provide research on tests; some also provide reviews of tests.
9. The test publisher's catalog is a key source of information about such matters as cost, availability of new or special editions, and scoring services.
10. Current users of tests can be helpful sources of information.
11. All the sources have their particular strengths and weaknesses.

Key Terms

Buros	MMY	TIP
ETS Test Collection	specimen set	*Test Critiques*
examination kit	*Tests*	

Exercises

Note: Many of these exercises can be divided among members of a class, and results can then be shared among them.

1. Access one of the websites listed in Key Points Summary 2.4.

    a. Enter key words and get a list of tests. Here are some sample key words: critical thinking, self-concept, diagnostic reading, aggression, depression. Or develop your own key words.

    b. Pick the name of a test from Chapters 8–15. Enter the test's title and see what information you get.

2. Visit a local library.

    a. Determine which of the comprehensive lists of tests and which of the systematic reviews the library has. (These books will usually be in the Reference section of the library.) Make note of their locations for use in later exercises.

    Buros MMY Location: _____

    Test Critiques Location: _____

    Tests in Print Location: _____

    Tests Location: _____

    b. Assuming you have found one of the editions of MMY and/or *Test Critiques,* read at least two reviews in one or both of these sources. Choose tests of interest to you. Note the length and style of the reviews.

    c. Assuming you have found one of the comprehensive lists (TIP, *Tests,* etc.), note the information contained in several entries. Then pick a topic such as self-concept or critical thinking and use the subject index to find tests for that topic.

3. Assuming you have access to Ovid's Mental Measurements Yearbook database, either CD or Internet:

   a. Conduct a search for a particular test title and access the full text of a review.

   b. Conduct a search based on key words—for example, self-concept, attention deficit disorder, or mathematics achievement. Then examine the records obtained. (When completing this exercise, set Display Options so that Full Text of reviews is not retrieved.)

4. For each of the following sources of information, review one of the books or journals—don't read them in detail—and make notes on what type of information the source provides:

   a. One of the special purpose collections covered on pp. 53–54.

   b. One of the books on single tests covered on pp. 54–55.

   c. One of the journals covered on pp. 55–57.

5. Using the web addresses for publishers given in Appendix C, try to access the publisher's catalog. Is the entire catalog presented? If so, what information is provided?

6. Pick any *three* of the journals listed on pp. 55–57 and determine if your local library has subscriptions to them or has full-text online access. Scan recent issues of the journals to see what topics and tests are treated. Please note that some of the articles will be very technical and you may not understand anything in them until after you have completed Chapters 3–6.

Note: The next two exercises are very substantial projects. They may be suitable for term projects. Unlike the previous exercises, they are not something you can complete in just a few minutes.

7. Using the format suggested in Appendix A: Test Reviewing and Selection, complete a formal test review. For this exercise, you will need a specimen set for the test. It will also be useful to have the publisher's catalog entry for the test.

8. Using the format suggested in Appendix A for test selection, complete a test selection exercise. Examples of areas in which this might be done include: diagnostic reading tests for elementary school students, creative thinking tests for college students, college admissions tests, measures of depression, anxiety, or eating disorders.

9. Several Internet sites feature laundry lists of psychological tests, including tests of intelligence and assorted personality variables. Be careful! Many of these tests have no information about reliability, validity, or norms: precisely the technical characteristics we take up in the next three chapters. We are *not* recommending that students take any of these tests. Nevertheless, the student may wish to look at some of these sites to see "what's out there." Examples of the sites are PsychTests.com, AllTheTest.com, Queendom.com, and Quincy's Online Psychological and Personality Tests.com. The following site has a collection of tests, used mostly for research purposes, available for inspection: http://www.atkinson.yorku.ca/~psyctest/.

CHAPTER 3

Test Norms

Objectives

1. Define the purpose of test norms.

2. Refresh your knowledge of these topics from descriptive statistics: types of scales, frequency distributions, terms for describing shapes of distributions, measures of central tendency, measures of variability, and z-scores.

3. Identify the various types of raw scores for tests.

4. Identify the meaning of theta.

5. Define each of these types of norms: percentiles and percentile ranks, standard scores, developmental norms.

6. Summarize the strengths and weaknesses of each type of norm.

7. Identify characteristics of each of these types of norm groups: national, convenience, user, subgroup, local, and institutional.

8. Distinguish between criterion-referenced and norm-referenced interpretation.

9. Describe how to determine the usefulness of a norm group.

Purpose of Norms

Matt got 36 items right on the vocabulary test. Is that good or bad? Meg answered "Yes" to 14 of the 30 items on a measure of test anxiety. Does that mean she is unusually anxious or unusually laid back about taking tests? Dan scored 52 items right on an 80-item reading test and 24 items right on a 40-item science test. Is he relatively better in reading or in science? These kinds of questions are addressed under the topic of *test norms*. The basic idea is to translate what is called the raw score into some type of normed score. The **raw score** is the more or less immediate result of an individual's responses to the test. In the **normed score** system, the individual's raw score is *compared with scores of individuals in the norm group*. Normed scores are also known as *derived* scores or *scale* scores. This chapter treats the two crucial questions about test norms. First, what are the commonly used types of norms? Second, what are norm groups, that is, where do the norms come from?

> Raw scores are determined, in part, by features of a test such as test length, choice of time limit, item difficulties, and the circumstances under which the test is administered. This makes raw scores difficult to interpret in the absence of further information. Interpretation and statistical analyses may be facilitated by converting raw scores into an entirely different set of values called *derived scores* or *scale scores. Standards* ...(AERA/APA/NCME, 1999, p. 49)[1]

Fundamental notions of norms are not peculiar to the field of psychological testing. We use the notions of raw score and relative position within a group in a variety of everyday circumstances. Consider these examples. Is 6 ft. 5 in. tall? That's not very tall for a tree. It is very tall for a human being. Even among humans, it is not terribly impressive for a player in the National Basketball Association, but it is utterly astounding for a student in grade 6. What about a pulse rate of 100? That's not remarkable for a newborn (human) baby or for an adult who has just completed vigorous exercise. However, it could be a danger sign for an adult in a resting state. What do you think of running the 100-meter dash in 24.01 seconds? For a high school or college track team, this is a dismal time. But Erwin Jaskulski ran this time in May 1999 and set a world record—in the 95 and older age category (*Runner's World,* 1999). These examples illustrate that we use the idea of comparisons within a group for many types of interpretations in ordinary life. In psychological testing, we operationalize these comparisons in the form of norms.

---

[1] In Chapter 1 we described the important role played by the Standards for Educational and Psychological Testing, published jointly by the American Educational Research Association, American Psychological Association, and National Council on Measurement in Education (AERA, APA, NCME; 1999). Chapters 3–6 contain brief excerpts from this document, abbreviated, as it often is in the literature, simply as the "Standards" to help illustrate points made in the text.

Here are some additional examples of raw scores. They provide context for our discussion of norms later in this chapter.

- Matt got *36* items right on the short-term memory test. How good is his memory?
- Meg answered "Yes" to *14* items on the test anxiety measure. Is she laid back or a basket case about taking tests?
- Dan got *32* items right on the reading test and *24* items right on the math test. Is he relatively better in reading or in math?
- Sheri is *62* inches tall. Is she especially tall, short, or about average?
- Tom's pulse rate is *71* beats per minute. Is that normal?
- Little Abigail was rated *7* on the 10-point scale of affability. Is she a delight or a beast?

Review of Statistics: Part 1

Test norms are based on elementary notions from descriptive statistics. It is assumed that the reader has had an introductory course in statistics. It is also assumed that the reader may need a refresher on some of the topics covered in that course. This section provides such a refresher. The section is not intended to repeat an entire statistics course or to teach one how to compute statistics. It is intended to be a quick review. The section treats key ideas from univariate statistics. Chapter 4 includes a refresher for bivariate statistics, that is, correlation and regression.

Examples in this section employ some small data sets to illustrate various statistics. In practice, we ordinarily have much larger data sets, often thousands of cases. We use computer software packages to apply statistics to these large data sets. Commonly used packages include SPSS, SAS, Minitab, and SYSTAT. There are many others. Microsoft's Excel software, oriented more toward other applications, also computes statistics. *Appendix D* provides several data sets that the reader may use to calculate any of the statistics reviewed in this section. Understanding the material in this chapter does not require familiarity with any of these statistical packages. However, some readers may find it helpful to apply one of these packages to the data sets in Appendix D.

TRY IT!

If you are not already familiar with one of the statistical packages listed in the preceding paragraph, find out which of them is available for your use. Exercises at the end of this and the next two chapters will allow you to apply the package.

Variables

How does the field of statistics interface with the field of psychological testing? To answer this question, we must understand the shades of meaning of the term

variable. A science is built around the variables it studies. Examples of variables in psychology are intelligence, extroversion, maladjustment, and visual acuity. The objects we study (humans, rats, etc.) *vary* along each of these variables from high to low, more to less, or some similar set of quantifiers. Variables can be described at three levels of generality. At the most general level, a variable is a **construct.** Here, we give verbal descriptions and definitions of the variable. For example, intelligence may be defined as the ability to manipulate abstract symbols; maladjustment may be described as either the feeling of or objective evidence of significant difficulties in conducting ordinary life activities.

At a second level, we *measure* the variable. This is the *operational definition* of the variable. The field of psychological testing deals with these measures. It studies the characteristics of the measures and catalogs existing measures. At the third level, we get *raw data*. These are the numbers that result from application of the measures.

Statistics operate on raw data, the most specific level for a variable. Since raw data come from our measures, statistics provide the summaries and treatments of the measures (tests) in which we are interested. Of course, all the while we are most interested in the variable at the level of a construct.

The two major divisions of statistics are descriptive and inferential statistics. In most studies, we get quite a bit of raw data. For example, we may have several test scores for hundreds of individuals. **Descriptive statistics** help to summarize or describe this raw data to aid our understanding of the data. Most frequently, the data come from a sample of individuals. We are mainly interested in knowing about the population from which this sample was drawn. **Inferential statistics** help us to draw conclusions—inferences—about what is probably true in the population based on what we discovered about the sample.

Types of Scales

Variables are measured on scales. Stevens (1951) presented a four-part classification of scales that is widely referenced in statistics and testing. Distinctions among these

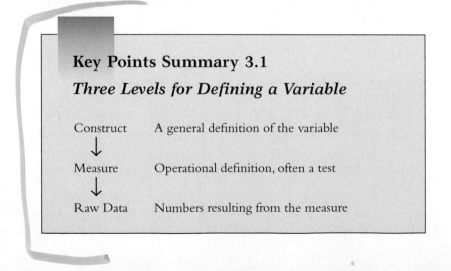

Key Points Summary 3.1

Three Levels for Defining a Variable

Construct   A general definition of the variable
↓
Measure   Operational definition, often a test
↓
Raw Data   Numbers resulting from the measure

types of scales are important because we can perform some types of arithmetical and statistical operations with some scales but not with others.

The classification of scales is in order of increasing level of sophistication. At the least sophisticated or most primitive level is the **nominal scale.** It simply distinguishes objects from one another by tagging each object with a number. The numbers do not signify more or less, bigger or smaller, or any other quantitative distinction. Examples are the numerals on basketball jerseys, Social Security numbers, or the codes 0 and 1 assigned to males and females, respectively, for purposes of computer coding.

On an **ordinal scale,** objects are assigned numerals that indicate an ordering, such as more or less of a trait, without specifying anything about the distances between objects on the scale. Rank orderings illustrate an ordinal scaling. For example, college football polls provide a ranking of the teams: 1, 2, 3, 4, … 25. Because these numbers are understood to be on an ordinal scale, one cannot infer that team 2 is as much better than team 3 as team 1 is better than team 2. In fact, teams 1 and 2 may be only slightly different, whereas team 3 may be vastly inferior to team 2.

The **interval scale** places objects in order and does so with equal intervals. Hence, on an interval scale, the distance between 2 and 4 is the same as the distance between 6 and 8 or between 20 and 22. However, the interval scale lacks a **true zero** point; it usually does have a zero point but this zero does not indicate complete absence of the variable being measured. The classic example of an interval scale is the Fahrenheit thermometer. On this scale, zero does *not* indicate the complete absence of heat. Addition and subtraction are legitimate operations on an interval scale. For example, the difference between 30° and 40° means the same as the difference between 50° and 60°. However, multiplication and division are not legitimate: 60°F does not represent twice as much heat as 30°F or half as much as 120°F. To make such statements, one would need to use the Kelvin scale, which does have a true zero point, a point where there is no heat at all.

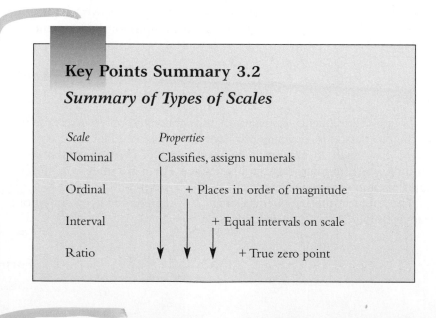

Key Points Summary 3.2
Summary of Types of Scales

Scale	*Properties*
Nominal	Classifies, assigns numerals
Ordinal	+ Places in order of magnitude
Interval	+ Equal intervals on scale
Ratio	+ True zero point

The **ratio scale,** the most sophisticated scale, places objects in order, does so with equal intervals, *and* has a true zero point. Most of our everyday physical measurements, such as length and weight, are on ratio scales. In contrast, most of our psychological measurements are on ordinal or interval scales.

What is the relevance of these seemingly arcane distinctions to our interest in psychological measurement? Consider the case of the familiar IQ scale. It is not a ratio scale—it does not have a true zero point. Hence, it is not legitimate to say that a person with an IQ of 150 is twice as smart as a person with an IQ of 75. Furthermore, if the IQ scale is only an ordinal scale, we cannot say that the difference between IQs of 80 and 100 means the same thing as the difference between IQs of 120 and 140. We do need to worry about the nature of our scales in order to make meaningful statements about our measurements or, conversely, to avoid saying stupid things about them. Stevens's (1951) method of classifying scales, though widely cited, is not the only way to think about scales. However, it is a very helpful way to think about scales.

Organization of Raw Data

When confronted with a mass of raw data, we often want to organize it. The most typical way to organize raw data is with a frequency distribution. The **frequency distribution** organizes the data into groups of adjacent scores. Figure 3.1 presents a set of raw data and a frequency distribution of the data. While it is difficult to make sense of the array of raw data, the frequency distribution readily reveals such features as the range of scores and the area where scores are concentrated. The frequency distribution in Figure 3.1 shows the score intervals into which scores are categorized, the frequency or count of scores falling in each interval, and the cumulative frequency (cum f), that is, the frequency at *and* below each interval.

A frequency distribution is often converted to graphic form. The two most common forms for this conversion are the **frequency histogram** and the **frequency polygon.** Figure 3.2 presents these graphs for the frequency distribution in Figure 3.1.

Central Tendency

Although the frequency distribution, histogram, and polygon are useful summaries of the raw data, it is convenient to have one index that best represents the complete set of data. Such an index is called a measure of **central tendency**—the center around which the raw data tend to cluster. There are three commonly used measures of central tendency: the mean, median, and mode.

The **mean** is the arithmetic average. It is represented by either M or $\overline{X}$ (read X-bar, or simply "mean"). Its formula is:

$$M = \frac{\Sigma X}{N}$$
                                                                            Formula 3-1

Scores (*N* = 100)									
102	110	130	99	127	107	113	76	100	89
120	92	118	109	135	116	103	150	91	126
73	128	115	105	112	138	100	158	103	86
114	134	117	91	92	98	96	125	155	88
129	108	99	83	149	103	95	95	82	133
91	121	103	147	110	90	122	94	124	65
71	101	93	88	78	105	145	90	94	87
102	79	99	111	117	98	115	112	116	80
96	114	106	111	119	101	123	109	132	100
105	77	100	131	106	108	113	143	102	88

Frequency Distribution

Interval	F	Cum F
150–159	3	100
140–149	4	97
130–139	7	93
120–129	10	86
110–119	18	76
100–109	23	58
90–99	19	35
80–89	9	16
70–79	6	7
60–69	1	1

FIGURE 3.1   Sample set of raw scores and frequency distribution.

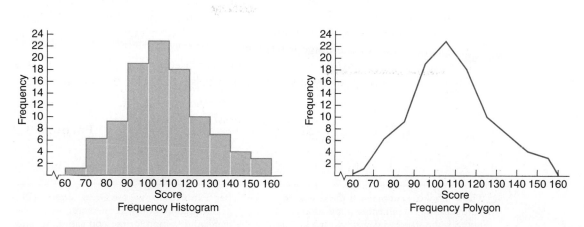

FIGURE 3.2   Frequency histogram and frequency polygon.

> Raw Data: 2, 5, 3, 6, 6, 7, 6, 4, 8, 3, 4
>
> Mean: $M = \Sigma X / N = 54/11 = 4.91$
>
> Median: 5   Mode: 6

FIGURE 3.3   Measures of central tendency for a small data set.

where
   X = score or raw datum
   N = number of scores
   Σ = summation sign, saying "add up all these things (X's)"

The **median** is the middle score when scores are arranged in order from low to high. The median divides the array of scores in half. The **mode** is the most frequently occurring score. Figure 3.3 gives examples of the three measures of central tendency for a small data set.

TRY IT! ....

Determine the three measures of central tendency for this set of test scores.

   Score: 2   5   4   5   3   4   5   2   6

   Mean = _____   Median = _____   Mode = _____

....

Variability

A measure of central tendency provides a very convenient summary of the data but robs us of any sense of **variability** in the data. For example, two sets of data may have the same mean but in one set all scores are within two points of the mean, whereas in the other set the scores are widely scattered. Therefore, to better describe the raw data, we provide an index of variability.

The simplest index of variability is the **range.** This is the distance from the lowest to the highest score. To indicate the range, one may list the lowest and highest scores or the difference between them. For the raw data in Figure 3.1, we may say the range is 65–158, or the range is 93.

The **standard deviation** is the most widely used index of variability. It is denoted in various contexts by any of these symbols:[2] *S, SD,* or σ. Its formula is:

$$SD = \sqrt{\frac{\Sigma(X-M)^2}{N}}$$ **Formula 3-2**

---

[2] The symbol σ, read sigma, is the Greek (lowercase) letter S. In statistics, we use Greek letters to designate measures for an entire population and English letters (e.g., *S*) to designate measures on samples. Thus, *S* is the standard deviation for a sample, σ is the standard deviation for the population. The distinction is not rigidly observed in the literature of psychological testing.

It is also often written as:

$$SD = \sqrt{\frac{\Sigma x^2}{N}}$$ **Formula 3-3**

where $x = X - M$. These formulas give the formal definition of the standard deviation. When SD is calculated on a sample but is intended as an estimate of SD in a population, the "N" in the formula is replaced by "$N - 1$."

The formula provides little intuitive insight into how the SD measures variability. However, it has mathematically felicitous consequences for later use, so one simply gets accustomed to its ungainly presence. The standard deviation is used heavily later in this chapter.

A closely related index of variability is the **variance**, which is simply SD^2. Conversely, SD is the square root of the variance. In some advanced work in statistics, the variance is used more than the standard deviation. In psychological testing, we use the standard deviation more frequently, though not exclusively. Figure 3.4 shows the standard deviation (SD), variance, and range for a small data set.

Scores:		6	9	4	5	5	1	$M = \Sigma X/N = 30/6 = 5$
$(X - M) = x$		1	4	−1	0	0	−4	
	$x^2 = 1$		16	1	0	0	16	$\sqrt{\Sigma x^2/N} = \sqrt{34/6} = 2.38$
$SD = 2.38$			Variance $= SD^2 = 5.66$					Range $= 1 - 9$

FIGURE 3.4 Measures of variability for a small data set.

TRY IT!

Calculate the standard deviation and range for this data set.

   Scores: 1   4   7
   $SD =$ _____   Range = _____

A fourth measure of variability is the **interquartile range.** As suggested by its name, it is the distance between the first and third quartiles. The first and third quartiles correspond to the 25th and 75th percentiles, respectively. If percentiles are already available, as is often the case with psychological test data, the interquartile range is easily determined.

z-scores

A **z-score** or, simply, z is defined as:

$$z = \frac{X - M}{SD}$$ **Formula 3-4**

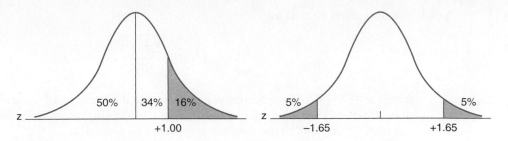

FIGURE 3.5   Examples of z-scores marking areas under the normal curve.

where X is an individual score or data point, M is the mean and SD is the standard deviation. The distribution of z-scores has a mean $= 0$ and $SD = 1$. Hence, no matter what the values of the original scores, when converted to z-scores, they always have the same mean and standard deviation.

z-scores are used to "map out" the normal curve in terms of areas under the curve. Figure 3.5 illustrates the use of z-scores to mark areas under the normal curve. Recall the tables of areas under the curve from elementary statistics. Because z-scores have a common mean (0) and standard deviation (1) regardless of values for original scores, z-scores play a crucial role in development of some test norms.

Shapes of Distributions

Psychological testing makes frequent reference to the shape or form of a frequency distribution of test scores. We should be familiar with the terms used to describe these shapes. The reference point or benchmark distribution is the **normal curve** or normal distribution. Its popular name is the bell curve, although it is only roughly the shape of a bell. The curve, generated by a rather unwieldy formula,[3] is a density function; that is, the area under the curve is filled in, actually packed with data points. The distribution in Figure 3.5 is a unit normal curve. It is laid out with a mean of 0 at its center and a scale established by standard deviation units (sometimes called σ-units) on its base. Note carefully the position of the standard deviation units.

This distribution is *unimodal:* It has one mode or "hump." It is *symmetrical* about its central axis, an imaginary line erected perpendicular to the base at the mean. Around this central axis, the left side is the mirror image of the right side of the curve. The curve's "tails" are *asymptotic* to the base. That is, they continue on to infinity, always getting closer to the base but never reaching it. Of course, this is true only in the theoretical normal curve. In practice, the data do stop at some finite point. Notice that nearly all area (about 99.8%) under the curve is contained within $+/- 3$ σ-units.

Distributions may "depart from normality," that is, be different from the normal curve, in several ways. Figure 3.6 depicts these departures from normality. The first departure is in terms of **kurtosis**, the "peakedness" of the distribution. A

---

[3] This equation generates the normal curve: $Y = (N/(\sigma\sqrt{2\pi}))(e^{-(X-\mu)^2/2\sigma^2})$.

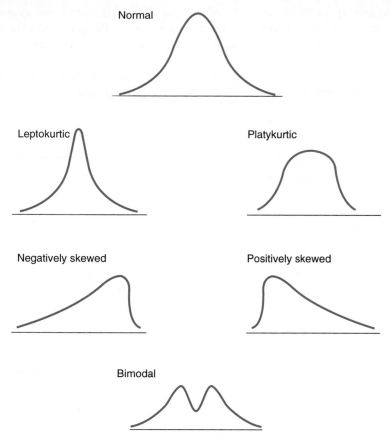

FIGURE 3.6   Examples of various distributions.

leptokurtic distribution is more peaked and a platykurtic distribution is flatter than the normal distribution.

Another type of departure from normality is in terms of **skewness,** the degree of symmetry for the right and left sides of the curve. *Negative* skewness or skewness to the left has a long tail to the left and a bulge in scores to the right. *Positive* skewness or skewness to the right has a long tail to the right and a bulge of scores to the left. A final type of departure from normality is in terms of the modality of the distribution. Whereas the normal distribution is unimodal, a distribution may have more than one mode, for example, a *bimodal* distribution, shown at the bottom of Figure 3.6.

Why is the normal curve important in psychological testing? Many naturally occurring phenomena tend to be normally distributed. For example, for people of a given sex and age, the following easily measured variables tend to be normally distributed: height, short-term memory span for digits, reaction time, grip strength, and so on for many other variables. This tendency toward normality is so ubiquitous that when the actual distribution of a variable is unknown, it is not unreasonable to assume that it is probably normal. Hence, many tests are built to yield a roughly normal distribution of scores. However, we sometimes deliberately build tests to yield positively or negatively skewed distributions, as we will discuss in Chapter 6. It is also the case that some naturally occurring distributions are distinctly nonnormal, for example the distributions of income, weight, and city population.

This is sufficient review of statistics to get us through the present chapter. We will extend the review of statistics at the beginning of Chapter 4.

The Raw Score

All test norms are transformations of *raw scores.* Hence, before defining types of test norms, it will be useful to consider the raw score. The **raw score** is the most immediate result from scoring a test. Raw scores arise in several different ways. The raw score may be the number of correct answers given to an achievement test. The raw score may be the number of questions answered in a certain direction, for example, "Yes" or "Agree" on a personality or interest inventory. The raw score may be the sum of numerically coded responses on a series of attitude items. For example, an attitude scale may have ten items. Each item calls for a response on a five-point scale, ranging from Strongly Disagree (1) to Strongly Agree (5). The raw score is the sum of the numerical responses to the ten items. Figure 3.7 gives an example of this type of raw score for a six–item measure of attitude toward mathematics. In this example, items with negative wording or connotation reverse the scale values for purposes of determining the raw score.

Anthropometric and physiological measures may also be thought of as raw scores. Sheri is 62 inches tall; Dan's pulse rate is 54 beats per minute; Amanda swims the 200-yard butterfly in 2:20. All these measures are raw scores. Placing these measures in a normative context will aid in their interpretation. Norms help to answer

	Response					
	Strongly Disagree				**Strongly Agree**	**(Item Score)**
Item	1	2	3	4	5	
1. Algebra is great fun.	[ ]	[X]	[ ]	[ ]	[ ]	(2)
2. Geometry is for the birds.	[ ]	[ ]	[ ]	[ ]	[X]	(1)
3. I like computing.	[X]	[ ]	[ ]	[ ]	[ ]	(1)
4. Math is very useful to me.	[ ]	[ ]	[X]	[ ]	[ ]	(3)
5. I love statistics.	[ ]	[X]	[ ]	[ ]	[ ]	(2)
6. Equations give me shivers.	[ ]	[ ]	[ ]	[X]	[ ]	(2)
				Raw Score = 11		

FIGURE 3.7   Deriving the raw score for an attitude toward math scale.

questions like these: Is Sheri very tall for her age? Is Dan's pulse abnormal? Is Amanda swimming at an Olympic-competition level?

> Typically, scoring begins with responses to separate test items, which are often coded using 0 or 1 to represent wrong/right or negative/positive, but sometimes using numerical values to indicate finer response gradations. Then the item scores are combined, often by addition but sometimes by a more elaborate procedure, to obtain a *raw score. Standards....* (AERA/APA/NCME, 1999, p. 49)

Scoring procedures for some tests call for a "corrected" or "adjusted" raw score. The most popular of these adjustments is the *correction for guessing*. This is applied to some ability and achievement tests that use a multiple-choice format. The theory is that on a multiple-choice test one can get some answers right by wild, blind guessing. More precisely, one should be able to get $1/K$ of the items correct by guessing, where K is the number of options in the multiple-choice item. Thus, the fraction $[W/(K - 1)]$, where W is the number of wrong answers, is subtracted from the obtained raw score to get the corrected raw score. The correction for guessing, once widely used, has faded in use.

The Special Case of Theta (Θ)

[handwritten: = weighted by level of difficulty]

Recall the discussion of item response theory (IRT) from Chapter 1. Whereas a test scored in the conventional way yields a raw score that is the sum of responses to all items in the test, a test scored according to IRT is not the simple sum of responses. The IRT score is a function of the *examinee's responses interacting with the characteristics of the items*. The IRT score is usually called **theta** (θ). Let us consider two examples of how θ may arise. In both examples it is *crucial* that the items be selected for unidimensionality and scaled for difficulty in a previous research program. We treat the IRT characteristics of items more fully in Chapter 6. Actual scoring of tests according to IRT procedures is complex, requiring sophisticated computer programs. It is not a simple matter of adding up correct responses. However, at this point, we can give a rough idea of how IRT methodology yields a theta score.

First, consider the data in Figure 3.8. Items are arranged in order of difficulty from left to right. The lower numbered items are very easy, the higher numbered items are very difficult. For example, if this were a test of arithmetic computation for elementary school students, item 1 might be 6 + 3 = ___, item 10 might be 740 − 698 = ___, and item 20 might be 0.56 × 1.05. Here we have simply labeled the items as easy, moderate, or hard. In an actual application, exact difficulty values would be used. (The test items need not be arranged in order of difficulty physically, but it is useful to show such an arrangement for our examples.) Each "x" in the figure represents a correct response. Mike is presented with items 1–10 and gets 7 items right. Ned is presented with items 11–20 and also gets 7 items right. Because Ned answered more difficult items, he receives a higher theta score, despite the fact that both examinees got 7 items right. Obviously, this procedure will not work unless the items are scaled on difficulty value first.

Item:	1	2	3	4	5	6	7	8	9	10	11	12	13	14	15	16	17	18	19	20
Item Difficulty:			Easy								Moderate					Hard				
Mike	x	x	x	x		x		x		x										
Ned											x	x	x	x		x		x	x	

x = a correct response

FIGURE 3.8   Deriving a theta score from different sets of items.

There is an excellent web-based demonstration of the interaction of examinee responses with characteristics of items employing IRT methodology. Go to: http://edres.org/scripts/cat/catdemo.htm. Log on and try your hand at the test. Watch how the "ability estimate" is adjusted after each response. Although scores will be reported as percentiles or some other normed score, these scores are transformations from theta, which is being updated after each response.

At least some applications of IRT methodology allow us to examine the *pattern of responses,* as well as the number of correct responses. The pattern of responses may lead to adjustments in the number of correct responses when determining theta. Consider the data in Figure 3.9. In this example, both examinees are presented with all 20 items. Again, item difficulty data are known and items are arranged in order of difficulty.

Jen, in general, is not performing at a very high level. Notice, however, that she did get one very difficult item (item 20) correct—probably a lucky guess. Kristen got nearly all the items correct, but missed one very easy item (item 2)—perhaps careless oversight. Many IRT scoring procedures take into account the total pattern of responses in determining the person's theta score. There are many specific procedures for scoring tests according to IRT methods. The procedures depend on the particular model used to fit the data. We will not review these models here. However, we will examine some IRT characteristics of items in Chapter 6.

Item:	1	2	3	4	5	6	7	8	9	10	11	12	13	14	15	16	17	18	19	20
Item Difficulty:			Easy								Moderate					Hard				
Jen	x	x	x	x		x		x		x										x
Kristen	x		x	x	x	x	x	x	x	x	x	x	x	x	x	x	x		x	x

x = a correct response

FIGURE 3.9   Patterns of responses may help determine a theta score.

Theta has some properties of a raw score and some properties of a normed score. It is like a raw score in that it is a relatively immediate result of examinee responses. Also, like a raw score, it has little meaning by itself. Theta is like a normed score in that it is not a simple summation of examinee responses. It depends not only on whether the answer is correct (or "Yes" or other such response) but also on the IRT values of the items to which responses are given. Theta locates the examinee on a trait or an ability presumed to underlie the total set of items in the test bank. However, the numerical values for the dimension are arbitrary and hence not easily interpreted. Although theta numerical values are arbitrary, they are usually established with 0.00 as a central value and a range of about −4.0 to +4.0. Hence, they may look like z-scores. However, they do not refer to a position within a well-defined norm group.

Although theta values may be the immediate result of examinee responses in an IRT environment, their practical interpretation is ordinarily accomplished through use of the normed scores presented in this chapter. That is, they are converted to percentiles, standard scores, grade equivalents, and so on. In fact, in a test score report, one may be looking at a percentile or T-score and not even realize that it is a transformation from a theta score rather than from a conventional raw score.

Types of Norms

This section discusses the types of norms commonly used with psychological tests. There are three major categories of norms, with several subcategories. In this section, we describe each type of norm. Then its strengths and weaknesses are identified. For many tests several types of norms are available, not just one type. Most of these types of norms are systematically related to one another. Thus, one can convert from one type of norm to another, although this cannot be done for all types of norms. These relationships are important. They are generally conceptualized in the context of the normal curve that was reviewed earlier in this chapter. Many of the relationships are displayed in Figure 3.10. This figure warrants careful study. Frequent reference will be made to it in subsequent sections of this chapter.

Key Points Summary 3.3
The Major Categories of Test Norms

- Percentile Ranks
- Standard Scores
- Developmental Norms

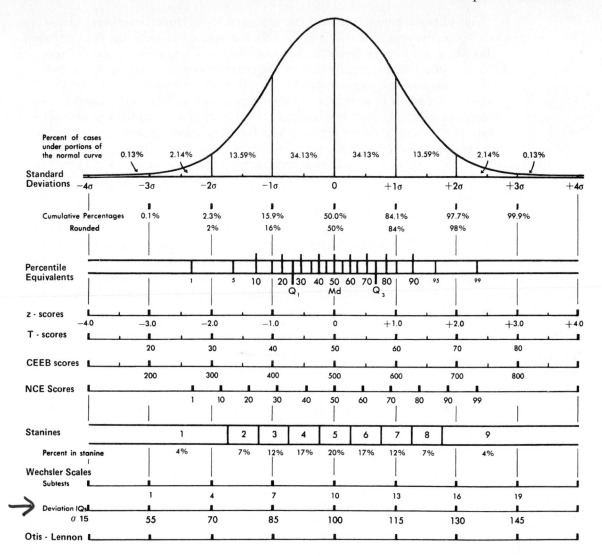

FIGURE 3.10 Equivalence of several types of norms in the normal curve.
Source: Reprinted from Seashore, H. G. Test service notebook 148: Methods of expressing test scores. With permission of the publisher, Psychological Corporation.

Many of the relationships depicted in Figure 3.10 are represented in tabular form in Table 3.1.

Percentile Ranks and Percentiles

One of the most common types of norms for psychological tests is the percentile rank or percentile. There is a technical distinction between these two terms. The **percentile rank** (PR) tells the percentage of cases in the norm group falling below a given raw score. Thus, if a raw score of 48 has a PR of 60, this means that

TABLE 3.1 *Percentile Equivalents of Several Standard Score Systems*

%ile	Stanine	NCE	IQ(15)	IQ(16)	W-sub	T-score	SAT	Z-score	%ile
99	9	99	133	135	17	74	740	2.4	99
98	9	93	130	132	16	70	700	2.0	98
97	9	90	129	130		69	690	1.9	97
96	9	87	127	128		68	680	1.8	96
95	8	85	125	126	15	66	660	1.6	95
94	8	83	123	125					94
93	8	81	122	124		65	650	1.5	93
92	8	80	121	122		64	640	1.4	92
91	8	78	120	121					91
90	8	77	119		14	63	630	1.3	90
89	8	76		120					89
88	7	75	118	119		62	620	1.2	88
87	7	74	117	118					87
86	7	73	116	117		61	610	1.1	86
85	7	72							85
84	7	71	115	116	13	60	600	1.0	84
83	7	70							83
82	7	69	114			59	590	0.9	82
81	7	68	113	114					81
80	7	68							80
79	7	67	112	113		58	580	0.8	79
78	7	66							78
77	7	66	111	112					77
76	6	65				57	570	0.7	76
75	6	64	110	111	12				75
74	6	64							74
73	6	63	109	110		56	560	0.6	73
72	6	62							72
71	6	62		109					71
70	6	61	108						70
69	6	60		108		55	550	0.5	69
68	6	60	107						68
67	6	59		107					67
66	6	59	106			54	540	0.4	66
65	6	58		106					65
64	6	58							64
63	6	57	105		11				63
62	6	56		105		53	530	0.3	62
61	6	56	104						61
60	6	55		104					60
59	5	55							59
58	5	54	103	103		52	520	0.2	58

(continued)

TABLE 3.1 *(continued)*

%ile	Stanine	NCE	IQ(15)	IQ(16)	W-sub	T-score	SAT	Z-score	%ile
57	5	54							57
56	5	53							56
55	5	53	102	102					55
54	5	52				51	510	0.1	54
53	5	52	101						53
52	5	51		101					52
51	5	50							51
50	5	50	100	100	10	50	500	0.0	50
49	5	50							49
48	5	49		99					48
47	5	48	99						47
46	5	48				49	490	−0.1	46
45	5	47	98	98					45
44	5	47							44
43	5	46							43
42	5	46	97	97		48	480	−0.2	42
41	5	45							41
40	5	45		96					40
39	4	44	96						39
38	4	44		95		47	470	−0.3	38
37	4	43	95		9				37
36	4	42							36
35	4	42		94					35
34	4	41	94			46	460	−0.4	34
33	4	41		93					33
32	4	40	93						32
31	4	40		92		45	450	−0.5	31
30	4	39	92						30
29	4	38		91					29
28	4	38							28
27	4	37	91	90		44	440	−0.6	27
26	4	36							26
25	4	36	90	89	8				25
24	4	35				43	430	−0.7	24
23	4	34	89	88					23
22	3	34							22
21	3	33	88	87		42	420	−0.8	21
20	3	32							20
19	3	32	87	86					19
18	3	31	86			41	410	−0.9	18
17	3	30		85					17
16	3	29	85	84	7	40	400	−1.0	16

(continued)

TABLE 3.1 *(continued)*

%ile	Stanine	NCE	IQ(15)	IQ(16)	W-sub	T-score	SAT	Z-score	%ile
15	3	28							15
14	3	27	84	83		39	390	-1.1	14
13	3	26	83	82					13
12	3	25	82	81		38	380	-1.2	12
11	3	24		80					11
10	2	23	81		6	37	370	-1.3	10
9	2	22	80	79					9
8	2	20	79	78		36	360	-1.4	8
7	2	19	78	76		35	650	-1.5	7
6	2	17	77	75					6
5	2	15	76	74	5	34	340	-1.6	5
4	2	13	74	72		32	320	-1.8	4
3	1	10	72	70		31	310	-1.9	3
2	1	7	70	68	4	30	300	-2.0	2
1	1	1	67	65	3	29	290	-2.4	1

IQ (15) is for IQ tests with $M = 100$ and $SD = 15$ (e.g., Wechsler Total Scores and Stanford-Binet 5th Ed.). IQ(16) is for IQ tests with $M = 100$ and $SD = 16$, such as SB 4th Ed. and Otis-Lennon. SAT covers any of the several tests that use $M = 500$ and $SD = 100$. W Sub is for Wechsler subtests and SB5 subtests, where $M = 10$ and $SD = 3$.

Reproduced from Hogan, T. P., Types of test scores and their percentile equivalents. In G. P. Koocher, J. C. Norcross, & S. S. Hill (Eds.). Psychologists' desk reference (2nd ed.) (pp. 111-116). Copyright © 2005 by Oxford University Press.

60% of the cases in the norm group scored at or below a raw score of 48. Of course, some cases in the norm group score exactly 48. This score is thought of as an interval from 47.5 to 48.5, with 48.0 being the midpoint of the interval. Hence, in some applications the PR is calculated to include one-half of the cases on the raw score interval.

A **percentile** (often abbreviated %ile) is a point on a scale below which a specified percentage of the cases falls. The difference between a percentile and a percentile rank may be summarized like this: For a percentile, one starts with a given percentage, then finds the raw score corresponding to this point. For a percentile rank, one starts with a given score, then finds the percentage of cases falling below this score. In practice, the terms *percentile* and *percentile rank* are often used interchangeably with no harm.

We sometimes encounter offshoots of the percentile system. These offshoots include deciles, quintiles, and quartiles. As implied by their Latin roots, these systems divide the distribution into tenths, fifths, and fourths, respectively. Correspondingly, we can think of percentiles as a system that divides the distribution into hundredths.

Figure 3.10 illustrates the place of percentile ranks in the normal curve. PRs range from a low of 1 to a high of 99, with 50 being the midpoint or median. The relationship between percentile ranks and z-scores is defined by the table of areas under the normal curve that is studied in introductory statistics.

TRY IT! ....

Use Figure 3.10 to answer these questions. Provide *estimates.* Fill in the approximate
z–score for each of these percentile ranks. Then use Table 3.1 to check the estimates.

PR	Estimated z (Figure 3.10)	z from table (Table 3.1)
50	_____	_____
84	_____	_____
16	_____	_____
25	_____	_____
99	_____	_____

....

Strengths and Weaknesses of Percentile Ranks

Percentile ranks have several attractive features. First, the concept of a percentile
rank is simple. It is easy to grasp, and it can be quickly explained even to a person
with no statistical training. Percentile ranks are also easy to calculate from a norm
group. For these reasons, percentile ranks are very widely used.

Percentile ranks have two main drawbacks. First, the layperson frequently
confuses the percentile rank with the **percentage–right score** used with many classroom tests. According to the time-honored tradition, in the percentage-right scoring
system, 90% is an A, 60% is failing, and so on. Thus, a percentile rank of 72, which is
above average performance, may be mistaken for barely passing performance. A percentile rank of 51, which is about average, sounds like horrible performance in the
percent-right system. The psychologist must distinguish carefully between percentile
ranks and percent-right scores, especially when interpreting scores to laypersons.

The second major drawback of the percentile rank is the marked inequality of
units at various points on the scale. Specifically, percentile ranks are "bunched up" in
the middle of the distribution and "spread out" at the two extremes of the distribution. At first, this peculiarity sounds like a trivial technicality. However, it has very
substantial practical implications. A given raw score difference, say 3 points, will
cover many percentile points in the middle of the distribution but only a few percentile points in either tail of the distribution. The phenomenon can be noted in
the percentile rank norms for any test. This difficulty is not a property of percentile
ranks but of the fact that they are applied to a variable that is normally distributed,
which is roughly true for most psychological tests. The difficulty would not arise in
the unusual circumstance in which the variable has a rectangular distribution; and
the phenomenon would actually reverse itself for a U-shaped distribution.

Figure 3.11 shows percentile norms for one of the facets on the NEO PI-R[4] Conscientiousness Scale. On these norms, going from a raw score of 10 to 13 results in negligible movement on the percentile scale, just one point, from a percentile of 2 to 3.

---

[4] The NEO PI-R is a widely used personality test. It is described in more detail in Chapter 12.

Raw Score	10 11 12 13 14 15 16 17 18 19 20 21 22 23 24 25 26 27 28 29 30...
Percentile	2 2 2 3 4 7 11 14 26 33 43 52 60 70 79 83 88 93 96 98 99

FIGURE 3.11   Raw score to percentile conversion for a NEO PI-R scale.
Source: Reproduced by special permission of the Publisher, Psychological Assessment Resources, Inc., 16204 North Florida Avenue, Lutz, Florida 33549, from the Revised NEO Personality Inventory, by Paul T. Costa, Jr., Ph.D. and Robert R. McCrae, Ph.D. Copyright © 1978, 1985, 1989, 1992 by PAR, Inc. Further reproduction is prohibited without permission of PAR, Inc.

However, going from a raw score of 20 to 23 corresponds to a percentile difference of 27 points (43–70). One can also observe this phenomenon by inspecting Figure. 3.10.

Standard Scores

Standard scores are another type of norm frequently used with educational and psychological tests. Standard scores constitute a family of norms. There are several widely used versions of standard scores and a potentially infinite variety of other versions. We first describe what is common to all standard scores, and then we identify the properties of specific versions. See Table 3.2 for examples.

A **standard score** system is a conversion of z-scores (reviewed earlier in this chapter) into a new system with an arbitrarily chosen mean *(M)* and standard deviation *(SD)*. The new *M* and *SD* are usually selected to be nice, memorable numbers like 50 and 10 or 500 and 100. In a few instances, as we will see, other desirable characteristics are sought.

To convert a raw score into a standard score, first translate the raw score into a z-score. Then multiply the z-score by the new (standard score) *SD* and add the new (standard score) mean. The steps are outlined in Figure 3.12. The following formula accomplishes these steps:

$$SS = \frac{SD_s}{SD_r}(X - M_r) + M_s$$

Formula 3-5

where SS = the desired standard score

SD_s = standard deviation in standard score system

SD_r = standard score in raw score system

TABLE 3.2   *Some Widely Used Standard Score Systems*

Test	Mean	SD
Wechsler and Stanford–Binet (SB) Full Scales	100	15
Wechsler and SB Subscale Scores	10	3
Law School Admissions Test	150	10
SAT and GRE	500	100

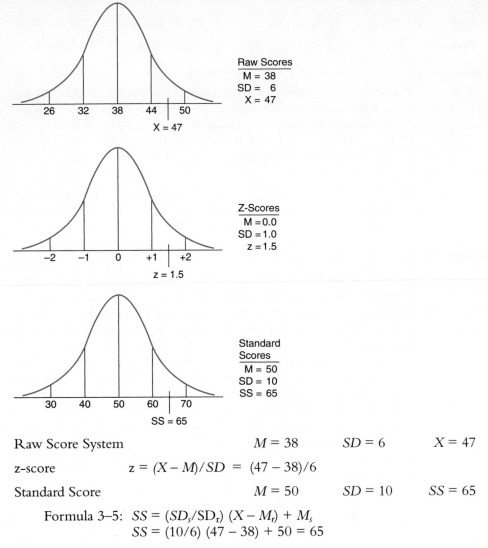

FIGURE 3.12   Illustration of converting a raw score system to a standard score system.

M_r = mean in raw score system

M_s = mean in standard score system

X = raw score

When the score (X) is translated into z-score form, the formula is:

$$SS = z\ (SD_s) + M_s$$ **Formula 3-6**

In ordinary practice, all these steps have already been completed and one simply uses a table in the test manual to convert a raw score to a standard score. Figure 3.13 provides an example of such a table. The figure includes only a section of the table, not the full range of scores.

Raw Score:	...	60	61	62	63	64	65	66	67	68	69	...
Standard Score:	...	55	56	56	57	58	59	60	61	62	63	...

FIGURE 3.13   Example of raw score to standard (T score) conversion.

Linear or Nonlinear

Most standard scores are **linear transformations** of raw scores. They follow Formula 3–5. However, some standard scores are derived by a **nonlinear transformation**. In such instances, Formula 3–5 and the example in Figure 3.12 do not apply. Nonlinear transformations may be used to yield a distribution of scores that is normal. Hence the result is sometimes referred to as a **normalized standard score**. The effect of the nonlinear transformation is illustrated in Figure 3.14. Ordinarily the nonlinear transformation is accomplished by relying on the relationship between z-scores and percentiles in areas under the normal curve. For this reason, a nonlinear transformation is sometimes referred to as an *area transformation*. Although it sounds complicated, the process is really quite simple. Throughout this chapter, we assume that standard scores are linear transformations, unless otherwise indicated.

T-scores

T-scores, sometimes called McCall's T-scores, are standard scores with $M = 50$ and $SD = 10$. Thus, the effective range of T-scores is from about 20 (corresponding to −3 z) to about 80 (+ 3 z). T-scores (capital T) should be distinguished from Student's t–values (lowercase t) used in tests of statistical significance. T-scores are widely used with personality tests, although they are used with other types of tests, too. For example, the Minnesota Multiphasic Personality Inventory (MMPI) described in Chapter 13 and the Strong Interest Inventory (SII) in Chapter 15 use T-scores. Figure 3.10 shows the distribution of T-scores.

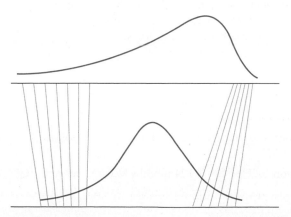

FIGURE 3.14   Illustration of nonlinear transformation of nonnormal distribution of raw scores into standard score system approximating a normal distribution.

Key Points Summary 3.4
Some Types of Standard Scores

T-scores
SATs and GREs
Deviation IQs
Stanines
Normal Curve Equivalents
Multilevel Standard (or Scaled) Scores

SATs and GREs

The SAT (formerly, Scholastic Assessment Test) and the Graduate Record Examinations (GREs) utilize a standard score system with $M = 500$ and $SD = 100$. These standard score systems apply to the main tests in these series: Verbal, Mathematics, and Writing for the SAT and Verbal, Quantitative, Analytic, and the various Advanced Tests for GRE. The tests are often combined to yield a total score. For example, a combined Verbal and Mathmatics score is often used for the SAT. When this is done, the means are additive but the SDs are not; that is, the mean for the combined or Total score is $500 + 500$, but the SD for the total score is not $100 + 100$. The SD for the total scores is less than 200 since the two tests being combined are not perfectly correlated. This phenomenon is not peculiar to the SAT and GRE. It will be true for any combination of tests that are not perfectly correlated.

Deviation IQs

The traditional definition of the IQ *(intelligence quotient)* is: IQ = (MA/CA) × 100, where MA is **mental age** (see page 89 for a description of mental age), CA is **chronological age**, and 100 is a multiplier to eliminate the decimal point. For example, Zelda's MA is 10 years, her CA 8 years, so her IQ is $(10/8) \times 100 = 125$. This is called a **ratio IQ** since it represents the ratio of MA to CA.

TRY IT!

Calculate ratio IQs for these cases.

> Matt's MA is 78 months (6 years, 6 months). His CA is 84 months (7 years, 0 months). What is his ratio IQ?

> Meg's MA is 192 months. Her CA is 124 months. What is her ratio IQ?

Ratio IQs were used with the earliest intelligence tests. However, it was observed that standard deviations of these ratio IQs were not the same at different age levels.

Specifically, the standard deviations tended to increase with age. Thus, a ratio IQ of 120 deviates less from the average (100) at age 18 than at age 6. Conversely, a ratio IQ of 70 deviates more from 100 at age 7 than at age 17. Such variation in the meaning of an IQ at different age levels is unfortunate and undesirable.

The IQs obtained from modern intelligence tests are *not* ratio IQs. They are standard scores with $M = 100$ and SD usually set at 15 or 16. These standard scores are often referred to as **deviation IQs.** The $M = 100$ is used in deference to the traditional (ratio) definition of IQ. Ratio IQs on the original Stanford–Binet test yielded a standard deviation of 16 at certain ages. This SD was adopted as *the SD* for the standard scores used with some intelligence tests. Other tests, most notably the Wechsler tests (WAIS, WISC, WPPSI), adopted $SD = 15$.

Some segments of the psychological community strive mightily to shun the term *IQ*, while retaining the tradition of using a standard score system with $M = 100$ and $SD = 15$ or 16. Hence, what we refer to here as the deviation IQ sometimes surfaces in test manuals and score reports under a variety of other names, for example, school ability index (SAI). Usually, such alternate names are easily recognized as standard score systems with the familiar M and SD.

Stanines

Stanines, a contraction of "standard nine," are a standard score system with $M = 5$ and $SD = $ (approximately) 2. Stanines were constructed to (a) divide the normal distribution into nine units and (b) have the units cover equal distances on the base of the normal curve, except for the units covering the tails of the distribution, that is, units 1 and 9. When these two conditions are met, the mean will obviously be 5 and the standard deviation will be slightly in excess of 2. These two properties of stanines are illustrated in Figure 3.10. See also Figure 3.15. Notice that units 2–8 cover equal distances on the base of the normal curve. Since the density of the curve varies in different sections, these equal distances cover varying percentages of the cases in the distribution. For example, stanine 2 covers 7% of the cases (from the 4th to the 11th percentile), while stanine 4 covers 17% of the cases (from the 23rd to the 40th percentile).

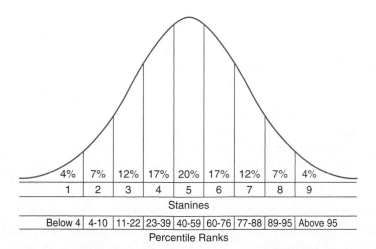

FIGURE 3.15 The distribution of stanines.

TRY IT! ....

Using Figure 3.10 or Figure 3.15, determine the stanine corresponding to each of
these percentiles:

Percentile:	2	36	52	90
Stanine:	_____	_____	_____	_____

....

Stanines are always derived by reference to the percentile divisions shown in Figure 3.15 rather than by Formula 3–5. Hence the stanines result in a nonlinear transformation of raw scores (unless the original distribution was already perfectly
normal). Stanines are used extensively for reporting scores on standardized achievement tests and some mental ability tests in elementary and secondary schools. They
are not employed much in other contexts.

Normal Curve Equivalents

The **normal curve equivalent** (NCE) is a standard score system developed so that
the NCEs are equal to percentile ranks at points 1, 50, and 99. When this condition
is met, the NCE system has $M = 50$ and $SD =$ (approximately) 21. NCEs are used
almost exclusively to meet certain federal reporting requirements for achievement
testing in public schools. Figure 3.10 shows the relationship between NCEs and
other norms.

Multilevel Standard Scores

A multilevel test is one that has at least partially distinct tests at different age or grade
levels. The primary examples of such tests are achievement batteries (see Chapter
11) and group-administered cognitive ability tests (see Chapter 9) used in elementary and secondary schools. Although one of these tests may have the same name
(e.g., *Metropolitan Achievement Tests* or *Otis-Lennon School Ability Test*) across a wide
age or grade span, obviously the same items are not used across the entire span. The
test is divided into a number of separate levels. One level may be used in grades 1–2,
another level in grades 3–4, and so on.

The raw scores obtained from different levels on such tests are often linked by a system of standard scores that span all levels. These standard scores are sometimes called
scaled scores. Multilevel standard scores are difficult to interpret. They have a convenient mean and standard deviation (e.g., 500 and 100) at one level, usually for a
grade or age in the middle of the range covered by the entire series, but the mean and
standard deviation will differ at other age or grade levels. Thus a seventh grade student's standard score of 673 on the reading test has no readily interpretable meaning.

Multilevel standard scores can be useful for measuring growth across grade or age
levels. The score system is usually developed to approximate an interval scale. However,
for ordinary test interpretation, these multilevel standard scores are not very useful.

Strengths and Weaknesses of Standard Scores

Standard scores provide a convenient metric for interpreting test performance in a
wide variety of circumstances. Since many traits of interest to psychologists are

presumably normally distributed, standard scores' connections to z-scores are help-ful. Standard scores avoid the percentile problem of marked inequality of units in various regions of the normal distribution. For this reason, standard scores are more amenable to statistical calculations.

Standard scores do have some drawbacks. First, it must be admitted that an exceedingly small fraction of the human race has any idea what the normal curve or a z-score is. Hence, relating standard scores to the context of the normal curve and z-scores has little value except when working with the cognoscenti. Second, to make sense of a standard score, one needs to be reminded of the M and SD for the system. Earlier paragraphs cited some of the well-known standard score systems where this problem is minimized, for example, $M = 100$ and $SD = 15$ for the devi-ation IQs on mental ability tests. However, there are many other standard score sys-tems—potentially an infinite variety, since one can choose any values for M and SD. For example, the Law School Admissions Test (LSAT) and the ACT college entrance test each have their distinctive standard score systems. What does a score of 130 mean on the LSAT? What does a score of 26 mean on the ACT? One doesn't have a clue without going to a test manual to look up the M and SD for these stan-dard score systems.

Special note should be made of stanines. They have the merit of simplicity for reporting individual scores. It is easy to explain, for example to parents, that a child's performance is reported on a scale from 1 to 9. Generally, no further explanation is needed about means, standard deviations, equal distances on the base of the normal curve, and so on. This simplicity is an advantage. On the other hand, stanines are rather gross for reporting group averages.

Normal curve equivalents (NCEs) are an unfortunate creation. As standard scores, they have no advantage over other standard score systems. However, they look like percentiles and are thereby easily confused with percentiles. As previously noted, in fact, NCEs match percentiles at three points in the distribution, but they are notably different at other points in the distribution.

Developmental Norms

When the trait being measured develops systematically with time, it is feasible to create what may be called a **developmental norm.** There are two commonly used developmental norms: **age equivalents** (AE) and **grade equivalents** (GE). AEs are used with some mental ability tests. In this context, the score is called a mental age (MA), easily the most well known of the age equivalents. GEs are used with many achievement tests. Developmental norms are meaningful only in the range where the trait being measured is developing or growing with time in the relevant popu-lation. In a developmental norm, a raw score is interpreted in terms of the age or grade for which the raw score is typical.

Mental Age (MA)

Mental ages are the primary example of age equivalents. MAs were one of the first types of norms used with psychological tests. They originated with the Binet scales. MAs are determined by finding the typical or median score for examinees

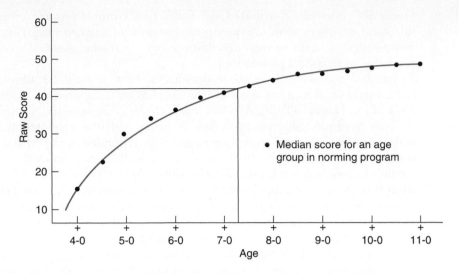

FIGURE 3.16   Illustration of curve to develop mental ages.

at successive age levels. Age groups may be formed by year, half-year, three–month intervals, or any other such grouping of individuals. The median score on the test is then determined for each group. The results are plotted and a smooth curve is fitted to the points as in Figure 3.16. Each "•" in the figure is a median obtained from the norming program for the test. The figure illustrates how to obtain an MA from a raw score. For example, a child who obtains a raw score of 42 has an MA of 88 months or 7 years–4 months (often written as 7–4 in the parlance of age equivalents). In practice, raw scores are converted to mental ages by way of a table prepared from the developmental curve. An example of such a table is shown in Figure 3.17.

TRY IT! ....

Using Figure 3.16, estimate the MA (mental age) corresponding to the following raw scores:

Raw Score   11   22   47

MA   _____   _____   _____

....

Raw Score	15	20	25	30	35	40	45
Mental Age	4-0	4-2	4-5	5-0	5-4	6-2	8-8

FIGURE 3.17   Portion of raw score to mental age table developed from Figure 3.16.

Sept	Oct	Nov	Dec	Jan	Feb	Mar	Apr	May	June
0.0	0.1	0.2	0.3	0.4	0.5	0.6	0.7	0.8	0.9

FIGURE 3.18 Division of the school year in the grade equivalent system.

Grade Equivalents (GE)

Grade equivalents are developed by administering a test to students in different grade levels. This is done in the norming program. The typical or median performance in each grade is then obtained. The medians are plotted and a curve is fitted to the points as in Figure 3.16, except with grades rather than ages on the base. Similar to the procedure for MAs, the GE for a raw score is read from the curve, and a table of raw score–GE conversions is prepared.

The convention for GEs is to divide the school year into tenths as shown in Figure 3.18. A GE is reported, for example, as 6.3, meaning the third month of grade 6. GEs above 12.9 (the last month of grade 12) are often reported as 12.9+ or with some verbal label such as Post High School (PHS). The GE scale is not ordinarily extended to college years.

Other Developmental Norms

Although mental ages and grade equivalents are the primary examples of developmental norms, brief mention should be made of two other examples. First, there are tests based on *stage theories* of human development. Well-known examples of such theories are Piaget's theory of cognitive development and Kohlberg's theory of moral development. Tests based on these theories yield results that place an individual at a certain stage. For example, a Piagetian task may place a child at the "pre-operational stage" of cognitive development. A Kohlbergian test may place an individual at the "conventional stage" of moral development. Such tests usually do not result in a numerical score. However, in some applications, these stages may also be related to ages at which the stages are typically attained. In any case, the fundamental notions involved in staged-based norms for these tests are essentially the same as the notions involved in MAs and GEs. Obviously, the usefulness of norms for stage-based theories depends on the validity of the stage-based theory as well as on the psychometric characteristics of the test.

A second example is anthropometric measurements such as height and weight. Such measurements are often interpreted in terms of developmental norms. These are essentially age equivalents. For example, a child is reported to be "as tall as the typical 6-year-old." Just as with mental ages, such statements are usually interpreted in relation to the child's chronological age, for example, "Mike is very tall for his age."

Strengths and Weaknesses of Developmental Norms

All developmental norms have some common strengths and weaknesses. On the positive side, developmental norms have a naturalness to their meaning that is quite attractive. To say that a 16-year-old functions mentally like a 3-year-old or that a student in grade 2 is reading at the grade 8 level—such statements seem to convey considerable meaning, free from the sterile, statistical jargon of percentile ranks and standard scores. Ideas about normal developmental patterns are deeply embedded in our thinking about humans. The basic notion of developmental norms is used in many situations. The adult throwing a temper tantrum is accused of "acting like a 2-year-old." It is noted that grade 6 students in Japan are doing algebra "usually reserved for grade 9 students in the United States." Mick is praised for "performing in his first game as a freshman like he was a veteran senior." Age equivalents and grade equivalents simply formalize these natural ways of thinking. They help to accomplish the goal of making raw scores meaningful.

A second advantage of developmental norms is that they provide a basis for measuring growth across multilevel tests. For example, during the elementary school years, a child may take the Primary I level of an achievement test in grade 1, the Elementary level in grade 4, and the Intermediate level in grade 7. Grade equivalents (developed in a scaling program, described on page 88) link all these levels of the test.

There are two principal drawbacks to developmental norms. First, they are applicable only to variables that show clear developmental patterns. Hence, they are not ordinarily applicable to areas such as personality traits, attitudes, and vocational interests. It does not mean anything, for example, to say that someone has the extrovertedness of a 10-year-old or a third grader. Furthermore, even those variables that do show developmental patterns at some levels do not ordinarily continue their growth patterns indefinitely. Mental ability as measured by many tests, for example, develops systematically to about age 18 but not thereafter. Reading ability develops rapidly in the elementary school years, but it does not continue to develop indefinitely. There is a useful distinction for purposes of test interpretation between the mental ability of a 5-year-old and a 15-year-old, but not between a 25-year-old and a 35-year-old. This is not an all-or-none affair. Developmental norms do not cease to be useful at a clearly defined point. Rather, they gradually lose their usefulness as the developmental curve (such as those in Figures 3.16) becomes less steep. When the curve becomes flat, developmental norms become completely meaningless.

A second disadvantage of developmental norms is their uncontrolled standard deviations. The *SD*s are usually not the same at different levels or on different tests. On many tests, the *SD*s tend to increase systematically with age or grade level. The *SD*s vary unsystematically between different tests within the same battery even when the norms are based on the same norm group. This may sound like a trivial, technical point. However, it has substantial practical implications. For example, a 5-year-old who is one year below average in mental ability (i.e., CA = 5–0, MA = 4–0) is much further below average in standard deviation units or in percentile units than a 16-year–old who is one year below average (i.e., CA = 16–0, MA = 15–0). The student in grade 1.5 who is reading at GE = 3.5 is practically out of the distribution of grade 1 students, whereas the student at grade 7.5 who has a reading GE of 9.5 is not all that unusual. Also, consider the student in grade 3.5 who has a GE of 4.5 in mathematics computation and a GE of 4.5 in reading. Relative to other students, this student is probably much more advanced in computation than in reading because the

Content Level:	Grade 2	Grade 3	Grade 4	Grade 5	Grade 6	Grade 7	RS	GE
Items	xxxxx	xxxxx	xxxxx	xxxxx	xxxxx	xxxxx		
Grade 3 Student	/////	/////	/////				15	6.5
Grade 6 Student	////	///	///	///	/	/	15	6.5

Each x is a test item. Each / is a correct answer.

FIGURE 3.19 Different ways of obtaining a GE of 6.5.

SD of GEs is typically smaller for computation than for reading. These differences in *SD*s for various tests are unsystematic. They may differ from one test series to another.

A third criticism is usually reserved for grade equivalents. It is noted that a student in, say, grade 3 may get a GE of 6.5 not by knowing the same material as the typical grade 6 student but by answering perfectly all the grade 2, grade 3, and grade 4 items, whereas the typical grade 6 student gets some but not all items right from across a grade span of 2 to 7. The situation is depicted in Figure 3.19.

This argument, usually mentioned only in connection with grade equivalents, can be applied to any type of normed score. Two students scoring at the 75th percentile or at a standard score of 60 did not necessarily answer the same items correctly. Tests constructed according to item response theory attempt to minimize this problem, but that is a function of the test construction method, not the type of norm used.

Examples of Norm Tables

Now that we have considered each of the major types of norms, it will be useful to observe how test manuals present norms. What does a norm table look like? Actually, norm tables come in an enormous variety. However, there are some standard patterns. After one sees a few examples, it is easy to decipher variations in the patterns.

Table 3.3 shows what a typical norm table looks like in a test manual. You always start with a raw score (RS), then convert to a normed score. In this example, you enter with a raw score in the left-hand column and then find any one of several normed scores: standard score (SS), deviation IQ (DIQ), percentile rank (PR), stanine (S), and normal curve equivalent (NCE). In many applications, the conversion

TABLE 3.3 *Example of a Norm Table Incorporating Many Types of Norms*

RS	SS	DIQ	PR	S	NCE
60	420	119	90	8	77
59	417	117	86	7	74
58	414	114	82	7	69

is performed by computer, and all you see is the normed score on a report. In practice, you will usually concentrate on just one type of normed score even though several are provided.

Narrative Reports and Norms

Recall that the basic purpose of norms is to provide an interpretive context for a raw score. Generally, normative information is quantitative: another set of numbers. Increasingly, however, test scores are being reported in the form of a computer-generated narrative. The user may see no numbers at all, although most reports provide both numbers—the usual kinds of norms—as well as a **narrative report**. How do these narrative reports originate?

The substance for narrative reports always begins with a test score, at least a raw score or theta, and most frequently with a normed score. From this beginning, narrative reports range considerably in complexity. At the simplest level, the narrative report may just translate a normed score into a verbal description. For example, a computer may have a table showing the following correspondence between standard scores (in a system with $M = 100$, $SD = 15$) and verbal labels:

130+	Exceptionally high
120–129	Well above average
110–119	Somewhat above average
90–109	Average
80–89	Somewhat below average
70–79	Well below average
Under 70	Exceptionally low

With this table, a profile of an individual's scores on Tests A, B, and C, may look like this:

Test	Score	Performance Level
A	98	Average
B	82	Somewhat below average
C	94	Average

The "Score" column may not even appear on the report, although the scores are at the root of the report. With a bit more sophistication in programming, the report may read like this: "Jim's performance on both Tests A and C was in the average range, whereas his performance on Test B was somewhat below average." Narrative reports often incorporate reference to the norm group. For example, "In comparison with other boys in his grade, Jim is at the 60th percentile in mechanical aptitude, which is slightly above average for boys in his grade."

Some narrative reports go well beyond translation of normed scores into verbal labels. They take into account information about the reliability and validity of the test. These issues are addressed in the chapters on these topics.

For use in a narrative report, devise a set of labels that distinguish between stanines 1–3, 4–6, and 7–9. Labels may be more than single words.

Stanine Group	Verbal Label
1–3	_____
4–6	_____
7–9	_____

Figure 3.20 shows portions of a narrative report for the NEO PI-R, a test described in detail in Chapter 12. The full narrative report goes on for five to six pages. The excerpt presented here gives the flavor of such a report. Note that the report begins with the normed scores, T-scores in this case. The report then proceeds to interpret these scores.

The Barnum Effect

When evaluating narrative reports of test scores, we must be particularly alert to operation of the Barnum effect. This effect is named after the circus promoter, P.T. Barnum, renowned for his ability to make people believe (and buy) anything. As applied in psychological testing, the **Barnum effect** refers to people's tendency to believe high-sounding statements that are probably true about everyone but contain no unique, specific information arising from the test. Consider these statements purportedly based on a personality test:

- Your scores indicate that with some groups you can be very extroverted. However, you do sometimes want to be by yourself.
- The combination of the first three scales indicates that you can usually control your temper, even though at times you are boiling inside.
- According to this test, there are times when you think it is unfair that people take advantage of one another.

Now consider these statements purportedly based on mental ability and achievement tests administered to elementary school students Ned and Abigail:

- The battery of tests shows that Ned is not equally good in all areas. His teacher needs to capitalize on his strengths while at the same time motivate him to do well in other areas.
- These test results can be especially helpful in dealing with a case like Abigail. She can certainly improve in a number of ways.

All the latter statements could be made about nearly everyone. The statements contain no information based specifically on the test results. In fact, we could construct an entire report based on these Barnum-like statements. These types of statements are not helpful—narrative reports should give information that uniquely characterizes the individual and that arise directly from the test results.

— **Validity Indices** —

Validity indices are within normal limits and the obtained test data appear to be valid.

— **Basis of Interpretation** —

This report compares the respondent to other adult men. It is based on self-reports of the respondent.

At the broadest level, personality can be described in terms of five basic dimensions, or factors. NEO-PI-R domain scores provide estimates of each of these five factors. More precise measures, however, are provided by NEO-PI-R factor scores, which may differ somewhat from the domain scores plotted on the individual's profile. The factor scores are as follows:

Scale		Factor T Score	Range
Neuroticism	(N)	53	AVERAGE
Extraversion	(E)	44	LOW
Openness	(O)	56	HIGH
Agreeableness	(A)	50	AVERAGE
Conscientiousness	(C)	50	AVERAGE

These factor scores are used to describe the individual at a global level. Factor scores are based on a composite of facet scale scores. To the extent that there is wide scatter among facet scores within a domain, interpretation of that domain and factor becomes more complex. In these cases, particular attention should be focused on the facet scales and their interpretation.

— **Global Description of Personality: The Five Factors** —

The most distinctive feature of this individual's personality is his standing on the factor of Extraversion. Such people are somewhat introverted, preferring to do many things alone or with a small group of people. They avoid large, noisy parties and tend to be quiet and reserved in social interactions. Those who know such people would probably describe them as retiring and serious [McCrae & Costa, 1987]. The fact that these individuals are introverted does not necessarily mean that they lack social skills—many introverts function very well in social situations, although they might prefer to avoid them. Note also that introversion does not imply introspection; these individuals are likely to be thoughtful and reflective only if they are also high in Openness.

This person is high in Openness. High scorers like him are interested in experience for its own sake. They enjoy novelty and variety. They are sensitive to their own feelings and have a greater than average ability to recognize the emotions of others. They have a high appreciation of beauty in art and nature. They are willing to consider new ideas and values and may be somewhat unconventional in their own views. Peers rate such people as original and curious.

Next, consider the individual's level of Neuroticism. Individuals scoring in this range are average in terms of their emotional stability. They experience a normal amount of psychological distress and have a typical balance of satisfactions and dissatisfactions with life. They are neither high nor low in self-esteem. Their ability to deal with stress is as good as the average person's.

This person is average in Agreeableness. People who score in this range are about as good-natured as the average person. They can be sympathetic but can also be firm. They are trusting but not gullible and are ready to compete as well as to cooperate with others.

Finally, the individual scores in the average range in Conscientiousness. Men who score in this range have a normal level of need for achievement. They are able to set work aside in pursuit of pleasure or recreation. They are moderately well-organized and fairly reliable and have an average amount of self-discipline.

— **Detailed Interpretation: Facets of N, E, O, A, and C** —

Each of the five factors encompasses a number of more specific traits, or facets. The NEO-PI-R measures six facets in, each of the five factors. An examination of the facet scores provides a more detailed picture of the distinctive way that these factors are seen in this person.

Neuroticism

This individual is anxious, generally apprehensive, and prone to worry. He sometimes gets angry at others and is prone to feeling sad, lonely, and dejected. Embarrassment or shyness when dealing with strangers is not a problem for him. He reports being poor at controlling his impulses and desires, but he can handle stress as well as most people.

FIGURE 3.20   Excerpts from narrative report for NEO PI-R.

Source: Reproduced by special permission of the Publisher, Psychological Assessment Resources, Inc., 16204 North Florida Avenue, Lutz, Florida 33549, from the Revised NEO Personality Inventory, by Paul T. Costa, Jr., Ph.D. and Robert R. McCrae, Ph.D. Copyright © 1978, 1985, 1989, 1992 by PAR, Inc. Further reproduction is prohibited without permission of PAR, Inc.

Norm Groups

All the types of norms treated earlier in this chapter are based on **norm groups.** The test is administered to the norm group in what is called a *norming program* or *standardization program.* The value of the norms for a test depends on the nature of the norm group. Interpretation of test scores is affected greatly by the norm group used for deriving norms, regardless of the type of norm derived. Hence, it is important to consider what kinds of norm groups one might encounter.

Norm groups for psychological tests display enormous variety. It is difficult to formulate distinct categories within this variety. We present here a categorization scheme that represents points along a continuum rather than clearly distinct approaches. In practice, one will find examples at intermediate points along the continuum.

National Norms

Some tests aspire to have **national norms**—that is, norms based on a group that is representative of the segment of the national population for whom the test is intended. This segment of the population may be all adults, all children in grades K–12, all persons applying for admission to college, or all persons who are legally blind. The target group—the population—is ordinarily defined along with the purpose of the test. Table 3.4 shows sample statements claiming nationally representative norms. Compare these statements with those in Table 3.5, which disavow representativeness for any well-defined group.

International Norms

In the context of international studies of school achievement, international norms have been developed in recent years. The norms are based on schoolchildren drawn from groups of countries—usually limited to economically advanced nations—that have chosen to participate in the studies. Most of the interpretations are based on comparisons of total scores and percentage of students correctly answering individual items. Hence, there is little use of norms such as percentile ranks or standard scores. For examples of such international norms, see Chapter 11.

TABLE 3.4 *Sample Statements Claiming Norms Representative of a Population*

Norms for the Scranton Test of Nonverbal Intelligence are based on samples carefully selected to be representative of children aged 3-16 in the U. S. population.

The University Attitude Scale has norms reflective of the nation's college student population.

TABLE 3.5 *Sample Statements NOT Claiming Norms Representative of a Population*

Norms for this test are based on all persons taking the test and having their scores processed by the publisher within the past three years.

The Scranton Anxiety Test norms are based on 236 cases completing the test at the Scranton Community Counseling Center.

Convenience Norm Groups

Some tests may aspire to have a national norm, but make no pretense about actually having such a norm. Rather, they have norms based on one or several **convenience groups** that are "conveniently" available for testing. Often such groups come from a single geographical location, are relatively homogeneous in cultural background, and may be limited in range of age, educational level, and other important variables.

Some tests will present several different norms based on different groups. For example, a self-concept test may present one norm based on 250 grade 8 students in a northeastern city, another norm based on 150 persons aged 15–18 referred for counseling, and another norm based on 200 adults who participated in a consumer attitude survey.

At best, the test user hopes the test manual will contain a frank and careful description of the characteristics of these ad hoc norm groups. Often, even that is not available. Norms based on such convenience groups must be interpreted with the utmost caution. The test user must refrain from assuming that such norms can be used as a fair substitute for a national norm or a clearly defined subgroup norm.

User Norms

Some tests employ what are called **user norms.** These norms are based on whatever groups actually took the test, usually within some specified time. As new groups take the test, the publisher simply adds these cases to the normative database.[5] The percentile rank norms on the SAT are user norms (see Chapter 9, pp. 356–357). They are based on all students who took the test within the most recent year. Norms on the Major Field Tests (see Chapter 11, p. 430) are based on all individuals who took the test within a three-year period.

With user norms there is no a priori attempt to ensure that the group is representative of any well-defined population. User norms are actually a type of convenience norm. As noted for convenience norms, one hopes a detailed description accompanies the user norm.

Subgroup Norms

Some tests provide **subgroup norms.** The subgroups are taken from the total norm group. For example, separate norms may be provided by sex, race, socioeconomic group, occupational group, or geographic region.

---

[5] Hence, this type of norm is usually encountered only in cases where the test publisher scores all or at least a substantial fraction of the tests administered.

Subgroup norms are potentially useful only if there are substantial differences between the subgroups on the variable measured by the test. If the subgroups do not differ on the variable, then the subgroup norms will not differ from the norm based on the total group.

Depending on the purpose of testing, one may prefer to use only a total group norm or only a subgroup norm. In many circumstances, the use of both a total group norm and a subgroup norm will enhance test interpretation. For example, it may be useful to know that Zeke's score is at the 60th percentile on the national norm but at the 30th percentile for persons in his occupational group.

Local Norms

A school uses the *Metropolitan Achievement Tests.* Students' scores in this school are reported in terms of the national norms. In addition, the school prepares a distribution of its own students' scores and interprets each student's score in relation to the scores of other students in this school. This is called a **local norm.** Such norms are almost always expressed as percentiles.

Consider another example. A company uses a quantitative aptitude test to select clerical employees. The company tests 200 job applicants each year. Although there are national norms on the test, the company uses the 200 applicants it tests to develop a local norm.

Local norms may be useful for some interpretive purposes. An advantage of local norms is that one certainly knows the characteristics of the norm group since it is precisely the people in the local situation. Of course, on a local norm, the typical person will be average. This has the potential to be misleading. For example, in the school testing situation previously mentioned, the typical student in each grade will be "at norm." This is not very informative since it is true by definition. One cannot determine on a local norm whether the typical individual is above or below average in terms of some external frame of reference.

Figure 3.21 provides an example. In this case, where the local group is somewhat above the national norm, a raw score of "X" is at the 55th percentile on the national norms but

Key Points Summary 3.5

Major Types of Norm Groups

- National Norms
- International Norms
- Convenience Norm Groups
- User Norms
- Subgroup Norms
- Local Norms
- Institutional Norms

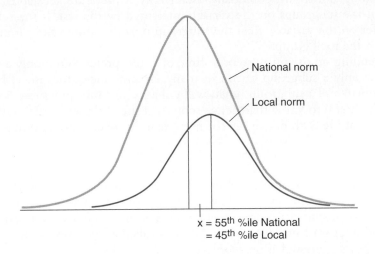

National norm

Local norm

x = 55th %ile National
 = 45th %ile Local

FIGURE 3.21 Sample comparison of national and local norms.

at the 45th percentile on the local norm. Much larger differences will be observed when the local group is very much above average or very much below average.

Institutional Norms

Some tests, especially achievement tests, provide norms based on institutions as well as norms based on individuals. The **institutional norms** are based on averages for individuals within institutions. For example, a test is administered to 5,000 students in 200 colleges. Average scores are determined for each of the 200 colleges. A frequency distribution of these averages is obtained, and a norm, usually a percentile norm, is developed for the averages. This is an institutional norm. It might be called a school norm, group norm, or some other such designation.

Ordinarily, the distributions of individual scores and group averages will have approximately the same center, but the individual scores will be substantially more varied than the group averages. Hence, a given raw score, except at the middle of the distribution, will be more deviant on the norm for institutions than on the norms for individuals. Above-average scores will be more above-average on the institutional norm than on the individual norm and vice versa for below average scores. The differences can be dramatic. Figure 3.22 depicts a comparison of individual and institutional norms. This is only an example. The actual degree of overlap between the two types of norms will vary with different tests and norm groups.

Much confusion may result if one does not distinguish carefully between individual norms and institutional norms. Consider, for example, the statement that "Southwest's score is at the 95th percentile on national norms." Many people would interpret this to mean that the typical student at Southwest scores better than 95% of students in the country. However, if that 95th percentile is based on institutional norms, it may very well be that the typical Southwest student scored better than only 70% of the nation's students.

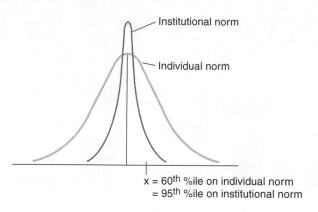

FIGURE 3.22   Individual versus institutional norms.

Criterion-referenced Interpretation

A 50-item test of basic computational skill is administered to a group of adults. The test includes such items as $7 \times 9 = $____, $417 + 236 = $____, and $2596 - 1688 = $____. An individual gets 30 items (60%) right. Such performance may be judged to be "unsatisfactory," perhaps by a teacher or a parent. This is an example of a **criterion-referenced** interpretation of test performance. In making the judgment that 60% correct was unsatisfactory, there was <u>no reference to any norm group</u>. Thus, criterion-referenced interpretation is contrasted with norm-referenced interpretation. **Norm-referenced** interpretation was the subject of all earlier parts of this chapter.

Tests themselves are sometimes characterized as criterion-referenced or norm-referenced. This terminology is inappropriate. It is not the test but the framework for interpreting test performance that is either criterion-referenced or norm-referenced. In fact, both kinds of interpretation can be used with a given test. For example, in the test described in the preceding paragraph, it might be noted that a raw score of 30 places the individual at the 75th percentile in a norm group representing the general adult population of the United States. In Figure 3.23, Calvin and his dad are having some disagreement about criterion-referenced interpretation of his performance in math. It might be useful to add a norm-referenced interpretation to their conversation.

Criterion-referenced interpretation is <u>usually applicable only</u> to some well-defined content domains such as computation, spelling, or all skills required by a certain occupation. We often apply criterion-referenced interpretation to scores on professional licensing exams and minimum competency exams for high school graduation. (We examine this topic in the section on "cutscores" in Chapter 11.) The less well defined the domain, the more difficult criterion-referenced interpretation becomes. The method of testing also becomes important when applying criterion-referenced interpretation. For example, in the computation test mentioned earlier, interpretation of performance may differ substantially depending on whether the test items were free-response or multiple-choice, whether a calculator was used, and whether a time limit was used. How might the interpretation of "60% correct" change if unlimited time was allowed or each item had to be completed in

FIGURE 3.23   Calvin and his dad try to interpret Calvin's performance.

10 seconds? Criterion-referenced interpretation often sounds like a simple idea, but it becomes problematic when examined more closely.

Criterion-referenced interpretation is often applied to classroom examinations. The familiar grading scheme "90% is an A, 80–89% is a B, … below 60% is failing" is an example of criterion-referenced interpretation. The content domain may be defined as "what the instructor covered in class" or "everything in Chapters 1–4 in the textbook." The judgment is that students should have learned all or nearly all of this material. Then the familiar grading scheme is applied. Of course, the grades may be "curved" so that the average score is a "C" and so on. Such "curving" is really a type of norm-referenced interpretation, specifically the application of a local norm.

The *proficiency levels* established for state assessments of achievement provide another good example of criterion-referenced interpretations. The levels are often referred to as *performance standards.* A common system uses these four categories: Advanced, Proficient, Basic, and Below Basic. Committees, commonly composed of teachers, school administrators, and representatives of the public, examine the test content and make judgments about what raw score level warrants calling a student "proficient" or "advanced" on the test. The division points are called "cut-scores." Thus, three cut-scores are needed to separate the four categories mentioned above. Numerous specific procedures have been developed to create such cut-scores, but they all come down to a criterion-referenced judgment about performance. See Cizek (2001b) for descriptions of a host of such methods and Cizek, Bunch, and Koons (2004) for a practical introduction to the methods. Use of these proficiency labels does not preclude the use of norms, too. For example, we might find that the cut-score separating the basic and proficient categories corresponds to the 45th percentile on the test.

The Standardization Group: Determining Its Usefulness

Individuals in the norm group are tested in what is called a norming program or **standardization** program. This is ordinarily one of the last steps in test development. Chapter 6 describes the full-test development process in detail. Here we treat the question of how one determines whether the standardization program is a good one. Competent use of psychological tests requires not only knowledge of the types of norms—percentiles, standard scores, and so on—but also the ability to judge the usefulness of the norms. Usefulness here means the extent to which the norms provide a meaningful framework for test interpretation. In most instances, this means having a norm that is (1) stable and (2) representative of some well-defined population. Hence, there are two issues: stability and representativeness.

The *stability* of a norm is determined largely by the size of the norm group, that is, the number of cases in the standardization program. This is rarely a problem. It does not take very many cases to achieve statistical stability. Several hundred cases will yield sufficient stability for most practical uses of norms. Consider the norm in a standard score system with $M = 100$ and $SD = 15$; with $N = 300$, the standard error of the mean is less than one point and the 95% confidence interval is $+/-1.7$ points. That is good stability. In practice, the norms for many tests are based on thousands of cases.

When considering the number of cases in a norm group, one needs to determine the size of the norm group on which a particular norm is based. The total number of cases aggregated over several norm groups is not the crucial number. For example, a test may boast that its norms are based on nearly 1,000 cases. However, suppose that the actual norms are given separately by gender and by grade over 10 grades. Thus, there are actually 20 norm groups, each with only about 50 cases. The important number here for determining stability is 50, not 1,000.

As noted, stability is rarely a problem and, in any case, is easily determined. However, stability does not guarantee representativeness. The difference between stability and representativeness is one of the most important distinctions to learn about norms. It is possible to have very large norm groups, yielding highly stable norms, that are very unrepresentative of the target population for a test.

How will we determine the *representativeness* of a norm group? Formulating an answer to this question depends on the test author's claims about the norms. There are two possibilities. First, the test author may claim that the norms are representative of a particular population. For example, the claim may be that the norm group is representative of all adults in the United States aged 20–80, or all students in grade 6, or all women in four-year colleges. Second, the test author may make no claim that the norms are representative of any particular population but simply presents the norm sample as a convenience or user group norm.

Let us consider how to judge the representativeness of the norm group in the first case where the claim is that the norm group is representative of a target population. From one perspective, determining the quality of a norm group intended to be representative of a population is a question for sampling theory. The reader is, no doubt, familiar with random sampling techniques used in introductory statistics courses. However, simple random sampling is rarely used in practice for norming tests. Ordinarily, some form of stratified cluster sampling is used in more sophisticated programs, for example, in the development of national or international norms. Sampling issues are complicated by the fact that participation in the norming program is usually voluntary. Thus, in practice, instead of concentrating attention on notions from sampling theory, we focus on evidence regarding the match between the norm group and the target population in terms of important characteristics. "Important" charcteristics in this context are characteristics that are related to the

TABLE 3.6   *Types of Information Helpful in Judging the Usefulness of a Norm Group*

Age	Racial/Ethnic Groups
Gender	Socioeconomic Status
Ability Level	Geographic Region
Educational Level	Size of City

variable being tested. Several demographic characteristics are frequently used to show the match between the norm group and the target population. Commonly used characteristics (see Table 3.6) are age, gender, racial/ethnic classification, socioeconomic status, and geographic region. Performance on other tests that themselves have well-documented norms may also be used. It should be shown that the norm group matches the target population reasonably well on such characteristics.

Often, when there is some mismatch between the norm group and the target population, cases in the norm group will be weighted to improve the match. Suppose, for example, that the population has 50% males and 50% females, whereas the norm group has 40% males and 60% females. Assigning a weight of 1.5 to each male (or .67 to each female) will yield a weighted norm group with the required 50–50 split on gender.

Figure 3.24 shows an example of a table comparing characteristics of a norm group with national statistics. The table gives some idea of what information the test user might expect to find for tests claiming nationally representative norms. Of course, the test manual will have additional information about the norming process.

> Reports of norming studies should include a precise specification of the population that was sampled, sampling procedures and participation rates, any weighting of the sample, the dates of testing, and descriptive statistics. The information provided should be sufficient to enable users to judge the appropriateness of the norms for interpreting the scores of local examinees. Technical documentation should indicate the precision of the norms themselves *Standards...* (AERA/APA/NCME, 1999, p. 55)

When the claim is made that a norm group is representative of a particular population, it is the test author's responsibility to provide sufficient information to justify the claim. The user needs to be especially wary of claims that the norm group is representative when only minimal information is presented about the match between norm group and population on important characteristics. For example, simply showing that a norm group for an intelligence test matches the national population in terms of age and gender is insufficient. What about the socioeconomic status and level of educational attainment of cases in the norm group?

Even when a norm group shows a good match with a target population on important characteristics, there are two problems that plague the process of establishing a good norm. The first is the effect of nonparticipation. It arises from the fact that participation in a norming program is nearly always voluntary, either for the individual or for an organization to which the individual belongs. What kinds of individuals or organizations declined to participate? What were their characteristics? What effect might their nonparticipation have on the norms? Often we do not have very good answers to these questions.

PPVT-III   Standardization Sample, by Age Group and Education Level, Compared to the U.S. Population

	Parent or Examinee Education Level[a]											
	Grade 11 or Less			High School Graduate			One to Three Years of College or Tech School			Four or More Years of College		
	PPVT-III Sample		U.S. Pop.[b]	PPVT-III Sample		U.S. Pop.[b]	PPVT-III Sample		U.S. Pop.[b]	PPVT-III Sample		U.S. Pop.[b]
Age Group	N	%	%	N	%	%	N	%	%	N	%	%
2–5	97	3.6	5.5	199	7.3	8.0	262	9.6	8.5	142	5.2	3.6
6–9	102	3.7	3.5	167	6.1	6.3	147	5.4	5.9	84	3.1	2.6
10–13	91	3.3	3.0	119	4.4	4.7	120	4.4	4.9	70	2.6	2.1
14–18	76	2.8	3.0	128	4.7	4.9	128	4.7	4.6	68	2.5	2.1
19–24	31	1.1	1.2	42	1.5	1.8	50	1.8	1.7	27	1.0	0.8
25–30	11	0.4	0.6	35	1.3	1.6	43	1.6	1.3	36	1.3	1.1
31–50	26	1.0	1.1	86	3.2	3.1	54	2.0	2.5	84	3.1	2.5
51–90+	31	1.1	1.9	78	2.9	2.7	48	1.8	1.4	43	1.6	1.3
Total Sample	465	17.1	19.9	854	31.3	33.1	852	31.3	31.0	554	20.3	16.0

[a] For examinees aged 24 and younger, if education level of both parents/guardians was not reported, education level of one parent/guardian was used.

[b] U.S. population data from *Current Population Survey, March 1994* [machine-readable data file] conducted by the Bureau of the Census for the Bureau of Labor Statistics. U.S. population percentages for the total sample are averages of the census percentages for each of the age groups, weighted by each age group's sample size in PPVT-III.

FIGURE 3.24 Demographic information for standardization program for *Peabody Picture Vocabulary Test,* 3rd Edition.
Source: From Dunn, L. M., & Dunn, L. M. Peabody Picture Vocabulary Test, (3rd Edition), Test Kit Form IIIA Examiner's Manual, p. 43. Copyright © 1997. With permission of the publisher, American Guidance Service, Inc.

Second, norming programs are research programs rather than ordinary uses of the tests. Participants usually know this. Under these circumstances it is difficult to ensure that participants' motivational levels are the same as they would be for ordinary use of the test. As for nonparticipation, we often do not know the effect of motivational levels on the norms. About the best one can hope for is a frank discussion of these problems in the test manual.

Now consider our second case: when no claim is made that the norm group is representative of a particular population. What criteria will we use to judge the quality of the norms in this second case? Basically, we reverse the process previously used. In the first case, we had a target population and tried to demonstrate that the norm group was representative of that population. The demonstration depended on the use of information about important characteristics. In the second case, we hope to have adequate information about the norm group so that we can project what population might be mirrored by the norm group. For example, if we have user norms for an achievement test used by colleges, we would want information about the colleges, such as their size, acceptance and retention rates, curricular emphases, gender and racial composition, and so on. Based on this descriptive information, we might infer that the norms provide good representation of small, selective, liberal arts colleges, but not good representation for large, urban, open-admissions colleges. If we have convenience norms for a self-concept test for high school students, we would want to know about the ability level, gender, racial/ethnic classification, and socioeconomic status of the participants. Based on this information, we might conclude that the norms are probably representative of low socioeconomic, highly urbanized schools, but certainly not a nationally representative group.

In either the first or second case, the user must be particularly cautious about norms for a derivative of the original test. For example, a "short form" may be created from an original, long test. Or, from a 300-item personality test measuring 10 traits, the 30 items measuring one trait may be administered as a separate test. One cannot assume that the norms for the original test are applicable to these derivative works. The change in context may have unpredictable effects on examinees' responses to the items. In these situations, the applicability of the original norms must be demonstrated empirically.

Summary

1. The raw score is usually the most immediate result of a test. Typical raw scores are the number of correct answers for cognitive tests and the number of answers in a certain direction on noncognitive tests.

2. Tests scored according to IRT methods, yielding a theta score (θ), take into account the difficulty level of items and sometimes the patterns of responses.

3. The distribution of raw scores in a norm group forms the basis for converting raw scores into normed scores. Normed scores help to give meaning to the raw scores.

4. To understand test norms, one needs to be familiar with the following topics from elementary statistics: frequency distributions and shapes of distributions, measures of central tendency and variability, and z-scores within the normal distribution.

5. Percentile ranks indicate the percentage of individuals in the norm group who score below a given raw score.

6. Standard scores are norms that convert the raw score distribution into a distribution with a new, convenient mean and standard deviation. There are several widely used standard score systems.

7. Developmental norms express performance in terms of the score that is typical for an age or grade level. The most common developmental norms are mental ages and grade equivalents.

8. Each of the major types of norms has its own advantages and disadvantages.

9. The quality of the norm is dependent on the characteristics of the norm group. The most important fact is the extent to which the norm group is representative of a well-defined population.

10. Common types of norm groups are national, convenience, user, and local norm groups. A few tests have international norms. There are also subgroup norms and institutional norms for some tests.

11. Some tests may use criterion-referenced rather than norm-referenced interpretation of scores. Criterion-referenced interpretation is a relatively direct judgment about the quality of test performance without reference to any norm group. Both types of interpretation may be used with some tests.

12. It is important to be able to judge the usefulness of a norm group. Information about the characteristics of the norm group is crucial for making such judgments. In judging the usefulness of a norm group, it is often helpful to compare the norm group with a population in terms of such characteristics as age, gender, racial/ethnic group, geographic region, and socioeconomic characteristics such as educational level and family income.

Key Terms

age equivalent	local norm	percentile rank
Barnum effect	mean	range
central tendency	median	ratio IQ
chronological age	mental age	ratio scale
construct	mode	raw score
convenience group	narrative report	scaled scores
criterion-referenced	national norm	skewness
descriptive statistics	nominal scale	standard deviation
developmental norm	nonlinear	standard score
deviation IQ	transformation	standardization
frequency distribution	norm group	stanine
frequency histogram	normal curve	subgroup norms
frequency polygon	normal curve equivalent	theta
grade equivalent	normalized standard	true zero
inferential statistics	score	T-score
institutional norm	normed score	user norms
interquartile range	norm-referenced	variability
interval scale	ordinal scale	variable
kurtosis	percentage-right score	variance
linear transformation	percentile	z-score

Exercises

1. Using the data in Figure 3.1, create a frequency distribution with a 5-point interval, starting with 65–69.

2. Calculate the mean, median, and standard deviation for these scores:

    5, 3, 6, 8, 8

    $M =$ _____

    Mdn = _____

    $SD =$ _____

3. If feasible, record the heights of everyone in your class. Create a frequency distribution. What shape does the distribution take in comparison with the models shown in Figure 3.6? Do the same exercise for pulse.

4. Using Figure 3.10, make *estimates* for the missing values.

    z-score = + 1.0   Percentile = _____   NCE = _____   Wechsler IQ = _____

    Percentile = 75   z-score = _____   Otis-Lennon = _____   stanine = _____

    T-score = 30   Percentile = _____   stanine = _____   z-score = _____

5. Using Table 3.1, fill in exact values for the same cases (*Note:* for Wechsler IQ, $SD = 15$, for Otis-Lennon IQ, $SD = 16$).

    z-score = + 1.0   Percentile = _____   NCE = _____   Wechsler IQ = _____

    Percentile = 75   z-score = _____   Otis-Lennon = _____   stanine = _____

    T-score = 30   Percentile = _____   stanine = _____   z-score = _____

6. Refer to Figure 3.12. Convert a raw score of 32 into the standard score system.

7. Using Figure 3.16, what is the estimated mental age for a person whose raw score is 35?

8. Use Table 3.4. What percentile rank and standard score (T-score) correspond to a raw score of 65?

9. Devise a set of labels for use in a narrative report for each quartile, that is, percentiles 1–25, 26–50, 51–75, 79-99, and so on. Labels may be more than one word. To avoid using the same label repeatedly for a given decile, give at least two equivalent labels for each decile. The computer program will then chose one at random for each instance of that decile.

Quartile Group	Verbal Label A	Verbal Label B
1-25	_____	_____
26-50	_____	_____
51-75	_____	_____
76-99	_____	_____

10. Enter the data from Appendix D1:GPA into the spreadsheet for a statistical package such as SPSS, SAS, or Excel. Run the program to obtain the means and standard deviations for each of the variables. For any two variables, run frequency distributions and histograms. How would you describe the shapes of the distributions?

CHAPTER 4

Reliability

Objectives

1. Define reliability as the term is used in psychological testing.

2. Refresh your knowledge of basic statistical concepts related to correlation and prediction, including factors that affect the magnitude of correlations.

3. Make the distinctions between reliability and validity, between several everyday uses of the term *reliability*, between real change and temporary fluctuations, and between constant errors and unsystematic errors.

4. Identify the major sources of unreliability in test scores.

5. Describe the components of true score theory.

6. For each of these reliability methods, tell how the study is conducted and what source of unreliability is treated: test-retest, inter-scorer, alternate form, internal consistency.

7. Define and calculate the standard error of measurement and a confidence band.

8. Distinguish the standard error of measurement from the standard error of the mean and from the standard error of estimate.

9. Define what precision of measurement means in IRT.

10. Describe what generalizability theory attempts to do.

11. State how factors affecting the correlation coefficient influence reliability data.

12. Provide benchmarks for acceptable levels of reliability.

Introduction

Jack takes the college admissions test on Saturday, October 2, after a really tough week in school capped off by a Friday night football game. Jill also takes the test on October 2, feeling sharp as a tack and ready to whip the world. Would Jack and Jill get substantially different scores if they were to take the test on Saturday, October 9, when their personal circumstances might be somewhat different?

Terry's chemistry class includes 700 freshmen. To discourage cheating during an exam, the professor takes 100 test problems and divides them randomly into four sets of 25 problems each. Call them forms A, B, C, and D of the exam. The forms are distributed randomly to the class. Would Terry's score differ much if he took form A rather than form B?

How much do scores on a personality test fluctuate from day to day? How similar are scores on an essay test depending on who scores the test? When two clinicians use a form to rate the severity of psychological maladjustment, are they likely to agree in their ratings?

All these latter questions relate to the topic of reliability. This chapter considers the ways that have been developed to answer these kinds of questions. Before beginning our formal treatment of reliability, four important distinctions should be made.

Four Important Distinctions

First, we should distingush at the outset between the *reliability* and *validity* of measures. Validity is treated more fully in the next chapter, but we can define it briefly here in order to contrast it with reliability. Validity deals with what a test measures, specifically whether it measures what it was intended to measure. **Reliability** deals only with the consistency of the measure, regardless of exactly what it is measuring. A measure may be reliable without being valid. For example, the chemistry test referenced earlier may be very reliable; but it may be more a measure of mathematical skill than knowledge of chemistry. There may be excellent agreement among clinicians in the ratings assigned for maladjustment, but the rating form may be more a measure of poor verbal skill than of maladjustment. Although a test can be reliable without being valid, a test cannot be valid unless it is reliable. In this chapter, we treat only the question of reliability.

FIGURE 4.1 Sir Rodney uses one definition of the term "reliable."

Source: From Parker, B. & Hart, J. The Wizard of Id. Copyright © 1998. By permission of Johnny Hart and Creators Syndicate, Inc.

Second, we should be aware of differences between *everyday uses of the word* reliability and the technical use of this word in psychological testing. In everyday parlance, the word *reliability* has several related meanings. A reliable machine starts and runs continuously when we push the ON button. A reliable employee arrives on time and is rarely absent. A "usually reliable source" (Figure 4.1) provides accurate information rather than rumors. A reliable car dealer has been in business for many years, is expected to stay in business, and gives good customer service.

All of these everyday meanings for the word *reliability* have some relevance to the concept of reliability in psychological testing. However, test reliability has a more technical and quantitative meaning. The best synonyms in English for the technical term reliability are consistency, replicability, and dependability. A reliable test, in the psychometric sense, is one that *consistently* yields the same or a similar score for an individual. The score can be *replicated* at least within a certain margin of error. We can *depend* on a reliable test to yield much the same score for an individual. This chapter deals with the technical, psychometric meaning of the word *reliability*.

Third, a distinction should be made between **real change** in the trait being measured and fluctuations in scores attributable to fleeting changes in personal

---

Key Points Summary 4.1

Four Important Distinctions for Reliability

1. Reliability versus Validity
2. Everyday Uses versus Technical Definition
3. Real Change versus Temporary Change
4. Constant Errors versus Unsystematic Errors

circumstances, the "luck of the draw" in what form of a test is taken, or differences due to who scores the test. Real changes in the trait being measured are not a source of unreliability. The other factors just mentioned would usually be considered sources of unreliability, although they may not be if one is trying to measure changes in mood or emotional state. There is no clear demarcation between short-term, temporary changes and long-term, real changes but the distinction is conceptually important.

Fourth, we need to distinguish between constant errors and **unsystematic errors** in our measurements. A **constant error** is one that leads to a person's score being systematically high or low quite apart from the constancy in the person's status on the trait being measured. For example, consider the intelligence level of a child whose native language is Spanish but who is tested in English. The child's intelligence level will probably be underestimated, and the underestimate will be relatively constant whether the child is tested on Tuesday or Wednesday. Or consider Jessica, who is "savvy" at taking tests. Jessica knows how to detect clues to the right answer even though she does not know much about the subject being tested. Jessica will tend to get a higher score than her real knowledge warrants and will do so regardless of when tested. Reliability does not account for these constant errors. Reliability deals only with unsystematic errors. Note that what we refer to as "constant" errors are not really constants but tendencies that move scores in a certain direction.

Review of Statistics: Part 2—Correlation and Prediction

Correlation coefficients and their offshoots—standard errors and prediction formulas—are crucial elements in our study of reliability and validity, the topics for this and the next chapter. Hence, it will be useful to provide a quick review of key concepts and procedures related to these statistical methods. As with our review of statistics in the previous chapter, it is assumed that the reader has had a thorough introduction to this material but needs a refresher to activate old memories.

Bivariate Distribution and Correlation Coefficients

The relationship between two variables may be represented by a **bivariate distribution,** also known as a **scattergram** or scatter plot. Figure 4.2 depicts several of these distributions. In each case, the X variable is on the horizontal axis, and the Y variable is on the vertical axis Each dot (·) in a distribution corresponds to the (X, Y) coordinates for a single case. For example, if X is a score on Form X of a test and Y is a score on Form Y of a test, then the (X, Y) coordinate for an individual is the person's scores on Forms X and Y.

The **correlation coefficient** *(r)* provides a numerical summary of the relationship depicted in a bivariate distribution. In giving formulas for *r*, we usually distinguish between a basic definition for *r* and a computing or raw score formula. The following are commonly used definitions and computing versions of the formulas. No doubt, you saw these in your elementary statistics course.

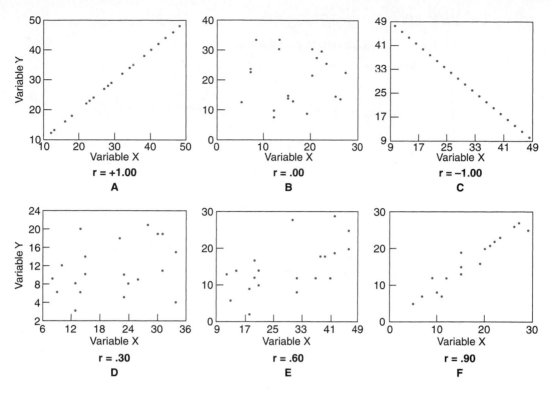

FIGURE 4.2   Examples of bivariate distributions and corresponding *r*'s.

Definition

$$r = \frac{\Sigma(X - \overline{X})(Y - \overline{Y})}{NS_X S_Y}$$

Formula 4-1

Computing formula $r = \dfrac{N\Sigma XY - (\Sigma X)(\Sigma Y)}{\sqrt{[N\Sigma X^2 - (\Sigma X)^2][N\Sigma Y^2 - (\Sigma Y)^2]}}$

Formula 4-2

   The value of *r* can range from −1.00 to + 1.00 An *r* of +1.00 represents a perfect positive linear relationship between two variables, as shown in panel A of Figure 4.2. An *r* of −1.00 represents a perfect negative linear relationship, as shown in panel C. An *r* of .00 represents lack of relationship between the two variables, as shown in panel B. In most practical work in psychological testing, we encounter *r*'s that are far from perfect. Figure 4.2 shows bivariate distributions for several intermediate values of *r*, specifically, for .30, .60, and .90.

TRY IT! ....

Estimate *r* for this bivariate distribution.

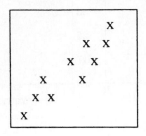

r = _____

In this box, fill in marks (★) to show a bivariate distribution corresponding to *r* = .40.

Compare your estimates for this exercise with answers developed by others students.

....

Most of the correlations encountered in psychological testing, as well as in other work in the social and behavioral sciences, are Pearson correlations. The formulas for *r* given earlier are for the Pearson correlation. However, there are many other types of correlation coefficients. Some are variations on the Pearson coefficient, applicable when the nature of the scale allows for computational simplification in the formula. For example, when one variable is a dichotomy and the only possible scores are 0 and 1, then $\Sigma X/N = p$, the percentage of cases scoring 1. This allows for simplifying the computational formula for *r*. Other types of correlation are not simple variations on the Pearson coefficient and are derived in other ways. However, all the correlation coefficients can be interpreted in much the same way as the Pearson coefficient. There are a few exceptions to this generalization, but the exceptions rarely have important practical implications. Table 4.1 lists several of the other types of bivariate correlation coefficients. Unless otherwise stated, throughout this book we assume that a correlation is of the Pearson type. In Chapter 5, we will examine multivariate correlation, specifically multiple correlation and partial correlation.

Regression Line

Once we establish the correlation *(r)* between two variables (*X* and *Y*), we can use the relationship to predict status on *Y* from a knowledge of *X* (or vice versa).

TABLE 4.1 *Examples of Types of Correlation Coefficients Other than Ordinary Pearson*

Biserial r (r_{bis})	Point biserial r (r_{pbis})
Tetrachoric r (r_{tet})	Phi coefficient (Φ)
Contingency coefficient *(C)*	Spearman rank order correlation (R)
Intraclass correlation *(ICC)*	Eta (η)
Kappa (κ)	Kendall's tau (τ)

Suppose we know the correlation between a college admission test *(X)* and grade point average *(Y)*. Now we have a student's *X* score and wish to predict his GPA (*Y'*, we use the ′ to indicate that this is a predicted *Y* rather than a known *Y*). The general form of the prediction equation is:

$$Y' = bX + a$$

where *b* is the slope of the **regression line**[1] and *a* is the intercept on the *y*-axis. This is the best fitting line according to the least squares criterion; it minimizes the quantity

$$\Sigma (Y - Y')^2$$

A convenient computing formula, algebraically equivalent to the latter formula, is:

$$Y' = r_{xy}\left(\frac{S_y}{S_x}\right)(X - \overline{X}) + \overline{Y} \qquad \textbf{Formula 4-3}$$

where

r_{xy} = the correlation between *X* and *Y*

S_x = the standard deviation of *X*

S_y = the standard deviation of *Y*

X = the person's score on *X*

$\overline{X}$ = the mean of *X* scores

$\overline{Y}$ = the mean of *Y* scores

TRY IT!

To make sure you understand how to compute *Y'*, substitute the following values in the formula and obtain *Y'*. You are predicting GPA *(Y)* from SAT *(X)* scores. For SAT, the mean is 500 and SD is 100. For GPA, the mean is 2.80 and *SD* is .50. The correlation between GPA and SAT is .65. What is the predicted GPA for an SAT of 650?

---

[1] The term *regression line* is not very descriptive. It would be nice to call it the "prediction line." However, the term *regression* was adopted early in the development of this methodology, originating with the work of Francis Galton. The term has had amazing but unfortunate staying power.

Figure 4.3 presents an example of a regression line. Each point in the figure represents the X, Y coordinates for a person. We use the line to predict status on Y from status on X. For example, follow the dotted line in the lower quadrant of the figure. For a person with an X score of 9, we predict a Y score of 29.

Of course, not all the actual Y scores fall exactly on the prediction line (except when $r = +1.00$ or -1.00). There is some scatter of actual Y scores around the line. The higher r is, the less the scatter. The lower r is, the more the scatter. Think of the scatter at one point on the prediction line, specifically for one value of X. We assume a normal distribution of the Y's; in fact, we assume equivalent normal distributions of Y's for each value of X all along the prediction line. The distribution in Figure 4.4 illustrates this situation. This distribution has a standard deviation. We call this particular kind of standard deviation the **standard error of estimate** or standard error of prediction. By using features of the normal distribution—for example, the fact that 68% of the cases are within +/− one standard deviation—we can make statements about the probability that actual scores will differ from predicted scores by a certain amount. The formula for the standard error of estimate is:

$$SE_{Y'} = SD_Y \sqrt{1 - r_{xy}^2}$$ **Formula 4-4**

where SD_y is the standard deviation on the test we are predicting

   r_{xy} is the correlation between the test to be predicted and the test we are predicting from

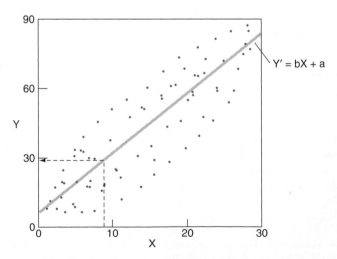

FIGURE 4.3   Regression line for predicting Y from X.

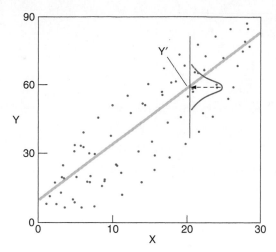

FIGURE 4.4 Distribution of actual *Y* scores around *Y'*.

Factors Affecting Correlation Coefficients

We need to be aware of several factors that affect the magnitude of correlations and their interpretation. First, the Pearson correlation coefficient, which is by far the most widely used type of correlation, accounts only for the degree of *linear* relationship between two variables. If there is some degree of nonlinearity, the Pearson correlation will underestimate the true degree of relationship. Figure 4.5 shows a

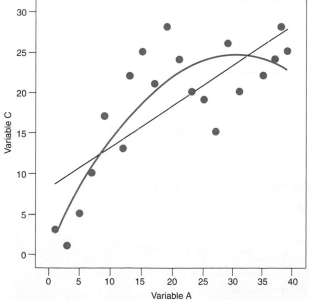

FIGURE 4.5 A bivariate distribution showing a curvilinear relationship.

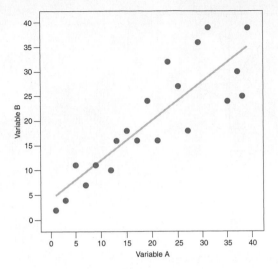

FIGURE 4.6 A bivariate distribution showing heteroscedasticity.

bivariate distribution that has a degree of curvilinearity. A Pearson correlation will account for the linear part of the relationship, as shown by the straight line, but not for the nonlinear trend shown by the curved line.

Second, as noted, we assume that Y scores are normally distributed around any predicted Y score (Y') and that the degree of scatter is equal for any point along the prediction line. This is known as the assumption of **homoscedasticity** (roughly, in Greek, equal scatter). However, it is possible for the bivariate distribution to display **heteroscedasticity** (different scatter), as shown in Figure 4.6. Notice that the data points cluster rather tightly around the trend line in the lower part of the distribution but the points scatter more widely toward the top of the distribution. In this case, the standard error is not equal throughout the range of the variables, although we calculate it as if it were equal throughout.

Key Points Summary 4.2

Four Factors Affecting the Correlation Coefficient

1. Linearity
2. Heteroscedasticity
3. Relative (not absolute) Position
4. Group Heterogeneity

TABLE 4.2   *Correlation Is a Matter of Relative Position, Not Absolute Score*

Case	1	2	3	4	5	6	7	8	9	10
Test A	80	85	92	90	86	96	100	105	107	110
Test B	80	86	85	92	90	96	105	100	107	110
Test C	90	95	102	100	96	106	110	115	117	120

$r_{AB} = .94$ $r_{BC} = .94$

$M_A = 95.1$ $M_B = 95.1$ $M_C = 105.1$

Third, correlation is strictly a matter of relative position within each group. Correlation does not require or imply equal absolute scores. Consider the data in Table 4.2. Obtain the correlations among these intelligence test scores for 10 cases. There is a nearly perfect correlation between the scores on Tests A and B, and the means are equal. For Tests B and C, there is the same correlation but the means differ by 10 points. One might be inclined to say that Test C does not correlate very well with Test B. However, $r_{AB} = r_{BC} = .94$. The relative positions of cases are the same for A versus B and B versus C, even though absolute scores are higher on C.

Fourth, we consider the effect of group variability on the correlation coefficient. The standard deviation or variance defines a group's variability. In this context, variability is often called **heterogeneity** (difference) or its opposite **homogeneity** (same). A very heterogeneous group yields an inflated correlation. A very homogeneous group yields a deflated correlation. Consider the data displayed in Figure 4.7. If we calculate r for the very heterogeneous group included within frame A, we get a very high r. If we calculate r for the more homogeneous group included within frame C, we get a much lower r. For cases in frame B, we get an intermediate value of r. The example given in Figure 4.7 is somewhat artificial because it suggests restricting range simultaneously on both the X and Y variables. In practice, range is usually restricted in just one way, but it has the same kind of effect as illustrated here.

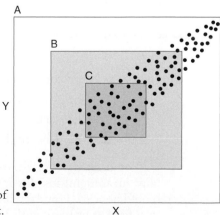

FIGURE 4.7 Illustration of the effect of range restriction on the correlation coefficient.

How might these situations arise in practice? Suppose we calculate the correlation between SAT scores and GPA only on students who graduate summa cum laude, that is, with GPAs in excess of 3.90. This group is very homogeneous with respect to GPA. We would be likely to get a very low correlation, perhaps near zero, between SAT and GPA for this group. It would be rash to conclude that as a rule GPA is unrelated to SAT scores. If we calculate the correlation between SAT and GPA for students with the full spectrum of GPAs, we will obtain a very different result. Or suppose we calculate the correlation between shoe size and reading test score for children in grades 1–8, a very heterogeneous group. We would get a much higher correlation than if we had determined the correlation between shoe size and reading test score only for students in grade 8.

Differences in group variability can have a very substantial influence on the magnitude of correlation. One needs to be constantly vigilant about this influence. There are formulas that allow for correction in r for increased or decreased variability in the group. The formulas are called "corrections for restriction in range." We provide here the most widely used formulas for such corrections. For a host of variations in the formulas for specialized cases, see Sackett and Yang (2000). Assume we know the variances (or standard deviations) for both the groups with restricted and unrestricted variability (or that we know one of the variances and can make a reasonable estimate of the other one). Then knowing r for the restricted group, we can estimate what r would be in the unrestricted group. Alternatively, knowing r in the unrestricted group, we can estimate what r would be in the restricted group. To estimate what r would be in a more heterogeneous group from an r obtained in a more homogeneous group, use Formula 4–5. To estimate what r would be in a more homogeneous group from an r obtained in a more heterogeneous group, use Formula 4-6. See Glass and Hopkins (1996) for further examples of the effects of range restriction on the correlation coefficient.

$$r_L = \frac{r_M(S_L/S_M)}{\sqrt{1 - r_M^2 + r_M^2(S_L/S_M)^2}}$$

Formula 4-5

$$r_M = \frac{r_L(S_M/S_L)}{\sqrt{1 - r_L^2 + r_L^2(S_M/S_L)^2}}$$

Formula 4-6

where r_L = the correlation in the *less* restricted group

r_M = the correlation in the *more* restricted group

S_L = the standard deviation in the *less* restricted group

S_M = the standard deviation in the *more* restricted group

For ordinary mortals, examination of Formulas 4–5 and 4–6 does not provide any meaningful insights into the effect of group homogeneity on the correlation coefficient *(r)*. However, it is easy to insert values into the formulas and observe the results. Let us work with Formula 4–5. This is the more widely used formula since

TABLE 4.3   *Sample Values for Applying Correction for Group Homogeneity (Formula 4–5)*

SD in more restricted group as % of SD in less restricted group	r in more restricted group	r in less restricted group
50%	.20	.38
50%	.50	.76
50%	.90	.97
70%	.20	.28
70%	.50	.64
70%	.90	.95
90%	.20	.22
90%	.50	.54
90%	.90	.92

many research projects employ groups that are more homogeneous than the general population. We want to know how *r* in our research project might change if we conducted the study with the entire population. Let us set *r* at values of .20, .50, and .90. Then let us set the *SD* in the more restricted group at 50%, 70%, and 90% of the *SD* in the less restricted group. For example, let *SD* in the less restricted group be 10 and *SD* in the more restricted group take on values of 5, 7, and 9, successively. Finally, apply Formula 4-5 to determine what *r* would be in the less restricted group. Table 4.3 shows the results.

From the data in Table 4.3, as well as from additional simulations, we conclude the following. First, the correction for group homogeneity has very substantial effects when variability is much less in the restricted group than in the unrestricted group. For example, when *SD* in the restricted group is only one-half of the *SD* in the unrestricted group, *r* may increase by more than 20 points. However, when the *SD* in the restricted group reaches about 90% of the *SD* in the unrestricted group, there is little effect on *r*. Second, the effect of the correction is most pronounced for moderate levels of correlation. This is an important conclusion because most of the correlations we work with in psychology are moderate. Very low correlations (e.g., under .10) and very high correlations (e.g., above .90) are not greatly affected by the correction for group homogeneity. In case it is not immediately obvious, we should note that the correction never results in a change in the direction of the relationship.

Major Sources of Unreliability

Before formulating specific methods for expressing the reliability of tests, it is important to consider potential sources of unreliability. What factors or conditions will lead to less than perfectly reliable measurement? It is these sources of unreliability that the indexes of reliability must address. Anything that results in *unsystematic* variation in test scores is a source of unreliability. No list of sources will be exhaustive. We identify here four major categories for these sources of unsystematic variation.

Test Scoring

Variation in test scoring as a source of unreliability is one of the easiest to understand. It is also one of great historical importance. Concern for differences in scores from one scorer to another—even on simple tests like spelling or arithmetic computation—was a major force in the development of multiple-choice items in achievement and ability testing.

Consider the simple cases presented in Table 4.4 and Table 4.5. For the responses on the dictated spelling test summarized in Table 4.4, both scorers 1 and 2 agree that the first two words are spelled correctly and that the third word is spelled incorrectly. However, scorer 1 credits "colour" as a legitimate alternate scoring of "color." Scorer 2 does not credit it. For the scoring of "achievement," scorer 1 gives the student the "benefit of the doubt" for the ambiguous "ie" in the middle of the word.

TABLE 4.4   *Responses to Dictated Spelling Test*

Dictated Word	Student Response	Scorer 1	Scorer 2
reliability	*reliability*	C	C
testing	*testing*	C	C
psychometrics	*cyconetrix*	W	W
color	*Colour*	C	W
achievement	*achievement*	C	W
Total Score		4	2

C = correct, W = wrong.

TABLE 4.5 *Responses to Arithmetic Computation Test*

Item	Student Response	Scorer 1	Scorer 2
6 + 2	8	C	C
10 − 5	5	C	C
3 × 3	6	W	W
4 + 3	⌐	C	W
35 − 12	20 +3	C	W
Total Score		4	2

C = correct, W = wrong.

Scorer 2 is not so kind. Thus, the person's score on these five items varies by two points (40%!) depending on who scored the responses.

Table 4.5 gives examples of responses for a simple arithmetic computation test. Scorers 1 and 2 agree that responses to the first two items are correct and that the response to the third item is incorrect. However, for the third item, scorer 1 credits the reversed 7, noting that the student obviously knows the result of the operation but just has trouble writing it correctly. Scorer 2 insists that the result be expressed correctly. On the fifth item, scorer 1 generously notes that the student's response is technically correct, though expressed in a nonstandard form. Scorer 2 dourly finds this nonstandard expression quite unacceptable.

The latter examples illustrate how variations in scoring criteria can affect even simple test items. Consider how much more variation may be encountered in scoring responses to items such as open-ended questions in an individually administered intelligence test, a scale for rating creativity, or a projective test of personality. Many intelligence tests, for example, include vocabulary items. The test administrator says a word, and the examinee is to give an acceptable definition. Table 4.6 gives two sample words and several responses for each word. Each response is scored as 0 (clearly wrong), 1 (partially correct), or 2 (clearly correct).

TRY IT! ....

Score the responses in Table 4.6. Compare your scores with those assigned by other students.

....

In summary, lack of agreement among scorers may result in unsystematic variation in persons' test scores. Machine scoring of "choice" items generally eliminates such variation, although even machine scoring may not be completely error-free. The more judgment required in scoring, the more worrisome this potential source

TABLE 4.6 *Sample Examinee Responses to Vocabulary Items*

Word	Examinee Responses	Score 0, 1, 2
Reliable	> like, you know, being consistent, dependable	( )
	> hard, difficult	( )
	> being the same, identical	( )
	> usual	( )
School	> a building	( )
	> a place students go to learn	( )
	> a group of fish	( )
	> a lot of books	( )
	> where the teacher lives	( )

of unreliability will be. When judgment is required, the goal is to have scoring directions that are sufficiently clear and explicit so that scorer variation is reduced to a minimum.

Test Content

Variations in the sampling of items in a test may result in unsystematic error in test scores. Consider the case of a mathematics test used for placing students in college math courses. The college has ten slightly different versions of the test to use with incoming students throughout the summer orientation sessions. One version of the test has two items on the Pythagorean theorem; another version has only one such item. A student who is particularly proficient with the theorem may get a slightly higher score on the first version than on the second version. Or consider two students preparing for an essay exam in history. The exam will cover six chapters. The professor will include on the test four questions from a potentially infinite number she carries around in her head. One student concentrates on the first four chapters and skims the last two. The other student skims the first two chapters and concentrates on the last four. Going into the exam the two students know the same total amount of material for the exam. However, three of the four essay questions are drawn from the last four chapters. How does this variation in content affect the two students' scores? What would happen if three of the four questions were drawn from the first four chapters?

These slight variations in the sampling of items in a test yield unsystematic errors. Individuals' scores increase or decrease, perhaps by only a few points, perhaps by more, not because of real differences in the trait being measured but because of more or less random changes in the particular set of items presented in the test.

Test Administration Conditions

A test should have standardized procedures for its administration. This includes such factors as the directions, time limits, and physical arrangements for administration.

However, it is impossible to control every conceivable detail of the administration. Yet these details may have some influence on test scores. For example, noise in the hallway outside the testing room or less than ideal lighting conditions might adversely affect scores in a certain administration of the test. If a test has a 30-minute time limit, one administrator may be a little more generous with the limit, giving perhaps 31 minutes while another is a little stingier, giving 29.5 minutes. All these slight variations in test administration may be sources of unreliable variance in test scores.

Personal Conditions

The temporary conditions of examinees may have unsystematic influences on their test scores. If tested on Tuesday, Jim may get a somewhat lower score because he has a bit of a headcold. If tested on Wednesday, when he's feeling much better, he might garner a few extra points. Jen is in a foul mood on Friday when she takes a personality inventory. If tested on Saturday, when she had mellowed, her score might be somewhat different. In both instances, there is no difference from one day to the next in the person's status on the underlying trait being measured, but the temporary personal condition has influenced the scores.

Variations in the factors just considered do not automatically result in unreliability. For example, variations in room lighting or a minor case of the sniffles may not affect test performance. The extent to which these factors affect test scores is an empirical question. It is precisely this empirical question that is addressed by the methods for determining and expressing test reliability. We now begin formal consideration of these methods.

Conceptual Framework: True Score Theory

The reliability of tests may be formulated within three somewhat different theoretical contexts: classical test theory (CTT), item response theory (IRT), and generalizability theory (GT). The great majority of the reliability information currently encountered in test manuals, professional journals, and test score reports relies on CTT. Hence, this chapter concentrates on that framework. However, IRT and GT approaches are gaining in popularity, so these frameworks are also presented at the end of the chapter.

The classical test theory approach begins with an interesting, useful conceptual framework. The key terms in this framework are *observed score (O), true score (T),* and *error score (E).* The **observed score** is a person's actual score on a test. Think of it as the person's raw score, for example, 30 right out of 45 items on a test of arithmetic problem solving, although the concept applies equally well to normed scores, for example, standard scores. This observed score may be affected, positively or negatively, by various sources of unreliability. For example, the observed score might be a little high due to some lucky guesses; or it might be a little low because the examinee was especially tired at the time of testing.

A person's **true score** is the score a person would get if all sources of unreliability were removed or canceled. It may be thought of as the average score obtained from many administrations (theoretically, an infinite number) of the test at different times and with slightly different conditions. Each variation in conditions may introduce some unreliability. When all the actual, observed scores are averaged, the mean should equal the true score. The true score is what we really want to know, although in practice we never know it for sure. We only get an observed score.

> To say that a score includes a component of error implies that there is a hypothetical error-free value that characterizes an examinee at the time of testing. In classical test theory, this error-free value is referred to as the person's *true score* for the test or measurement procedure. It is conceptualized as the hypothetical average score resulting from many repetitions of the test or alternate forms of the instrument. *Standards…*
>
> (AERA/APA/NCME, 1999, p. 25)

The **error score** is simply the difference between the true score and the observed score. *E* may be either positive or negative. It is the summation of all the unsystematic influences on a person's true score that were considered under sources of unreliability above. Formula 4–7 expresses the relationships among the observed, true, and error scores.

$$T = O +/-E \qquad\qquad \textbf{Formula 4-7}$$

The formula could also be written as:

$$O = T +/-E \qquad\qquad \textbf{Formula 4-8}$$

or

$$+/-E = T - O$$

Of course, the three formulas are algebraically equivalent. Each gives a slightly different way of thinking about the relationship. Notice that the error score can be either positive or negative.

True score theory may also be expressed in terms of variances of test scores. Recall that the variance is simply the standard deviation squared. In this formulation:

$$\sigma_o^2 = \sigma_T^2 + \sigma_E^2 \qquad\qquad \textbf{Formula 4-9}$$

or

$$\sigma_T^2 = \sigma_o^2 - \sigma_E^2$$

That is, the variance of observed scores is the sum of true score variance and error score variance; or true score variance is observed variance with error variance subtracted. These relationships are depicted in Figure 4.8. Panel A shows a test for which the true variance represents only about half of the observed variance; the remainder is error variance. Panel B shows a test for which the error variance is a relatively small fraction of the total observed variance; most of the variance is true variance. In other words, the test in panel B has much better reliability than the test in panel A.

Using the symbolism adopted here, we may define reliability (r) as:

$$r = \frac{\sigma_T^{\,2}}{\sigma_o^{\,2}} \qquad\qquad \textbf{Formula 4-10}$$

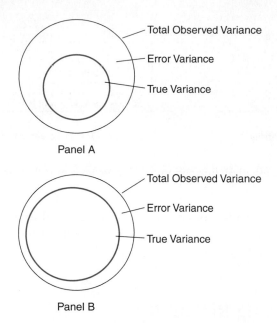

Panel A

Panel B

FIGURE 4.8 Relationships among observed, true, and error variances.

that is, as the proportion of observed score variance that is true variance. Alternatively, the latter formula can be presented as:

reliability

$$r = \frac{\sigma_o^2 - \sigma_E^2}{\sigma_o^2}$$

Formula 4-11

This formula becomes important in some more advanced treatments of reliability.

As suggested earlier, it is convenient to think of a person's true score as the average of many observed scores. Figure 4.9 shows examples of distributions resulting from many administrations of two tests. In frame A, the test is very reliable; observed scores cluster tightly around the true score *(T)*. In frame B, the test is not very reliable; observed scores scatter widely around the average or true score *(T)*. The difference between any observed score *(O)* and *T* in these distributions is the error *(E)* in the measurement. It is usually assumed that the observed scores are normally distributed around the true score. Figure 4.9 uses this assumption, which will have convenient consequences later in the chapter (see The Standard Error of Measurement, p. 140).

Ordinarily, in a practical testing situation, we get *only one* observed score. The distribution of observed scores as illustrated in Figure 4.9 is purely hypothetical. This is the way observed scores would distribute themselves, we presume, *if* many scores were obtained for an individual. Our study of reliability will help to operationalize this presumption.

As noted earlier, we never know a person's true score, although that is what we wish to know. We always have only an observed score. The various methods for

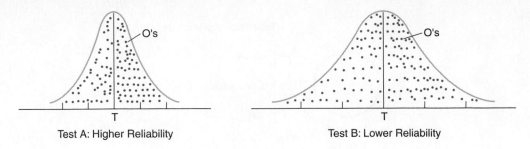

Test A: Higher Reliability   Test B: Lower Reliability

FIGURE 4.9 Hypothetical distributions of observed scores *(O)* around true scores *(T)*.

determining reliability, to be considered next, are designed to estimate how much difference there might be between a person's observed score and true score—that is, how much error there might be.

Methods of Determining Reliability

A variety of methods can be used to determine the reliability of a test. Each method treats one or more of the sources of unreliability previously described. Here we consider the more frequently used methods for determining test reliability. Throughout this section, we will operate within the conceptual framework of classical test theory.

Test-Retest Reliability

One of the easiest types of reliability to understand is called **test–retest reliability.** As suggested by the name, this reliability coefficient is obtained by administering the same test to the same individuals on two separate occasions. The two occasions are typically one day to one month apart. The reliability coefficient is simply the correlation (usually a Pearson correlation) between scores on the first and second testing. It is often called a stability coefficient. Table 4.7 presents an array of data for a study of test-retest reliability.

What sources of unreliability, as outlined earlier, does test-retest reliability address? Clearly, it helps to assess the influence of changes in personal conditions. Clearly, it does *not* address the influence of changes in test content since exactly the same test is used. Test-retest reliability may or may not address variations due to test administration, depending on whether the test is administered in the same room, by the same person, and so on, on both occasions. Also, it may or may not address inter-scorer variation, depending on whether the test is scored by the same person or process on both occasions.

Determining reliability by the test-retest method has three principal drawbacks. First, the method obviously does not account for unsystematic error due to variations in test content. Second, for any but the simplest, shortest tests, it is a nuisance to obtain test-retest reliability. Who wants to take the same four-hour test twice within

TABLE 4.7   *Array of Data for Determining Test-Retest Reliability*

Examinee	Test	Retest
1	85	81
2	92	79
3	76	75
4	61	69
5	93	93
—	—	—
—	—	—
—	—	—
100	80	82

$r = .85$

two weeks? Third, there is concern about the effect of the first test on the second test. Perhaps the examinee will remember responses from the first test and consciously give the same answers the second time for the sake of consistency, even if he or she thinks differently at the time of the second test. This would tend to inflate the reliability coefficient. If an item calls for novel problem solving, the examinee may fail the item on the first test but "figure it out" in a few days and get the item right on the second test. On items calling for information, the examinee might look up the correct answer between the first and second testings. The extent to which such factors might influence scores on the second test is largely a matter of judgment.

The timing between first and second tests is a matter of concern for test–retest reliability. On the one hand, the inter-test interval should be long enough so that the first test has minimal influence on the second test. On the other hand, the interval should not be so long that the trait being measured is likely to undergo real change between the two testings. To take an extreme example, if the inter-test interval were five years, one might suppose that the correlation between first and second testings was more a function of real changes in the trait rather than the test's reliability. In practice, test-retest reliability studies usually employ an inter-test interval of a few days to a few weeks. However, there is no definite rule regarding this matter.

Inter-scorer Reliability

Inter-scorer reliability is easily understood. It assesses unsystematic variation due simply to who scores the test. "Who" in this case usually means two different people, although it could mean two different machines or one machine versus one person or any other such combination. Inter-scorer reliability is sometimes called inter-observer or inter-rater reliability, depending on what the "scorer" is actually doing in the testing situation. For example, two persons may rate the creativity or severity of maladjustment of individuals. The shortened names of *scorer reliability, rater reliability,* or *observer reliability* are often used for this type of reliability.

Inter-scorer reliability is easily obtained. A test taken by a group of examinees is scored twice. The inter-scorer reliability coefficient is simply the correlation, usually a Pearson correlation, between the scores obtained by the first and second scorers. For a data array in an inter-scorer reliability study, refer to Table 4.7 and simply replace the headings Test and Retest with Scorer A and Scorer B.

It is important that the two (or more) scorers or raters work independently. That is, one scorer should not be influenced by the other scorer or rater. For example, if scorer B knows what score has been assigned to an item or entire test by scorer A, then scorer B might be inclined to assign the same or a similar score, thus inflating the resulting reliability coefficient. Of course, it is conceivable that scorer B detests scorer A and hence deliberately disagrees in assigning scores, thus deflating the reliability coefficient. Whatever the case, the influence of one scorer on another contaminates the study of reliability. The scorers should work independently.

In some studies, more than two scorers or raters are used. For example, after the initial interview with each of 50 clients four clinicians independently rate the degree of maladjustment. Ratings are made on a 20-point scale, ranging from "severely maladjusted" to "no noticeable maladjustment." Table 4.8 presents the ratings for a few of the clients. How is the inter-rater agreement expressed in this situation? It would be possible to compute correlations among all possible combinations of raters (A vs. B, A vs. C, A vs. D, B vs. C, B vs. D, C vs. D), then average the correlations. In fact, this is sometimes done. However, the more appropriate analysis for this situation is the **intraclass correlation coefficient.** The coefficient is abbreviated as r_I or ρ_I in statistics books but is usually written simply as ICC in other sources. The ICC is computed from mean squares (MSs) developed in an analysis of variance (ANOVA). There are a surprising number of ways to define and compute an ICC. For discussion of these variations, see Shrout and Fleiss (1979) or Winer (1991). For our purposes, the important point is that the ICC is interpreted like the familiar Pearson correlation coefficient *(r)*. In treatments of reliability, the ICC's usual application is for determining inter-scorer or inter-rater reliability.

TABLE 4.8 *Array of Data for Study of Inter-rater Reliability with More than Two Raters*

	Clinician			
	A	B	C	D
Client	Ratings of Maladjustment			
1	15	12	13	14
2	8	7	7	6
3	12	18	8	10
4	14	10	14	9
—	—	—	—	—
—	—	—	—	—
50	6	4	5	3

> ### Key Points Summary 4.4
> ### *Methods of Determining Reliability*
>
> - Test-retest
> - Inter-scorer
> - Alternate Form
> - Internal Consistency

Inter-scorer reliability obviously provides information about unsystematic errors arising from variation in scorers. It does not provide information on any other source of error. Inter-scorer reliability information is particularly important when judgment enters the scoring process.

Alternate Form Reliability

Also sometimes referred to as parallel form or equivalent form reliability, **alternate form reliability** requires that there be two forms of the test. The two forms should be the same or very similar in terms of number of items, time limits, content specifications, and other such factors.[2] The alternate form reliability study consists of administering both forms of the test to the same examinees. The alternate form reliability is the correlation, usually Pearson, between scores obtained from the two forms. Refer to Table 4.7. Replace the column headings, Test and Retest, with Form 1 and Form 2. That is the basic design for an alternate form reliability study.

The alternate forms of the test may be administered in immediate succession if they are relatively brief and undemanding. Otherwise, an inter-test interval similar to that used for test-retest reliability—a few days to a few weeks—may be employed. In the simplest case of alternate form reliability, when the two forms are administered in immediate succession, the method measures only unreliability due to content sampling. For lengthier tests, the alternate forms are usually administered with an inter-test interval of a few days to a few weeks. In this case, the method measures unreliability due to content sampling and, as in test-retest reliability, changes in personal conditions and variations in administrative conditions.

Alternate form reliability is not used very frequently for the simple reason that most tests do not have alternate forms. It is hard enough to build one good test, let alone two or more alternate, more or less equivalent, forms of the test. Alternate forms are usually available only for some of the most widely used tests.

---

[2] Technically, distinctions are made among several types of alternate forms, for example, strictly parallel, τ-equivalent, and essentially τ-equivalent forms. Differences among these types of forms have implications for some advanced psychometric issues. See Lord and Novick (1968), Feldt and Brennan (1989), and Nunnally and Bernstein (1994) for elaboration on these distinctions.

Traditionally, three broad categories of reliability coefficients have been recognized: (a) coefficients derived from the administration of parallel forms in independent testing sessions (alternate-form coefficients); (b) coefficients obtained by administration of the same instrument on separate occasions (test-retest or stability coefficients); and (c) coefficients based on the relationships among scores derived from individual items or subsets of the items within a test, all data accruing from a single administration (internal consistency coefficients). Where test scoring involves a high level of judgment, indexes of scorer consistency are commonly obtained. *Standards...*

(AERA/APA/NCME, 1999, p. 27)

Internal Consistency Reliability

Internal consistency reliability is one of the most frequently used methods of expressing test reliability. There are numerous methods for determining a test's internal consistency reliability. We will describe three of the most widely used methods: split-half, Kuder-Richardson, and coefficient alpha. All these methods, both those we describe here and other methods described elsewhere, attempt to measure the common characteristic of the test's internal consistency.

The internal consistency methods, like the other methods considered thus far, yield a reliability coefficient in the form of a correlation. However, exactly what is happening with the internal consistency methods is less obvious than for the other methods. Once described, the test-retest, inter-scorer, and alternate form methods seem intuitively clear. Not so with the internal consistency methods. We should begin, then, by describing the rationale for these methods, starting with the split-half method.

Split-half Reliability

Recall the alternate form method from the previous section. Think specifically of the case in which the two forms are administered in immediate succession. Now think of the administration of a single test, but one we will score in halves, as if each half were an alternate form of the test. Then we correlate scores on the two halves of the test. This is like a "mini-alternate forms" measure of reliability. This is essentially what happens with **split-half reliability.**

There are two important expansions on the latter scenario. First, the test is usually *not* split into the first and second halves of the test. The second half of a test often has more difficult items; examinees may be more fatigued toward the end of the test; and, if there is any effect of timing, it is more likely to influence the second half than the first half of the test. So, how will the test be split in half? One frequently used method is to divide the test into odd-numbered and even-numbered items. In this case, the result is sometimes referred to as **odd-even reliability.** Other types of splits may be useful for certain types of test items, but the odd-even split is clearly the most widely used.

Second, the correlation between the two halves of the test does not give the reliability of the full-length test. The correlation gives the reliability of a test half the length of the test one is really interested in. A correction must be applied to the correlation between the two halves of the test to yield the reliability of the full-length test. The appropriate correction is called the **Spearman-Brown correction.** Its formula is:

$$r_c = \frac{2r_h}{1+r_h}$$

Formula 4-12

where r_c = the corrected, full-length reliability

r_h = the correlation between the two half-length tests

The Spearman-Brown formula has a more general form that allows one to determine the estimated effect on internal consistency reliability of any change in test length. The more general form is:

$$r_c = \frac{nr_o}{1+(n-1)r_o}$$

Formula 4-13

where n = the factor by which test length is changed

r_c = the corrected reliability

r_o = the original reliability

In this formula, n may be a fraction. For example, one may estimate a corrected reliability for a test one-fourth ($n = .25$) the length of the original test. Or one may estimate the effect of tripling ($n = 3$) the length of the test. One may also set r_c at some desired value, then solve for n to determine what change in test length is required to obtain r_c, given a starting value of r_o. For all these changes in test length, the Spearman-Brown formula assumes that the items added (or lost, in the case of shortening the test) are equivalent to other items in the test.

TRY IT!

Practice using the Spearman-Brown formula with the following example.
A 20-item test has an original internal consistency reliability of .75. Suppose the test is doubled in length (i.e., $n = 2$). What is the reliability of the double-length test?

Kuder-Richardson Formulas

A series of formulas developed by G. Fredrick Kuder and M. W. Richardson (1937) provide other measures of internal consistency. Two of these formulas, numbers 20 and 21, commonly referred to as **KR-20** and **KR-21**, have been widely used and are presented here. KR-20, the more widely used of the two formulas, is defined as follows:

$$r_{KR-20} = \left(\frac{K}{K-1} \right)\left(1 - \frac{\Sigma pq}{S_X^{\,2}} \right)$$

Formula 4-14

where K = the number of items in the test

p = percentage correct and q is $(1 - p)$

S_X = the standard deviation of test scores

What is pq? For dichotomously scored items, such as correct–incorrect or yes–no items, the possible scores for each item are 1 and 0. P is the percentage of cases getting a "1" on the item—that is, answering correctly or "Yes." Q is simply $(1 - p)$. We obtain pq for each item and then sum these values over all items in the test. Table 4.9 presents a simple example.

Here is a curious property of KR-20. Recall the discussion of splitting a test in half. A commonly used method is to divide the test into odd and even items. However, many other splits are possible. For example, on a 10-item test, one could use items 1–5 versus 6–10; or items 1, 2, 5, 6, and 9 versus 3, 4, 7, 8, and 10; or items 1, 2, 3, 9, 10 versus 4, 5, 6, 7, and 8; and so on. The KR-20 formula yields the average correlation among all possible split-halves for the test.

Starting with the formula for KR-20, assume that all "p's" are equal. That is, all the items have the same percentage of "Correct" or "Yes" responses. Recall that summation of a constant (C) over n objects equals $n \times C$. For example, let the constant be 3; summing that constant over five objects yields $3 + 3 + 3 + 3 + 3 = 5 \times 3$. Applying this principle to "pq" when all "p's" are equal, $\Sigma\, pq$ becomes npq. Since $np = M$ (the mean of the test scores), under the assumption that all "p's" are equal, the KR-20 formula can be written as KR-21:

$$r_{KR-21} = \left(\frac{K}{K-1} \right)\left(1 - \frac{M(K-M)}{KS_X^{\,2}} \right)$$

Formula 4-15

where n = the number of items

M = the mean of total scores on the test

S_X = the standard deviation of test scores

The assumption that all "p's" are equal is quite unrealistic. If the assumption is approximately true, the use of KR-21 could be attractive because it is easier to compute than KR-20. Computational ease was a relevant criterion in the pre-computer age, but it is no longer an important criterion. Hence, one will encounter KR-21

TABLE 4.9 *Sample Data Array for Determining KR-20 Reliability*

Examinee	Item					Total Score
	1	2	3	4	5	
A	1	1	1	1	1	5
B	1	1	1	1	0	4
C	1	0	1	0	0	2
D	1	1	0	0	0	2
E	1	1	1	1	1	5

reliabilities in older test manuals and journal articles but not in more contemporary work. Nevertheless, it is useful to remember KR-21. It allows for an estimate of reliability when only M and S_x are available (they usually are) and no other estimate of reliability has been provided. Thorndike (1982) notes that KR-21 closely approximates KR-20 even when "p's" are quite varied.

Coefficient Alpha

The Kuder-Richardson formulas require dichotomously scored items. There is a more general formula that does not have this restriction. Items can have any type of continuous score. For example, items on an attitude scale might be on a five-point scale, ranging from strongly disagree (1) to strongly agree (5). The more general form is **coefficient alpha,** often called **Cronbach's alpha** (see Cronbach, 1951). Do not confuse this alpha with the alpha used in significance tests. They have nothing to do with one another. Two equivalent versions of the formula for coefficient alpha are:

$$\alpha = \left(\frac{K}{K-1} \right) \left(\frac{S_X{}^2 - \Sigma S_i{}^2}{S_X{}^2} \right) \qquad \textbf{Formula 4–16}$$

and

$$\alpha = \left(\frac{K}{K-1} \right) \left(1 - \frac{\Sigma S_i{}^2}{S_X{}^2} \right)$$

where K = the number of items in the test

S_X = the standard deviation of test scores

S_i = the standard deviation of item scores

Note the similarity in symbolism between these formulas and that for KR-20. In fact, when items are scored dichotomously, $\alpha = r_{KR-20}$, since for dichotomously scored items (0,1), $S_i^2 = pq$, so $\Sigma S_i = \Sigma pq$. Check an elementary statistics book to verify that the variance of a percentage is pq or $p(1-p)$. Coefficient alpha is very widely used in contemporary testing. Hogan, Benjamin, and Brezinski (2000) found that coefficient alpha was reported for over two-thirds of the tests included in the *Directory of Unpublished Experimental Mental Measures.* Thus, although coefficient alpha is not easy to understand, it is important for the psychology student to be familiar with it.

What does coefficient alpha indicate? A formula that is an alternative to those presented previously helps to answer this question. Assuming that all items are "standardized," that is, converted to a form so that each has a mean = 0 and $SD = 1$, then the following formula applies:

$$\alpha = \frac{K(\bar{r}_{ij})}{1 + (K-1)\bar{r}_{ij}} \qquad \textbf{Formula 4–17}$$

where r_{ij} = the correlation between items i and j

K = the number of items

What is this formula doing? It is certainly not obvious from inspection of the elements in the formula. Recall the rationale for the split–half method. It was like creating alternate mini-forms. Now extend this reasoning to individual items. Each item may be thought of as a mini-form of the test. We can then ask how each of these mini-forms (items) agrees with all the other mini-forms (items) in the test. Then we can sum all this information into a measure of internal consistency reliability. In this formula $\bar{r}_{ij}$ is the average intercorrelation among all the items. It is certainly not a convenient formula to use for practical computing purposes. However, it does give a better idea than the earlier formulas about what KR-20 and coefficient alpha indicate.

Application of the latter formula provides some practical guidance about how the internal consistency of tests works. Insert sample values for K and $\bar{r}_{ij}$ into the formula and note the consequences. In Table 4.10, we let K take the values 5, 20, and 50, and let $\bar{r}_{ij}$ take the values .10, .25, and .40. Then we calculate α. What do we observe? First, as the number of items increases, reliability increases. Second, as the average interitem correlation increases, reliability increases. Furthermore, when there are relatively few items (say, 5), reliability is very low when inter-item correlations are low; when inter-item correlations are high, reliability is much higher but still not very high. When there are a large number of items (say, 50), reliability is quite respectable even when inter-item correlations are relatively low. Thus, the formula shows that alpha depends on the average correlation among the items. The number of items is also very important. Alpha indicates the extent to which items in the test are measuring the same construct(s) or trait(s). It is sometimes called a measure of *item homogeneity,* that is, the extent to which the items are the same in terms of what they are measuring. Note that individual items are not very reliable by themselves. Hence, the intercorrelations among items will seem unusually low. For example, a correlation of .25 is usually considered quite low, but it is a respectable level for a correlation among individual items.

TABLE 4.10 *Effect of Number of Items (K) and Average Interitem Correlation ($\bar{r}_{ij}$) on Coefficient Alpha*

K	$\bar{r}_{ij}$	α
5	.10	.36
5	.25	.63
5	.40	.77
20	.10	.69
20	.25	.87
20	.40	.93
50	.10	.85
50	.25	.94
50	.40	.97

In an outburst of psychometric exuberance, Nunnally and Bernstein (1994, p. 232) observe, "It is hard to overestimate the importance of [Formula 4-17] to the theory of measurement error." They point out that this formula is also a general form of the Spearman–Brown formula presented in connection with our treatment of split–half reliability.

In relation to the sources of unreliability outlined previously, coefficient alpha relates to unreliability due to content sampling. It does not measure unreliability due to changes in test administration, personal conditions, or scoring. This same generalization applies to all the internal consistency methods of determining reliability.

TRY IT!

Substitute these values in Formula 4-17: $K = 30, \bar{r}_{ij} = .10$.
What is α?

The various measures of internal consistency are *not* appropriate for *speeded tests*. They are entirely inappropriate if the test is primarily a speed test, such as a test of reading rate or clerical speed. Some "power" tests are partly speeded in that some examinees may not finish all items. To the extent that speed does affect scores, the measures of internal consistency will yield inflated estimates of reliability. To deal with this problem, it is possible to split tests in terms of times rather than number of items, but this tends to create a rather artificial testing situation. When speed is a significant factor in determining scores, it is best to simply use other methods for determining reliability.

Three Important Conclusions

As noted earlier, it is not easy to see exactly what the formulas for internal consistency measures are doing. However, it is easy to deduce three important conclusions from inspection of the formulas. First, test length is important. The number of test items always enters the formulas. In general, the longer the test, the more reliable it will be. Very short tests are often unreliable. In the limiting case, single items almost always have quite limited reliability. As a general rule, to increase reliability, increase test length.

The second conclusion is that reliability is maximized when the percentage of examinees responding correctly in a cognitive ability test or responding in a certain direction (e.g., "Yes") in a noncognitive test is near .50. Notice that "pq" is at a maximum when $p = .50$; pq decreases as p moves away from .50. This is the reason that standardized tests in the cognitive domain often seem so hard. The test developer is trying to maximize reliability. Actually, taking into account the effect of guessing the correct answer, the target p-value for items is usually set somewhat above .50, but still at a difficult level. However, Thorndike (1982) shows that little reliability is sacrificed by departing substantially from $p = .50$. We take up this topic again in Chapter 6.

Third, the correlation among items is important. Observe the effect of the average inter-item correlation in Table 4.10. The practical lesson to be learned is this: To get good internal consistency reliability, use items measuring a well-defined trait.

The Standard Error of Measurement

A reliability coefficient provides important information about a test. However, its practical implications for test interpretation are not immediately evident. For practical interpretation, we depend on the **standard error of measurement**, usually abbreviated SEM. The *SEM* is defined as:

$$SEM = SD_x \sqrt{1 - r_{xx}}$$ **Formula 4-18**

where r_{xx} is the test's reliability and SD_x is the test's standard deviation for the group on which the *r* was determined.

The *SEM* is the standard deviation of a hypothetically infinite number of obtained scores around the person's true score. Refer to Figure 4.9. Each of these distributions has a standard deviation. This particular kind of standard deviation is called a standard error of measurement. The distribution on the right in Figure 4.9 has a relatively large *SEM*. The distribution on the left has a relatively small *SEM*. Observe some of the consequences of the formula for *SEM*. If test reliability is perfect ($r = 1.00$), *SEM* = 0—that is, there is no measurement error. What is SEM if the test reliability is .00, that is, completely unreliable? In that case *SEM* is the *SD* of the test.

TRY IT! ....

Determine SEM for the following cases:

The reliability of the WAIS Verbal IQ score is .92; *SD* is 15. What is *SEM*?

Suppose the reliability were .70, while *SD* remains at 15. What is *SEM* now?

....

Confidence Bands

The SEM can be used to create a confidence interval, which in testing parlance is sometimes called a **confidence band,** around the observed score. Since the SEM is a standard deviation of a distribution assumed to be normal, all the customary relationships apply. Refer to the normal curve in Figure 3.10 as a refresher. For example, in 68% (about two-thirds) of the cases, the true score will be within +/− 1 *SEM* of the observed score. Conversely, in about one-third of the cases, the observed score will differ from the true score by at least 1 *SEM*.

Computer-generated score reports often use the confidence band. Table 4.11 gives an example. The confidence band for Test A ranges from 9 to 17, centered around an observed score of 13. Test B has a band ranging from 24 to 36, centered around an observed score of 30. Such reports usually give the "band" as +/− 1 *SEM*—essentially a 68% confidence interval, although it is easy to use a 95% band (+/− 1.96 *SEM*) or 99% band (+/− 2.58 *SEM*).

TABLE 4.11 *Illustration of Score Report Using Confidence Bands*

Test A			xxxXxxx							
Test B						xxxxxxXxxxxxx				
0	5	10	15	20	25	30	35	40	45	50

Test Score

Appropriate Units for SEM

The *SEM* should be expressed in the score units used for interpretation. Test manuals often give the *SEM* only in raw score units. If interpretation employs normed scores, then the raw score *SEM* must be converted to the normed score. This can easily be done for normed scores that are linear conversions of raw scores, such as linear standard scores. The task is much trickier for nonlinear conversions. For example, percentile ranks are nonlinear conversions because of the marked inequality of percentile units (assuming a roughly normal distribution of scores).

> The standard error of measurement ... should be reported both in raw score or original scale units and in units of each derived score recommended for use in test interpretation. *Standards...*
>
> (AERA/APA/NCME, 1999, p. 31)

Consider the following examples for a 100-item test. Figure 4.10 shows the distribution of scores on this test in terms of raw scores ($M = 75$, $SD = 5$), standard scores ($M = 500$, $SD = 100$), and percentiles. The test's reliability is .80. Thus, in raw score units, $SEM = 5 \sqrt{1 - .80} = 2.2$. This many raw score units (2.2) equals 44

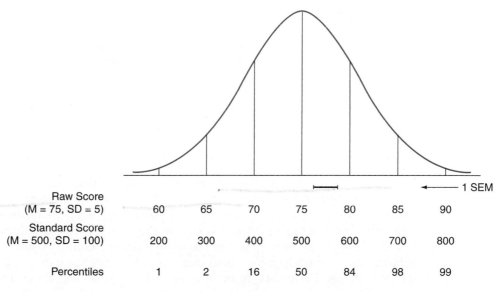

Raw Score (M = 75, SD = 5)	60	65	70	75	80	85	90
Standard Score (M = 500, SD = 100)	200	300	400	500	600	700	800
Percentiles	1	2	16	50	84	98	99

FIGURE 4.10 *SEM* in different score units.

units in the standard score system, that is, $100\sqrt{1 - .80}$. Obviously, the raw score SEM is not useful if the interpretation is based on standard scores. There is no such simple conversion for percentile ranks. However, we can estimate the effect of applying $+/- 1$ *SEM* in raw score units at various points along the percentile scale. Around the 5th (or 95th) percentile, $+/- 2.2$ raw score units covers about 10 percentile points. Around the 50th percentile, $+/- 2.2$ raw score units covers 34 percentile points! This difference arises for the same reason as discussed in Chapter 3 in connection with the interpretation of percentile scores, but here is applied to the interpretation of the *SEM*.

Standard Error of the Difference

The preceding section described the standard error of measurement for a single score. What about the case of comparing two scores? How should one apply the concept of error of measurement in such a case? Add the standard errors for the separate scores? Take their average? The answer to these questions, which is not intuitively obvious, is given by the following formula:

$$SEM_{diff} = \sqrt{SEM_1^2 + SEM_2^2} \qquad \textbf{Formula 4-19}$$

where SEM_{diff} = the **standard error of the difference** between two scores
$\quad\quad SEM_1$ = the *SEM* for the first test
$\quad\quad SEM_2$ = the *SEM* for the second test

Recall that $SEM_1 = SD_1 \sqrt{1 - r_{11}}$ and $SEM_2 = SD_2 \sqrt{1 - r_{22}}$. It is often the case that $r_{11} = r_{22}$ and $SD_1 = SD_2$. In that case the formula for SEM_{diff} simplifies to:

$$SEM_{diff} = SD \sqrt{2(1 - r)} \qquad \textbf{Formula 4-20}$$

where SD = the common standard deviation
$\quad\quad r$ = the common reliability coefficient

The distribution of differences between scores is assumed to be normal, and SEM_{diff} is the standard deviation of this distribution. Hence, all the customary statements about the standard deviation apply here: 68% of the cases fall within $+/-$ one SD, 5% fall outside $+/- 1.96$ SD, and so forth.

Standard Errors: Three Types

The *standard error of measurement* must be carefully distinguished from two other types of standard errors: the *standard error of the mean* and the *standard error of estimate*. The distinctions are a source of great confusion for novice psychometricians, especially since each of these entities may be referred to simply by the abbreviated name "standard error" and one is expected to know from the context which one actually applies. All three really are standard deviations, but they are standard deviations of different things. Let us briefly outline the differences among these three types of standard errors.

> **Key Points Summary 4.5**
>
> *Three Types of Standard Errors*
>
> 1. *Standard Error of Measurement:*
>   Index of error due to unreliability (Formula 4-18)
> 2. *Standard Error of the Mean:*
>   Index of error due to random sampling (Formula 4-21)
> 3. *Standard Error of Estimate:*
>   Index of error in predicting *Y* from *X* (Formula 4-4)

The standard error of measurement is the standard deviation of a hypothetical population of observed scores distributed around the true score for an individual person. Examples of such distributions are given in Figure 4.9. The relevant formula is formula 4-18. The **standard error of the mean** is the standard deviation of a hypothetical population of sample means for samples (of a given size) distributed around the population mean. The standard error of the mean is used for tests of significance, for example, *t*-tests and *z*-tests, and for confidence intervals for means of samples. Recall from elementary statistics that the standard error of the mean is:

$$S_{\bar{X}} = \frac{S_X}{\sqrt{N}}$$ **Formula 4-21**

where S_X = the standard deviation of scores

N = the sample size

The **standard error of estimate** (also sometimes called the standard error of prediction) is the standard deviation of actual *Y* scores around the predicted *Y* scores when *Y* is predicted from *X*. We encountered the standard error of estimate in our review of statistics earlier in this chapter. Its formula is Formula 4-4.

It is important to keep these distinctions in mind. The differences among these three types of standard errors have very real practical consequences. This is not just a nit-picky, academic nuance.

Some Special Issues in Reliability

Reliability in Narrative Reports

Reliability information is usually provided in precise, quantitative terms, that is, in the form of reliability coefficients and standard errors of measurement. Increasingly, however, test performance is being reported in narrative form. Such narrative reports can greatly ease the task of interpreting test scores. Unfortunately, narrative reports are not readily adapted to the traditional tools of reliability analysis. Some narrative reports neatly incorporate the concepts of reliability and errors of measurement. Other reports do not. The reports may give the impression that reliability is not an issue. In fact, reliability is always an issue. The reader of the narrative report must ensure that he or she is (a) familiar with the reliability information about the test, and (b) utilizes this information when interpreting the report. Every narrative report should incorporate the concept of error of measurement.

Reliability of Subscores and Individual Items

Reliability information must be provided for the "score" that is actually being interpreted. Consider the following case. A test battery has four separate tests; the test manual provides reliability information for each test. Each test has quite good reliability, say, $r > .90$. However, score reports for the test battery may give information about individuals' performance on clusters of items or even individual items within the tests. One cannot assume that these clusters or individual items have the same reliability as the total scores on the tests. In fact, it is quite certain that performance on the clusters or individual items will be substantially less reliable than the total scores. Reliability of item clusters, say three or four items, is notoriously low, at best usually around $.30 - .40$. One would generally not even consider using a test with a reliability of .30. Unfortunately, item clusters with reliabilities in this neighborhood are reported rather routinely. Performance on individual items is even less reliable. Beware!

Reliability of Profiles

Profiles of test scores are often the basis for test interpretation. Figure 4.11 gives sample profiles for a four-test battery. What may be of interest here is not the absolute level of the scores on Tests A–D but the *patterns* displayed by the profiles. For example, the "V" formed by scores on Tests A–C for Sue and Fred may be of particular interest. The reliability of such patterns is not easily represented, but is certainly less reliable than the reliability of the individual tests. The issue is related to the standard error of difference treated earlier. We noted that the error of measurement for differences combines the errors for the individual scores. This compounding of unreliability is even greater when a profile of three or more scores is the basis for interpretation.

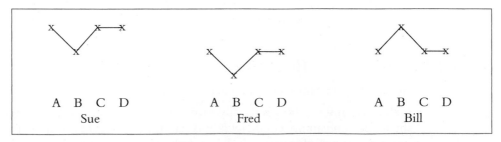

FIGURE 4.11   Sample profiles of test scores on Tests A, B, C, and D.

Reliability of Criterion-referenced Tests

Recall the distinction between a criterion–referenced test (CRT) and a norm-reference test (NRT) from Chapter 3. The key difference is in the method of interpretation. The methods of determining reliability may have to be different for CRTs, depending on the distribution of scores on the test and the uses for the scores. The classical approaches to reliability considered in this chapter assume a normal distribution of test scores. At a minimum, there must be a reasonable distribution of scores. Otherwise, the correlation coefficient does not work. Consider the extreme case in a test-retest study where all scores are the same, say, perfect scores, on the retest. The formula for the correlation coefficient will lead to $r = .00$.

Concern about inadequate variability in test scores *may* be applicable to some mastery testing situations where the score distributions have marked negative skewness, that is, an accumulation of scores at or near a perfect score. The distribution of CRT scores in relation to a "cut-score" may also affect interpretation of the reliability of a CRT. Numerous methods have been developed to express the reliability of CRTs in these special circumstances. For various methods to deal with reliability in these special cases, see Berk (1984), Crocker and Algina (1986), Feldt and Brennan (1989), and Nunnally and Bernstein (1994). One does not encounter these specialized methods very frequently in practice.

Reliability in Item Response Theory

Reliability is an issue for tests constructed according to item response theory (IRT), just as it is for tests constructed according to classical test theory (CTT). Our treatment of reliability has concentrated on the CTT approach because the vast majority of extant tests use that approach. However, an increasing number of tests use an IRT approach. Hence, we should examine reliability in the IRT context. Note first that IRT's unique approach to reliability treats only internal consistency. Even if a test is constructed and scored according to IRT, if the concern is with

---

Key Points Summary 4.6

Special Issues in Reliability

- Narrative Reports
- Subscores and Individual Items
- Profiles
- Criterion-referenced Tests

temporal stability or scorer consistency, then methods described earlier in this chapter should be used to determine reliability.

For purposes of internal consistency analysis, IRT provides a different approach from those already described. Like coefficient alpha, IRT reliability analysis depends on the functioning of items within the test. However, in IRT the items function independently, whereas in CTT internal consistency analysis, items function interdependently.

In IRT, the standard error is expressed as:

$$SE(\Theta) = \frac{1}{\sqrt{I(\Theta)}}$$ **Formula 4-22**

where Θ is the ability or trait score (theta), as described in Chapter 3, and $I(\Theta)$ is the test information function, which is simply the sum of item information functions. Item information functions arise from characteristics of the items. These item characteristics are described in more detail in Chapter 6.

The standard error $SE(\Theta)$ in IRT is often referred to as an index of the **precision of measurement.** It has a major advantage over the *SEM* in CTT. In CTT, the *SEM* is assumed to be the same at all score levels.[3] Consider an IQ test with $SD = 15$ and $\alpha = .89$, so that $SEM = 5$. This *SEM* applies throughout the entire range of IQs: at 80, 100, 150, and so on. Furthermore, this *SEM* is dependent not only on the homogeneity of the test items but also on the heterogeneity of the individuals on whom α was determined. $SE(\Theta)$ does not suffer from these limitations. It is determined specifically for each score level, that is, for each level of theta. Thus, for a particular test, $SE(\Theta)$ may be relatively less for low scores and relatively greater for high scores; or vice versa, depending on how items are functioning for various levels of the trait. We give an example of this application for the GRE-General Test in Chapter 9 (p. 368); on this test, error is greater for midlevel scores than for extreme scores. On other tests, $SE(\Theta)$ may be less for midlevel scores. Further details regarding reliability in IRT can be found in Hambleton and Swaminathan (1985) and Hambleton, Swaminathan, and Rogers (1991). For detailed treatment of reliability for computer-adaptive tests based on IRT, see Thissen (2000).

Generalizability Theory

From the treatment of various types of reliability earlier in this chapter, it should be clear that there is no such thing as *the* reliability of a test. There are many sources of unreliability. Each method of determining reliability attempts to treat one or just a few of these sources. Hence, we may say that a test has a test-retest reliability of .85, an alternate form reliability of .78, and a coefficient alpha of .92. Each of these types of reliability may be determined in a separate study. **Generalizability theory** (GT) is an attempt to assess many sources of unreliability simultaneously.

---

[3] Thorndike (1982) suggests a procedure for avoiding this assumption, but his suggestion is not widely used.

GT begins with the same basic notion as classical test theory, that is, that each person has a true score. In GT, the true score is often called a **universe score** or domain score. Think of a person being tested on many occasions, with many different forms and many different scorers. The person's true score or universe score is the average score across all occasions, forms, and scorers. Now imagine 500 people undergoing these multiple assessments. For any particular pair of assessments, we could determine one of the classical measures of reliability. For example, the correlation between scores on two occasions would be the test-retest reliability. However, it would be very useful if we could determine, *in a single study,* reliability for several occasions, several forms, and several scorers. This is what GT attempts to do.

Analysis of variance (ANOVA) provides the basic framework for a generalizability study (G-study). Recall that ANOVA allows for studying the effect of several independent variables simultaneously on a dependent variable. ANOVA also allows for the study of interactions, the unique effect created by the combination of two (or more) independent variables over and above their separate effects.

[G]eneralizability theory permits the researcher to specify and estimate various components of true score variance, error variance, and observed score variance. Estimation is typically accomplished by the application of the techniques of analysis of variance. Of special interest are the separate numerical estimates of the components of overall error variance. *Standards…*
(AERA/APA/NCME, 1999, p. 28)

Suppose we are measuring anxiety. We have a sample of 50 people. We examine them on five different occasions. On each occasion, we present them with two tasks that might increase anxiety. We have four judges rate the degree of anxiety manifested. This design allows us to investigate consistency.

- Across occasions (as in test-retest reliability)
- Between tasks (as in alternate form reliability)
- Among judges (as in inter-rater reliability)

This gives rise to a $5 \times 2 \times 4$ factorial ANOVA design: occasions $\times$ tasks $\times$ raters. In this design, we can study variance due to each factor, as well as interactions among the factors.

The GT literature distinguishes between a generalizability study (G-study) and a decision study (D-study). The G-study analyzes the components of variance, including interactions. The D-study utilizes results of a G-study to *decide* how the measurement might be improved by changes in one of the components. Consider our anxiety study. We used four judges. Does that provide sufficient stability in the results? Would we have sufficient stability if we used only two judges? Answers to such questions can help to refine and improve the measurement process.

Details of conducting a generalizability analysis would take us well beyond the scope of this book. The interested reader should consult Shavelson, Webb, and Rowley (1989) for a good overview of the topic; Shavelson and Webb (1991) for a more detailed treatment; and Brennan (2001b) for a very complete exposition. Brennan (2001a) provides a historical analysis showing development of GT from earlier methods of reliability analysis. Brennan (2000) also cautions that the

ANOVA framework previously described for GT can be taken too literally. Nevertheless, this framework provides a good introduction to GT.

Generalizability theory offers an exceptionally useful framework for thinking about the reliability of measures. However, at present, it is not widely used in practical applications. This is probably because even simple reliability studies are a nuisance to conduct (except for internal consistency studies). Who wants to take the same test twice on two different occasions? Or take two different forms of a test? Conducting a study that varies in, say, time of administration, number of forms, and scoring procedures becomes very difficult from a practical viewpoint. We do encounter generalizability studies for a few tests and we are likely to see at least some increase in the use of this methodology in the future. For the moment, the most important point is the perspective the methodology gives us on the whole topic of reliability.

Factors Affecting Reliability Coefficients

Recall our discussion earlier in this chapter of four factors affecting correlation coefficients. Since reliability is usually expressed as a correlation coefficient, these factors may affect reliability data. Let us consider each of these four factors.

First, the fact that correlation is a matter of relative position rather than absolute scores is *not* a significant concern for reliability. Second, curvilinearity is generally not an issue for reliability data. Although it is theoretically possible to have a curvilinear trend in reliability data, it does not usually occur in practice. In any case, it is easy to check on the assumption of linearity by examining a bivariate distribution of the reliability data. Any standard statistical software package will run a bivariate distribution for inspection.

Third, heteroscadasticity may very well be a problem for the standard error of measurement. Again, the solution is to run a bivariate plot to check on the assumption of homoscedasticity. It should be noted that the precision of measurement statistic in IRT, $SE(\Theta)$, provides different standard errors for different score levels, hence adjusting for any lack of homoscedasticity.

Finally, group variability is *often* a problem when interpreting reliability data. Reliability data may have been developed for a group much more homogeneous or much more heterogeneous than the group considered relevant for one's interpretive framework. The solution to this problem is to use Formulas 4-5 and 4-6 to correct for excessive homogeneity or heterogeneity. These corrections are used frequently in practical work. We discuss specific examples in Chapter 9 on the use of tests to predict success in college, graduate school, and jobs.

How High Should Reliability Be?

After even the briefest exposure to the topic of reliability, one's inclination is to ask: How high should a test's reliability be? There is no simple answer to the question, other than: It depends. Specifically, it depends on what you want to do with the test. It is like asking "How high should a ladder be?" It depends. Do you need to change a light bulb that is just barely out of reach, or do you need to get on the roof of a three-story building?

If you need to make a very important decision for which the test information weighs heavily—for example, in granting a license to practice in some professional field—then you want a highly reliable test. If a test is just one of many sources of information giving you an approximate idea about a person's overall level of adjustment, then a more moderate degree of reliability may be satisfactory. If a test is used in a research project in which group averages are the focus of attention, then an even lesser degree of reliability may be sufficient.

Everyone agrees on the generalizations just cited. However, it is still useful to have some benchmark figures in mind for reliability. Here are some benchmarks that may be helpful. Nunnally and Bernstein (1994, p. 265) state that "If important decisions are made with respect to test scores, a reliability of .90 is the bare minimum, and reliability of .95 should be considered the desirable standard." These authors also note: "Group research is often concerned with the size of correlations and with mean differences among the experimental treatments, for which a reliability of .80 is adequate." Groth-Marnat (2003, p. 13) states: "Ideally, clinicians should hope for correlations [reliabilities] of .90 or higher in tests that are used to make decisions about individuals, whereas a correlation of .70 or more is generally adequate for research purposes." Kaplan and Saccuzzo (2005, pp. 123–124) state that "it has been suggested that reliability estimates in the range of .70 to .80 are good enough for most purposes in basic research … [and] for a test used to make a decision that affects some person's future, evaluators should attempt to find a test with a reliability greater than .95." Murphy and Davidshofer (2001, p.142) characterize different reliability levels in these terms: "… in the neighborhood of .90 … is likely to be regarded as a high level of reliability. Reliability estimates of .80 or more are typically regarded as moderate to high … around .70 are likely to be regarded as low … reliability estimates lower than .60 usually are thought to indicate unacceptably low levels of reliability."

Here are three important supplements to the discussion about how high reliability should be. First, one sometimes encounters the argument that reliability is not an important issue for a particular type of test or a particular score on a test. Never believe this claim! Reliability is always important. Information that is unreliable or of unknown reliability cannot be used. Second, recall our discussion of the relationship between test length and reliability: Short tests are usually rather unreliable. One sometimes encounters a test author or even a test reviewer claiming that a test has quite good reliability given how short it is. Beware of this claim. A test with a reliability of .60—whether short or long—is a test with a reliability of .60, which is not very good. If such a test is to be used for serious purposes, its reliability must be increased, probably by lengthening the test. Third, some test authors report the statistical significance of reliability coefficients, often gleefully noting that the coefficient is highly significant. Such reports are not very helpful. We have much higher standards for reliability coefficients, as noted, than simple statistical significance.

More important than the reliability of the test is its validity. Although a test with no reliability cannot have any validity, it is possible to have a highly reliable test that is not valid for the purpose we have in mind. Furthermore, a test with moderate reliability and moderate validity is preferable to a test with high reliability and low validity. These brief observations provide a transition to the crucial topic of the next chapter: test validity.

Summary

1.   Reliability, one of the most important concepts in testing, deals with the consistency or replicability of test scores.
2.   We distinguish between reliability and validity, the psychometric sense of reliability and several everyday uses of the term, real change and temporary fluctuations in measures, and constant errors and unsystematic errors.
3.   The correlation coefficient *(r)* is the most typical method for expressing reliability; hence, it is important to understand correlations and factors influencing them.
4.   The major sources of unreliable variance are test scoring, test content, test administration conditions, and personal conditions of the examinee.
5.   Classical test theory utilizes the concepts of true score, error score, and observed score.
6.   Among the commonly used methods for determining reliability are test-retest, alternate form, inter-scorer, and several types of internal consistency measures. Each method treats some but not all sources of unreliability.
7.   The standard error of measurement *(SEM)* and confidence bands help to translate reliability coefficients into practical interpretation.
8.   The concept of standard error applies not only to interpretation of single scores but also to differences between scores and profiles of scores.
9.   The standard error of measurement must be distinguished from the standard error of the mean and from the standard error of estimate.
10. Concepts of reliability and standard error apply equally to narrative and quantitative reports of test performance.
11. Reliability is important for criterion-referenced interpretation, but the situation sometimes requires alteration in the usual approaches to determining reliability.
12. Item response theory (IRT) uses the concept of precision of measurement, which can differ for various points along the scale.
13. Using the techniques of analysis of variance, generalizability theory attempts to apportion several sources of unreliability in a single study.
14. Factors affecting correlation coefficients, especially group variability, must be taken into account when interpreting reliability data.
15. The type of test usage determines the desired level of reliability for a test. For important decisions, reliability should be at least .90. In instances where a test is one of several types of information considered jointly, reliability of at least .80 is desired.

Key Terms

alternate form reliability	intraclass correlation	standard error of the
bivariate distribution	coefficient	difference
coefficient alpha	KR-20	standard error of
confidence band	KR-21	estimate
constant error	observed score	standard error of
correlation coefficient	odd-even reliability	measurement
Cronbach's alpha	precision of	standard error of the
error score	measurement	mean
generalizability theory	real change	test-retest reliability
heterogeneity	regression line	true score
heteroscedasticity	reliability	universe score
homogeneity	scattergram	unsystematic error
homoscedasticity	Spearman-Brown	
internal consistency	correction	
inter-scorer reliability	split-half reliability	

Exercises

1. Use any software package with which you are familiar (e.g., SPSS, Minitab, SAS, or Excel) to obtain the correlation for these data.

Examinee	Test X	Test Y
1	20	24
2	18	12
3	23	27
4	34	37
5	19	15
6	33	45
7	16	10
8	35	42
9	15	10
10	22	24

2. Prepare a bivariate distribution for the scores in the previous problem.

3. Using any electronic database in your library, do a key word search on *test reliability*. What kind of references do you get? (*Note:* It is likely that you will find references in fields in addition to those related to psychological testing.)

4. Use the Spearman-Brown formula (p. 135) with the following examples. A 20-item test has an original internal consistency reliability of .75.

a. What is r_c if the test is quaprupled in length (80 items, $n = 4$)?

b. What is r_c if the test is made half as long (10 items, $n = .5$)?

c. You want r_c to be .90. How many items should the test have? (Solve for n, then multiply n by 20, the original test length.)

5. For the data given in Table 4.9, what is "p" for item 2? What is "pq"?

$p = $ _____ $pq = $ _____

6. Calculate r_{KR-20} for the following data. Entries in the box are correct (1), incorrect (0) responses. Some of the calculations are already completed for you.

Item	1	2	3	4	5	Total Score
Examinee						
A	1	1	1	1	1	5
B	1	1	1	1	0	4
C	1	0	1	0	0	2
D	1	1	0	0	0	2
E	1	1	1	1	1	5
F	1	0	1	1	1	4
G	1	1	1	0	1	4
H	0	0	0	1	0	1
I	0	1	0	0	0	1
J	0	0	0	0	0	0
$p = $	.7	.6	.6	.5	.4	$M = 28/10 = 2.8$

$$S_x = 1.81$$
(using $n - 1$ in denominator)

$\Sigma pq = (.7x.3)+(.6x.4)+(.6x.4)+(.5x.5)+(.4\ x.6) = 1.18$

7. Calculate coefficient alpha for the following test data. Entries in the box are examinee responses to attitude items, each scored on a 5-point scale.

Item	1	2	3	4	5	Total Score
Examinee						
A	5	4	5	3	5	22
B	4	4	3	4	4	19
C	4	3	3	4	4	18
D	3	3	3	4	3	16
E	3	3	3	3	3	15
F	3	3	3	2	2	13
G	2	2	2	2	2	10
H	2	1	2	1	2	8
I	1	2	2	1	1	7
J	1	1	2	1	1	6
$S_i = $	—	—	—	—	—	$S_x = $ ____

8. Using Formula 4–17 for α, complete the following table. (This will take some simple algebra.)

K	$\bar{r}_{ij}$	α
10	.15	—
25	—	.90
—	.20	.80

9. Consider these data for a test: reliability = .90, SD = 15.

   a. What is the standard error of measurement (SEM)?

   b. What is the probability that the person's true score is within +/- one SEM of the person's obtained score?

   c. What is the 95% confidence band for these data?

10. Assume two tests have the same SD = 10 and the same reliability (r) = .80. What is SEM_{diff} for these tests? (Use Formula 4–20.) Assume the common SD = 10 and r = .60. Now what is SEM_{diff} for these tests?

11. Use the data in Appendix D2 to determine the test-retest reliability of the measures. Simply run the correlations between first test and second test using your statistical software package. What do you conclude about these reliabilities?

CHAPTER 5

Validity

Objectives

1. Compare the "standard" and "refined" definitions of test validity.

2. Discuss validity using the concepts of construct underrepresentation and construct irrelevant variance.

3. Identify the three traditional categories for describing validity evidence.

4. Define face validity.

5. Define content validity and discuss its typical uses.

6. Define criterion-related validity and discuss its three typical uses.

7. Discuss the effects of the reliability of both the test and the criterion on criterion-related validity.

8. Illustrate the use of multiple correlation in demonstrating incremental validity.

9. Define convergent and discriminant validity and use of the multitrait-multimethod matrix.

10. In the context of criterion-related validity, illustrate the concepts of false positives, false negatives, base rates, selectivity and specificity.

11. Define construct validity and give several examples applying this concept.

12. Describe the purpose of factor analysis.

13. Define the role of studying response processes in construct validity.

14. Discuss the meaning of consequential validity.

15. Show how criterion-related validity is used to study test bias.

16. Discuss the meaning of validity generalization and meta-analysis in considering test validity.

Introduction

Let us begin with these very practical situations and questions related to test validity.

- Ivy College uses the Western Admissions Test (WAT) to select applicants who should be successful in their studies. What type of evidence should we seek to determine if the WAT satisfies its purpose?

- Dr. Heidi considers using the Scranton Depression Inventory to help identify severity of depression and especially to distinguish depression from anxiety. What evidence should Dr. Heidi use to determine if the test does what she hopes it will do?

- The newly published Diagnostic Wonder Test promises to identify children with a mathematics learning disability. How will we know whether the test does so or is simply a slickly packaged general ability test?

- Mike is reviewing a narrative report of his scores on the Nifty Personality Questionnaire (NPQ). The report says he is exceptionally introverted and unusually curious about the world around him. Can Mike have any confidence in these statements? Or should they be dismissed as equivalent to palm readings at the county fair?

- A school system wants to use an achievement battery that will measure the extent to which students are learning the curriculum specified by the school. How should the school system proceed in reviewing the available achievement tests?

Refining the Definition of Validity

All these questions relate to the validity of tests. In this chapter, we refine our thinking about this topic and examine methods used to answer the questions. The customary definition of **validity** is the *extent to which a test measures what it purports to measure*. We used this definition in Chapter 1 when discussing the fundamental questions in psychological testing. This definition is often used in introductory psychology books. At an elementary level, we are encouraged to ask the question: Is this test valid? However, now that we have the opportunity to treat the topic of validity in more detail, we need to refine our thinking. We need to rephrase the question in three ways.

> It is the interpretations of test scores required by proposed uses that are evaluated, not the test itself. When test scores are used or interpreted in more than one way, each intended interpretation must be validated. *Standards...*
>
> (AERA/APA/NCME, 1999, p. 9)

First, we note that it is imprecise to refer to the validity of a test. What we need to establish is the validity of a test score when used for a particular purpose. Even more accurately, we should refer to the *interpretation of a score for a particular purpose or use.* Notice that in the scenarios sketched at the beginning of the chapter we always stated a purpose for the test. A score may be appropriately used for one purpose but not for another. We cannot define the validity of a test score in the abstract—only with respect to a particular use. Thus, we should not ask such questions as: Is the Rorschach valid? Or is the SAT valid? Rather, we should ask such questions as: Is the Depression Index from the Rorschach valid for identifying the severity of depression? Or is the SAT Verbal score valid for predicting GPA at the end of the college freshman year?

Second, we note that validity is a *matter of degree;* it is not an all-or-none affair. Some tests may have no validity for a particular purpose. There are probably no test scores that are perfectly valid for a given purpose. Most of the test scores we use have some validity. The validity may be very slight, moderate, or considerable. Our concern will be determining the extent of validity. From a practical viewpoint, we want to know if the validity is sufficient to make use of the test worthwhile. Thus, we further refine our questions as: *To what degree* is the Rorschach Depression Index valid for determining the severity of depression? Or *to what extent* is the SAT Verbal score valid for predicting freshman GPA?

Third, we must distinguish between validity and the accuracy of norms for a test. It is entirely possible to have a test with good validity but also have norms that are well off the mark. When this occurs, some people conclude, erroneously, that the test is not valid. Consider the following scenarios. Tests A and B are both "IQ" tests used to predict college GPA. Both tests correlate .65 with GPA. In both instances the average GPA is 3.0. On Test A, the average IQ is 110, while on Test B the average is 80. The user might conclude that Test B is "not valid" because it makes no sense to think that students with an average IQ of 80 would have an average GPA of 3.0. Note, however, that the validity coefficient ($r = .65$) is the same for both tests. They are equally valid for predicting GPA. The problem is with the accuracy of the norms, not with the test validity. Of course, the converse may also be true. That is, a test may have excellent norms but little or no validity.

Construct Underrepresentation and Construct Irrelevant Variance

As we formalize our treatment of validity, two technical terms will aid our thinking. Before introducing these terms, let us consider the overlap between the *construct* we

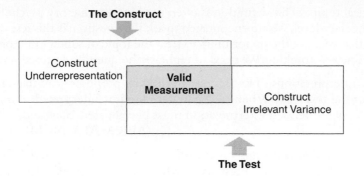

FIGURE 5.1   Geometric representation of the concepts of construct underrepresentation and construct irrelevant variance.

wish to measure and the *test* we hope will measure that construct. The **construct** is a trait or characteristic. For example, the construct might be depression or mathematical reasoning ability. We may have a simple, 20-item questionnaire to measure depression and a 50-item multiple-choice test to measure mathematical reasoning. We represent the relationship between the construct and the test by overlapping geometric forms as in Figure 5.1. Overlap between the construct and the test represents validity: measuring what we want to measure. The part of the construct *not* covered by the test we call **construct underrepresentation.** The construct of interest is not fully covered by the test. On the other hand, the test, in addition to measuring part of the construct of interest, may measure some characteristics other than what we want to measure. This "other" measurement we call **construct irrelevant variance.**

Let us first consider some concrete examples, then examine how they can be represented graphically. Suppose we conceptualize depression as having three components: cognitive (thoughts about depression), emotional (feeling depressed), and behavioral (doing or not doing things symptomatic of depression). Our questionnaire may do an excellent job of covering the cognitive and emotional components, yet gives no information about the behavioral component. Thus, the complete construct of depression is underrepresented by the test, specifically by omission of the behavioral component. This analysis assumes that the three components are at least partially independent, not simply different names for the same characteristic. It may also be that, to some extent, the questionnaire scores reflect a tendency to give socially desirable responses. This is not what we want to measure. This aspect of the scores is construct irrelevant variance.

Apply these concepts to the mathematical reasoning test. We expect mathematical reasoning to be manifested in the ability to solve both conventional and novel problems. However, the test items cover only conventional problems. Thus, the part of the construct related to novel problems is underrepresented. (We assume that reasoning about novel problems is not perfectly correlated with reasoning about conventional problems. If they are perfectly correlated, or nearly so, it does not make any difference which type of problem we use.) Furthermore, the test requires a very high level of reading ability. We do not want this test to be a reading test. That part

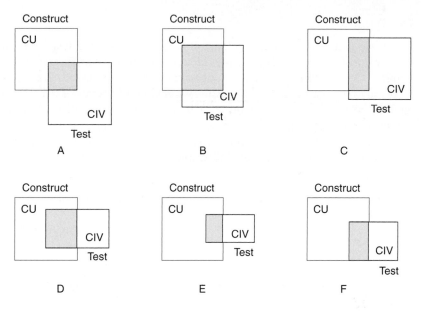

CU = Construct Underrepresentation   CIV = Construct Irrelevant Variance

FIGURE 5.2   Illustrations of varying degrees of construct underrepresentation and construct irrelevant variance.

of the test scores determined by reading ability rather than mathematical reasoning ability is construct irrelevant variance.

We can have an infinite variety of relationships between the construct and the test. The test may cover much of the construct, yet also have much irrelevant variance. The test may have little irrelevant variance, but also cover little of the construct. Figure 5.2 shows several different possibilities. Of course, the ideal case is complete overlap of the construct and the test. We do not ordinarily attain that ideal in practice. The notions of construct underrepresentation and construct irrelevant variance will be useful as we examine different methods of investigating the validity of tests.

> Construct underrepresentation refers to the degree to which a test fails to capture important aspects of the construct. ... Construct irrelevant variance refers to the degree to which test scores are affected by processes extraneous to the intended construct. *Standards*...
>
> (AERA/APA/NCME, 1999, p. 10)

TRY IT!

Which of the examples in Figure 5.2 shows the highest degree of test validity? Which example shows the greatest degree of construct irrelevant variance?

The Basic Issue

The basic issue is providing evidence that the score(s) on a test are indicative of the trait or construct of interest. This evidence undergirds our interpretation of the test score(s). Our treatment of test validity considers the types of evidence that seem to be persuasive regarding this basic issue. We review the types of evidence presented to establish test validity. We also, necessarily, discuss special cautions in interpreting this evidence and introduce the special terms psychologists have developed for this topic. There is universal agreement that validity is the single most important feature of a test. Good norms, high reliability, and other desirable features are important, but they become rather meaningless in the absence of good validity.

> Validity is ... the most fundamental consideration in developing and evaluating tests. *Standards*...
>
> (AERA et al., 1999, p. 9)

The Traditional and Newer Classifications of Types of Validity Evidence

There is a traditional, tripartite system for classifying types of validity evidence. It is used in the 1985 *Standards* and is well-entrenched in the psychometric literature. The 1999 *Standards* partially abandon this system in favor of a more diversified representation of types of validity evidence. However, the traditional system is not likely to go away soon. We introduce here both the traditional and the newer systems. Table 5.1 outlines the two systems. The contemporary reader should be familiar with the terminology of both systems.

We treat each of these categories of validity evidence in subsequent sections of this chapter. But, first, we provide a comparison of the terminology in the traditional and newer outlines summarized in Table 5.1. Content validity has much the same meaning in the two systems. Criterion-related validity in the traditional system corresponds approximately to the newer category of "relationships to

TABLE 5.1 *Outline of the Traditional and Newer Systems for Classifying Types of Validity*

Traditional Outline	Newer Outline
Content	Content
Criterion-related	Relations to Other Variables
Concurrent	Convergent and Discriminant
Predictive	Test-criterion Relationships
Construct	Response Processes
	Internal Structure
	Consequences

other variables," especially to the "test-criterion relationships" subcategory. The distinction between concurrent and predictive validity is made in both the 1985 and 1999 *Standards,* but without being made distinct subcategories. We represent them as separate subcategories here because this distinction is so often made in test manuals, journal articles, and similar documents. The concepts of convergent and discriminant validity are reflected in the traditional system, but they are made much more explicit in the newer system. Similarly, studies of response processes and internal structure are represented in the traditional system, but under the general category of construct validity. Construct validity is not a major category in the newer system, although the 1999 *Standards* are suffused with the notion of construct validity. Consideration of "consequences," as we note later in this chapter, is quite a new topic.

In subsequent sections of this chapter we cover all the major elements in both systems. However, we emphasize here, and again at the end of the chapter, that establishing validity is not a matter of checking off boxes in a classification scheme. Rather, it involves presenting an integrated, multifaceted array of evidence regarding appropriate interpretation of a test score. In addition to the *Standards*, an essential resource for all types of validation efforts in the employment context is the *Principles for the Validation and Use of Personnel Selection procedures*, prepared by the Society for Industrial and Organizational Psychology, Inc. (SIOP, 2003).

The Issue of Face Validity

When psychologists refer to test validity, they mean some *empirical demonstration* that a test measures what it purports to measure and, more specifically, that scores on the test can be interpreted meaningfully for a particular purpose. We contrast this empirical approach with the notion of face validity. **Face validity** refers to whether a test *looks like* it measures its target construct. Face validity has its advocates and detractors. The detractors scoff at face validity primarily because it is often used as a substitute for empirical demonstration of validity. It can be alluring and deceptive. A test author may say: "Inspection of items on the Scranton Anxiety Test clearly indicates that the test measures the major facets of anxiety." In the absence of any other support, this claim is not helpful. On the other hand, advocates for face validity note that we do work with real people in the real world. We should certainly have empirically demonstrated validity. However, in most circumstances it is also helpful if the test appears to be a valid measure.

We offer the following advice about face validity. Face validity is never a substitute for empirical validity. You cannot simply look at a test and know whether it has any degree of validity. However, face validity may be useful. If two tests have equal empirically established validity, it is usually preferable to use the one with better face validity. When constructing a test, it is prudent to aim for face validity but never at the expense of empirical validity. Perhaps most important, we need to be always aware of the difference between face validity and empirically demonstrated validity.

Content Validity

Content validity deals with the *relationship between the content of a test and some well-defined domain of knowledge or behavior.* For a test to have content validity there must be a good match between the content of the test and the content of the relevant domain. Application of content validity often involves the notion of sampling, that is, the test content covers a representative sampling of all the possible contents of the domain. This is not necessarily the case. The test may cover all material in the domain. However, ordinarily, the domain is too large to make saturation coverage feasible, so we rely on sampling. Content validity has two primary applications: educational achievement tests and employment tests. In each of these areas, there is a well-defined body of content. We want to determine the extent to which the test content matches the content of the relevant educational area or job.

Application to Achievement Tests

Content validity is generally considered the most important type of validity for achievement tests. The usual purpose of such tests is to determine the extent of knowledge of some body of material. Table 5.2 lists examples of bodies of material that might be targets for an achievement test.

The process of establishing content validity begins with careful definition of the content to be covered. This process usually results in a table of specifications or blueprint. Consider some of the entries in Table 5.2. The table of specifications for "high school chemistry" may arise from examination of content in the five most widely used textbooks in this field. The table of specifications for "Chapter 5 in this book" may arise from the list of learning objectives at the beginning of the chapter and the list of key terms at the end of the chapter. "Mathematical concepts covered in grades 1–3" may be defined by the curriculum guides from several states. Most frequently, written documents serve as the basis for the table of specifications.

TABLE 5.2 *Examples of Bodies of Knowledge as Targets for Achievement Tests*

Mathematical concepts covered in grades 1–3

High school chemistry

First course in psychological testing

Chapter 5 in this book

Geography lessons in Mrs. Vasguez's class last week

Typical elementary school spelling words

Addition, subtraction, multiplication, and division number facts

History of the Civil War

Basic writing skills

TABLE 5.3   *Statements of Test Purpose Oriented Toward Content Validity*

"... the Major Field Tests ... are designed to measure basic knowledge and understanding achieved by senior undergraduates in their major field of study. [They] are designed to assess mastery of concepts, principles, and knowledge expected of students at the conclusion of an academic major in specific subject areas." (ETS, 2005, p. 1)

"The *Stanford Achievement Test* Series ... assesses students' school achievement in reading, mathematics, spelling, language, science, social science, and listening ... the test items included in Stanford 10 reflect extensive review of national and state instructional standards, content-specific curricula, and educational trends as developed by national professional educational organizations." (Harcourt Assessment, 2003, p. 5)

Table 5.3 cites statements about the content bases for two standardized achievement tests: the *Major Field Tests,* college-level achievement tests in 14 disciplines, and the *Stanford Achievement Test,* a multilevel battery for grades K–12. Notice how references to content define the tests' orientation.

In many instances, a content area is represented by a *two-way table of specifications.* The first dimension of the table covers the content topics. The second dimension of the table represents mental processes such as knowledge of facts, comprehension of concepts, and ability to apply or synthesize material.

The most well-known scheme for representing processes is called Bloom's taxonomy. This is an outgrowth of the work of Benjamin Bloom and his colleagues. They produced three taxonomies or classification schemes: one in the cognitive domain (Bloom, 1956), one in the affective domain (Krathwohl, Bloom, & Masia, 1964), and a little-used one in the psychomotor domain (Harrow, 1972). Table 5.4 outlines the major categories in the cognitive taxonomy. The cognitive taxonomy is the most widely cited of the three taxonomies. It is also the most relevant to our discussion of the content validity of achievement tests. Although the full cognitive taxonomy is sometimes used, people often reduce the six major categories to three, while still calling it Bloom's taxonomy. Attempts to validate the distinctions made in Bloom's cognitive taxonomy, that is, to show that the various categories represent relatively distinct mental processes, have generally failed (Kreitzer & Madaus, 1994; Seddon, 1978). Nonetheless, Bloom's taxonomy or some variation of it is frequently encountered in tables of specifications, as well as in discussions of content validity.

We use a reduced Bloom-type system in Table 5.5 to illustrate a two-way table of specifications for the content of Chapter 4: Reliability in this book. Entries in the cells of Table 5.5 show the relative weight assigned to each cell in percentage form.

TABLE 5.4   *Major Categories in Bloom's Taxonomy for the Cognitive Domain*

Knowledge	Comprehension	Application
Analysis	Synthesis	Evaluation

TABLE 5.5   *Example of a Two-way Table of Content Specifications Based on Material in Chapter 4: Reliability in This Book*

Content	Process			
	Facts	Concepts	Applications	Total
Sources of unreliability	5	5	—	10
Test-retest method	3	5	5	13
Inter-rater reliability	3	3	3	9
Internal consistency	5	10	5	20
Standard error	5	5	5	15
Criterion-referenced tests	3	3	2	8
Generalizability theory	2	3	—	5
Factors affecting r	5	5	10	20
Total	**31**	**39**	**30**	**100**

For example, approximately 10% of the content deals with concepts related to internal consistency. Therefore, about 10% of the test items should deal with concepts related to internal consistency; in a 50-item test, that would mean 5 items on this topic. If there were only 1 item on this topic or as many as 20 items on this topic, the test would have poor content validity to that extent. In terms of marginal totals in Table 5.5, we would expect about 20% of the test items (10 in a 50-item test) to be on "factors affecting *r.*"

After preparing a table of specifications for a content area, we determine the content validity of a test by matching the content of the test with the table of specifications. This is ordinarily done on an item-by-item basis. This analysis should show (a) areas of content not covered by the test and (b) test items that do not fit the content specifications. Notice that these two areas correspond closely to the notions of construct underrepresentation and construct irrelevant variance introduced earlier.

The latter description applies when determining the content validity of an existing test. A similar process is used when an achievement test is being developed. However, now one prepares test items specifically to match the content blueprint. Pages 206–226 in Chapter 6 describe the test development process in more detail.

> Test developers often work from a specification of the content domain. The content specification carefully describes the content in detail, often with a classification of areas of content and types of items. *Standards …*
>   (AERA/APA/NCME, 1999, p. 11)

Given how we determine content validity for an achievement test, one would think we could summarize the result numerically. That is, we could express the percentage of the domain covered by test items and the percentage of test items not reflected in the domain. In practice, this is rarely done. Rather, after matching the test content to the domain content, a judgment is rendered that the test does or does not have sufficient content validity.

Instructional Validity

A special application of content validity is the notion of instructional validity, also known as curricular validity. Whereas content validity asks whether the test content fairly matches a well-defined body of content, **instructional validity** asks whether the content has actually been taught. For a test to have instructional validity, there must be evidence that the content was adequately covered in an instructional program. We sometimes call this the "opportunity to learn." In some contexts, we ask whether the students taking the test have actually been exposed to the material covered in the test.

The concept of instructional validity applies primarily to educational achievement tests. Consider the topic of square roots. This topic may be listed in the school's curriculum guide and in the math textbook used in the school. Therefore, the school's achievement test includes items on square roots. That is good content validity. Suppose, however, that none of the teachers in the school ever covers square roots in class or in homework assignments. Then the square root items do not have good instructional validity. There was no "opportunity to learn" about square roots.

The notion of instructional validity is not well established as something distinct from content validity. The *Standards* document does not include the term *instructional validity*, although there is brief discussion of the concept of opportunity to learn. In effect, the notion of instructional validity simply references the "well-defined body of content" to what is actually taught rather than to what is supposed to be taught. This is a useful distinction, but it does not introduce an entirely novel type of validity. Nevertheless, the term *instructional validity* or *curricular validity* has emerged. It was a prominent concept in one famous court case, *Debra P v. Turlington,* treated in Chapter 16.

Application to Employment Tests

The second major application of content validity is to employment tests. The essential notions are the same as for educational achievement tests. For employment tests, the content domain consists of the knowledge and skills required by a particular job. When constructing the list of job specifications, it is customary to restrict the list to knowledge and skills required by the job, particularly at the entry level. Such factors as motivation and personality traits are not ordinarily included. These other factors might be assessed in the job selection process, but they would be assessed by tests other than the employment tests we are discussing here. Furthermore, these other tests would be subject to validation through methods other than content validation. The process of developing the list of knowledge and skills required by a job is often called a **job analysis.** After completing the job analysis, we match the test content to the job content. As with achievement tests, we may be matching an existing test with a set of job specifications, or we may be constructing a new test to match the job specifications.

Although there are many similarities in applying content validity to achievement and employment tests, there are two interesting differences. First, for achievement tests, print documents such as textbooks or curriculum guides usually serve as the basis for content specifications. For employment tests, very often panels of experts develop the specifications. For a detailed description of such a process, see Knapp and Knapp (1995); these authors also provide a useful review of court cases on the necessity of test content validity and adequate job analysis. Second, although a percentage-agreement figure is rarely used with achievement tests, use of such a figure does occur for the evaluation of employment tests. Lawshe (1978) presented a methodology for expressing the percentage of test content that a panel of experts judged essential for job performance, resulting in what he called a content validity ratio. Schmidt, Ones, and Hunter (1992) and Borman, Hanson, and Hedge (1997) provide useful reviews of research related to job analysis. Raymond (2001) applies the concept of job analysis to licensure and certification exams.

> Evidence based on content can also come from expert judgments of the relationships between parts of the test and the construct. For example in developing a licensure test, the major facets of the specific occupation can be specified, and experts in that occupation can be asked to assign test items to the categories defined by those facets. *Standards* ...
> (AERA, APA, NCME, 1999, p. 11)

Content Validity in Other Areas

As noted earlier, content validity has its primary applications in the areas of educational achievement tests and employment tests. Its application to other areas, for example, intelligence and personality, is limited because few other areas are susceptible to clear specification of the domains to be covered. What, for example, is the content outline for intelligence or for extroversion? Although we may have simple definitions of these constructs, it is difficult to specify a detailed outline of what they encompass. Hence, content validity does not apply very neatly to them. However, in a few instances content validity may have some limited use in these areas. For example, it may be helpful to show that a test designed to measure a certain personality disorder covers all the traits specified for this disorder in the *Diagnostic and Statistical Manual of Mental Disorders: DSM—IV* (American Psychiatric Association, 2000). We cover precisely this point for some of the tests treated in Chapter 13: Clinical Instruments and Methods. However, we ordinarily rely on other methods of demonstrating validity for such tests.

Problems with Content Validity

Establishing content validity always seems like a very simple process. Conceptually, it is basic: specify the content of the domain, then check how well the test matches this content. However, in practice, the process nearly always turns out to be much more complicated. Complications arise from three sources. First, except in a few very simple cases, getting a clear specification of the content domain is often difficult. Consider these examples from Table 5.2. We said that the content for "mathematics concepts in grades 1–3" could be determined by checking the curriculum guides from several states. But state curriculum guides differ somewhat. Suppose we

TABLE 5.6 *Different Test Items Matching a Single Content Category*

Content Objective: Basic Multiplication Facts

Possible Test Items

1. $5 \times 4 = $ _____
2. $5 \times [\ ] = 20$
3. $5 \times 4 = $ (a) 9   (b) 20   (c) 25   (d) 7
4. $5 \times [\ ] = 20$ $[\ ] = $ (a) 15   (b) 4   (c) 5   (d) 25
5. Jack bought 4 pieces of candy at 5 cents each. How much did he spend?
6. Jack bought 4 pieces of candy at 5 cents each. How much did he spend?

       (a) 9   (b) 20   (c) 25   (d) Not Given

7. Jack paid 20 cents for 4 pieces of candy. What was the cost per piece?

check guides from five states. Three states may include knowledge of metric units in grades 1–3, but two other states may delay this topic until grade 4. How do we handle this? In specifying content for "Chapter 5 in this book," what depth of knowledge do we want: a passing acquaintance with major topics or a thorough grasp of every detail? We can ask a similar question about the knowledge and skills listed in specifications for an employment test.

The second difficulty in applying content validity comes in judging how well test items cover elements of the content specifications. Items with a common classification can vary widely in the skills they require. Consider the examples in Table 5.6. Many different items apply to a content category such as "basic multiplication facts." Are all these items equally appropriate? Do they all measure the content category equally well? Probably not. The example of a content category used here— basic multiplication facts—is a simple one. Imagine how much more complicated the situation becomes with a more complex topic, such as knowledge of the Civil War or elementary writing skills. In a listing of test content, all the items in Table 5.6 might be categorized as "basic multiplication facts." The person judging content validity must examine the actual test items and not rely exclusively on a listing of categories. In the final analysis, content validity requires a judgment, not just checking off boxes in an outline.

TRY IT!

Write two more test items that apply to the content objective listed in Table 5.6: "basic multiplication facts."

A third difficulty with content validity is that it does not refer in any way to actual performance on the test. All other methods of determining validity refer, at least in some way, to empirical performance. Thus, content validity leaves us unanchored to the real world of examiness' interaction with the test.

Criterion-related Validity

The essential feature of **criterion-related validity** is establishing the *relationship between performance on the test and on some other criterion* that is taken as an important indicator of the construct of interest. There are three common applications of criterion-related validity and two general contexts for these applications. In all these cases, we are attempting to establish the relationship between performance on the test and standing on some other criterion.

The two general contexts for criterion-related validity are predictive validity and concurrent validity. In **predictive validity**, the test aims to predict status on some criterion that will be attained in the future. For example, we may use a college entrance test, taken in the senior year of high school, to predict GPA at the end of freshman year in college. Or we may use a personality inventory to predict likelihood of attempting suicide at some future time. In **concurrent validity**, we check on agreement between test performance and current status on some other variable. For example, we may determine the relationship between performance on a standardized achievement test and a teacher-made test, where both tests are administered at approximately the same time. Or, we may determine the relationship between score on a test of depression and clinicians' ratings of current depression level. The difference between predictive and concurrent validity is strictly one of time for the criterion variable. From all other perspectives, the two concepts are the same.

> Historically, two designs, often called predictive and concurrent, have been distinguished for evaluating test-criterion relationships. *Standards …*
> (AERA/APA/NCME, 1999, p. 14)

The three common applications of criterion-related validity involve use of (a) an external, realistic criterion defining the construct of interest, (b) group contrasts, and (c) another test. Fundamentally, these three approaches reduce to the same thing. However, they have some practical differences, so we will treat them separately.

Key Points Summary 5.1

Three Common Approaches to Criterion-related Validity

1. External, Realistic Criterion
2. Group Contrasts
3. Another Test

External, Realistic Criterion

In some circumstances, we have an **external criterion** that provides a realistic definition of the construct of interest. The external criterion is what we would really like to have information about. The natural question is: If we really want information for the external criterion, why not get that information rather than rely on the test? There are two reasons. First, it may be that we cannot get information on the criterion until some time in the future and we would like to predict, now, what a person's future standing might be on the criterion. Second, it may be that getting information on the criterion is very time-consuming or expensive and we would like to have a simpler method of estimating what the person's standing might be. In either case, we will determine if the test provides useful information about the person's probable standing on the external criterion. Let us first consider some examples of this type of criterion-related validity and then examine exactly how the degree of validity is expressed. Table 5.7 lists several examples of using a test to estimate standing on some external criterion. For example, as noted earlier, we may use a college entrance test to predict GPA at the end of freshman year in college. Similarly, we may use a test to predict job performance as defined by supervisor's ratings at the end of six months on the job. We may want to determine severity of depression. We could have three clinicians interview each client for one hour and judge the degree of depression. This is expensive. We may want to know how well a 15-minute test of depression will indicate the degree of depression. In each of these instances, we have some external criterion that defines what we really want to know. We can think of the test we are validating as a potential substitute for the external criterion.

In these situations, we usually express the validity of the test as a correlation coefficient. Most often, we use the familiar Pearson correlation coefficient, although other types of coefficients may be used, depending on the nature of the scales for the criterion and the test. When the correlation coefficient is used in this way, it is called a **validity coefficient**. Ordinarily, a validity coefficient is simply a correlation coefficient used to express test validity. Hence, everything you have learned about correlation coefficients applies to validity coefficients. Figure 5.3 shows a bivariate distribution and the resulting correlation coefficient used to express the validity of a college admissions test.

Recall from the review of correlations in Chapter 4 that once we know the correlation between two variables, we can use the correlation to predict status on

TABLE 5.7 *Examples of External Criteria Used to Establish Criterion-related Test Validity*

Test	Criterion
College admissions test	Freshman year GPA
Depression inventory	Clinicians' ratings of severity of depression
Clerical aptitude test	Supervisors' ratings of job performance
Creative thinking test	Panel rating of creativity displayed in artistic products
Salesperson personality scale	Dollars of insurance sold annually

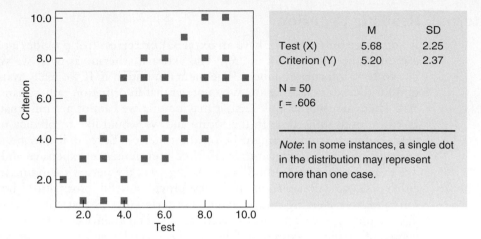

	M	SD
Test (X)	5.68	2.25
Criterion (Y)	5.20	2.37

N = 50
r = .606

Note: In some instances, a single dot in the distribution may represent more than one case.

FIGURE 5.3 Bivariate distribution illustrating relationship between a test and an external criterion.

variable Y from standing on variable X. (We use the term *predict* here to apply to both predictive and concurrent forms of criterion-related validity.) In the context of criterion-related validity, Y is the external criterion and X is the test. Hence, we can apply the usual regression equation:

$$Y' = bX + a \qquad \textbf{Formula 5-1}$$

where Y' = predicted status on the criterion

X = score on the test

b = the slope of the regression line

a = the intercept on the Y variable

When we have means and standard deviations for the X and Y variables and the correlation between X and Y, a convenient computing formula for the regression equation is:

$$Y' = r_{XY} (S_Y/S_X) (X - M_X) + M_Y \qquad \textbf{Formula 5-2}$$

where r_{XY} = the correlation between test and criterion

S_Y = standard deviation of the criterion

S_X = standard deviation of the test

X = score on the test

M_X = mean of the test

M_Y = mean of the criterion

Using the regression equation is often puzzling for students. They wonder: If we already have X and Y scores to determine r_{XY}, why do we need to make a prediction about Y? The answer is that we determine r_{XY} in a research study. Then, in

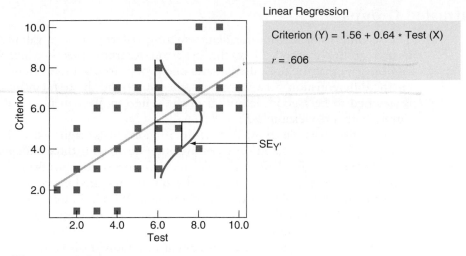

FIGURE 5.4 The prediction line and the scatter around the line.

another situation, when we do *not* already have the *Y* scores, we use the information from the research study and our knowledge of the regression equation to predict *Y*.

Recall, also, the concept of the standard error for this regression equation. This is the **standard error of estimate** (*SE*$_{Y'}$), expressed as follows:

$$SE_{Y'} = S_Y \sqrt{1 - r_{XY}{}^2}$$ **Formula 5-3**

where S_Y = the standard deviation of criterion scores

r_{XY} = the correlation (the validity coefficient) between the criterion *(Y)* and the test *(X)*

This is the same as Formula 4-4 in Chapter 4. Remember to distinguish between the three types of standard errors we have encountered so far: the standard error of the mean used in connection with sampling variability, the standard error of measurement used with reliability, and this standard error of estimate. For comparison of the formulas, see pp. 142–143.

This standard error of estimate *is* a standard deviation. It is the standard deviation of actual criterion scores around their predicted scores. Using the assumption of homoscedasticity and our knowledge of the normal curve, we can apply this formula to estimate probabilities that individual cases will exceed or fall short of their predicted status on the external criterion by certain amounts. Figure 5.4 shows the model for making such predictions.

TRY IT! ....

For the data given in Figure 5.3, what is the standard error of estimate? Use Formula 5-3 for SE.

....

Contrasted Groups

The second major method for demonstrating criterion-related validity is the con-trasted groups method. Here the criterion is group membership. We wish to demonstrate that the test differentiates one group from another. Generally, the bet-ter the differentiation between groups, the more valid the test. Group membership is assumed to be a good definition of the criterion. We can illustrate the method simply with a few examples.

In the first example, group A contains 50 individuals diagnosed with schizophre-nia. The diagnosis is based on extensive interviews with three independent clini-cians, so we are confident of the diagnosis. Group B contains 50 individuals who have no history of major psychological problems and are known to be functioning normally in their family and work environments. We administer a personality inven-tory to all 100 individuals. We want to show that the test sharply distinguishes between the two groups.

In the second example, group A contains 35 individuals who have completed a course in computer programming with flying colors. Group B contains 35 individ-uals who did not perform well in the course. We had administered a programmer aptitude test to all 70 individuals at the beginning of the course. We want to estab-lish that the aptitude test clearly distinguishes between those who were successful and those who were unsuccessful in the course.

When viewing the results of a contrasted-groups study of test validity, it is impor-tant to consider the degree of separation between the groups. Simply reporting that there was a "statistically significant difference" between the groups, as is often done in test manuals, is not sufficient. With a large number of cases in the study, it is not difficult to obtain a significant difference between the groups. The important point is whether the test differentiates between the groups to an extent that is useful in practice. Statistical significance is a necessary but not a sufficient condition for such practical use.

Consider the degree of differentiation between groups in the two examples in Figure 5.5. In example A, although there is a significant difference in mean scores between the criterion and the contrast groups, there is nearly complete overlap in

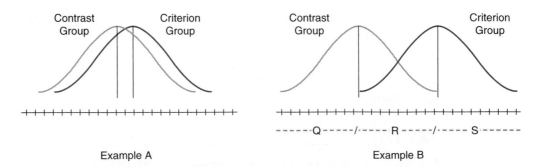

FIGURE 5.5   Examples of poor and good differentiation in use of the contrasted groups method.

the distributions of scores. For almost any score on this test, it is difficult to surmise whether the examinee is more like the criterion group or more like the contrast group. In example B, there is good differentiation between the groups. An examinee scoring in the range marked Q is like the contrast group, not the criterion group. An examinee scoring in the range marked S is like the criterion group, not the contrast group. It is only in the range marked R where the test information is not useful.

The examples in Figure 5.5 naturally bring to mind the notion of **effect size** from elementary statistics. It would be useful to apply this notion to contrasted group studies of criterion-related validity. Unfortunately, measures of effect size are rarely used for this purpose. However, we will encounter some analogous notions in the section on decision theory later in this chapter.

As noted in Chapter 3, the results of contrasted group studies serve as the basis for some statements in narrative reports of test information. For example, a statement such as "Persons who score like John often display difficulties in interpersonal relations" probably arose from a study showing different score distributions for persons with and without difficult interpersonal relations.[1] A statement such as "Jill's score on scale A suggests a favorable prognosis for short-term therapy" probably arose from a study of differences on scale A for persons who did or did not profit from short-term therapy. Obviously, the validity of such statements depends partly on how well the test differentiates between groups.

The perceptive reader will note that the contrasted groups approach can be converted into a form of the external, realistic criterion approach simply by assigning values of 0 and 1 to membership in the groups. The statistically inclined person can easily make the conversion. However, in practice, the two approaches are usually treated as distinct cases.

Correlations with Other Tests

A third method for establishing criterion-related validity is showing the correlation between the test to be validated and some other test that is known or presumed to be a valid measure of the relevant construct. For simplicity, let us call the test to be validated the "new" test. In this application, the other test becomes the criterion, analogous to the external criterion treated above. On first encountering this method, one is inclined to ask: If the other test is known or presumed to be valid, why not use it rather than the new test? There are several reasons why we might want to establish the validity of the new test. The new test may be shorter or less expensive that the criterion test. For example, we may have a 15-minute test of intelligence that we want to validate against the *Wechsler Intelligence Scale for Children*, which takes about one hour to administer. The new test may have better norms or more efficient scoring procedures. For example, we may wish to show the correlation between a new edition of a test of depression—enhanced by computer scoring,

---

[1] In these examples, we assume that authors of the narrative reports are using empirical evidence for statements. However, some reports are based on wishful thinking or hypotheses rather than evidence.

updated items, and new national norms—and the old edition of the test. Why? Because we may have 20 years of research studies on the old edition. It is a venerable, time-tested measure, richly embedded in the research literature on depression. We hope our new edition will correlate highly with the old edition. For any of these or similar reasons, we may want to establish the validity of the new test rather than rely on the criterion test.

Using another test to establish criterion-related validity is simple. It is also very widely used (Hogan & Agnello, 2004). The correlation (usually Pearson) between the new test and the criterion test expresses the validity. Thus, the methodology is the same as that described above for use of an external, realistic criterion.

When considering test validity, we must be alert that we do not confuse words with reality. Many years ago, Kelley (1927) described what he called the *jingle fallacy* and the *jangle fallacy*. Simply put, the jingle fallacy is thinking that using the same or similar words for two things means that they really are the same. As applied to tests, supposing that both the Wisconsin Intelligence Test and the Scranton Intelligence Test measure the same trait simply because they both use the word "intelligence" is an example of the jingle fallacy. The two tests may or may not measure the same trait; for example, they may correlate only .45, suggesting that they are at least partly measuring different traits. The jangle fallacy is thinking that two things are really different because they use different words. As applied to tests, supposing that the Non-verbal Test of Intelligence and the Test of Verbal Fluency measure different traits because they use different words in their titles is the jangle fallacy. These two tests may or may not measure different traits; for example, they may correlate .95, strongly suggesting that they are measuring the same trait. Guarding against the jingle fallacy and the jangle fallacy calls for empirical evidence. Information about the correlations among tests is especially relevant, although it is not the only relevant information. Reference to the jingle and jangle fallacies is particularly relevant when considering validity as demonstrated by correlations among various tests, but it is relevant to all considerations of validity.

The most common index for reporting criterion-related validity is the correlation coefficient. The degree of correlation may be depicted with bivariate distributions like those in Figures 5.3 and 5.4. A special application of this type of array is the *expectancy table*, which has a structure very similar to that of the bivariate chart. Entries for each row in an expectancy table are percentages of cases in that row. Thus, entries and combinations of entries easily translate into probabilities. In the precomputer era, expectancy tables facilitated interpretation of criterion-related validity data. The ready availability of computer-generated predictions, using the methods described earlier in this chapter, render the expectancy table largely obsolete. However, older test manuals still contain such tables.

Special Considerations for Interpreting Criterion-related Validity

At first glance, criterion-related validity appears clean and simple. In many ways it is. However, under the veneer of simplicity lurk a number of problems and issues that merit special attention. We now take up these special issues.

Conditions Affecting the Correlation Coefficient

When reviewing the correlation coefficient (r) in Chapter 4, we noted several conditions that affect the magnitude of r. Since the validity coefficient is simply a type of correlation coefficient, all these conditions are relevant to consideration of criterion-related validity. Specifically, linearity, group homogeneity, and heteroscedasticity are all important matters.

If the relationship between test and criterion is *nonlinear,* the Pearson correlation will underestimate the true degree of relationship. When using a correlation coefficient to express criterion-related validity, one should always examine the bivariate distribution (scatterplot) for the two variables. Nonlinearity of relationship is *not* a common problem when studying test validity. Correlations of tests with other variables are not ordinarily strong enough to manifest distinctly nonlinear trends. Nevertheless, it is easy enough to check the bivariate distribution for the presence of a nonlinear trend. Simply examine the bivariate plot (scattergram), usually prepared with SPSS, SAS, Excel, or similar software to determine if a nonlinear trend is present.

Difference in group *heterogeneity* is a common problem when interpreting validity coefficients. A validity study may be conducted on a very heterogeneous group, yielding a relatively high validity coefficient, when we want to apply the result to a much more homogeneous group. For example, the validity of a college admissions test for predicting freshman GPA may be established in a multicampus study, including a wide range of abilities. We want to use the test at a single campus where there is a much narrower range of ability. Almost certainly the validity will be less for our single campus. Contrariwise, we may conduct the study on a single campus with a narrow range of talent. Surely, the test will have greater predictive validity for schools with a much wider range of ability. In Chapter 4 we gave formulas to make the appropriate adjustments for differences in group heterogeneity. These formulas are used routinely in the study of criterion-related validity.

Homoscedasticity, as described in Chapter 4, refers to the assumption that data points are approximately equally scattered around the prediction line throughout the range. See Figure 5.4. This is *not* generally a problem when examining test validity. Correlations between test scores and other criteria are not often high enough to warrant concern on this point. However, as with nonlinearity, it is easy enough to check the scatterplot to determine if there is a problem in this regard.

The Reliability-Validity Relationship

The validity of a test depends to some extent on the reliability of the test. The test's validity is also dependent to some extent on the reliability of the criterion. Thus, limited reliability of either the test or the criterion will limit the criterion-related validity of the test. These reliability-validity relationships are usually treated in the context of criterion-related validity, a practice we follow here. However, the fundamental notions extend more broadly to all types of validity. *The concepts covered in this section are among the most important in all of psychometric theory.*

We will first express some of the relationships between reliability (of both test and criterion) and validity in narrative form. Then we will examine the relationships in a more formal manner, specifically with formulas that express the relationships. If a test has no reliability whatsoever—the test scores are simply random error—then the test can have no validity. However, a test can be perfectly reliable and still have no validity; that is, the test is reliably measuring something other than what we want to measure. If the criterion has no reliability—status on the criterion is simply random error—then the test can have no validity with respect to the criterion, even if the test is perfectly reliable. We formulated all the latter statements in terms of extremes: no reliability and perfect reliability. Of course, in practice, we usually deal with less extreme cases. Tests usually have some degree of reliability. Criterion measures usually have some degree of reliability. How do we treat these in-between cases?

Fortunately, there are formulas that express the effect of limited reliability on criterion-related validity. And, fortunately, they are simple formulas, although they are not intuitively obvious. Before listing the relevant formulas, let us introduce the specialized terms used for this topic. **Attenuation** is the technical term for the limit placed on validity by imperfect reliability. Attenuation simply means "lessened" or "reduced." From the obtained validity coefficient, we can calculate the *disattenuated* validity coefficient. This is also called the validity coefficient *corrected for unreliability*. We can correct or disattenuate the validity coefficient for unreliability in either the test or the criterion or both. These corrections give the estimated validity coefficient if reliability (for the test, criterion, or both) is perfect, that is, +1.00. Here are the symbols we use for the correction formulas:

Y is the criterion

X is the test

r_{XY} is the correlation between test and criterion (the validity coefficient)

r_{XX} is the reliability of the test

r_{YY} is the reliability of the criterion

Here are the appropriate formulas. We use a prime ($'$) on either X, Y, or both X and Y to indicate we have corrected for unreliability in the variable(s).

$$r_{X'Y} = r_{XY}/\sqrt{r_{XX}}$$ **Formula 5–4**

Formula 5-4 gives the validity coefficient corrected for unreliability in the *test (X)*. One arrangement of this formula gives rise to the pithy generalization that the validity coefficient cannot exceed the square root of the reliability of the test *(X)*. It is perhaps more important to simply remember that test validity is limited by test reliability.

$$r_{XY'} = r_{XY}/\sqrt{r_{YY}}$$ **Formula 5–5**

Formula 5-5 gives the validity coefficient corrected for unreliability in the *criterion (Y)*.

$$r_{X'Y'} = r_{XY}/\sqrt{r_{XX}\, r_{YY}}$$ **Formula 5–6**

Formula 5-6 gives the validity coefficient corrected for unreliability in *both* the test and criterion. For further details on these formulas, see Gulliksen (1950), Lord and Novick (1968), or Nunnally and Bernstein (1994).

Consider this example. The correlation between a test *(X)* designed to predict job success as defined by supervisor's rating of on-the-job performance (*Y*, the criterion) is .60. The test reliability is .75. If the test were perfectly reliable, the test–criterion correlation (the validity coefficient) would be $.60/\sqrt{.75} = .72$. Suppose the reliability of the supervisor's rating is .65. Correcting for unreliability in both the test and the criterion yields a validity coefficient of $.60/\sqrt{.75 \times .65} = .86$. Thus, the validity coefficient (.60), which is moderate, is limited considerably by the imperfect reliability of the test and the criterion.

TRY IT! ....

Apply the correction for unreliability (only for unreliability in the test, Formula 5-4) to these data:

$$r_{XY} = .40 \qquad\qquad r_{XX} = .70 \qquad\qquad r_{X'Y} = \underline{}$$

In most practical applications of these procedures, we correct only for unreliability in the test. We assume that the criterion's reliability is unimpeachable or, more realistically, that there is nothing we can do about it. However, it is sometimes useful to apply the correction to the criterion, too. It is important to emphasize that applying these corrections does not actually change the validity coefficient determined in a specific study. However, the corrections help us to think about the effects of imperfect reliability on the validity coefficient.

The correction for unreliability is usually applied to bring the test to a level of perfect reliability (1.00). Although this procedure is useful for theoretical purposes, it is quite unrealistic. It is more realistic to set the reliability at a figure such as .85 or .90. This can be done by including the more realistic figure as a multiplier in the denominator of the formulas given above. For example, the first formula may be written as

$$r_{X'Y} = r_{XY}/\sqrt{.90(r_{XX})} \qquad\qquad \textbf{Formula 5-7}$$

This will give the estimated validity coefficient (r_{XY}) with the assumption that the reliability of the test (r_{XX}) is brought to .90.

Validity of the Criterion

When discussing criterion–related validity, we tend to focus attention on the test. How well does the test predict or correlate with the criterion? Indeed, the test should be the focus of attention because we are trying to assess the test's validity. However, from another perspective, we need to examine the validity of the criterion, specifically the operational definition of the criterion. Is the operational definition of the criterion appropriate?

Let us consider a few examples. We want a college admissions test to predict "success in college." We use freshman GPA as the operational definition of success in college. How good is this operational definition? Freshman GPA is only one possible definition of success in college. Another definition is GPA upon graduation. Another definition is active participation in extracurricular activities. Yet another definition is a composite of GPA and extracurricular participation. What about success as a salesperson? Total dollar volume sold might be a definition of success. But this may not be the best definition. Some salespersons may be assigned to market segments that naturally have high volume. Perhaps number of new accounts acquired would be a better definition of success. Or the sales manager's rating might serve as a definition of success. Obviously, we could multiply examples of different ways to define any criterion that might be used for test validation. The important point here is that when considering criterion-related validity of a test, we also need to think about the validity of the operational definition of the criterion.

Criterion Contamination

When we are trying to establish the validity of a test by correlating it with an external criterion, **criterion contamination** refers to a situation in which performance on the test influences status on the criterion. An example will make the concept clear. Using a sample of 50 cases, we attempt to establish the validity of the Cleveland Depression Scale (CDS) by showing that it correlates highly with ratings of depression made by three clinicians. The clinicians have access to the CDS scores and base their ratings of depression, at least in part, on these scores. This will lead to inflation of the correlation between the test and the criterion. (It is conceivable that the influence could go in the opposite direction, that is, that the correlation would decrease. For example, if the clinicians despised the CDS, they might deliberately disagree with it. However, this seems unlikely. Criterion contamination ordinarily leads to an increase in the correlation between test and criterion.)

When conducting a criterion-related validity study, it is important to design the study to avoid criterion contamination. When reviewing a criterion-related validity study, one must be alert to detecting the possible presence of criterion contamination. There are no analytical methods or formulas that estimate the effect of criterion contamination.

Convergent and Discriminant Validity

Two useful concepts for thinking about criterion-related validity are convergent validity and discriminant validity. **Convergent validity** refers to a relatively high correlation between the test and some criterion thought to measure the same construct as the test. For example, to demonstrate the validity of a test of depression we may want to show that the test has a high correlation with another test already known to be a good measure of depression. In contrast, we may want to show that our test of depression is *not* simply a measure of general maladjustment. Thus, we want to show that it does *not* have a high correlation with such constructs as anxiety or stress. This is **discriminant validity**, which shows that the test has a relatively low correlation with constructs other than the construct it is intended to measure.

> Relationships between test scores and other measures intended to assess similar constructs provide convergent evidence, whereas relationships between test scores and measures purportedly of different constructs provide discriminant evidence. *Standards…*
>
> (AERA/APA/NCME, 1999, p. 14)

The concepts of convergent and discriminant validity are widely used in the field of personality measurement. The concepts are *not* widely used, in practice, for ability and achievement tests, although the concepts certainly have potential applications in these areas. Here is an example of the use of the concepts of convergent and discriminant validity in the personality domain. Suppose we are trying to establish the validity of the Scranton Test of Anxiety (STA). We may wish to show that the STA is highly related to other measures of anxiety, but is *not* highly related to measures of depression. We administer the STA along with the Taylor Manifest Anxiety Scale (TMAS) and the Beck Depression Inventory (BDI). We assume that the TMAS is a reasonably valid measure of anxiety and that the BDI is a reasonably valid measure of depression. A favorable result would be a correlation of .75 between STA and TMAS (convergent validity) and a correlation of .20 between STA and BDI (discriminant validity). Suppose that the correlation between STA and BDI were .75. We would conclude that the STA is not discriminating between anxiety and depression. This type of analysis and reasoning is very common in discussions of the validity of personality tests. See the statements from test manuals in Table 5.8 using these concepts.

The Multitrait-Multimethod Matrix

A special application of the concepts of convergent and discriminant validity is the multitrait-multimethod matrix. In a classic article, Campbell and Fiske (1954) recommended the use of such a matrix for analyzing convergent and discriminant validity of several tests. The matrix is just a correlation matrix. Variables in the matrix

TABLE 5.8 *Sample Statements about Convergent and Discriminant Validity from Test Manuals*

"Of special importance is the finding that the BDI-II [Beck Depression Inventory-II] was more positively correlated ($r = .71$) with the Hamilton Psychiatric Rating Scale for Depression (HRSD) … than it was with the Hamilton Rating Scale for Anxiety (HARS) ($r = .47$) … These findings indicate a robust discriminant validity between depression and anxiety." (Beck, Steer, & Brown, 1996, p. 28)

"Correlations of the STAI [State-Trait Anxiety Inventory] scales and other measures of personality provide evidence of the convergent and discriminant validity of the STAI. In general, larger correlations would be expected with measures of emotional disturbance and psychopathology, and smaller correlations would be expected with unrelated constructs." (Spielberger, 1983, p. 35)

"A study … compared the Piers-Harris [Children's Self Concept Scale] to the Coopersmith Self-Esteem Inventory … The two measures correlated at $r = .78$, which established convergent validity. Discriminant validity was assessed by correlating self-concept scores with variables representing academic achievement, socioeconomic status, special-education placement, ethnicity, grade placement, gender, and age. Multiple correlation coefficients with these conceptually distinct variables did not exceed .25, which provides evidence of discriminant validity" (Piers & Herzberg, 2002, p. 66).

TABLE 5.9 *Simple Example of a Multitrait-Multimethod Matrix*

	D-1	D-2	A-1	A-2
D-1	r			
D-2	H	r		
A-1	L	VL	r	
A-2	VL	L	H	r

include tests that purport to measure several different traits—this is the multitrait part—using several different methods—the multimethod part. Different traits might be anxiety and depression, as in the example used earlier. The different methods might include self-report questionnaires, projective techniques, and ratings based on clinicians' interviews. The essential purpose of the **multitrait-multimethod analysis** is to demonstrate that correlations within a trait but cutting across different methods are higher than correlations within methods cutting across different traits, and, of course, higher than correlations cutting across both traits and methods. Table 5.9 presents a schematic for understanding a multitrait-multimethod matrix. In this example, we attempt to measure depression and anxiety (two presumably different traits). For each trait we have a projective measure, say a score derived from the Rorschach Inkblot Test, and a score from a self-report inventory, say the MMPI-2. Call the traits D and A and the methods 1 and 2. In Table 5.9, the correlations *(r)* in the diagonal are reliability coefficients. The other entries are also correlations coded in terms of our expectations about their levels. An "H" means we expect to find a high correlation. For example, we want to obtain a high correlation between the two measures of depression even when they are measured by different methods, here the Rorschach and the MMPI-2. An "L" means we expect to find a low correlation and "VL" means a very low correlation. We want to find a low correlation between depression and anxiety, even though both are measured by the Rorschach. Of course, we expect to find a very low correlation between depression measured by the MMPI-2 and anxiety measured by the Rorschach.

Table 5.10 inserts illustrative data for the multitrait-multimethod matrix in our example. In this example, the correlations reflect favorably on the tests. That is, they show appropriate convergent and discriminant validity.

We emphasize that this is a very simple example used for pedagogical purposes. Campbell and Fiske (1954) employ examples involving three traits and three

TABLE 5.10 *Illustrative Data for a Multitrait-Multimethod Matrix*

	D-1	D-2	A-1	A-2
D-1	.84			
D-2	.75	.87		
A-1	.32	.17	.79	
A-2	.09	.49	.65	.81

methods and even more; the correlation matrix rapidly becomes large. The method is widely cited in the psychometric literature. However, it is *not* widely used in practice. In a follow-up to the classic 1954 article, Fiske and Campbell (1992) lament that, while the 1954 article received thousands of citations, "We have yet to see a really good matrix" (p. 393). Nevertheless, the approach helps us to think more clearly about our methods for validating tests.

Combining Information from Different Tests

Up to this point, we have referred to criterion-related validity as the relationship between a single test and a criterion. However, in some contexts we want to use several tests to predict status on a criterion. The usual method for dealing with this situation is multiple correlation. **Multiple correlation** is a technique for expressing the relationship between one variable (the criterion) and the optimum combination of two or more other variables (in this case, several tests). For example, we may want to predict freshman GPA from a combination of an admissions test, high school rank, and a test of academic motivation. The trick is to get the optimum weights for the other variables so as to maximize the correlation between the criterion and the combination of tests. These weights depend not only on the tests' correlations with the criterion but also on the relationships among the predictor tests.

There are two main purposes for multiple correlation procedures. The first is the very practical purpose of yielding the best possible prediction of a dependent variable, such as job success or academic performance, from several other variables and to do so as economically as possible, that is, by not including any more variables than necessary. The second purpose is to understand theoretically which variables contribute effectively to prediction of a dependent variable and which variables are redundant.

There are two end products from multiple correlation procedures. The first is a multiple correlation coefficient, represented by R (note capital). The R is subscripted to indicate what is being predicted and from what. For example, if variable 1 is predicted from variables 2, 3, and 4, we show $R_{1.234}$. This R is interpreted the same as the Pearson r, which we now call a zero-order correlation coefficient.

The second product of multiple correlation procedures is the weights assigned to the predictor variables. These come in two forms: b's and β's (betas). "b's" are applied to raw scores, β's are applied to the scores in "standardized" form, that is, z-scores. The equation showing a prediction from a multiple correlation, called **multiple regression equation**, is like this for three predictors:

$$\text{Raw score form: } Y' = b_1 X_1 + b_2 X_2 + b_3 X_3 + c \qquad \textbf{Formula 5-8}$$

$$\text{z-score form: } z_y = \beta_1 z_1 + \beta_2 z_2 + \beta_3 z_3 \qquad \textbf{Formula 5-9}$$

Note the difference between b's and β's. "b's" just tell how much to weight each raw score variable. They compensate for differences in the scales used for the raw scores. Variables with "big" numbers usually get small weights, variables with "little" numbers often get large weights. In z-score form, all variables have $M = 0$ and $SD = 1$. Hence, beta weights are directly comparable; they tell directly which variables are receiving the most weight.

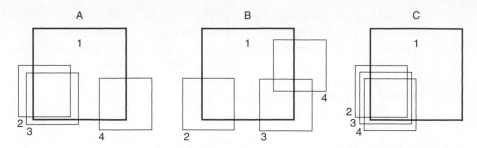

FIGURE 5.6 Illustrations of multiple *R* situations.

We also use *R*-squared (R^2), that is, the percent of variance in *Y* accounted for or overlapping with variance in the predictors. This leads to an interesting and pedagogically useful way of interpreting contributions of different variables to *R*.

Consider the examples in Figure 5.6. The box labeled "1" represents the criterion we are trying to predict. The degree to which the other boxes (2, 3, and 4) overlap with box 1 is proportional to their respective correlations with the criterion. More specifically, the degree of overlap with the criterion corresponds to r^2 for each of the other variables. Similarly, the degree of overlap between boxes 2, 3, and 4 is proportional to their respective intercrorrelations. In these examples, we want to use Tests 2, 3, and 4 to predict the criterion (1).

Now consider Example A. Tests 2 and 3 show substantial overlap with the criterion. However, they are themselves highly correlated. After we enter one of them into the formula for predicting the criterion (i.e., the multiple regression equation), the other one adds little new information. Suppose Test 2 enters the equation first. It will have the greatest weight (β, beta). Test 4 will have the next greatest weight even though Test 3 has a higher correlation with the criterion than does Test 4. Test 4 provides more new or unique information after Test 2 is in the equation. Note that Test 4 is uncorrelated with Tests 2 and 3 (no overlap).

In Example C, Tests 2, 3, and 4 all have about the same degree of correlation (overlap) with the criterion. Furthermore, Tests 2, 3, and 4 are highly correlated, as indicated by their degree of overlap with one another. After one of these tests enters the equation, the other two add little new information. From a practical viewpoint, it would probably not be worth administering all three of these tests for purposes of predicting the criterion. For example, to predict freshman GPA, it would not be useful to administer three separate tests of general verbal ability, even though all three tests have substantial correlation with GPA.

Important questions in multiple correlation are (1) the order in which variables enter the equation, (2) the overlap between predictors, and (3) when new variables do not add any predictive power. Thus, multiple correlation procedures may show that certain variables are not valuable predictors once other predictors are taken into account.

Multiple correlation is a crucial technique for determining incremental validity. **Incremental validity** refers to how much new, unique information a test (or other source of information) adds to an existing body of information. The general notion of incremental validity is important quite apart from multiple correlation. We are always trying to determine how much new information a test or procedure provides, how difficult and how expensive it is to get the new information, and whether the new information is worth the extra effort and cost. In some circumstances, we may have a test with good validity, but we do not need to use the test because we already have good information about the trait of interest. In other circumstances, we may have virtually no information on the trait of interest; hence we are glad to use a test that has only modest validity—but it gives us at least some useful information. See Hunsley and Haynes (2003) for practical applications of the notion of incremental validity in clinical contexts.

The procedures of multiple correlation and regression supply the mathematical details for the concepts we have illustrated with Figure 5.6. One can understand the general concepts involved without intimate knowledge of the mathematical procedures. That is sufficient for our purposes. Multiple regression procedures allow for different ways of adding variables into the equation. One procedure is to enter *all* variables, even if some will have insignificant weights. Another is to move forward stepwise, adding in variables until the next one doesn't add anything significant to the prediction. Another method is to start with all the variables and then "back-out" those that don't contribute significantly. The procedures are tedious when done by hand. They are easy to use in statistical packages such as SPSS and SAS. For an excellent introduction to multiple correlation, see Licht (1995). For more technical development, see Glass and Hopkins (1996).

Multiple correlation is the multivariate statistical technique most frequently used when combining information from different tests. However, it is not the only multivariate technique used for this purpose. Other techniques, such as discriminant functions, canonical correlations, and structural equation models are beyond the scope of this book. For further information on these techniques, see Tabachnik and Fidell (2006).

Statistical versus Clinical Prediction

In the previous section, we described the statistical methodology for combining information. With multiple correlation techniques, we determined empirically what information to use, what weights to apply to what we do use, and what information to discard. As an alternative, we could combine the information based on clinical intuition and experience. Which method is better for combining information: the statistical or clinical? Some sources call this the statistical versus clinical issue, whereas other sources call it the actuarial versus clinical issue. Reference to clinical experts is not limited to clinical psychologists. The reference includes any type of professional, for example, counselors, criminal justice experts, and so on. Consider the following two scenarios.

First, we want to predict freshman GPA for a group of 100 students. We can make a statistical prediction based on high school rank and SAT scores, using multiple correlation methodology. We can also ask a group of admissions counselors to make predictions. The counselors have the high school rank and SAT information. They also have the students' folders with letters of recommendation, transcripts of high school courses, and records of extracurricular and work activities. The counselors can combine all this information in any way they wish and make a clinical judgment about probable success, as defined by the freshman GPA. Which prediction will be more accurate: the purely statistical one based on multiple regression or the clinical one based on intuitive use of all the information?

Here is a second scenario. We have a group of 50 patients at a state hospital. Half of them have been diagnosed with condition A and half with condition B. These diagnoses are based on very extensive testing and multiple interviews with several psychologists. We are very confident that the diagnoses are correct. We now want to see how accurately we can classify these individuals with (a) statistical method and (b) clinical review. We develop a multiple regression equation using only the profile of MMPI scores to get the statistical prediction of group membership, A versus B. We have three clinical psychologists interview the patients to make a determination. In addition to the interview information, the clinicians also have the MMPI scores. Which will make the better prediction of group membership: the statistical formula or the clinical judgment?

Numerous studies have been conducted using designs similar to the two scenarios previously described. In general, the statistical predictions at least equal and usually beat the clinical predictions. This finding makes clinicians wince. On the other hand, it makes statisticians giddy. Meehl (1954) was the first to document the superiority of statistical over clinical prediction in a variety of studies. Other reports have amply confirmed the result. For a particularly thorough and readable review of the literature on this matter see Dawes (1994, especially Chapter 3). Can we replace clinicians with formulas? Sometimes yes, sometimes no. Development of the formulas requires an adequate database. When we have an adequate database, we should rely on it. But we do not always have an adequate database. In that case, we must rely on clinical judgment to make the best of the situation. Furthermore, we need clinicians to develop the original notions of what should be measured to go into the formulas. There may also be situations in which clinical judgment *firmly* guided by statistical formulas can be better than the formulas themselves. See Grove and Meehl (1996), Kleinmuntz (1990), and Swets, Dawes, and Monahan (2000) for thoughtful discussions of this matter.

Decision Theory: Basic Concepts and Terms

Decision theory is a body of concepts, terms, and procedures for analyzing the quantitative effects of our decisions. As applied to testing, the decisions involve using tests, especially in the context of criterion-related validity, for purposes such as selection, certification, and diagnosis. In applying the theory, we usually want to optimize the results of our decisions according to certain criteria. The criteria might involve savings in cost or time. Formal applications of decision theory rapidly become quite complex mathematically and go beyond the scope of this book. However, a simple introduction of some of the basic concepts and terms from decision theory will aid our thinking about validity, especially criterion-related validity.

Hits, False Positives, and False Negatives

First, let us introduce the notions of hits, false positives, and false negatives. Observe the data array in Figure 5.7. As in Figure 5.3, we are using a college admissions test to predict freshman GPA. At many colleges, falling below a GPA of 2.0 results in academic probation, so 2.0 is a natural cut-score to use for GPA. Here GPA is the criterion *Y* variable. Our college admissions test, the *X* variable here, has a mean of 50 and standard deviation of 10. We decide to use a score of 40 to select students for next year's freshman class. Thus, 40 is the test cut-score.

A **hit** is a case that has the same status with respect to both the test and the criterion. That is, hits include cases that exceed the cut-scores on the criterion and the test, as well as cases that fall below the cut-scores on both criterion and test. These cases are in the upper right and lower left quadrants of Figure 5.7. Obviously, a high hit rate indicates good criterion-related test validity. However, unless the correlation between test and criterion is perfect (1.00), there will be some errors in prediction. The errors are labeled as follows. **False positives** are cases that exceed the test cut-score but fail on the criterion. These cases are in the lower right quadrant of Figure 5.7. **False negatives** are cases that fall below the test cut-score but are successful on the criterion. These cases are in the upper left quadrant of Figure 5.7.

Note: It is easy for the psychometric novice to place "hits" in a chart like Figure 5.7, but false positives and false negatives are often confused. Here is a way to keep these terms straight. Always draw the chart so that the test is on the bottom axis and the criterion on the left axis. Then, draw the cut-score lines. Place the "hit" labels; that's easy. To place the false positive and false negative labels, remember that on a number line "positive" values are to the *right,* negative values to the *left.* Thus, in the two remaining boxes, false positives are to the right and false negatives to the left.

Two factors affect the percentages of hits, false positives, and false negatives. The *first* factor is the degree of correlation between the test and the criterion.

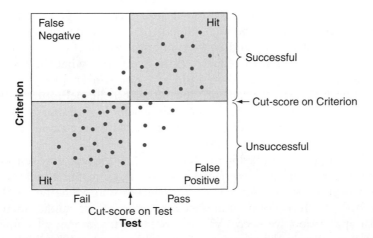

FIGURE 5.7 Hits, false positives, and false negatives in the relationship between test and criterion.

The limiting cases are a perfect correlation and zero correlation. For a perfect correlation, there will be no false positives or false negatives; all cases will be hits. For a zero correlation, the sum of false positives and false negatives will equal the number of hits.

The *second* factor is placement of the cutoff score on the test. Changes in this cutoff score affect the relative percentage of false positives and false negatives. Refer back to Figure 5.7. Notice the placement of false positives and false negatives. Now move the cut-score one half inch to the right. You decrease the false positives, but increase the number of false negatives. Now, from its original position, move the cut-score one-half inch to the left. Notice the effect. Here is a general rule when the test-criterion correlation is less than perfect (in practice, always the case): There is a trade-off between the false positive rate and the false negative rate. In setting the test cut-score, the test user must decide what result is preferable: a relatively high false positive rate or a relatively high false negative rate. For example, when using a test to select successful airline pilots, we might want to minimize false positives: those who pass the test but are not qualified to fly. This would result in increasing the false negatives, that is, those who are qualified to fly but fail the test. On the other hand, in some circumstances, we might want to minimize false negatives (e.g., persons likely to commit suicide but with low suicide-prone test scores), while allowing an increase in false positives.

Base Rates

Base rate is a crucial concept in understanding test validity, especially in relation to the concepts of false positives and false negatives. The **base rate** is the percentage of individuals in the population having some characteristic. For example, the base rate for schizophrenia in the general population is about 1%. The base rate for males aged 25–29 who are single is 45%. The base rate for adults who have attained a bachelor's degree is about 21%. When a base rate is extreme, either very high or very low, it is difficult to show that a test has good validity for identifying individuals in the target group. Consider a characteristic possessed by only 0.5% of the population (1 in 200 people). Unless the test for identifying such individuals has exceptionally high validity, we minimize errors in classification by simply declaring that no one has the characteristic, no matter what the test score. Good test validity is easiest to attain when the base rate is near 50%. It is important to note that the base rate may change depending on the definition of the population. For example, the base rate for a certain psychological disorder may be 1% in the general population, but the rate may be 30% for the population of persons who voluntarily seek help at a clinic.

In a classic publication, Taylor and Russell (1939) explain how test validity interacts with base rates for a given selection ratio. They provide a lucid description of the interaction, as well as a set of tables for selected values. The Taylor-Russell tables indicate how much *improvement* in selection results as test validity increases. In this particular application, we need a validity coefficient, a known selection ratio, and a base rate. For example, the selection ratio may be selecting 40% of job applicants for employment or admitting 80% of applicants to a college. We also need to know the base rate for success, for example, the percentage of cases that would be successful in employment or successful as students in the absence of using a test. With this information, the tables indicate how much improvement we get by use of a test with a given validity in contrast to not using the test.

Selectivity and Specificity

Selectivity and specificity are terms closely related to the notions of false positives and false negatives. We apply these terms when a test is used to classify individuals into two groups, such as alcoholics and nonalcoholics or suicide attempters and suicide nonattempters. Suppose we want to use a test to identify persons who are likely to attempt suicide. Our criterion group for validating the test is a group of people who have, in fact, attempted suicide. We have a contrast group of individuals who suffer depression but have not attempted suicide. We want a test and a cutoff score on the test that will (a) identify the criterion group (suicide attempters in this example) but (b) will *not* identify the contrast group (suicide nonattempters). The test's **selectivity** is the extent to which it correctly identifies the criterion group (suicide attempters). The test's **specificity** is the extent to which it does *not* identify or avoids identifying the contrast group (nonattempters). Both selectivity and specificity are usually expressed as simple percentages. In the language of the previous section, both selectivity and specificity represent "hits."

Data in Table 5.11 illustrate selectivity and specificity for distributions of test scores for suicide attempters and nonattempters. The four examples show two different degrees of separation between groups. Examples A and B show rather good separation whereas Examples C and D show less separation between groups. The examples also show two different cut-scores for each degree of separation. Observe the changes effected by the changes in cut-scores. Comparing Examples A and B (for which the degree of separation is the same), moving the cut-score from 6+ to 5+ increases selectivity from 74% to 88%, while specificity decreases. The *combination* of selectivity and specificity is better for Examples A and B than for Examples C and D because group separation is more marked for A and B.

TRY IT! ....

In Example C, what would selectivity and specificity be if the cut-score were set at 3^+ rather than 6^+?

....

Two factors affect the selectivity and specificity for a test: the degree of separation between the groups and placement of the cut-score. Generally, the greater the degree of separation between the groups, the better both selectivity and specificity. That is, the better the test discriminates between the groups, the higher both selectivity and specificity will be. For a fixed degree of separation between the groups, moving the cut-score will make selectivity and specificity vary inversely. That is, as selectivity increases, specificity decreases and vice versa.

When considering discrimination between groups, it is important to have meaningful contrasts. For example, it is more useful to contrast suicide attempters with

TABLE 5.11   *Distributions Illustrating Varying Degrees of Selectivity and Specificity*

Test Score	Example A Att.	Example A Nonatt.	Example B Att.	Example B Nonatt.	Example C Att.	Example C Nonatt.	Example D Att.	Example D Nonatt.
10	2		2		2		2	
9	4		4		4	1	4	1
8	5	1	5	1	5	3	5	3
7	11	3	11	3	11	2	11	2
6	15	2	15	2	15	8	15	8
5	7	8	7	8	7	14	7	14
4	3	14	3	14	3	11	3	11
3	2	11	2	11	2	4	2	4
2	1	4	1	4	1	5	1	5
1		5		5		2		2
0		2		2				
Selectivity	74%		88%		74%		88%	
Specificity		88%		72%		72%		54%

There are 50 cases in each distribution.

—★ indicates cut-score.

nonattempters who are suffering from depression than to contrast attempters with the general population. The first contrast is more useful because it corresponds to the type of distinction one is ordinarily trying to make in practice. However, this more useful distinction may lead to less separation between the groups. The distributions of scores for attempters versus nonattempters suffering from depression may be more like those in Example C in Table 5.11, whereas the distributions for attempters versus the general population may be more like those in Example A. It would be possible to get very good separation between a group of suicide attempters and a group of individuals who were very well adjusted. But that is not the type of distinction the clinician is ordinarily trying to make in practice. Thus, when examining data about selectivity, one must be sensitive to the nature of the groups involved in the comparison.

As noted previously, selectivity and specificity vary inversely for a fixed degree of separation. A natural question follows. Is it better to have relatively high selectivity while sacrificing some specificity? Or is it better to have relatively high specificity while sacrificing some selectivity? Of course, this is similar to the question about the trade-off between false positives and false negatives. And the answer is the same: It depends. It depends on relative risks, costs, and other such factors involved in the trade-off. In the case of suicide-attempters, we would probably opt for an increase in selectivity; that is, we would want to identify most of the suicide-attempters— and provide them with help—even if this means capturing more nonattempters. In other situations, we may tilt in the other direction, that is, decreasing selectivity while increasing specificity.

Note: For the novice psychometrician, the terms selectivity and specificity are unfortunate. They look and sound nearly the same, yet mean nearly the opposite. Try this simple device to keep the terms straight. "Selectivity" means *selecting* the people you want to select. "Specificity" is *not* selectivity: It means *not selecting* the people you do not want to select. Practice this simple distinction to keep the terms straight.

Note also, to add the difficulty of keeping the terms straight, that some sources use the term *sensitivity* as equivalent to selectivity.

Construct Validity

Among the traditional categories of validity (see Table 5.1), construct validity is, at first, the most difficult to comprehend. The basic notion of construct validity can be described as follows. A test attempts to measure some construct. Sometimes this construct has no obvious reference points, such as a clearly defined body of content or an external criterion. Nevertheless, a variety of kinds of evidence can be adduced to support the proposition that the test measures the construct. **Construct validity** encompasses all these methods.[2] As noted in the 1985 edition of the *Standards* for educational and psychological testing, "Evidence for the construct interpretation of a test may be obtained from a variety of sources" (AERA et al., 1985, p. 10). In fact, starting from this line of reasoning, we may think of construct validity as subsuming content validity and criterion-related validity. The content matching involved in content validity and the test-criterion correlation are simply cases—relatively clear cases—of demonstrating the extent to which the test measures a construct. The 1999 edition of the *Standards* does not list construct validity as a major category. Rather, it lists several different methods of demonstrating validity in addition to content validity and criterion-related validity. Table 5.1 lists these other sources of evidence. Actually, the list of "other" sources is endless. Any evidence that plausibly supports the proposition that the test measures its target construct is relevant. However, there are certain types of evidence that recur in discussions of construct validity, and we present these types in this section.

Internal Structure

Evidence regarding the internal structure of a test aids our understanding of the test's validity. The 1999 *Standards* identifies two subcategories under the general topic of internal structure: internal consistency and factor analysis.

In the context of validity, internal consistency means the same thing as it did when considered under reliability in the previous chapter (cf. pp. 134–140). A high degree of internal consistency, for example, a high KR-20 or alpha coefficient, indicates that the test is measuring something in a consistent manner. Thus, high internal consistency supports a claim that a test measures a particular construct or trait. Alternatively, it is difficult to maintain such a claim if internal consistency is low.

---

[2] See Kane (2001) for a useful summary of the evolution of the concept of construct validity.

Internal consistency provides only weak, ambiguous evidence regarding validity. It is probably best to think of internal consistency as a prerequisite for validity rather than as validity evidence itself. High internal consistency indicates that a construct is being measured, but other evidence is required to suggest what that construct might be.

Factor Analysis

Factor analysis is a family of statistical techniques that help to identify the common dimensions underlying performance on many different measures. These techniques are widely used in the construction and validation of tests. They play a particularly prominent role in personality inventories and intelligence tests. In fact, the development of factor analytic methodology is intimately connected with the classic debates on the nature and measurement of intelligence. One can hardly understand the world of personality testing or intelligence testing without some familiarity with factor analysis. When we refer to factor analysis as a "family" of techniques, we use the term in a broad sense—like an extended family—to include what is called principal components analysis, various rotation procedures, stopping rules, and related topics.

Factor analytic techniques can become quite complex. Detailed exploration is certainly beyond the scope of this book. However, we can summarize the purpose and general approach without getting bogged down in details. For an excellent semitechnical description of factor analysis, see Bryant and Yarnold (1995). For detailed, technical treatment, see Tabachnik and Fidell (2006).

Factor analysis, like all statistical techniques, begins with raw data. However, from a practical perspective, we can think of factor analysis as beginning with a correlation matrix. Consider the correlations in Table 5.12. Variables *A* and *B* are intercorrelated, .95. Well, we might just as well speak about one underlying dimension for these two variables. It is not fruitful or economical to think of two *different* variables here. Now expand the case to four variables. The correlation r_{CD} is also very high, .93. Again, consider it one variable or dimension. The *r*'s for *A* and *B* with *C* and *D* are fairly low, for example, $r_{AC} = .20$. So we cannot collapse *A* and *B* with *C* and *D*. But we started out with four variables and have concluded that there are really only two underlying dimensions. This is, intuitively, what factor analysis does. If we expand the case to 20 variables and all their interrelationships, you can see that our ability to keep track of things would soon deteriorate. For these more extensive cases we need the help of formal, mathematical procedures. These are the procedures of factor analysis.

TABLE 5.12   *Sample Correlation Matrix for Factor Analysis Discussion*

Variable	A	B	C	D
A	—	.95	.13	.03
B		—	.20	.17
C			—	.93
D				—

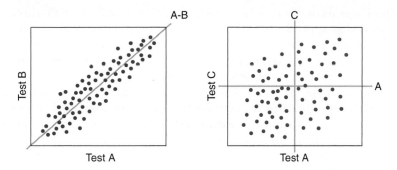

FIGURE 5.8 Factor analysis illustrated in geometric form.

It is useful to construct some geometric versions of what factor analysis is doing. Consider the examples in Figure 5.8. In the bivariate distribution on the left, scores on Tests A and B are so highly correlated that we need only one dimension—the *AB* vector—to describe performance. That is, we do not need separate *A* and *B* dimensions. In the example on the right, we *do* need two dimensions—the *A* and *C* *vectors*—to describe the array of scores. Here we use the terms *dimension* and vector as equivalent to the term factor in "factor analysis." These geometric illustrations show, roughly, how the mathematical procedures of factor analysis operate.

Results of factor analysis are usually represented as a factor matrix. This shows the weight that each of the original variables has on the newly established factors. The weights are actually correlations between the original variables and the factors. Table 5.13 shows a sample factor matrix. In the language of factor analysis, these correlations are called "loadings." The custom is to consider loadings in excess of .30 as noteworthy. Of course, the higher the loading, the more noteworthy it is.

Factors are "named" and interpreted rationally. For example, examination of Table 5.13 suggests that Factor I is a verbal dimension, with highest loadings on Vocabulary and Reading. Factor II appears to be a quantitative dimension. It is revealing that Arithmetic Problems loads more highly on Factor I than on Factor II, suggesting that understanding the verbal presentation of the problem is more influential in determining one's score on this test than is skill in mathematics. Factor III can be dismissed as meaningless—nothing loads very highly on this factor. Thus, it appears that two underlying dimensions explain this set of five tests.

TABLE 5.13 *Sample Factor Matrix*

Test	Factor I	Factor II	Factor III
Vocabulary	.78	.07	.22
Reading	.83	.13	.06
Arithmetic Problems	.54	.36	.16
Computation	.23	.89	.21
Quantitative Estimation	.46	.67	.09

The latter example illustrates the use of factor analysis with entire tests. Factor analysis is also applied to test items. The results show how the items group themselves according to underlying dimensions. This technique is very widely used in the construction and interpretation of personality and interest inventories. See Chapter 6 for further discussion of this point.

There are many different ways to "extract" factors. They differ in the mathematical criteria used to extract. After factors are extracted, it is customary to "rotate" the axes to aid interpretation. Several rotation procedures are available. Varimax rotation is the most common. There are also several different criteria to decide when to discontinue extracting factors. Computational procedures for factor analysis and rotation are horrendous. However, it is easy to do with statistical packages such as SPSS or SAS. It is not so easy to interpret the printout. It is often easy—and actually fun—to figure out what the factors are. In this chapter, we are not concerned with all the alternative procedures for conducting factor analysis. The important point is that this family of techniques helps us understand the structure of tests. Hence, the techniques are an important source of information for construct validity. For example, the results of a factor analysis may suggest that a measure of depression actually has two factors: one defined by items related to the emotional component of depression and another defined primarily by items related to behavioral indicators of depression.

Response Processes

Study of how examinees go about responding to a test, their **response processes,** may provide evidence regarding the validity of the test. For example, when studying a test of quantitative reasoning, it may be useful to know that examinees typically go through several steps to arrive at an answer rather than applying a memorized formula. We could determine that examinees employed a multistep approach by using a "talk-aloud" administration of the test. For investigating a test purporting to measure creative thinking ability, a talk-aloud administration may help to support the argument that the test measures flexibility in thinking rather than simply extent of vocabulary.

Study of response processes may also employ mechanical or electronic recordings. For example, Exner (2003) reported studies of eye movements as examinees responded to the Rorschach Inkblot Test. The results shed light on how examinees approach the ambiguous stimulus, the inkblot.

Evidence from response processes does not ordinarily provide strong, highly persuasive evidence regarding test validity. Furthermore, such evidence is not widely used for establishing validity. However, study of response processes does sometimes provide useful insights about what a test may or may not be measuring.

Effect of Experimental Variables

The effect of experimental variables can help to demonstrate the validity of a test. Consider these examples. We want to establish the validity of the Scranton Test of

Anxiety (STA). We administer the test to a group of 25 individuals, subject them to an anxiety-producing situation, and then readminister the STA. We would expect the scores to increase (high scores indicate anxiety on the STA). We want to establish the validity of the Bechtoldt Creativity Test (BCT). We administer the BCT to 50 individuals, give them 10 hours of instruction in techniques for creative thinking, then readminister the BCT. We would expect an increase in BCT scores. (In both studies, we should have control groups to rule out the possibility that any increase in scores is simply the result of a practice effect.)

Studying the effects of experimental variables is similar to the contrasted groups method treated earlier under criterion-related validity. In fact, logically they are the same. Contrasted group studies ordinarily employ naturally occurring groups (e.g., depressed and nondepressed persons), whereas the groups considered under construct validity are created specifically to study test validity.

Developmental Changes

Another potential source of information regarding construct validity is developmental changes. We expect children at successively higher ages to have increased mental ability. Showing that a mental ability test reflects these increases helps to establish the validity of the test. We would certainly puzzle over a mental ability test that showed the same scores on average for 8-, 9-, and 10-year-old children. Demonstrating changes in the average scores for children at successively higher ages was one of the major methods used by Binet in arguing for the validity of his test items. Increases in test scores and in performance on individual test items at successively higher grades are used to argue for the validity of achievement tests. We expect performance in reading, mathematics, and so on to increase from grade 3 to 4 to 5, and so on. Study of developmental changes, like the study of the effect of experimental variables, may be thought of as a variation on the contrasted groups approach. In this instance, we are contrasting groups at different ages or grades.

Key Points Summary 5.2

Some Important Ways to Study Construct Validity

- Internal Structure
- Factor Analysis
- Response Processes
- Effect of Experimental Variables
- Developmental Changes

We have now reviewed several different procedures that help to establish the construct validity of a test. As noted earlier, the list of possible ways to establish construct validity is endless. Any evidence that persuades us that the test is measuring its target construct is relevant and useful.

Consequential Validity

Consequential validity references the test to the consequences of its uses and interpretations. The concept includes both intended and unintended consequences. What are the consequences, results, or implications of using a test? For example, what are the consequences of systematic use of a college admissions test? What are the "spin-offs"? Notice that this question is different from the question of whether the test usefully predicts freshman GPA. We might inquire about whether the test improves (or detracts from) the quality of instruction at the college where the test is used. We might also ask what is the effect of requiring the test on the high school students who must take the test. Here is another example. Suppose we use a test to identify students for remedial instruction in mathematics. We might ask whether the test adequately covers the content of the mathematics curriculum. That is a question about the content validity of the test. We might also ask whether use of the test leads to educational benefits for the students identified for remedial instruction. That would be a question about consequential validity.

At least two separate issues need consideration here. The first issue relates to explicit claims regarding consequences made by the test authors. The second relates to consequences that may occur regardless of explicit claims by the test authors. Let us consider the first issue. Recall that the validity of a test is defined with respect to its purpose. The test authors formulate the purpose. If the purpose explicitly states an intended consequence, then certainly the validation process should address the consequence. For example, if the authors of the college admissions test state that use of the test will improve instruction at the college or will make high school students more diligent, then validity evidence regarding these claims should be collected. Suppose that the authors of a depression inventory claim that it not only validly measures depression but also leads to more effective therapy. Then evidence regarding improved therapy as a consequence of using the inventory should be provided.

The second issue becomes more tangled. Suppose the test authors make no claim regarding consequences, for example, about improving instruction or influencing high school students. The authors only claim that the test usefully predicts GPA. Are the consequences for instructional improvement and high school students' diligence still a matter of test validity? Furthermore, suppose that the test authors make no claim other than regarding the prediction of GPA, but the college president claims that use of the test ultimately improves the quality of instruction at the college. Does the college president's claim make the matter of consequences an issue of test validity? If so, whose responsibility is it to collect the validity evidence?

Evidence about consequences can inform validity decisions. Here, however, it is important to distinguish between evidence that is directly relevant to validity and evidence that may inform decisions about social policy but falls outside the realm of validity. *Standards...*

(AERA/APA/NCME, 1999, p. 16)

Both the term and the general concept of consequential validity are relatively recent entries in the psychometric lexicon. The term does not appear in the 1985 *Standards for Educational and Psychological Tests.* The 1999 *Standards* does introduce the term, in fact, devoting an entire section to the concept of consequential validity. However, the treatment is guarded, even tentative. Messick (1993) gives the earliest systematic development of the notion of consequential validity. He argues that it is an important evolution in our thinking about test validity. Incidentally, he also provides a concise, useful summary of the general evolution of thinking about all the types of validity we have covered in this chapter.

There is by no means agreement regarding the place of consequential validity in the psychometric universe. Some authorities agree with Messick that it is essential (e.g., Linn, 1997; Shepherd, 1997). Other authorities feel that consequences are a matter of politics and policy-making, not test validity (e.g., Mehrens, 1997; Popham, 1997). Still others ponder, if consequential validity is a legitimate psychometric concept, how one would gather relevant evidence (e.g., Green, 1998; Lane, Parke, & Stone, 1998; Linn, 1998; Moss, 1998; Reckase, 1998; Taleporos, 1998). For example, in the case of the college admissions test, can one reasonably identify all of the consequences of using the test? In Chapter 9, we will examine an unintended use of college admissions tests and observe some of the consequences. In Chapter 16, we will see how some court cases have used consequences of testing in reaching a legal decision. For those consequences that can be identified, how does one judge whether the sum of all possible consequences is salutary or pernicious? It seems clear that the debate over consequential validity will continue for some time.

Differential Validity in the Study of Test Bias

Test bias is one of the hottest topics in all of psychology today. It is basically a question of test validity. **Test bias** means that a test functions differently for different groups. A test is biased if it measures different constructs or predicts differentially. Hence the methods we have discussed in this chapter are directly relevant to studying this topic. We will also discuss the topic in Chapter 6 when we examine the test development process.

A simple difference in average performance between groups does not constitute bias. There is bias only if the difference in averages does not correspond to a real difference in the underlying trait the test is attempting to measure. Consider the contrast between students who do and do not study for an exam in a psychological testing course. Persons in Group A study the textbook 20 hours per week and attend all lectures. Persons in Group B study the textbook 20 minutes on the night before the exam and have erratic attendance records. On the exam, the Group A average score is appreciably higher than the Group B average score. That difference does not mean that the exam is biased against Group B. In fact, we would be shocked if the average scores for the two groups were not appreciably different. Why? Because we presume there is a real difference between the groups in the underlying trait of knowledge about the subject matter. Furthermore, if performance on this exam is intended to be predictive of performance on the GRE Subject Exam in Psychology, it will, no doubt, predict higher scores for persons in Group A than in Group B. This, too, does not indicate that the exam is biased. Why? Because we presume that people who study more will do better on the GRE than people who study less.

> The idea that fairness requires overall passing rates to be comparable across groups is not generally accepted in the professional literature. Most testing professionals would probably agree that while group differences in testing outcomes should in many cases trigger heightened scrutiny for possible sources of test bias, outcome differences across groups do not in themselves indicate that a testing application is biased or unfair. *Standards…*
>
> (AERA/APA/NCME, 1999, p. 75)

For tests designed to make predictions, criterion-related validity methods, as described earlier in this chapter, provide an important mechanism for studying test bias. Do the tests function in the same way for different groups, even if the groups vary in average performance related to real differences in the underlying trait? An unbiased test should yield equally good predictions for various groups. That does not mean predicting the same performance on the criterion. It means predicting equally well for two (or more) groups. In the following discussion, we will always refer to a contrast between two groups, although the methodology easily extends to comparison of any number of groups.

In the context of criterion-related validity, especially predictive validity, we identify two types of potential bias: intercept bias and slope bias. Note that these terms relate to the two parameters in the regression equation (Formula 5-1). **Intercept bias** means that the intercepts of the regression lines differ for two groups. Figure 5.9 shows an example of intercept bias. Notice that the slopes of the lines are the same for the two groups. As suggested by its name, **slope bias** means that the slopes of the regression lines differ for the groups. Figure 5.10 shows an example of slope bias.

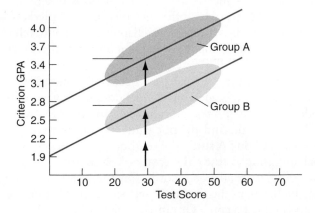

FIGURE 5.9   Illustration of intercept bias.

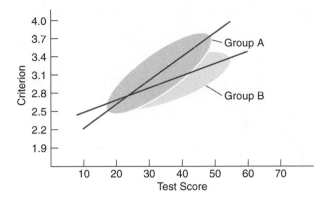

FIGURE 5.10 Illustration of slope bias.

Let us consider these two concepts in more detail. We use an example of predicting GPA from an admissions test score. In Figure 5.9, notice how the intercepts differ. The intercept for Group A is at about 2.8, for Group B at about 1.9. A person in Group A who gets a test score of 30 is predicted to have a criterion score (GPA) of about 3.5. A person in Group B who gets a test score of 30 is predicted to have a criterion score of about 2.8. This is a most undesirable situation. Ordinarily, the regression line would be determined for the groups combined. However, this differential validity is lurking behind the overall group results. Note that the correlation between the test and the criterion in this case would be the same for Groups A and B. This is an example of intercept bias.

Now consider Figure 5.10, the case of slope bias. Here the magnitude of the correlation is different for the two groups. The difference in slopes means that there will be overprediction for some cases in Group A and for some cases in Group B. Similarly, there will be underprediction for some cases in each group. This, too, is a very undesirable situation. This is an example of slope bias. Of course, it is possible to have both slope and intercept bias.

> When tests are used for selection and prediction, evidence of bias or lack of bias is generally sought in the relationships between test and criterion scores for the respective groups. Under one broadly accepted definition, no bias exists if the regression equations relating the test and the criterion are indistinguishable for the groups in question. *Standards*…
>
> (AERA/APA/NCME, 1999, p. 79)

Figure 5.11 shows the case in which there is a difference in average performance for the two groups but no difference in either intercept or slope. Notice that a given score, say, 40, predicts the same criterion performance regardless of group membership. This is the case of students who did and students who did not study for their exam in psychological testing. Group A studied. Group B did not study. Group A scores higher than Group B. The test has equal validity in predicting GPA.

Investigation of differential validity of tests, particularly for tests of mental ability, became very active in the late 1960s. At that time, mental ability tests came

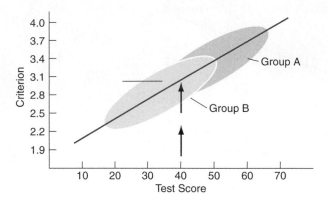

FIGURE 5.11   Illustration of lack of test bias for criterion-related validity: equal slopes and intercepts but difference in means.

under scrutiny especially for racial/ethnic bias, although sex bias was also an issue. A flurry of studies resulted in the conclusion that the tests did not evidence differential validity. Studies also suggested that the structure of the tests, as determined, for example, by factor analysis, were highly similar across various groups. Perhaps the most frequently cited reference is Jensen (1980), who concluded, after an exhaustive investigation of the topic, that "most current standardized tests of mental ability yield unbiased measures for all native-born English-speaking segments of American society today, regardless of their sex or their racial and social-class background. The observed mean differences in test scores between various groups are generally not an artifact of the tests themselves, but are attributable to factors that are causally independent of the tests" (p. 740). At about the same time, Hunter, Schmidt, and Hunter (1979) completed a summary of 39 studies investigating possible differential validity by race for employment tests. They concluded that "true differential validity probably does not exist" (p. 721). With a more recent summary of the research on test bias, Reynolds (1994) says: "Only since the mid-1970's has considerable research been published regarding race bias in testing. For the most part, this research has failed to support the test bias hypothesis, revealing instead that (1) well-constructed, well-standardized educational and psychological tests predict future performance in an essentially equivalent manner across race for American-born ethnic minorities; (2) the internal psychometric structure of the tests is essentially not biased in favor of one race over another; and (3) the content of the items in these tests is about equally appropriate for all these groups" (p. 177). In a more recent review, Reynolds and Ramsay (2003) concluded: "Test bias exists but is small. ... It most often overestimates or overpredicts minority examinees' performance, so that its social consequences may be very different from those typically ascribed to it" (p. 87). However, the question of differential validity continuously needs treatment as new tests are developed.

The Practical Concerns

By now it should be clear that test validity is no simple matter. There are numerous ways to study validity. Each way has its special limitations. For many tests, a multitude of validity studies have been conducted, with results varying from one study to another. There may be legitimate reasons for a test's validity to vary from situation to situation. For example, depression may have a somewhat different complexion in younger adults and older adults, thus altering the validity of the Scranton Depression Inventory for these groups. The Western Admissions Test may have somewhat different validity at Ivy College and at Behemoth State University, not because of differences in group heterogeneity but because of differences in courses at the two institutions. In this final section of the chapter, we try to formulate some advice about dealing with these issues.

Integrating the Evidence

In the final analysis, the professional test user must weigh all the available evidence and make a judgment about the probable validity of a test for use in a particular set of circumstances. The process of weighing all the evidence and judging the relevance of extant studies to a specific anticipated use is called **validity generalization**. Intelligent application of validity generalization requires (a) knowledge of the relevant content area (e.g., depression, reading achievement, college performance), (b) familiarity with the research already conducted with the test and with similar tests, (c) understanding of the concepts and procedures treated in this chapter, and (d) perceptive analysis of local circumstances for an anticipated use of the test.

> An important issue in educational and employment settings is the degree to which evidence of validity based on test-criterion relations can be generalized to a new situation without further study of validity in that new situation.... statistical summaries of past validation studies in similar situations may be useful in estimating test-criterion relationships in a new situation. This practice is referred to as the study of validity generalization. *Standards*...
>
> (AERA/APA/NCME, 1999, p. 15)

The 1999 *Standards* treats validity generalization as a subtopic under test-criterion relations. For example, you must judge the similarity of your college to other colleges where the relationship (predictive validity) between a college admissions test and freshman GPA has already been determined. However, the concept of validity generalization applies to all types of validity determinations. For example, a test manual reports the results of a factor analysis, indicating that a test seems to measure four distinct factors. That study was conducted with a particular group of examinees: a certain age distribution, gender breakdown, socioeconomic status, and so on. The professional test user must judge the extent to which those results apply to a local situation.

Many of the more widely used tests, such as the SATs, Rorschach, and MMPI-2, have been the subject of thousands of studies. Some of these studies concentrate on validity, others on reliability, and still others on other features of the tests. Summarizing all the relevant studies on one aspect of a single test, for example, the validity of the Rorschach, can be a daunting task. However, conducting such reviews is part of the task of integrating validity evidence for a test.

The traditional method for conducting such reviews involves a narrative description and synthesis. The reviewer locates relevant studies, reviews and comments on each one, and attempts to draw conclusions. The more contemporary approach to such reviews is called meta-analysis. **Meta-analysis** is a technique for summarizing the actual statistical information contained in many different studies on a single topic. For an excellent introduction to this topic, see Durlak (1996). The result of a meta-analysis is a statistic such as a correlation coefficient or a measure of effect size that represents a generalization from all the studies on the topic. Meta-analysis is currently the preferred technique for summarizing information such as validity or reliability for a test arising from many different studies. Following are some examples of meta-analyses completed on widely used tests: Finger and Ones (1999) on the MMPI computer version; Hiller, Rosenthal, Bornstein, Berry, and Brunell-Neulieb (1999) on the Rorschach and MMPI; Morrison and Morrison (1995) on the Graduate Record Examination; and Parker, Hanson, and Hunsley (1988) on the MMPI, Rorschach, and WAIS. Any one of these will give the reader a good idea of how meta-analysis helps with validity generalization.

In the Final Analysis: A Relative Standard

At the conclusion of Chapter 4, we raised the question about how high reliability should be. Although no single, definitive answer was provided, we did identify some guidelines for answering the question. Now at the conclusion of this chapter on validity, we should ask a similar question: How high should validity be? Unfortunately, the answer to this question is necessarily even less definitive than the answer to the corresponding question about reliability. In the final analysis, the answer to the question about validity is a relative one. We need to ask whether one test is more or less valid than another. Both may have low validity, but we will choose the one that is relatively better. Sometimes the practical question is whether to use a test or nothing. In that circumstance, we may be satisfied if the test shows any degree of validity. The alternative may be to base a decision on no information at all—equivalent to flipping a coin. In ordinary practice, we have to take the best we can get, while striving to develop ever better sources of information.

Summary

1. Validity refers to the extent to which interpretation of a test score is appropriate for a particular purpose. Validity is the most important characteristic of a test.

2. The concepts of construct underrepresentation and construct irrelevant variance are useful when considering the degree of overlap between a test and the construct it is intended to measure.

3. Face validity refers to whether a test looks like it is valid. It is not an empirical demonstration of validity. It is useful primarily for public acceptance of the test.

4. Content validity deals with the match between test content and a well-defined body of knowledge or skill. It is used primarily with achievement and employment tests.

5. Criterion-related validity expresses the relationship between test scores and status on some other criterion reflecting the construct of interest. Status on the criterion may be determined at approximately the same time as the test is administered (concurrent validity) or at some time in the future (predictive validity).

6. In criterion-related validity, the criterion may be an external, realistic criterion; a group contrast; or another test.

7. When criterion-related validity is expressed as a correlation (r_{XY}) between test and criterion, we call the correlation a validity coefficient. Having established r_{XY}, we can use this validity coefficient to predict status on the criterion from a test score. Furthermore, we can determine the standard error of estimate and use this to determine probabilities about the accuracy of the estimate.

8. All the factors affecting interpretation of the correlation coefficient, including linearity, homoscedasticity, and group heterogeneity, also affect interpretation of validity coefficients.

9. Reliability of both the test and the criterion affects the validity coefficient. Some simple formulas allow correcting the validity coefficient for limited (attenuated) reliability.

10. The criterion of interest must be operationally defined. There are usually alternative operational definitions that should be considered.

11. Criterion contamination refers to an undesirable situation in which test scores influence status on the criterion, thereby unfairly inflating the validity coefficient.

12. Convergent and discriminant validity are useful concepts when thinking about criterion-related validity. Convergent validity means that the test correlates highly with other tests or sources of information that measure the test's target construct. Discriminant validity means that the test shows low correlation with other tests or sources of information that are indicative of a different construct.

13. Multiple correlation is a statistical technique for combining information from several tests (or other sources of information) to predict status on a criterion. To obtain the best possible prediction, multiple correlation procedures assign weights to the tests in accordance with their unique contributions to the prediction. Multiple correlation procedures are especially important for studying incremental validity. Where adequate databases exist, statistical formulas are usually equal to or better than clinical judgment in combining information for decisions.

14. Decision theory is a body of concepts and procedures for analyzing the quantitative effects of decisions. As applied to criterion-related validity, decision theory includes the concepts of hits, false positives, and false negatives.

Test selectivity and specificity are two other useful concepts. Base rates and the placement of test cut-scores have important consequences within this framework.

15. Construct validity was originally defined as a miscellaneous collection of techniques considered relevant to validity other than content validity and criterion-related validity. Construct validity is now considered an overarching concept encompassing all types of validity evidence. Types of evidence usually listed under construct validity include a test's internal structure, especially as revealed by factor analysis; the study of response processes; the effect of experimental variables; and developmental changes. Any type of evidence that persuades us that a test is, at least to some extent, measuring its target construct for a particular purpose can be considered construct validity.

16. Consequential validity references the test to the ultimate consequences of its use and interpretation. The notion encompasses both intended and unintended consequences. Consequential validity is a relative newcomer to discussions of validity. At present, there is no consensus as to whether consequences should be considered a psychometric property or placed in some other category.

17. Differential validity studies the similarity of slopes and intercepts for regression lines in the investigation of test bias. In general, studies of test bias over the past three decades have indicated that well-constucted mental ability tests are reasonably unbiased.

18. The test user must integrate validity evidence from a variety of sources to arrive at a judgment about the extent to which a test fulfills its purpose. In the final analysis, when reaching this judgment, the user tries to answer the question: Am I better off using this test as a source of information or not using it?

Key Terms

attenuation
base rate
concurrent validity
consequential validity
construct
construct irrelevant
  variance
construct
  underrepresentation
construct validity
content validity
convergent validity
criterion contamination
criterion-related validity

discriminant validity
effect size
external criterion
face validity
factor analysis
false negative
false positive
hit
incremental validity
instructional validity
intercept bias
job analysis
meta-analysis
multiple correlation

multiple regression
  equation
multitrait-multimethod
  analysis
predictive validity
response process
selectivity
slope bias
specificity
standard error of estimate
test bias
validity
validity coefficient
validity generalization

Exercises

1. Confirm your understanding of the concepts of construct underrepresentation and construct irrelevant variance. Draw pictures like those in Figure 5.1 to show these cases:
    a. A construct includes 12 components. A test covers 6 of them. In addition, test scores are just slightly influenced by factors other than these 6 components.
    b. A test aims to measure creative thinking, but the test is almost entirely just a measure of vocabulary. (Assume for this exercise that vocabulary and creative thinking ability have a low correlation.)

2. Identify a job with which you are familiar. Create a table of specifications for the job. This table will be used to examine the content validity of a test designed to select employees for the job.

3. The validity coefficient for the Western Admissions Test (WAT; the X variable) for predicting freshman GPA (the Y variable) is $r_{XY} = .60$. Here are the means and *SD*s for X and Y.

	M	*SD*
X	50	10
Y	3.00	.40

    a. What is the predicted GPA for a WAT score of 65? Use Formula 5-2.
    b. What is the standard error of estimate for these data? Use Formula 5-3.
    c. For a person with a WAT score of 35, what is the probability of attaining a GPA below 2.00?

4. There are 50 cases in this bivariate distribution.

    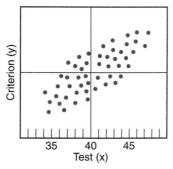

    a. With the cut-score on X set at 40, as shown, how many hits, false positives, and false negatives are here?
    b. Move the cut-score on X to a higher level, say 42, so as to decrease the number of false positives. Now count the number of hits, false positives, and false negatives.

5. For purposes of predictive validity studies, success in college is often defined as GPA at the end of the freshman year. What other operational definitions of "success in college" can you devise? Would any of these alternate definitions lead to use of different college admissions tests?

6. Test A and Test B both purport to predict college GPA. Test A is a rather short test with a reliability of .60. Its correlation with GPA is .45. Test B, a very long test, has a reliability of .95 and correlates .50 with college GPA. Apply the correction for unreliability to both tests' correlations with GPA. Correct for unreliability in the test, but not in the criterion (Formula 5-4). What are the corrected correlations with GPA for Tests A and B? Based on these results, would you conclude that it might be worthwhile revising Test A to make it more reliable? How might you make Test A more reliable? (*Hint:* See page 139 in Chapter 4.)

7. Refer to Figure 5.6. Using a diagram like those presented there, illustrate this verbal description. Tests X, Y, and Z may be used to predict a criterion, C. Tests X and Y are highly correlated with C. Tests X and Y are very highly correlated with one another. Test Z shows a moderately low correlation with both Tests X and Y, as well as with the criterion, C.

8. Using either electronic or hard copy sources, access reviews of any test from a recent edition of Buros' *Mental Measurements Yearbook*. What do the reviewers say about the test's validity? What types of validity evidence are discussed?

9. What would you use as the *operational definition of "success"* for each of these occupations?

    College teacher _____

    Baseball player _____

    Lawyer _____

10. For the data in Appendix D1: GPA, use SPSS or another statistical package to determine the correlation between SAT Total score and GPA. According to the terminology in this chapter, what would we call this correlation coefficient? Also create a bivariate distribution (scatterplot) for the data. See if you can use the line-fitting function to generate the regression line for the scatterplot.

CHAPTER 6

Test Development and Item Analysis

Objectives

1. List the steps involved in developing a test.

2. Identify issues that must be treated in the preliminary design of a test.

3. Identify common examples of selected-response items.

4. Identify common examples of constructed-response items.

5. Cite some of the approaches to scoring constructed-response items.

6. Discuss the relative merits of selected-response and constructed-response items.

7. Give examples of some item writing rules for selected-response, then constructed response items.

8. Identify the two main types of traditional item statistics.

   9. Describe the features of an item characteristic curve.

   10. Define what is meant by differential item functioning.

   11. Cite guidelines for selecting items.

   12. Outline the array of materials that should be available upon publication of a test.

Introduction

This chapter outlines the steps ordinarily taken in developing a test. The chapter title makes special mention of "item analysis" because these analytic procedures play a crucial role in test development. However, item analysis procedures are only part of the complete test development enterprise. There are six major steps in test development.[1] Figure 6.1 outlines the steps. This chapter describes each of these steps. The steps are not always entirely discrete. In practice there will often be some overlap and recycling among steps. This is especially true between steps 1 and 2 and between steps 3 and 4, as will become apparent in our description. However, this list of steps gives both the logical progression and typical chronological order for test development work.

> The process of developing educational and psychological tests commonly begins with a statement of the purpose(s) of the test and the construct or content domain to be measured. *Standards*...
>
> (AERA/APA/NCME, 1999, p. 37)

Defining the Test's Purpose

Test development begins with a clear **statement of purpose** for the test. This statement includes delineation of the trait(s) to be measured and the target audience for the test. The statement should be formulated with an eye toward the kind of interpretation ultimately intended for the test score(s). Table 6.1 contains the statements of purpose for several widely used tests. Statements of purpose are usually quite simple, often consisting of a single sentence.

From a practical point of view, after the purpose of the test has been clearly stated, one should *not* proceed immediately to build the test. The next step should

---

[1] This list differs slightly from that given in the *Standards for Educational and Psychological Tests* (AERA/APA/NCME, 1999). The *Standards* includes four steps. The first two are essentially the same as those used here. The *Standards* combines our steps 3 and 4 into a single step; we list these steps separately because they are logically and chronologically quite distinct. Inexplicably, the *Standards* does not include our step 5, although it cross-references the test development chapter to the chapters on norms, validity, and reliability. The *Standards'* step 4 is the same as our step 6.

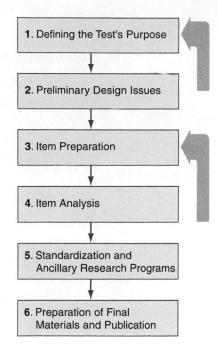

FIGURE 6.1   Major steps in test development.

TABLE 6.1   *Statements of Purpose for Several Widely Used Tests*

"The *Revised NEO Personality Inventory* ... is a concise measure of the five major dimensions, or domains, of personality and some of the more important traits or facets that define each domain. Together, the 5 domain scales and 30 facet scales of the NEO PI-R allow a comprehensive assessment of adult personality." (Costa & McCrae, 1992, p. 1)

"The *Wechsler Memory Scale-Revised* (WMS-R) is an individually adminsitered, clinical instrument for appraising major dimensions of memory functions in adolescents and adults." (Wechsler, 1987, p. 1)

"The *Minnesota Multiphasic Personality Inventory-2* (MMPI-2) is a broad-band test designed to assess a number of the major patterns of personality and emotional disorders." (Hathaway & McKinley, 1989, p. 1)

"The *Otis-Lennon School Ability Test* (OLSAT), Seventh Edition ... is designed to measure those verbal, quantitative, and figural reasoning skills that are most closely related to scholastic achievement." (Otis & Lennon, 1997, p. 1)

"The *Edwards Personal Preference Schedule* (EPPS) was designed primarily as an instrument for research and counseling purposes, to provide quick and convenient measures of a number of relatively independent *normal* personality variables ... [having] their origin in a list of manifest needs presented by H. A. Murray and others." (Edwards, 1959, p. 5)

> ## Key Points Summary 6.1
>
> ### *The First Two Crucial Steps in Test Development*
>
> 1. Clearly Define Purpose: Target Variable(s) and Target Group
> 2. Consider Preliminary Design Issues, including Such Matters as:
>   Mode of Administration, Length, Item Format, Training, Number of Scores, and Score Reports

be to determine whether an appropriate test already exists. Utilizing the sources of information outlined in Chapter 2 can help make this determination. Building a new test—at least a good one—is a long, difficult, expensive task. A word to the wise: Take time to determine whether an existing test will serve your purpose before attempting to build a new one.

TRY IT!

Select a trait of interest to you. Suppose you are going to develop a test to measure this trait. Formulate a statement of purpose for your test. Include reference to the target population for the test in your statement.

Preliminary Design Issues

In the earliest stages of test development, the test author must make a number of decisions about the design of the test. These decisions are based on the test's purpose and intended score interpretations as well as practical considerations. The following **design issues** must be treated.

*   *Mode of administration.* Will the test be individually administered or amenable to administration to a group? Group administration will be more efficient, but individual administration allows for more adaptability in item formats and for clinical observation of the examinee.

*   *Length.* About how long will the test be? Will it be short, with an administration time of about 15 minutes, or longer, taking as much as 45 minutes or even several hours? Short is obviously more efficient, but it may mean very limited reliability and only one score. Length is not simply a matter of the number of test items and testing time. Length relates intimately to the issue of how sensitive the test will be. Will the test be a broad-brush, global measure of the trait to be tested? Or will the test provide a basis for a sensitive, diagnostic analysis of the trait?

- *Item Format.* What item format will be used: multiple-choice, true-false, agree-disagree, constructed-response? A constructed-response format allows for a richer response and greater flexibility, but it will almost inevitably be harder to score and, therefore, more expensive to use. We treat these issues in more detail later in this chapter.

- *Number of Scores.* How many scores will the test yield? This question is necessarily related to the question about test length. More scores allow for additional interpretations, but more scores require more items and, therefore, more testing time.

- *Score Reports.* What kind of score reports will be produced? Will there be a simple, handwritten record of the score or an elaborate set of computer-generated reports, possibly including narrative reports? Exactly what will be reported: just a total score for the test or also reports of performance on clusters of items?

- *Administrator Training.* How much training will be required for test administration and scoring? Will test administrators need extensive professional training to administer, score, and interpret the test? If extensive training is required, how will it be provided?

- *Background Research.* At the preliminary design stage, one may need to conduct background research on the area to be tested unless one is already thoroughly familiar with the area. This research should include the standard literature search. If the test is intended for widespread practical application, the research should also include discussions with practitioners (e.g., clinicians, counselors, school psychologists, etc.) in the fields in which the test might be used.

Many treatments of test development start with "item writing." But item writing cannot (or, at least, should not) begin until these preliminary design considerations have been thoroughly explored. The design considerations will determine what kind of items and how many items will be written. Poor decisions regarding the original design of the test cannot be remedied at the item writing or item analysis stages of test development.

Deliberations regarding these preliminary design issues may result in some refinement in the statement of the test's purpose. This is the reason for the reverse arrow going from step 2 to step 1 in Figure 6.1. For example, a decision to make the test shorter rather than longer may lead to a more restrictive statement of purpose. Or discussions with practitioners may lead to expanding the intended target audience for the test.

TRY IT!

For the test whose purpose you stated in the last exercise (p. 208), answer the following questions about the design of your test:

How many items will the test have?

How many scores will it report?

Will it be individually or group administered?

About how many minutes will it take to complete?

What type of items will it have (e.g., multiple-choice, constructed-response)?

Origin of New Tests

Before proceeding to the next step in test development, let us pause to consider this question: What motivates the development of new tests? There is no simple, definitive list of motivators for test development projects. However, an analysis of existing tests suggests *three principal sources* of test development work.

First, many of the most widely used tests arose in response to some *practical need*. Binet's intelligence test, forerunner of the *Stanford-Binet Intelligence Scale*, was developed to identify children in Parisian schools who might need what we would now call special education. The Stanford-Binet itself was developed to provide a Binet-type scale for use with Americans. The *Wechsler-Bellevue Intelligence Scale,* which gave rise to today's panoply of Wechsler scales, was developed to provide an intelligence test more suitable for adults than the Stanford-Binet. The first group-administered intelligence tests, Otis's Army Alpha and Beta, were developed to measure mental ability for the large number of recruits to military service in World War I. Screening a large number of military recruits in the war was also the motivation for developing the *Woodworth Personal Data Sheet,* the prototype for many subsequent personality tests. The *Minnesota Multiphasic Personality Inventory* (MMPI) was developed to aid in classification of mental patients in clinical practice at the University of Minnesota hospitals. These are just a few examples of the fact that many tests originate in response to a very practical need.

Some tests are developed from a *theoretical base.* For example, the *Thematic Apperception Test* (TAT) was intended to provide a measure of Murray's personality theory. Thurstone's *Primary Mental Abilities* test, the prototype for many subsequent multifactor intelligence tests, was designed to support Thurstone's theory of multiple intelligences. Initially such tests are often used strictly for research purposes but later become used in applied contexts.

Finally, a large amount of test development work is devoted to *revising* or *adapting existing tests.* For example, each of the major achievement batteries has a new edition every 5 to 10 years. Tests such as the SAT and ACT are under more or less continuous revision. New editions of such tests as the Wechsler scales and popular personality tests appear regularly. Another type of revision calls for modifying a test for use with special populations. For example, many tests originally developed in English are also made available in Spanish or other languages. There are also adaptations of tests for persons with various disabilities. Thus, development of new editions or adaptation of existing editions of tests constitutes a third major source of test development efforts.

Item Preparation

Item preparation includes both item writing and item review. Item writing should not proceed until the purpose of the test is well defined and preliminary design considerations have been thoroughly explored. Assuming these first two steps are satisfactorily completed, item preparation begins. It may be useful to start this

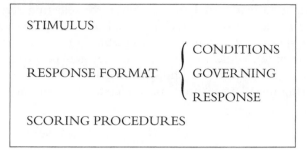

FIGURE 6.2 The anatomy of a test item.

section by asking: Exactly what is a test item? A test item has four parts. See Figure 6.2. First, there is a *stimulus* to which the examinee responds. Second, there is a *response format* or method. Third, there are *conditions* governing how the response is made to the stimulus. Fourth, there are *procedures for scoring* the response, sometimes called the scoring rubrics. Let us briefly describe each of these components.

The *stimulus,* often called the **item stem,** may be a question, such as those illustrated in Table 6.2. The first is from an intelligence test, the second from an achievement test, the third from an attitude survey, and the fourth from a personality inventory. The stimulus may also be a picture, accompanied by an oral question. For example, the Rorschach presents a picture along with a question about what the examinee sees. The stimulus may also be an apparatus such as the hand dynamometer; but the "item" is not complete without a direction, such as "Take it in your right hand and squeeze as hard as you can."

The *response format* includes such factors as whether this is a multiple-choice or constructed-response item. For example, any of the stimuli in Table 6.2 could have a set of choices, or they could call for a constructed-response. We treat various response formats more fully in the next section.

Perhaps not so obvious as the first two components of an item, the third component is crucial for understanding the nature of an item. *Conditions governing the response* include such factors as whether there is a time limit for responding, whether the test administrator can probe ambiguous responses, and exactly how the response is recorded, for example, on an answer sheet or in the test booklet.

Finally, the *procedure for scoring* is a critical part of the item. For a multiple-choice test of ability or achievement, each item might be scored as correct/incorrect.

TABLE 6.2 *Examples of Stimulus Parts of Test Items*

What does "prodigal" mean?

Solve for x: If $6x + 10 = 14$, $x =$ _____

Do you like meeting new people?

Complete this sentence: Today I'm feeling especially _____.

Alternatively, it might be that partial credit is given for selecting certain options. For constructed-response items in parts of the *Wechsler Adult Intelligence Scale*, a very good answer merits two points, an acceptable but not particularly good answer receives one point, while an incorrect answer gets no points. Procedures for scoring responses to projective techniques can be very elaborate. Thus, the procedure for scoring must be specified and understood when considering a test item.

Types of Test Items

Test items come in an enormous variety. Items are usually classified in terms of the items' response format, the second component of a test item previously considered. At a very general level, items can be classified as *selected-response or constructed-response*.[2] We present here only the more common examples of these two types of formats, with brief commentary about usual applications and their strengths and weaknesses.

Selected-response Items

In **selected-response items** the examinee is presented with at least two, but no more than a reasonably small number of options from which to choose a response. Selected-response items are also called multiple-response, multiple-choice, or forced-choice items.

For the most widely used tests, the selected-response format is clearly the most popular. Most group-administered ability and achievement tests use a *multiple-choice* format with four or five options for each item. Every reader is certainly familiar with this type of item. A special case of the multiple-choice item is the *true-false* item, which is really a multiple-choice item with just two options: True or False. Table 6.3 illustrates multiple-choice and true-false items for an achievement test.

Selected-response formats are most familiar from the realm of ability and achievement testing. However, selected-response formats are also widely used with tests of personality, interests, and attitudes. For example, the *Strong Interest Inventory* uses "Like," "?" (uncertain), and "Dislike" for most of its items. The MMPI-2 uses a true-false format for its items. Table 6.4 illustrates multiple-choice and true-false items for interest and personality inventories.

A special case of a selected-response format used in many attitude measures is the **Likert format**.[3] Table 6.5 illustrates items using this format. These items

---

[2] As noted in the text, there are a variety of alternative terms for selected-response and constructed-response formats.

[3] Technically, the Likert format refers to the method of constructing the entire scale. However, it is common to refer to the response format itself as a Likert format. See Chapter 15 for further discussion of this topic

TABLE 6.3 *Examples of Multiple-Choice and True-False Items of Achievement*

A Multiple-Choice Item

Which of these is a method for determining test reliability?

    A. test-retest   B. stanine   C. validity   D. criterion-referenced

A True-False Item

    T   F   The stanine is a method for determining test reliability.

TABLE 6.4 *Example of Multiple-Choice and True-False Items of Interests and Personality*

Multiple-Choice Items

For each item, mark whether you Like (L), Dislike (D), or are unsure (?) about the activity.

	L	?	D
Working with numbers	O	O	O
Doing subtraction problems	O	O	O

True-False Items

For each item, mark whether it is True (or mostly true) or False (or mostly false) for you.

    T   F   I feel depressed most of the time.
    T   F   Things have been going very well for me lately.

TABLE 6.5 *Example of Likert Format for Attitude Items*

SA = Strongly Agree   A = Agree   ? = Uncertain   D = Disagree   SD = Strongly Disagree

	SA	A	?	D	SD
I love algebra.	O	O	O	O	O
Square roots are neat.	O	O	O	O	O
I can't wait to take statistics.	O	O	O	O	O
Arithmetic problems are fun.	O	O	O	O	O
I like to do geometry.	O	O	O	O	O

employ the five-point Strongly Agree … Strongly Disagree scale for each response. A test might use a three-point, nine-point, or any other finite number of points. In one variation, responses may be marked anywhere along a continuum between two poles; marks are then converted to numerical form at a later time. This procedure, sometimes called a **graphic rating scale** (Guilford, 1954) or a visual analogue scale (Barker, Pistrang, & Elliott, 1994), is illustrated in Figure 6.3. The respondent can mark anywhere along the line. Later, responses are converted to numerical form (1–10 in this example) by applying the scale

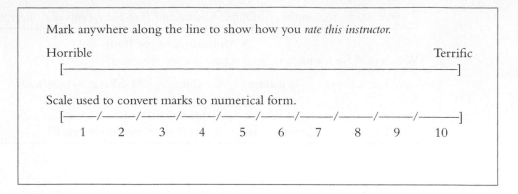

Mark anywhere along the line to show how you *rate this instructor.*

Horrible   Terrific

[——]

Scale used to convert marks to numerical form.

[——/——/——/——/——/——/——/——/——]
  1   2   3   4   5   6   7   8   9   10

FIGURE 6.3   Illustration of a graphic rating scale.

shown. An interesting application of this response format is the **semantic differential** in which an object (e.g., idea, person, or organization) is rated on a series of scales bracketed by polar opposite adjectives such as "hard-soft," "hostile-friendly," "hot-cold," and "competent-incompetent."[4] Figure 6.4 illustrates this approach.

Scoring Selected-response Items

In the realm of ability and achievement tests, most selected-response items are simply scored correct/incorrect; one point is awarded for a correct response, zero points for an incorrect response. Then, the score on the test is the total number of correct responses. However, there are other ways to score these items. One variation involves awarding partial credit for selecting an option that is not the best possible answer and yet is not clearly wrong. Another variation involves giving extra weight to items that are especially important. For example, for purposes of computing the total score on the test, a correct response to certain items might be worth three points, to other items two points, and for the remaining items one point. Still another variation in scoring items for which there is a correct answer involves application of the correction for guessing (see Chapter 3, pp. 74–75). Comparisons of the simple 0/1 scoring method with these more complicated methods have been the subject of much research. The question is whether the more complicated scoring systems yield more reliable and/or more valid scores than the simpler 0/1 scoring. The answer comes in two parts. First, the more complicated systems usually yield only slightly better (more reliable or more valid) scores. On the second part of the answer, authors differ. Some say that with such marginal gains, it is not worth bothering with the more complicated systems (see, e.g., Nunnally & Bernstein,

---

[4] Sometimes reference is made to *the* semantic differential, as if it were a specific test. However, as noted in the classic work on this topic (Osgood, Suci, & Tannenbaum, 1957), semantic differential refers to a general technique, not a specific test.

Rate *this school* on each of the scales listed below. Put a mark anywhere along each line.

[HOT _____ COLD]
[FRIENDLY _____ HOSTILE]
[COMPETENT _____ INCOMPETENT]
[HARD _____ SOFT]

FIGURE 6.4 Example of a semantic differential approach.

1993). Others say that with the ease of modern computer scoring, the so-called complications are trivial, so any gain in reliability or validity is worthwhile. For description of some of these item- and option-weighting procedures, see Millman and Greene (1993).

Scoring selected-response items on personality, interest, and attitude tests occurs in a variety of ways. In some applications, each item is scored 1 or 0 in a manner analogous to the correct/incorrect procedure for ability tests. However, the 1/0 scoring does not imply a right or wrong answer but a response in a certain direction, for example, more anxious, more depressed, better adjusted, or more interested in some activity.

Alternatively, it is not uncommon to assign varying numbers to the different responses for items in personality, interest, and attitude measures. For example, on the Like-?-Dislike scale, we might assign scores of 3, 2, and 1 or + 1, 0, and −1 to the various responses. On the five-point Strongly Agree—Strongly Disagree scale, one might assign points of 5, 4, 3, 2, and 1 or +2, +1, 0, −1, and −2 to the different responses. Notice that it would be possible to assign a score of 1 to responses of Strongly Agree or Agree and 0 to all other responses. The method of scoring these items is determined as part of the preliminary design considerations in test development.

Constructed-response Items

The **constructed-response item** presents a stimulus but does not constrain the examinee to select from a fixed set of responses. The examinee must create or construct a response. *Free-response* is another common name for this format. Although the examinee's response is "free" in the sense that he or she is not limited to a fixed set of alternatives, there are still conditions governing the response. For example, responses are to be given orally within a certain time period or responses are to be written in essay form. Individually administered intelligence tests ordinarily use a constructed-response format. For example, an examinee might be asked. "What does 'prodigal' mean?" Or, "If each pencil costs 15¢ and Jim buys 5 pencils, how much does he pay?" In each instance, the examinee constructs a response "from scratch." The response might be given orally or in writing. A very simple version of a constructed-response item is the *fill-in-the-blank* format. Here a key word or phrase is omitted from a sentence. The examinee must supply the missing word(s). For example: Stanines are a type of _____ score. Note that for questions such as these, it would be easy to use exactly the same item stem but with a selected-response format.

One of the most familiar examples of the constructed-response format is the **essay test.** The test item presents a situation or topic and the examinee writes a response that might range from a few sentences to several pages of text. The essay test might be considered one example of the more general category of performance assessment. In a **performance assessment,** the stimulus is supposed to be a realistic situation such as a science problem, a library assignment, or an artistic production. The response involves solving the problem, completing the assignment, or producing the artwork. At present, performance assessments are receiving much attention in the educational assessment arena as an alternative to multiple-choice measures of achievement. A popular application of performance assessment is the use of portfolios. As suggested by the name, the **portfolio** is essentially a collection of a person's work. A portfolio might be constructed for a student's written work or science lab projects or statistical analyses completed. The collection might take place over a few months or a few years. Like other performance assessments, the contents of the portfolio become an assessment tool when their quality is judged on some relevant dimension.

The constructed-response format is widely used for personality testing. Table 6.6 illustrates two relatively simple examples of such items. Of course, the classic examples of constructed-response measures of personality are the projective techniques like the Rorschach and TAT. In these tests, each item presents an ambiguous stimulus, and the examinee has considerable freedom in constructing a response. We consider these techniques in more detail in Chapter 14.

Certain behavioral tests can also be classified as constructed-response items. For example, the *leaderless group technique* and the *in-basket technique* are constructed-response items. In the leaderless group technique, a person is placed in a situation

---

TABLE 6.6   *Examples of Simple Constructed-Response Items Measuring Personality*

Word Associations

I'll say a word and you say the first word that comes to your mind.

　　Hot...
　　School...
　　Summer...
　　Mother...

Sentence Completions

Complete each sentence.

　　My favorite game is...
　　Families are...
　　The biggest problem is...

(e.g., a committee meeting,) where there is no obvious leadership or authority structure. The question is how the person will behave in this situation. An observer rates the person's behavior. The in-basket technique presents the individual (typically the candidate for a job) with contents of an in-basket. The person indicates how each paper or other item should be treated. Again, someone needs to rate how the person handles the items.

Scoring Constructed-response Items

Scoring constructed-response items presents special challenges precisely because the responses can be so diverse. In nearly all instances, scoring requires some judgment. There are *two key factors* in developing useful scores for constructed-response items. The first is ensuring inter-rater reliability; the second is conceptualizing a scheme for scoring.

Since the scoring of constructed-response items ordinarily requires judgment, the degree of agreement between raters (those rendering the judgments) is crucial. If there is inadequate agreement among raters, then no meaningful scores will result from the testing. Of course, inter-rater reliability does not establish the validity of the scores, nor even other types of reliability, for example, test-retest reliability. However, in the absence of inter-rater reliability all else is lost. The point here is that inter-rater reliability is a special concern for constructed-response items.

Conceptualizing a scheme for scoring the items is an even greater challenge. The types of schemes vary widely. It does not seem feasible to provide a comprehensive list. Let us rather give examples of some of the approaches that have been developed, considering first some examples from the realm of achievement tests, then turning our attention to personality testing.

Several different methods have evolved for scoring essays. One common distinction is between *holistic* and *analytic* scoring. In **holistic scoring,** the reader—the person scoring the essay—forms a single, overall, holistic judgment about the quality of the essay. The score assigned to the essay reflects this overall judgment. The score scale may have any number of points, for example, 1–4, 1–10, or 1–100. The reading is typically done rapidly, with no corrections or notes written on the paper. What quality of the essay is rated? That depends on the specific application. The essay might be rated in terms of the quality of written expression for an English composition test or knowledge of subject matter for a history test. The key feature of holistic scoring is that there is just one overall score based on the total quality of the essay.

In **analytic scoring,** the same essay is rated on several different dimensions. Analytic scoring requires advance specification of the important dimensions of the quality of the essay. The separate ratings may be completed by the same rater or by different raters, one for each dimension. The essay for English composition might be rated separately for (a) grammatical correctness, (b) organization, and (c) use of vocabulary. The history essay might be rated separately for use of historical facts, identification of major themes, and quality of writing. From a measurement perspective, analytic scoring obviously assumes that there is some meaningful

Key Points Summary 6.2

Some Methods for Scoring Essays and Other Products

- Holistic
- Analytic
- Point System

independence among the traits specified in the analytic scoring scheme. Often such independence seems to be lacking, as indicated by the extremely high correlations among the scales of various analytic schemes. Some degree of independence among the scales should be established before adopting an analytic scoring system.

A final method for scoring essays is a **point system.** Here, there are certain points to be included in a "perfect" answer. The scorer simply determines the presence or absence of each point. The simplest example of the point system is a sheer memory test—for example, "State the ten commandments." One point is awarded for each commandment. Of course, even in the point system, except for the most trivial examples, scorer judgment is required. Does "Go to church on Sunday" qualify as a correct answer for the third commandment? Must the commandments be given in the traditional order?

The various methods for scoring essays can also be applied to a wide variety of *product evaluations.* In fact, essays are just one type of product. The methods can be applied to performance assessments of artistic productions, science projects, public speaking skill, and many other products. To score a portfolio, a decision must be made not only about the method of scoring but also the feature of the portfolio to score. One could score all entries in the portfolio, only the best entries, or the amount of progress shown from earlier to later entries.

We have emphasized a number of times that scoring constructed-response items requires judgment. This is time-consuming, expensive, and potentially fraught with problems of rater reliability. Researchers are now investigating the application of expert computer systems—called **automated scoring**—to the scoring of constructed responses. Automated scoring should not be confused with simple machine scoring of responses to multiple-choice items on a "bubble" form. Automated scoring, as the term has developed in the research literature, involves development of sophisticated computer programs that simulate the process of applying human judgment to free-response items. For example, one project applied automated scoring systems to a performance assessment of physicians' patient management skills (Clauser, Swanson, & Clyman, 1999). Another project applied an automated scoring system to assessment of architects' responses to a constructed-response architectural problem (Williamson, Bejar, & Hone, 1999). Some of the earliest work along these lines was Ellis Page's computer-generated scores for the quality of writing displayed in essays. Wresch (1993) provides a historical account of these efforts. For a semi-popular account of Page's current work with Project Essay Grade (PEG), see Page and Petersen (1995). The key issue with all of these projects is whether the automated system approximates expert human judgment. The *Graduate Management Admissions Test* now uses a computer to generate one of the scores on the essay part of the test; the "computer score" is combined with a human rating of the essay. We are likely to see rapid expansion in the use of a variety of automated scoring systems for constructed-response items in the future. See Shermis and Burstein (2003) for an excellent collection of chapters on this fascinating topic; and Rudner and Gagne (2001) for a brief summary.

In the realm of personality testing, projective techniques provide classical examples of constructed-response items. We consider projective techniques more systematically in Chapter 14. Here we simply illustrate a few of the techniques for scoring them.

Common methods for scoring the Rorschach rely on specifying categories, counting the number of responses falling within these categories, then forming ratios among these counts. Table 6.7 shows one commonly used category: location, that is, the location on the card used as a reference point for the response. The scorer (most often the clinician who administered the test) classifies each response to each card according to these categories. The conceptual scheme here consists of (a) the list of categories, (b) the notion of counting statements, and (c) forming ratios. Of course, it is the business of validity studies to determine whether any of these ratios relate to personality characteristics or pathological conditions.

The *Rotter Incomplete Sentences Blank* (RISB; Rotter, Lah, & Rafferty, 1992) provides another example of a conceptual scheme for scoring a projective test. The Rotter consists of 40 incomplete sentences similar to those given in Table 6.6. What will one do with the responses to such items? Each response is scored on a six-point scale for the *degree of maladjustment* manifested. Ratings on the 40 items are then summed to yield a total adjustment score. The RISB manual gives specific directions regarding indicators of adjustment/maladjustment. Thus, the conceptual scheme is to look at the responses in terms of indications of adjustment, to rate the responses on a simple numerical scale, then to sum these ratings for a total score.

TABLE 6.7   *Sample Categories for Scoring "Location" Responses to a Rorschach Card*

Determine the location on the card used as reference point for the response:

Whole	Whole inkblot used to formulate response
Common detail	A well-defined, commonly seen part
Unusual detail	An unusual part is used
Space	Response defined by white space

TRY IT! ....

The RISB is scored for degree of maladjustment indicated by responses. Can you think of another conceptual scheme that might be used to score responses?

....

In some applications, constructed-response items in the personality domain are not scored in any formal way. Responses are simply considered as starting points for discussion between clinician and client or to give the clinician ideas about topics to explore in more detail. However, the most typical applications involve formal scoring. The scoring procedures can be quite simple or very elaborate. The key feature of these procedures involves coding elements of responses in relation to some well-defined dimension.

The *test manual* plays an essential role in assuring that constructed-response items yield meaningful scores. The manual should clearly specify what type of training is required to score the items. The test manual must also explain the rationale for scoring the items. Examples of the application of the rationale should be provided. The directions for scoring constructed-response items, often with examples of responses at different levels, are often called scoring *rubrics*. The manual should also report results of inter-rater reliability studies.

The Pros and Cons of Selected-response versus Constructed-response Items

The relative merits of selected-response and constructed-response items are hotly contested in both the psychometric literature and the public media. Let us try to summarize the main points in these arguments. When discussing the pros and cons of selected-response versus constructed-response items, we should first note that this distinction in response formats is not the same as the distinction between group-administered and individually administered tests. It is true that the selected-response format is typical for group-administered tests. However, any test that can be administered to a group can also be administered individually. Although many individually administered tests use the constructed-response format, a constructed-response format can also be used for group-administered tests. For example, essay tests can obviously be administered to large groups. Even projective measures such as the TAT can be administered to groups, provided the "story" responses are written rather than spoken.

Selected-response items have three principal advantages. The first is scoring reliability. Because scoring requires little or no judgment, one major source of unreliable variance is eliminated. Inter-scorer or inter-rater reliability is essentially perfect for selected-response items. In contrast, inter-scorer reliability for constructed-response items may be a substantial problem. This concern about reliability was the stimulus for development of the earliest multiple-choice versions of achievement tests in the early twentieth century. These multiple-choice tests were not developed to accommodate machine scoring, as is often thought. In fact, there were no machines to score the tests at that time. The multiple-choice item became the preferred format because it yielded more reliable scores than constructed-response items. For an historical account of factors leading to the development of early multiple-choice measures of achievement, see Ebel (1979).

The second major advantage of selected-response items is *temporal efficiency*. In a given amount of time, an examinee can usually complete more selected-response items than constructed-response items. For example, in 20 minutes an examinee might easily complete 30 multiple-choice vocabulary items. In this same time period, the examinee might complete only 10 vocabulary items in constructed-response format. For a measure of achievement, in 20 minutes a person might complete one essay versus 30 multiple-choice items. Because reliability generally increases as a function of the number of items, this second advantage, like the first advantage discussed earlier, comes down to a matter of reliability. And these advantages also relate to validity because of the relationship between reliability and validity.

The third advantage of selected-response items is *scoring efficiency*. A clerk or an electronic scanner can score these items very rapidly. This advantage was the main stimulus for the development of the earliest group-administered mental ability and personality tests in World War I. Note that this advantage is logically independent of the matter of scorer reliability.

Three main advantages are often cited for constructed-response items. First, they allow for easier *observation of test-taking behavior and processes.* In some ways, this advantage relates more to the mode of administration (individual rather than group) than to the response format. However, the constructed-response format facilitates observation of examinee motivation, anxiety, approaches to problems, and so on in ways that selected-response items would not, even if the selected-response items were administered on an individual basis.

A second advantage of the constructed-response format, especially in the realm of personality testing, is that the format allows for *exploring unusual areas* that might never come to light with a selected-response format. Of course, the relevance of this argument depends on the comprehensiveness of the selected-response test. If it really is comprehensive, then it should, by definition, bring to light all important information. The question is whether those measures are, in fact, comprehensive in their measurement of personality.

In the realm of achievement testing, some authors believe that the type of test item used influences the *development of students' study habits.* More specifically, it is felt that use of multiple-choice items encourages rote memorization and an atomistic approach to learning subject matter, whereas constructed-response items encourage a more holistic and meaningful approach to study.

For summaries of the research on selected-response versus constructed-response items, see Hogan (1981, 2007), Traub (1993), and Rodriguez (2002, 2003). Current developments in automated scoring systems may significantly influence future evaluations of the relative advantages and disadvantages of selected-response versus constructed-response items.

Suggestions for Writing Selected-response Items

There are numerous lists of suggestions for writing selected-response items, especially multiple-choice items for achievement tests. Haladyna and Downing (1989a, 1989b) prepared a taxonomy of these so-called item-writing rules, gleaned from a survey of 46 textbooks and similar sources. Subsequently, Haladyna (1994, 1999, 2004) devoted an entire book to elaboration of these rules and research regarding

TABLE 6.8 *Guidelines for Writing Selected-Response Items*

Content concerns
1. Every item should reflect specific content and a single specific mental behavior, as called for in test specifications (two-way grid, test blueprint).
2. Base each item on important content to learn; avoid trivial content.
3. Use novel material to test higher level learning. Paraphrase textbook language or language used during instruction when used in a test item to avoid testing for simply recall.
4. Keep the content of each item independent from content of other items on the test.
5. Avoid over specific and over general content when writing MC items.
6. Avoid opinion-based items.
7. Avoid trick items.
8. Keep vocabulary simple for the group of students being tested.

Formatting concerns
9. Use the question, completion, and best answer versions of the conventional MC, the alternate choice, true-false (TF), multiple true-false (MTF), matching, and the context-dependent item and item set formats, but AVOID the complex MC (Type K) format.
10. Format the item vertically instead of horizontally.

Style concerns
11. Edit and proof items.
12. Use correct grammar, punctuation, capitalization, and spelling.
13. Minimize the amount of reading in each item.

Writing the stem
14. Ensure that the directions in the stem are very clear.
15. Include the central idea in the stem instead of in the choices.
16. Avoid window dressing (excessive verbiage).
17. Word the stem positively, avoid negatives such as NOT or EXCEPT. If negative words are used, use the word cautiously and always ensure that the word appears capitalized and boldface.

Wording the choices
18. Develop as many effective choices as you can, but research suggests three is adequate.
19. Make sure that only one of these choices is the right answer.
20. Vary the location of the right answer according to the number of choices.
21. Place choices in logical or numerical order.
22. Keep choices independent; choices should not be overlapping.
23. Keep choices homogeneous in content and grammatical structure.
24. Keep the length of choices about equal.
25. None-of-the-above should be used carefully.
26. Avoid All-of-the-above.
27. Phrase choices positively; avoid negatives such as NOT.
28. Avoid giving clues to the right answer, such as
    a. Specific determiners including always, never, completely, and absolutely.
    b. Clang associations, choices identical to or resembling words in the stem.
    c. Grammatical inconsistencies that cue the test-taker to the correct choice.
    d. Conspicuous correct choice.

    e. Pairs or triplets of options that clue the test-taker to the correct choice.

    f. Blatantly absurd, ridiculous options.

29. Make all distractors plausible.

30. Use typical errors of students to write your distractors.

31. Use humor if it is compatible with the teacher and the learning environment.

Source: Haladyna, T.M., Downing, S.M., & Rodriguez, M.C. (2002). A review of multiple-choice item-writing guidelines for classroom assessment. *Applied Measurement in Education,* 15, 309–334. (Table 1, p. 312). Copyright © 2002 by Lawrence Erlbaum Associates. Reproduced by permission.

their validity. The current edition of this book is easily the best source of advice for writing selected-response items and whether the suggestions make any difference in the quality of items. Anyone in need of help on writing selected-response items should consult this source. We could hardly do better than to provide Haladyna's list, reproduced here in Table 6.8. Haladyna (2004, p. 98) noted, "Item writers should apply these guidelines judiciously but not rigidly, as the validity of some guidelines still may be in question." In fact, some authors conclude their lists of item-writing rules with this rule: Disregard any of these rules when there seems to be good reason to do so.

Most of the rules in Table 6.8 are self-explanatory. We can illustrate a few of them with this sample item:

Test validity_____

    a. is the single most important feature of a test.

    b. determined in just one way.

    c. is the same as reliability.

    d. All of the above.

This item violates several of the rules. It violates rule 15 in that the stem does not contain enough content. It violates rule 24 since the correct answer (a) stands out by its length. It violates rule 26 by including option d. If an examinee can determine that just one of the options is incorrect or untrue, then "All of the above" can be eliminated as a possibility. The item also violates rule 28c since option b does not complete a grammatically correct sentence and hence cannot be the correct option, even though the examinee may not know whether validity is determined in just one way.

Rule 9 in Table 6.8 introduces some unfamiliar terminology. A multiple true-false item (MTF) is one that attaches several true-false items to a single scenario. A complex MC (Type K) item is one that presents several pieces of information and then offers choices that are various combinations of the pieces of information. A conventional MC item is the common one with a stem and set of options, one of which is considered the best answer.

We are loath to invent yet another list of item-writing rules. However, we will venture the opinion that nearly all the extant rules reduce down to these three: *Get the content right, don't give away the right answer,* and *keep it simple and clear.* Furthermore, the first two of these are restricted to ability and achievement tests, leaving only the third for personality, interest, and attitude measures.

Suggestions for Writing Constructed-response Items

As previously indicated, textbooks and articles are replete with suggestions for writing selected-response items. Suggestions for writing constructed-response items are more limited. Perhaps the very open-ended nature of these items makes it more difficult to formulate specific advice. Interestingly, the first bit of advice that many experienced test developers give is to try to avoid constructed-response items and use selected-response items instead, principally because of the scorer reliability issue already discussed. That having been said, we can offer the following advice about preparing constructed-response items.

1. *Make sure the task is clear.* With selected-response items, the examinee's task is clarified by looking at the possible responses. Such guidance is lacking in the constructed-response item. Hence, greater care is needed in formulating and clarifying the directions for these items.

2. *Be specific about the scoring system at the time the item is prepared.* A common practice for the constructed-response format is to prepare the item, administer it, and assume that the method of scoring will become clear later. That strategy is an invitation to psychometric disaster. The way the item will be scored, preferably with sample responses, should be clear before the item is administered. This suggestion applies regardless of the generality of the response. It is equally important in scoring fill-in-the-blank items as well as scoring lengthy essays, performance assessments, or projective techniques.

3. *Use a sufficient number of items.* There is a tendency with constructed-response items to consume all the available testing time with just a few items, perhaps only one item. The reliability and validity of the measurement are generally better served by including more items. If there is only one item and, for some reason, an examinee misunderstands it or "makes a wrong turn" with it, there is no way to counterbalance the situation with responses to other items. Although the constructed-response format usually allows for fewer items than the selected-response format, one should lean toward more rather than fewer items when using constructed-response items.

Some Practical Considerations in Writing Items

We consider here a few practical matters about writing items for tests. First, if one is preparing a set of items for tryout, how many items should be written? This question has no definitive answer. The answer depends partly on making good decisions at the preliminary design stage, for example, about the appropriate type of item to use and thoroughly researching the area to be tested. The answer also depends on doing a reasonable job of informal tryout to make sure the prototypes of intended items will work. With these qualifications in mind, a common rule of thumb is to prepare two to three times as many items as needed for the final test. Thus, if the final test will have 50 items, one would prepare 100 to 150 items for tryout. Consider these extreme departures from the rule of thumb. If the final test will have 50 items and only 55 items are tried out, it is almost certain that the item analysis will reveal more than 5 items with undesirable characteristics. With room to discard only 5 items, you will be forced to include some items in the final test that are not very good. At the other extreme, suppose you prepare 500 items for tryout. First, it should be noted that preparing 500 items on almost any topic is a difficult task. More important, if you select 50 items from a pool of 500 items, it is very likely that you will be capitalizing on some chance factors that would not survive a cross-validation process. If you need to try out 500 items to get 50 usable items, you probably need to rethink your approach to the test.

Item Editing and Review

In major test development projects, once items are written they are subject to review from several perspectives. First, they are reviewed for clarity, grammatical correctness, and conformity with the item-writing rules covered earlier. Second, for achievement test items, there is review for content correctness. Experts in the relevant content field conduct these reviews.

Third, in recent years it has become customary to review items for possible gender, racial, or ethnic bias. Individuals representing the referenced groups typically conduct these reviews. The question is whether anything about the item unfairly disadvantages a member of the group. By "unfairly" we mean that members of the group are likely to respond inappropriately not because they are low on the trait being measured but because of their group membership. If an item is suspected of unfairly affecting the test performance in this way, the item would ordinarily be eliminated from the item pool even before item tryout. For example, suppose that most items prepared for a reading test deal with topics from a male-dominated sport such as football, including paragraphs about the nickel defense, crack-back blocking, and the two-minute drill. Girls might score lower on the test not because of poor reading ability but because they have not spent Saturday and Sunday afternoons listening to these topics being discussed endlessly. Such items should be eliminated or perhaps counterbalanced by items working in the other direction. Later in this chapter we will look at some statistical methods for examining this same issue.

Item Analysis

One of the crucial steps in test development is **item analysis.** This involves the statistical analysis of data obtained from an item tryout. Items are selected for inclusion in the final test based on the item analysis. Thus, what we have labeled here as Item Analysis actually consists of three closely related processes: item tryout, the statistical analysis, and item selection. We discuss each of these processes in this section.

Why is item analysis important? As noted previously, the great majority of educational and psychological tests consist of a collection of individual items. Test items are like building blocks. We control the characteristics of a test by controlling the items that make up the test. If we want an easy test, we use easy items. If we want a test with high internal consistency reliability, we use items that are highly correlated with one another. Item analysis is the collection of procedures that allow us to exercise this control. Furthermore, because item characteristics determine important features of a test, test

---

Key Points Summary 6.3

The Three Phases of Item Analysis

1. Item Tryout
2. Statistical Analysis
3. Item Selection

---

manuals frequently refer to the results of item analysis. Hence, to be an informed reader of test manuals, one must be familiar with the concepts and techniques of item analysis.

TRY IT! ....

Access a test review in any edition of Buros's *Mental Measurements Yearbook*, either electronically or in hard copy. Scan the test review to see what is said about the test construction process. Be especially alert to references to item statistics. What item statistics are mentioned?

....

Item Tryout

There are two stages of item tryout: informal and formal. Item analysis data are based on the formal tryout. However, before conducting the formal tryout, it is customary and prudent to carry out *informal tryout* of the test items. This is typically done with only a few cases, say five to ten individuals similar to those for whom the test is intended. Often, the items are not even scored in any formal way. Individuals completing the informal tryout are asked to comment on the items and test directions. The individuals may be asked to "think aloud" while answering the items. Think-aloud tryouts can be especially helpful with novel formats or approaches. This helps the test developer to identify ambiguous wording, unexpected interpretations of an item, confusion about methods for responding, and other such anomalies. Informal tryouts can prevent wasting resources in the formal tryout phase. There is no sense collecting data from several hundred examinees and conducting elaborate statistical analyses on items that examinees do not understand in the first place.

The *formal item tryout* involves administration of new test items to samples of examinees. The samples should be representative of the target population for the test. For example, if the test is intended for use with normal children aged 3–6, the tryout sample should be representative of this group. If the test is intended for college applicants, the tryout sample should be representative of college applicants.

Item tryout samples are often not as large as the samples used for establishing norms for a test. However, the samples obviously need to be large enough to yield stable data. Samples of several hundred individuals are generally adequate when using classical item analysis procedures, as defined later. Use of item response theory procedures may require much larger samples.

There are three common practices for conducting a formal item tryout. We label these the *independent study* procedure, the *attachment* procedure, and the *continuing analysis* procedure. The independent study procedure involves conducting a study exclusively for the purpose of item analysis. Samples of examinees complete items in circumstances approximating the conditions intended for the final test. However, test length may vary—either longer or shorter—and there may be no time limit to ensure that all examinees have the opportunity to try all items. The independent study approach is the most common practice for item analysis.

The attachment procedure involves including tryout items in the regular administration of some existing test. Examinees are ordinarily told that the test contains some "experimental" items, but the examinees are not told which items these are. The tryout items do not count toward examinees' regular test scores. This procedure is often used with large, national testing programs in which tests are administered on only a few dates.

The continuing analysis procedure requires that a test or pool of items be used repeatedly, with new items (usually just a few) being added in each use. The new items are subjected to item analysis. They are retained, modified, or discarded based on the item analysis. They may or may not count in the test score. Some previously used items may be retired from the item pool not because of poor item statistics but just to keep the pool of items fresh. Instructors often use this procedure in order to have information about the quality of their items without using exactly the same test repeatedly.

Item Statistics

Much of the vocabulary used in item analysis originates with applications to achievement and ability tests, especially for multiple-choice items. In these domains, there is a correct option and several incorrect options. However, the item analysis procedures also work with tests in other domains, for example, with personality tests or attitude surveys. The terminology developed within the cognitive domain often carries over to these other domains, although the usage is sometimes a bit strained. Figure 6.5 shows terminology commonly used for such items.

Item Difficulty

The formal item tryout results in a set of item statistics. Traditional item analysis procedures, those arising from classical test theory, depend on two concepts: the item difficulty index and the item discrimination index. **Item difficulty** refers to the percent of examinees answering the item correctly for items scored correct/incorrect; or responding in a certain direction for items where there is no correct answer, for example, responding "agree" to an attitude item. In the case of

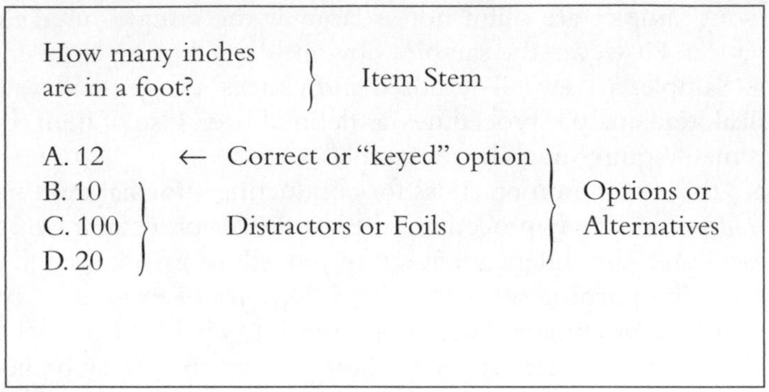

How many inches
are in a foot?   } Item Stem

A. 12   ← Correct or "keyed" option ⎫
B. 10   ⎫   ⎪ Options or
C. 100   ⎬   Distractors or Foils   ⎬ Alternatives
D. 20   ⎭   ⎭

FIGURE 6.5   The anatomy of a multiple-choice item.

items scored correct/incorrect, item "difficulty" is really an index of item "ease," that is, the percent answering correctly. However, the term *item difficulty* is well entrenched in the psychometric literature.

Item difficulty levels are usually called **p-values,** where p stands for percentage or proportion. Thus an item with a p-value of .85 is an easy item: 85% of examinees answered it correctly. An item with a p-value of .25 is a very difficult item: only 25% of examinees answered it correctly.

Item Discrimination

Item discrimination refers to an item's ability to differentiate statistically in a desired way between groups of examinees. The term *discrimination* here does not refer to sociological or juridical discrimination based, for example, on race, gender, or religion. Because of potential misunderstanding on this point, we would be better off using some other term for this statistical differentiation. However, like the term *item difficulty*, the term *item discrimination* is well entrenched in the psychometric literature and is not likely to go away.

What kind of discrimination or differentiation do we want in a test item? Generally, we want the test item to differentiate between individuals with more of the trait we are trying to measure from individuals with less of the trait. Since items are the building blocks for a test, items that differentiate this way will make for a good test. The following paragraphs describe (a) how to define the groups with more or less of the trait and (b) how to express the extent to which the item differentiates.

To determine whether an item differentiates between those with more or less of the trait that we want to measure, we need to identify groups with more or less of the trait. There are two methods commonly used for this identification. We call the first method the *external method* and the second the *internal method*. The reference point for the terms *external* and *internal* here is the test itself. In the external method, the basis for identification of groups is external to the test; in the internal method, the basis is internal to the test. The external method depends on having two (or more) groups differentiated on the relevant trait according to some external criterion. Consider these two examples of externally defined groups. First, suppose we are developing a questionnaire designed to measure depression. We have a group of 50 individuals diagnosed by a team of psychologists to be suffering from depression and another group of 50 individuals identified as experiencing mild phobic reactions but with no other significant clinical symptoms. We want test items that discriminate or differentiate between these two groups, that is, items that differentiate the depressed from the nondepressed group. Second, suppose we are developing a test of proficiency in using Microsoft Access, a software package for creating databases. We have a group of 100 individuals who have completed a three-week training course in Access and another group of individuals who are generally computer literate but have not been trained in Access. We expect our test items to discriminate between these two groups.

In the internal method for creating groups who have more or less of the trait we are trying to measure, we score the entire test, then identify those who scored higher on the test and those who scored lower. The assumption is that the entire test is a reasonably valid measure of the trait. Then we determine the extent to which an individual item differentiates between high scorers and low scorers. Essentially, we determine the extent to which the item differentiates among people in the same way as the total score differentiates. For many traits we wish to measure we do not have a good external indicator of the trait, or it is very difficult to obtain the external indicator. Hence, the internal approach is far more commonly used than the external approach in test development work.

In the internal method, one of several possible splits between high scorers and low scorers may be made. We start with the distribution of total scores[5] on the test. Then **"high" and "low" groups** may be defined as the top and bottom halves of the distribution, the top and bottom thirds, or top and bottom quarters. Another commonly used split is top and bottom 27%.[6] For completeness of analysis, when top and bottom 25%, 27%, or 33% are used, it is customary to also examine performance of the intermediate groups, although performance of these intermediate groups does not enter into the discrimination analysis. (All cases enter into determination of the difficulty index.)

---

[5] In different applications, total score on the test may be defined in several different ways. For example, it may be based on all items in the test, all items excluding the one being analyzed, or all items in a subset within a larger battery.

[6] Although 27% seems like a strange number there is good reason for it. When contrasting groups, we want to optimize two conditions that generally work against one another. On the one hand, we want the groups to be as different as possible. According to this principle, a contrast between the top and bottom 5% or top and bottom 10% would be better than, say, a constrast between the top and bottom 50%. On the other hand, to get stable data, we want the groups to be as large as possible. According to this principle, the top and bottom 50% groups are preferable. In a famous analysis first published in 1928 but subsequently corrected, Truman Kelley (1939) showed that the optimum solution to this problem was to use the top and bottom 27%. Hence, this 27% has become the "industry standard" for splits. The top and bottom 25% or 33% are often used as reasonable approximations to 27%, with the added benefit of allowing for analysis of one or two middle groups equal in size to the extreme groups.

Whereas item difficulty almost always has just one universal indicator—the p-value—item discrimination can be expressed in several different ways. Most commonly, the degree of discrimination is represented by D (for difference or discrimination) or by r (the correlation between performance on the item and on the external criterion or total test score). D is usually defined as the simple difference in percent right in the "high" and "low" groups. In practice, one encounters several different types of correlation coefficients (r's) to express the item-test or item-criterion relationship. The type of r depends on certain assumptions made in a particular case about the nature of the variables involved; r's in common use include the biserial r (r_{bis}) and the point biserial r (r_{pbis}). In the psychometric literature, one will also find reference to the tetrachoric correlation (r_{tet}) and phi coefficient (Φ) One also encounters the term *corrected-r*. This term is used when the correlation between item and total test is based on a total test score that excludes the item being analyzed. All the methods give much the same information about the discriminating power of an item. In addition to finding a variety of ways of determining item discrimination, one encounters a variety of ways of naming the index. Regardless of the particular method used to determine the index, it may be called the discrimination index, the item-total correlation, or the item validity index.

Distractor Analysis

The main products of an item analysis are the item difficulty index *(p)* and item discrimination index (*D* or *r*). However, item analysis data are also used for what is called "distractor[7] analysis." A **distractor** is an incorrect or nonpreferred option in an item. An item analysis usually provides information not only about performance on the correct or preferred option—this information yields *p* and *D* or *r*—but also on each of the other options in the item. Obviously, distractor analysis applies only to items that have more than two options.

Distractor analysis may yield useful information about examinees' understanding or misunderstanding of an item. Some authors suggest that distractor analysis might provide a basis for revising an item. For example, one "incorrect" option might actually behave like a correct option; that is, more people in the "high" group than in the "low" group select the option. This might suggest that people in the high group are interpreting the question somewhat differently from what the test author intended. Perhaps the item stem or options could be modified to avoid such misinterpreation.

Examples of Item Statistics

Table 6.9 presents data for five items from an achievement test. Let us examine these data to illustrate what can be learned from an item analysis. The left-hand column,

---

[7] Most dictionaries give "distracter" as the correct spelling of this word. However, for some reason the psychometric literature prefers the alternative "distractor."

TABLE 6.9   *Sample Item Analysis Data for Items from an Achievement Test*[a]

| | Item Statistics | | | Statistics on Alternatives | | | | |
| | | | | | Prop. Endorsing | | | |
Item	Prop. Correct	Disc. Index	Point Biser.	Alt	Total	Low	High	Key
6	.56	.50	.43	1	.56	.36	.87	★
				2	.26	.45	.07	
				3	.10	.09	.07	
				4	.05	.00	.00	
10	.62	.10	.04	1	.05	.00	.00	
				2	.62	.64	.73	★
				3	.00	.00	.00	
				4	.31	.36	.27	
23	.26	.40	.37	1	.03	.09	.00	
				2	.08	.18	.00	
				3	.26	.00	.40	★
				4	.56	.55	.60	
28	.97	.09	.24	1	.00	.00	.00	
				2	.03	.09	.00	
				3	.00	.00	.00	
				4	.97	.91	1.00	★
29	.69	.05	.03	1	.69	.55	.60	★
				2	.08	.09	.13	
				3	.15	.27	.20	
				4	.08	.09	.07	

[a] Format adapted from ITEMAN™, a component of the Item and Test Analysis Package developed by Assessment Systems Corporation, with permission.

labeled "Item," gives the item number. There are three entries under "Item Statistics": Prop. Correct (proportion getting the item correct), Disc. Index (the item discrimination index), Point Biser. (the point biserial correlation coefficient between performance on this item and total score on the test for top and bottom 27% of the cases).

Under "Statistics on Alternatives," we find the following entries: Alt (alternative or option; in this test each item had four options); Prop. Endorsing (proportion endorsing or choosing each option) for each of the following groups: Total group (the total group of students), Low group (students in the lowest 27% on total score), and High group (students in the top 27% on total score). Under "Key" in the far right column, an asterisk (★) indicates which of the alternatives was keyed as the correct answer.

For item 6, Prop. Correct is .56; that is, 56% of the students got this item right. Notice that this is the same figure as Prop. Endorsing Total for Alt 1, that is, the proportion of the total group that selected the correct answer. The Disc. Index for item 6 is .50. This is the difference (with some rounding error) between Prop. Endorsing High and Prop. Endorsing Low for alternative 1. Thus, on this item, 87% of students who scored best on the test as a whole selected the correct option, whereas only 36% of students who scored the lowest selected the correct option. This item was quite effective in separating the high and low groups. Option 2 was rather attractive for students in the Low group, with almost half of them choosing this option. Even a few students—but only a few—in the High group chose option 2. The Point Biser. correlation (.43) cannot be determined directly from data given here, but it is the correlation between total score on the test and performance on this item. The biserial correlation and the discrimination index will usually be similar, as illustrated by the examples in Table 6.9.

Item 10 had about the same difficulty level as item 6 (.62 vs. .56, not much difference), but item 10 had much less discriminating power than item 6. Whereas 64% of the Low group chose the correct option (Alt 2), only a slightly greater percentage (73%) of the High group chose this option. About one-third of each group chose option 4. These data suggest that item 10, especially option 4, should be reviewed carefully.

Item 23 is a very difficult item. Only 26% of the total group answered this item correctly. None of the students in the Low group got the item right. Although the item shows excellent discrimination, the fact that more students in the High group than in the Low group chose option 4 makes one wonder about that option.

Item 28 is a very easy item. Nearly everyone answered it correctly. As a validation that students learned the content of the item, it is useful. However, it contributes little to distinguishing between those who know more or less of the material, as indicated by its low item discrimination index.

Item 29 is moderately difficult (p-value = .69) but the distribution of responses across the options is puzzling. The discrimination index and point biserial correlation are near zero. The split between High and Low groups is roughly the same on each option. Wording of this item should be examined.

TRY IT! ....

Following are some item data arranged in the same way as the data in Table 6.9. Fill in the missing figures for "Prop. Correct" and "Disc. Index."

| | Item Statistics | | | Statistics on Alternatives | | | | |
| | Prop. | Disc. | Point | | Prop. Endorsing | | | |
Item	Correct	Index	Biser.	Alt	Total	Low	High	Key
3	_____	_____	.48	1	.00	.00	.00	
				2	.15	.36	.13	
				3	.85	.64	.87	★
				4	.00	.00	.00	

Item Statistics in Item Response Theory

The discussion of item statistics in the previous section was based on classical test theory (CTT). The item difficulty index and the item discrimination index in CTT are often called *traditional* item statistics. Item response theory (IRT) also utilizes item statistics, but the concepts and terminology are somewhat different from those in CTT.

A key feature of item analysis in IRT is the **item characteristic curve (ICC)**. The **ICC** relates performance on an item to status on the trait or ability underlying the scale. Performance on the item is defined as the *probability of passing* an item. Passing means getting the correct answer on an ability or achievement test, or answering in a certain direction on a personality, interest, or attitude test. Status on the trait is defined in terms of theta (θ), as discussed in Chapter 3. (IRT terminology originates primarily from work with ability and achievement tests. The terminology is often transferred directly, with some strain in meaning, to personality, interest, and attitude measures. Thus, theta represents an "ability" even if the construct is depression or interest in politics; performance on the item is "passing" even if the response is "Yes" or "Like." Some authors use the more generic terms "trait" and "probability of keyed response.") Theta values are somewhat arbitrary, but they usually range from about −4.0 to +4.0, where negative values represent less of the trait and positive values represent more of the trait. The ICC is a plot of the relationship between these two constructs.

Figure 6.6 depicts four ICCs. With increasing levels of θ (i.e., moving from left to right along the base of each plot), the probability of passing the item increases for these items. This is true for all four ICCs. Notice the dotted lines associated with the ICC for item A. The horizontal dotted line shows where the curve crosses the point of 50% probability of passing. The vertical dotted line shows where this point is on the theta scale (−1.5 in this example). That is, theoretically, persons at −1.5 on the trait have a 50–50 chance of passing the item. On item A,

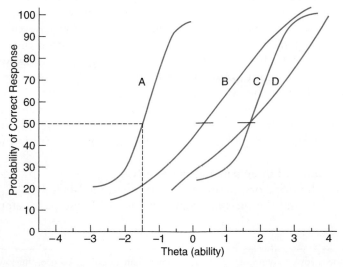

FIGURE 6.6 Examples of item characteristic curves (ICC) in item response theory.

persons with a θ of −2.5 have only about a 20% chance of passing the item, whereas those with a θ of 0.0 have about a 95% chance of passing the item. We use the original theta values here. In practical work, we usually add a constant (e.g., +5) to eliminate negative numbers.

In the most commonly used IRT models, the item's *difficulty parameter* is the point at which the ICC crosses the mark for 50% probability of passing the item. The concept is very similar to the item difficulty index (p-value) in CTT. However, the difficulty paramter in IRT is represented by its corresponding θ value.

Notice the "tick" marks on the ICCs for items B, C, and D in Figure 6.6. These marks show where the curves cross the 50% point on the *y*-axis. Item B is more difficult than item A. One needs a higher level of ability (θ) to have a 50–50 chance of passing item B than of passing item A. Items C and D cross the 50% mark at the same place, and both of these items are more difficult than items A and B.

The ICCs in Figure 6.6 do not all have the same shape. The ICC shapes for items A and C are quite similar. They are very "S-shaped." They rise steeply in the middle of the curve. The ICCs for items B and D rise more gently. The formal term for this steepness is **slope.** The slope of the curve shows how sharply the item differentiates among persons of differing abilities (θ values). Reference to "differentiating" reminds us of the item discrimination index in CTT. Indeed, the slope of the ICC does correspond closely to the notion of the item discrimination index.

Item A shows sharp differentiation from about −2.0 to −.5 on the θ scale. Item C has the same slope as item A, but item C functions best (i.e., discriminates most sharply) in the range of 1.0 to 3.0. This illustrates an important feature of ICCs: They help the test developer identify items that function differently at different points along the ability spectrum.

There is a third feature of the ICCs in Figure 6.6. The lower end of the curves for items A and C flatten out around the 20% level on the *y*-axis. Technically, this "flattening out" is known as the lower asymptote. Thus, no matter how low a person is on θ, there is about a 20% chance of passing the item. At first, this may seem inexplicable. However, consider the case of a five-option multiple-choice item. No matter how little one knows about the subject matter being tested, one has about a 20% chance of passing the item by wild guessing. Some IRT models account for this lower asymptote with a **guessing parameter.**[8] For a ten-option item, the guessing parameter might be at the 10% level. Notice that the lower end of the ICC for item B does approach zero on the *y*-axis, illustrating that not all items are affected by guessing. Generally, upper asymptotes for ICCs are near 100%; hence no separate parameter is introduced for upper asymptotes.

We have examined three parameters of an ICC: difficulty, slope, and guessing. In IRT parlance, the slope or discrimination parameter is labeled as "a," the difficulty parameter as "b," and the guessing parameter as "c." These parameters give rise to

---

[8] There may be a lower asymptote for reasons other than guessing. Hence, the lower asymptote is sometimes referred to as the pseudo-guessing parameter.

three IRT models, often referred to as 1P, 2P, and 3P models: the one-parameter, two-parameter, and three-parameter models. The one-parameter model takes into account only the difficulty parameter (b). This model assumes that all items are equal in slope (discriminating power) and that guessing is not a significant factor. The most popular one-parameter model is the **Rasch model,** named after George Rasch who developed it (Wright, 1997). The one-parameter Rasch model is probably the most widely used IRT model for test development work. The two-parameter model takes into account both difficulty and discrimination, but not guessing. The three-parameter model takes into account difficulty, discrimination, and guessing.

Figure 6.7 shows ICCs for two items from an actual test development project using the Rasch model. The connected dots show the actual performance of subgroups in the research program. The ICCs are fit to these empirical points. Item 40 is a relatively easy item, with a difficulty parameter (b) of −2.70. Item 352 is a more difficult item, with b = 1.67.

TRY IT!

Using a straight-edge, for the ICCs in Figure 6.7, verify that theta values are −2.70 and 1.67 at "probability of keyed response" equal .50.

To aid in understanding ICCs, it may be useful to introduce some examples that are theoretically possible but not likely to occur in practice. Figure 6.8 gives these examples. Item E shows a case in which everyone below a certain ability level ($\theta = -2.0$) fails the item and everyone above that ability level passes the item. From many points of view, this is an ideal item. A series of items like this but at

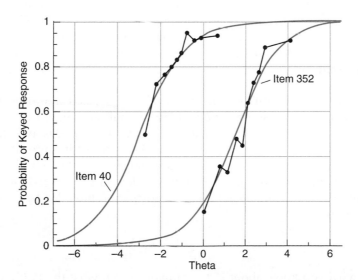

FIGURE 6.7 Examples of ICCs for items using the Rasch model.

Source: Reproduced with permission of Renaissance Learning, Inc.

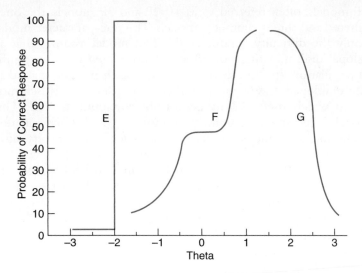

FIGURE 6.8 Some theoretically possible but improbable ICCs.

different θ levels would give a very efficient test. Item F shows a case in which the item differentiates positively up to a certain point, then loses its differentiating power, then again accelerates. One does sometimes encounter a pattern like this, but it is probably more a matter of unstable fluctuations in the sample of cases used than a true phenomenon. Item G shows the odd case where the probability of passing the item actually decreases with an increase in ability level. This would correspond to a *negative* item discrimination index in CTT: More people in the lower group than in the higher group got the item right. Actually, the plot for item G is not as bizarre as it may first appear. In practical situations this is precisely the kind of plot that occurs for incorrect options on a selected-response item. That is, as ability level increases, the probability of selecting a certain incorrect option decreases.

Parameters of an ICC can be translated into what is called an **item information function.** This function shows where along the trait continuum (θ) an item provides relevant measurement information. Figure 6.9 presents two hypothetical information functions. The function for Item B shows that it is providing a moderate amount of information throughout the range from 0.0–3.0; the amount of information is roughly uniform through the middle of this range. Item A is sharply focused around $\theta = -1.0$. The amount of information provided by item A falls off rapidly away from −1.0.

TRY IT! ....

Based on what you know about ICCs, can you sketch what the ICCs might be for the items whose information functions are shown in Figure 6.9?

....

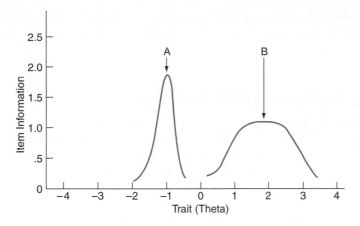

FIGURE 6.9 Item information functions for two hypothetical items.

IRT models had their first practical applications for test development work in the 1970s. Since that time, these models have become increasingly popular, first with ability and achievement tests and more recently with personality tests. Research on the characteristics of various IRT models and development of new models must be described as explosive in the past 30 years.[9] Our treatment of the item statistics in IRT has necessarily been brief. For a more detailed explanation, with excellent examples, see Hambleton, Swaminathan, and Rogers (1991).

The relative value of IRT and CTT item statistics is somewhat controversial. Most contemporary test developers employ IRT item statistics, suggesting that experts find value in the IRT data. However, traditional (CTT) item statistics continue to be used in the same test development projects. This appears to be more than just a matter of holding on to an old security blanket. Practicing test developers find value in the traditional test statistics as well as in the IRT statistics.

Formal criticisms of IRT methods concentrate on three concerns. First, from a very practical point of view, obtaining stable estimates of IRT parameters requires rather large samples. Second, the IRT model assumes that the trait being measured is unidimensional. However, many tests are not unidimensional; hence the IRT model does not apply. Of course, one could argue that in these circumstances the appropriate course of action would be to decompose the test into a number of unidimensional subtests, then apply the IRT model to each subtest. Finally, it might be noted that while the Rasch model is the most widely used IRT model, this model's assumption that all items have equal discriminating power is patently false in nearly every test development project. See Nunnally and Bernstein (1994) for a general

---

[9] See Wright, B. (1997) for a history of the Rasch IRT methodology.

critique of IRT methodology. See Green, Yen, and Burkett (1989) for a comparsion of CTT and IRT approaches to test development from the perspective of a major test publisher.

Factor Analysis as an Item Analysis Technique

In Chapter 5, we described factor analysis as a method used to help demonstrate a test's construct validity. In that application, the test was already established and the factor analytic results indicated its structure. However, factor analysis is also used in the item analysis phase of test development to help select items that will yield relatively independent and meaningful scores. This approach is widely used in the construction of multitrait personality, interest, and attitude scales.

In this application of factor analysis, a large number of items apparently relevant to the traits intended for measurement are administered to a sample of examinees. Intercorrelations among the items are factor analyzed. Underlying dimensions (factors) are identified. Then, items with high loadings on the factors are selected for inclusion in the final test. The final test yields separate scores for each of the factors with items that should be relatively pure and efficient measures of the factors.

Table 6.10 shows part of the results of the factor analysis of a pool of items designed to measure children's interests in various school subjects. Items with loadings in bold print might be selected for the final scales. In this process, item loadings on the factors serve a purpose similar to item discrimination indexes (D's). However, in order to determine D, we need a total score to split the tryout sample into high and low groups. In the factor analytic approach, we do not have any total scores to begin the process. Rather, we generate factors and determine the relationship between items and these factors.

TABLE **6.10**   *Partial Results from Factor Analysis for Items on an Interest Inventory*

Item	Factor: I	II	III	IV
			Item Loadings[a]	
1	10	**76**	−07	06
2	05	16	10	**73**
3	08	29	**59**	**39**
4	19	**39**	67	−05
5	**51**	26	47	−11
6	**36**	51	33	**−31**
7	12	**44**	40	17
8	03	24	**65**	−01
9	09	06	**55**	16
10	**58**	**45**	23	01

[a] Decimal points omitted.

Some authors hesitate to factor analyze groups of items, as opposed to groups of tests. Nunnally and Bernstein (1994), for example, express grave concern regarding typical item-level factor analyses. Henryssen (1971) provides a more benign treatment of the topic. Rather than join the fray on this matter, we simply note that we reference factor analysis as an item analysis technique because it is, in fact, often used.

Differential Item Functioning (DIF)

The item analysis stage of test development provides the context for the study of **differential item functioning,** usually referred to by its acronym **DIF.** Item bias is an older term for this topic, but the current literature prefers the more neutral and perhaps more descriptive term *differential item functioning.* DIF addresses the question of whether test items function differently for different groups of examinees for reasons other than actual differences on the trait being measured. Of particular interest are differences by race, ethnic, and gender groups. However, the basic question can be addressed for any group comparisons, for example, between persons of different ages, height, or handedness. In our earlier discussion of item preparation, we referred to review of items to eliminate potential racial, ethnic, and gender bias (p. 225). Those review procedures were purely judgmental. DIF procedures aim to detect bias by statistical analysis.

> Differential item functioning is said to exist when test-takers of approximately equal ability on the targeted construct or content domain differ in their responses to an item according to their group membership. *Standards...*
> (AERA/APA/NCME, 1999, p. 40)

The most important point to understand in the discussion of differential item functioning is that a simple difference in item difficulties is not necessarily an indication of bias in an item. Consider this case. We will examine performance on one test item—item 23—on a test of academic aptitude. On test item 23, 60% of Group A responds correctly[10] and 80% of Group B responds correctly. This does not mean that the item is biased against Group A. Suppose that on some external criterion of performance on the trait we determine that Group B is, in fact, substantially higher than Group A on the trait. For example, we may know that Group A has grade point average (GPA) of 2.75, whereas Group B has an average GPA of 3.68. Then we would expect Group B to do better than Group A on item 23. We would take the difference of 60% versus 80% as a reflection of a real difference on the trait. We would be puzzled if the two groups performed equally on item 23. Suppose, on the other hand, that, according to the external criterion, Groups A and B were equal on the trait we were

---

[10] Once again, the basic terminology comes from the realm of ability and achievement testing, but the concepts apply equally well to personality, interest, and attitude measures. Hence, we refer here to "responds correctly," but it could just as well be "responds affirmatively" or "responds Yes." Note that the statement from the *Standards* refers to "equal ability" but, by extension, it means "equal on the trait."

trying to measure: both have an average GPA of 3.20. Then we would not expect the groups to differ on item 23. We would be disinclined to include that item on the final test.

Numerous methods have been proposed to study DIF. The field has clearly not settled on a single best approach. Berk's (1982) edited collection of papers provides an excellent introduction to a variety of methods, although it is now somewhat dated. Cole and Moss (1993) provide a more recent review of the methods for studying DIF. However, new developments are rapidly appearing in the research literature. A review of all the methods or even most of them would take us well beyond an introductory text such as this. However, we will briefly mention two of the more popular DIF methods.

TRY IT!

If you have access to an electronic index of current research literature in psychology, education, or the social sciences, conduct a search using the key words DIFFERENTIAL ITEM FUNCTIONING. Observe the variety of group differences being studied.

In the example given above with Groups A and B, we established the groups' equivalence on the trait in terms of an external criterion. In the most typical applications of DIF, the equivalence of the groups is based on total score on the test or estimated theta. Ordinarily, the larger group or majority group is called the *reference group*. The smaller or minority group is called the *focal group*, that is, the group we are focusing our attention on. Then, performance on individual items is examined. The **Mantel-Haenszel procedure** begins by dividing the reference and focal groups into subgroups based on total test score. Think of a 50-item test. Divide the total score on the test into intervals as shown in Table 6.11. Then for each item in the test, determine the number of cases in the reference and focal groups that got the item right or wrong. The Mantel-Haenszel statistic is derived from this type of data array. Within a given score interval, say, from 31 to 40, the two groups are considered equal on the trait. The question is whether they differ in performance on an individual item. The full groups, combined across all intervals, may very well have a mean difference on the trait while still allowing for analysis of differences on single items. For example, in Table 6.11, average performance is higher for the reference group than for the focal group. However, within any score range, the ratio of right

TABLE **6.11** *Part of the Data Array for Mantel-Haenszel Analysis of DIF*

Total Score Group	1–10		11–20		21–30		31–40		41–50	
Performance on Item 23[a]	+	–	+	–	+	–	+	–	+	–
Reference Group	14	16	30	30	56	28	64	22	10	2
Focal Group	10	12	20	20	15	8	10	4	2	0

[a] + = Right, – = Wrong.

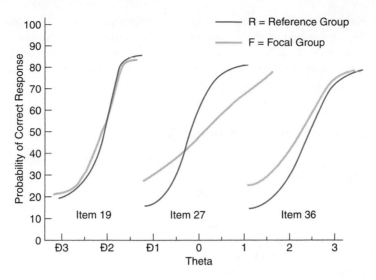

FIGURE 6.10 DIF analysis via ICCs for two groups on three items.

to wrong answers is about the same for the two groups.[11] The most obvious case is within the score range 11–20 where the ratios of right to wrong answers are exactly the same for the two groups. Forty percent of the Focal group scores in this lower range, while only 22% of the Reference group is in that range. However, the item p-value is exactly .50 for both groups within that range.

TRY IT!

Calculate the overall p-value for the item in Table 6.11 for the Reference and Focal Groups. To get p for one of the groups, sum all the "+" responses and divide this by the sum of all "+" and "−" responses for the group. How do the overal p-values compare?

The latter description suggests an analysis very much like an item characteristic curve (ICC). Indeed, IRT methodology is one of the main approaches to DIF. Specifically, ICCs are developed for each item for the groups being compared. The parameters for these curves—difficulty, slope, and guessing—can also be examined for DIF. Figure 6.10 illustrates this application. ICCs that overlap, or nearly so, indicate lack of DIF, as indicated by item 19. Item 27 shows noticeably different ICCs—that is, substantial DIF. Item 36 illustrates an item with noticeable DIF at the lower levels of the trait (θ) but no difference at the upper levels. Note that these analyses do not say anything about the overall performance of the two groups. It may be that the average score for the two groups differs by 20 points.

---

[11] Technically, the Mantel-Haenszel procedure performs a chi-square analysis on the data array. Score intervals would typically be narrower than those given in Table 6.11 and may be in unit intervals throughout the distribution.

DIF analysis for racial, ethnic, and gender differences is typically conducted at the item analysis stage of test development. However, many DIF studies are conducted after a test is published. Some of these studies apply new or revised DIF methods. Other studies apply existing methodologies to new subgroups. The number of subgroups that can be analyzed is virtually endless.

Item Analysis for Criterion-Referenced Tests

Item analysis procedures, for both CTT and IRT, assume that a test's purpose is to measure *differences* among people. The procedures help to identify items that contribute to this differentiation. Items that do not differentiate are useless.

Criterion-referenced tests aim to determine if a certain criterion has been met. It is immaterial whether the test differentiates among people. Perhaps everyone taking the test will achieve a perfect score. In this case, all item discrimination indexes would be zero. Such a result would be quite acceptable, provided that the test validly measures the construct of interest. Thus, from a theoretical perspective, one can claim that item analysis statistics are irrelevant for criterion-referenced tests.

However, item analysis can be useful for criterion-referenced tests in two circumstances. First, if the test is measuring the effects of training or some other treatment, item analysis can employ the external criterion approach described earlier, where the external criterion is exposure versus nonexposure to the training or treatment. The earlier example of training in use of Microsoft Access illustrates this case.

Second, even in the absence of a relevant external criterion, the internal criterion of split on total test score can be useful. It is rare to find an application in which all examinees achieve perfect scores (or scores of zero) on a test. There is nearly always some differentiation, even if that is not the purpose of the test. When there are any differences in scores, item analysis procedures can yield useful information about items in the test.

Cross-validation and Validity Shrinkage

Consider this scenario. You try out 100 items to get the 10 best items for your test. There are 20 cases in your tryout sample. In this situation—a relatively small sample and a small percentage of items to be selected—the item data for the 10 best items will be unduly influenced by chance factors. For example, almost certainly the 8th, 9th, 10th best items would be different with a different tryout sample. To get a good idea of the true item statistics for the 10 items selected, they should be tried out again on a second sample. This process is called **cross-validation.** The loss in the validity of the items goes by the quaint name of **validity shrinkage.** In the context of item analysis, "validity" refers to the item discrimination index, which, as noted earlier, is sometimes called the item validity index. However, the item difficulty index can also be affected by factors considered here. The item data on the second sample will not look as favorable as they did on the first sample. The extent of this problem depends primarily on two factors: the size of the tryout sample and the selection ratio for items. When the tryout sample is large, say, 200 or more cases and the selection ratio is no less than 25%, validity shrinkage should not be a significant problem. You should be particularly wary of a test that has a tryout sample of less than 50 cases and reports item data without cross-validation. Cross-validation and validity shrinkage are important issues regardless of the item analysis procedures used.

Item Selection

The final phase of the item analysis process is item selection. From all the items prepared and tried out, one selects the items that will appear in the test to be standardized.[12] Selection of items takes into account the original purpose and design of the test, relevant content specifications, and item analysis data. We identify here several guidelines for the item selection process. These guidelines are outgrowths of principles developed in the chapters on norms, reliability, and validity. Item selection does not occur in a vacuum. Characteristics of a good test govern the item selection process.

1. The total number of items in the test is often the most important determinant of the test's reliability. Of course, everyone likes a short test. But short tests are usually not very reliable. As a general rule, to increase a test's reliability, increase the number of items. However, there is a point of diminishing returns where the addition of new items does not significantly increase reliability.

Consideration of the desired number of items must focus on the score(s) to be reported, not simply the total number of items in the test. Suppose a test has 100 items but the important scores are based on six clusters of items, one of which has 50 items and each of the other five clusters has 10 items. The 50-item cluster is likely to yield a reliable score, but the other clusters are likely to yield rather unreliable scores. The fact that the total test has 100 items is largely irrelevant.

2. The average difficulty level of the test is a direct function of the item p-values. The mean score on the test is simply the sum of the p-values. Another way to express this is that the mean score on the test is the average p-value times the number of items on the test. As noted earlier, the p-value is really an index of item ease rather than item difficulty. Hence, to get an easy test, use items with high p-values; to get a hard test, use items with low p-values. Whether an easy or hard test is desired depends on the purpose of testing. An easy test will provide the best discrimination at the lower end of the distribution of test scores. A hard test will provide the best discrimination at the upper end of the distribution. An easy test might be desired for a diagnostic reading test designed to give good information about students who are having trouble reading. Figure 6.11, Test A, illustrates the distribution of scores for such a test. In this distribution, spread among cases is greatest in the lower portion of the distribution. This type of distribution results from having many items with high p-values. On the other hand, one might want a test that spreads cases out at the top of the distribution, for example, for selecting scholarship candidates. The desired distribution for this

---

[12] In some applications, item analysis and standardization will be accomplished in a single research program. However, this is not the customary practice. Combining item analysis and standardization requires exceptional caution and expertise (and, perhaps, luck) to accomplish successfully.

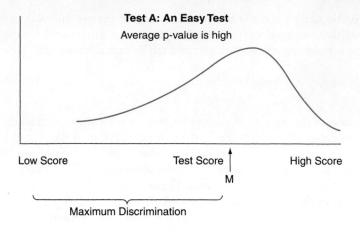

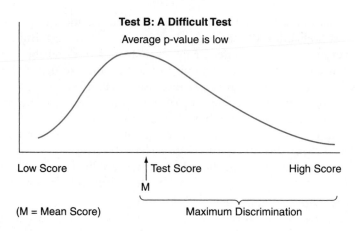

FIGURE 6.11   Distributions resulting from selecting items with high or low p-values.

case is shown in Figure 6.11, Test B. This type of distribution results from having many items with low p-values. In statistical terminology, the distribution for Test A is negatively skewed or skewed to the left while the distribution for Test B is positively skewed or skewed to the right. It should be clear that there is no rule that a psychological test inevitably leads to a normal distribution of scores.

   3. In general, we want items with high discrimination indexes.[13] Such items help contribute to the measurement of the trait. What is "high" for a discrimination index? Whereas we usually think of a "high" correlation as .80 or higher, good (high) discrimination indexes are often no higher than about .50 and an index

---

[13] There is a limit to this generalization. If the trait we are trying to measure is very narrowly defined and sharply focused, then very high discrimination indices are desirable. If the trait is more broadly defined, diffuse, and complex, then moderate (but still clearly positive) discrimination indices may be desirable. In practice, one rarely has to worry about having discrimination indices that are too high.

of .30 is quite respectable. One needs to remember that a single item has very limited reliability; hence, it is not likely to have an extremely high correlation with any other variable. However, a collection of many items with item discrimination indexes of .30–.50 will make for a very good test. This guideline applies regardless of the method of determining item discrimination. Negative discrimination indexes should certainly be avoided. Items with discrimination indexes near zero contribute nothing to measurement of the trait. For an exception to this generalization, see the comments under Item Analysis for Criterion-Referenced Tests (p. 242).

When factor analysis is used as an item analysis technique, the goal is usually to obtain several tests, corresponding to factors, that are relatively "pure" measures of the factors. Hence, one selects items that have high loadings on a single factor and relatively low loadings on all the other factors.

4. There is an important relationship between an item's p-value and the maximum possible discrimination index (D). Specifically, D can take on its maximum value when p is at its midpoint. Consider the examples given in Table 6.12 for a total group of 200 cases. For these data, D is based on a split of the total group into top and bottom 50%, giving 100 cases in the low group and 100 in the high group. The table shows the number of cases in each group getting the item right (No. Right), then translates this number into a proportion (Prop.) for each group. Recall that the discrimination index is the difference between proportion correct in the High and Low groups. If $p = 1.00$, that is, everyone answered the item correctly, then it is also the case that 100% of the upper group and 100% of the lower group answered correctly. Therefore, D = .00. A similar analysis can be made if everyone answered incorrectly: the p-value is .00 and D = .00. If the p-value is .50, then the proportion of cases in the upper group can be 1.00 and in the lower group .00, yielding a maximum D = 1.00. If p = .50, the maximum difference can be obtained between the high and low groups. Examine other combinations in Table 6.12 to confirm the relationship between p and D.

TABLE 6.12   *Examples of the Relationship between an Item's p-value and the Maximum Possible Discrimination Index*

Total Group (N = 200)		Low Group (N = 100)		High Group (N = 100)		Maximum
No. Right	Prop. (p)	No. Right	Prop.	No. Right	Prop.	Possible D
200	1.00	100	1.00	100	1.00	.00
150	.75	50	.50	100	1.00	.50
125	.625	25	.25	100	1.00	.75
100	.50	0	.00	100	1.00	1.00
60	.30	0	.00	60	.60	.60
40	___	___	___	___	___	___
0	.00	0	.00	0	.00	.00

TRY IT! ....

To make sure you understand Table 6.12, fill in the missing values across from 40.

....

Two points should be made about the relationship between p and D. First, the relationship refers to maximum *possible* D. It could certainly be the case that p = .50 and 50% of cases in both the high and low groups answered correctly, yielding D = .00. The p-value determines how high D *can be*, not how high it will actually be. However, it is generally the case that in practical test development work there is an actual relationship between p and D.

Second, when we set the midpoint value of p = .50, we assume there is no effect of guessing. In practice, for multiple-choice tests there is usually some effect of guessing. For purposes of the kind of analysis included in Table 6.12, the midpoint is defined as the halfway mark between a perfect score and a chance score. For example, for a test composed of five-option items, where chance score is 20%, the midpoint value for p is .60, not .50.[14]

Having considered the relationship between p and D, let us return to the issue of the distribution of p-values desired for the test. Since D can be maximized by having p = .50 (or appropriately adjusted upward for guessing), the recommendation is sometimes made that items with p = .50 should be selected for the test. This has been an influential recommendation in the world of testing. It helps to explain why tests of ability and achievement seem so difficult to many examinees. Getting half the items wrong on a test is an unsettling experience.

Not all experts agree on the recommendation to select most items with p-values = .50. The recommendation is applicable only when one wants to make the maximum discrimination in the middle of the distribution of scores. This is sometimes desirable, sometimes not. In many testing situations, one wishes to make reasonably good discriminations throughout the range of the trait tested. This suggests scattering the p-values from low to high. With this strategy, essentially what one is trying to do is get reasonably good discriminations at many points while sacrificing maximum discrimination at one point. This analysis again illustrates the influence that the purpose of the test has on how the test gets developed.

5. Statistical criteria need to be tempered by nonstatistical considerations in the selection of items. Certain items may be included in an achievement test to satisfy demands of the test's content specifications, that is, to ensure content validity. For example, the test blueprint for a math test may call for 10 items on concepts and 10 items on computation. Even if the item statistics are more favorable for the concepts items than for the computation items, one would not exclude the computation items.

Items might also be included for motivational purposes. For example, it is common to begin ability tests with very easy items in order to get examinees off to a good start. The items may have p-values of .99 and, therefore, D values near .00. However, the

---

[14] Analyses such as these assume that examinees are guessing at random whenever possible. In fact, examinees often do not guess randomly and may not guess at all when they do not know the answer to a question.

items still serve a useful purpose in the test. In personality and interest inventories, items are sometimes deliberately repeated in order to check on response consistency.

Recycling to the Item Preparation Stage

Recall that the outline of steps in the test development process (Figure 6.1) showed the possibility of reversing course between step 3 (item preparation) and step 4 (item analysis). In fact, when the item analysis process is completed, it may very well be that the test author will decide to prepare more items. It may be that an insufficient number of high-quality items survived the item analysis process. It may also be that insights were gained in the item analysis stage that suggest some new directions for item development. Such new insights may even affect the overall design of the test. Common practice is to proceed from item analysis to standardization. However, recycling back to item preparation does sometimes occur.

Standardization and Ancillary Research Programs

The **standardization program** yields the norms for the test. The program is sometimes called the standardization program, sometimes the norming program. This program is a major part of the complete test development enterprise. It is undertaken after items are selected in the final phase of the item analysis stage. The test that is standardized should be the exact test that is finally published. All the directions, the number of items, time limits, and so on should be fixed; otherwise, the norms resulting from the standardization may be compromised.

We described the nature of standardization programs in Chapter 3 in connection with the treatment of norms. We need not repeat that presentation here. We simply note the place of standardization in the test development process.

Either as part of the standardization program or occurring at about the same time, there will usually be other research programs conducted with the final version of the test but before publication. The nature and extent of these ancillary research programs depend on the scope of the test. Here we mention just some of the possible programs that might be conducted.

Some research programs will be conducted simply by analyzing data from the norming program. These programs are logically independent of the development of norms—the principal purpose of the norming program—but they do not require any new data collection. Analysis of test scores by gender, race, age, geographic region, and other such demographic classifications is often completed with the norming data. Studies of the test's validity may be conducted. The test's relationships with other tests or with ratings by supervisors, clinicians, or teachers may be obtained for subsamples of the norm group. The factor analytic structure of the test may be determined with the norming data.

Several types of reliability studies may be conducted now. For example, studies of test-retest reliability might be undertaken. It is generally not feasible to conduct such a study with everyone in the norming program. However, a subsample of the norming group might be retested at a later date. Since test-retest studies are burdensome, such a study might be conducted with a sample completely independent of the norming group. If the test has more than one form, an alternate form reliability study might also be carried out in conjunction with the norming program or in an independent study at about the same time as the norming program. Measures of internal consistency, for example, coefficient alpha, are easily completed on the entire norming sample; this is simply a statistical analysis, not requiring any new data collection.

There are three types of **equating programs** that might be conducted as part of or, at least, at the same time as the standardization program. First, if there are alternate forms of the test, in order for the norms to apply to all forms, the forms must be equated. Sometimes all forms are normed directly but more commonly one form is normed and the other form(s) equated to the first form in a separate research program. Second, if the test has more than one level, for example, an achievement test spanning grades K–12, then the different levels must be equated. This is often called a "scaling" program, resulting in the development of a continuous scale covering all levels of the test. Third, if the newly standardized test is a revision of a previously standardized test, it may be desirable to provide tables equating the norms on the new and old editions. Such tables allow scores from the older edition to be compared directly with scores from the newer edition of the test.

Preparation of Final Materials and Publication

The final step in the test development process is publication. What exactly is published? In everyday usage of the term *published*, we tend to think of the printing of a test booklet or set of stimuli, such as TAT cards. But publication of a test involves much more than printing a test booklet or set of stimuli. Publication also involves directions for administering and interpreting, technical manuals, scoring reports, and other supplementary materials. For fairly simple tests with limited use, the array of materials may be quite modest: a test booklet, a scoring key, and a 20-page manual covering directions for administering and technical characteristics of the test. For complex tests that are widely used, the array of materials may be staggeringly large. The array may include several types of manuals, supplementary interpretive materials, special technical reports, complex computer programs for scoring and reporting, and versions of the test in foreign languages, large print, or Braille editions.

A published test should have a *technical manual*. This manual is the key source of information about the test's purpose, rationale, and structure. The manual should include information about the test's reliability, validity, and norming procedure. Finally, the manual should include guidelines for interpreting the test's score(s). Some tests may cover all these matters in one manual while other tests may have more than one manual covering these topics.

Many tests today have elaborate *score reports*. The reports may involve graphical presentation of scores and/or translation of numerical scores into narrative form. The more widely used group-administered tests of achievement and ability yield computer-generated reports not only for individuals but also for groups, for example, for classrooms, school buildings, entire school systems, or even entire states.

Finally, publication may entail a variety of *supplementary materials.* For example, some tests have "locator" tests to help test administrators determine which level of a multilevel test is most appropriate for an examinee. Some tests provide special booklets on test score interpretation for students and parents.

Actually, it may be somewhat misleading to identify publication as the last step in the test development process. The process is never complete. Upon publication, no test has an exhaustive demonstration of its validity. Furthermore, there are always more questions about applicability of the test to various special populations. And no matter how perfect the norming program, the norms are time-bound. Thus, there is continuing concern about whether the norms have become outdated due to changes in the target population. For all these reasons, a published test will be subject to additional research even after its publication. Some of this development will originate with the test author(s) and publisher. Other interested users will also undertake studies of the test. Some of these studies will be published in journals devoted to testing as identified in Chapter 2.

> Tests and their supporting documents… are reviewed periodically to determine whether revisions are needed. Revisions or amendments are necessary when new research data, significant changes in the domain, or new conditions of test use and interpretation would either improve the validity of the test scores or suggest that the test is no longer fully appropriate for its intended use. *Standards…*
>
> (AERA/APA/NCME, 1999, p. 42)

Summary

1. The first step in test development is formulating a clear statement of purpose. The statement identifies the variable or construct to be measured and usually includes reference to the target group.
2. Next the general design of the test must be considered. Preliminary design considerations include such matters as test length, item format, number of scores, scoring procedures, and background research on the variable.
3. Among currently used tests, many originated to meet some practical need. Others originated for theoretical purposes. Much test development work involves adaptation or revision of current tests.
4. Selected-response items, with a variety of specific formats, are widely used in testing. The multiple-choice format is the most widely used selected-response type of item.
5. Constructed-response items, also widely used, include essays, oral responses, and performance assessments. These items present special challenges for scoring.
6. There are a variety of suggestions for writing good test items, both selected-response and constructed-response.
7. Item analysis refers to the collection of procedures for empirical tryout and statistical treatment of individual items. There are three phases: the item tryout program, statistical analysis, and item selection.

8. Traditional item statistics include the item difficulty index (p) and item discrimination index (D or r).

9. In IRT methodology, the item characteristic curve and its parameters, especially the difficult and slope parameters, are important factors in selecting items.

10. Factor analysis of items is sometimes used as an item analysis technique.

11. Potential bias in items, which is not simply a matter of group differences in item difficulty, is addressed by judgmental review as well as by several types of statistical analysis. Differential item functioning (DIF) is a common type of analysis for this purpose.

12. Item analysis concepts are approached somewhat differently for criterion-referenced tests, although the traditional methods of analysis often work well with these tests.

13. When item tryout samples are small and selection ratios are small, cross-validation is necessary to avoid or minimize validity shrinkage.

14. Item analysis data are used, along with other criteria such as content specifications, to select items for the final test.

15. There is a relationship between an item's p-value and its maximum possible discrimination index.

16. Norms are developed for the final test in the standardization program. Several other research programs may occur concurrently with the standardization.

17. Final publication involves the actual test as well as manuals, scoring services, and other supplementary materials.

18. Research on the test usually continues after publication. Some of this research will be conducted by the test's author and publisher, while independent investigators also conduct research with the test.

Key Terms

analytic scoring
automated scoring
constructed-response
    item
cross-validation
design issues
differential item
    functioning (DIF)
distractor
equating programs
essay test
graphic rating scale
guessing parameter

high and low group
holistic scoring
item analysis
item characteristic curve
    (ICC)
item difficulty
item discrimination
item information
    function
item stem
Likert format
Mantel-Haenszel
    procedure

performance assessment
point system
portfolio
p-value
Rasch model
selected-response items
semantic differential
slope
standardization program
statement of purpose
validity shrinkage

Exercises

1. Refer to the statements of test purposes in Table 6.1. How might any of these statements be improved?

2. You plan to develop the world's best, most definitive test of self-concept for college students. Answer the following questions about the design of your test:

   How many items will the test have? _____

   How many scores will it report? _____

   Will it be individually or group administered? _____

   About how many minutes will it take to complete? _____

   What type of items will it have (e.g., multiple-choice, constructed-response)? _____

3. Observing the guidelines for writing good test items, for the material covered in this chapter:
   - Write 5 multiple-choice items.
   - Write 5 true-false items.
   - Write 5 essay questions.
   - Have another student critique your items.

4. Suppose you want to measure attitude toward capital punishment, that is, the extent to which a person is in favor of it or opposed to it.
   - Write 5 Likert-type items for this topic.
   - Create 5 items using a graphic rating scale.
   - Have another student critique your items.

5. Refer to the data in Table 6.9.
   - What is the p-value for item 10?
   - What percentage of students in the Low group answered item 23 correctly?
   - Which is the easiest item in the table?
   - What is the difference between High and Low groups in percentage answering correctly for item 29?

6. Refer to Table 6.11. For item 23, determine the p-value for the entire Reference group, then for the entire Focal group.

7. Review the item analysis data given below. D is the discrimination index and p is the item difficulty index.

   Which two items would you eliminate if you wanted to make the final test easier?

   Which two items would you eliminate if you wanted to make the final test harder?

   Which two items would you eliminate to increase the internal consistency of the test?

Item	p	D
1	.60	.20
2	.75	.25
3	.55	.05

4	.90	.15
5	.35	.30
6	.65	.35
7	.60	.40
8	.40	.15
9	.80	.25
10	.85	.10
11	.70	.30
12	.50	.25

8. Refer to the item statistics in Exercise 7. Suppose you were creating a five-item test and you selected items 2, 4, 9, 10, and 11. Assume the item statistics are based on a representative sample. Would the distribution of scores on the five-item test look more like that of Test A or Test B in Figure 6.11?

9. Access, in either electronic or hardcopy form, a review of any test in a recent edition of Buros MMY. What does the review say about the standardization program for the test? How large was the standardization group? Was it representative of the target population for the test?

10. Use the item data in Appendix D3 to generate item statistics (p and D) using any software package.

PART II

Introduction

Part I of this book concentrated on fundamental principles and procedures applicable to all types of tests. Part II proceeds to an examination of particular types of tests, dividing tests into the main categories reviewed in Chapter 1. Following an introduction to theories of intelligence in Chapter 7, Chapters 8-11 cover tests primarily in the cognitive domain. Chapters 12-15 cover tests primarily in the non-cognitive realm. Each chapter in Part II outlines the major uses of tests in a specific category. Then each chapter identifies widely used tests within that category. Next, a few of the widely used tests are given detailed treatment. Within most of the major categories of tests, there are literally hundreds of examples that could be introduced. In accord with our practical orientation, we have usually selected for presentation only the most widely used tests. We definitely avoid the abhorrent practice of cataloging numerous tests with only the barest description of each. One can get such lists of tests from the sources of information presented in Chapter 2. Finally, each chapter or major section of a chapter concludes with some observations or questions about the current status of testing within the category being treated.

CHAPTER 7

Intelligence: Theories and Issues

Objectives

1. Describe the meaning of the term *intelligence* and its practical correlates.

2. Describe key features of the following theories of intelligence:

   Spearman's "g"

   Thurstone's Primary Mental Abilities

   The Hierarchical Model

   Developmental theories

   Information processing/biological models

3. Describe the relationship between theories of intelligence and tests of intelligence.

4. For each of these group comparisons, identify the major research results: sex, age, socioeconomic status, racial/ethnic groups.

5. Summarize the major results for studies of the heritability of intelligence.

Intelligence: Areas of Study

The psychologist's study of intelligence falls broadly into four interrelated but recognizably distinct areas of interest. The first is *theories* about the nature of intelligence. Second is the methodology, both theoretical and applied, for the *measurement* of intelligence. Third is the area of *group differences* in intelligence: by age, gender, socioeconomic level, racial/ethnic groups, and so on. Fourth, there is the question of *hereditary and environmental* influences on development of intelligence. Our principal concern in this book, obviously, is with the second topic: the measurement of intelligence. Chapters 8 and 9 are devoted entirely to this topic. We need to study the first topic, theories of intelligence, because of its interplay with measurement procedures. Good theories help to direct measurement. Measurement helps to stimulate and undergird theoretical developments. In this book, we do not really need to study the third and fourth topics. Nevertheless, the student of psychological testing usually has an intense interest in the matters of group differences and hereditary and environmental influences on intelligence. Hence, in the final part of this chapter, we give an overview of these topics. We do not intend to provide exhaustive treatment of the topics. We will outline major conclusions and point to sources for more detailed coverage of the topics. Before taking up each of these topics, we should pause to consider the meaning of the term *intelligence*, varying names for this term, and general findings about the correlates of intelligence.

The Meaning of Intelligence

What is intelligence? The question has occupied psychologists since the early twentieth century, when Spearman first theorized about its structure and Binet introduced the first practical measurement of it. It is not unusual to encounter statements that we do not know what the term *intelligence* means. Actually, among those who study the topic diligently, there is quite good agreement about the meaning of intelligence, at least for the human species and in Western cultures. In fact, there is probably better agreement about the meaning of the term *intelligence* than there is for many psychological constructs, for example, "personality." To be sure, there is not universal agreement on the definition of intelligence. And we can find authors who give unusual definitions of intelligence, but among psychologists who regularly study this area, there is surprisingly good agreement on what intelligence is, and this agreement has spanned many years.

Several sources provide useful lists of the elements (or manifestations) of intelligence. A series of articles in the *Journal of Educational Psychology* (1921), featuring such legendary authors as Terman, Thorndike, and Thurstone, addressed, in part, the

Think abstractly   **Solve problems**

Identify relationships

Learn quickly   **Memory functions**

Speed of mental processing

Learn from experience   **Plan effectively**

Deal effectively with symbols

FIGURE 7.1 Terms commonly used in the definition of "intelligence."

definition of intelligence.[1] Sixty-five years later, Sternberg and Detterman (1986) undertook a similar effort with another distinguished panel of experts. Although their effort to summarize the viewpoints expressed in the two symposia was fuzzy at best, the principal point of agreement in both cases was concentration on "abstract reasoning, representation, problem solving, decision making" (Sternberg & Detterman, p. 158). Snyderman and Rothman (1987) surveyed 661 psychologists and educational specialists deliberately selected to represent those with expertise in the area of intelligence. More than 95% of respondents agreed with these descriptors of intelligence: abstract thinking or reasoning, problem-solving ability, and capacity to acquire new knowledge; and 70 to 80% agreed that intelligence included memory, adaptation to one's environment, and mental speed. Neisser et al. (1996, p. 77), summarizing the thoughts of a task force appointed by the American Psychological Association to develop a consensus statement on a host of issues related to intelligence, referred to "ability to understand complex ideas, to adapt effectively to the environment, to learn from experience, to engage in various forms of reasoning, to overcome obstacles by taking thought." A panel of 52 leading researchers of intelligence endorsed this definition: "Intelligence is a very general mental capacity that, among other things, involves the ability to reason, plan, solve problems, think abstractly, comprehend complex ideas, learn quickly and learn from experience" (Gottfredson, 1997, p. 13). These sources usually emphasize that intelligence is not simply expertise in some field. Figure 7.1 summarizes the terms commonly used in the definition of intelligence.

---

[1] It was called a "symposium" but was actually just a series of brief articles scattered over three issues of the journal, with an editorial promise for a later wrap-up treatment which, in fact, never appeared. Thus, calling it a "symposium" perhaps suggests more than it really was. We reference here only the editorial introduction.

The Real-World Correlates of Intelligence

Does intelligence, as defined earlier in this chapter, make any difference in people's lives? Answering this question calls for some empirical analysis, some perspective on the empirical results, and some perspective on life itself. Dealing with the first topic is fairly easy; dealing with the second is somewhat more difficult but still within a realm where psychometric and statistical concepts are applicable; and dealing with the third moves us into regions of philosophy and religion where our competence thins.

A vast number of studies have addressed the first question, usually by showing the correlation between performance on an intelligence test and standing on some external criterion; or showing differences in group averages. The external criteria of interest include academic achievement, defined by such indexes as grades, achievement tests, or progression to higher levels of education; job performance, defined by such indexes as supervisors' ratings and promotions; socioeconomic status, defined by such indexes as income and occupational prestige; and general "quality-of-life" issues, defined by such indexes as health status, law-breaking, and family integrity. In general, intelligence is positively related to all these external criteria. Correlations with academic achievement are the highest, ranging from the .80s when the criterion is an achievement test to the .50s when the criterion is grades. Correlations with job performance, for a wide range of occupations but especially at the skilled and professional levels, tend to range in different studies from the .30s to .60s. Correlations (or group differences) with a wide variety of health-related and quality-of-life issues vary considerably but are clearly in a positive direction. For summaries of relevant research on these matters, see Gottfredson (2004), Kuncel, Hezlett, and Ones, D. S. (2004), and Schmidt and Hunter (2004), as well as the book-length, general treatments of intelligence, for example, Brody (1992) and Mackintosh (1998).

Regarding all of this correlational research, the reader should be aware that the research techniques routinely include the various corrections for attenuation (imperfect reliability) given in Chapter 5 and the corrections for range restriction given in Chapter 4 of this book. Those corrections are not just ethereal technicalities; they really are used.

There is very good agreement regarding the general magnitude of the relationship between intelligence and the types of criteria just outlined. Opinion begins to diverge on interpretation of the data. To one interpreter, a correlation of .50 is a "strong" relationship, even exceptionally strong for the types of relationships usually encountered in the behavioral world. To another interpreter that same $r = .50$ is not all that impressive—after all, it accounts for only 25% of the variance. Similarly, a correlation of, say, .30 between an intelligence test and some index of job performance may justify the statement that intelligence is "the most powerful predictor known" for job performance, but at the same time, $r = .30$ is simply not a very powerful predictor. These simple examples remind us that the bare facts about the correlates of intelligence are subject to varying interpretation. On the one hand, intelligence, as measured by the types of tests described in the next two chapters, clearly has noteworthy relationships with a wide variety of variables usually considered important in life. Anyone who denies that is not paying attention to the facts. On the other hand, intelligence does not tell the complete story about anything.

Anyone who implies that it does is also not paying attention to the facts. Other factors that make a difference include education and experience; personality, motivation, and effort—and sheer chance.

What to Call Them?

Perhaps more so than for any other type of test, the tests considered in the next several chapters seem to be in a perpetual identity crisis. Psychologists are content to call a personality test a personality test and an achievement test an achievement test. However, they become anxious and ambiguous about naming the tests covered in Chapters 8 and 9.

In earlier days, the standard labels for these tests were intelligence, mental ability, or aptitude. Some of the tests retain use of these terms. However, a host of alternative terms has emerged in recent years. There are two reasons for the change. First, theories about the structure of human intelligence have evolved over time. The next section examines this issue. Hence, test authors have sought terms more clearly aligned with the specific purpose of the test. For example, the *Otis-Lennon Mental Ability Test* (successor to the *Otis Intelligence Scale*) is now the *Otis-Lennon School Ability Test*. That is, rather than address exactly what "mental ability" means, the test emphasizes that it attempts to measure the abilities needed in school. Second, there has been great fear that people assume that intelligence or aptitude is innate or exclusively hereditary. To counter this assumption, test authors have chosen terms emphasizing that the test measures developed abilities, not innate aptitudes. For example, the *Scholastic Aptitude Test* became the *Scholastic Assessment Test*, and later simply the SAT. Thus, we now encounter a bewildering array of terms such as "cognitive assessment," "differential abilities," or simply "vocabulary" in the titles of tests generally considered measures of intelligence or mental ability. In this and the next chapter, we use the terms *intelligence* and *mental ability* on the assumption that the reader will keep the latter cautions in mind.

Key Points Summary 7.1

Four Major Areas for Psychologists' Study of Intelligence

1. Theories about Intelligence
2. Measurement of Intelligence
3. Group Differences in Intelligence
4. Hereditary/Environmental Influences on Intelligence

Theories of Intelligence

Theories about the nature of what we are trying to measure play a more prominent role in the area of intelligence testing than in any other area of testing. Hence, before describing particular tests, we summarize major theories about intelligence—just enough to provide the necessary background for understanding the development and application of intelligence tests. For more thorough discussion of theories of intelligence, see Brody (1992), Mackintosh (1998), Wolman (1985), and various articles in the *Encyclopedia of Human Intelligence* (Sternberg, 1994a).

References to theories about intelligence are common in the manuals for intelligence tests. Read the sample statements from such manuals presented in Table 7.1. We need some familiarity with the theories to understand the tests. For example, what is the "g" referenced in the Wechsler manual? What is a higher-order factor? What is Vernon's "hierarchical theory" in the Otis-Lennon manual? Notice, again, the reference to "g." What are the "fluid and crystallized abilities" in the description of the Stanford-Binet? These citations refer to elements of various theories of intelligence.

The historical interaction between theories of intelligence and development of specific tests has been peculiar. Many of the most widely used tests developed with only an informal theoretical base. Once developed, the tests stimulated research about their theoretical implications. Relatively few tests have been direct outgrowths of a particular theory about intelligence. However, recently developed tests, both revisions of older tests and entirely new tests, seem to be more influenced by

TABLE 7.1   *Sample Statements Referring to Theories of Intelligence in Test Manuals*

From the manual for the *Wechsler Intelligence Scale for Children*, Third Edition:
"Approaches to isolating the g contained within the Wechsler scales and other tests have included the extraction of an unrotated first factor … second order factor analysis … identification of a higher-order factor through hierarchical factor analysis … and use of the Full Scale IQ score based on its correlation with the general factor." (Wechsler, 1991, p. 180)

From the *Otis-Lennon School Ability Test, Eighth Edition, Technical Manual*:
"The most satisfactory theoretical framework for the OLSAT series is the Hierarchical Structure of Human Abilities … [the] "general factor" (g) is placed at the top of the hierarchy. One level below are the two major group factors. … Immediately below these are the minor group factors and specific factors. (Otis & Lennon, 2003, p. 5)

From the *Technical Manual* for the *Stanford-Binet Intelligence Scales, Fifth Edition* (SB5):
The use of a hierarchical model of intelligence (with a global g factor and multiple factors at a second level) . . . is repeated in SB5. (Roid, 2003b, p. 6)

From the *Wechsler Adult Intelligence Scale. Third Edition—Wechsler Memory Scale, Third Edition Technical Manual*:
"Several theories of cognitive functioning emphasize the assessment of fluid reasoning … The new WAIS-III subtest, Matrix Reasoning, has been added to enhance measurement of this domain." (Wechsler, 1997, p. 12)

theoretical considerations. We note these influences when describing particular tests in Chapters 8 and 9.

Two Classical Theories

There are two classical theories of intelligence. They have dominated the literature on the nature of intelligence. We begin the description of various theories with these two classical approaches.

Spearman's "g"

Charles **Spearman** (1904, 1927a, 1927b), an Englishman, developed what is generally considered the first formal theory about human mental ability. Chapter 1 contained a brief description of this theory. Spearman based his theory on examination of the correlations between many tests of simple sensory functions. He thought that these correlations were sufficiently high to conclude that performance on the tests was mostly dependent on one general mental ability. He called this general ability **"g"** (always lowercase g). Of course, the correlations among the various measures were not perfect. Each test had some unique or specific variance, independent of "g." Thus, any set of tests had a series of "s" factors and one "g" factor. Spearman also relegated error variance to the "s" factors. Hence, each "s" contained some variance unique to a specific ability plus error variance. However, many summaries of Spearman's theory mention only "g" and "s."

Figure 7.2 depicts Spearman's theory. Each oval in the figure represents a test. The degree of overlap between the ovals represents the degree of correlation between them. The large area in the center corresponds to "g," the general factor in mental ability. Each oval also has an area that does not overlap with other ovals. The areas of nonoverlap are the "s" factors, specific to that particular test.

Since the theory has two types of factors (g and a series of s's), Spearman called it the **two-factor theory.** However, the essential factor in the theory is "g." The "s's" are not of much interest. Hence, despite Spearman's use of the two-factor

---

Key Points Summary 7.2
Major Theories of Intelligence

- Two Classical Theories
  Spearman's "g"
  Thurstone's Primary Mental Abilities
- Hierarchical Models
- Developmental Theories
- Information Processing and Biological Models

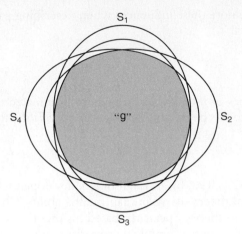

FIGURE 7.2 Illustration of Spearman's theory of "g."

terminology, the theory is usually called a one-factor or unifactor theory of intelligence. Sometimes it is simply called the theory of "g."

In the process of developing his theory of human intelligence, Spearman worked out the elements of factor analysis. We reviewed this statistical technique earlier (p. 190). By today's standards, his methods were quite primitive. However, he showed remarkable insight regarding how to think about the relationships among many tests, thus pointing the way for a wide variety of applications in testing and other social sciences.

Spearman's "g" remains a central concept in psychologists' thinking about intelligence. It serves as a common reference point in test manuals, as well as in other theories about intelligence. We should note that Spearman's original works, though now dated in many respects, provide a rich source of insights for the modern student of psychology. Many contemporary summaries of Spearman's work oversimplify his thinking. For example, in addition to "g," he credited "w" (will) and "c" (character) with effects on test performance. However, "g" is the central concept with the most enduring influence in the field.

Thurstone's Primary Mental Abilities

Throughout the early years in the debate over the nature of intelligence, the American psychologist L. L. **Thurstone**, at the University of Chicago, provided the main competition to Spearman's theory of "g." Whereas Spearman said that the correlations among different tests were high enough to think that they were mostly measuring one common factor, Thurstone (1938) believed that the correlations were low enough to think they were measuring several largely independent factors, thus yielding a **multiple-factor theory**. Figure 7.3 depicts Thurstone's theory. As with the illustration of Spearman's theory, the degree of overlap among the ovals represents the level of correlation. Thurstone emphasized the separation between ovals, whereas Spearman emphasized the overlap. Each of the *"P's"* in Figure 7.2 is a relatively independent factor. Like Spearman, in the process of developing his theory, Thurstone made major contributions to factor analytic methodology. His books,

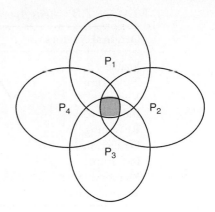

FIGURE 7.3   Illustration of Thurstone's theory of primary mental abilities.

The Vectors of the Mind (Thurstone, 1938), and especially its revision, *Multiple-Factor Analysis* (Thurstone, 1947), helped define modern factor analysis.

In his most famous study, Thurstone (1938) administered a battery of 60 tests (15 hours of testing!) to 240 students. (The sample was highly selective: all males and nearly all students at the University of Chicago.) Thurstone extracted twelve factors, nine of which he considered interpretable. He called these group factors or **primary mental abilities.** The latter term stuck. Table 7.2 lists the nine factors originally identified by Thurstone, with brief descriptions of each factor.

TABLE 7.2   *Thurstone's Original Nine Primary Mental Abilities*

S	Spatial	Spatial, especially visual, ability as in doing mental rotations of geometric figures or counting hidden blocks
P	Perceptual	Perceptual, especially speed of visual perception, as in scanning a printed page to identify letters or comparing columns of numbers
N	Numerical	Numerical, especially, speed and accuracy of computation
V	Verbal	Verbal, including verbal analogies, antonyms, reading comprehension
M	Memory	Rote, short-term memory, as in paired-associate learning
W	Words	Word fluency, especially dealing with isolated words, as in the disarranged word test or word fluency test
I	Induction	Finding a rule or principle to solve a problem, as in number series, figure classification, or pattern analogies
R	Reasoning	Reasoning, especially when dealing with a closed-solution problem as in arithmetic reasoning
D	Deduction	A factor weakly defined by several tests calling for application of a rule

TABLE 7.3   *Tests Appearing in Different Versions of Primary Mental Ability (PMA) Tests*

Original Factors	In Most PMA Tests	In Some PMA Tests
Spatial	X	
Numerical	X	
Verbal	X	
Induction		
Reasoning	X	
Deduction		
Perceptual		X
Memory		X
Word fluency		X

Interestingly, Thurstone was the only major theorist who authored mental ability tests that attained any widespread use. There were editions from different publishers and for different age levels. None of the tests is currently in use. Understandably, all the tests included the tag "primary mental abilities" (PMA), which we will use as a generic descriptor here. The various versions of the PMA test covered only five of the original nine factors—but not always the same five! Thus, there are many references in the literature to Thurstone's five factors, but one easily becomes confused trying to identify exactly what the five factors are. As summarized in Table 7.3, of the original nine factors, four factors appear in nearly all versions of PMA tests: spatial, numerical, verbal, and reasoning. The original induction, reasoning, and deduction factors collapse into a single reasoning factor. The perceptual, memory, and word fluency factors appear in some PMA tests but not in others, always bringing the total number of tests to five. Of these last three factors, the perceptual factor most frequently appeared as the fifth factor in a PMA test.

Thurstone was not the only person to propose a multifactor theory of intelligence. In what he called the structure of intellect model, J. P. Guilford (1956, 1959b, 1967, 1985, 1988) presented what is undoubtedly the most extreme version of a multifactor theory of intelligence. According to Guilford, mental ability manifests itself along three principal axes: contents, products, and operations. Each of these axes contains further subdivisions—five for content, six for products, and six for operations. The three axes may be depicted in the form of a cube, with the subdivisions forming cells, thus yielding $5 \times 6 \times 6 = 180$ cells, which Guilford posited to be relatively independent of one another.[2]

---

[2]For contents operations, and products, respectively, the first version of Guilford's model had $4 \times 5 \times 6 = 120$ cells (Guilford, 1956). The second version had $5 \times 5 \times 6 = 150$ cells (Guilford, 1959b). The latest version, described here, had 180 cells. Various sources might cite any one of these versions without mentioning the evolution of the model.

Guilford's theory has not stood the test of time (and research). But one of the distinctions built into the model has endured, that is, the distinction between divergent production and convergent production. These were subdivisions along the operations axis. **Divergent production** involves producing alternative or unusual solutions. **Convergent production** involves identification of a single correct answer. That is, in convergent thinking, the mind converges on one answer. In divergent thinking, the mind diverges from the usual path to seek diverse possibilities. This reference to divergent thinking distinction helped stimulate a great deal of research on creative thinking.

TRY IT! ....

Answer these questions. They illustrate the difference between convergent and divergent thinking.

Convergent: What is the most common use for a brick? (One correct answer.)

Divergent: In how many different ways can you use a brick? (Many possible answers.)

....

Hierarchical Models

The "one versus many" argument, as framed by Spearman and Thurstone, has proved to be one of the enduring battles in psychology. **Hierarchical models** of intelligence seek a compromise position. They admit that there are many separate abilities but note that these many abilities are arranged in a hierarchy with just one or a few dominant factors at the top of the hierarchy. Several hierarchical models have been advanced. We will examine three of them.

First, let us add this aside. As previously noted, the development of Spearman's and Thurstone's theories went hand-in-hand with developments in factor analysis. So, too, with the hierarchical models. Especially important for these theories were the notions of oblique (as opposed to orthogonal) rotation of axes, second-order (and even higher order) factors and, more recently, confirmatory factor analysis and structural equation modeling. Explanation of these more advanced topics would take us too far afield for this introductory book. However, the reader should be aware that the hierarchical models depend on these methodologies.

Cattell's Fluid and Crystallized Intelligence

Roughly contemporaneous with Guilford's work, R. B. Cattell[3] entered the theoretical fray with his theory of fluid and crystallized intelligence. In his earliest work on the subject (Cattell, 1940), he excoriated Binet for producing a test that was too verbal and too dependent on schooling. He proposed a "perceptual intelligence test" based mostly on figural items such as matrices and mazes. He called it a culture-fair test. Later, Cattell (1963) elaborated and refined (Horn & Cattell, 1966) the Gf-Gc theory. Gc, a

---

[3] No relation to James McKeen Cattell, considered the father of mental testing (see pp. 23–24).

general **crystallized intelligence,** is the sum of everything one has learned: a fund of information, relationships, and mental skills developed through education, experience, and practice. Gf, a general **fluid intelligence,** might be thought of as raw mental horsepower. It probably has some neurological substrate. The difference between Gf and Gc corresponds roughly, although not exactly, to the difference between hereditary and environmental influences on intelligence. The difference might also be thought of as the difference between the common terms "potential" and "actual."

Both Gf and Gc are composed of a number of more specific factors. That is, there are several components to Gf and several components to Gc. Thus, the theory qualifies as a hierarchical model. There is some difference of opinion as to whether Gf and Gc ultimately merge into a kind of super "g." For recent summaries of the theory, see Kline (1991, 1994) and Horn (1994).

Cattell completed much of his work on this theory in collaboration with J. L. Horn. Hence, the theory is sometimes called the Cattell-Horn theory More often, it is known as Cattell's theory of fluid and crystallized intelligence or, simply, Gf-Gc theory. Whatever its label, the theory has proved enormously appealing to psychologists. Gf is of special interest. Can we measure this raw mental horsepower, unaffected by cultural influences, education, home background, and so on? But how do you get at Gf except through the manifestation of developed abilities, which by definition are Gc? Some of the information processing models considered in the following sections attempt to address precisely this question.

Vernon's Model

Philip Vernon (1950, 1961, 1965) elaborated what has become perhaps the most widely cited hierarchical theory of intelligence. Unlike most of the other theorists cited here, Vernon himself did little original research. He tried to summarize in a convenient way the enormous amount of research completed by others until about 1950 and to bring some unity to conflicting theoretical orientations. His first summary was published in 1950. It was just slightly updated in 1961 and received some further elaboration in 1965. Figure 7.4 shows Vernon's widely cited summary. Vernon actually had several other summaries, some of which are much more detailed than the one shown here (see, e.g., Vernon 1947, 1965) However, we use only Figure 7.4 since it is the summary most often referenced in the professional literature.

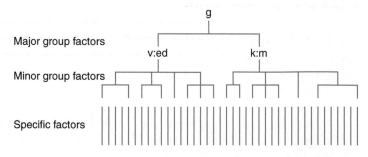

FIGURE 7.4   Vernon's hierarchical model of intelligence.

Source: From Vernon, P. E. The Structure of Human Abilities (2nd ed.). Copyright © 1961 by Taylor & Francis. Reproduced by permission of Thomson Publishing Services.

According to this model, there are a series of narrowly defined abilities. The vertical lines at the bottom of the figure represent these specific abilities. These abilities tend to cluster under a number of "minor group factors." (To say that some specific abilities "cluster" means that some are more highly correlated among themselves.) The minor group factors, then, cluster in two major group categories or factors. Vernon called these v:ed (verbal: educational) and k:m (spatial: mechanical). The k:m factor is sometimes called the "practical" factor. The two major group factors are themselves somewhat related and form an overall, general mental ability. This is Spearman's "g."

Vernon did not attempt to specify exactly how many minor group factors there are. He did mention what at least some of these minor group factors are. Prominent among the minor group factors under v:ed in Vernon's model are such factors as verbal and numerical abilities. Minor group factors under k:m include spatial ability, mechanical information, and psychomotor abilities. Some aspects of mathematical abilities also fit under k:m.

Carroll's Summary

John Carroll has labored in the factor analytic vineyard for many years. In the 1980s, he undertook to summarize the hundreds of factor analyses completed on human abilities. His monumental work, *Human Cognitive Abilities: A Survey of Factor Analytic Studies* (Carroll, 1993), concludes with his own summary of a hierarchical model. Figure 7.5 presents Carroll's model.

Carroll uses three strata. In fact, he calls it the **three-stratum theory**. General intelligence is at the highest level. This is Spearman's "g." Carroll incorporates Cattell's Gf and Gc at the second level. However, there are a number of other second-level group factors in addition to Gf and Gc. Some of these other second-level factors correspond rather well with some of Thurstone's primary mental abilities (see Table 7.2). Finally, at stratum I, there are a host of more specific, narrowly defined abilities. Carroll notes that some of these specific abilities are factorially complex, thus contributing to more than one group factor. In Figure 7.5, the length of the lines from the box for general intelligence to the boxes for the group factors is roughly indicative of the relationship between "g" and a group factor: the shorter the line, the greater the relationship. For example, the line from Gc to g is relatively short. Gc is highly related to overall g, although not as highly related as Gf. There is a long line from g to 2R: Broad Retrieval Ability because 2R is less related to g. Carroll's summary in Figure 7.5 is worthy of careful study. It is probably the best current summary of all the factor analytic approaches to the definition of human intelligence. Sternberg and Kaufman (1998) stated that Carroll "does masterfully integrate a large and diverse factor-analytic literature, thereby giving great authority to his model" (p. 488). Lubinski (2004, p. 98) noted that "Carroll's (1993) three stratum model of cognitive abilities is unquestionably the most definitive treatment."

Developmental Theories

All the theories previously treated, the classical and the hierarchical, are sometimes called **psychometric theories** of intelligence. They depend heavily on the analysis of the relationships among specific tests. However, some theories of human

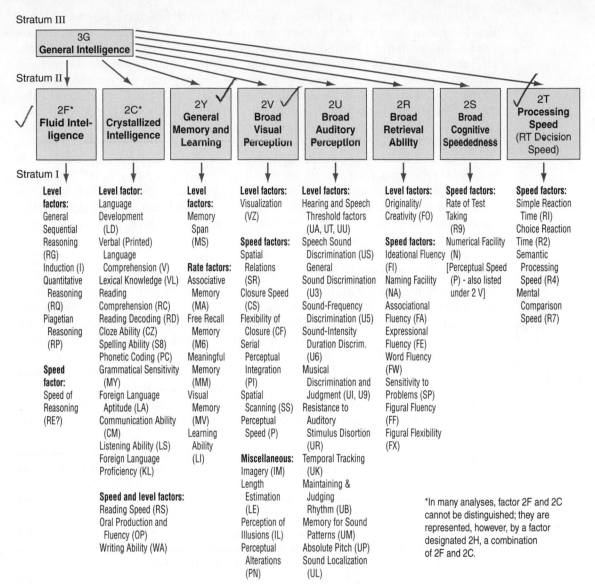

FIGURE 7.5   Carroll's three-stratum hierarchical model of human intelligence.

Source: From Carroll, J. B. Human cognitive abilities: A survey of factor analytic studies (p. 626). Copyright © 1993. Reprinted with the permission of Cambridge University Press.

intelligence arise from other considerations or perspectives. One such perspective is development. The key element in these **developmental theories** is how the mind develops with age and experience.

Before examining specific developmental theories, let us note that such theories, whether about intelligence or some other trait, tend to have the following

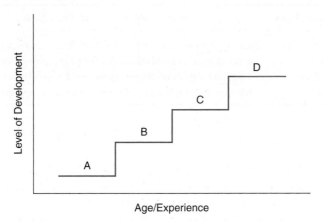

FIGURE 7.6   Illustration of stage-based theories.

characteristics. Figure 7.6 helps to summarize these characteristics. First, these theories are **stage-based**. Development proceeds through a serious of stages. Each stage has special features that make it qualitatively different from other stages. Hence, development is not simply accumulating more of the same thing, for example, more information or more vocabulary. It's like the caterpillar and the butterfly: The butterfly is not just a bigger caterpillar. That is why development in Figure 7.6 proceeds as a series of discrete steps rather than as the typical, continuous growth curve. Second, the sequencing of stages is invariant. Everyone passes through the stages in the same order, though not necessarily at the same age. Thus, one cannot skip a stage. If there are four stages in the theory (assuming the theory is correct), you must move from stage A to B, then B to C, and so on. You cannot go from stage A immediately to stage D.

Third, the stages are irreversible Once having reached stage C, you will not fall back to stage B. You can go from caterpillar to butterfly but not from butterfly to caterpillar. Finally, there is usually (though not always) a relationship between progression through the stages and age. For example, on average, children may reach stage C at age 7 or stage D at age 12. There may be variability around this average. This progression by age usually assumes certain common experiences. A child who grows up in a closet will not develop. Of course, all these characteristics are idealized. In practice, a good stage theory will approximate these conditions but may not meet them exactly.

Stage-based theories occur in areas of psychology other than intelligence. For example, there are stage-based theories of personality development, the best known being Erikson's theory of psychosocial development. There is also the well-known stage-based theory of grief.

Piaget's Theory of Cognitive Development

Without doubt, the most prominent of the developmental theories of intelligence is that of Jean **Piaget**. Piaget's theory has been enormously influential in

TABLE 7.4   *Piaget's Main Stages of Intellectual Development*

Name of Stage	Typical Ages	Some Behaviors at This Level
Sensorimotor	Birth–2 yrs	Limited to sensory input, lack of object permanence
Preoperational	2–6 yrs	Uses words to symbolize. Lacks principles of conservation
Concrete Operational	7–12 yrs	Uses principles of conservation and reversibility
Formal Operational	12+ yrs	Mature adult thinking in terms of hypotheses, cause and effect

developmental psychology and early childhood education. According to Piaget, the human mind develops through four main stages (see, e.g., Piaget, 1950, 1983; Piaget & Inhelder, 1969). Table 7.4 outlines these stages.

Although Piaget's theory of cognitive development has been very influential in psychology and education in general, it has not had much influence on the field of testing. Piagetian research has its own cadre of test-like tasks. However, they have not found their way into the kinds of tests psychologists use for clinical testing. This is rather curious because the tasks are simple and could easily be incorporated into the types of individually administered intelligence tests we examine in the next chapter. Some of the tasks are even amenable to a multiple-choice format that could be used in a group-administered test. However, the simple fact of the matter is that Piagetian tasks have remained largely the province of laboratory research projects.

TRY IT!

Can you identify any way in which you think fundamentally differently now than you did, say, 10 or 15 years ago—not just having more information, but a radically different way of thinking about the world? If you can identify such a transformation, this may represent part of a stage-based theory of mental ability.

Information Processing and Biological Theories of Intelligence

Information processing and biological theories of human intelligence are partially distinct but also intersect with one another at a number of points. An **information processing model** emphasizes not the content of what is known but how that content is processed. Computer processing often serves as an analogy for information processing models. **Biological models** emphasize brain functioning as the basis for understanding human intelligence. That is, whatever human intelligence is, it must function through the brain. Thus, we need to study what the brain does in order to understand intelligence. Of course, the neural networks in the brain are often compared to computer processing. Hence, the two types of models are not entirely distinct.

Elementary Cognitive Tasks (ECTs)

Within many of the information processing approaches to understanding human intelligence, an essential element is the **elementary cognitive task** or **ECT**. An ECT is a relatively simple task that calls for some type of mental processing. Researchers hope that performance on the ECT will provide a window on mental functioning. In fact, the ECT may provide a relatively direct measure of the efficiency of mental processing, something at the root of intelligence. Because the tasks are relatively simple, they at least give the appearance of being free from educational and other cultural experiences For this reason, some researchers hope that performance on the tasks will provide a culture-free, unbiased measure of intelligence.

The research literature contains a host of ECTs. Let us give examples of a few of them. One is *simple reaction time*. A person responds to the onset of a light in the center of the box, as shown in Figure 7.7, by depressing a switch. Consider what must happen. The onset of the light must be observed. Then the person must "decide" to press the switch. Finally, a motor response must occur. Although this does not seem like intelligent behavior, the speed with which the person can execute all these functions may provide the substratum of human intelligence.

Next, consider what is called *choice reaction time*. Refer again to Figure 7.7. A light may occur on either the left or the right. The person depresses a switch if the light occurs on the right but not if it occurs on the left. Consider what must happen. The person must sense a light, then decide if it is the target light (right), and finally execute an action. The task can be made somewhat more complicated, although still very simple, by adding more lights. Another variation on this task is to have the person's finger already depressing the switch, then move from that switch to the light when it comes on. In this version, we separately measure the time

FIGURE 7.7   Reaction time device.

Source: Lafayette Instrument Company, Inc. Reproduced by permission.

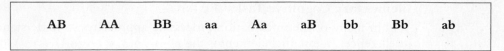

FIGURE 7.8   Examples of letter pairs used in an ECT.

required for the motor response (moving the hand) and other aspects of the total reaction.

Here is another example of an ECT. The person is presented with two letters, appearing on a computer monitor. See Figure 7.8 for examples of pairs of letters. The task is to indicate whether the letters are physically identical. For example, letters "aa" are physically identical; the letters aA are not physically identical. Or task may be to indicate whether the letters have name identity; that is, they name same letter (e.g., aA), although they are not physically identical.

Yet another ECT utilizing letters is the semantic verification task. It uses the three letters A, B, and C in different orders. Then a statement is paired with the letters, for example, "A after B" or "C between A and B." The person must indicate whether the statement is True or False. See Figure 7.9 for examples. The items appear in succession on the screen in rapid order.

A final example of an ECT is inspection time. In this task, the subject sees two parallel lines flashed rapidly on a tachistiscope or computer monitor. The task is simply to tell which line is longer. Again, the now familiar paradigm: sensory input, coding, determining, comparing, reacting. Stokes and Bohrs (2001) provide an example of an inspection time task using letters. See Deary and Stough (1996) for further description of inspection time tasks and their relationship to intelligence.

In all these examples, the researcher can measure over several trials not only the average reaction time but also the variability (standard deviation) in reaction time. Of course, with enough time—and not very much time is needed—almost anyone would get perfect scores on these tasks. But how well can one perform when the items appear rapidly? It is also possible to contrast scores on different versions of the tasks, for example, on the physical identity versus name identify versions of letter matching.

We have provided here several examples of the types of tasks used in the information processing approach to studying intelligence. The essential point is that in all these tasks the researchers hope that processing the information will tell us something

Letters on Screen	Statement	Mark True (T) or False (F)	
B C A	B between C and A	T	F
C B	B after C	T	F
A C B	A before C and B	T	F

FIGURE 7.9   Examples of items in the semantic verification task.

about the basic nature of intelligence and do so free from cultural influences. This is what Brody (1992) calls "the search for the holy grail" (p. 50).

Jensen's Theory

One of the principal proponents of an information processing approach to intelligence is Arthur **Jensen**. Jensen is most famous (or infamous) for his article in the *Harvard Educational Review* on black–white differences in intelligence (Jensen, 1969). In most of his research, published in numerous articles, he has concentrated on the relationships between ECTs and general intelligence. In *The g Factor: The Science of Mental Ability*, Jensen (1998) provided a comprehensive summary of his research and theoretical position.

Figure 7.10 summarizes Jensen's model. The direction of the arrows indicates causality in the figure. At the bottom of the figure are reaction time tasks, an assortment of ECTs. Various information processes (P_1, P_2, etc) determine performance on these tasks. In turn, the P's are determined by a general information processing factor (IP), as well as by a pure speed of reaction time (RT) factor. Fluid intelligence determines the IP factor, but not the RT factor. In the other direction, it is fluid

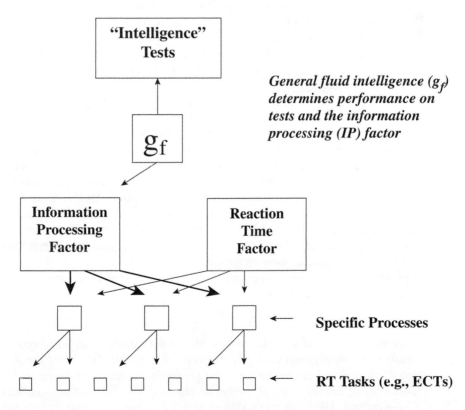

FIGURE 7.10 Schematic illustration of Jensen's information processing model of intelligence.

Source: After Jensen, 1998.

intelligence that determines performance on psychometric tests, such as those we study in Chapters 8 and 9.

What is of principal interest is "g," specifically fluid intelligence. The "g" will determine performance on tests. However, performance on the RT tasks, according to Jensen's reasoning, also reflects "g," as mediated by some intermediate processes. In Jensen's model, performance on ECTs provides the avenue to "g."

Sternberg's Triarchic Theory

In a prolific series of books, articles, and presentations, **Sternberg** has propounded his **triarchic theory** of intelligence. The first full exposition of the theory was given in *Beyond IQ: A Triarchic Theory of Intelligence* (Sternberg, 1985). For a useful summary of the theory, consult Sternberg (1994b). According to this theory, intelligence has three facets. Each facet, in turn has a number of subdivisions. A host of triads populate the theory. The theory has three subtheories: componential, experiential, and contextual. This is the triarchy in the theory's title. The *componential* subtheory refers to mental processes. It includes three types of processes. First, there are three metacomponents: planning, monitoring, and evaluating. Such processes are sometimes called executive functions. They govern other operations. The second componential process is performance. This involves the actual solution of a problem, under the watchful eye of the metacomponents. The third mental process specified in the componential subtheory is knowledge-acquisition. It, too, has three parts: encoding (encoding the information), combination (combining elements of what has been encoded), and comparison (comparing elements that have been encoded). The *experiential* subtheory deals with task familiarity, ranging from the completely novel to tasks that are so familiar that their performance is automatic. The *contextual* subtheory stipulates three ways of dealing with the environment: adapting to it, changing it, or selecting a different one.

The componential subtheory has been the most widely cited part of the triarchic theory. Because this part of the theory concentrates on processes, we classify the theory with other information processing theories. Although it is not technically a part of the triarchic theory, descriptions of the theory often include a methodology called **componential analysis.** This method attempts to break down parts of the approaches to a problem, then measure the time involved in executing each part. As a spin-off from the triarchic theory, Sternberg sometimes emphasizes what he calls "tacit knowledge" (Sternberg & Wagner, 1986) and "practical intelligence," a notion very similar to that of adaptive functioning that we consider in Chapter 8.

Gardner's Theory of Multiple Intelligences

In a veritable flood of publications, Howard **Gardner** has advanced his theory of **multiple intelligences or MI theory.** We classify Gardner's theory in the biological category because he refers frequently to brain functioning and evolutionary concepts in his writings, although he also uses other criteria. Gardner (1983; see also Gardner, 1986) first announced seven intelligences: linguistic, musical, logical-mathematical, spatial, bodily-kinesthetic, intrapersonal, and interpersonal. Another book (Gardner, 1993) reproduced some of these expositions and further elaborated the theory, particularly regarding educational applications. However, the theory remained basically the same. Linguistic, logical-mathematical, and spatial intelligence are well represented in other theories. Musical, bodily-kinesthetic, intrapersonal, and interpersonal as types of intelligence are mostly peculiar to Gardner's theory. Most people would consider these functions as something distinct from intelligence, for example as part of a psychomotor domain or as part of personality.

More recently, Gardner (1999) has announced the addition of three and possibly four additional types of intelligence. They include naturalist, spiritual, existential, and moral intelligence. For example, Gardner defines naturalist intelligence as "expertise in the recognition and classification of the numerous species—flora and fauna—of [the] environment" (p. 48). Under spiritual intelligence, Gardner mentions concern with cosmic or existential issues, encountering higher truth, and having an effect on other people.

Gardner's MI theory has been enormously popular in educational circles. In some cases, the theory has spawned entire school curricula. The theory is purveyed at educational meetings as if it were the final word, perhaps the only word, on theories of intelligence.[4] In terms of educational implications, the main thrust of Gardner's MI theory seems to be twofold. First, maximize everyone's potential. Second, everyone is good at something. These may be useful maxims for approaching education. However, they do not constitute an adequate theory of intelligence.

Simultaneous and Sequential Processing: The PASS Theory

The **PASS theory**, elaborated by Das, Naglieri, and Kirby (1994), is an information processing model with explicit reference to biological foundations, specifically to various areas of the brain. Essential elements of the theory originated with the work of the Russian neuropsychologist A. R. Luria on mentally retarded and brain-injured individuals. Figure 7.11 provides a simplified outline of the PASS theory. The theory postulates three functional units. Each unit's activity occurs in specific cerebral areas. The first unit is *attention* or arousal. Quite simply, the person has to be awake and paying attention for information to get into the system. The second functional unit receives and processes information. A key feature of the theory is that there are two types of processes: sequential and simultaneous. **Simultaneous processing** deals with holistic, integrated material. That

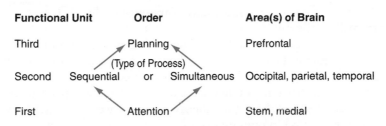

Functional Unit — **Order** — **Area(s) of Brain**

Third — Planning — Prefrontal
(Type of Process)
Second — Sequential or Simultaneous — Occipital, parietal, temporal
First — Attention — Stem, medial

FIGURE 7.11   Outline of the PASS model.

---

[4] The four recent additions to Gardner's list of types of intelligence have not yet been the subject of much discussion in the research or popular literature.

is, the material is dealt with all at once or simultaneously. Test items might include verbal meaning, arithmetic reasoning, and spatial relations. **Sequential processing** deals with temporally ordered or chain-like events. Test items might include spelling and short-term memory. Das (1994) notes that sequential and simultaneous processing are the same as serial and parallel processing in computer terminology. The third functional unit involves *planning*. More generally, this unit includes what other theories call the executive functions: monitoring, evaluating, directing, and so on. Das et al. (1994) suggest that "planning is the essence of human intelligence" (p. 17). Nevertheless, some descriptions of the theory and tests based on it concentrate almost exclusively on the two processes: simultaneous and sequential.

The order of letters in the PASS acronym may lead to confusion. Figure 7.11 shows the order dictated by the theory: First A (attention), then either S or S (sequential or simultaneous processing), then P (planning). However, that order does not yield a simple acronym.

Two tests explicitly use PASS theory for their development and interpretation: The *Kaufman Assessment Battery for Children* (K-ABC; Kaufman & Kaufman, 1983) and the *Cognitive Assessment System* (CAS; Naglieri & Das, 1997).

Current Status of Testing in Relation to the Theories

In contemporary practice, we note the following generalizations regarding the relationship between theories of intelligence and the everyday practice of mental ability testing.

1. Clearly, among the most widely used tests, some version of a hierarchical model predominates. In the classic battle between "one" (Spearman) and "many" (Thurstone), both are winners (or losers, depending on your point of view). Today, all the major tests give a total score, usually acknowledging it as indicative of "g." All the major tests also give a number of subscores corresponding to broad group factors. Commonly reported group factors are verbal, nonverbal, spatial, memory, and numerical or quantitative. Vernon's model, Gf-Gc theory, and Carroll's three-stratum theory are all widely cited in the manuals for contemporary mental ability tests. Thus, the psychologist must have some knowledge of hierarchical models in order to make sense out of today's mental ability tests.

Just because a test manual says it is using a particular theory does not mean that the test actually uses that theory or that the theory is a valid one. In some instances a test manual claims to use a particular theory, but connection between the theory and the test's content and structure is tenuous. Even where there appears to be a reasonable match between test and theory, the theory may be a weak one. It is always necessary to examine the test on its own merits.

2. Information processing and biological models, to date, have not had a great influence on testing. This is surprising. Discussion of and research on these models dominates current literature on intelligence. For example, the work of Sternberg and Gardner is widely cited, in both professional and popular sources. Work on elementary cognitive tasks (ECTs), for example, the work of Jensen and others, abounds in journals. Yet we do not see much practical effect of these models on everyday testing by psychologists. (One minor exception to this generalization is use of the PASS model by a few tests.) If major changes are to come in the measurement of human intelligence, they are likely to come from the information processing models. However, it has not happened yet. The simple fact of the matter is that performance on the processing tasks does not correlate very highly with the more established measures of intelligence. Furthermore, the processing tasks are rather clumsy for ordinary use.

3. Developmental theories of intelligence have not exerted much influence on practical measurement of mental ability. This, too, is surprising. Piaget's work has dominated thinking about mental ability in developmental psychology for decades. Yet, it has had little effect on testing. Piagetian tasks remain largely confined to laboratory use.

Group Differences in Intelligence

Few topics in psychology generate more curiosity, and controversy, than group differences in intelligence. People in Western cultures have a particular fascination with these differences, probably more so than is healthy: It borders on an obsession. Our review of group differences in intelligence should begin with a consideration of *three perspectives.* These perspectives help diffuse some of the emotional charge often associated with these differences. Actually, these perspectives are important regardless of whether we are considering differences in intelligence or any other trait. They apply to group differences in personality and other traits as well as to differences in intelligence.

First, an *overlap in distributions is the rule.* Research reports usually convey group differences in the form of averages. Let us consider trait X. It might be intelligence, introversion, or height. Typical statements include these: Group A is significantly higher than Group B on X. Men and women differ on X. Asian-Americans have more of X than do Hispanics. All of these statements refer to differences in average or mean performance on trait X. The unsophisticated listener may infer that everyone in Group A is higher than everyone in Group B; that all

Key Points Summary 7.3

Three Major Perspectives in the Study of Group Differences

1. Overlap in Distributions is the Rule.
2. Group Difference Itself Doesn't Reveal the Cause.
3. Differences May Change with Time.

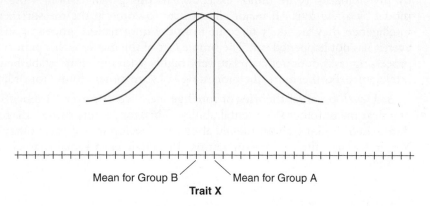

FIGURE 7.12   Example of overlapping distributions on trait X for groups A and B.

men are different from all women; and so on. However, in general, what we find is that (a) there is great variability within each group and (b) the distributions of the two groups overlap substantially. Figure 7.12 shows such **overlapping distributions**. Notice that many people in Group B exceed the mean (average) performance of people in Group A. Many people in Group A fall below the mean performance of people in Group B.

The situation depicted in Figure 7.12 prevails in virtually all studies of group differences. The preferred method for reporting differences is in standard deviation *(SD)* or sigma (σ) units. In the language of statistics, we call this an **effect size**.[5] For example, Group A is .2 σ above Group B. The effect size is .2. This type of reporting, assuming roughly equivalent σ's for the two groups, allows one to think about the difference in a form similar to Figure 7.12. Unfortunately, many reports simply say there is a difference (e.g., Group A is higher than Group B). Such unsophisticated reporting is, perhaps, understandable in the popular media, but one also encounters it in the psychological literature. Noting that a difference is "significant" or even "highly significant" does not evade the overlapping distribution phenomenon. A difference between groups can be highly significant and the distributions still overlap very substantially. This is especially true when the numbers of cases are very large, which is often the situation in studies of group differences in intelligence.

TRY IT! ....

Based on your personal knowledge about the differences in height between men and women, sketch the degree of overlap in the distributions for this trait.

....

---

[5] The term *effect size* is unfortunate because it suggests causality. As noted in the next paragraph, this suggestion is not appropriate when examining group differences.

The second important perspective is that the *group difference itself does not reveal the cause of the difference.* We have a natural tendency to infer that the difference between Group A and Group B on trait X has something to do with inherent characteristics of each group. This is a classic case of inferring causation from correlational data. Group differences are really correlational data. They represent the correlation between the trait (X) and group membership, which can be coded as 0 and 1 for A and B.[6] Knowing that Groups A and B differ on trait X, we cannot infer that the difference is directly due to the group membership. In fact, it may be due to some other variable that is indirectly associated (correlated) with group membership. Consider this admittedly silly example. Say men and women differ on personality trait X. Our first inclination is to think that there is something specific to being a man or woman that causes this difference. However, the key causal factor may be height. Men tend to be taller than women. It may be the "height" factor rather than the gender factor that causes the difference in personality trait X. How would we disentangle such causal relationships? Usually through an enormous amount of research. The point is that the simple report of a group difference does not tell us anything about causal links.

The third major perspective is that *differences may change with time.* That is, a difference well established 30 years ago may be gone or, at least, greatly diminished today. A difference well established now may not last forever. For several of the differences we describe, there is ample evidence that the difference has changed over time. For a good example of how some group differences have changed in the past 30 years, see Lee (2002).

Keep these three perspectives in mind as we review the following group differences in intelligence. Most research has concentrated on differences by gender, age, socioeconomic status, and racial/ethnic membership. We take up each in turn. Some differences formerly of interest, for example, between geographic regions and between urban and rural residents, are no longer of much interest, so we do not review them.

Differences by Sex

Do men and women, or boys and girls, differ in intelligence? Yes and no. In terms of total scores on tests of general mental functioning, the differences seem to be minimal. For more specific abilities, there are some noteworthy differences. The most pronounced difference is a male superiority on some tests of spatial ability. The effect size for this difference is about 0.5 to 0.7. Especially during the developmental years, females outpace males in verbal skills, but this difference disappears by late adolescence. Even within the verbal area, there are some more subtle differences in the way males and females function. Sex differences in mathematics show unusually complex patterns, both by age levels and subareas within mathematics. By subarea, for example, females tend to be better in computation and males in

---

[6] In fact, given reasonable assumptions about standard deviations, there are simple formulas that allow one to convert a group difference into a correlation coefficient *(r)* and vice versa.

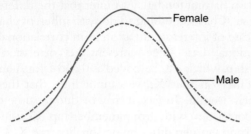

FIGURE 7.13 Illustration of difference in variability with the same average scores for males and females.

problem solving, although even within the problem-solving domain somewhat different patterns manifest themselves for certain types of problems.

One of the most intriguing findings about sex differences in intelligence is that variability is greater for males than for females. Figure 7.13 illustrates this type of difference. The practical effect of this difference is most evident at the extremes of the distribution. There are more males than females at the very highest levels *and* at the very lowest levels of the intelligence distribution. When this result combines with any difference in the average for a specific ability, the results at the extremes of the distribution can be quite dramatic.

For summaries of the vast literature on sex differences in intelligence, see Brody (1992; especially Chapter 10), Jensen (1998; especially Chapter 13), Neisser et al. (1996), and Halpern (2000).

Differences by Age

We study differences in intelligence by age by plotting average scores on intelligence tests for successive age groups. Figure 7.14 outlines the major trends.

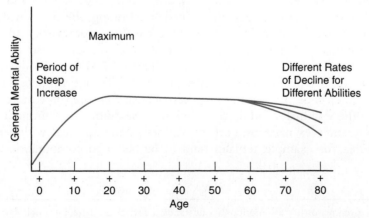

FIGURE 7.14 Generalized trends for age changes in intelligence.

Examination of these plots reveals the following trends. For general intelligence, the growth curve is very steep throughout approximately the first 12 years. It then moderates but continues to increase to around 20 years. Some estimates place the maximum as low as age 16, others as high as 25. The averages then remain approximately the same but with slight decline until around age 60. At that point, decline becomes much more noticeable. The rate of decline increases in the later years.

The most important point about declines in later adulthood is the differential rates of decline for specific abilities or tests. Tests such as vocabulary and information show less decline. Tests of short-term memory and perceptual and spatial abilities decline more rapidly. When studying age differences in intelligence, we must be careful to distinguish between cross-sectional and longitudinal studies. In cross-sectional studies, the older groups differ from younger groups not only in age but also in such factors as educational levels, nutritional histories, and so on. Hence, cross-sectional studies (which are easier to conduct) generally show more declines in old age than longitudinal studies.

All the latter results relate to changes in group averages. There is also the question of the stability of relative intelligence across the life span. Notice that this question refers to relative level of intelligence. On average, everyone is increasing in intelligence up to early adulthood, then generally declining thereafter. However, what about an individual's standing within his or her age group? Is the high-IQ two-year-old destined to be the high-IQ adult? Is an IQ of 90 in grade 4 predictive of a similar IQ level in high school?

Relative levels of intelligence begin to stabilize around age 6. Stability increases until around age 16, by which time we observe a high degree of stability. Of course, this stability is never complete. Some people continue to increase their relative position, while others are decreasing their position. The later the ages, the more the stability. For example, we can make a better prediction about intelligence at age 25 from a measure taken at age 16 than from one taken at age 12; a better prediction from age 12 than from age 10; and so on. In addition, the closer together the two ages at which measurements are taken, the greater the similarity in scores. For example, a prediction over a two-year period will be better than a prediction over a four-year period. Before age 6, relative levels of intelligence are not very stable. Thus, infant IQ tests are not very predictive of later intelligence. For summaries of the research on age changes in intelligence, see Brody (1992), Hayslip (1994), Lindenberger and Baltes (1994), Neisser et al. (1996), Hoyer and Touron (2003), and O'Connor and Kaplan (2003).

Population Shifts over Time

Another way to think about the stability of intelligence is in terms of entire populations. Is the average IQ any higher today than it was, say, 50 years ago? Apparently, the answer is "Yes," and by a rather astounding amount. Relevant data come from national testing programs, especially from military testing with universal draft and from re-standardization of tests. Several researchers noted the trends, almost as a sidelight, over the years. James Flynn, an Australian psychologist, has done a wonderful job of summarizing the data from a variety of sources from 20 countries over the past 60 years (Flynn, 1984, 1987, 1994, 1999). Hence, the steadily increasing levels of IQ have been dubbed the **"Flynn effect."** Some sources refer to the changes with the title of "secular trends" in intelligence. Flynn's summaries show differential amounts of gain for tests presumed to test fluid versus crystallized intelligence. The more fluid-related tests (e.g., figural and spatial reasoning) show an average increase of about 15 points per generation. (There is no exact quantification for the term "a generation." It generally refers to a period of about 20–25 years.) The more crystallized measures (e.g., vocabulary and verbal comprehension) show average gains of about 9 points per generation. Let us say, averaging across the two areas, there is about a 12-point gain per generation. That means an IQ of 100 today would have been an IQ of 124 in your grandparents' day (i.e., two generations ago). In the other direction, an IQ of 100 in your grandparents' day would be an IQ of 76 today. Those are very large differences. Numerous hypotheses have been advanced to explain these results (see Neisser, 1998). None have met with universal acceptance. Is it more schooling? Better nutrition? Flynn does suggest that perhaps test scores (IQs) are increasing without any real change in intelligence levels; or at least, the changes in underlying intelligence are not as great as the changes in IQ. No doubt, the search for explanations of the Flynn effect will continue. Of course, we are all anxious to know if the trend will continue. If the trend does hold for another four or five generations, the average person at the end of the twenty-first century will have an IQ of about 160 according to today's norms!

Differences by Socioeconomic Level

The two previous variables—age and sex—are easily defined. Socioeconomic status (SES) is a more complex variable. Various studies define it in terms of family income, occupation, or educational level. Combinations of these variables are also used. Also, some studies treat socioeconomic status as a continuous variable while other studies create groups, for example, high, middle, and low SES. Whichever definition is used, there is a clear relationship between intelligence levels and SES. When SES is represented as a continuous variable, the correlation with intelligence test score is about .30. Many researchers use five SES groups. When the SES variable is represented in this manner, average differences between successive groups are usually about 5 to 10 points of IQ. Figure 7.15 presents a generalized version of this summary. The regression line through the medians of the five groups corresponds to the correlation between SES and IQ of approximately .30. The figure is another good illustration of overlapping distributions. Notice that there is a distinct trend but also substantial overlap.

The reason for the relationship between IQ and SES status is hotly contested. Do brighter people move to the top of the SES ladder? Or are the tests more a measure of SES culture than of brightness? While this debate about the roots of the differences rages on, there is little question about the magnitude of the differences themselves. For summaries of information on these SES differences, see Brody (1992), Gottfredson (2004), Herrnstein and Murray (1994), Jencks (1979), Jensen (1998), Neisser et al. (1996) and Turkheimer (1994). Some of these authors take a distinct tack on the explanation for the differences by SES level, but they all supply the basic information about the magnitude of the differences.

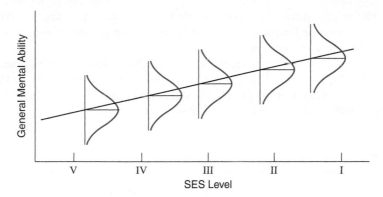

FIGURE 7.15 Generalized relationship between IQ and SES status with SES represented by groups.

Differences by Racial/Ethnic Group

Even more contentious than the differences in intelligence by SES group are the differences by race/ethnic group. However, as with the SES differences, the controversies relate primarily to causes. Regarding the magnitude and direction of differences, there is good agreement. We must note that overlaid on the discussion is a question about the legitimacy of the concept of race. Some writers believe the concept of race does not have sufficient biological validity to make it useful. Other writers note that, even if there is some validity to the concept, the groups to which we apply the terms *race* or *ethnic group* are too heterogeneous to be meaningful. For example, the term *Hispanic* subsumes people coming from a wide range of cultures and geographic areas. Asians include Chinese, Japanese, Vietnamese, Cambodians, and a many other subgroups. These are all good points. However, the simple fact of the matter is: There is an enormous amount of research reporting differences between whites, blacks, Hispanics, and Asians, as well as a host of other groups defined by appearance and/or geographic origin. We will try to summarize points on which there seems to be good agreement.

In most of the reported studies, whites, specifically, American or West European Caucasians, constitute the majority group to which other groups are compared. Furthermore, most of the tests used in the research have whites as the majority group in their norms, hence making the average IQ for whites approximately 100. Blacks generally average about one standard deviation (1 σ-unit) below whites. This tends to be true on more specific abilities, too, although the difference may be somewhat less on performance-type tests than on more verbally oriented tests. There is some evidence that this difference may be narrowing with time. Hispanics tend to be close to the mean for whites on performance and nonverbal tests but about one-half to one full standard deviation below on verbal tests. Of course, a crucial issue for testing many Hispanics is the language for the testing. Native Americans show a pattern similar to that for Hispanics. Asians tend to be approximately at the mean for whites on verbal tests. On nonverbal tests, especially tests of figural and spatial abilities, Asians tend to be about one standard deviation above the white mean. The vast majority of research on Asians involves only persons of Chinese or Japanese origin; the research on persons from other Asian cultures and regions is very thin.

For summaries of the research on racial/ethnic differences in intelligence, see Brody (1992), Herrnstein and Murray (1994), Jencks and Phillips (1998), Jensen (1994, 1998), Neisser et al. (1996), Rushton and Jensen (2005), Suzuki and Gutkin (1994a, 1994b, 1994c), and Vraniak (1994).

Heredity and Environment

If you like controversy, go into this field. Few topics in all of science, let alone psychology, stir such impassioned debate as the influences of heredity and environment on intelligence. The arguments have proceeded for at least 100 years, sometimes tilting in one direction, sometimes in the other direction. There is no end in sight. However, there are some well-established perspectives and basic facts. We will summarize these, leaving the less certain matters for others to handle. It must also be noted that knowledge in this area is growing at a dizzying pace with the unfolding of the Human Genome Project and its spin-offs.

Common Misconceptions

Let us begin by dispelling some common misconceptions. First, no one who has seriously studied this issue believes that either heredity or environment by itself completely determines intelligence. The question is no longer heredity *or* environment. All scholars agree that intelligence results from an **interaction** of hereditary and environmental influences. The combined influences are not additive. It is more like a multiplicative relationship. (See Exercise 2 at the end of the chapter for an illustration of the multiplicative effect.) No matter what the hereditary influence, if the environment is completely negative, intelligence will not develop. Raise the child of two geniuses in a closet and the child's intelligence will not develop. Send a frog to Ivy College and the frog will be none the wiser. Today, the questions are about the relative contributions of heredity and environment and about how the interplay between them works. Beware of writers who attack "psychologists who believe that intelligence is hereditary" or "psychologists who believe that intelligence is environmentally determined" with the implication that either position refers to an exclusive influence. These are straw men. No psychologist today believes either of these positions.

A second common misconception is that hereditary traits are present at conception or birth whereas environmental influences develop later. That is not necessarily the case. Consider baldness. It is heavily influenced by heredity but does not manifest itself until midlife or thereafter. Development of facial hair in the male and breasts in the female are largely hereditary but do not manifest themselves until puberty. On the other hand, fetal alcohol syndrome is environmentally determined (by the intrauterine environment) and is present at birth. A third misconception, related to the latter one, is that hereditary influences are permanent and unchangeable, whereas environmental influences are impermanent and changeable. Even traits heavily influenced by heredity are subject to change.

For example, a person may have a hereditary disposition toward some disease yet can avoid the disease through medication. Furthermore, a trait may be largely hereditary, but the entire population may be influenced by environmental factors. For example, height is largely hereditary, but the average height in the population has increased due to improved nutrition and health care. On the other hand, brain damage due to trauma or the amputation of a leg are environmentally determined, yet their effects are very permanent.

A fourth misconception is that intelligence may have some hereditary component, but personality characteristics are determined by environmental influences, especially by family and other early experiences. However, the evidence suggests that heredity plays a role in personality characteristics just as it does in intelligence.

Methodology and Terms

The primary methodology for studying the relative influences of heredity and environment on intelligence is familial genetic distance. Of special interest is study of identical or **monozyotic** (MZ) twins. These twins, coming from one fertilized egg (one zygote), are nature's laboratory for observing two individuals with the same genetic endowment. Within this subgroup, interest focuses on twin pairs raised in substantially different environments. Getting appropriate samples for such studies is a very tall order. There are relatively few identical twins, and an exceedingly small number of them have been raised in separate environments. Hence, the number of credible studies of this sort is very small. Nevertheless, there have now been a sufficient number to yield meaningful, cross-checked results. Studies of other degrees of family resemblance are also relevant. Siblings, including **dizygotic** (DZ; nonidentical) twins, have half their genes in common. We can determine degrees of shared genetic background for other relationships, too.

The proportion of variance for a trait that is attributable to genetic factors in a population is designated by the **heritability index,** labeled h^2. The remaining variance $(1 - h^2)$ includes environmental influences and errors of measurement. Among the environmental influences, there is special interest in within-family factors. This is called **shared family variance** and often labeled c^2. The question is: How different are environments for the individuals within a family unit? When addressing this question, it is especially important to remember that the "environment" begins with the intrauterine environment. There is also between-family environmental variance, that is, environmental differences from one family unit to another.

Major Results

We identify here four major conclusions from studies of the heritability of intelligence. First, estimates of heritability of intelligence range from about .40 to .80. When summarizing results from several studies, many authors use a midpoint of this range, that is, .60 as a good estimate. Some authors round down to .50. Second, the evidence now seems quite solid that heritability increases with age. Reasonable estimates are that heritability is around .40–.60 for youth, but the figure rises to .60–.75 for adults. Third, most of the studies have defined intelligence with a measure of general intellectual functioning, reasonably interpreted as "g." Studies using tests tapping more specific abilities suggest that these more specific abilities have somewhat lower heritability indexes. For example, in an excellent summary of the research on this topic, Plomin and DeFries (1998) concluded that heritability is about 60% for verbal ability and 50% for spatial ability. However, there have not been a large number of genetic studies with the multiplicity of specific abilities referenced in Carroll's summary (Figure 7.5). Fourth, many authors comment about the surprisingly small contribution of between-family variance. Within-family variance seems to be more important than between-family variance. Furthermore, even the within-family variance decreases in influence with increases in age.

Let us note several cautions about drawing conclusions regarding the genetics of intelligence. First, nearly all authors emphasize that we know very little about the mechanisms by which either genes or environment work their respective influences on intelligence, although this is an area of intense research at the moment (see Plomin et al., 2003). Second, estimates of heritability apply within gene-pool populations. It is hazardous to generalize across gene pools. And it is difficult to define exactly when one has crossed into a new gene pool. Third, and related to the second point, we note that the great majority of studies on this topic have been conducted with American and Western European populations. The standard reference on the genetics of intelligence is *Behavioral Genetics* (Plomin et al., 2001), now in its fourth edition. A summary and modest update of that work is provided by Plomin and Spinath (2004).

Summary

1. Study of intelligence falls into four broad categories: theories, measurement, group differences, and hereditary/environmental influences.

2. Over the years, psychologists have used the terms *intelligence*, *mental ability*, *aptitude*, and a variety of other terms for the trait(s) we study in this and the next several chapters. Although some sources say that psychologists do not agree on the meaning of the term *intelligence*, there is actually quite good agreement. Intelligence does correlate with important practical variables, but authorities differ on the the interpretation of the magnitude of the correlations.

3. It is important to be familiar with theories of intelligence because current intelligence tests draw heavily on those theories.

4. Spearman's theory of "g" was the first formal theory of intelligence. It posits one dominant, general factor, plus a host of more specific factors.

5. For many years, the main competitor to Spearman's theory was Thurstone's theory of primary mental abilities or multiple-factor theory. This theory provided for 5 to 10 relatively independent factors. In a more extreme version of a multiple-factor theory, Guilford thought there were as many as 180 relatively independent abilities.

6. Hierarchical models combine the one-factor and multiple-factor positions by noting that the multiple factors can form a hierarchy, with "g" at the apex. Well-known models of this type include Vernon's, Carroll's, and Cattell's models. Cattell's model introduces the notions of fluid and crystallized intelligence.

7. Another way to think about mental ability is in terms of developmental models. Piaget's theory of cognitive development has been very influential.

8. In recent years, information processing and biological models have dominated the research literature. Among the more well-known theories in this camp are those of Jensen, Sternberg, and Gardner. The PASS theory, incorporating simultaneous and sequential processing, is another model in this category. Research using elementary cognitive tasks is particularly active at present.

9. Current tests rely mostly on one of the hierarchical models. The developmental and information processing models, while attractive from many perspectives, have not yet exerted much practical influence on mental ability testing.

10. When considering group differences in intelligence, it is important to remember the rule of overlapping distributions, the fact that causes of the differences can be elusive, and that the differences may change with time.

11. For general mental ability, sex differences are negligible. There are some sex differences in more specific abilities. Greater variability for males is an intriguing difference.

12. General mental ability increases rapidly with age until puberty, then begins to moderate in rate of growth, and peaks in early adulthood. With aging during the adult years, specific abilities decline at different rates.

13. The Flynn effect describes a general upward drift in intelligence test performance in many countries over the past few generations. The reasons for the upward drift are not clear.

14. Socioeconomic status is significantly related to intelligence test scores. The relationship is moderate, and there is much overlap between SES levels.

15. There is reasonable agreement about the direction and magnitude of differences among various racial/ethnic groups on mental ability tests, but significant controversy remains over the reasons for the differences.

16. Estimates of the heritability of general intelligence center around .60. When studying hereditary versus environmental influences on intelligence (or any other trait), one should avoid certain common misconceptions.

Key Terms

Terms

biological model
componential analysis
crystallized intelligence
convergent production
developmental theories
divergent production
dizygotic
effect size
elementary cognitive
    tasks (ECT)
fluid intelligence
Flynn effect
"g"

heritability index
hierarchical model
information processing
    model
interaction
monozygotic
multiple intelligences
    (MI)
multiple-factor theory
overlapping distributions
PASS theory
primary mental abilities
psychometric theories
sequential processing
shared family variance

simultaneous processing
stage-based theories
three-stratum theory
triarchic theory
two-factor theory

People

Gardner
Jensen
Piaget
Spearman
Sternberg
Thurstone

Exercises

1. Refer to Table 7.2. Which of these abilities do you think are important for success in college?

2. In the discussion of heritability, we recommended thinking of heredity and environment in a multiplicative relationship. Think of the genetic factor on a scale of 1–10 and the environmental factor on another scale of 1–10. On both scales, 10 is high or favorable. Fill in the values in the table to see the result of the multiplicative relationship.

Case	*Heredity*	*Environment*	*Result*
1	5	6	—
2	1	10	—
3	10	1	—
4	4	8	—
5	7	7	—

3. Compare the stratum II factors in Carroll's three-stratum model with Thurstone's primary mental abilities. Where do these two models align nicely? Where do they not agree?

4. To observe the variety of terms used for "intelligence," access the ETS Test Collection site (sydneyplus.ets.org) and do a DescriptorSearch on "intelligence" as a key word. List ten terms you find, describing or naming the resulting entries.

5. Recall the distinction between convergent and divergent thinking (p. 265). Where does divergent thinking fit in Carroll's model of intelligence (p. 267)?

6. Read again about the elementary cognitive tasks (pp. 271–273). Where does performance on these tasks fit in Carroll's model?

7. Look at Figure 7.12, showing overlapping distributions. Estimate the effect size for these overlapping distributions. Compare your estimate with someone else's.

CHAPTER 8

Individual Tests of Intelligence

Objectives

1. List the typical uses of individual intelligence tests.

2. Describe the common characteristics of individual intelligence tests.

3. Identify major features of the WAIS-III, including its structure, types of scores, norming, reliability, validity, and profile interpretation.

4. Identify the major features of the Stanford–Binet.

5. Identify the major features of the PPVT-III.

6. Describe the major features and principal uses of the WMS-III.

7. Describe the concept of adaptive behavior and how it relates to defining mental retardation.

8. Describe significant trends in the development and use of individual intelligence tests.

Some Cases

- Bill, a sixth grader at Highland School, has struggled with his schoolwork since second grade. His older brother and sister excelled in their studies and now attend prestigious colleges. Bill's Mom and Dad wonder whether Bill is not trying or, perhaps, is trying, but just doesn't have the same degree of mental acuity as his older siblings. Perhaps there is a learning disability requiring a different approach to instruction for Bill. Mom and Dad ask the school psychologist to assess Bill's level of mental ability.

- According to her friends, Mrs. Kelly, age 75, used to be "sharp as a tack." She doesn't seem to be so anymore. Partly it's memory lapses, but there are other telltale signs, too. Mrs. Kelly is referred to a clinical psychologist specializing in geriatric cases for an overall assessment of her mental functioning. Perhaps the changes are quite normal for her age, perhaps not.

- Fred, a homeless, middle-age mute, winds up at the Midtown Social Service Center. As part of his in-processing, staff members want to know if he may be mentally retarded. One can often make an informal determination on this point simply through conversation with the individual. However, Fred's inability to speak prevents this assessment. Is there a reasonably quick but reliable and valid way to assess Fred's mental ability?

- In a recent car accident, Sue sustained a severe concussion. Is there any evidence that the accident affected her level of intelligence? How will we answer this question?

All these cases illustrate situations in which the psychologist might want to use an individually administered mental ability test. In this chapter, we explore the types of tests psychologists often use with such cases.

Uses and Characteristics of Individual Intelligence Tests

The individually administered intelligence test is a staple in the fields of clinical, counseling, and school psychology. In a wide variety of cases, the psychologist needs some measure of the individual client's general mental ability. The intelligence test will ordinarily be used with other sources of information, such as an interview and other types of tests. The other tests will depend greatly on the nature of the presenting problem. They may include personality tests and/or tests of more specialized mental functions. However, some measure of general mental ability will often serve as an essential source of information. Individual intelligence tests also play an important function in research. Some of this research deals directly with the nature of intelligence. However, a measure of general mental ability is also desired in other areas of research, for example, research on family environments or personal characteristics because general mental ability is such an important human characteristic.

Individually administered intelligence tests have a number of common characteristics. Before describing specific tests, it will be useful to identify these common

FIGURE 8.1 Typical arrangement for administration of individual intelligence test.

Source: Ray Stott/The Image Works.

features. We list eight such common features. Most obviously, these tests are *individually administered*. There is one examiner and one examinee (see Figure 8.1). In the nostalgic terminology of experimental psychology's early days, test manuals sometimes refer to the examinee as the "subject"—a term now frowned on. The examiner presents questions, items, or stimuli to the examinee. The examinee responds in some way. The response might be oral (e.g., defining a word), manual (e.g., assembling a puzzle), or pointing (e.g., with the finger or even with the eyes).

Second, administration of these tests requires *advanced training*. Observing the administration of one of these tests gives the impression that it is easy, almost like a casual conversation. However, this appearance comes from much practice and careful study of the test manual. It is like a well-executed ballet or football play. It looks easy, but it requires hours of practice, instruction, and effort.

Third, these tests usually cover a *very wide range of age and ability*. For example, a single test might cover ages 3–16 and, within that age range, from mentally retarded to genius level. Within this broad span, items usually progress from easiest to hardest. However, a single examinee completes only some of these items. The test manual provides **start- and stop-rules** for determining which items the examiner actually presents. For example, the start-rule may say, "Begin with items typical for persons one year younger than the examinee." The stop-rule may say, "Discontinue testing

Key Points Summary 8.1

Eight Common Characteristics of
Individually Administered Intelligence Tests

1. Individual Administration
2. Requires Advanced Training to Administer
3. Wide Range of Ages and Abilities (with Start- and Stop-Rules)
4. Establishing Rapport
5. Free-response Format
6. Immediate Scoring of Items
7. About One Hour for Administration
8. Opportunity for Observation

when the examinee fails 5 items in succession." The examiner must be thoroughly familiar with these rules in order to achieve a standardized administration.

Fourth, the examiner must *establish rapport* with the examinee. **Rapport** is testing's semitechnical term for a warm, comfortable relationship between examiner and examinee. To establish rapport, the examiner may need to spend some time just chatting with the individual before testing begins. It is important to maintain this relationship throughout the examination.

Fifth, most individually administered intelligence tests use a *free-response format* rather than a selected-response format. As we will see in our review of specific tests, some items may employ a selected-response format, and some brief tests may be entirely multiple-choice. The general rule for the more widely used individual intelligence tests is to use the free-response format. However, a movement toward more use of selected-response items is detectable.

Sixth, individual tests typically require *immediate scoring of items.* That is, the examiner scores each response as the examinee gives it. Proper use of the start- and stop-rules requires this immediate scoring. For example, if testing discontinues after five successive failures, the examiner must know immediately when the fifth failure occurs. Furthermore, since most tests use a free-response format, the examiner needs to decide immediately whether to ask for clarification of a particular response. The examiner's ability to apply immediate scoring is one of the most important reasons for advanced training in the use of these tests. Immediate scoring is required for individual items, but not for total scores. Total scores and conversion of scores into various types of norms can be completed after the test administration.

Seventh, administration of the more widely used individual intelligence tests usually requires *about one hour.* An exact time is not specified because different examinees complete different items and the exact selection of items is determined during the actual administration. Some examinees may complete the test in as little

TABLE 8.1 *Examples of Comments an Examiner Might Record during Administration of Individual Intelligence Test*

- JK★ seemed very deliberate and methodical in approaching tasks. Often articulated a "plan" for doing an item.
- EB made many excuses for his performance ... even when correct or successful. Seemed defensive.
- LN often asked to have a question repeated. May be an attention problem or could be hearing problem. Need to have hearing checked.
- BV had exceptional problem concentrating. Eyes darting about the room. Easily distracted by even minor noises in the hallway.

★ Initials of examinee.

as 45 minutes, while others may require 90 minutes. One hour is about average. This one hour does not include time for summarizing scores, converting raw scores to norms, and so on. There are some briefer individually administered tests designed for completion in about 15 minutes. We describe some of these later in this chapter.

Finally, the individual intelligence test allows *opportunity for observation,* quite apart from the formal scoring of the test. This is one of the chief advantages of the individually administered test in comparison with a group-administered test. The examiner can observe approaches to tasks, note mannerisms, infer something about personality, and so on. The test record, where the examiner records responses, usually provides space to make notes about such observations. Table 8.1 shows examples of observations that might be made during the test administration. These observations do not enter the formal scoring of the test. However, they may be useful when preparing a report about the individual. The report typically goes beyond a simple report of scores. The report usually includes an integration of information from a variety of sources, including the intelligence test and other tests.

Typical Items in an Individual Intelligence Test

How do individually administered intelligence tests attempt to measure intelligence? From a practical perspective, this question translates into: What kind of items do the tests have? Later in this chapter, we will examine specific tests. First, let us consider some typical items, examples that we might find in a variety of tests.

We start by trying to identify some simple tasks that we believe are indicative of intelligent behavior. What sorts of things can be done by people we consider smart or bright that cannot be done by people we consider intellectually dull or slow? We need to find tasks that are not overly dependent on specific cultural experiences. There are two common approaches for this purpose. One approach is to use very novel material, material that virtually no one has experienced. Another approach is to use very common material, material that almost everyone would have experienced, at least within a very broadly defined culture, such as "everyday America."

Table 8.2 lists types of items commonly appearing in individual intelligence tests. Examine each item type. Try to determine what mental functions each item calls on. After examining these items, note the following cautions about these examples.

These are just examples of the types of items encountered in individual intelligence tests. Other types are found, too, although these examples are encountered frequently. Obviously, each item type can accommodate an enormous range of difficulty. These examples have not undergone empirical tryout and editorial review. Some of them might turn out to be poor items. Also, we have not specified scoring rules for these items. For example, what will we accept as an adequate definition of "arrogant"? Will

TABLE 8.2   *Examples of Items Included in Individual Intelligence Tests*

Category	Examples	Comment
Vocabulary	• What does angry mean? • What does arrogant mean?	Vocabulary items are very common in intelligence tests. Vocabulary usually correlates highly with total scores based on many kinds of items. Some tests consist entirely of vocabulary items.
Verbal Relations	• What is the opposite of tardy? • How are a bus and a car alike? • Father is to son as mother is to what?	This category includes antonyms, similarities, analogies, and other items dealing with the relationships between words and concepts.
Information	• Show me your elbow. • How many days are there in a week? • Name one planet in our solar system other than the earth.	It is important to get items that are not too culturally bound or overly dependent on formal schooling. The emphasis is on common, everyday information.
Meaning, Comprehension	• Make a sentence from these words: the, Ed, car, drove. • Why do we have speed limits on highways? • Examiner reads a paragraph, then asks for a summary of its main point.	These items deal with meaning other than single words. The items emphasize connections, concepts, relationships, usually of a verbal nature.
Arithmetic	• Jim bought 2 pencils for 10 cents each. How much did he pay? • Jim bought 5 pencils for 12 cents each and 2 notebooks for 80 cents each. How much did he pay?	These are good, old-fashioned word problems. The items avoid very complicated computations (e.g., $1 \frac{3}{4} \times \frac{2}{3}$). The items concentrate on mental manipulation of fairly simple numbers.

(continued)

TABLE 8.2 *(Continued)*

Category	Examples	Comment
Short-term memory	• Listen, then repeat the numbers I say: numbers: 9–4–7–2–6 • Listen: dog, house, cow, table. (Pause.) What was the second word I said?	The first item is called **digit span**. It can employ any number of digits. It can also be used with digits repeated backward. Obviously, the lists can become very long. Some items call for immediate repetition; for other items there may be a delay of several minutes.
Form Patterns	Use the blocks to make a building like this picture. 	There are a great variety of items using puzzles, form boards, and blocks. Many of these items are modeled on entire tests developed in the early days of testing, e.g., Kohs Block Design, Porteus Mazes, and Seguin Form Board.
Psychomotor	 Fill in as quickly as possible: 	These items are usually speed tests. The example here requires only one row, but actual tests might have 20 such rows. The basic tasks are simple. The tasks require eye-hand coordination and concentration. Another example is comparing columns of numbers.
Matrices		Matrices have become increasingly popular as nonverbal reasoning items. They are usually presented as multiple-choice items. They can become very complex.

we give bonus points for speed of response to the arithmetic items or score them only as correct/incorrect? These scoring rules become part of the item.

TRY IT!

Pick one of the categories of items listed in Table 8.2. Construct an item that you think would measure mental ability for 10-year-olds.

The Wechsler Scales: An Overview

Historical Introduction

As noted later in our description of the Stanford–Binet, for many years that test was the most popular method for assessing intelligence. Although it was originally designed for use with children, it was also used with adults. David Wechsler, a clinical psychologist working at New York City's Bellevue Hospital, was not happy with the child orientation of the Stanford–Binet, nor with the fact that it yielded only one, global score. Wechsler worked primarily with adults. Furthermore, he wanted separate scores for what seemed to him to be somewhat separate manifestations of mental ability. He created what came to be known as the *Wechsler-Bellevue Intelligence Scale,* first published in 1939. The Wechsler–Bellevue struck a resonant chord with clinicians and rapidly rose in popularity. It was revised in 1955, under the new name **Wechsler Adult Intelligence Scale (WAIS)**, a name it retains today.

In an odd twist, after expressing dissatisfaction with the child-oriented Stanford–Binet, Wechsler created a downward extension of the WAIS: the **Wechsler Intelligence Scale for Children (WISC)** for ages 6–16, first published in 1949. The WISC's structure generally followed that of the WAIS. Later, the WISC was pushed even lower, with publication of the **Wechsler Preschool and Primary Scale of Intelligence (WPPSI)** for ages 2½–7, first published in 1967. Figure 8.2 gives a time line for successive editions of the WAIS, WISC, and WPPSI.

1930			
		1939 Wechsler-Bellvue	
1940			
		1949 WISC	
1950			
	1955 WAIS		
1960			
			1967 WPPSI
1970			
		1974 WISC-R	
1980	1981 WAIS-R		
			1989 WPPSI-R
1990		1991 WISC-III	
	1997 WAIS-III		
2000			2002 WPPSI-III
		2003 WISC-IV	
2005			

FIGURE 8.2 Time line for original and revised editions of the WAIS, WISC, and WPPSI.

TABLE 8.3   *The Wechsler Family of Tests*

Test Title	Publication Date	Acronym
Wechsler Adult Intelligence Scale, 3rd ed.	1997	WAIS-III
Wechsler Intelligence Scale for Children, 4th ed.	2003	WISC-IV
Wechsler Preschool and Primary Scale of Intelligence, 3rd ed.	2002	WPPSI-III
Wechsler Memory Scales, 3rd ed.	1997	WMS-III
Wechsler Abbreviated Scale of Intelligence	1999	WASI
Wechsler Individual Achievement Test, 2nd ed.	2001	WIAT-II
Wechsler Test of Adult Reading	2001	WTAR

David Wechsler died in 1985. However, his name continues in use on new editions of his tests and even on entirely new tests devised since his death. Table 8.3 shows the current panoply of Wechsler tests. The most recent additions to the family, the WIAT and WTAR, fall outside the realm of intelligence tests.

Psychologists usually pronounce the acronyms for the main Wechsler tests. It is a mark of professional maturity, albeit a very minor one, to use this lingo. Here is a brief pronunciation guide for the Wechsler (Wex-ler) tests: WAIS rhymes with "face," WISC rhymes with "brisk," WPPSI rhymes with "gypsy."

Weschsler's Concept of Intelligence

Throughout the various editions of the Wechsler intelligence scales, Wechsler consistently defined intelligence as "the aggregate or global capacity of the individual to act purposefully, to think rationally and to deal effectively with his environment" (Wechsler, 1958, p. 7). He also emphasized that intelligence involved more than intellectual ability, although "the capacity to do intellectual work is a necessary and important sign of general intelligence" (Wechsler, 1958, p. 12). General intelligence or, more precisely, intelligent behavior depends on such variables as "persistence, drive, energy level, etc." (Wechsler, 1949, p. 5). See Wechsler (1974) for more extended treatment of

TABLE 8.4   *Wechsler's and Binet's Definitions of Intelligence*

"the aggregate or global capacity of the individual to act purposefully, to think rationally and to deal effectively with his environment." (Wechsler, 1958, p. 7)

"It seems to us that in intelligence there is a fundamental faculty, the alteration or the lack of which, is of the utmost importance for practical life. This faculty is judgment, otherwise called good sense, practical sense, initiative, the faculty of adapting one's self to circumstances. To judge well, to comprehend well, to reason well, these are the essential activities of intelligence." (Binet, 1905)[a]

[a] This statement originally appeared in an article by Binet and Simon entitled "New Methods for the Diagnosis of the Intellectual Level of Subnormals," published in *L'Anee Psychologique* in 1905. Here we use the translation by E. S. Kite in Binet and Simon (1916).

his views. As noted earlier, Spearman made similar points about the nature of intelligence. Unfortunately, these points are often lost in the descriptions of both Wechsler's and Spearman's thoughts about intelligence. Wechsler hoped that his combination of tests, which we will examine shortly, would tap this "aggregate" of abilities and traits. Table 8.4 gives the classic definitions of intelligence from both Wechsler and Binet.

Wechsler Adult Intelligence Scale—Third Edition

Among individually administered intelligence tests, the *Wechsler Adult Intelligence Scale*—Third Edition (WAIS-III; Wechsler, 1997a, 1997b) is the most widely used test for both applied and research purposes. Its familiarity to psychologists and its influence on the field are truly remarkable. It is fitting, therefore, that we examine this test in some detail.

Structure and Administration

One of the hallmark features of WAIS-III is its structure. It includes a series of Verbal and Performance subtests, as listed in Table 8.5. The test yields separate **Verbal and Performance IQs,** as well as a **Full Scale IQ.** The professional literature often abbreviates these scores as VIQ, PIQ, and FSIQ. In addition, each subtest yields a normed score. In the interpretation of WAIS-III scores, as described later, much is made of the comparison of Verbal and Performance scores and the profile of subtest scores. Table 8.6 provides a brief description of each subtest. Figure 8.3 gives examples of items for some subtests. These examples are *not* actual

TABLE 8.5   *List of WAIS-III Subtests and Composite Scores*

Index Scores:	Verbal Comprehension	Working Memory	Perceptual Organizaton	Processing Speed	Not in Index
Verbal Subtests					
2. Vocabulary	X				
4. Similarities	X				
6. Arithmetic		X			
8. Digit Span		X			
9. Information	X				
11. Comprehension					X
13. Letter-Number Sequencing		X			
Performance Subtests					
1. Picture Completion			X		
3. Digit Symbol-Coding				X	
5. Block Design			X		
7. Matrix Reasoning			X		
10. Picture Arrangement					X
12. Symbol Search				X	
14. Object Assembly					X

TABLE 8.6 *Descriptions of the WAIS-III Subtests*

Subtest	Description
Picture Completion	A set of color pictures of common objects and settings, each of which is missing an important part that the examinee must identify
Vocabulary	A series of orally and visually presented words that the examinee orally defines
Digit Symbol-Coding	A series of numbers, each of which is paired with its own corresponding hieroglyphic-like symbol. Using a key, the examinee writes the symbol corresponding to its number
Similarities	A series of orally presented pairs of words for which the examinee explains the similarity of the common objects or concepts they represent
Block Design	A set of modeled or printed two-dimensional geometric patterns that the examinee replicates using two-color cubes
Arithmetic	A series of arithmetic problems that the examinee solves mentally and responds to orally
Matrix Reasoning	A series of incomplete gridded patterns that the examinee completes by pointing to or saying the number of the correct response from five possible choices
Digit Span	A series of orally presented number sequences that the examinee repeats verbatim for Digits Forward and in reverse for Digits Backward
Information	A series of orally presented questions that tap the examinee's knowledge of common events, objects, places, and people
Picture Arrangement	A set of pictures presented in a mixed-up order that the examinee rearranges into a logical story sequence
Comprehension	A series of orally presented questions that require the examinee to understand and articulate social rules and concepts or solutions to everyday problems
Symbol Search	A series of paired groups, each pair consisting of a target group and a search group. The examinee indicates, by marking the appropriate box, whether either target symbol appears in the search group
Letter-Number Sequencing	A series of orally presented sequences of letters and numbers that the examinee simultaneously tracks and orally repeats, with the numbers in ascending order and the letters in alphabetical order
Object Assembly	A set of puzzles of common objects, each presented in a standardized configuration, that the examinee assembles to form a meaningful whole

Source: From WAIS®-III Administration and Scoring Manual (p. 2). Copyright © 1997 by Harcourt Assessment, Inc. Reproduced by permission. All rights reserved.

Matrix Reasoning   **Picture Completion**

Pick the box that completes the series

1   2   3

What is missing in this picture?

4   5

Digit Span

       Examiner says: *5 − 2 −9*
       Examinee repeats back.

       Examiner says: *7 − 1 − 3 − 6 − 9 − 2 − 5 − 4*
       Examinee repeats back.

Information
What is the distance in miles from Chicago to Los Angeles?

Comprehension
Why do we have speed limits on highways?

Letter–Number Sequencing
       Examiner says: L − 5 − B − 2
       Examinee says (with numbers in ascending order, letters in alphabetical order):
       2 − 5 − B − L

FIGURE 8.3   Simulations of some Wechsler-type items.

test items from WAIS-III; they simply illustrate in a very general way the nature of the tasks in the subtests. Notice the variety of tasks presented. This is in accord with Wechsler's strong belief that intelligence is multifaceted and its measurement requires many different approaches.

    A new feature of WAIS-III, not found in any previous editions, is provision of four **Index Scores:** Verbal Comprehension, Working Memory, Perceptual Organization, and Processing Speed. Each Index Score comes from a combination of two to three subtests, as indicated in Table 8.5. The Index Scores are subscores within the broader Verbal and Performance areas. Some of the subtests do not enter into any Index Scores. The Index Scores are outgrowths of factor analysis of the Wechsler subtests. Numerous studies have examined the factor structure of the Wechsler, usually identifying either three or four factors. The publisher has finally adopted the four-factor model, partly dependent on introducing modest adjustments in the complete set of subtests.

The numerals preceding subtest names in Table 8.5 show the order for their administration. Notice the alternation of Verbal and Performance subtests in actual administration of the test. Scores on all Verbal subtests combine to yield the Verbal IQ. Similarly, all Performance subtests combine to yield the Performance IQ. Then, all subtests combine to yield the Full Scale IQ. Index Scores result from the subtests marked in Table 8.5. Some subtests are optional for determining IQ scores (but not for Index Scores); they are administered in instances in which one of the other subtests has been "spoiled"; that is, something has gone awry in the administration of the other subtest. Letter-Number Sequencing, Symbol Search, and Object Assembly are the optional subtests that substitute for selected other subtests.

Most of the subtests in WAIS-III are the same as those in previous editions of the test. Approximately half of the items are new and half remain from WAIS-R. However, there are three entirely new subtests: Letter-Number Sequencing, Matrix Reasoning, and Symbol Search. Addition of these subtests was important for development of the Index Scores.

Administration of WAIS-III follows the patterns previously outlined for common characteristics of individually administered intelligence tests. The examiner and examinee sit at a table across from one another. The examiner has test materials and the test record form, for recording responses, on the table. The examiner spends some time "establishing rapport." For each subtest, there is a start-rule for determining where to begin. If there is initial failure, the examiner moves backward to easier items. The examiner scores each item as it is presented. Some scoring is very simple, as in the multiple-choice Matrix Reasoning test or the Digit Span test. Items in other subtests (e.g., Vocabulary) require some judgment by the examiner. Also, responses on some subtests are timed by the examiner with a stopwatch. Administration of the subtest proceeds until determined by the stop-rule. The examiner then moves on to the next subtest. Total administration time is typically 45 to 90 minutes.

In earlier days, provision of separate Verbal and Performance scores and a profile of subtest scores distinguished the Wechsler approach from the Stanford-Binet approach, with its single, total score. However, as described later, the Stanford-Binet now uses a multiscore approach. As we will see in Chapter 9, the granddaddy of group-administered mental ability tests, the Otis test, has followed a similar route. Clearly, some version of a hierarchical model of intelligence has won the day among test publishers.

Scores and Norms

Scoring the WAIS-III begins with determining the raw score for each subtest. Subtest raw scores are converted to standard scores. The standard score system for the subtests has $M = 10$ and $SD = 3$. In the WAIS, these standard scores are called Scaled Scores. There are separate raw score to scaled score conversions for 13 age

TABLE 8.7   *Raw Score to Scaled Score Conversions for Vocabulary and Block Design Subtest of WAIS-III for Two Age Groups*

Subtest:		Vocabulary		Block Design	
	Age:	20–34	85–89	20–34	85–89
Scaled Score					
−3 SD	1	0–5	0–1	0–2	0–1
	2	6–8	2–5	3–6	2
	3	9–12	6–8	7–10	3–4
−2 SD	4	13–16	9–12	11–14	5–7
	5	17–20	13–16	15–19	8–10
	6	21–24	17–20	20–24	11–13
−1 SD	7	25–28	21–24	25–29	14–16
	8	29–32	25–28	30–34	17–19
	9	33–37	29–32	35–39	20–22
Mean	10	38–42	33–37	40–43	23–25
	11	43–46	38–42	44–48	26–27
	12	47–49	43–46	49–52	28–29
+1 SD	13	50–52	47–50	53–55	30–32
	14	53–55	51–53	56–58	33–35
	15	56–58	54–56	59–61	36–38
+2 SD	16	59–61	57–58	62–63	39–41
	17	62–63	59–60	64–65	42–44
	18	64–65	61–62	66–67	45–47
+3 SD	19	66	63–66	68	48–68

Source: From WAIS®-III Administration and Scoring Manual, Table A.2. Copyright © 1997 by Harcourt Assessment, Inc. Reproduced by permission. All rights reserved.

groups, with age intervals varying from 2 to 10 years (e.g., 16–17, 20–24, 55–64, 85–89). There is also a Reference Group that includes ages 20–34.

Using separate raw score to scaled score conversions for each age group means that scaled scores obscure any differences in performance by age. In the previous edition (WAIS-R), the typical procedure was to convert raw scores to scaled scores for the common Reference Group, thus preserving any changes by age when representing performance in scaled scores. This has important consequences for score interpretation. Let us pause to illustrate this point. Table 8.7 shows the raw score to scaled score conversions for two subtests for the Reference Group (ages 20–34) and for the 85- to 89-year-old age group. Consider a raw score of 23 on the Block Design subtest. The raw score of 23 converts to a scaled score of 6 for the Reference Group, more than one *SD* below the mean or a percentile rank of approximately 10. However, that same raw score of 23 converts to a scaled score of 10 for the 85–89 age group: an average score. Thus, the same raw score appears average with respect to one norm group, but indicates a substantial deficit with respect to another norm group. Now let us consider an example for the Vocabulary subtest. Take a raw score of 37. It converts to a scaled score of 9 for the Reference Group and to a scaled score of 10 for the 85–89 age group: very little difference. A raw score of 50 converts to a scaled score of 13 in both age groups. These examples help to emphasize that the person interpreting test scores must understand the technical characteristics of the test. Failure to understand these technical characteristics can lead to serious misinterpretation.

TRY IT!

Use Table 8.7 to make these conversions from raw scores to scaled scores.

	Raw Score	Scaled Score Reference Group	Age 85–89
Vocabulary	46	___	___
Block Design	29	___	___

Suppose these scores are for Mr. McInerney, age 85. What do you conclude about Mr. McInerney?

Subtest scaled scores are added, then converted to WAIS-III composite scores. The composite scores include the three IQ scores (Verbal, Performance, Full Scale) and four Index Scores (Verbal Comprehension, Perceptual Organization, Working Memory, and Processing Speed). All these composite scores are standard scores with $M = 100$ and $SD = 15$. The WAIS-III manual provides tables for converting these standard scores to percentile ranks. However, most of the WAIS-III materials employ the standard scores as the basis for interpretation.

Standardization

WAIS-III was standardized on a stratified sample of 2,450 adults selected to be representative of the U.S. population aged 16–89. Stratification variables included age, sex, race/ethnicity, education level, and geographic region. The basic age groups for development of norms were 16–17, 18–19, 20–24, 25–29, 30–34, 35–44, 45–54, 55–64, 65–69, 70–74, 80–84, and 85–89. There were 200 cases per age group, except for somewhat smaller numbers in the two oldest groups. The WAIS-III manuals carefully document the representativeness of the age groups in terms of the stratification variables. Commendably, the manuals also explicitly identify criteria for excluding certain types of cases. For example, persons with Alzheimer's dementia, schizophrenia, color-blindness, uncorrected hearing loss, or upper extremity disorder affecting motor performance were excluded. Thus, it would be best to think of the norms as representing the population of adults free from significant sensory defects and in reasonable physical and mental health. The WAIS-III manuals do not address the problem of unrepresentativeness of the norms due to self-selection. Of course, individuals had to be invited to participate in the standardization, and then agree to do so. As is typically the case when soliciting volunteers for such a project, it is difficult to estimate the effect of self-selection. What types of individuals would not be invited, other than for the explicit exclusionary criteria mentioned? Which individuals, once invited, would decline? Such problems are by no means peculiar to the WAIS-III standardization process. The problem haunts nearly all norming procedures. With the latter cautions in mind, the WAIS-III norming process appears to be excellent. The user should be able to depend on the WAIS-III norms with confidence.

Reliability

The WAIS-III manuals provide exceptionally thorough treatment of reliability. They report internal consistency (split-half) and test-retest coefficients separately by age group for IQs, Index Scores, and subtest scores. Standard errors of measurement are also reported for all scores. As noted, WAIS usage often entails comparison of Verbal and Performance IQs, various Index Scores, and analysis of subtest profiles. In recognition of this fact, the WAIS manuals, laudably, provide explicit treatment of standard errors of differences between scores.

Internal consistency and test-retest reliabilities of the Full Scale and Verbal IQs average about .95 or higher. That is, these scores are very reliable. The Verbal Comprehension Index (VCI) shows a similar degree of reliability. The three other Index Scores (Perceptual Organization, Working Memory, and Processing Speed) and the Performance IQ tend to have somewhat lower reliabilities, averaging around .90—still very high levels of reliability. Standard errors of measurement for the three IQ scores and the four Index Scores average 3–5 scaled score points.

Internal consistency reliabilities for the WAIS subtests range generally from the upper .70s to low .90s, with an average of about .85. Test-retest reliabilities for the subtests average about .80. In general, reliabilities of the Performance subtests are lower than for the Verbal subtests. Among the Verbal subtests, reliabilities for Vocabulary and Information are especially high: generally in the mid-.90s, in terms of both internal consistency and test-retest.

Validity

The array of validity information for the WAIS is breathtaking in both its breadth and depth. The array includes thousands of studies on nearly every conceivable aspect of the test. The WAIS-III manuals reference content, criterion-related, and construct validity. As is true for most intelligence tests, the discussion of content validity is not very useful since there is no well-defined body of content that we can call "intelligence." Under criterion-related validity, the WAIS-III manuals report correlations with a great variety of other mental ability tests. Under construct validity, the manuals treat the factor structure of the test and what the manuals call comparison studies. Information on factor structure generally supports the use of the four Index Scores as recognizably distinct. The comparison studies show the patterns of WAIS-III scores for a host of special groups, for example, Alzheimer's, Parkinson's, learning disabled, and brain injured cases.

Profile Interpretation

Interpretation of the WAIS depends heavily on analysis of the profile of scores, including subtests and composite scores. Figure 8.4 shows the Profile Page from the WAIS-III test record booklet. It provides space to plot the scaled scores from the subtests, as well as the IQ and Index Scores. Another page allows for calculating "discrepancy comparisons" between Verbal and Performance IQs and among the four Index Scores. Yet another page provides space to show the difference between subtest scores and mean scores on all subtests. For all these comparisons, the summary spaces provide room to record the statistical significance of the difference and the frequency of the difference in the standardization samples, based on tables of

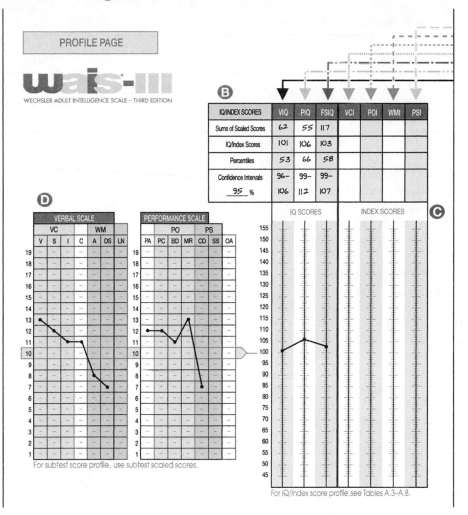

FIGURE 8.4 Profile page from the WAIS-III test record.

Source: From WAIS®-III, Administration and Scoring Manual (p. 56). Copyright © 1997 by Harcourt Assessment, Inc. Reproduced by permission. All rights reserved.

data in the test manuals. These summaries emphasize the need for the test interpreter to be conversant with the concept of errors of measurement, which we treated in Chapter 4. To the neophyte, such concepts may appear to be so much window dressing. However, they play a very real role in the ordinary work of the psychologist.

Groth-Marnat (2003) outlines a five-level process for reviewing WAIS-III performance. The first level concentrates on the Full Scale IQ. The second level deals with comparisons between the Verbal and Performance IQs and the Index Scores. The third level analyzes the profile of subtest scores. The fourth level involves

TABLE 8.8   *Subtests in the Wechsler Abbreviated Scale of Intelligence*

Subtest	Vocabulary	Similarities	Block Design	Matrix Reasoning	Yields
Version					
Four-subtest	x	x	x	x	VIQ, PIQ, FSIQ
Two-subtest	x			x	FSIQ

analysis of performance within a single subtest. The fifth and final level deals with the behavioral observations made during the course of test administration. Many-interpretations employ this type of approach, although perhaps not as formally as represented in Groth-Marnat's scheme. House (1996) provides a good example of the interpretation of WAIS scores, with an interesting case study.

Abbreviated Forms

Administration of the WAIS-III usually requires 60 to 90 minutes. That's a lot of time for both examiner and examinee. Over the years, numerous proposals have been offered for abbreviated or short forms of the WAIS. Generally, the intent of these abbreviated forms is to yield the VIQ, PIQ, and FSIQ, but in a much shorter time. Most proposals involve a selection of the subtests. A few proposals call for administration of only selected items within subtests. The number of subtests included in a short form depends on how diagnostic the proposer wants to be. The less diagnostic, the fewer the subtests. The more diagnostic, the greater the number of subtests. There have been proposals for two, three, four, and seven subtest forms. For a summary of various proposals, see Groth-Marnat (2003) and House (1996).

The publisher of the Wechsler scales, the Psychological Corporation, has itself recently issued the *Wechsler Abbreviated Scale of Intelligence* (WASI; Psychological Corporation, 1999). There are actually two versions: a four-subtest version and a two-subtest version. Table 8.8 shows the subtests employed in each version. The two-subtest version, requiring about 15 minutes of administration time, yields only the Full Scale IQ. The four-subtest version, requiring about 30 minutes to administer, yields Verbal, Performance, and Full Scale IQs. The WASI does not yield Index Scores. The WASI has norms for ages 6–89, thus spanning both WISC-III and WAIS-III ages. It is too early to tell how popular the WASI will be. If the numerous attempts to produce Wechsler short forms give any indication, then it seems likely that the WASI will become very popular.

Wechsler Intelligence Scale for Children—Third Edition

The *Wechsler Intelligence Scale for Children*—Fourth Edition aims to assess the intellectual ability of children in the age range 6–0 to 16–11. Today, WISC-IV is clearly the most widely used individual intelligence test for children, having displaced the Stanford-Binet from its lofty position. It will be convenient to describe WISC-IV by comparing it to WAIS-III.

WISC-IV versus WAIS-III

Originally conceived as a downward extension of the WAIS, the WISC, understandably, is highly similar to its parent instrument in purpose and structure. Most of what we said about the WAIS-III applies to the WISC-IV. In fact, there is much cross-referencing between the manuals for these two tests. At a very basic level, the most obvious difference between the tests is in the difficulty level of items. For example, in the Vocabulary subtest, WISC-IV might ask the meaning of "dictionary" while WAIS-III might ask the meaning of "bibliography." In arithmetic, WISC-IV might ask, "How much will you spend if you buy 2 pencils at 5 cents each?" while WAIS-III might ask "How much will you spend if you buy 4 pencils for 12 cents each and 2 notebooks for 90 cents each?" Of course, there is substantial overlap in difficulty level between the upper end of WISC-IV and lower end of WAIS-III.

In terms of structure, WISC-IV and WAIS-III are highly similar, but there are some differences. Table 8.9 lists the subtests and scores for WISC-IV. Compare this table with Table 8.5 for WAIS-III. We note the following *similarities:*

- Both tests yield a Full Scale IQ, four Index Scores (also reported in the IQ metric), and 10 to 15 subtest scores.

- Most of the subtests are the same, though appearing in somewhat different order. There are also a few differences in which subtests are supplementary. Descriptions of the WAIS-III subtests in Table 8.5 serve as adequate descriptions of the WISC-IV subtests, keeping in mind the differences in difficulty levels. However, this similarity does not necessarily mean that the subtests measure exactly the same traits at all age/ability levels.

The *differences* between WISC-IV and WAIS-III are as follows:

- WISC-IV abondons the Verbal IQ and Performance IQ scores, a distinction represented in all previous editions of both WAIS and WISC. The Index Scores are the new kid on the block, the conquest of factor analysis!

TABLE 8.9 *List of Subtests and Index Scores in WISC-IV*

Index Score	Core Subtests	Supplementary Subtests
Verbal Comprehension	Similarities Comprehension Vocabulary	Information Word Reasoning
Perceptual Reasoning	Block Design Matrix Reasoning Picture Concepts	Picture Completion
Working Memory	Digit Span Letter Number Sequencing	Arithmetic
Processing Speed	Coding Symbol Search	Cancellation
Full Scale IQ (FSIQ)	Sum of the four Index scores	

- Subtest composition of some Index Scores is slightly different between the two tests. Overall, however, the Indexes are very similar in composition. On a very minor note, the name is Perceptual Organization in WAIS-III but Perceptual Reasoning in WISC-IV.

- A type of expanded version of WISC-IV is the *WISC Integrated*. It provides additional subtests, many in multiple-choice format, designed to explore various cognitive processes, especially for children with disabilities.

WISC-IV versus WISC-III

WISC-IV is highly similar to its immediate predecessor, WISC-III. Well over one-half of the items remain unchanged or just slightly modified. The publisher attempted to update and enhance artwork for the items. There is some change in the order of administration for subtests. The most significant differences between the two editions are (a) a complete re-norming (b) elimination of the Verbal Performance IQs, thus adding to the prominence of the Index Scores, and (c) some change in subtests. Specifically, the following subtests were dropped from WISC-IV: Mazes, Object Assembly, and Picture Arrangement. The following subtests (some modeled on WAIS or WPSSI subtests) were added: Picture Concepts, Letter–Number Sequencing, Matrix Reasoning, Word Reasoning, and Cancellation. Development of the new edition also entailed additional study of item bias, new reliability studies, equating of norms for the two editions, and other ancillary research programs.

Performance on WISC-IV is highly correlated with performance on WISC-III. This is important in order to generalize validity studies from the earlier to the more recent edition. However, Full Scale IQs average about 3 points lower on WISC-IV than on WISC-III. Assuming that standardization programs for the two tests were equally good, which seems a reasonable assumption, this means that the population of children in the United States is about 3 points of IQ brighter in 2003 than in 1991. This is in addition to a 5-point increase from 1974 to 1991, making for an 8-point increase—approximately one-half standard deviation—over the 30 years from 1974 to 2003, roughly one generation. A variety of studies have confirmed such increases in the measured ability of entire populations, as we described in Chapter 7. This may seem like a trivial technical point, but it has substantial practical implications. Consider the difference it may make in classification of a person as being mentally retarded. Some who meet the IQ criterion for mental retardation on today's norms would not meet the criterion on norms for an earlier edition. That might affect the disposition of a death penalty case!

Psychometric Characteristics of WISC-IV

The WISC-IV manual offers an excellent presentation on the psychometric characteristics of the test. The standardization program involved 2,200 cases carefully selected to represent the U.S. population of children in the age range 6–16 years by gender, geographic region, race/ethnicity, and level of parents' education. Both the array of reliability data and the general level of reliability are similar to those for the

WAIS-III, as described earlier. In terms of internal consistency measures, the Full Scale IQ (FSIQ) rather uniformly shows $r = .97$, the Index Scores' reliabilities range generally in the low .90s, and subtest scores in the mid-.80s. For test-retest stability, the FSIQ averages .93, the Index Scores generally hover in the high .80s, and subtest scores in the mid-.80s. Inter-rater reliabilities for some subtests is virtually perfect, but even for those subtests requiring some judgment in scoring, the reliabilities are at least .95. Overall, this is a very reliable test, with the usual precaution that the shorter the test, the less reliable. As with the WAIS-III, the WISC-IV manual provides excellent advice about score comparisons. Validity data include correlations with a wide variety of other tests, factor analyses supporting the composite scores, and descriptions of performance by a host of different groups, for example, mentally retarded, learning disabled, and so on. All together, the validity data support use of the WISC-IV for its intended purposes. However, one needs to repeat—like a mantra—that no intelligence test is perfect, caution is always warranted in interpretation, and other sources of information must be secured when drawing conclusions about a person.

The Stanford-Binet

For many years, the *Stanford-Binet Intelligence Scale* reigned supreme as *the* measure of human intelligence. Today, in terms of frequency of use, it is clearly overshadowed by the Wechsler scales and rivaled even by several other individually administered mental ability tests. However, the **Stanford-Binet** is still widely used in clinical practice. More important, it holds a special place in the history of testing.

Recall from Chapter 1 that the Frenchman Alfred Binet, in collaboration with Simon, created the original Binet-Simon scales in 1905. For its day, when most theorists were concentrating on perceptual and sensory processes, Binet's conception of intelligence was revolutionary. It focused on what today we would call "higher mental processes," such as judgment and reasoning (see Binet & Simon, 1916). Table 8.4 gives Binet's famous definition of intelligence. Binet's test did not have a formal name; he simply called it a scale. Revisions appeared in 1908 and 1911.

Several Americans prepared English versions of the Binet-Simon scales. The most famous revision was the one prepared by Lewis Terman, then working at Stanford University. Terman published his first revision in 1916. It was a very substantial revision of Binet's work. What seemed to distinguish it from several other American revisions was the provision of a national norm, developed in a way that was very advanced for its time. It also introduced the ratio IQ, an entity destined to enter the national consciousness. Like Binet, Terman did not originally have a formal name for his test, but it soon came to be known as the Stanford-Binet. In informal discourse, the test is often called simply "the Binet." A first revision of the 1916 test appeared in 1937, with two parallel forms, designated L and M, and a new set of national norms. A version published in 1960 combined the two forms, known as Form L-M, but without any re-standardization. However, this revision abandoned the ratio IQ in favor of a standard score IQ. There was a re-standardization, but with minimal change in the content of Form L-M, in 1970.

TABLE 8.10 *Milestones in Development of the Stanford-Binet*

1905, 1908, 1911	Editions of the original Binet-Simon Scales
1916	Stanford revision of the Binet Scales, ratio IQ used
1937	Forms L and M, new standardization
1960	One form (L–M), no re-standardization, standard score IQ
1972	New standardization
1986	Fourth edition (SB4), multiple scores, new standardization
2003	Fifth edition (SB5), more scores, new standardization, change in SD for IQ

Transition to New Structure: SB4 and SB5

A new, fourth edition of the Stanford–Binet appeared in 1986 (Thorndike, Hagen, & Sattler, 1986); and another revision (SB5) in 2003 (Roid, 2003a, 2003b).[1] Table 8.10 summarizes some of the milestones in the history of the Stanford–Binet. Ordinarily, a new edition of a test introduces some minor adjustments in structure and updating of content, norms, and research programs. This was not the case with the newer editions of the Stanford–Binet. They did update content and norms, but they also included a radical departure from previous editions in two important ways. Both of these hallmark features stretched back to the original Binet scale. First, the classic Binet-type scale organized items by age level. Each age level contained items of diverse content, but similar in difficulty level. For example, age-level 6 might contain a few vocabulary items, a digit span item, some similarities, and an arithmetic problem, all appropriate in difficulty for this age level. Second, the classic Binet-type scale yielded a single, global score. In Binet's original work, this was a mental age. It evolved into the now-familiar IQ in the Stanford–Binet.

SB4 and SB5 abandon both features. Although they retain some items from their immediate predecessor, they are essentially an entirely new test rather than an evolution from the previous edition. In SB4 and SB5, items are organized by subtest in the tradition of the Wechsler scales. They also present multiple scores, in addition to a total score. It is important to recognize these structural changes because many references to "the Binet" or "the Stanford–Binet" describe the old, traditional structure rather than the current test.

Table 8.11 outlines the structure of SB5. Recall from Chapter 7 our discussion of a hierarchical model of intelligence, especially as represented in Carroll's model. The SB5 manual (Roid, 2003a) quite explicitly adopts this model, though acknowledging that SB5 does not cover all facets of the model. Table 8.11 should be viewed as a matrix: rows x columns. The matrix reveals the types of scores SB5 yields. At the highest level is a Full Scale IQ (FSIQ), much like the Wechsler scales. And, as with the Wechsler scales, FSIQ means "g." SB5, as suggested by the outline, also yields two other types of composite scores. First, it yields Verbal and Nonverbal IQs. These arise from summation of content down the two columns of the table. Second, it yields Index Scores, notably:

---

[1] Various sources refer to the Stanford-Binet Fourth Edition as SB-IV, SB-FE, or SB4. For the fifth edition, SB5 seems to be standard.

TABLE 8.11   *Organization of the Standford-Binet, Fifth Edition*

		Domains	
		Nonverbal (NV)	**Verbal (V)**
Factors	**Fluid Reasoning (FR)**	*Nonverbal Fluid Reasoning** Activities: Object Series/Matrices (Routing)	*Verbal Fluid Reasoning* Activities: Early Reasoning (2–3), Verbal Absurdilies (4), Verbal Analogies (5–6)
	Knowledge (KN)	*Nonverbal Knowledge* Activities: Procedural Knowledge (2–3) Picture Absurdities (4–6)	*Verbal Knowledge** Activities: Vocabulary (Routing)
	Quantitative Reasoning (QR)	*Nonverbal Quantitative Reasoning* Activities: Quantitative Reasoning (2–6)	*Verbal Quantitative Reasoning* Activities: Quantitatives Reasoning (2–6)
	Visual-Spatial Processing (VS)	*Nonverbal Visual-Spatial Processing* Activities: Form Board (1–2), Form Patterns (3–6)	*Verbal Visual-Spatial Processing* Activities: Position and Direction (2–6)
	Working Memory (WM)	*Nonverbal Working Memory* Activities: Delayed Response (1), Block Span (2–6)	*Verbal Working Memory* Activities: Memory for Sentences (2–3), Last Word (4–6)

Note: Names of the 10 Subtests are in ***bold italic***. Activities are shown with the levels at which they appear. *Routing Subtests

- Fluid Reasoning
- Knowledge
- Quantitative Reasoning
- Visual-Spatial Processing
- Working Memory

These Index Scores result from summations of content across the rows of the table. That is, each one has a verbal and a nonverbal component. The Index Scores are not called IQs, but they employ the familiar IQ metric: $M = 100$, $SD = 15$. On this matter, we note that SB5 has capitulated by adopting $SD = 15$, the Wechsler tradition, after eons of using $SD = 16$. Finally, like the Wechsler scales, SB5 yields scores for each of the cells in the matrix: a total of 10. These subtest scores use $M = 10$ and $SD = 3$.

An important feature of SB5 is the use of "routing tests"; these are marked (★) in the table. They are the Object Series/Matrices subtest in the Nonverbal domain and Vocabulary in the Verbal domain. All of the tests are organized into levels: five for nonverbal and six for verbal. The examiner administers these routing tests first and uses the results to determine the appropriate level of other tests to administer. Figure 8.5 illustrates how the routing tests work. Incidentally, use of the two routing tests by themselves serves as the SB5 Abbreviated IQ scale.

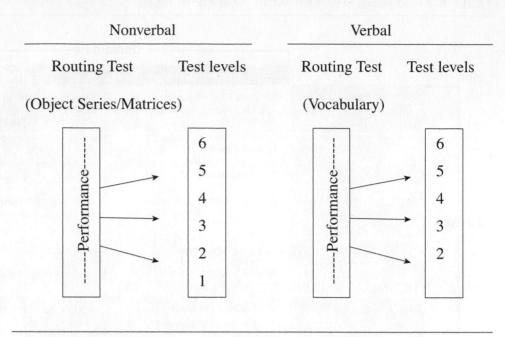

FIGURE 8.5   Use of a "routing test" in SB5.

Another very important feature of SB5, not apparent from Table 8.11, is its exceptionally broad target age range: ages 2 to 85+. Thus, whereas the Wechsler series provides different tests (WPPSI, WISC, WAIS—similar, although not identical in structure) across this age range, SB5 spans the entire range. Obviously, the difficulty level of items varies across the range, but there are also some changes in the types of items.

Psychometric Characteristics of SB5

In general, psychometric characteristics—norming, reliability, validity evidence—for SB5 are excellent. The array of data is very comparable to that already presented for the Wechsler scales. The rationale for the structure of the test is carefully presented. Norms are based on carefully selected and meticulously described samples throughout the 2–85+ age range. Great pains were taken to assure fairness, that is, absence of bias. Internal consistency reliabilities are generally in the .90s for the various total scores: full scale, Verbal, Nonverbal, and five index scores. Test-retest stability coefficients are only slightly lower. As is always the case, subtest reliabilities are lower but generally in the respectable range. Finally, as was true for the Wechsler scales, the SB5 manual presents a plethora of validity-related information: correlations with earlier editions and other tests, as well as group differences, for example, for samples of gifted, mentally retarded, learning disabled, and other such groups. All together, the SB5 manual provides a model of professional presentation. The perennial question is: Which is better, the Wechsler or the Stanford-Binet? We leave the answer to others. One thing is certain: The two series are much more similar today than they were in the past.

TRY IT

Compare the SB5 structure shown in Table 8.11 with Carroll's hierarchical model shown on page 268. What parts of Carroll's model are covered? What parts are not covered?

Brief Individually Administered Tests of Mental Ability

Among individually administered tests of mental ability, the most widely used tests require 60 to 90 minutes for administration and include a wide variety of item types. However, there are also individually administered tests that feature brevity and simplicity. Such tests are used when the clinician needs a quick, global assessment of mental ability. Sometimes the effort required for a lengthier, more detailed assessment does not seem justified. Subsequent work with a client may suggest the need for more detailed assessment of mental ability. However, a quick assessment may be sufficient initially.

Tests in this "brief" category usually require less than 15 minutes to administer and sometimes as little as 7 to 8 minutes. The tests usually yield a single, global score. They often consist of only one type of item. Validity information for these tests concentrates on showing that they have a reasonably high correlation with lengthier measures of mental ability.

Peabody Picture Vocabulary Test

The **Peabody Picture Vocabulary Test**—Third Edition (**PPVT**-III) provides an excellent example of a brief, simple test of mental ability. It requires 12 to 15 minutes to administer. Norms are available for ages $2\frac{1}{2}$ to 90+ years, an exceptionally wide age range for a single instrument. The test consists of 204 items. In each item, the examiner reads a single word. The examinee selects from among four pictures the one that best represents the word. Thus, though individually administered, the test items use a multiple-choice format.

The PPVT has risen steadily in popularity since its first publication in 1959. A revised edition (PPVT-R) appeared in 1981. The most recent edition, described here, appeared in 1997. Several surveys show that the PPVT now outranks the Stanford–Binet in usage, although it is a distant second to the WAIS and WISC (see, e.g., Watkins, Campbell, Nieberding, & Hallmark, 1995; Hutton, Dubes, & Muir, 1992; Lubin, Larsen, & Matarazzo, 1985). Even more impressively, among all types of tests, the PPVT ranked sixth overall in terms of number of references included in *Tests in Print-V* (Murphy, Impara, & Plake, 1999).

Purposes

The PPVT-III Examiner's Manual presents an exceptionally guarded statement of purpose. It states, "First, the PPVT-III is designed as a measure of an examinee's receptive (hearing) vocabulary. In this sense, it is an achievement test. ... Second, [it] serves as a screening test of verbal ability, or as one element in a comprehensive test battery of cognitive processes" (Dunn & Dunn, 1997a, p. 2). It appears that the typical use of the PPVT is as a short test of mental ability. The clear majority of validity studies abstracted from the professional literature, as reported in the Technical References (Williams & Wang, 1997), deal with the relationship between the PPVT and lengthier measures of intelligence, such as the Stanford–Binet and Wechsler scales. No one is trying to use the PPVT as a substitute for the *Stanford Achievement Test*. Many people are apparently attempting to use it as a substitute for the Stanford–Binet. The PPVT capitalizes on the fact that knowledge of words, whether tested as receptive or expressive vocabulary, is highly correlated with lengthier, more complicated measures of intelligence. Why vocabulary is such a good measure of "g" is not entirely clear. However, many studies show a high correlation between simple knowledge of words and other measures of intelligence. Thus, for example, the WAIS Vocabulary subtest appears in both versions of the *Wechsler Abbreviated Scale of Intelligence*. The utility of the PPVT depends on this relationship.

Materials

The PPVT-III consists of the following materials:

- *The Test Kit.* This includes the pictures to which examinees respond. There are separate kits for Forms IIIA and IIIB. Figure 8.6 shows how the kit is displayed for actual administration.

- *The Performance Record.* The examiner uses this six-page booklet to record responses, scores, identification information, and behavioral observations.

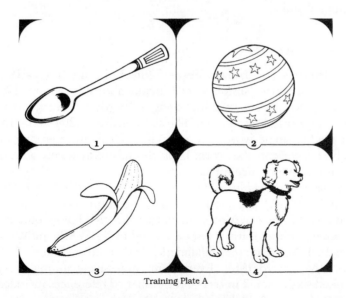

Training Plate A

Examiner displays card and says: Show me _____ or Point to _____

FIGURE 8.6 Sample item from the PPVT-III.

Source: From Dunn, L. M., & Dunn, L. M. Peabody Picture Vocabulary Test, (3rd Edition), Test Kit Form IIIA Training Plate A. Copyright © 1997. With permission of the publisher, American Guidance Service, Inc.

- *Examiner's Manual.* The 68-page manual describes the purposes and uses of the PPVT-III, provides instructions for administration and scoring, and summarizes technical characteristics of the test.
- *Norms Booklet.* This booklet consists entirely of norm tables for the test.
- *Technical References.* This 95-page book provides more detailed treatment of technical characteristics than is contained in the Examiner's Manual. Various sections cover test development, standardization, reliability, and validity. It includes references to studies of earlier editions of the test.

This array of materials is typical for brief measures of mental ability. The norms booklet is often included directly in the examiner's manual. Sometimes the last three items mentioned (examiner's manual, norms booklet, technical references) appear in a single book.

Administration

Physical arrangements for administration of the PPVT-III are essentially the same as for longer tests, as displayed in Figure 8.1. The examiner is seated with the examinee at a table. The examiner must establish rapport. There are sample items to introduce the task. The examinee looks at the pictures on a page of the test kit. The examiner says a word. The examinee indicates a response by pointing or giving the number of the picture.

The examiner must select a starting point, then establish a basal and a ceiling level. The 204 test items are arranged in 17 blocks of 12 items each. The 204 items are steeply graded in difficulty, from words that would be in the working vocabulary of most preschool children to words that would be considered highbrow in a master's thesis. This organization is apparent to the examiner but not to the examinee. The examiner selects a Start Item, the first item in one of the 17 blocks of items, based on the examinee's age. The examiner may select a higher or lower Start Item if there is good reason to suppose that the examinee is well above average or below average. The examiner then establishes a Basal Set, the lowest block of 12 items in which the examinee gets no more than one wrong. The examinee receives credit for all items below the Basal Set. Administration proceeds until the Ceiling Set is reached. The Ceiling Set is the highest block of 12 items in which there are at least 8 incorrect responses. After reaching the Ceiling Set, testing stops. Using these procedures, according to the Examiner's Manual, the typical individual responds to five blocks, that is, 60 items.

Our description of the administrative procedures for the PPVT-III illustrates an important point. Even for a fairly simple test like the PPVT, procedures for administration can be very detailed. It is essential that the procedures be followed for the test to be considered standardized. Violation of the procedures may render the norms inapplicable. For example, suppose the examiner continued to administer items after reaching the Ceiling Set. No doubt the examinee would get some items correct by chance, thus adding perhaps 5 or 6 points of raw score. That addition could lead to a serious overestimate of the person's ability.

Scores, Norms, and Standardization

Within the Ceiling Set, the examiner notes the highest item number, called the Ceiling Item. The raw score on the test is the Ceiling Item number minus the number of incorrect responses. This raw score converts to a normalized standard score and/or age equivalent. The standard score system has $M = 100$ and $SD = 15$, thus the same system as the Wechsler IQs. (In development of the standard scores, the raw score to standard score conversion actually involved an intermediate step, transparent to the user, whereby the raw scores convert to an IRT-based scale before translation to the normalized standard score.) The PPVT manuals never refer to this standard score as an IQ, but one has to wonder why this particular standard score system would be used other than to hint at an IQ. Separate standard score systems are developed for each age group at varying age intervals from 2–6 to 90–11. Standard scores may be converted to percentile ranks, stanines, and normal curve equivalents by means of a table similar to Table 3.1.

The age equivalent scores, based on median performance for successive age groups, range from "<1–9" (under one year and nine months) to "22+" (beyond age 22). Recall that age equivalents become quite meaningless when the trait being measured stops increasing (see p. 92). Figure 8.7 from the PPVT-III Examiner's Manual (Dunn & Dunn, 1997) provides a clear example of this phenomenon. This figure plots the median raw score for age groups in the PPVT-III standardization. Note that the curve rises steeply from age 2 to about 15, then rises slowly to about age 25, and is nearly flat throughout the adult years.

TRY IT ....

Use what you know about determining age equivalents with Figure 8.7. What age equivalent corresponds to a raw score of 130? If you have access to a PPVT-III Norms Booklet (Dunn & Dunn, 1997b), check the accuracy of your estimate by consulting Table 4 on page 46.

....

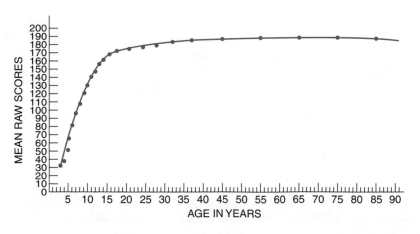

FIGURE 8.7   Growth curve on the PPVT-III.

Source: From Dunn, L. M., & Dunn, L. M. Peabody Picture Vocabulary Test, (3rd Edition), Test Kit Form IIIA Examiner's Manual, p. 47. Copyright © 1997. With permission of the publisher, American Guidance Service, Inc.

PPVT-III norms are based on samples of 100–150 cases per age group for 25 age groups from 2–6/2–11 to 61–90+ years, for a total of 2,725 cases. Cases were selected to be representative of the U.S. population in terms of age, gender, geographic region, race/ethnic group, and socioeconomic status, with the latter characteristic indicated by educational level. See Figure 3.27 for an example of the information provided. The manuals carefully document the representativeness of the standardization samples on these variables. Examiners excluded cases that could not adequately speak and understand English. There is no indication of how many cases were excluded for this reason.

Reliability

PPVT-III manuals provide an excellent array of reliability data. They include two types of internal consistency (split-half and alpha), alternate form, and test-retest. The internal consistency and alternate form reliability coefficients are based on all cases in the standardization program previously described. The test-retest data derive from subsamples of the standardization group retested approximately one month later. Internal consistency and alternate form reliabilities for the various age groups are nearly all in the mid-.90s, with medians of .94–.95. Test-retest reliabilities range from .91 to .94.

Reliability data for the PPVT-III illustrate an important general principle in psychological testing. With a narrowly defined trait (knowledge of vocabulary), an adequate number of items (an average of about 60 per examinee), and thorough test development procedures, one can get a very stable measurement even in a relatively brief period of testing time.

Validity

PPVT-III manuals address content, construct, and criterion-related validity, the last-named category receiving by far the most attention. Most of the criterion-related studies report correlations between the PPVT and other tests, especially the lengthier intelligence tests such as the Wechsler scales and the Stanford-Binet. The manuals also summarize studies with special populations, for example, mentally retarded, learning disabled, and gifted students. Separate sections of the manuals report studies of the new edition (PPVT-III) and the previous edition (PPVT-R). The section on PPVT-R presents abstracts of 122 published validity studies. Many of the studies report correlations with the WISC, SB-IV, and similar comprehensive tests of mental ability. This pattern suggests that, at least in the published literature, the principal interest is in use of the PPVT as a quick substitute for the lengthier measures of intelligence.

How highly does the PPVT correlate with the lengthier measures of intelligence? On average, the correlations are very high. Understandably, the correlations are especially high with more verbal measures, such as the Wechsler Verbal IQ. Correlations with performance and nonverbal measures are lower. Although results obviously vary across the dozens of criterion-related validity studies, it is not unusual to find PPVT correlations of .80 with such measures as the Wechsler VIQ or the Stanford-Binet Composite.

The PPVT-III illustrates that for at least some purposes a very simple, brief instrument yields reliable, useful information. In fact, it really seems quite remarkable that in a matter of about 15 minutes one can obtain a fairly good approximation to the information provided by the total score on a test like the SB-IV or WISC-III. Of course, the PPVT-III does not allow for profile analysis, discrepancy scores, and so on. But sometimes one does not need all that detail.

Two Other Entries

To illustrate individual tests of intelligence, we have provided descriptions of the WAIS-III, WISC-IV, SB5, and PPVT-III. There are many other individually administered tests of intelligence, far too many to list. However, two others merit mention because they are frequently cited in the literature on intelligence testing. They are the *Woodcock-Johnson Tests of Cognitive Abilities*, Third Edition (WJ-III), and the *Kaufman Assessment Battery for Children* (K-ABC). The reader is encouraged to consult the usual sources for further information about these two tests; to begin, check the publishers' websites in Appendix C.

A Test of a Specific Mental Ability: The Wechsler Memory Scale—III

Tests such as the WAIS-III, WISC-IV, and SB5 attempt to measure general intellectual functioning. They do so with an amalgam of content covering such areas as verbal meaning, quantitative reasoning, spatial relations, perceptual acuity, memory, and other intellectual tasks. They are like a market basket: a jar of this, a bag of that, a dozen of these, two pounds of those, and so on. Sometimes the psychologist wants to measure one area in more depth. The specific ability that receives the most attention is memory. Memory is crucial for learning, which, in turn, is a basis for further intellectual development. Memory seems particularly sensitive to changes in brain functioning. Such changes may result from head trauma, aging, and other conditions. Figure 8.8 depicts the relationship between measurement of general mental ability and the specific mental ability of memory. A measure of general mental ability consists of a variety of subareas. Without attempting to be exhaustive, we have marked vocabulary (V), verbal relations (VR), quantitative reasoning (Q), spatial relations (S), perceptual ability (P), and memory (M). There are several other subareas unmarked to indicate that our catalog is not complete; that is, other subareas may be included. Furthermore, memory itself can be broken down into several more specific areas, as indicated in Figure 8.8. We will identify some of these specific areas in the description of the next test.

A variety of tests are directed specifically at measuring memory. Clearly the most widely used is the **Wechsler Memory Scale**, Third Edition (**WMS-III**). This test is not only the most common measure of memory, but it is also one of the

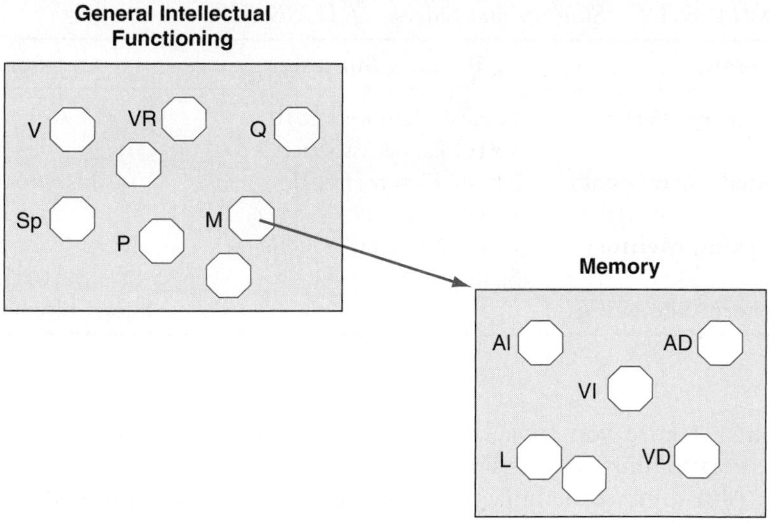

FIGURE 8.8 Relationship between measure of general mental functioning and measure of memory.

most popular tests in the psychologist's entire repertoire. Among all tests used by clinical psychologists, WMS-III ranks ninth; for neuropsychologists, it ranks third (Camara, Nathan, & Puente, 2000). For neuropsychological assessments, WMS-III is tied for second place in overall usage by both groups of psychologists (Camara, Nathan, & Puente, 1998). Because of this widespread usage, we provide a brief description of this instrument. For a history of the successive editions of the test, see Figure 8.2. We will see applications of the use of WMS-III in Chapter 10: Neuropsychological Assessment.

Structure and Items

As implied by the preceding paragraphs, WMS-III aims to measure memory in a clinically relevant way by tapping a variety of memory functions. The test is designed for ages 16–89. The same technical manual describes WMS-III and WAIS-III. In fact, standardizations for the two tests overlap. Administration of WMS-III is similar to the administration of individual intelligence tests. That is, there is an examiner who establishes rapport and presents stimulus materials to the examinee seated at a table. The examiner scores items immediately, uses start- and stop-rules, and records behavioral observations. The examiner must be trained to administer the test. WMS-III requires about 45 minutes to administer.

It is primarily a measure of short-term memory. The memory tasks range from immediate recall to recall over a 30-minute span. Except very indirectly, it does not attempt to measure long-term memory, for example, how much you remember

TABLE 8.12 *Structure and Subtests of WMS-III*

Domain	Primary Subtests	Optional Subtests
Auditory/Verbal	Logical Memory I & II Verbal Paired Associates I & II	Word Lists I & II
Visual/Nonverbal	Family Pictures I & II Faces I & II	Visual Reproduction I & II
Working Memory	Letter–Number Sequencing Spatial Span	Mental Control
General Screening		Information and Orientation

from a course you took last year. How would you approach testing short-term memory? Think of some simple tasks you encounter daily that draw on your memory. Also, think of memory tasks you may have seen demonstrated in the psychology lab. Take all these kinds of tasks and cast them in the form of test items, with standardized directions, very specific scoring criteria, and a test booklet to record answers. And, of course, add norms, studies of reliability, and demonstrations of validity. That is essentially what the WMS-III does. We will observe examples of specific memory tasks in the next section.

Table 8.12 outlines the structure of WMS-III. There are Primary and Optional Subtests. All Primary subtests must be administered to obtain the Primary Index scores. These Index Scores are like the Index Scores for WAIS-III, as described earlier. That is, they are based on combinations of subtests to yield more stable and coherent measures of some presumed underlying trait. From the brief descriptions of subtests in the figure, what the tasks are may not be perfectly evident. Let us give a few examples. We will not attempt to give detailed descriptions of all the subtests, but just enough to give the flavor of the test. The full array of subtests (both Primary and Optional) and scores for WMS-III is rather overwhelming. There are 18 subtests and 41 scores, including 8 primary indexes, 4 auditory process composites, and 23 supplemental scores.

The WMS-III uses two important distinctions. The first distinction is between auditory and visual input. On some items, the examinee hears the stimulus. On other items, the examinee sees the stimulus. Most important information in everyday life comes to us through one of these modalities. The test does not use the other sensory modalities. The second distinction is between **immediate** and **delayed memory**. In WMS-III, immediate memory means recall within a few seconds after presentation of the stimulus. It does not mean recall within milliseconds, as in study of afterimages and other such phenomena. Delayed memory means recall in 20 to 30 minutes after presentation of the stimulus. It is within the same testing period. Delayed recall does not mean recall after days, months, or years. Figure 8.9 outlines these two distinctions. Many of the subtests in WMS-III simply fill in the boxes in this figure. Notice that combinations of these two dimensions give rise to the specific areas identified in Figure 8.8; for example, AI is Auditory Immediate. Notice also that auditory input implies verbal material, whereas visual input implies nonverbal material.

	Length of Recall	
Type of Input	Immediate	Delayed
Auditory		
Visual		

FIGURE 8.9   Two important distinctions within WMS-III: Type of input and length of recall.

As we describe some of the subtests, notice the contrast with items from tests of general mental ability. There is no conceptual difficulty with memory items: no difficult words as in a vocabulary test, no abstractions as in a similarities or analogies test, no complicated manipulations of quantitative material. On their face, memory items are quite simple. The question is: Can you remember this simple stuff?

The label *Logical Memory* is a bit of a misnomer. There is no logic involved. The test stimulus is simply a detail-filled paragraph of about 50 words read to the examinee. The examinee is asked to repeat the story back to the examiner. The examiner checks off how many of the details the examinee repeated. For example, the examiner reads the passage in Figure 8.10. After the examiner is finished, the examinee repeats as much as he or she can remember. The test manual gives criteria for acceptable answers. There is also a "delayed" version of this task in which the examinee is asked to repeat the story again 30 minutes later. These delayed versions are the "II's" shown in Table 8.12.

Observe the *Visual Reproduction* item in Figure 8.10. This is a simple item. Obviously, much more complicated figures can be presented. These items, like the Logical Memory and Paired Associates items, can be administered in the "delayed" mode, too. The *Letter-Number Sequencing* task is the same as that used in WAIS-III (see Figure 8.3). The *Information and Orientation* subtest is optional, but it is ordinarily the first subtest administered. It asks for basic information about the individual (name, home address, etc.) and orientation in space and time (where are you now, what day is it, etc.). The examiner may not score these items, but poor performance on such basic information may indicate that it is not feasible to proceed with the remainder of the test.

Primary Index Scores are obtained from various combinations of subtests. For example, the Auditory Immediate Index comes from Logical Memory I and Verbal Paired Associates I. The Visual Immediate Index comes from Faces I and Family Pictures I. Then the Immediate Memory Index is the combination of all four of these subtests—that is, combining Auditory and Visual Indexes. The Working Memory Index is the sum of scores on Letter-Number Sequencing and Spatial Span.

Psychometric Characteristics

As indicated earlier, WMS-III was normed in conjunction with WAIS-III. This was an excellent standardization program. WMS-III Primary Index scores use the

Logical Memory Paragraph

Examiner reads:

Ned and Abigail went by train from New York to Washington. Although the train ride usually takes only 3 hours, they were delayed by a snow storm, so they did not arrive until almost midnight. Ned lived east of the train station and Abigail west of the station. There was only one cab, so they had to take that, dropping off Abigail first, then taking Ned in the opposite direction.

Then, examinee is asked to repeat the story. Examiner checks off how many items in the story were included in the response.

Verbal Paired Associates

Examiner reads these pairs once.

| pencil—down | car—baby | bake—four | foot—green |
| hill—print | paper—floor | tree—open | block—towel |

Examinee is asked to give the correct paired word when examiner reads one, e.g., "bake," then "tree," etc. The stimulus words do not follow the order of original presentation. Then examiner says the pairs a second time, and follows with stimulus words. The cycle is repeated several more times.

Visual Reproduction

Examinee is shown a figure for 10 seconds. The figure is removed and the examinee is asked to reproduce it. Here is a sample figure.

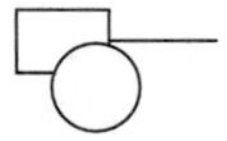

Mental Control

Count backward by 4's, starting with 37.

FIGURE 8.10   Examples of memory-type items similar to those on WMS-III.

now-familiar standard score system with $M = 100$ and $SD = 15$. As with WAIS-III, interpretation of WMS-III begins with conclusions about the general level of performance in comparison with national norms, then proceeds to profile analysis and discrepancy analysis, that is, identifying strengths and weaknesses.

Table 8.13 summarizes internal consistency and test-retest reliabilities for WMS-III Primary Subtests and Primary Indexes for selected groups. The WMS-III technical manual provides these data for separate age groups. It is evident that WMS-III subtests are, in general, not as reliable as the WAIS-III subtests. Even some of the Index Scores, based on combinations of subtests, show marginally acceptable levels of reliability. The person interpreting WMS-III profiles obviously needs to be aware of these limitations.

TABLE 8.13 *Reliability Coefficients for WMS-III Primary Subtests and Primary Indexes for Selected Groups*

Subtest/Index	Internal Consistency for Reference Group	Test-retest for Ages 16–54
Subtests		
Logical Memory I	.88	.74
Faces I	.76	.70
Verbal Paired Associates I	.92	.81
Family Pictures I	.84	.63
Letter–Number Sequencing	.79	.71
SpatialSpan	.85	.72
Logical Memory II	.75	.76
Faces II	.76	.63
Verbal Paired Associates II	.86	.77
Family Pictures II	.84	.68
Auditory Recognition Delayed	.76	.62
Indexes		
Auditory Immediate	.94	.85
Visual Immediate	.84	.77
Immediate Memory	.92	.85
Auditory Delayed	.87	.83
Visual Delayed	.83	.75
Auditory Recognition Delayed	.76	.62
General Memory	.92	.87
Working Memory	.88	.79

Source: Adapted from WAIS®-III/WMS®-III Technical Manual. Copyright © 1997 by Harcourt Assessment, Inc. Reproduced by permission. All rights reserved.

Validity information for WMS-III consists of correlations with other tests, group differences in average scores, and factor analytic results. In general, validity information supports the use of WMS-III as a measure of short-term memory. Correlations with other tests indicate that WMS-III is not simply a measure of general intelligence (discriminant validity) and gives reasonable correlation with other measures of memory (convergent validity). Reports of group differences show that WMS-III is sensitive to identification of groups that would be expected to have memory loss. The factor analytic results, in general, support the Index structure of the test, although there is some evidence that the factor structure may be somewhat different in different age groups.

Mental Retardation and the Concept of Adaptive Behavior

Individually administered intelligence tests play a crucial role in the definition of mental retardation. As noted in our discussion of the history of testing (pp. 20–31), several early developments in testing related to identification of the mentally retarded. In the early 1900s, the definition of mental retardation relied almost exclusively on intelligence tests. IQ ranges defined levels of retardation. According to one widely used system, there were three levels of retardation, defined by the following IQ ranges: 50–70, moron; 20–50, imbecile; below 20, idiot. In today's lexical world, these terms seem derogatory and insensitive. However, in the field of mental retardation, terminology that we now find objectionable fills even relatively recent history. Terms such as feebleminded, defective, lunatic, moron, imbecile, and idiot were common in the scientific (and legal) literature. These were simply the technical terms of the day. We should not assume that the writers were heartless. In fact, many of the writers devoted their entire professional lives to improving the lot of the mentally retarded. No doubt, a future generation will find some of the terms we use today in the mental health field to be terribly offensive. For useful summaries of the history of defining mental retardation, see Scheerenberger (1987), Smith (1997), and Editorial Board (1996). For the history in a British context, see Clarke and Clarke (1985).

The Concept of Adaptive Behavior

Increasingly, definitions of mental retardation have depended on the concept of **adaptive behavior**. Let us first explore this notion in general. In the next section, we will see how it becomes incorporated into formal definitions of mental retardation. Adaptive behavior refers to how well a person copes with ordinary life. Equivalent terms characterizing this notion are adaptive skills, adaptive functioning, functional skills, everyday functioning, and even practical intelligence. In earlier sources, common terms were social maturity and social competence. The key idea is: What does it take, at least at a simple level, to get along in ordinary life? Table 8.14 lists some behaviors that define adaptive functioning at different levels.

There are, obviously, age differences in these adaptive behaviors. For example, we expect a 10-year-old to be able to tie his shoelaces, but not a 3-year-old. We expect a 16-year-old to go to the store to buy bread, but not a 5-year-old. There are also cultural differences. Being able to dial 911 in an emergency might be important in one culture but irrelevant in another. Later, we examine specific tests that attempt to gauge these adaptive behaviors.

TRY IT!

Think of a 4-year-old boy, call him Frank. List a few things you think Frank needs to be able to do to get through his day.

TABLE 8.14   *Examples of Adaptive Behaviors at Three Levels*

Level 1	Feeding self, clothing self, climbing stairs, saying "hello," "goodbye"
Level 2	Telling time, making change, reading simple words
Level 3	Taking bus or subway, following news on TV, buying own clothes

> **Key Points Summary 8.2**
>
> *Three Criteria for Mental Retardation*
> *(All three must be met)*
> 1.　Significantly Subaverage Intellectual Functioning
> 2.　Limitations in Adaptive Behaviors
> 3.　Onset before Age 18

Definition of MR

Let us move now to formal definitions of mental retardation. Currently, the most common source for a definition of mental retardation is the **American Association on Mental Retardation (AAMR)**.[2] AAMR's (2002) book *Mental Retardation: Definition, Classification, and Systems of Support* (sometimes referred to as the AAMR manual, although the term *manual* does not appear in the title) uses the following definition (p. 8):

> Mental retardation is a disability characterized by significant limitations both in intellectual functioning and in adaptive behavior as expressed in conceptual, social, and practical adaptive skills. The disability originates before age 18.

TRY IT! ....

To see summaries of the AAMR definition of mental retardation, as well as the range of issues of interest to the organization, visit this website: www.aamr.org.

....

Notice that there are three criteria and all three must be met for the case to be considered one of mental retardation. The *first criterion* is significantly subaverage intellectual functioning. There are two issues here. (1) What is intellectual functioning? (2) What is significantly subaverage? In practice, intellectual functioning is nearly always defined by performance on one of the widely used individual intelligence tests, such as WISC. Definition of "significantly subaverage" has varied over the years, but it usually references standard deviation units in a standard score

---

[2] Before 1988, AAMR was AAMD: American Association on Mental Deficiency. Some sources still use the AAMD tag. Increasingly, the organization is using the term *intellectual disabilities* in place of "mental retardation."

system with $M = 100$ and $SD = 15$. The most common practice is to use two SDs below the mean, hence 70, as the cutoff point. Furthermore, minus three SDs takes us to 55, minus four SDs to 40, and minus five SDs to 25. These SD-defined cutoffs help to define levels of retardation. An estimated standard error of measurement of 5 points for the IQ is often overlaid on these cutoffs, resulting in ranges such as 70–75, 50–55, and so on as part of the definitions. This brief description illustrates the importance of knowing the concepts of standard scores, SD-units, and standard errors of measurement in order to understand the origins of such definitions.

The literature on mental retardation refers unabashedly to "IQ" and "IQ tests." Both AAMR and DSM-IV (see later) sources even use specific IQ scores for the criterion of intellectual functioning. Thus, while the rest of psychology squeamishly tries to remove the term IQ or, at least, rename it, the field of mental retardation evidences no such qualms.

AAMR's *second criterion* refers to limitations in adaptive skill areas. Three such areas are referenced: conceptual, social, and practical. The operational definition of mental retardation calls for performance at least two SDs below average in at least one of the three areas or on an overall score based on all three areas. (AAMR's 1992 definition included 10 areas, but the relentless application of factor analytic studies, as in so many other applications, led to the reduction to three areas.)

The *third criterion* is age. The condition must manifest itself before age 18. From a practical perspective, this is not ordinarily much of an issue because the assessment usually occurs well before age 18. However, from a technical perspective, it is important to note that if the first two criteria are met but the condition has not developed until, say, age 30, it would not be classified as mental retardation. In this case, the diagnostic classification would be something else. Mental retardation, by definition, is a condition that arises during the developmental years, operationally defined as before age 18. (A few sources extend this operational definition to age 22. However, the essential point remains that there is a developmental criterion.)

An important feature of the AAMR definition of mental retardation is the specification of levels. As noted earlier, traditional levels depended primarily on IQ ranges. However, AAMR defines levels in terms of "patterns and intensities of needed support." AAMR uses four levels of needed support: intermittent, limited, extensive, and pervasive. The emphasis is on adaptive functioning. The terms are largely self-explanatory and, obviously, represent shades of difference along a continuum. For example, the intermittent category means the person only occasionally needs help with basic adaptive behaviors. The pervasive category means the person is completely dependent, even for such basic functions as toileting.

The *Diagnostic and Statistical Manual of Mental Disorders*, Fourth Edition, Text Revision (DSM-IV) of the American Psychiatric Association (APA, 2000) adopts the AAMR definition of mental retardation. However, DSM-IV uses a different system for specifying degrees of severity. Table 8.15 shows the DSM-IV levels. Notice that these levels depend heavily on the IQ score. Notice also the labels: mild, moderate, severe, and profound. For most other conditions, DSM-IV uses only the first three levels. However, the "profound" category is well entrenched in the literature of mental retardation, so the DSM-IV system incorporates it. There is also a category for

TABLE 8.15 *DSM-IV Diagnostic Criteria for Mental Retardation*

A. Significantly subaverage intellectual functioning: an IQ of approximately 70 or below on an individually administered IQ test (for infants, a clinical judgment of significantly subaverage intellectual functioning).

B. Concurrent deficits or impairment in present adaptive functioning (i.e., the person's effectiveness in meeting the standards expected for his or her age by his or her cultural group) in at least two of the following areas: communication, self-care, home living, social/interpersonal skills, use of community resources, self-direction, functional academic skills, work, leisure, health and safety.

C. The onset is before age 18 years.

Code based on degree of severity reflecting level of intellectual impairment:

317	Mild Mental Retardation:	IQ level 50–55 to approximately 70
318.0	Moderate Mental Retardation:	IQ level 35–40 to 50–55
318.1	Severe Mental Retardation:	IQ level 20–25 to 35–40
318.2	Profound Mental Retardation:	IQ level below 20 or 25
319	Mental Retardation, Severity Unspecified: when there is strong presumption of Mental Retardation but the person's intelligence is untestable by standard tests	

Source: Reprinted with permission from the Diagnostic and statistical manual of mental disorders, Fourth Edition, Text Revision (Copyright 2000) American Psychiatric Association.

"severity unspecified," used when clinical judgment suggests retardation but there has been no formal assessment. Many sources also refer to a "borderline" category of retardation, usually corresponding to an IQ in the 70–80 range or from one SD to two SDs below the mean.

DSM-IV takes pains to emphasize the importance of distinguishing mental retardation from other conditions such as dementia, severe emotional disorder, and learning disabilities. Some of these other conditions may coexist with mental retardation, while others are mutually exclusive. Tests may be useful in making some of these distinctions.

Vineland Adaptive Behavior Scales

The most widely used measure of adaptive behavior is the **Vineland Adaptive Behavior Scales** (**VABS**; Sparrow, Balla, & Cicchetti, 1984; Sparrow, Cichetti, & Balla, 2005). These are revisions of the venerable *Vineland Social Maturity Scale* (VSMS; Doll, 1935, 1965). Its author, Edgar Doll, through his development of the VSMS and his other work based at the Vineland (NJ) Training School, helped pioneer the concept of adaptive behavior. Both the original scale and its more recent editions are usually known simply as "the **Vineland**." The 1984 revision often went by its acronym (VABS), whereas the publisher has tagged the 2005 revision as "Vineland–II." In this chapter we describe mainly the Vineland II, although we usually refer to it simply as the Vineland. The Vineland is among the top 20 tests used by clinical psychologists. It is the top-ranked test for both adaptive/functional assessment and developmental assessment among both clinical psychologists and neuropsychologists (Camara, Nathan, & Puente, 1998, 2000). We presume the Vineland II will gradually replace the earlier edition, although it is interesting to note that the original VSMS still experiences significant use.

The Vineland follows closely in the footsteps of its predecessor, the VSMS, in what it is attempting to measure and the general methodology for measurement. The Vineland differs from the VSMS primarily in the number of scores it yields, its greater sophistication in test development, and its greater variety of supplementary materials. The most important point to be learned here is how the concept of adaptive behavior, so crucial in the definition of mental retardation, becomes operationally defined.

The Vineland uses two approaches that distinguish it from measures of intelligence considered earlier in this chapter, for example, the WAIS, WISC, and SB5. (These differences generally apply to other measures of adaptive behavior, too.) First, the Vineland aims to measure *typical performance* rather than maximum performance. For example, on the WISC we want to test the limits of the child's vocabulary. On the Vineland, we want to know what kinds of words the child typically uses. Second, the Vineland obtains information from an *external observer* (e.g., a parent) rather than by direct questioning of the individual.

Versions

There are four versions of the Vineland. Each version yields scores for a number of Domains and Subdomains, as well as an Adaptive Behavior Composite score. Table 8.16 provides capsule descriptions of contents for the various parts.

The *Survey Interview Form* requires about 45 minutes to administer and an additional 15 to 30 minutes to score. This is the standard, most widely used version. The target age group goes all the way from birth to 90 years of age, a substantial expansion in years from the previous edition. There are 433 items, but not all items are used in all interviews because of the basal and ceiling rules. A trained examiner interviews a caregiver, usually a parent for a child, who is very familiar with the person being assessed. In many ways, procedures for administration are very similar to those for an individual intelligence test. The procedure is also similar to that of the semistructured interview described in Chapter 14. The examiner must establish rapport, have intimate familiarity with the standardized administrative directions, score items immediately, probe when needing clarification, determine basal and ceiling levels within subdomains, and so on.

Each item identifies a specific behavior. The items are arranged in hierarchies within clusters. The clusters, in turn, occur within the subdomains, as shown in Table 8.17. Based on the caregiver's description, the interviewer scores the item according to this system:

2 = Usually [does this]

1 = Sometimes or partially

0 = Never [does this]

N = No opportunity [to observe]

DK = Don't Know

TABLE 8.16   *Content Descriptions of Vineland Items by Domain and Subdomain*

Domain and Subdomain	Content
Communication	
Receptive	What the individual understands
Expressive	What the individual says
Written	What the individual reads and writes
Daily Living Skills	
Personal	How the individual eats, dresses, practices personal hygiene
Domestic	…household tasks the individual performs
Community	…uses time, money, telephone, job skills
Socialization	
Interpersonal Relationships	How the individual interacts with others
Play and Leisure Time	…plays and uses leisure time
Coping Skills	…demonstrates responsibility and sensitivity to others
Motor Skills	
Gross	…uses arms and legs for movement and coordination
Fine	…uses hands and fingers to manipulate objects
Adaptive Behavior Composite	A composite of the above areas
Maladaptive Behavior (Optional)	Undesirable behaviors which may interfere with the individual's adaptive functioning

Source: Adapted from: Sparrow, S. S., Cicchetti, D. V., & Balla, D. A., Vineland Adaptive Behavior Scales, Second Edition, Survey Forms Manual, Table 1.1, p. 3. Copyright © 2005. With permission of the publisher, Pearson Assessments.

Note: The Motor Skills domain may be omitted for some adult cases where it does not seem useful. If omitted, the manual provides directions for substituting scores in determining the Adaptive Behavior Composite.

Table 8.17 shows a Vineland-like item. This is not an actual item but illustrates the structure and administration of an item.

The *Expanded Interview Form* includes all of the Survey items, plus additional items to provide a more detailed description of the individual. It has approximately twice as many items and takes twice as long to administer. Administration procedures are the same as for the Survey Form. The Expanded Interview Form provides additional information for planning a developmental program for the individual and follow-up evaluation of the program.

The *Parent/Caregiver Rating Form* uses the same items as the Survey, but it is completed directly by the parent/caregiver. However, a person trained in administration of the Vineland must review responses with the parent/caregiver after the form has been completed in order to arrive at final scores. This form is new with the 2005

TABLE 8.17 *Simulated Example of Items Related to Adaptive Behavior*

Interviewer: Tell me about how Jack follows the news.

Caregiver: Gives narrative description.

Interviewer scores each of the following items: 2, 1,0, N, DK.

Interviewer probes caregiver's description, as needed, in order to score each item.
Shows awareness of major current events, e.g., presidential election   _____
Listens to news reports on radio or TV   _____
Reads daily newspaper   _____

edition of the Vineland. Time will tell whether it is a viable and useful addition to the series.

The *Teacher Rating Form* (formerly the Classroom Edition) of the Vineland is completed by a teacher, based on observations in an educational setting. It does not require an interviewer. Completion time is about 20 minutes. The target group is children aged 3 to 22 years.

In effect, the four different versions are four separate tests, each with its own test materials, development procedures, norms, and scores. They have in common a conception of adaptive behavior and, for the most part, the same domains and subdomains. An allied instrument is the *Vineland Social-Emotional Early Childhood Scales* (Vineland SEEC) aimed at children from birth through 5 years. As suggested by its title, this instrument concentrates only on the areas of social and emotional functioning.

The Vineland yields the usual panoply of normed scores for the four Domains and the Adaptive Behavior Composite: standard scores ($M = 100$, $SD = 15$), percentile ranks, and stanines. Note that the standard score system is the same as for the Wechsler scales. The Subdomains yield standard scores (called v-scale scores) with $M = 15$ and $SD = 3$. Rather oddly, the Vineland gives age equivalents for subdomains but not for domains and gives percentile ranks for domains but not subdomains.

The Vineland norms have two special features. First, the Vineland reports *adaptive behavior levels*. Initially, these may appear to be criterion-referenced definitions of adaptive functioning. They are not. They are strictly norm-referenced, defined in SD or percentile rank (PR) units as follows:

Adaptive Level	SD units	PR units
Low	Below −2	2 and below
Moderately Low	−1 to −2	3–17
Adequate	+1 to −1	18–83
Moderately High	+1 to +2	84–97
High	Above +2	98 and above

The term *adequate* for the middle category does smack of a criterion-referenced interpretation. It is an unfortunate usage, since there appears to be no basis for declaring this category or any other category either adequate or inadequate. It should also be noted that a middle (adequate) category, covering the 18th to 83rd percentiles, is a very broad range.

A second special feature of the Vineland norms relates to the Maladaptive Behavior Domain. Actually, this entire part of the Vineland warrants special comment. The Maladaptive Behavior Domain does not enter the Adaptive Behavior Composite. Moreover, its use is optional. High scores in the Maladaptive Behavior Domain are undesirable, whereas high scores in all other Vineland areas are desirable. The Maladaptive Behavior Domain includes 11 "internalizing" items, 10 "externalizing" items, 15 "other" items, and 14 "critical items." Separate *v*-scale scores are provided for Internalizing, Externalizing, and the (total) Maladaptive Behavior Index, which includes the internalizing, externalizing, and other items. The critical items stand on their own, not entering into any score. This domain yields Maladaptive levels, defined as follows:

Maladaptive Level	*SD units*	*v–Scale Score*
Average	Up to +1	Below 18
Elevated	+1 to +2	18–20
Clinically Significant	Above +2	21–24

The 1984 edition of the Vineland provided separate, abbreviated norms for a variety of clinical groups (e.g., emotionally disturbed children, ambulatory mentally retarded adults). The 2005 edition does not provide such norms.

Technical Characteristics

The technical characteristics of the Vineland are, on the whole, excellent. Norms are based on what appear to be well-defined and competently selected samples. The manual reports internal consistency, test-retest, and inter-rater reliability. In general, internal consistency and test-retest reliabilities are excellent, with some exceptions. Many of the inter-rater reliabilities are in the .70s, sometimes below, thus giving special urgency to the call for caution in interpreting scores. The Vineland has an excellent array of validity information, including correlations with other tests, factor analyses, and performance of relevant subgroups. Factor analyses provide support for the domain structure of the Vineland, although it must be admitted that a one-factor (general adaptive behavior) solution provides nearly as good a fit to the data. As usual, interpretation of all data in the manual for the many group contrasts and correlations with a multiplicity of other tests presents a daunting challenge for the reader.

Other Adaptive Scales

The Vineland is clearly the benchmark instrument for adaptive functioning. Its earlier editions almost single-handedly defined the entire field of adaptive behavior and, in the process, significantly shaped contemporary definitions of mental retardation. There are, however, numerous other measures of adaptive behavior. In general, these other measures tend to follow the basic patterns established by the Vineland: concentrating on everyday skills and behavior, assessing typical performance, and relying on reports by another person. The alternatives differ from the Vineland in such matters as specific domains assessed and level of detail. There is also wide variation in the richness of developmental research with these other instruments.

TRY IT! ....

To examine the variety of adaptive behavior measures, go to the ETS Test Collection site (sydneyplus.ets.org). Enter as key words adaptive behavior, adaptive functioning, or social maturity.

....

Infant and Early Childhood Tests

We will not review a specific example of a test designed for infants and very young children. However, we will briefly discuss some important characteristics of such tests. There are three main points to consider. First, the general categories of test items for these very young ages are similar to the categories used for older ages: words, memory, psychomotor tasks, quantitative material, and so on. However, the tasks are at such a simple level that it is not clear whether they measure the same dimensions as those measured at older ages. For example, being able to recognize the difference between many marbles and just one marble may not be on the same dimension as solving an arithmetic word problem, although both items are quantitative in nature. Recognizing the meaning of "hand" may not be on the same dimension as defining "arrogant," although both items deal with word meanings. Second, emphasis for these young ages is on developmental status rather than intelligence. In fact, we probably do not have a very clear idea of what intelligence means for, say, a 2-year-old. Perhaps both of these first two points help explain the negligible predictive power of infant tests (see pp. 280–281). Third, tests for these very young ages serve primarily a screening function. For the general population there is not a high correlation between measured intelligence at later ages (say, age 6 and beyond) and measures at very young ages. However, there is a high correlation for cases at the lowest end of the distribution. For example, moderate and severe retardation manifests itself at a young age. Hence, there is interest in screening cases that may need detailed evaluation. For young children following a normal course of development, there is no value in trying to measure intelligence at these very early ages. Among the most popular measures of early development are the *Bayley Scales of Infant Development* for ages 1 month to 42 months, the *McCarthy Scales of Children's Abilities* for ages 2–6 to 8–6, and the classic *Gesell Developmental Schedules* for ages 4 weeks to 6 years.

Other Applications

In a preceding section, we observed how one aspect of general intellectual functioning (memory) could be explored in more detail. In another section, we saw how a measure of general intellectual functioning could be paired with measurement of another construct (adaptive behavior) to help define a condition (mental retardation). These examples could be expanded almost indefinitely. Other examples might include measures applicable to learning disabilities, attention deficits, Alzheimer's dementia, creativity, hearing impairment, quantitative genius, and so on. Needless to say, space does not permit treatment of all these applications in an introductory text. However, we note that, regardless of the application, the questions are always the same.

- How do we conceptualize the issue (e.g., mental retardation, memory, dyslexia)?
- What tests or combination of tests (and nontest information) might be useful?
- Is the test providing reliable information?
- What evidence is there that the test is valid?
- Are the test norms reflective of some well-defined group?

If we follow this line of thought, we should be able to approach any area of interest with some success. In Chapter 10, we will examine additional applications to a variety of other conditions.

TRY IT!

To see how mental ability tests might apply to one of the areas mentioned in the last paragraph, enter one of the terms (e.g., dyslexia) as a keyword in PsychInfo. List the tests that are used to help assess the area.

Trends in Individual Intelligence Testing

Several trends can be detected in the nature and use of individually administered tests of mental ability in recent years. Newer editions of the widely used tests as well as the emergence of several newer tests show these trends. Some of the trends also characterize group-administered tests of mental ability, although we concentrate here on the individually administered tests. We will identify six trends, some of which have partially distinct elements within them.

First, the tests increasingly use some version of a *hierarchical model* of intelligence as a theoretical framework. Such models are not used rigidly but as a rough guide to test development and interpretation. References to Vernon's, Cattell's, and Carroll's hierarchical models are now common in the manuals for individually administered mental ability tests. In fact, the test user must have some familiarity with these models in order to follow the discussions of test interpretation in the manuals.

Second, among the comprehensive tests, there is a trend toward *greater complexity* in both the structure of the tests and ways in which scores are used. The increased complexity results partly from use of a hierarchical framework. Such a framework almost inevitably leads to production of more scores. Recent legal demands also lead to a need for more scores. We will examine some of these legal demands in Chapter 16. However, we can note here that if the definition of mental retardation refers to deficits in at least two of ten areas, this certainly suggests that one had best assess ten areas. Furthermore, the identification of learning disabilities depends heavily on comparing scores in different areas, hence suggesting use of a multiscore instrument. The Stanford-Binet provides perhaps the clearest example of this multiplication of scores. Whereas this test provided only one global score for its editions published over 70 years (1916–1986), the 1986 edition yields one total score, four major subscores, and 15 minor subscores. The most recent editions of the Wechsler scales have also added scores. However, quite apart from the production of more scores, the tests have become more complex in how the scores are used. Test manuals contain recommendations for more comparisons among scores. Computer scoring systems facilitate multiplication of score comparisons. All these factors interacting put additional strains on the test interpreter. Recall, for example, that the standard error of the difference between two test scores is not simply the sum of the standard errors for the separate tests. This is just one example of the fact that a proliferation of scores requires greater sophistication in the interpretation of those scores. The ready availability of computer-generated narrative reports, which easily spin out numerous comparisons, can be a boon to the user but also calls for extra caution.

Third, *materials for remedial instruction* increasingly accompany the tests. That is, once a profile of strengths and weaknesses has been determined with the tests, there are instructional materials aimed at capitalizing on the strengths and remediating the weaknesses. This is a direct outgrowth of the use of multi-score tests with persons with learning disabilities, ADHD, mental retardation, and other such conditions. Although this practice has a long history in achievement testing, it is a remarkable development for mental ability testing. We have not examined these instructional materials when presenting the tests because they would take us too far afield. However, the trend is unmistakable.

Fourth, although traditional scales like WISC and WAIS still predominate among individually administered tests of mental ability, there does seem to be *growing use of briefer instruments*. The major reason for this growth is the increased demand for efficiency in providing services within the health care industry (see Daw, 2001;

Key Points Summary 8.3

Recent Trends for Individually Administered Intelligence Tests

- Use of Hierarchical Model for Structure
- Increased Complexity
- Provision of Remedial Materials
- Growing Use of Briefer Tests
- Sophistication in Norming
- Attention to Test Bias

Piotrowski, 1999; Thompson et al., 2004). If service is to be covered by a third party, the third party does not want to pay for a 90-minute test if a 10-minute test gives the necessary information. This type of demand now pervades most of the health care industry. Provision of psychological services simply reflects this broader trend. A secondary reason for this trend may be the increased complexity already mentioned. That is, the longer instruments may have become too complex.

Fifth, almost without exception, the more widely used tests in this category feature *excellent norms.* The process of developing national norms for tests has become very sophisticated and standardized. Although some of the lesser-known tests may still rely on convenience sampling for preparation of norms, such a practice does not typify the more widely used tests. Not only the norming process itself but also the description of the process in test manuals has now reached a high level of excellence. Whereas the description of the norming process in earlier editions of these tests might consume only one or two pages in the test manual, the descriptions now typically cover a dozen or more pages.

Finally, *attention to test bias* has become highly explicit in the preparation of these tests. Items in the latest editions of these tests routinely undergo review by panels of minority representatives. Test publishers regularly use statistical procedures to detect item bias, as described on pages 239–242, in the test development process. Furthermore, discussion of test score interpretation gives much more attention now than in earlier times to possible effects of environmental and cultural factors. Virtually no one today would claim that performance on these tests is exclusively attributable to "innate" ability. Vastly increased attention to concerns about minority groups and persons with disabilities have motivated much of the development in this area. See Chapter 16 for details regarding this matter.

Summary

1. Psychologists use individually administered intelligence tests in a wide variety of practical applications.

2. Individual intelligence tests have the following common characteristics: individual administration, requiring advanced training to administer, covering a wide range of ages and abilities, the need to establish rapport, use of a free-response format, immediate scoring of items, needing about one hour for administration, and providing the opportunity for observation.

3. Many of the tests use items from these categories: vocabulary, verbal relations, information, meaning (comprehension), arithmetic reasoning, short-term memory, form patterns, and psychomotor skill. Some tests use only one or a few of these categories.

4. The Wechsler scales constitute a family of tests, several of them among the most widely used in psychology.

5. The *Wechsler Adult Intelligence Scale* (WAIS), now in its third edition, features Verbal and Performance scales, as well as four new Index Scores. We examined the nature of the subtests in some detail. The WAIS-III

norming, reliability, and validity studies are all of high quality. In the interpretation of WAIS-III scores great importance is accorded to profile analysis and discrepancy analysis. These procedures require special caution.

6. The *Wechsler Intelligence Scale for Children* (WISC), now in its fourth edition, is very similar to the WAIS-III in structure, purpose, and technical quality. However, there are some differences, especially in the list of subtests.

7. The fifth edition of the venerable Stanford-Binet adopted significant changes in structure from its predecessors. It continues to yield an overall score, but it now also yields scores in four major areas (verbal, quantitative, abstract/visual, and short-term memory abilities) and a host of more specific areas.

8. For some purposes, a brief measure of mental ability is sufficient. An excellent example of such a measure is the *Peabody Picture Vocabulary Test, Third Edition* (PPVT-III). This test relies entirely on auditory vocabulary, requires only 15 minutes to administer, and uses a multiple-choice format. It correlates highly with lengthier, more globally defined measures of intelligence.

9. The *Wechsler Memory Scale, Third Edition* (WMS-III), illustrates how one aspect of general mental ability can be measured in greater depth. The WMS-III is very widely used by clinical psychologists and neuropsychologists because of the sensitivity of memory functions to a variety of debilitating conditions.

10. Mental retardation, once defined almost exclusively by IQ, now depends partly on the notion of adaptive behavior.

11. The most widely used measures of adaptive behavior are the editions of "the Vineland." This test attempts to measure typical performance through reports from an individual familiar with the person being evaluated. The Vineland helped to re-define our understanding of mental retardation.

12. We identified six trends for individually administered intelligence tests: (1) use of hierarchical models of intelligence for determining the test's structure; (2) increases in the complexity of test structure, numbers of scores, and methods of reporting; (3) provision of remedial materials to follow up on low scores; (4) growing use of brief tests, primarily as a result of pressures from managed care; (5) great sophistication in norming the tests; and (6) greatly increased attention to test bias in the test development process.

Key Terms

AAMR	PIQ	VIQ
adaptive behavior	PPVT	WAIS
delayed memory	rapport	WISC
digit span	Stanford-Binet	WMS
FSIQ	start-and stop-rules	WPPSI
immediate memory	VABS	
index score	Vineland	

Exercises

1. Note the list of subtests in the WAIS-III in Table 8.5. Assign each subtest to one of the Level 2 strata in Carroll's hierarchical model (p. 268). Compare your assignment with someone else's assignment.

2. Among the items commonly used in individual intelligence tests are vocabulary, information, and arithmetic word problems. For each of these areas, prepare three test items that would be suitable for 6-year-old children.

3. The American Association on Mental Retardation (AAMR) is the main source for the definition of mental retardation. The organization also pursues legislative initiatives. To check on the latest developments in AAMR, go to www.AAMR.org.

4. Using the ETS Test Collection (sydneyplus.ets.org), identify any three adaptive behavior tests. Fill out this table:

Test	Test Title	Age Range	Scores
1			
2			
3			

5. For the *Vineland Adaptive Behavior Scales* (see p. 329), note the subdomains of receptive and expressive communication. Identify two examples of each skill area that might be used in the test. Remember, these skills must be displayed typically, and they must be observable to the person being interviewed.

6. You are going to administer the WISC to a 6-year-old girl. The first thing you have to do is establish rapport. What might you say or do to accomplish this? What about for a 16-year-old boy?

7. Refer to the sample items in Table 8.2. For each category, write two items that might be used in an individual intelligence test: one for age 6 and one for age 20.

8. Figure 8.8, at the beginning of the section on the Wechsler Memory Scale, illustrated how one realm within general intellectual functioning (memory) could be expanded into a more detailed test. Pick one of the other areas, for example, verbal or quantitative ability. List subtests you might create to provide more detailed measurement of this other area. Compare your list with someone else's list.

9. Return to Table 8.7. The table shows portions of the norm tables for WAIS–III Vocabulary and Block Design for two age groups. Using what you know about the normal distribution and standard scores (the scaled score in the left column of the table), draw overlapping distributions for the two age groups. Make two drawings: one showing the two groups on Vocabulary and the other showing the two groups on Block Design.

CHAPTER 9

Group Tests of Mental Ability

Objectives

1. Identify the major categories and applications of widely used group mental ability tests.

2. List the eight common characteristics of group mental ability tests, especially in contrast to individually administered mental ability tests.

3. For each of these tests, give the full title, purpose, target group, score scale, and brief summary of its reliability and validity: OLSAT8, SAT, ACT, GRE-G, and ASVAB.

4. Describe the intent of attempts to build culture-fair tests of mental ability and give examples of the types of items used in those tests.

5. Discuss the five generalizations regarding group mental ability tests.

Some Cases

- Mrs. Vasquez teaches grade 5 at St. Cecilia's School in Exeter. She is new to the school this year, hence does not know any of the children. At the end of grade 4, the students took a standardized achievement test and mental ability test. Mrs. Vasquez plans to work all of her students to the maximum. However, she is particularly concerned about identifying two types of students. First, does she have any students who are very bright, but achieving at a mediocre level? If so, she wants to find out how to motivate them in a special way so that they "really take off" this year. Second, does she have any students with quite low mental ability? She wants to make sure these students don't become discouraged by her no-nonsense approach to school work. Mrs. Vasquez scans the printouts of test scores with these questions in mind.

- Ivy College prides itself on its traditional, liberal arts curriculum. Lots of reading. Lots of writing assignments. There are also lots of applicants from private high schools and high socioeconomic suburban public schools. Ivy College would also like to attract students from lower socioeconomic and rural schools—students who never had an AP course, never traveled to Europe, never went to a museum. At the same time, Ivy College wants to make sure that these students have the basic ability to be successful within its high-powered curriculum. Is there a test of this "basic ability" that will help select these students?

- The U.S. Army will recruit 100,000 young men and women this year. They will fill about 300 jobs, including radar operator, fireman, intelligence officer, auto/truck mechanic, mess hall server, and so on. Is there anything about the mental abilities of these recruits that will help assign them to these various positions? What would you include in a test of their mental abilities?

All these cases illustrate situations calling for the application of group-administered mental ability tests. In this chapter we examine the characteristics of these tests and describe several specific examples.

Uses of Group-Administered Mental Ability Tests

The group-administered mental ability tests examined in this chapter are among the most widely used of all tests. Although no exact count is available, it seems safe to estimate that about 50 million of these tests are administered annually just in the United States. By the time the typical individual becomes an adult, at least in the United States and many other Western countries, he or she will have taken a half-dozen or more of these tests. These widely used mental ability tests fall naturally into four major groups. We will use these groups as an organizational scheme for this chapter.

The *first* major use is in elementary and secondary school settings. In these settings, group-administered mental ability tests are usually given in conjunction with a standardized achievement test as part of the school testing program. (See page 421 for a description of a typical school testing program.) Results of the mental ability and achievement tests are compared to determine if a student's achievement is reasonably consistent with his or her mental ability. The mental ability test may also be used as one of several criteria to select students for special programs, for example, a gifted student program or special education program.

A *second* major use of group-administered mental ability tests is for predicting success in college, graduate school or professional school. Examples of such tests include the SAT, ACT, GRE, and LSAT—initials familiar to most readers of this book. This category has two major subcategories. There are the two dominant tests used for college selection and placement: the SAT and ACT. A variety of tests are used for selection for graduate and professional schools.

A *third* major use of group-administered mental ability tests is for job selection or placement in military and business settings. Every inductee into the U.S. military service completes at least one mental ability test. Recall from Chapter 1 (p. 26) that testing large numbers of military recruits stimulated the development of the first group-administered mental ability test. Applicants for many federal and state jobs take "civil service" tests. Many businesses also use mental ability tests as one criterion in selecting employees.

Fourth, group-administered mental ability tests are widely used for research in the social/behavioral sciences. Some of this research relates directly to the nature of mental ability and its relationship to other variables, such as age, income, educational outcomes, or personality variables. We referred to some of these tests, for example, the Primary Mental Abilities Test, in the description of theories of intelligence in Chapter 7. In other instances, a measure of intelligence is included simply to describe the sample used in a research project. Individually administered tests are also used for research purposes. However, group-administered tests are used more frequently because they are so much easier to use.

Key Points Summary 9.1
Major Uses of Group Mental Ability Tests

- Elementary and Secondary Schools, with Achievement Tests
- Predicting Success in:
    College
    Graduate and Professional School
- Job Selection or Placement in Military and Business
- Research

Common Characteristics of Group Mental Ability Tests

Group-administered mental ability tests share a number of characteristics. Particularly noteworthy are the ways in which these tests differ from the individually administered tests described in the previous chapter.

First, and most obviously, these tests can be *administered to a large group.* Theoretically, there is no limit to the size of the group. A typical situation would involve 20 to 50 examinees and one test administrator. Larger groups of several hundred can be accommodated with one main administrator and several proctors. The main administrator reads the directions, while proctors circulate to maintain order, prevent cheating, and so on. Note that any test that can be administered to a large group can also be administered to an individual and this is sometimes done.

TRY IT!

List any group-administered mental ability tests you have taken in the past five years.

_____   _____   _____   _____

See if the tests you have taken fit the characteristics we outline in this section.

Second, group-administered tests are nearly always composed of *multiple-choice items.* Thus, the tests are amenable to *machine-scoring.* These characteristics (multiple-choice items and machine-scoring) particularly distinguish group administered from individually administered. There are, of course, exceptions. A few individual tests, such as the PPVT-III, use multiple-choice items. A few group-administered tests use a free-response format, thus usually requiring some "human scoring." However, the exceptions are very few.

Third, despite the latter differences in format, the *content of group and individual tests is very similar.* In the group tests, we will find vocabulary, verbal analogies, arithmetic reasoning, information, and many of the other kinds of items we

Source: Paul Thomas/The Image Bank/Getty Images, Inc

observed in individual tests. This similarity in content is hardly surprising. Recall that Otis created the first group-administered mental ability test to simulate the Binet. In addition, authors of both group and individual tests draw on the same research base about the nature of intelligence to create their tests.

Table 9.1 shows examples of items in both free-response and multiple-choice formats for content that often appears in both individual and group tests. The free-response items come from Table 8.2, where they were used as examples of items that might appear in individually administered intelligence tests. The most obvious difference between the two formats is the presence of optional answers for the multiple-choice version. Not so obvious is the fact that the item is spoken in the individually administered free-response format, whereas the examinee reads the item in the group-administered multiple-choice format (except for tests below grade 3).

There are two exceptions to this generalization about the similarity in content between group and individual tests. First, group tests usually do not include items measuring short-term memory. Second, group tests usually do not include manipulative items involving blocks, puzzles, and so on. The group administration venue ordinarily precludes use of both of these types of items.

Fourth, there is a *fixed time limit* and *fixed number of items* for these tests. For example, a group test may have 80 items and a time limit of 50 minutes. All examinees see all items, although not all examinees may answer all the items. Everyone works within the same time limit. These arrangements contrast with the individually administered test, with its start- and stop-rules leading to varying amounts of testing time for each individual. Some group-administered tests are becoming available in computer adaptive mode. In this mode, there may not be a fixed time limit or fixed number of items. However, it is still the case that the great majority of group-administered tests are administered in the conventional format. *Administration times* for typical group-administered tests show a peculiar bimodal

TABLE 9.1   *Examples of Items in Free-response- and Multiple-choice Format*

Typically Used In	Individually Administered Test	Group Administered Test
Format	*Free-response*	*Multiple-choice*
Vocabulary	What does arrogant mean?	Arrogant means (a) stingy (b) obese (c) haughty (d) malevolent
Verbal Relations	Father is to son as mother is to what?	Father is to son as mother is to (a) sister (b) niece (c) daughter (d) uncle
Arithmetic Reasoning	Jim bought 5 pencils for 12 cents each and 2 notebooks for 80 cents each. How much did he pay?	Jim bought 5 pencils for 12 cents each and 2 notebooks for 80 cents each. How much did he pay? (a) $2.20 (b) $1.20 (c) $2.32 (d) 99¢

distribution. Many have administration times in the 45–60 minute range. Others are in the $2\frac{1}{2}$–3 hour range.

In terms of numbers of scores, group tests are similar to individual tests. They usually yield a *total score plus several subscores,* for example, verbal and quantitative scores, or verbal and nonverbal scores. Some of the tests yield as many as 10 or 12 subscores. Each subscore usually has 25 to 50 items and requires 20 to 50 minutes administration time. Of course, there are variations on these patterns, but the patterns are remarkably common across a great variety of group-administered mental ability tests.

Among the more widely used group mental ability tests, the research base for norming, equating, determining reliability, and so on is *very large,* usually much larger than for individually administered tests. Whereas the norm group for an individually administered test may involve 2,000 cases, the norm group for a group test may involve 200,000 or even a million cases.

Virtually all the tests in this category have as their *principal purpose prediction.* Some aim to predict performance in school, ranging from the earliest grades in primary school on up to graduate and professional school. Of course, from a practical perspective, prediction often translates into selection, for example, selection for graduate school. Other tests aim to predict success on the job. Hence, predictive validity studies hold a premier place in the research literature about these tests. The effect of restriction in range on correlation coefficients is particularly acute in these predictive validity studies. In order to interpret **predictive validity** data for these tests, especially those at the upper range of ability, the reader may wish to review this topic (restriction in range) on pages 175–177. The effect of imperfect reliability in the criterion (see pp. 176–177) is also important in these studies. An ancillary purpose for many of the tests is to aid in placement within educational or job settings in order to maximize success, but prediction or selection remains the primary purpose.

Key Points Summary 9.2

Common Characteristics of Group-Administered Mental Ability Tests

- Can Be Administered to Large Groups
- Multiple-choice, Machine-scored Items
- Content Generally Similar to Individual Tests
- Fixed Time-limit, Fixed Number of Items
- Administration Times: 1 *or* 3 Hours
- Total Score Plus Several Subscores
- Research Bases Very Large
- Principal Purpose: Prediction

Mental Ability Tests in School Testing Programs

As previously noted, one major use of group-administered mental ability tests is in school testing programs. Although there are an enormous number of group mental ability tests, only a few fall in this category. However, each of these is itself very widely used. Table 9.2 lists the major entries in this category: the **Otis-Lennon School Ability Test (OLSAT)**, the *Test of Cognitive Skills,* and the *Cognitive Abilities Test.* Each is paired with one of the major standardized achievement batteries, as described later in Chapter 11. We describe below one of these series of tests, the Otis-Lennon. The three tests listed in Table 9.2 are very similar in many ways. Hence, many of our observations about the Otis-Lennon apply to the other tests listed in Table 9.2.

One of the special features of all these tests is their multilevel structure. Notice the second column in Table 9.2 indicating the number of levels. Recall that individually administered tests allowed for covering a wide range of ages and abilities by having start- and stop-rules. That strategy obviously will not work for a group-administered test in which everyone takes the same items. A **multilevel test** structure accommodates individual differences—which are particularly dramatic during the younger ages—by having different levels of the test for different ages or grades. The various levels are then linked statistically to allow for continuous score scales throughout the range covered by the test.

Otis-Lennon School Ability Test

The *Otis-Lennon School Ability Test,* Eighth Edition (OLSAT8; Otis & Lennon, 2003) is the most recent version in the long line of Otis intelligence tests. Recall

TABLE 9.2　*Group-Administered Mental Ability Tests Used in School Testing Programs*

Test	Levels/Grades	Scores	Publisher[a]	Related to
Otis-Lennon School Ability Test (OLSAT)	7 levels K–12	Verbal, Nonverbal, Clusters, Total	Harcourt Assessment	Stanford Achievement Test Metropolitan Achievement Tests
Test of Cognitive Skills (TCS)	6 levels, 2–12	Verbal, Nonverbal, Memory, Total	CTB/McGraw Hill	Terra Nova
Cognitive Abilities Test (CogAT)	11 levels, K–12	Verbal, Quantitative, Nonverbal, Composite	Riverside Publishing	The Iowa Tests

[a] See Appendix C for publisher contact information, including website.

from Chapter 1 that Otis's effort to create a group-administered form of the Binet-type test represented a milestone in the history of testing. The successive editions of Otis's tests have been among the most widely used tests in the world for nearly 100 years. According to the OLSAT8 Technical Manual, "OLSAT8 is designed to measure those verbal, quantitative, and figural reasoning skills that are most closely related to scholastic achievement. The OLSAT series is based on the idea that to learn new things, students must be able to perceive accurately, to recognize and recall what has been perceived, to think logically, to understand relationships, to abstract from a set of particulars, and to apply generalizations to new and different contexts" (Otis & Lennon, 2003, p. 5).

OLS AT8 finds its primary use in school testing programs. It is jointly normed with *Stanford Achievement Test,* Tenth Edition.

Structure and Items

Table 9.3 outlines the OLSAT8 structure. The structure is similar, though not identical, across the seven levels of the series. An examinee takes one of these levels. The selection depends on the examinee's grade in school, age, and/or estimated ability. Table 9.3 shows the grades in which a level of OLSAT8 would typically be used. However, given the way the test was developed, it is feasible to use atypical levels. A school administrator makes the decision about what level of the test to administer to a group of students. For example, a very bright group of grade 2 students might be measured more effectively with Level D than with the more typical Level C; the students might "top out" on Level C. Figure 9.1 illustrates how the various levels cover different areas of the full-ability spectrum. At the left of the ability spectrum are students of lower ability and/or younger ages. At the right of the ability spectrum are the students with greater ability and/or higher grade levels. Notice that the test levels overlap in their coverage. For example, the upper reaches of Level A cover the same areas as the middle reaches of Level B, and so on. This multilevel arrangement approximates the use of stop- and start-rules for individually administered tests.

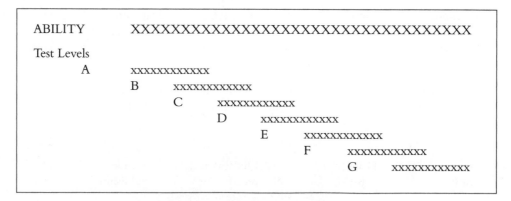

FIGURE 9.1 Illustration of how a multilevel test covers the ability spectrum.

TABLE 9.3 OLSAT Structure

Verbal Comprehension

Verbal Reasoning — } Verbal }

Pictorial Reasoning [a]

Figural Reasoning — } Nonverbal — Total

Quantitative Reasoning [b]

[a] Occurs only at the three lowest levels (A, B, C).

[b] Occurs only at the three highest levels (E, F, G).

Next, note the categories of test items. OLSAT8 yields a total score, based on all items at a given level (60–72 items); verbal and nonverbal subscores, based on 30–36 items per area at each level; and cluster scores. The clusters include verbal comprehension and verbal reasoning within the verbal area; pictorial reasoning, figural reasoning, and quantitative reasoning within the nonverbal area. There is further subdivision of items within clusters (e.g., aural reasoning and arithmetic reasoning within the verbal reasoning cluster), but these further subdivisions do not yield any type of score.

TRY IT!

Look at the items in Figure 9.2. How would you classify each item in the outline of leftmost subcategories listed in Table 9.3? Compare your classifications with someone else's. Do you agree?

Provision of a number of different scores is a relatively recent development within the Otis series. The earliest editions yielded only a single, global score, although they incorporated a variety of item types. The OLSAT8 manual explicitly adopts Vernon's hierarchical model of intelligence (see Figure 7.4) as a framework for test development. The manual notes that OLSAT8 attempts to measure only the v:ed portion of the model. However, it is apparent that OLSAT8 uses Vernon's model only roughly. In fact, the model does not use a distinction between verbal and nonverbal, certainly not within the v:ed portion of the model. In any case, the outline in Table 9.3 certainly illustrates a hierarchical model.

Test items for a group-administered mental ability test typically appear in a test booklet of about 12 to 20 pages. Such is the case for OLSAT8. See Figure 9.2 for a

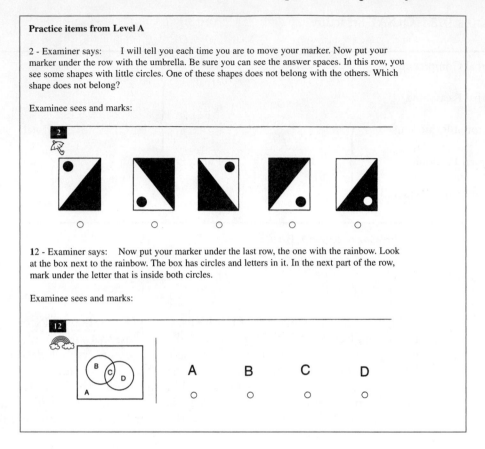

Practice items from Level A

2 - Examiner says: I will tell you each time you are to move your marker. Now put your marker under the row with the umbrella. Be sure you can see the answer spaces. In this row, you see some shapes with little circles. One of these shapes does not belong with the others. Which shape does not belong?

Examinee sees and marks:

12 - Examiner says: Now put your marker under the last row, the one with the rainbow. Look at the box next to the rainbow. The box has circles and letters in it. In the next part of the row, mark under the letter that is inside both circles.

Examinee sees and marks:

Practice items from Level F

3   The numbers in each box go together by following the *same* rule. Decide what the rule is, and then choose the number that goes where you see the question mark.

| 4, 10, 8 | 3, 9, 7 | 7, 13, ? | **A** 9   **B** 10   **C** 11   **D** 14   **E** 19

4   Which word does *not* go with the other four?

F   manager   **G**   participant   **H**   leader   **J**   director   **K**   commander

9   The opposite of **guilty** is —

A   innocent   **B**   brave   **C**   unselfish   **D**   proud   **E**   friendly

FIGURE 9.2   Examples of types of items in OLSAT7.

Source: From Otis, A.S., & Lennon, R.T. Otis–Lennon School Ability Test, Seventh edition. Copyright © 1996 by Harcourt Assessment, Inc. Reproduced by permission. All rights reserved.

sampling of the types of items included in OLSAT8. Similar items occur in most other group-administered mental ability tests. In test administration, the examiner would precede the actual test items with practice items, instructions regarding how to mark answers, and so on.

Scores, Norms, Standardization

Like most tests, OLSAT8 first yields a raw score or, actually, several raw scores: Total, Verbal, and Nonverbal. These are converted to Scaled scores, a type of score used primarily to convert scores from all the levels into a common score system. These Scaled scores themselves are rarely used for practical interpretation. Rather, they are converted to the School Ability Index (SAI). The SAI is a standard score with $M = 100$ and $SD = 16$. This is the same score system as the old IQ used in previous editions of the Otis series. As noted earlier in this chapter, test publishers have made an effort to abandon IQ terminology—obviously without giving it up wholly. SAIs are determined separately for age groups in three-month intervals from ages 5 to 19. Note that there are no separate norms for adult groups, as there are for tests like WAIS-III and PPVT-III.

SAIs can be converted into percentile ranks and stanines, either by age group or grade group. Normal curve equivalents (NCEs) can be derived simply from the percentile ranks. Cluster scores are converted to a simple three-category scale: below average, average, above average, corresponding to stanines 1–3, 4–6, and 7–9, respectively.

In the typical use of OLSAT8, a computer would complete all these conversions and the user would be given a computer printed report. Of course, it is also possible to complete the conversions, laboriously, by hand using the norms booklet provided with the test materials. Conversions of SAIs into percentile ranks, stanines, and NCEs are made using tables similar to Table 3.1.

Figure 9.3 shows a sample score report containing OLSAT8 scores. As noted earlier, a test such as OLSAT8 is ordinarily used in conjunction with a standardized achievement test. The report in Figure 9.3 contains scores for OLSAT8 as well as for *Stanford Achievement Test,* a test we examine in Chapter 11. OLSAT8 scores appear in the middle portion of the report. Note that the scores include SAIs, percentile ranks, and stanines. OLSAT performance also enters the report in another way. The report incorporates *Anticipated Achievement Comparisons* **(AACs)**. OLSAT8 is used to predict performance on each of the Stanford tests. Then, predicted performance is compared with actual performance on the Stanford tests. In the column labeled AAC Range, the report notes the result of this comparison. "High" means that the achievement score was in the top 23% of cases for the student's OLSAT stanine. "Middle" means that the achievement score was in the middle 54% of cases. "Low" means that the achievement score was in the bottom 23% of cases. This is done separately for each achievement test. Figure 9.4 illustrates how the comparison works. Of course, all the computations are done "in the computer" and only the result appears on the report. There is nothing very special about this methodology. It is a straightforward application of expectancy tables. All of the mental ability tests listed in Table 9.2 provide a report that performs essentially these same operations, although the exact methodology and terminology may differ from the report shown here.

TRY IT! ....

For the case shown in Figure 9.3, what is the student's SAI? This score corresponds to approximately what z-score?

....

Development of OLSAT8 norms demonstrates the kind of expertise that major test publishers can bring to bear on the task today. OLSAT8 norms are empirically derived for each of grades K–12, separately for fall and spring periods within each year. Approximately 275,500 students participated in the spring norming and 135,000 in the fall norming. Adding cases that were in ancillary research programs, approximately one-half million cases contributed to the research base for OLSAT8.

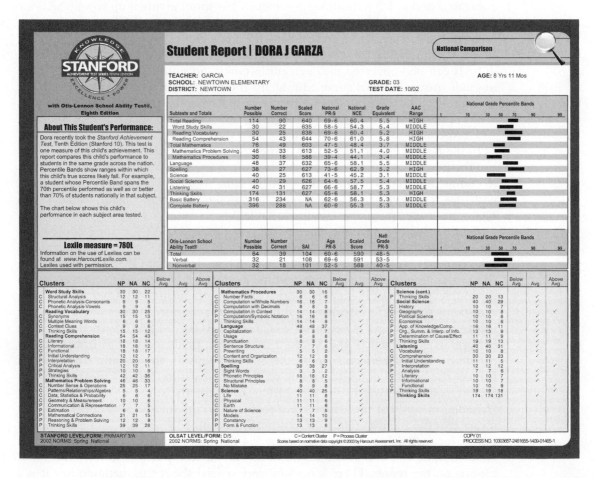

FIGURE 9.3 Sample report including OLSAT8 scores and Anticipated Achievement Comparisons.

Source: From Stanford Achievement Test Series, Tenth Edition. Copyright © 2003 by Harcourt Assessment, Inc. Reproduced by permission. All rights reserved.

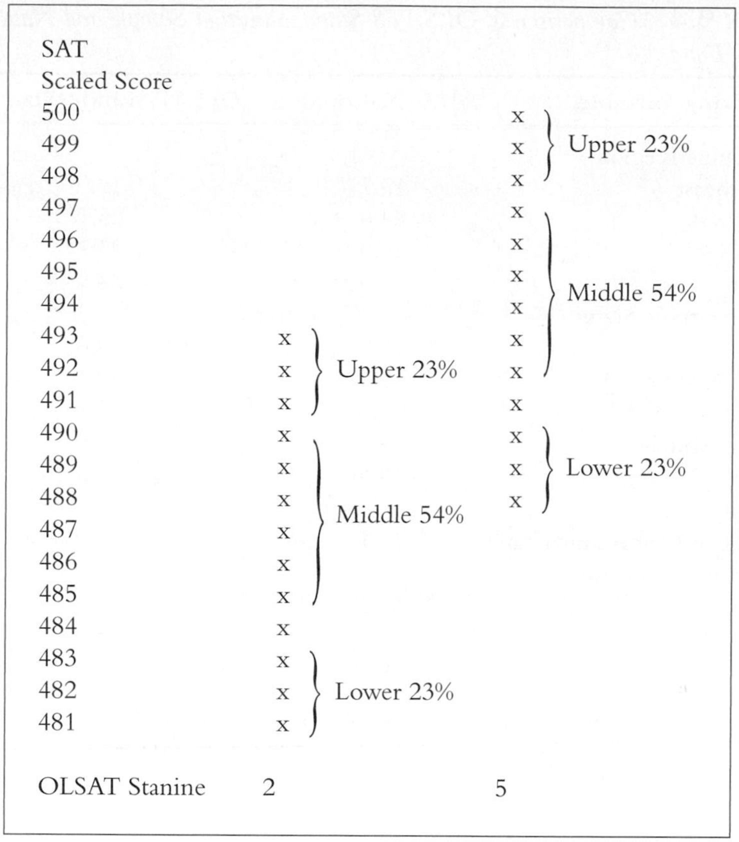

```
SAT
Scaled Score
500                                    x  ⎞
499                                    x  ⎬ Upper 23%
498                                    x  ⎠
497                                    x  ⎞
496                                    x  ⎟
495                                    x  ⎟
494                                    x  ⎬ Middle 54%
493                 x  ⎞               x  ⎟
492                 x  ⎬ Upper 23%    x  ⎠
491                 x  ⎠               x
490                 x  ⎞               x
489                 x  ⎟               x  ⎞ Lower 23%
488                 x  ⎟               x  ⎠
487                 x  ⎬ Middle 54%
486                 x  ⎟
485                 x  ⎠
484                 x
483                 x  ⎞
482                 x  ⎬ Lower 23%
481                 x  ⎠

OLSAT Stanine      2                   5
```

FIGURE 9.4 Methodology used to obtain Anticipated Achievement Comparison (AAC) between mental ability test and achievement test (simulated distributions).

For both fall and spring norm groups, cases were stratified by socioeconomic level, urbanicity, and ethnicity. Cases were also weighted to improve the fit with total population characteristics. Table 9.4 summarizes the fit between the OLSAT8 fall standardization group and national population data for several of the stratification variables. Notice that the fit between national data and standardization sample is very close.

Standardization data for most of the widely used group-administered mental ability and achievement tests follow patterns similar to those outlined here for OLSAT8. From earlier days of sometimes haphazard or ill-conceived norming procedures, the field has attained a high level of sophistication in determining norms. However, several significant issues still lead to cautionary notes. There are two principal concerns. First, we often do not know what percentage of students a school system has excluded from the normative testing. Certainly some students are excluded. The percentage is probably around 5%. More important, we usually know little about the motivation level of students in the norming program. This may be a particularly troublesome issue in the upper grades, where students are typically less compliant. However, we do not know much about this issue.

TABLE 9.4   *Comparison of OLSAT8 Standardization Sample and National Census Data*

Stratifying Variable	U.S. National	OLSAT Standardization
Geographic Region		
Northeast	19.7	17.0
Midwest	24.0	25.1
South	24.0	23.7
West	32.3	34.9
Socioeconomic Status		
Low	19.8	19.8
Low–Middle	19.6	20.1
Middle	21.0	22.2
High–Middle	19.7	18.6
High	19.9	19.3
Ethnicity		
Black or African American	15.1	15.0
Hispanic or Latino	15.0	14.3
White	65.2	67.0
Asian	3.8	3.5
Other	0.9	0.2

Source: From Otis, A. S., & Lennon, R. T. Otis-Lennon School Ability Test, Eighth Edition. Copyright © 2003 by Harcourt Assessment, Inc. Reproduced by permission. All rights reserved.

Reliability

The OLSAT Technical Manual (Otis & Lennon, 2003) provides several types of reliability information. KR-20 reliabilities for Total scores at various grades fall in a narrow band from .89 to .94. We can use .92 as a convenient summary index for the internal consistency reliability within a grade. KR-20 reliabilities for the Verbal and Nonverbal scores range for various grades from .81 to .90, with a median of .84 for Verbal and .86 for Nonverbal. We can use .85 as a convenient summary index for the internal consistency reliability within a grade for these subscores.

The OLSAT8 manual also provides KR-21 reliability coefficients for Total score, Verbal and Nonverbal subscores, and cluster scores. These data are provided separately by grade for fall and spring standardization periods. It is odd to see KR-21 reliability coefficients for a recently developed test. The KR-21 formula is an estimate that was useful in the pre-computer era but is now obsolete. More important, the KR-21 data show that the cluster scores are often quite unreliable and probably should not be reported as separate scores. Although some of the cluster reliabilities are quite respectable, many are in the .50s and .60s—clearly substandard for ordinary usage.

The extensive tables of KR-20 and KR-21 reliability data also contain standard errors of measurement *(SEM)* for the scores. The *SEMs* are all given in raw score units. This is unfortunate because one virtually never interprets scores on such a test in raw score units. Happily, the manual provides a separate table with *SEMs* for Total, Verbal, and Nonverbal scores in School Ability Index (SAI) units. All these *SEMs* are in the range of 5.5–5.8. That is, the *SEMs* in SAI units are all about one-third of a standard deviation (recall that the OLSAT8 *SD* = 16). This is a good rule of thumb: For a well-constructed test of reasonable length, the *SEM* will usually be about one-third of the standard deviation.

The OLSAT8 manual does not report test-retest reliability data. This is a significant omission. At a minimum, the manual should have reported test-retest data for earlier versions of the test. The manual does argue for the continuity of the successive editions and even presents correlations between the seventh and eighth editions.

Validity

The OLSAT manual addresses validity under content, relations to other variables, and internal test structure. It claims content validity based on simple inspection of the items. This is more a matter of face validity: Do the items look like they are measuring school-related ability? Use of content validity presumes the existence of some well-defined body of material against which we can match test content. We do not have a well-defined body of material called school-related ability (or intelligence or mental ability, the predecessor terms in the Otis series). The manual also argues that the correlations between the seventh and eighth editions demonstrate content validity. That line of argument is hard to follow.

Under relationships with other variables, the manual includes data on the correlations of OLSAT scores with *Stanford Achievement Test*, Tenth Edition, a test we take up in detail in Chapter 11. Table 9.5 presents a selection of these correlations.

TABLE 9.5   *Selected Correlatons between OLSAT8 and SAT9*

		OLSAT		
Grade	Stanford	Total	Verbal	Nonverbal
K	Total Reading	.68	.65	.61
	Total Mathematics	.73	.72	.62
3	Total Reading	.76	.78	.60
	Total Mathematics	.75	.72	.66
6	Total Reading	.69	.67	.63
	Total Mathematics	.73	.63	.73
9	Total Reading	.71	.70	.65
	Total Mathematics	.70	.61	.70

Source: Adapted from Otis, A. S., & Lennon, R. T. Otis-Lennon School Ability Test, Eighth Edition. Copyright © 2003 by Harcourt Assessment, Inc. Reproduced by permission. All rights reserved.

Unfortunately, the OLSAT manual provides minimal interpretation of these data. Also in this category, the manual references changes in mean p-values between grades served by a common level of the test.

Under test structure, the manual presents correlations between adjacent levels, correlations between verbal and nonverbal scores, and median biserial correlations. The reasoning and analysis used in these sections of the manual are not well developed. Also, considering the claims for a hierarchical structure in the test, it is remarkable that no factor analytic results are presented.

For a description of the circumstances surrounding the development of the original Otis tests, including excerpts from a revealing interview with Arthur Otis, see Lennon (1985). Robertson (n.d.) recounts the development of successive editions of the Otis tests through the first six editions.

College Admissions Tests

The second major category of group-administered mental ability tests is college admissions tests. Two entries exhaust the field of entries in this category, at least for the United States: the SAT and the ACT. The principal purpose of tests in this category is to aid in selection of students for college. Applicants come from a wide diversity of high school experiences. School grading practices and individual student experiences in courses, job demands, and extracurricular commitments may differ substantially. The college selection tests provide a uniform yardstick to measure students' capabilities and probabilities for success in college. The two tests in current use go about the process somewhat differently, but their fundamental purposes are very similar. These tests may also be used to help place students in courses within a college after their admission.

The SAT

Few tests match the **SAT** in name recognition and publicity. It has a storied history, going back to the very foundations of testing as a recognizable discipline. Each year millions of high school students (and their parents) anxiously prepare for and then await the results of this test. The newspapers fill with reports of fluctuations in state and national averages on the SAT. It is a classic example of high-stakes testing—more so than necessary given the way colleges actually use the scores, but high-stakes nonetheless.

Let us start the description of the SAT by making some distinctions among terms. More so than for any other test, people become confused by terms surrounding the SAT. Let us examine the sources of confusion and be sure we are making the appropriate distinctions regarding the name of the SAT, the College Board, and ETS.

The *SAT* is a *test*. From its inception until 1988, SAT was an acronym for *Scholastic Aptitude Test*, then *Scholastic Assessment Test*. Many sources and popular references still use these titles. The substitution of "assessment" for "aptitude" resulted from the profession's effort to avoid the implication that the traits being measured were somehow innate.

The SAT is actually a cluster of tests. First, there is the *SAT Reasoning Test*, which is actually three tests, as described later. This is the widely used college admissions test, the one people usually mean when they refer to the SAT. Second, there are the *SAT Subject Tests*, a series of separate tests in fields such as biology, history, chemistry, and a host of languages. Popular reference to the SAT usually implies the SAT Reasoning Test. Our description below concentrates on it. To further complicate matters regarding the name of the SAT, the most widely used standardized achievement battery is *Stanford Achievement Test*: also SAT. Thus, the initials SAT sometimes refer to this achievement test, which has no relationship to the SAT college admissions test. One simply needs to be alert to the possible confusion between these two SATs.

The **College Board** is *an association* of about 3,000 colleges and secondary schools focused on the school-to-college transition. This association, headquartered in New York City, sponsors and oversees development of the SAT, as well as a number of other testing programs. Originally, the association's name was College Entrance Examination Board or CEEB, an acronym still encountered frequently. The CEEB was organized in 1900 specifically to coordinate college entrance testing among more selective schools, all of which used to operate their own admissions testing programs (Johnson, 1994). The upshot of this coordinating effort was the SAT, first administered in 1901. The test was entirely in essay form until 1926, when it adopted the multiple-choice format. Because the College Board sponsors development of the SAT, some people call the test "the College Boards."

ETS stands for Educational Testing Service. It is a nonprofit *test development organization,* headquartered in Princeton, New Jersey. ETS actually develops the SAT and organizes its far-flung administration. ETS does this under contract with the College Board. ETS develops and sells many other tests. Examples include the *Test of English as a Foreign Language* (TOEFL) and the *Graduate Record Examinations.* In addition, just as ETS develops the SAT under contract with the College Board, it develops other tests under contract with other associations. For example, ETS develops the *Graduate Management Admissions Test* (GMAT) under contract with the Graduate Management Admissions Council, an association of business schools.

Structure and Items

For many years, College Board publications emphasized that the SAT attempts to measure highly generalized abilities developed over a long period of time. That is, the tests are not measures of "innate aptitude." In recent years, some attempt has been made to show that the test content is based on skills that should be developed in school, thus making it sound more like an achievement test than a test of generalized abilities that transcend specific school learning (Lawrence et al., 2002).

SAT Reasoning consists of three tests: Critical Reading, Mathematics, and Writing. This three-test structure was introduced in 2005. For many years prior to 2005, the SAT consisted of two tests: Verbal and Mathematics. No doubt, many sources will continue to refer to SAT-Verbal and SAT-Math for years to come. In fact, at the time the three-test structure was introduced, many institutions that use the SAT to assist with college admissions decisions declared that they would take a "wait-and-see" attitude toward use of the Writing test. Table 9.6 outlines the number of items and types of items in the three SAT Reasoning Tests. In addition, there is an experimental section, used for research and development purposes. The experimental items do not contribute to the student's score.

TABLE 9.6   *Structure of the SAT Reasoning Test*

Area	Item types	Time (mins) Sections	Total
Critical Reading	Sentence completions Reading passages	25, 25, 20	70
Mathematics	Multiple-choice Grid-in	25, 25, 20	70
Writing	Multiple-choice Essay	35, 25	60
Total			200 (3 hrs., 20 min.)[a]

[a] Total time includes time for the experimental section, but not for distributing materials, reading directions, and other such administrative matters.

Traditionally, all items in the SAT have been of the multiple-choice variety. In recent years, the Mathematics test has also included some student-produced **grid-in items**, where the student determines a numerical answer (e.g., 524) and marks the answer in a bubble grid. The most recent (2005) SAT has eliminated two types of items that were "famous" in the SAT: verbal analogies and quantitative comparisons. And, of course, the recent edition has the entirely new Writing test, which includes an essay. The essay is scored by two "human" raters using the holistic method, as described in Chapter 6.

Score Scale and Norms

Along with the IQ scale, the scale for the SAT is one of the most well known in the psychometric universe. The scaled score system for each of the tests ranges from 200 to 800, with $M = 500$ and $SD = 100$. The situation is not quite that simple, but these generalized values are useful benchmarks. National percentile ranks are also provided for each of the SAT Reasoning Tests. Both the scaled scores and percentiles are user-norms. That is, they are based on whoever takes the SAT and are not necessarily representative of any well-defined population.

Under the previous two-test structure (Verbal and Mathematics), each with its 200–800 scale, it was customary to combine the scores into a SAT-Total. This was not an official SAT score, but the practice of using it was widespread. Thus, a student with "Boards of 1500" was an intellectual prize, probably scoring in the 700–800 range on each of the SAT tests (Verbal and Math). With the new three-test structure, it is not yet clear how people might combine the scores. "Boards of 1500" based on three tests, each having standard (scaled) score systems with $M = 500$ and $SD = 100$, indicates perfectly average rather than superior performance. The situation illustrates the importance of knowing exactly what tests and what score systems are being used when interpreting test performance.

**Hoping to impress the chicks, Daryl had his
SAT scores tattooed on his right arm.**

Source: Close to Home © 2000 John McPherson. Reprinted with permission of Universal Press Syndicate. All Rights Reserved.

The SAT scaled score norms and percentile rank norms have different bases. The scaled score norms were determined for a national group in 1994. As new tests are administered each year, the new tests are equated to and reported in terms of these national norms. Hence, the actual national average can fluctuate on the 200–800 scaled score system. This provides the basis for news reports on SAT scores increasing or decreasing. On the other hand, the SAT percentile norms are continually adjusted on an annual basis. New percentile norms arise from each annual crop of test-takers. A norming program conducted in 1941 served as the basis for scores on the 200–800 scale until 1994. When the new (1994) norms were introduced, the old (1941) norms were equated to the new norms in what was called a "recentering" project, thus allowing for conversion of old scores into the new system.

The ACT

As with the SAT, we begin with some clarifications. The initials **ACT** stand generally for American College Test. The initials designate both an organization and a test. The organization is ACT, Inc., headquartered in

Iowa City, Iowa. The test is the *ACT Assessment*. ACT, Inc. creates and distributes the test. ACT, Inc. also develops other tests and conducts sponsored research programs mostly at the college and pre-college levels. The *ACT Assessment* is ACT, Inc.'s hallmark enterprise. Technically, the *ACT Assessment* includes the academic tests and several ancillary sources of information: a profile of student background characteristics, a self-report of high school courses and grades, and a brief interest inventory. Reference to the ACT usually implies the *ACT Assessment* rather than the organization or any of its other products. Furthermore, the reference to ACT is usually to the academic tests rather than to the full package including the ancillary materials.

Structure and Items

ACT's approach is somewhat different than SAT's. Whereas the SAT has tradition-ally emphasized highly generalized abilities, (although, as noted earlier, this empha-sis has been changing), the ACT has always emphasized assessment of school-based skills. In its original form, ACT gave scores in English, mathematics, social studies, and science. It was essentially an upward extension of the *Iowa Test of Educational Development,* a traditional achievement test for use in secondary schools. Today, the tests are just slightly different; however, the basic approach remains the same. There is an emphasis on the school curricular base for the test.

Given this orientation, one might ask: Why do we classify this test under mental ability rather than under achievement tests? That's a good, legitimate question. The determining factor in classifying the ACT with other mental ability tests is its prin-cipal use. It is used primarily to make predictions about future performance, specif-ically performance in college. Its validity depends mainly on how well it makes these predictions. That is why we classify it with mental ability tests.

Table 9.7 outlines the ACT structure. There are four major tests: English, Mathe-matics, Reading, and Science Reasoning. Three of these major tests have subtests.

TABLE 9.7   *Structure of the ACT*

Area	Subtests	Items	Time (mins)
English		75	45
	Usage/Mechanics		
	Rhetorical Skills		
Mathematics		60	60
	Pre-algebra/Elementary Algebra		
	Intermediate Alg./Coordinate Geometry		
	Plane Geometry/Trigonometry		
Reading		40	35
	Social Studies/Sciences		
	Arts/Literature		
Science Reasoning (no subtests)		40	35
COMPOSITE		215	2 hrs, 55 mins
Writing Test (optional)		–	30

English

Choose a change in the underlined part or indicate that it should remain unchanged.

After *the final performance of one last* practice landing, the French instructor nodded to the African-American woman at the controls and jumped down to the ground.

A. NO CHANGE   B. one finally ultimate

C. one final   D. one last final

Mathematics

$3 \times 10^{-4} =$

A. −30,000   B. −120   C. 0.00003   D. 0.0003   E. 0.12

How many solutions are there to the equation $x^2 - 15 = 0$?

A. 0   B. 1   C. 2   D. 4   E. 15

Reading

Read a passage of 90 lines, then answer questions such as:

According to the narrator, Mrs. Sennett wears a hat because she:

A. is often outside   B. wants to look like a literary figure

C. has thin hair   D. has unique taste in clothing

As it is used in line 3. the word composed most nearly means:

A. contented   B. unexcited

C. satisfied   D. constituted

Science Reasoning

Study a chart (not given here) and answer questions such as:

According to Figure 2, pioneer plant(s) showing a progressive increase in summed diameter of stems per unit area over the course of several years of succession is (are):

A. horseweed only   B. broomsedge only

C. aster and broomsedge only   D. horseweed, aster, and broomsedge

FIGURE 9.5 Sample items from the ACT Assessment.

Source: From the ACT sample test website. Copyright © 2001 by ACT, Inc. Reproduced with permission.

There is also a Composite score. The Composite is the simple average of scores on the four major tests. Most references to ACT scores are to the Composite score. For example, if a college states that normal admission requires an ACT of 22, this refers to the Composite score. Figure 9.5 shows examples of ACT items. The figure does not contain the full set of directions for each item, but gives a general idea of the nature of some items. In 2005, the ACT added a Writing Test. This test is optional and does not enter into the Composite.

TRY IT! ....

To see samples of the topics used for the essay writing parts of the SAT and ACT, including examples of scoring rubrics, go to these websites:
ACT: www.actstudent.org/writing/sample/index.html
SAT: www.collegeboard.com/student/testing/sat/about/sat/writing.html

....

Score Scale and Norms

Scores for each of the four major ACT tests are placed on a scale of 1 to 36. This is surely one of the most unusual scales in the psychometric universe. It defines itself with a range rather than with a mean and standard deviation. Inspection of the norm tables for the ACT shows that the scale has a mean of approximately 20 and standard deviation of approximately 5. These values fluctuate slightly from one test to another. However, the values of $M = 20$ and $SD = 5$, though not the basis for the scale, are useful to remember.

The Composite score is the simple average of the scores on the four major tests, rounded to the nearest whole number. The mean and standard deviation for the Composite are approximately the same as for the four tests: $M = 20$, $SD = 5$. The subtests have an equally unusual score scale, ranging from 1 to 18. Inspection of norm tables reveals that the means and standard deviations for these scales hover around 10 and 3, respectively.

Norms for the ACT are simple user-norms. That is, the norms are based on whoever takes the test within an annual cycle, generally about one million students. Scores are given in the 1–36 (or 1–18) scale and in percentile rank form. Figure 9.6 shows a sample report for the ACT. The report contains not only the test scores but also the ancillary information collected as part of the complete ACT Assessment.

Generalizations about the Reliability of SAT and ACT Scores

Reliability of the traditional scores for the SAT and ACT has been studied extensively. The new essay-writing portions have not been as extensively studied. Reliability data for the two test series are sufficiently similar that we can provide a single summary. Table 9.8 shows typical results for reliability studies of these test series (see ACT, 1997; Breland et al., 2004; College Board, 2006; Ewing et al., 2005). The typical results are largely predictable from the number of

TABLE **9.8** *Typical Results for Studies of Reliability of SAT and ACT*

Type of Score	r
Total Scores (e.g., ACT Composite, SAT-CR + SAT-M)	.95
Main Tests (e.g., ACT Reading, Math, SAT-CR, SAT-M)	.85–.90
Subscores (clusters within main tests)	.65–.85
Writing (essay portion, inter-rater reliability)	.60

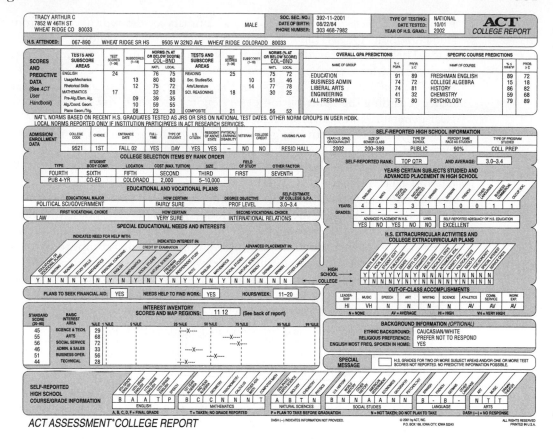

FIGURE 9.6 Sample report of ACT scores.

Source: Copyright © 2005. Reproduced with permission of ACT, Inc.

items entering a particular score. The total scores, based on over 150 items, are highly reliable, usually in the neighborhood of .95. The main tests, typically based on at least 40 items, tend to have reliabilities of at least .85 and often slightly over .90. The total scores and main tests are the principal reporting vehicles for SAT and ACT. In some applications, an attempt is made to provide subscores below the level of the main tests. Some of these subscores have reliabilities below desirable levels. The reliabilities are largely predictable from the number of items in the cluster. Then there is the case of the writing tests. As noted earlier, reliabilities of these tests —at least the essay portion—have not been as routinely studied. However, currently available data show that the inter-rater reliabilities are problematic.

Generalizations about the Validity of SAT and ACT

The principal method for studying the validity of the SAT and ACT is predictive validity. Literally thousands of such predictive validity studies have been conducted with each of these tests. We offer here a summary of the typical results from these studies. Results for SAT and ACT are sufficiently similar to allow for a single summary. The summary is drawn primarily from Burton and Ramist (2001) and Bridgeman, McCamley-Jenkins, and Ervin (2000) for the SAT and the *ACT Assessment Technical Manual* (ACT, 1997) for the ACT. At present, there is insufficient evidence regarding the contribution of writing tests to predictive validities to warrant clear generalizations. Therefore, the writing tests are not treated here.

The design of the studies generally follows this pattern. The most common criterion (to be predicted) is *first-year college GPA*, designated *FYGPA*. The predictors are the tests. The studies usually represent the tests separately (SAT Verbal and Math, the four ACT tests) as well as in terms of total scores. We will concentrate on total scores and simply refer to SAT and ACT as the *admissions test* **(AT)**. The studies invariably include high school grades, too. The high school record may be represented by high school GPA, either self-reported or taken from the high school transcript; by some specially computed high school GPA, for example, one based only on relevant college-prep courses; or by high school rank. We will use *HS* to designate this *high school record*, regardless of how it was determined.

The typical study reports the following:

- Correlation between the admission test (AT) and FYGPA
- Correlation between high school record (HS) and FYGPA
- Multiple correlation of AT + HS and FYGPA

The effect of **range restriction** on the resulting correlations is a matter of special concern in these studies. The studies are conducted with students who have already been selected and, therefore, ordinarily have less variability than the full set of applicants to the college. In Chapter 4, we reviewed the nature of this problem and how to correct for it. Studies of the predictive validity of college admissions tests usually report both the uncorrected and corrected correlations. Imperfect reliability of the criterion (FYGPA) is also a matter of concern. Some studies introduce corrections for this imperfect reliability.

Table 9.9 provides a summary of typical results from the numerous studies of predictive validity of college admissions tests conducted as outlined earlier. Data for correlations corrected for range are in bold because these data are probably the most realistic estimate of how the tests function. We note the following generalizations:

TABLE 9.9 *Typical Results from Studies of Predictive Validity of College Admissons Tests*

	Correlations		
Variables	**Uncorrected**	**Corrected for Range**	**Corrected for Range and Reliability**
FYGPA—AT	.40	**.50**	.55
FYGPA—HS	.40	**.50**	.55
FYGPA—(AT+HS)	.50	**.60**	.65

1. AT and HS correlate about equally with FYGPA.

2. The combination of AT and HS is always better than either alone in predicting FYGPA. This combination uses multiple correlation methodology. It is not the simple sum of the two variables. The incremental validity for the combination is about .10.

3. Examination of original data indicates that the correlations shown in Table 9.9 are approximately the same for different racial/ethnic groups. There are some differences by gender, college major, and type of college. However, one is struck more by the similarities across these various categories than by the differences. Nevertheless, for practical use, each college should conduct its own studies of validity.

What do we conclude about the utility of college admissions tests from this summary? Those who favor use of the tests emphasize that a correlation of .50 is a very respectable validity coefficient. In fact, it is rather remarkable that results from a few hours of testing would correlate that highly with the FYGPA that summarizes an entire year of effort. In addition, the AT nearly always adds predictive power to the HS index. Those who are ill disposed toward college admissions tests point out that a correlation of .50 accounts for only about 25% of the variance in FYGPA, leaving 75% to other factors. Similarly, these opponents argue, the incremental validity of the admissions test, adding .10 to the predictive power of the HS index, is hardly worth the grief associated with the high-stakes testing. These arguments, pro and con, will probably go on forever.

Correspondence between SAT and ACT

In popular conversations about college admissions tests, the ACT has a much lower profile than the SAT. However, the ACT is taken by a very large number of students each year. Approximately one million students take the ACT and somewhat more take the SAT annually. There are probably three reasons for the disparity in name recognition. First, the SAT has a much longer history, stretching back to 1901, whereas the ACT started in 1959 (for a brief history of the ACT, see Maxey, 1994). Second, the SAT is dominant in the media-rich East and West coast states, while the ACT is dominant in the midwestern and southern states. When something happens with the SAT in New York or California, the entire country hears about it. When something happens with the ACT in Ohio or Louisiana, no one really cares.

A third reason for a difference in name recognition between the two tests can be appreciated only by the psychometrically sophisticated. It results from the difference in standard deviations on the tests: approximately 100 for SAT and 5 for ACT. To the naked eye, a change in SAT scores is much more noticeable than a change in ACT scores. A one-point change in ACT score, say, from 20 to 21, does not look like much of a change. However, that change (one-fifth of an *SD*) is equivalent to a change of 20 points on the SAT scale, which sounds very substantial. Each year brings reports of changes in the national averages for SAT scores. A change of 5 points in the national average, say, from 510 to 515 or to 505 is big news! The equivalent change on the ACT scale is .2 (say, from 20.4 to 20.6), which hardly seems noteworthy.

From a practical viewpoint, probably the greatest difference between the SAT and ACT is the difference in geographic usage noted earlier. Although the two tests have somewhat different philosophies in terms of content development, the practical consequences of this difference are minimal. The tests have very similar reliabilities and predictive validities. Dorans (1999) gives a correlation of .92 between the SAT Total and the ACT Composite. Maxey (1994) gives the correlation as .89. These figures are only slightly lower than the reliabilities for the tests. Correcting the correlation for imperfect reliability yields a near perfect correlation between the SAT and ACT.

The numerical values of SAT and ACT scores are obviously different. SAT Verbal and Math scores range from 200 to 800, with $M = 500$ and $SD = 100$, approximately. ACT scores range from 1 to 36, with $M = 20$ and $SD = 5$, approximately. Knowledge of z-scores allows one to make conversions between the two score systems. However, that method of conversion assumes equivalence of the norming bases and shapes of distributions for the two tests. More exact, empirically based conversions result from use of **concordance tables**.[1] These tables allow users to convert scores from one test to another. This is useful in the admissions process because many schools accept scores from both tests, but depend primarily on one of the tests for most of the school's work. With the concordance tables, a school that uses an SAT Composite score of 1200 as a benchmark knows that this score corresponds to an ACT Composite of 26; or that an ACT Composite of 15 converts to an SAT Total of 710–750. For the full set of SAT-ACT concordance tables, see Dorans, Lyu, Pommerich, and Houston (1997). The tables are reproduced in Dorans (1999).

A Third Use of College Admissions Tests

As noted at the beginning of this section, the principal purpose of these tests is to aid in the college's selection process. A secondary purpose is for placement within courses. However, the tests have come to serve a tertiary purpose, one not intended by the test developers but one that is important to the colleges using the tests. This tertiary purpose (or purposes) is to describe the college itself, to help define its image, and to serve a marketing function for the college. This purpose is never announced as a formal reason for using the test. It is, nevertheless, very real. We have not yet developed methods for studying the validity of these tests for this purpose.

TRY IT! ....

If you are a student, do you know the average SAT or ACT for your school? Do you know the averages for any other schools? To see an example of how scores for SAT and ACT are used to describe a school—a use that is unrelated to making predictions about individual student performance—check the list of scores at this website: www.usnews.com/college.

....

---

[1] Tables were prepared using the equi-percentile method, a method commonly used to equate different levels and forms of tests.

Graduate and Professional School Selection

A third major application of group-administered mental ability tests is selection for graduate and professional school. The audience, obviously, is prospective graduate or professional school students. A person's undergraduate preparation (as indicated by the undergraduate GPA), experience in the field, motivation to pursue graduate study (as documented in letters of recommendation), and a host of other factors will aid in selecting the most promising students. However, there is also a widespread feeling that, beyond these other factors, general mental ability is important. Tests in this category aim to assess general mental ability for this purpose. Table 9.10 lists some of the major tests in this category. We will illustrate this application by describing just one example, the *Graduate Record Examination: General Test*. However, the observations made about this test, for example, regarding its reliability and validity, apply surprisingly well to most of the other tests in Table 9.10. We should note that some of the tests listed in the Table are best classified, at least in part, as achievement tests rather than tests of general ability. For example, the MCAT and DAT cover a mixture of subject matter knowledge (e.g., physiology and physics) and more general abilities (e.g., verbal ability). For more detail on any of the tests listed in Table 9.10, check their websites, as well as the usual sources such as Buros' *Mental Measurements Yearbook*.

TRY IT!

Access one of the websites listed in Table 9.10. Find the test listed. What purpose is stated for the test?

TABLE 9.10   *Examples of Tests used for Graduate and Professional School Selection*

Acronym	Test	Applicants to:	Website
GMAT	Graduate Management Admission Test	Business school, especially MBA	www.gmac.com/gmat
GRE	Graduate Record Examinations	Graduate school, especially doctoral	www.gre.org
LSAT	Law School Admission Test	Law school	www.lsac.org
MCAT	Medical College Admission Test	Medical school, especially MD, DO	www.aamc.org/students/mcat
MAT	Miller Analogies Test	Graduate school	www.milleranalogies.com
DAT	Dental Admission Test	Dental school	www.ada.org/prof/ed/ testing/dat/index.asp

Graduate Record Examinations: General Test

The **Graduate Record Examinations (GRE)** encompass the General Test and the Subject Tests. The Subject Tests include 8 achievement tests, based on content typically covered in a college major such as biology, mathematics, or psychology. We discuss achievement tests in the next chapter. The GRE General Test, described here, provides a good example of a general mental ability test designed for a very specific purpose and audience. The purpose is to aid in the selection of applicants to graduate school, especially for entrance into doctoral programs.

Structure and Items

The *GRE General Test* is actually three separate tests, the Verbal Reasoning, Quantitative Reasoning, and Analytical Writing tests, usually designated GRE-V, GRE-Q, and GRE-A, respectively.[2] The *GRE Guide to the Use of Scores* notes that all three tests are intended to be measures of "developed abilities that have been acquired over a long period of time" (ETS, 2005a, p. 4). Figure 9.7 shows examples of the items for each test.

Verbal Reasoning	**Quantitative Reasoning**
Antonyms	Quantitative Comparisons
Analogies	Problem Solving – Discrete
Sentence Completion	Problem Solving – Data Interpretation
Reading Comprehension	

Analytical Writing (2 essays)

Present Your Perspective on an Issue

Analyze an Argument

FIGURE **9.7** Outline of types of items in GRE: General Test.

---

[2] The Analytical score was added in 1977, then converted to Analytical Writing in 2003. Prior to 1982, the GRE: General Test was known as the GRE Aptitude Test. A surprising number of sources still use this title and make no reference to the Analytical score.

TRY IT! ....

To see additional items for the GRE General Test, go to www.gre.org/codelst.html. You can download and take an entire practice test.

....

The traditional format for the GRE-G is a paper-and-pencil, fixed-length set of tests. In this format, the Verbal test has 76 items, the Quantitative test 60 items, and the Analytical test 50 items. In recent years, a computer-adaptive version of the GRE-G has replaced this traditional format, at least in the United States. An examinee goes to one of the worldwide network of Sylvan testing centers to take the GRE-G. The GRE-Subject tests continue to use the traditional paper-and-pencil format, although computer-adaptive versions are under development. The number of items in the computer-adaptive version of the test are GRE-V 30 items and GRE-Q 28 items—that is, about half the number used in the paper-and-pencil test. This illustrates the efficiency of computer-adaptive testing.

Scores and Norms

GRE-V and GRE-Q each yield a scaled score and percentile rank. The scaled score is from a standard score system with $M = 500$ and $SD = 100$, thus having an effective range of 200–800. This standard score system was developed many years ago. The means and standard deviations on the GRE tests have drifted over the years so that today the national norms are no longer 500 and 100. Table 9.11 shows means and standard deviations for contemporary test-takers. The table also shows the percentile rank corresponding to a scaled score of 500, illustrating the extent to which average performance has drifted since the original scale was established. This is a situation similar to what we observed for the SAT, except that the GRE has not been recentered.

On the recently introduced Analytical Writing test, two raters score each essay on a 6-point holistic rubric (see www.gre.org/writing.html). The scores are averaged and reported in half-point increments, for example, 4.0, 4.5, 5.0. Percentiles are also provided. The percentile changes by score level are truly staggering in the middle of the scale, increasing by 15 to 20 points for each half-point increment in score level. For example, scores of 4.0, 4.5, and 5.0 correspond to percentiles of 31, 51, and 70, respectively.

TABLE **9.11**   *Means and Standard Deviations for GRE-General Tests for Recent Examinees*

	Verbal	Quantitative
Mean	469	597
Standard Deviation	120	148
Percentile Rank for 500	59	25

Source: GRE Guide to Use of Test Scores (ETS, 2005).

TABLE 9.12   *Average Scores on GRE-V and GRE-Q for Two Fields of Study*

	Verbal	Quantitative
Computer and Information Sciences	469	704
English Language and Literature	559	552

Percentile rank norms for the GRE provide a classic example of "user norms." Refer to page 98 for a description of this type of norm. The norms are based simply on all persons who actually took the test within a certain period of time. The GRE norms are updated each year, based on test-takers within the most recent three-year period. For example, the percentile ranks for the 2005–2006 year are based on approximately 1,250,000 examinees tested in 2001–2004. Each year a new set of percentile ranks arises, adding in new cases from the immediately preceding year and dropping cases from three years ago.

The GRE manual also provides data on the performance of examinees from various fields of intended graduate study. From some perspectives, this provides another type of norm. Table 9.12 shows mean scores from two fields, Computer and Information Systems (CIS) and English Language and Literature (EEL), on the Verbal and Quantitative tests. Note that a Verbal score of 500 is above average for CIS students but below average for EEL students. On the other hand, a Quantitative score of 600 is below average for CIS students but above average for EEL students. This information reinforces an important point. The purpose of norms is to enhance interpretation of test scores. Having multiple normative frameworks often helps to serve this purpose. It takes a little extra time to look at these multiple frameworks, but it is usually worthwhile spending that time.

Reliability and Validity

Notice that the Analytical Writing test has noticeably lower reliability than the other two tests, and lower than the previous (multiple-choice) Analytical test. Internal consistency reliabilities (KR–20) for the GRE General Tests are: Verbal .92, Quantitative .91, and Analytical .72. Notice that the Analytical Writing test has noticeably lower reliability than the other two tests, and lower than the previous (multiple-choice) Analytical test. The resulting standard errors of measurement (SEMs) on the scaled scores are in the range of 30–40 points. Applying IRT methodology (see p. 146), *SEMs* can be reported for various parts of the score range. These *SEMs* tend to be smallest at the extremes of the score ranges and greatest for midlevel scores. For example, on the GRE-V the *SEM* is only about 20 points for a score of 250 or 800, but the *SEM* rises to about 35 for scores in the 450–550 range. This is useful interpretive information.

As with all tests, the most important question for the GRE General Test concerns its validity. The first step in answering this question involves deciding on a criterion. What defines success in graduate school? Is it grades in graduate school? Or graduate professors' ratings of overall success regardless of grades? Or eventual productivity as a scholar as indicated by number of publications 10 years after completing the program? Or perhaps some other criterion?

TABLE 9.13 *Correlations between First-year Graduate GPA (FYGPA) and GRE General Tests (Verbal, Quantitative, Analytical), plus Undergraduate GPA (U)*

Type of Department	V	Q	A	U	VQA	VQAU
All Departments	.30	.29	.28	.37	.34	.46
Natural Science	.28	.27	.26	.36	.31	.44
Engineering	.27	.22	.24	.38	.30	.44
Social Sciences	.33	.32	.30	.38	.37	.48
Humanities & Arts	.30	.33	.27	.37	.34	.46
Education	.31	.30	.29	.35	.36	.47
Business	.28	.28	.25	.39	.31	.47

Source: Adapted from *GRE Guide to Use of Scores* (ETS, 2005, p. 22).

The most typical criterion used for GRE validity studies is the first-year GPA in graduate school (FYGPA). Literally thousands of studies have used this criterion. In addition, fewer but still a substantial number of studies have used a variety of other criteria. Table 9.13 shows the correlations between FYGPA and GRE General tests, plus undergraduate GPA (U). Data for "all departments" represent over 1,000 departments and over 12,000 examinees. The table also shows correlations between FYGPA and composites of the variables using multiple correlation methodology. The data were collected in 1986–1990 (ETS, 2005). It is important to note that the Analytic test was the "old" multiple-choice test, not the Analytic Writing test. Burton and Wang (2005) reported more recent data, quite similar to that reported here, but they did not use any version of the GRE-A. To date, there is surprisingly little validity information for the Analytical Writing test.

Data in Table 9.13 suggest the following conclusions about predicting FYGPA from the GRE General Test:

1. All three of the GRE General tests have some modest degree of predictive validity. People who favor use of the tests emphasize that these correlations are highly significant and that any degree of validity is better than chance selection. People ill disposed toward the tests emphasize that the tests still leave much of the variance in FYGPA unpredicted.

2. The three tests (V, Q, A) have remarkably similar predictive validities.

3. The composite, V+Q+A, is slightly better—but only slightly—as a predictor than any one of the tests. No doubt, this fact results from the substantial inter-correlation among the three tests. The correlations are: V–Q = .45, V–A = .60, Q–A = .66.

4. The undergraduate GPA (U) is a better predictor than any one of the tests and roughly equal to the composite (VQA) in predictive power.

5. The combination of all three tests *and* the undergraduate GPA (VQAU) is clearly superior to either the tests alone or the undergraduate GPA alone in predicting FYGPA. The incremental validity is about .10.

6. The latter generalizations are approximately the same across all types of departments.

7. We are not examining the GRE Subject Tests here. However, we should note that data similar to those in Table 9.13 show that the Subject tests are better predictors of FYGPA than are the General tests, on average across different fields by about .10. Furthermore, in some fields, the Subject tests are better predictors than the undergraduate GPA, while in other fields the two predictors are approximately equal.

Kuncel, Hezlett, and Ones (2001) reported an extensive meta–analysis of 1,521 studies of the GRE's validity, including both General and Subject tests. The study included the following eight criteria for defining success in graduate school:

- First-year graduate GPA (the same as FYGPA above)
- Final graduate GPA
- Score on comprehensive examinations in graduate school
- Faculty ratings of success
- Degree completion (yes or no)
- Time to degree completion
- Number of publications
- Citation count for publications.

TRY IT! ....

Can you think of any other criteria that might be used to define *success in graduate school* beyond those listed?

....

For the criteria of first-year GPA, final GPA, comprehensive exam score, and faculty ratings, their conclusions are much the same as those listed above based on Table 9.13. For the other criteria, predictive validities of the GRE tests were marginal or negligible. Kuncel et al. emphasize that even a moderate degree of predictive validity, as for the first four criteria, is better than chance selection.

Military and Business Selection Tests

The military and business provide a third major application of group mental ability tests. The rationale is much the same as for the first two applications. The intent is to select individuals with sufficient general mental ability to be successful on the job or in a training program. One widely used test in this category is the *General Aptitude Test Battery* (GATB), sponsored by the U.S. Employment Service. Businesses use a wide diversity of tests. The *Differential Aptitude Test* (DAT) is used primarily in high schools, but also experiences significant use in industry. Some tests in this category are derivatives of the Otis tests, for example, the *Wonderlic Personnel Test*. As the result of court cases regarding the predictive validity of tests for employment purposes,

TABLE 9.14　*Some Group Mental Ability Tests Widely Used in Business and Military Settings*

Initials	Full Title	Source
GATB	General Aptitude Test Battery	U.S. Employment Service
DAT	Differential Aptitude Test	Psychological Corporation
WPT	Wonderlic Personnel Test	Wonderlic, Inc.
ASVAB	Armed Services Vocational Aptitude Battery	U.S. Dept. of Defense

businesses have increasingly turned to tests of more specific abilities. See Chapter 16 for a review of these cases and their effect on testing. However, tests of general mental ability are still used in business. They may even be making a return to popularity (Schmidt, Ones, & Hunter, 1992). We next examine the main test used in the military setting.

Armed Services Vocational Aptitude Battery

The **Armed Services Vocational Aptitude Battery (ASVAB)** is used by all branches of the United States military for selection of recruits and placement in specific jobs. The military administers approximately two million ASVABs annually. The roots of the ASVAB go back to World War I. Recall from the history of testing, covered in Chapter 1, the initial use of group-administered mental ability tests, the Army Alpha and Army Beta, to screen military draftees. Following that initial use, all branches of the military began to use group mental ability tests routinely. For many years, each branch of the service used its own test. Perhaps the most famous of these was the *Army General Classification Test* (AGCT). Beginning in 1976, all services began using the single ASVAB. For a brief history of the ASVAB and its predecessors, see Larson (1994) and Sands and Waters (1997). In the late 1990s, a project team undertook creation of a computer-adaptive version of the ASVAB. Sands, Waters, and McBride (1997) provide a particularly thorough description of this project. Currently, the test is available in both forms: computer-adaptive and paper-and-pencil. The Department of Defense also makes forms of the ASVAB available to high schools for use at no cost to the school.

Structure and Items

Table 9.15 outlines the structure of the ASVAB. There are 10 subtests. Total administration time, including directions, is approximately three hours.

TRY IT! ....

To see examples of items for each ASVAB subtest go to www.goarmy.com/util/asvabl.htm

TABLE 9.15   *ASVAB Structure*

Subtest	Items	Time (mins)	Description
AR Arithmetic Reasoning	30	36	Arithmetic word problems
WK Word Knowledge	35	11	Synonyms, word meaning in context
MK Mathematics Knowledge	25	24	High school level math
PC Paragraph Comprehension	15	13	Reading paragraphs
GS General Science	25	11	Science: physical (13 items), biological (12 items)
MC Mechanical Comprehension	25	19	Mechanical and physical principles
EI Electronics Information	20	9	Principles of electronics, radio, electricity
AS Auto & Shop Information	25	11	Terms and practices for auto, tools, shop
CS Coding Speed	84	7	Matching code numbers to words: speeded
NO Numerical Operations	50	3	Simple arithmetic computations: speeded

Source: Adapted from Larson (1994) and Sands and Waters (1997).

Examination of the list of ASVAB subtests is instructive. First, we note that this is a very strange mixture of content, especially for something called an aptitude test. Some of the subtests, for example, Word Knowledge and Arithmetic Reasoning, are classic entries in general aptitude tests. Other subtests, for example, Electronics Information and Auto and Shop Information, are highly specific areas of knowledge. Second, on a related point, one wonders about the underlying traits measured by the ASVAB. Are there really 10 rather distinct abilities covered by the test? No. Research indicates that there are four factors: Verbal (WK, PC, GS), Quantitative (AR, MK), Technical (EI, MC, AS), and Speed (CS, NO) (Sands & Waters, 1997). That result is certainly consistent with other research on the structure of human abilities. Third, note that some of the subtests are very short. One would expect these short subtests to have quite limited reliability. They do.

Technical Characteristics

Although the ASVAB yields scores for each of the subtests listed in Table 9.15, perhaps the most important score is the **AFQT**. At an earlier time, preceding the adoption of the ASVAB, there was the **Armed Forces Qualification Test**, consisting of verbal, quantitative, and spatial items. That test was abandoned in favor of the ASVAB, but the initials AFQT were retained to designate a special score coming from the ASVAB. This AFQT score consists of a combination of WK, PC, AR, and MK subtests. Hence, it is a classic "g"-type measure, combining verbal and quantitative domains. The AFQT score is the one used to actually make selection decisions for military recruits. The score converts to a list of six categories shown in Table 9.16. Notice that the verbal descriptors for the categories are in terms of "level of trainability," indicating one intended use of the AFQT score.

In general, Category V scores disqualify a person from selection into the military and Category IV scores have very restricted selection. One might expect the percentile norms for the ASVAB to be user-norms, like those for the SAT, ACT, and

TABLE 9.16   *Categories of AFQT Scores Obtained from ASVAB*

AFQT Category	Percentile Range	Level of Trainability
I	93–99	Well above average
II	65–92	Above average
IIIa	50–64	Average
IIIb	31–49	Average
IV	10–30	Below average
V	1–9	Well below average

GRE. However, that is not the case. ASVAB norms came from a carefully controlled national study of 12,000 men and women aged 18–23. This was the National Longitudinal Study of Youth Labor Force Behavior (NLSY79) conducted in 1979 by the U.S. Department of Defense and Department of Labor. Hence ASVAB has norms that should be reasonably representative of the national population. However, these norms are now somewhat dated.

In both computer-adaptive and paper-and-pencil versions, reliabilities of the ASVAB subtests are largely predictable from their lengths (see Moreno and Segall, 1997). As a general rule, short tests are not very reliable. Particularly problematic among the ASVAB subtests is Paragraph Comprehension (15 items in 13 minutes), with reliability around .50. The two short speeded tests (CS and NO) have reliabilities around .70. All other subtests have reliabilities around .80. Of course, the composite AFQT score is highly reliable.

The military setting provides many opportunities for studying the validity of the ASVAB as a predictor of success in a variety of training programs. Studies in numerous military training programs demonstrate respectable validity for the ASVAB, especially for the AFQT composite score. Across many training programs (e.g., air traffic controller, electronics technician, and radioman), the AFQT composite showed average range-corrected correlations of .615–.630 with final grades in training school (Wolfe, Moreno, & Segall, 1997). The single, 30-item Arithmetic Reasoning subtest is not far behind the AFQT composite in predictive validity. Virtually every reviewer of the ASVAB (see, e.g., Murphy, 1984) has noted with chagrin the lack of differential validity of the various subtests.

Culture-fair Tests of Mental Ability

Here is one of the great dilemmas in the psychometric universe. On the one hand, common definitions of intelligence emphasize the ability to succeed within one's environment. This suggests testing with the ordinary symbols, conventions, and artifacts of the culture. On the other hand, we would like a "pure" measure of intelligence, untrammeled by the specifics of a particular culture. The desire for such a "pure" measure has seemed particularly urgent as concerns about minority group performance have increased. We should note, however, that psychologists' pursuit of the "pure" measure predates contemporary concerns about minority group scores. The pursuit originated, as we will see, in the late 1930s, whereas concerns about minority group performance arose primarily in the 1960s.

Tests like the Stanford–Binet, Wechsler scales, Otis series, and SAT are obviously steeped in Western cultural practices. They are heavily verbal, specifically in standard English. Are there ways to measure intelligence without dependence on a particular culture and language? This is the question addressed by what we call culture-free or **culture-fair tests**. The term *culture-fair* is currently preferred, although a few sources use the term *culture-reduced*. Culture-free was the original tag for these tests. Not long after this pursuit began, it became perfectly apparent that no test could be entirely free from all cultural trappings. For example, using paper, assuming a left-to-right and top-to-bottom orientation on a page, giving direct answers to questions, being responsive to time constraints—all of these are culturally bound practices. Perhaps, however, we can create a test that is equally fair across cultures. Let us examine some efforts to accomplish this. We should note that, while we treat this topic under group mental ability tests, the topic is also directly relevant to individually administered tests.

Raven's Progressive Matrices

Probably the best known example of a test purporting to be culture-fair is **Raven's** *Progressive Matrices* (RPM). This is a very important example because it is so widely cited in the research literature on intelligence. Recall from our discussion of theories of intelligence the central role played by "g," general intelligence. Many people consider the RPM to be a particularly useful measure of "g." It often serves as a benchmark in factor analytic studies of intelligence. Therefore, students of psychological testing should have a basic familiarity with this test.

Many sources refer to "the Raven's" or "Raven's Matrices" as if it were a single test. However, Raven's matrices actually constitute three different test series, as summarized in Table 9.17. First, there is the *Coloured Progressive Matrices* (CPM), designed for younger children, the mentally retarded, and in general the lower end of the intelligence distribution. The test uses color to enhance interest level. Second, there is the *Standard Progressive Matrices* (SPM). This is the classic version, consisting of 60 items. It is intended for persons in the middle of the mental ability spectrum. Its most recent edition is the "Extended Plus" version, released in 1998. Third, there is the *Advanced Progressive Matrices* (APM), designed for the upper 20% of the mental ability distribution. A single test, *Raven's Progressive Matrices,* the forerunner of SPM,

TABLE 9.17   *The Three Versions of Raven's Progressive Matrices*

Title	Time (min)	Target Groups
Coloured Progressive Matrices (CPM)	15–30	5–11 yrs, lower 20%
Standard Progressive Matrices (SPM) (Extended, Plus Version)	20–45	6–16 yrs, general population
Advanced Progressive Matrices (APM)	40–60	12–17+ yrs, upper 20%

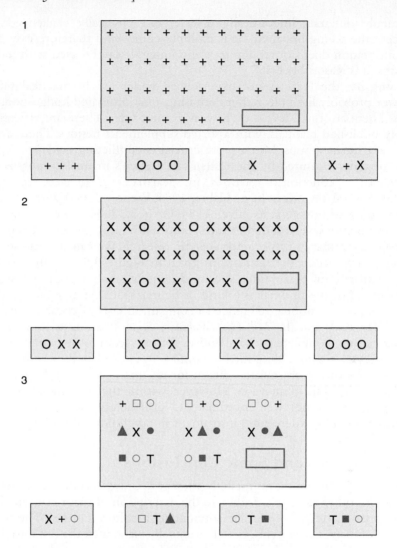

FIGURE 9.8   Simulations of Raven-type items.

was published in 1938. Recall from the previous chapter that Cattell published his seminal article proposing a culture-free test, based mostly on matrix-type items, in 1940.

Figure 9.8 shows simulations of Raven's items at several levels of difficulty. The item "stem" shows a pattern (matrix) with a part missing. The examinee's task is to select the option that completes the pattern. The important point for our presentation here is to observe the nature of these **matrix-type items**.

The Raven's has several desirable features. It is completely nonverbal. Even the directions can be given in pantomime if necessary. Hence, it is attractive for use with culturally different, linguistically diverse, and physically challenged individuals (except the seeing impaired). It is multiple-choice and therefore easy to score. Its administration does not require special training. It can be used with individuals or groups. It is reasonably brief.

Why has the Raven's not experienced wider use in practical settings? The answer, probably, lies in its rather confusing, uncoordinated hodge-podge of materials. There are three levels, each with distinct titles. There are at least five separately published manuals, with assorted supplements besides. There are a host of different norm groups. Much more crucial is conflicting evidence regarding the trait or traits measured by the test(s). The Raven's manual emphasizes measurement of the "eduction of relations" in Spearman's "g" (Raven, Raven, & Court, 1993). Several reviewers (e.g., Llabre, 1984; Vernon, 1984) agree. On the other hand, some authors (e.g. Esquivel, 1984; Gregory, 2004) note that factor analytic studies identify several different traits, even within a single level. Gregory gives an excellent summary of this factor analytic research. We can surmise some of these different traits from the simulations given in Figure 9.8. The first item seems to rely primarily on perception. The third item calls for analogical reasoning. Shot through all of the findings is a kind of figural/spatial ability. Finally, the Raven's manuals make continual reference to companion tests of vocabulary: the *Crichton Vocabulary Scale* and the *Mill Hill Vocabulary Scale*. These tests sometimes seem to be part of the complete package and sometimes seem to be completely unrelated to the Raven's, thus adding further confusion. The vocabulary scales are intended as measures of the crystallized dimension of intelligence, while the matrices are aimed at the fluid dimension. However, within the Raven's complex, the two types of tests are not well coordinated. Nevertheless, the Raven's, in its various incarnations, is a widely cited instrument in psychological testing.

Other Culture-fair Tests and Some Conclusions

The Raven's is by no means the only attempt to provide a culture-fair test. There are numerous other examples. Earlier, in the description of theories of intelligence, we mentioned Cattell's 1940 article announcing a culture-fair test. The test consisted mostly of matrix-type items. Cattell eventually elaborated the test into the regularly published *Culture Fair Intelligence Test* (CFIT). Early work with these matrix-type items served as part of the foundation for Cattell's distinction between fluid and crystallized intelligence. The CFIT was supposed to tap the fluid dimension, while more verbally oriented tests tapped the crystallized dimension. Many other authors have constructed tests using matrix-type items, figural relationships, geometric designs, and other nonverbal stimuli. Figure 9.9 shows examples of such items. The hope, nearly always, is that the test will be culturally fair.

We should note that the elementary cognitive tasks (ECTs) used in information processing models of intelligence (see pp. 271–274) have been proposed as culture-fair (even culture-free) measures of intelligence. It is an intriguing notion. However, application of these ECTs has been largely confined to laboratory usage. Furthermore, they have a long way to go to prove their worth as measures of intelligence.

The following three conclusions emerge from a review of the work on culture-fair tests. First, the tests tend to be measures of figural and spatial reasoning ability. This may be of some use, especially when there is no reasonable prospect

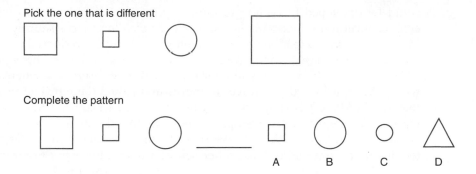

FIGURE 9.9 Examples of nonverbal items other than matrix-type items.

of using a more conventional measure of mental ability. However, these tests are obviously not measuring the same abilities as the benchmark tests of general intellectual functioning, tests in the tradition of the Wechsler and Otis tests. We must be wary of claims by test authors and publishers about "a nonverbal, culture-fair test of intelligence" on two counts. First, the "intelligence" referenced in the statement is of a very narrow variety. If the statement implies that this nonverbal test can serve as a substitute for, say, a WISC-III, then the statement is misleading. Second, we can determine by simple inspection that a test is largely nonverbal. We cannot determine by inspection that the test is culture-fair. The fact that a test is nonverbal does not automatically make it culture-fair. To determine that a test is culture-fair requires research showing that the test functions equivalently in a variety of cultures.

Second, when used to predict success in such areas as schools or jobs, tests that are primarily measures of figural and spatial reasoning are clearly inferior to verbally oriented tests. Furthermore, the figural/spatial tests add little, if any, predictive power to simple verbal tests for these predictive purposes. (There are some very limited exceptions to this generalization, for example, predicting success in architecture.) The reason for the superiority of verbal measures is probably quite simple. Most academic activities and jobs have more verbal demands than figural/spatial demands.

Third, the hope that culture-fair tests would eliminate differences in average scores between majority group and minority group examinees or between culturally different groups has not been fulfilled. Some research shows that these differences are reduced somewhat on nonverbal tests, in comparison with more conventional, verbally loaded tests. Other research shows that the group differences are approximately the same on the verbally loaded and the nonverbal tests. This search for the golden fleece will have to continue.

Intelligence Tests for Micro-cultures

At the other extreme from attempts to build culture-fair tests are intelligence tests based on a highly specific subculture, what we might call a micro-culture. Not infrequently, one hears about such an "intelligence" test. For example, such a test could be developed for sailing terminology (port, tack, starboard, coming about, etc.); baseball (bunt, Texas leaguer, sacrifice fly, etc.); or a city's subway system (the MTA, the D train, etc.). These tests are often put forward to discredit conventional mental ability tests, such as the WAIS or SAT. Some wag will note that a person with a WAIS IQ of 150 (who lives in Chicago) failed the subway test, whereas a person with a WAIS IQ of 90 (who lives in the Bronx) passed the test. The implication is that the WAIS IQ is unimportant. The public media are fond of touting such reports. The implication is transparent nonsense. We know a great deal about the generalizability of the WAIS IQ. We must ask the same questions about the subway test as about the WAIS. To what other behavior does subway test performance generalize? What does it correlate with? What are the norms for the test? Is the score reliable? Ordinarily, no such information is available for these micro-culture tests.

Generalizations about Group Mental Ability Tests

Our survey of group mental ability tests suggests the following six generalizations. These generalizations must be tempered with the more specific information about each test and its particular applications. However, some clear trends cut across the various tests we have reviewed.

1. *Content.* Despite the variety of target groups and specific purposes for these group tests, there is remarkable similarity in their content. Of course, they differ in difficulty level. However, allowing for that, we commonly find items on vocabulary, verbal relationships, reading, quantitative reasoning, and, to a lesser extent, spatial reasoning.

2. *Reliability.* Total scores on the widely used group tests are usually very reliable. Internal consistency reliability coefficients are usually about .95 and test-retest reliabilities about .90. Subscores are less reliable. Some of the tests provide too many subscores, based on too few items, and these subscores do not have acceptable levels of reliability for interpretation of individual scores. Some people think that group-administered tests are generally less reliable than individually administered tests. The data do not support that position. For appropriately developed tests, total scores on group tests are at least as reliable as scores on individually administered tests. The principal advantage for individual tests is the opportunity to observe the examinee's performance first-hand. This is especially crucial where there is concern about a possible disability, maladaptive behavior, or other unusual condition.

3. *Predictive validity.* Predictive validity of group mental ability tests is remarkably similar, although certainly not identical, across a wide range of practical applications. We examined criteria for performance in school and in jobs. Predictive validities for total scores in the range of .30–.60 are very common. Except when predicting performance on another test (where the correlations are very high), predictive validities rarely exceed .60. On the other hand, they rarely fall below .30.

    There is good room for thought here. To the age-old question of whether general mental ability makes any difference or is irrelevant in life's course, the answer is "Yes." Does mental ability make a difference? Yes. Do effort, determination, and character make a difference? Yes. Do circumstances make a difference? Yes. Does luck enter the picture? Yes. Is there error in the measurements? Yes, for both test and criterion. Life is complex. So, too, the relationships among all these variables are complex. We make this point here in the chapter on group mental ability tests, but it applies equally well to the individually administered tests covered in the previous chapter.

4. *Differential Validity.* Hope springs eternal regarding differential validity of subtests in these group mental ability tests. In general, various combinations of subtests do not yield validity coefficients higher than those obtained with total scores. We made this point explicitly about the ASVAB. A similar conclusion develops for a wide range of applications of tests to job selection (Borman, Hanson, & Hedge, 1997; Schmidt, Ones, & Hunter, 1992). The same point might be made with respect to college, graduate school, and professional school admissions. In general, a relatively brief but reliable test—say, a single 50-item test with reliability of .90–.95—provides nearly all the predictive power of a three-hour battery with multiple subtests. It is certainly feasible to develop a 50-item test, aimed mostly at measuring "g," having a reliability of .90–.95. In fact, it is not terribly difficult to do so. Why, then, do people continue to use three-hour, multiscore batteries?

5. *Range Restriction and Imperfect Reliability.* Research on and applications of group mental ability tests almost invariably involve some type of predictive situation. In these situations, we need to remember the effect of unreliability in the criterion and, even more so, the effect of restriction in range. It is not easy to remember these factors. They are not intuitively obvious. The statistical adjustments are not simple, although they are not tricky. However, they have very real consequences for our understanding of how the tests are functioning.

Key Points Summary 9.3

Generalizations about Group Mental Ability Tests

- Content: Vocabulary, Verbal Relations, Reading, Quantitative, Spatial
- Reliability: Total Scores Very High, Subscores Moderate (some very low)
- Predictive Validity: Usually in the .30–.60 Range
- Differential Validity: Generally Poor
- Two Special Statistical Issues: Range Restriction and Imperfect Reliability
- Culture-free Tests: Elusive So Far

6. The search for a culture-free test has not been successful to date. Tests labeled culture-fair tend to be nonverbal tests of spatial and figural reasoning ability which do not measure the same construct(s) as the typical measures of general intellectual functioning.

Summary

1. Group mental ability tests find their most common uses in schools, at all levels from elementary school to graduate and professional schools, and in military and business settings. Their primary purpose is usually to make predictions about future success in school or on the job. Group mental ability tests are also used for research purposes.

2. Group mental ability tests have eight common characteristics. Obviously, they are group administered, although they can be administered individually. They use multiple-choice, machine-scored items. Their content generally parallels that of individual tests. They usually have fixed time limits and numbers of items, although computer-adaptive tests without these characteristics are growing in popularity. Administration times fall into two camps: about one hour and about three hours. Most of these tests yield a total score and several subscores. The tests tend to have very large research bases. For nearly all of the tests, the principal purpose is prediction.

3. A group-administered mental ability test is often used in conjunction with a standardized achievement test in school testing programs. We described the *Otis-Lennon School Ability Test,* Eighth Edition, the latest in the long line of Otis tests, as an example of such tests.

4. The SAT and ACT are both widely used predictors of success in college. Although somewhat different in their philosophies, histories, and score scales, these two tests are very similar in purpose, reliability, and validity.

5. Another use of group mental ability tests is for selecting students for graduate and professional school. We described the *Graduate Record Examination—General Test* (GRE-G) as an example of tests in this category.

6. Group mental ability tests are also used to predict success in military and business settings. The *Armed Services Vocational Aptitude Battery* (ASVAB) illustrates this type of use. The ASVAB structure brings into stark relief the issue of using a multiplicity of subscores for these types of tests.

7. Psychologists have long sought culture-fair tests of mental ability. To date, the tests resulting from this effort are mainly measures of figural/spatial reasoning. The widely cited *Raven's Progressive Matrices* provides a good example of such a test.

8. We developed generalizations about group mental ability tests related to their content, reliability, predictive validity, and lack of differential validity. We also

called special attention to the need for sensitivity to two matters when using tests to make predictions: restriction in range and imperfect reliability of the criterion.

Key Terms

ACT	ETS	predictive validity
AFQT	GRE	range restriction
ASVAB	grid-in items	Raven's
College Board	matrix-type item	SAT
concordance table	multilevel test	
culture-fair test	OLSAT	

Exercises

1. To observe the diverse ways in which intelligence tests are used in research, enter "intelligence" as a key word for a search in any electronic database of articles in the social/behavioral sciences (e.g., PsychInfo). To avoid getting too many references, limit the search to just one or two years. For a few of the articles obtained in the search, try to determine exactly which test was used.

2. To try a computer adaptive test prepared by the publisher of the GRE, go to www.ets.org/cbt/cbtdemo.html. Recall that there was also a computer adaptive test introduced on page 37 in this book.

3. Learn to use websites to access technical data about tests. As an example, access information about the SAT from the College Board's website. Go to www.collegeboard.com. Click on Site Search. In the Keyword box, enter "reliability." Examine some of the reports. Then enter "validity" as a key word and examine some of those reports. You can also access the latest national and state data for the SAT.

4. On page 343 we gave a few examples of items converted from free-response to multiple-choice form. Look at the sample items in Table 8.2. Try to write your own multiple-choice versions of some of these items.

5. Look at the report of OLSAT8 scores in Figure 9.3. What is the student's SAI? What conclusions do you draw about this student from the pattern of Anticipated Achievement Comparisons?

6. In the TRY IT exercise on page 342, you listed one or two group mental ability tests you have taken in the past five years. Pick one of these tests. Align it with the eight common characteristics of group mental ability tests listed on page 344. How well does the test you chose correspond to these eight characteristics?

7. Access the website for the ACT Assessment, www.act.org. How does the site describe the purpose of the ACT? Can you find information about the reliability of the ACT tests?

8. On page 135 we noted the low reliabilities of some of the short ASVAB tests. For example the 15-item Paragraph Comprehension test has a reliability of approximately .50. Using what you have learned about the relationship between reliability and test length (see p. 135), how many items should this test have to bring the reliability to approximately .85?

9. Use data set D1: GPA Data in Appendix D Using your preferred statistical package, prepare the bivariate distribution (scatterplot) for SAT Total vs. GPA. Also, get the correlation between SAT and GPA. What conclusions do you draw from these data?

CHAPTER 10

Neuropsychological Assessment

Contributed by
Brooke J. Cannon

Objectives

1. Trace the history of clinical neuropsychology.

2. Identify reasons for a neuropsychological assessment.

3. Describe basic issues in neuropsychological assessment.

4. Differentiate between a fixed battery and a flexible battery approach.

5. Name the cognitive domains tapped in a flexible battery approach.

6. List the characteristics of pseudodementia.

7. Describe techniques used to assess effort/motivation.

8. Describe what types of supplemental information should be gathered when doing a neuropsychological evaluation.

9. Name two types of dyslexia and how they differ in spelling and reading errors.

Neuropsychological assessment is one of the most rapidly developing sectors in the world of testing. In this chapter, we trace the origins of this type of assessment and describe the types of problems it treats. We will find that it draws on many of the concepts and specific tests covered in earlier chapters. In fact, you will see how important it is to know the earlier material in order to conduct a competent neuropsychological assessment. Let us begin with three cases that call for neuropsychological assessment. We will conclude the chapter by seeing what assessments were actually obtained for these cases.

Case Examples

- Case #1. Nancy O'Roarke, a recently widowed, 74-year-old woman, complains of memory loss, trouble concentrating, and an inability to perform her usual daily activities. Does she have Alzheimer's disease?

- Case #2. Jack Davis, a 42-year-old construction worker, was injured on the job when a cement block struck him in the head. Since that time, he has had headaches, memory loss, poor attention span, and depressed mood. He is involved in a lawsuit against his employer. Does he have brain damage?

- Case #3. Billy Zollinger, a 10-year-old boy in fourth grade, has been receiving failing grades in school. His mother reports that he often loses things, forgets to do what she asks, or fails to complete the job. He also takes excessive amounts of time to do his homework, often being distracted by outside noises or other stimuli. Does he have Attention Deficit Disorder?

Focus on the Brain: The Road to Clinical Neuropsychology

Today it is hard to imagine that the brain was not always considered to be the site of the mind. Ancient Egyptians thought that the guts, or viscera, were responsible for thought, carefully packaging them with mummies for use in the afterlife—and tossing the brain aside! The first recorded "brain hypothesis" is attributed to Alcmaeon of Croton (ca. 500 B.C.), who proposed that the brain controlled mental abilities. More specific awareness of the relationship between the human brain and the ability to reason came about 2,000 years ago, where Roman physician **Galen** (A.D. 129–ca. 210) tended to wounded gladiators. Through his work and his exposure to different types of wounds, he determined that the brain was a critical organ, responsible for sense, language, and thought.

Once this brain–behavior relationship was known, attempts were made to understand where in the brain different abilities resided. **Franz Josef Gall** (1758–1828) developed the concept of **phrenology,** the study of the relationship between one's moral, emotional, and intellectual behaviors and variations of the skull's surface (Fig. 10.1). Although phrenology did not hold up under scrutiny, Gall did spark the search for localization of function within the brain.

"The left side of your brain is good at math and science. The right side is creative and playful. You'll get a raise as soon as you have the right side surgically removed."

Source: © 1998 by Randy Glasbergen. Reproduced with permission.

The late 1800s witnessed significant advances in the localization of language abilities. Through an intensive case study, **Paul Broca** (1824–1880), a French surgeon, first documented the site of brain damage associated with an inability to speak, but with preserved language comprehension. **Carl Wernicke** (1848–1904), a German neuroanatomist, described a language disturbance involving impaired comprehension but preserved speech, although it was non-meaningful. This second form of language disorder was found to be associated

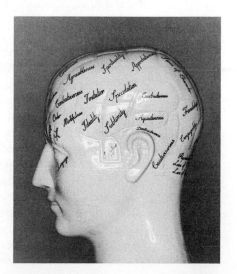

FIGURE 10.1   Areas on the skull according to phrenology theory.

Source: Stone/Getty Images, Inc.

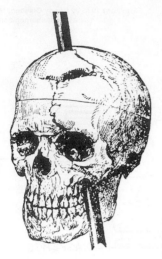

FIGURE 10.2   Phineas Gage, whose brain injury led to personality changes.

Source: From M. B. MacMillan: Brain and Cognition, 1986, p. 85. Reproduced with permission of Academic Press.

with a different area of the brain. Problems in communication, like those described by Broca and Wernicke, are known as **aphasias,** deficits in the ability to express or comprehend written or spoken communication as a result of brain injury.

One of the most famous case studies of personality change after brain injury is that of Phineas Gage, a railroad worker who, in 1848, suffered damage to the brain when an explosion sent a tamping iron through his head (Figure 10.2). The bar, over 3 feet in length and a little over 1 inch in greatest diameter, entered point-first through his left cheek and exited out the top of his head, damaging the left frontal portion of his brain. Prior to the accident, Gage was responsible, efficient, and with a good mind for business; after the injury, Gage was obnoxious and impatient (Macmillan, 2000). He began to use profane language and was unable to follow any of the plans of action that he devised.

Initially, the field of **neuropsychology,** defined as the study of brain–behavior relationships, was the domain of physiological psychologists, working primarily with animal models of brain functioning. Arthur Benton (1909–) may be credited with the birth of **clinical neuropsychology,** a distinct professional specialty that combines human neuropsychology with clinical psychology. The clinical neuropsychologist applies brain–behavior principles to the assessment and treatment of the individual patient. Benton began training doctoral students in clinical neuropsychology at the University of Iowa, with the first two neuropsychological dissertations completed in 1954 (Benton, 1997). See Table 10.1 for a timeline of major events in the history of clinical neuropsychology.

Clinical neuropsychologists are called upon to answer many different referral questions. We can identify six main reasons for neuropsychological assessment. Testing may be requested for *diagnosis.* Neuropsychological tests may demonstrate cognitive impairment when other medical examinations (X-rays of the head, etc.) are normal. With the evolution of brain scanning, the general question of "Is there brain damage?" is no longer asked of the clinical neuropsychologist. The

TABLE 10.1 *Key Events in the Development of Neuropsychology*

500 B.C.	Alcmaeon of Croton proposes that mental abilities are controlled by the brain.
A.D. ~180	Galen determines brain is critical for sense, language, and thought.
1798	Gall develops phrenology.
1848	Phineas Gage has a metal rod pass through his head.
1861	Broca reports the site of brain damage associated with expressive language deficits.
1874	Wernicke discovers site of brain damage associated with language comprehension.
1954	Benton supervises first doctoral dissertations in clinical neuropsychology.
1967	International Neuropsychological Society established.
1979	APA Division 40, Clinical Neuropsychology, established.
1996	Clinical neuropsychology officially recognized by APA as a specialty.

introduction of computerized axial tomography scans, or CT scans, allows for a quick, detailed examination of the brain. Magnetic resonance imaging (MRI) technology provides for an even greater clarity of brain structures, particularly for small changes caused by poor blood flow through the brain. More recently, positron emission tomography (PET) and the less expensive single photon emission computed tomography (SPECT) scanning give a window to the activity of the brain, rather than simply snapshots of its structures. With these advanced technologies it is possible to see which brain areas are being used during various

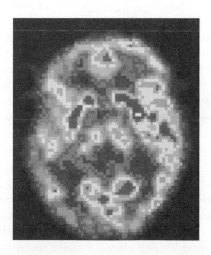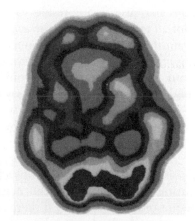

FIGURE 10.3 Images of a PET and SPECT scans.

Source: (left photo) Hank Morgan/Photo Researchers; (right photo) Oullette/Theroux/Publiphoto/ Photo Researchers

activities. Through the study of normal brain functioning, it is then possible to determine what areas of the brain are less active in different diseases or injury states. Although these brain-imaging technologies can demonstrate that there is damage in a certain brain structure, or that there is lower than normal metabolic activity, they may not be able to tell us exactly what the behavior of the patient is like. By simply looking at a CT scan or MRI of the brain, one cannot tell if the patient is behaving at all—the patient could be dead!

Neuropsychological testing no longer answers the "brain damage or not" question; however, questions about diagnosis must still be answered by neuropsychological evaluations and not by brain scans. For example, "Does this patient have dementia?" CT or MRI scans of early dementia may be normal in the presence of abnormal cognitive testing. A person may present as unimpaired during a cursory medical examination, but a more detailed cognitive evaluation would uncover deficits. Neuropsychological testing is valuable in documenting this impairment. See, for example, McKhann, Drachman, Folstein, Katzman, Price, and Stadlan (1984) on the criteria for Alzheimer's disease diagnosis, which requires neuropsychological testing.

Many times the diagnosis is already known, such as a stroke confirmed by neurological examination and brain scanning. Now the question asked of the clinical neuropsychologist may be, "What are this patient's *strengths and weaknesses* now, after sustaining a brain injury?" Here neuropsychological testing can document areas of preserved functioning and areas of impairment. Such knowledge is useful for *vocational planning,* as the patient attempts to return to work or is deciding upon an educational path. Someone who has suffered a stroke resulting in poor visual attention should not become an air traffic controller!

While the patient is in the hospital, the clinical neuropsychologist may be asked to assist in *treatment planning.* For example, testing may demonstrate that the patient remembers information better when it is verbal. A patient may be impulsive or have memory deficits that would inhibit independent living. The clinical neuropsychologist may use testing results to help hospital staff in the ward manage the patient. Not all treating staff may be aware of the possible behavior changes associated with brain injury. For example, a nurse became upset that a patient was constantly cursing at her and never said anything nice. It turned out that the patient had aphasia from a stroke and the only words which he could still utter were swear words. He might have been trying to say "Good Morning," but instead it came out as "#%@★$^!" Once the nurse was aware of the association between the patient's behavior and his brain injury, she learned to look to his nonverbal communication and to ignore his vocabulary.

Another area where neuropsychological testing has been utilized is in the *forensic* arena. Clinical neuropsychologists may be hired by the defense or prosecuting attorneys or by the court. Often a neuropsychological examination is requested to determine if there are cognitive deficits present and if they are consistent with the brain injury sustained by the client. Finally, neuropsychological testing is used in *research* to study normal cognitive functioning as well as the behavior of someone with known or suspected brain impairment. Testing also may help to determine the cognitive effects of a medical treatment or a new drug.

Key Points Summary 10.1

Reasons for Neuropsychological Evaluation

Diagnosis	Treatment Planning
Identifying Strengths and Weaknesses	Forensics
Vocational Planning	Research

Two Main Approaches to Neuropsychological Assessment

There are two main approaches to neuropsychological assessment. The first is the **fixed battery** approach, in which the same set of tests (a battery) is used for each examinee. The battery consists of many subtests. The second approach is called the **flexible battery.** The flexible battery allows the clinician to choose the subtests he or she believes are best suited to assess each examinee. It is important to remember that the subtests in both approaches are self-contained. Individual tests in a fixed battery (e.g., the *Trail Making Test*) can be used as part of a flexible battery.

Fixed Battery Approach

Approximately 15% of clinical neuropsychologists use a standardized, fixed battery approach to neuropsychological assessment (Sweet, Moberg, & Suchy, 2000). The two batteries most commonly used are the **Luria-Nebraska Neuropsychological Battery** and the **Halstead-Reitan Neuropsychological Battery.**

Luria-Nebraska Neuropsychological Battery

The *Luria-Nebraska Neuropsychological Battery* (LNNB; Golden, Purisch, & Hammeke, 1985) arose from "Luria's Neuropsychological Investigation" (Christensen, 1984), a collection of qualitative analyses of patient behavior built on the work of Russian neuropsychologist Aleksandr R. Luria (1902–1977). The LNNB was modified to produce scores for 11 clinical scales, 2 sensorimotor scales, 6 additional localization scales, and 5 summary scales (see Table 10.2). Twenty-eight additional factor scales allow for determination of more specific cognitive and sensory functioning. There are two essentially equivalent forms of the test, with Form II having an additional clinical scale. This test is designed for individuals aged 15 and older. There is also a children's form for use with ages 8–12 years. It includes the same clinical and optional scales as the adult form, but with no localization scales and only three summary scales. There are 11 additional factor scales for the children's version.

TABLE 10.2   *Scales of the Adult Form of the Luria-Nebraska Neuropsychological Battery*

Clinical Scales	Localization Scales	Summary Scales	Optional Scales
Arithmetic	Left Frontal	Left Hemisphere	Motor
Expressive Speech	Left Sensorimotor	Right Hemisphere	Writing
Intellectual Processes	Left Parietal-Occipital	Pathognomonic	Spelling
Intermediate Memory	Left Temporal	Profile Elevation	
(Form II only)	Right Frontal	Impairment	
Memory	Right Sensorimotor		
Motor Functions	Right Parietal-Occipital		
Reading	Right Temporal		
Receptive Speech			
Rhythm			
Tactile Functions			
Visual Functions			
Writing			

Administration of the LNNB requires 1.5 to 2.5 hours. Scoring can be done by hand or by computer. The test battery is portable and may be given at bedside if necessary.

Validation of the LNNB focuses on differentiating brain-damaged patients from other groups. It seems to distinguish brain-damaged from normal individuals quite accurately. Golden and the other test authors have provided several reports of the diagnostic accuracy of the LNNB (e.g., Golden, Hammeke, & Purisch, 1979; Golden, 1981, 1984). However, several studies contradict these findings (e.g., Adams, 1980, 1984; Crosson & Warren, 1982). Criticisms of the LNNB include its inability to detect mild impairment and the inaccuracy of the localization scales. In addition, the memory scales have been found to be affected by attentional deficits, such that a clear conclusion of the presence of memory impairment cannot be drawn. Furthermore, because many of the items require verbal processing, the presence of a language deficit may create test bias (Franzen, 2000).

Advantages of the LNNB include its ease of administration, portability, and brevity. However, beyond confirming the presence of brain damage, its utility is questionable. Although the LNNB has avid supporters, it is not as popular as other neuropsychological assessment approaches. A recent review of 100 neuropsychological evaluations conducted for forensic purposes found that only 10% used the LNNB (Lees-Haley, Smith, Williams, & Dunn, 1996).

Halstead-Reitan Neuropsychological Test Battery

The **Halstead-Reitan Neuropsychological Battery** (HRNB; Reitan & Wolfson, 1993) is used with adults. There also is a version for older children ages 9–14.

TABLE 10.3   *Components of the Halstead-Reitan Neuropsychological Battery*

Aphasia Screening Test	The patient must perform several different tasks that are rather simple. They include naming, spelling, writing, and reading; identifying body parts; simple arithmetic; right-left differentiation; and copying simple geometric shapes. The assumption is that a normal person could perform these items easily; if there are errors, then it indicates brain dysfunction.
Category Test	The patient responds to a series of figures flashed on a screen (or shown in a stimulus booklet) by pressing one of four levers. Either a bell (correct) or a buzzer (incorrect) sounds after each response. Each set of stimuli has some unifying principle, which the patient is to determine by the feedback received from prior responses.
Finger Tapping Test	This is a measure of motor speed. The patient is to tap on the apparatus (as shown in Figure 10.4) with his index finger as quickly as possible for 10-second trials. Both the dominant and the nondominant hands perform this test.
Grip Strength	The apparatus used for this test is the "hand dynamometer," which the patient holds with arm straight at the side and squeezes the grip. Again, each hand performs this task.
Rhythm Test	Using an audiotape, the patient is presented with several pairs of rhythmic beats that are to be identified as the same or different.
Sensory-perceptual Examination	This assessment includes a subbattery of measures that assess the patient's perception of sound, touch, and vision. In particular, there are unilateral stimuli, which occur on one side of the body, and others that are bilateral. Patients with certain types of brain damage may perform well on unilateral stimuli, but poorly on bilateral.
Speech-sounds Perception Test	Again using an audiotape, 60 spoken nonsense words are presented, which the patient is to identify from among four choices on an answer sheet.
Tactile Form Recognition Test	Here the patient is to identify by touch various plastic pieces of different shapes, such as a square or triangle.
Tactual Performance Test	For this test, the patient is blindfolded before being presented with a vertical board containing cutouts of various shapes with corresponding blocks. First with each hand and then with both, the patient is to place the correct block in each hole. Then the materials are hidden and the blindfold is removed. The patient is then asked to draw the board with the blocks in the correct places.
Trail-Making Test	There are two components to this test: Part A and Part B. Each is presented on a standard size sheet of paper. Part A includes circles containing numbers up to 25. The patient is to connect the circles, in order, with a continuous line as quickly as possible. Part B is similar, but contains the numerals 1–13 and the letters A–L. Again, the circles must be connected in order, but this time the patient must alternate between numbers and letters (1–A–2–B).

The battery consists of 10 tests (see Table 10.3). Performance on five of these tests determines the **Impairment Index** (Category Test, Tactual Performance Test, Seashore Rhythm Test, Speech Sounds Perception Test, Finger Tapping Test). This Impairment Index provides a cutoff point to represent the presence or absence of neurological deficits. The *Wechsler Adult Intelligence Scale* and the *Minnesota Multiphasic Personality Inventory* generally also are administered, but do not contribute to the Impairment Index. Memory testing also is necessary, as there is no memory test component in the HRNB battery. A larger number of variables (42) are used to obtain the **General Neuropsychological Deficit Score,** which reflects the severity of neuropsychological deficit. That is, the Impairment Index is used to determine the presence of deficits and the Neuropsychological Deficit Score reflects the degree of impairment.

Several studies of the HRNB and its indexes have demonstrated the battery's ability to discriminate brain-damaged subjects from normals (Russell, 1995), with an overall index accuracy rate of 80%. The HRNB has been found to have good test-retest reliability (Russell, 1992). Drawbacks include the battery's lack of a memory test and its administration time (4–5 hours for an experienced examiner). Originally, the battery was designed to determine the presence or absence of impairment, as reflected by the Impairment Index. Indeed, the authors' empirical investigation of one of the test components reflects its utility as "a general indicator of brain functions" (Reitan & Wolfson, 1989) rather than for finer discriminations. Others have found a lack of unique diagnostic contributions of some of the battery's tests (Sherer, Parsons, Nixon, & Adams, 1991).

FIGURE 10.4 The traditional mechanical finger tapping apparatus (left) and an electronic version (right).

Source: (left photo) Lafayette Instrument Company, Inc. Reproduced by permission; (right photo) Courtesy Western Psychological Services.

> ## Key Points Summary 10.2
> ### *Two Main Approaches to Neuropsychological Assessment*
>
> 1. Fixed Battery Approach
> 2. Flexible Battery Approach

Some Useful References. For reviews of the Luria-Nebraska, see Ayers and Burns (1991), Franzen (1985a, 1985b), Hooper (1992), Snow (1992), and Van Gorp (1992). For reviews of the Halstead-Reitan, see Dean (1985), Meier (1985), and Whitworth (1984). A more extensive review, with case study, of the Halstead-Reitan is given by Macciocchi and Barth (1996). For detailed descriptions of the administration procedures as well as normative data from a variety of sources for many of the tests mentioned under flexible batteries below, see Spreen and Strauss (1998).

Flexible Battery Approach

In contrast to the fixed batteries described earlier, the flexible battery approach allows the clinical neuropsychologist to select tests according to the patient and the referral question. Adopting such an approach precludes the use of an impairment index obtained from the fixed batteries. As neuropsychology has moved away from the "brain damaged or not" question, the flexible battery has been adopted to better tailor the assessment to address the reason for assessment and to give a more detailed description of the deficits present. A recent survey (Sweet, Moberg, & Suchy, 2000) found that 70% of clinical neuropsychologists use a flexible battery approach. This reflects an increase from 61% in 1995.

Test selection typically follows planned assessment of various cognitive domains. Table 10.4 contains examples of tests used in each of these domains. We'll discuss some of these later. Table 10.5 lists the tests most frequently used in neuropsychological assessment. Notice that some of these, for example, the Wechsler scales and MMPI, are covered in other chapters and are used in contexts in addition to neuropsychological assessment.

Mental Status

When one is considering which tests to give a patient, it is necessary first to obtain a general picture of that patient's gross cognitive functioning. If the patient has dementia, for example, one would not want to administer tests that are too difficult. This would waste both the patient's time and the examiner's. It is better to screen for significant cognitive impairment first. The measure typically used for this purpose is the

TABLE 10.4   *Examples of Tests Used to Assess Various Cognitive Domains*

Attention
Continuous Performance Test
Paced Auditory Serial Addition Test
Symbol Digit Modality Test
Trail-Making Test

Achievement
Peabody Individual Achievement Test-Revised
Wide Range Achievement Test 3
Wechsler Individual Achievement Test-II

Effort/Motivation
Rey Fifteen-Item Memory Test
Test of Memory Malingering
21-Item Test
Victoria Symptom Validity Test

Executive Functions
Behavioral Assessment of the Dysexecutive
   System
California Sorting Test
Category Test
Design Fluency Test
Stroop Test
Wisconsin Card Sorting Test

Intelligence
Kaufman Brief Intelligence Test-2
Microcog: Assessment of Cognitive
   Functioning
Raven's Progressive Matrices
Wechsler Intelligence Scales

Language
Boston Naming Test
Controlled Word Association
Peabody Picture Vocabulary Test-III
Token Test

Memory
Auditory Consonant Trigrams
Autobiographical Memory Interview
Benton Visual Retention Test, 5th Ed.
Buschke Selective Reminding Test
California Verbal Learning Test
Rey Auditory Verbal Learning Test
Wechsler Memory Scale-III

Mental Status
Mini-Mental State Exam

Motor
Finger Tapping Test
Grooved Pegboard Test
Hand Dynamometer
Purdue Pegboard Test

Personality/Psychological State
Beck Depression Inventory-II
Child Behavior Checklist
Geriatric Depression Scale
Minnesota Multiphasic Personality Inventory-2
Neurobehavioral Rating Scale
Neuropsychology Behavior and Affect Profile
Profile of Mood States
Vineland Adaptive Behavior Scales-II

Visuospatial/Perceptual
Clock Drawing
Embedded Figures Test
Facial Recognition Test
Hooper Visual Organization Test
Rey/Osterrieth Complex Figure Test
Right-Left Orientation

Mini-Mental State Exam (MMSE; Folstein, Folstein, & McHugh, 1975; Folstein, Folstein, McHugh, & Fanjiang, 2000). The MMSE consists of 30 points. Items measure general orientation (e.g., "What is today's date?"), memory (e.g., "Remember these 3 words—TABLE, FISH, BOX"), language (e.g., hold up pencil and ask patient to name the object), mental control (e.g., "spell 'world' backwards"), visuoconstructive skills

TABLE 10.5 *Top Ten Tests Used by Neuropsychologists*

Rank	Test
1.	Minnesota Multiphasic Personality Inventory/MMPI-2
2.	Wechsler Adult Intelligence Scale-Revised
3.	Wechsler Memory Scale-Revised
4.	Trail-Making Test, A & B
5.	Controlled Oral Word Association Test
6.	Finger Tapping Test
7.	Halstead-Reitan Neuropsychological Test Battery
8.	Boston Naming Test
9.	Category Test
10.	Wide Range Achievement Test-Revised and WRAT-3

Source: From Camara, Nathan, & Puente (2000).

(copying a geometric design), and the ability to follow a multiple-step command. Although scores below 24 are considered to be indicative of significant impairment in gross cognitive functioning, scoring at the normal level does not mean that the patient is free of impairment. Tombaugh and McIntyre (1992) provide a comprehensive review of the research on the MMSE.

Intelligence

The Wechsler intelligence scales are most frequently used as measures of intelligence. As these were covered in Chapter 8, they will not be described again here. The clinical neuropsychologist looks at the summary IQ scores, as well as performance on the individual subtests. A large difference between Verbal and Performance IQs, for example, may reflect relative impairment in language or in nonverbal functioning. Relative strengths and weaknesses within the verbal and nonverbal subtests also are determined. The patient's age-corrected subtest scores are averaged, and the clinical neuropsychologist looks for subtest deviation 3 points or greater from the average. Estimates of **premorbid** (before the onset of impairment) IQ levels can be determined through the use of formulas based on such factors as the patient's sex, age, occupation, and educational achievement. Education records often contain estimates of premorbid IQ, as many children completed an intelligence test in school.

Achievement

Another indication of a patient's premorbid cognitive level may be that individual's ability to read, spell, and complete written arithmetic problems. The Wide Range Achievement Test-3 (WRAT-3) often is used to assess academic achievement, with subtests assessing these three areas. Patient performance also gives information about possible learning disabilities. Spelling and reading errors, for example, may reflect dyslexia. Mistakes on the math problems might be related to attention deficits, such as adding instead of subtracting. The patient's performance on the WRAT-3 is reported in percentiles and grade equivalents.

Attention/Concentration

The flexible battery approach often includes several tests with attention/concentration components. Performance on subtests of the WAIS-III is considered. For example, the Digit Span subtest is a measure of auditory attention. Often patients are able to repeat digits forward without difficulty. It is when they are requested to repeat the numbers in reverse order that problems with concentration and mental control become apparent. Similar problems may occur on the Letter-Number Sequencing subtest. Visual attention deficits may be reflected by low performance on Picture Completion or Symbol Search.

TRY IT!

Have a friend read the following number sequences to you at the rate of one number per second, going from the shortest to the longest string of numbers. After each number string is read, repeat the digits in the same order. What is the longest string of digits you recalled without error? Now have your friend read each set again, but this time repeat the digits in reverse order.

4-2-7	6-9-8-3	2-1-7-4-8
8-6-2-5-9-7	9-3-7-5-6-2-4	7-1-4-2-8-3-6-9-5

Was that harder? Most people can recall 7 +/− 2 digits forward and about 2 digits less when recalling the digits backward.

The Trail-Making Test is one component of the Halstead-Reitan Neuropsychological Battery often administered as part of a flexible battery approach. The test is a measure of visual scanning, writing speed, and attention/concentration. See Table 10.3 for a description of the test. The more difficult Part B requires connecting the circles in order while alternating number-letter-number-letter. So the correct responses would be 1-A-2-B-3-C, and so on. Patients with brain injury may have a very hard time completing this task. Often they **perseverate,** or are unable to switch between patterns of thought.

Language

Impairment in communication may be obvious, such as when a patient has aphasia, or there may be more subtle deficits. Language involves both expressive and receptive abilities. Talking and writing are expressive skills. Comprehending another's speech and reading are receptive skills. An example of a measure of expressive language is the Boston Naming Test. This test is comprised of 60 line drawings of objects, arranged in increasing order of difficulty. That is, the first item would be as easy as "chair," and the last could be as difficult as "rivet" (you know, those metal things on the pockets of your jeans). A person with confrontational naming impairment may be unable to name the picture spontaneously. However, if prompted by a phonemic cue (e.g., "starts with 'ch'"), the person may respond correctly.

Another expressive language test can be performed either orally or in writing. This is the Controlled Word Association Test, also known as word fluency or verbal fluency. Here the task is to list as many words as possible within one minute that begin with a certain letter. Aphasics perform poorly on this task, as do some patients who have difficulty organizing and searching for information. A patient may begin to look around the testing room for objects that begin with the designated letter. This is not a particularly productive strategy. Other patients may show perseveration, such as saying the following when asked for "A" words: "apple, apricot, peach, orange." Here they started correctly, but they perseverated on the category of fruit.

If it was apparent during testing that a patient had trouble understanding spoken directions, formal testing for receptive language deficits might be conducted. The Token Test is a commonly used measure that assesses a patient's language comprehension. Plastic tokens varying in size, shape, and color are placed before the patient. Commands increasing in complexity are given. For example, one might be asked to point to the red square. Then one may be asked to point to the red square after touching the yellow circle. This test has been found to have very good discrimination between aphasic and nonaphasic patients. There also is a children's version.

Visuospatial/Perceptual

Subtests of the Wechsler intelligence tests provide useful information about visuospatial and perceptual functioning. Object Assembly, for example, requires a patient to put together puzzle pieces. A patient may perform poorly on this test because of **constructional apraxia,** which is an inability to assemble or copy two- or three-dimensional objects. The manual component can be removed by administering the Hooper Visual Organization Test. It is composed of 30 items, each a common object that has been cut into pieces. The patient's task is to assemble the pieces in his or her head and then name the object. So, one might have a patient who performs normally on the Hooper Visual Organization Test and poorly on Object Assembly. This would reflect the patient's difficulty in the construction of the item, rather than in perception. Such patients might comment while performing Object Assembly that they "know it is a horse," but that they "can't make the pieces go together the right way."

The Block Design subtest of the WAIS-III also requires visuospatial skills and construction abilities. Here the task is to reproduce a demonstrated pattern with red and white blocks. The design is either a 2×2 or 3×3 square.

Another test of visuospatial skills, as well as organizational abilities, is the Rey/Osterreith Complex Figure Test. The patient is requested to copy a geometric design that has many details. Scoring is determined according to the presence or absence of critical components, the accuracy of placement of the feature, and degree of distortion. Often a clinical neuropsychologist will also consider the qualitative components of the patient's performance. Did they approach drawing the figure in a sensible way? Did they copy the figure in a piecemeal fashion, resulting in a distorted drawing? Did they complete the drawing quickly, or were they very slow and meticulous?

For patients who may have dementia, another type of drawing task can be used. Guess what you do in the Clock Drawing Test? That's right. The patient either is given a predrawn circle or is asked to draw a circle and then is told to place the numbers in the circle to form a clockface. Often the instructions are to place the hands at "ten after eleven." As can be seen in Figure 10.5, some patients have problems with spacing the numbers, others perseverate and put in too many numbers, and still others have trouble drawing the hands. Some even place the numbers in the opposite direction. Sometimes visuospatial testing uncovers the presence of **spatial neglect,**

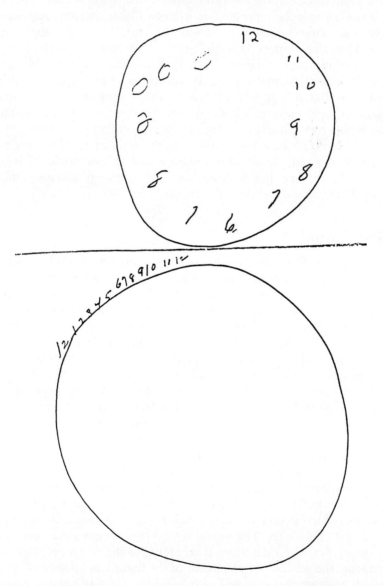

FIGURE 10.5 Samples of clock drawing by patients with dementia.

Source: Courtesy of Brooke J. Cannon, Marywood University.

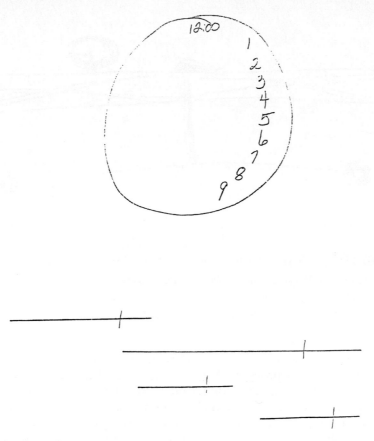

FIGURE 10.6　Clock and line bisection by patient with right hemisphere damage.

Source: Courtesy of Brooke J. Cannon, Marywood University.

usually for the left visual field, as a result of damage to the right hemisphere (see Figure 10.6).

TRY IT!

We can use drawing tasks to assess cognitive functioning. Some clinicians ask their patients to draw a bicycle. Go ahead and draw one now and then come back to the text.

Okay. How did you do? Lezak (1995) has devised a 20-point scoring system for bicycle drawing. She considers whether there are two wheels (you probably have those), spokes, a seat, and handlebars. Also, is there a drive chain? Is it properly attached? Are there gears? How about fenders? Don't worry if you've missed these. The average score reported for 20- to 24-year-old blue-collar workers is 13.95, with a standard deviation of 4.03 (Nichols, as cited in Lezak, 1995). See Figure 10.7 for the bicycle drawn by a patient with a frontotemporal dementia. Note the steering wheel.

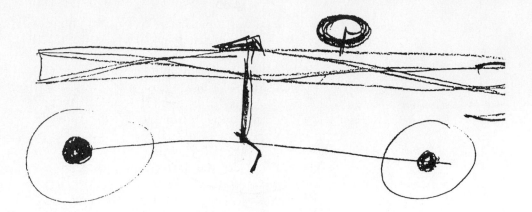

FIGURE 10.7   Bicycle drawn by patient with frontal lobe dementia.

Source: Courtesy of Brooke J. Cannon, Marywood University.

Memory

Memory deficits are probably the most frequently reported complaints by patients being referred for neuropsychological evaluations. Impairment in memory can have a variety of causes, such as head injury, stroke, vitamin deficiency, depression, and dementia. There are both verbal and nonverbal memory tests. Verbal memory tests may involve remembering a short story or word pairs, as in the Wechsler Memory Scale-III, or a long list of words, such as the Rey Auditory Verbal Learning Test (RAVLT). In the RAVLT, a 15-item word list is presented, after which the patient is to recall as many words as possible in any order. The list is presented a total of five times, with the patient recalling all the words he or she remembers after each administration. A distracter list of 15 new words is then presented for the patient to recall. At this point, the patient is now asked to recall the words from the first list.

Delayed recall of the original list also is requested 20 to 30 minutes later. Recognition memory is assessed by having the patient identify words from the original list from among distracter words. By looking at the patient's performance across the first five trials, one can see whether or not learning has occurred. Most people learn about five words from trial 1 to trial 5. They often "lose" two words when recalling the words after the presentation of the distracter list. Retention is typically good after the delay, with patients displaying good recognition memory.

Visual memory often is assessed by having the patient draw figures from memory. The Wechsler Memory Scale-III contains various subtests to assess nonverbal memory. There is a task requiring the memory of faces, another that assesses the patient's recall of the details of pictures presented earlier, and another where the patient is to touch the same sequence of blocks touched by the examiner.

Motor Functioning

Three areas of motor functioning typically are assessed by clinical neuropsychologists: motor speed, fine motor coordination, and grip strength. Motor speed can be reflected indirectly by the patient's performance on other tasks requiring a motor response, such as the Trail-Making Test, some of the WAIS subtests, and so on. The Finger Tapping Test was discussed earlier, as part of the Halstead-Reitan Neuropsychological Battery. This test is administered to each hand, with the dominant hand usually performing about 10% better than the nondominant hand. The Grooved Pegboard Test (see Figure 10.8) requires the patient to place small metal pegs one at a time into a series of holes much like keyholes, but oriented in varying directions. Time to complete the whole board determines the score, with attention also paid to the number of times the patient dropped a peg. Grip strength, as measured by a hand **dynamometer**, may also be assessed. (Pronunciation of this psychometric tongue twister bedevils the novice. Use this guide to get it right. The first part of the word is just like the first part of dynamite. The second part rhymes with thermometer. So, we have: dyna-mometer (*dyna*-mite + ther-*mometer*.) If all else fails, call it the "grip strength" test. Again, differences between dominant and nondominant hands are considered. The hand dynamometer (see Figure 10.9) also is part of the Halstead-Reitan Neuropsychological Battery.

Executive Functions

Additional tests measure what often are referred to as **executive functions**. Brain damage may disrupt these skills, particularly when the lesions are in the frontal lobes.

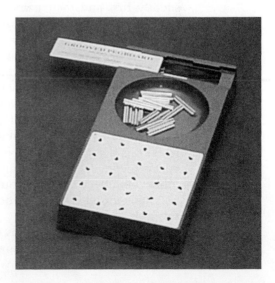

FIGURE 10.8 The grooved pegboard.

Source: Lafayette Instrument Company, Inc. Reproduced by permission.

FIGURE 10.9   The hand dynamometer.
Source: Lafayette Instrument Company, Inc.
Reproduced by permission.

TRY IT! ....

Do you know what it takes to be a successful *executive*? List the skills you think would be important. What could you ask a patient to do in order to assess these abilities?

....

Tests that require **cognitive flexibility,** the ability to switch cognitive sets, often are used to measure "executive functions." One measure, which is sensitive to impairment in executive functions, is based on the **Stroop effect.** First reported by Stroop in 1935, the Stroop effect originally referred to the slower naming of ink colors when the stimulus is an incongruent color name. The patient's task is to name the color of the ink and ignore the word. Because reading is an automatic behavior when presented with a word, the slowed color naming results from response interference. Often, one has to read the word silently first and then name the color. The Stroop Color-Word Test (Golden, 1978) is one of several forms of this test. Here there are three stimulus sheets, each composed of five columns of 20 stimuli. The first sheet is simply the words "red," "blue," and "green" printed in black ink. The patient is to read as many words as possible in 45 seconds. The second sheet contains XXXXs printed in red, blue, or green ink. Now the patient is to name the ink color of each stimulus, as many as possible in 45 seconds. On the final sheet are the interference stimuli, with each of the color names (red, blue, green) printed in an incongruent ink color. Again the patient is to name the color of the ink. Degree of interference is determined by the difference between the color naming of XXXXs versus incongruent color names, while taking reading speed into account. This inhibition effect has been found to be increased in patients with brain damage, although mood state (e.g., depression, anxiety) also decreases performance on this task.

Some interesting variations on the Stroop effect have been created for use with clinical populations. For example, phobics are slower at naming the ink color of words related to their fears. When this phenomenon is applied for noncognitive purposes, it is referred to as the "emotional Stroop effect" (see Williams, Mathews, & MacLeod, 1996, for a thorough review).

TRY IT! ....

Divide these six stimuli into two groups according to some characteristic. Now divide them into two new groups, by using a different strategy. Can you come up with a third way to separate them into two groups?

....

Another example of a measure of executive functioning is the Wisconsin Card Sorting Test. Here the patient is provided with four stimuli that vary from each other in three ways. The patient is given a set of cards, each of which is to be matched to one of the stimuli in some way. As you did earlier, it could first be by shape, then maybe by shading, or by color. After each card is placed, the patient is told whether the response was right or wrong; this information can then be used to determine where to place the next card. For example, if the first response was according to shape, but the correct category was shading, the examiner would say, "wrong." Once the required number is matched according to a predetermined criterion (e.g., first to shape), the examiner then changes the rule so that now another criterion is correct. Patients with deficits in executive functions have a very hard time with this switching of cognitive set. One patient with a dementia affecting the frontal lobes placed all 128 cards according to the same criterion, despite being told "wrong" over and over! He simply could not change his cognitive set and see the stimuli in a new way. The Category Test of the Halstead-Reitan Neuropsychological Battery uses a similar strategy of providing feedback to the patient to determine whether a correct strategy is being used.

Personality/Psychological State

Most clinical neuropsychologists add some sort of personality assessment to their test battery. Objective measures of personality, as discussed in Chapter 12, are used most frequently. Projective measures, as discussed in Chapter 13, are rarely used by clinical neuropsychologists. According to a survey by Sweet, Moberg, and Suchy (2000), for those who do use projectives, the majority (70%) use them when there is a suspected psychiatric diagnosis, as opposed to a suspected or known neurological diagnosis (10%).

Among the objective measures of personality, the *Minnesota Multiphasic Personality Inventory* (MMPI-2) typically is used. The MMPI is the most frequently used test by neuropsychologists (Camara, Nathan, & Puente, 2000). We describe this test in more detail in Chapter 13. The MMPI-2 may be administered to aid in differential diagnosis (e.g., psychiatric disorder versus "organic" disorder), to reflect possible personality changes after brain injury (e.g., significant paranoia), to assess the validity of the patient's report and his or her motivation (e.g., questionable validity scale configuration), and to determine the impact of the brain dysfunction on the patient's psychological state (e.g., reactive depression).

The MMPI uses the notion of 2-point codes (see Chapter 13). Some 2-point codes relate to brain injuries. Graham (2000) suggests that a 1–9 (hypochondriasis-mania) profile reflects poor coping in a person who has suffered a brain injury. A 2–9 (depression-mania) profile might reflect impaired emotional control or overactivity in an attempt to cope with the results of a brain injury. However, Graham emphasizes that the MMPI should not be used to diagnose brain damage. Groth-Marnat (1999) notes that "some code types, such as 28/82, occur more frequently among brain-damaged groups … [but] do not occur frequently enough, however, to be diagnostic of CNS involvement" (p. 593).

As the MMPI tests are self-report, it is assumed that the patient is able to give an accurate portrayal of his or her psychological state. Many neurological conditions, however, cause a lack of insight or the denial or unawareness of deficits. Think back to the story of Phineas Gage, the railroad worker who had the spike blown through his head. If he were to complete the MMPI, he would probably deny having any problems, yet we know that his deficits were significant. His friends, however, would tell a completely different story. This is why obtaining information from significant others about a patient's functioning may be critical.

One type of personality assessment tool that allows for the report of significant others is the *Neuropsychology Behavior and Affect Profile* (NBAP; Nelson, Satz, & D'Elia, 1994). This scale consists of 106 statements (see Table 10.6) assessing depression, mania, indifference, inappropriateness, and pragnosia, defined as "a defect in the pragmatics of communication style" (Nelson et al., p. 267).

For each statement, the respondent, usually a family member, indicates whether or not the target behavior was present before the injury and now. In this way, it is possible to see which areas have changed from pre-injury levels.

Although the NBAP was originally developed to be completed by a significant other, a self-report version also is available. The items remain the same, but are reworded into the first person (e.g., "I seem depressed, sad, or blue."). Cannon (2002) compared the self- and other-rated forms of the NBAP and found that both

TABLE 10.6   *Sample Items from the Neuropsychology Behavior and Affect Profile (NBAP)*

Item	Scale
My relative seems depressed, sad, or blue.	Depression
My relative's enthusiasm is almost continuous or unceasing.	Mania
My relative seems unconcerned about events around him.	Indifference
My relative behaves in a manner that causes others to wonder why he acts that way.	Inappropriateness
In beginning and ending conversations, my relative doesn't use the right everyday phrases.	Pragnosia

patients with mild traumatic brain injuries and their significant others reported that the patients had more problems with Depression and Inappropriateness after the injury than before it. Of particular interest was the finding that the patients reported significantly more problems with prognosia after the injury, as compared to the ratings by the significant others. This suggests that for mild injuries, the patient may be the best informant. These findings demonstrate the importance of gathering data from multiple sources.

Psychological state may be assessed through such widely used self-report measures as the *Beck Depression Inventory-II* (see pp. 501–502), and also through structured interviewing designed to determine the presence of any diagnosable psychiatric disorder.

Effort/Motivation

Until recently, many clinical neuropsychologists relied on only the validity scales of the MMPI to ascertain the motivation of the patient. Extreme elevations on the F scale in someone who, for example, does not have obvious psychosis, might suggest that the patient is faking bad. Elevations on the Lie scale might suggest a naïve attempt to fake good. Because the MMPI was not designed to assess neurocognitive dysfunction, it has not proven a reliable method for detecting faking of neuropsychological symptoms. The F and K scales are sensitive to the feigning of unusual, typically psychotic, symptomatology. If the patient had suffered a mild head injury, he or she might very well be **malingering,** faking deficits for secondary gain, but the problems reported usually are in memory and other cognitive functions, areas not included in the MMPI.

Attempts have been made to use the MMPI to detect malingering. A **"Fake Bad Scale"** from the MMPI-2 has been developed to help detect personal injury claimants who are exaggerating or simulating emotional distress (Lees-Haley, English, & Glenn, 1991). See Chapter 13 for descriptions of the various MMPI-2 validity scales: L, K, F, TRIN, VRIN, and so on. All these scales may enter the picture when interpreting a neuropsychological assessment case.

As noted, malingering on a neuropsychological assessment typically involves feigning of cognitive symptoms, rather than psychiatric disturbance. Most notably, patients fake memory impairment. Some of the earliest standardized techniques to assess the truthfulness of a patient's memory complaints used statistical probability and are referred to as *symptom validity testing*. For example, if I were to flip a coin 100 times and asked you to guess whether it would be heads or tails, by chance alone on average you would be right 50 times. By using a forced-choice test, typically with only two options, the probability of the correct/incorrect response being given can be calculated. So, I might show a patient either a red pen or a blue pen and ask the patient to remember the color. I might wait 10 seconds and then ask the color of the pen I had just shown. Now, if I did this 100 times (actually, it typically is done via computer), even if the patient had severe memory impairment, his or her performance should be at least 50% correct. Now imagine that the patient was faking a memory deficit. Having no real impairment, the patient would easily remember the accurate response but then would intentionally provide the wrong answer. Thus, if the patient gives the correct answer less than 50% of the time (actually, outside of a calculated confidence interval), then it is likely that the patient is intentionally providing the wrong answer—because only with effort could a patient perform below chance.

Other tests also look at accuracy on easy and hard items, as well as response latency, which is often measured by having the patient respond via a computer keyboard. It should take longer to identify the correct response and then choose the wrong answer than to answer honestly. This phenomenon, however, is likely to be obscured if the malingerer also fakes cognitive and motor slowing.

TRY IT!

Imagine that you are faking brain damage from a car accident. You are suing the other driver and have been sent for a neuropsychological evaluation. How would you perform on the different assessment measures previously described? Do you think that you could fake a believable injury? Are there any cognitive areas in which you would perform normally?

Supplementary Information

A complete neuropsychological assessment involves more than administering and interpreting tests. We describe here, very briefly, other types of information typically examined when undertaking a neuropsychological assessment.

Medical History

It is critical to get a complete medical history of the patient when conducting a neuropsychological evaluation. When a clinical neuropsychologist is working in an inpatient setting, these data typically are readily available. Review of the medical chart would find a history and physical completed by the treating physician. Here the clinical neuropsychologist would learn of any possible medical contributions to the patient's cognitive and psychological state. For example, thyroid dysfunction may be related to depressed mood, or significant vitamin deficiency may mimic dementia. A history of cardiovascular disease, such as irregular heart beat, past heart surgeries, or heart attacks may put the patient at risk for strokes. Visual deficits might impede the patient's ability to see test stimuli. A history of neurological disease or past brain injury also would be critical information. Family medical history also is significant, particularly for disorders that may be inherited, such as Huntington's disease.

Reading the progress note entries by all treating staff also can be enlightening. It can be learned if unusual behaviors have been demonstrated, if the patient has shown any signs of psychosis or paranoia, or if there have been periods of confusion during the day or night. In some cases of dementia, "sundowning" occurs: the patient is reasonably well oriented during the day but becomes quite confused at night. The medical chart also will allow the clinical neuropsychologist to determine what medications the patient is taking. Ideally, reports of a CT scan or MRI of the brain will be available. In addition, the ward social worker often completes a very detailed psychosocial history. Thus, by reviewing the chart prior to seeing the patient, much information can be gathered and hypotheses can be generated.

Many patients are not seen in the hospital, and, therefore, this same information needs to be gathered as an outpatient. If the patient has not had a recent physical, he or she should have one prior to the neuropsychological assessment. Records might be requested from the treating physician, and history forms are completed by the patient and/or a family member, with information gathered and clarified during an interview prior to assessment.

Psychiatric History

The clinical neuropsychologist must inquire about any past or present treatment for a psychiatric condition. Has the patient ever been hospitalized for psychiatric reasons? Has the patient ever engaged in psychotherapy or been treated by a psychiatrist? A history of electroconvulsive therapy (ECT), or "shock treatments," might also be relevant to a patient's reports of memory impairment.

Some patients may report a history of psychological disturbance but have never received treatment. Through detailed interview, the clinical neuropsychologist could attempt to determine possible diagnoses and severity of the difficulties. Again, family psychiatric history is important information to gain.

Psychosocial History

It is important to know the patient's educational background. How far did he go in school? What sort of grades did she get? Did he receive any special education? Was he ever held back, suspended, expelled? What were her favorite and least favorite subjects?

The clinical neuropsychologist would ask about the patient's family of origin and the current status of parents and siblings. Other information to gather includes the patient's occupational history, marital status, and number of children. Drug and alcohol use, both current and remote, is necessary to determine. Any history of legal problems also might be relevant. The patient's leisure activities, volunteer work, and so on may give further insight into current and remote status. In particular, changes in the level of activity are important to note.

School Records

Particularly for younger patients, school records provide a wealth of information. Often, intelligence testing was conducted, national achievement test scores are available, and teacher comments about the patient's behavior may be valuable. Grades provide evidence of areas of strength and weakness. It always is interesting to compare the patient's self-report ("I was a B student") with the person's actual transcripts; rarely do people state that they were worse than they really were—it usually is the reverse. So, school records can provide information about premorbid status, history of special education, and a validity check of the patient's self-report.

Collateral Information

As noted when discussing the NBAP, gathering information from the patient as well as from another source can be very useful in creating a full picture of the patient's status. Particularly in cases in which the patient no longer has insight into his or her functioning, family members provide critical information. Consider an early dementia case who denied having any memory difficulties or other problems. He was pleasant and socially appropriate. On the surface, he seemed fine. Only when his wife was interviewed, and then later during testing, were the significant areas of deficit apparent.

Behavioral Observations

Another important component of a neuropsychological evaluation is observation of the patient's behavior. Typically, clinical neuropsychologists include behavioral observations in their written reports. Such descriptions may help illustrate the type of errors the patient made. For example, the way a patient approaches a test may tell more than simply that he or she passed or failed the item. It might be noted that when asked to copy a very complex design, the patient failed to use a common strategy, constructing it in a haphazard fashion. Or, when completing the Block Design subtest on the Wechsler intelligence scales, the patient failed to maintain the 2×2 or 3×3 square configuration. Sometimes a patient actually stacks the blocks, forming a three-dimensional figure.

If a patient is not being cooperative with testing, or appears to be distracted and unable to focus on the tasks, this information should be included in the report. Any other unusual behaviors witnessed during the evaluation might be important in diagnostic considerations, such as evidence of seizure activity, hearing or visual impairment, or deficits in spontaneous speech.

Case Examples Revisited

Now let's revisit those cases described at the start of the chapter. In each case, we will see how certain neuropsychological tests or patterns of results would help to answer the referral question. That only certain tests are offered as evidence is not meant to imply that these would be the only measures administered; space does not allow us to discuss all the information that would be gathered or provide all the test results.

Case #1

Nancy O'Roarke, a recently widowed, 74-year-old woman, complains of memory loss, trouble concentrating, and an inability to perform her usual daily activities. Is this Alzheimer's disease?

Let's imagine that Mrs. O'Roarke has a clean bill of health. No history of significant medical problems or drug/alcohol use; no prior psychiatric disturbance or treatment.

Key Points Summary 10.3

Supplemental Information Gathered in a Neuropsychological Evaluation

- Medical History
- Psychiatric History
- Psychosocial History
- School Records
- Collateral Information
- Behavior Observations

She has had a recent physical that was normal. Her childhood was normal, with no medical or psychiatric problems in the family. She reports that she was valedictorian of her high school and earned high marks in college. Mrs. O'Roarke is a retired elementary schoolteacher. She has one child, a 45-year-old daughter, who works as an accountant and resides with her husband nearby. The patient was married for 48 years; her husband died suddenly of a heart attack two months ago. For the past four weeks, she has been complaining of forgetfulness, trouble concentrating, and an inability to carry on with her usual volunteer work and household chores.

So, what are the possibilities? Could this be early dementia? It is not unusual for patients to be referred for neuropsychological evaluation to assess for dementia after the loss of a spouse. In many cases, the patient had been having cognitive problems for a long period of time that went unnoticed, as the capable spouse handled all responsibilities. It is only on the loss of the spouse, leaving the patient alone, that it becomes apparent that the patient cannot manage independently.

On neuropsychological testing, Mrs. O'Roarke's performance was inconsistent. Her verbal memory, when tested by having to remember a story, was mildly impaired. In contrast, when she was required to learn a long list of words, she showed an average to high-average learning curve. Her delayed recall of these words, however, was moderately impaired, yet she had normal recognition memory. Visual memory was average to superior for both immediate and delayed recall. Attention was impaired on most measures. Language skills were high average to superior, and visuospatial skills were average, although she was somewhat slow on timed tasks. Motor testing was normal. When given a Wechsler intelligence test, Mrs. O'Roarke's Verbal IQ was 117, high average; her Performance IQ was 108, average. It was noted that she failed to receive any bonus points for quick completion on the performance tasks.

So, what do you think of the test results? Is there memory impairment? What about the attention deficits and motor slowing? Is this dementia?

Mrs. O'Roarke completed the MMPI-2. Her resulting profile showed a tendency to deny problems. All the clinical scales fell within the normal range, with the exception of Depression and Social Introversion, each of which was elevated into the clinically significant range.

The patient's daughter reported that her mother had been an active, social woman until the death of her father. Mrs. O'Roarke was busied after his death with funeral arrangements and financial paperwork. Once all these were completed, she simply stopped engaging in any activities outside the home. She failed to eat properly, she lost weight, and she complained of having trouble sleeping at night. When the patient's daughter would talk with her, the patient would have trouble paying attention to the conversation, being unable to concentrate.

Now what do you think? Certainly, the presence of depression is likely. This is supported by the MMPI-2, the daughter's report, the recency of her husband's death, and the presence of symptoms common to depression in the elderly, such as sleep disturbance, loss of appetite, weight loss, and loss of interest in usual activities.

But can depression account for the cognitive deficits? The answer in many cases is "YES!" Based on these data, a diagnosis of dementia would be inappropriate for Mrs. O'Roarke. It appears that she has **pseudodementia,** cognitive impairment that is similar to a dementia like Alzheimer's disease, but related to a psychiatric condition, typically depression. Patients with suspected pseudodementia should be referred for depression treatment, including antidepressant medications and/or psychotherapy. With resolution of the depression, typically the cognitive deficits disappear.

Mrs. O'Roarke shows the typical pattern of test results related to pseudodementia (see Table 10.7). She showed inconsistent performance in memory, at times being normal, at other times being impaired. If this were dementia, all testing would be impaired, with no variation. Also, Mrs. O'Roarke showed a significant difference in her spontaneous recall of information, which was impaired, as compared to her recognition memory (which was normal). This is like the difference between fill-in-the-blank questions and multiple-choice questions. If you don't know the answer, you do equally poorly on each type of question. This is the same as the dementia patient. He would have trouble storing information, so that it is not "in there" to be retrieved. If you *do* know the answer but can't remember it just then, you will fail a fill-in-the-blank question but are likely to be able to answer a multiple-choice question correctly, as you recognize the right answer from among the options. This

TABLE **10.7** *Neuropsychological Testing Features of Pseudodementia*

Frequent "I don't know" responses

Tendency to give up easily, but will persist with encouragement

Errors of omission instead of commission (i.e., they give no answer, whereas dementia patients give the wrong answer)

Better recognition memory than recall memory

Impaired attention/concentration

Disorientation

No language impairment

Depressed mood

is like the depressed elderly patient who appropriately stored the information but had trouble retrieving it.

Case #2

Jack Davis, a 42-year-old construction worker, was injured on the job when a cement block struck him in the head. Since that time, he has had headaches, memory loss, poor attention span, and depressed mood. He is involved in a lawsuit against his employer. Does he have brain damage?

At the time of the injury, Mr. Davis was wearing a safety helmet when the cement block fell from 20 feet above him, striking him in the helmet and knocking him to the ground. He was taken to the emergency room of the local hospital. At no time did he lose consciousness. His medical examination revealed a normal MRI of the brain and no neurological deficits. Mr. Davis has been in reasonable health until the accident. He smokes a half-pack of cigarettes per day and drinks beer socially. There is no prior psychiatric disturbance or treatment.

Even without signs of brain damage on the MRI, could he have sustained an injury that would account for his deficits? Let's find out more.

Mr. Davis reports a normal childhood, with no medical or psychiatric problems in the family. His parents are alive and well, and his two sisters are both married with children. Mr. Davis was an athlete in school, participating in varsity wrestling and football. He stated that he was the state wrestling champion. When asked about his grades, the patient stated that he was an "average" student. He denied having any significant problems in school but acknowledged that he only enjoyed sports.

The patient currently is going through the process of a divorce, due to "irreconcilable differences"; (he has been separated from his wife for the past year. He has two sons, ages 12 and 15. He reports that his 12-year-old was diagnosed with Attention Deficit Disorder and takes Ritalin. He denies having had any legal problems prior to the filing of this lawsuit.

When asked about the accident, Mr. Davis described in an angry tone how he had told the foreman not to knock down the wall without the retaining net, but that "he didn't listen!" Mr. Davis described how his friend had driven him to the hospital, where he was examined by a rude nurse and was "kept waiting for 90 minutes" before seeing a doctor. The patient also listed the various medical examinations he has had since the accident, some ordered by his own attorney and some by the attorney for the construction company. He has not returned to work since the accident and has filed for workers' compensation.

Mr. Davis would not give consent for his wife or his employer to be contacted to provide additional information. He did allow for his school transcripts to be obtained. These revealed that he was truant several times and suspended once for fighting. His grades typically were C's and D's, with A's in automechanics, wood shop, and gym. Intelligence testing conducted in grade school revealed an IQ of 95. Achievement testing found that he fell further and further behind his expected levels with increasing years.

Test results indicated generally average to low average performance on the intelligence testing subtests, with the exception of Digit Span, Arithmetic, and Digit Symbol, which were moderately impaired. Visuospatial testing was normal. Naming abilities were average, but his verbal fluency (as measured by word list generation) was severely impaired. Verbal and visual memory testing was severely impaired for both immediate and delayed recall. He showed no learning curve on the Key Auditory Verbal Learning Test, and his recognition memory was poor with many false identifications. Motor testing was high average with each hand. Achievement testing reflected significantly impaired spelling and reading skills, corresponding to the fifth-grade level, and low average written arithmetic.

What do you make of these findings so far? Is this consistent with what you would imagine could be caused by such an injury? Certainly, closed head injuries result in attention/concentration deficits and memory impairment.

On the MMPI-2, Mr. Davis endorsed many items indicating psychological distress, with his F scale quite high and his K scale much lower. All clinical scales, except Masculinity/Femininity (low scores indicate stereotypical male interests) and Social Introversion were significantly elevated. The Beck Depression Inventory-II then was administered, with the resulting score suggesting a moderate level of depression.

Symptom Validity Testing was performed, using a forced choice, two-option procedure. Mr. Davis was correct on 40% of the trials. He complained frequently about his inability to remember even the simplest things.

Now, with these data, we might hypothesize that Mr. Davis is feigning his memory impairment. Despite the fact that he scored in the impaired range on tests of memory, he was able to provide very accurate and detailed information about his accident and subsequent medical treatments. He overreported symptoms on the MMPI-2, at a level that would be indicative of psychosis, malingering, or a "cry for help." Testing of effort/motivation suggests that he was intentionally providing the wrong answer.

School records suggest that Mr. Davis was not academically gifted. He may have been allowed to pass through school on his athletic merits. His achievement testing, both in school and during the current evaluation, may indicate the presence of a learning disability. His son has been diagnosed with Attention Deficit Disorder, which may run in families. Therefore, some impairment on testing, unrelated to the accident, might be expected. However, it appears that Mr. Davis is exaggerating his deficits.

So, is Mr. Davis just being greedy and trying to gain a financial settlement when he has no real injury? This is possible. We must also consider his current situation. He is in a bitter divorce proceeding, is not working, and has no income. According to his Beck Depression Inventory-II results, he may also be experiencing moderate levels of depression (this scale does not contain an indication of the validity of the patient's responses).

Therefore, the information fails to conclusively support brain injury resulting from the accident. Symptom validity testing suggests intentional feigning or exaggeration of deficits. The inability to obtain collateral information certainly makes it more difficult to determine changes from his pre-accident state. There is a suggestion that he may be suffering from a situational depression and also has a premorbid learning disability.

The last case example will allow us to further explore evaluations of learning disabilities.

Case #3

> *Billy Zollinger, a 10-year-old boy in fourth grade, has been receiving failing grades in school. His mother reports that he often loses things, forgets to do what she asks, or fails to complete the job. He also takes excessive amounts of time to do his homework, often being distracted by outside noises or other stimuli. Does he have Attention Deficit Disorder?*

Billy's medical history reflects birth complications. He was a "blue baby," suffering hypoxia, a decrease in oxygen, and requiring placement in the neonatal intensive care unit (NICU) where he was intubated. He remained in the NICU for one week. Following discharge and during his preschool years, there were no delays in achieving developmental milestones, such as walking, talking, and so on. He did suffer a few "bumps on the head," according to his mother, mostly related to his enjoyment of climbing trees, and active, risk-taking play behavior, such as hanging by his feet from the monkey bars. He suffered a fractured wrist from a fall on the playground at age 7. Although he enjoys physical activities, his mother describes him as "somewhat uncoordinated."

Other medical tests reflect normal vision and hearing. There are no vitamin deficiencies, lab work is normal, and Billy is of normal height and weight for his age. He is left-hand dominant; there are no other left-handed members of his immediate or extended family.

Billy's teachers report that he is a pleasant young boy, but that he has difficulty following directions given to the class and often needs the instructions to be repeated to him individually. Often he cannot finish his work during the allotted time. His work reflects minor errors, such as adding instead of subtracting.

The results of neuropsychological testing reflect average to high average intellectual abilities, but significant deficits in attention-related WISC-III subtests, including Arithmetic, Digit Span, Symbol Search, and Picture Completion. His academic achievement finds Billy places well behind his expected grade level on spelling and mathematics. His written math errors often reflect simple mistakes. The Halstead-Reitan Neuropsychological Test Battery showed deficits consistent with auditory attention problems, difficulty with speech sound perception, and relative impairment with the right hand, when compared to the left. Assessment of written language found that Billy's handwriting was quite sloppy and there were errors in spelling and the omission of some words. Reading assessment revealed generally intact functioning, but simple errors, such as reading "duck" instead of "dock." Personality and mood assessment revealed no abnormalities.

This brief description of Billy's assessment highlights the results often found in a child with Attention Deficit Disorder-Inattentive Type. All tests with a strong attention/concentration component reflect impairment, for both visual and auditory stimuli. Language testing reflects the presence of dyslexia, a learning disability marked by poor spelling and reading errors. The child's pattern of testing performance determines the specific type of learning disability that may be present (see Table 10.8).

The original definition of a learning disability required a significant discrepancy between a child's level of intelligence and achievement. A recent revision of federal law regarding education of students with disabilities now focuses more on a

TABLE 10.8 *Definitions of Three Specific Learning Disabilities*

Disability Term	Definition
Dyseidetic dyslexia	Inability to read words as a whole, so that the child must sound out the word. Reading errors occur on irregular words, such as "yacht." Spelling errors are phonetic, such as "sikollojee" for "psychology."
Dysphonetic dyslexia	Inability to sound out words, so reading is by whole words and dependent on sight vocabulary. Spelling errors are nonphonetic, such as "instuite" for "institute." Reading errors are substitutions of visually similar words, such as "scratch" for "stretch."
Dyscalculia	Mathematical abilities that are lower than expected for age, education, and intelligence. Deficits may include difficulties understanding math concepts, recognizing numerical symbols, appropriately carrying over numbers, and performing arithmetic operations.

student's failure to respond to traditional educational approaches (Individuals with Disabilities Education Improvement Act of 2004, 20 U.S.C.; IDEA 2004). See Chapter 16 for further discussion of IDEA 2004.

The child's pattern of testing performance determines the specific type of learning disability that may be present (see Table 10.8). Prevalence rates of learning disabilities are estimated at 2–10%, with 5% of public school children diagnosed with a learning disability (American Psychiatric Association, 2000).

Summary

1. The brain was not always thought to control behavior. Through contributions by Alcmaeon of Croton, Galen, Gall, Broca, and Wernicke, the critical role played by the brain was revealed.
2. The field of clinical neuropsychology developed during the twentieth century. The profession has blossomed over the past 50 years.
3. Reasons for a neuropsychological assessment include diagnosis, assessment of cognitive strengths and weaknesses, assistance in treatment or vocational planning, use in forensic settings, and research.
4. Neuropsychological assessment may be conducted with a fixed battery or a flexible battery approach. The Luria–Nebraska Neuropsychological Battery and the Halstead–Reitan Neuropsychological Battery are examples of fixed batteries. The flexible battery allows the clinician to choose tests he or she believes are best suited to assess the client.
5. Cognitive domains that may be tested during a neuropsychological evaluation include attention, achievement, effort/motivation, executive functions, intelligence,

language, memory, mental status, motor skills, personality/psychological state, and visuospatial/perceptual.

6. A patient's medical history, school records, psychiatric history, collateral information, psychosocial history, and behavioral observations are important in gaining a complete neuropsychological picture.

7. Pseudodementia may present in some ways as a true dementia but leads to a different pattern of results on neuropsychological testing.

8. Some patients may fake cognitive deficits, particularly for secondary gain. There are neuropsychological assessment approaches that may help detect malingering.

9. Three examples of common learning disabilities are: dyseidetic dyslexia, dysphonetic dyslexia, and dyscalculia.

Key Terms

aphasia
Broca, Paul
clinical neuropsychology
cognitive flexibility
constructional apraxia
dynamometer
dyscalculia
dyseidetic dyslexia
dysphonetic dyslexia
executive functions
Fake Bad Scale
fixed battery

flexible battery
Galen
Gall, Franz Josef
General Neuropsychological Deficit Score
Halstead-Reitan Neuropsychological Battery
Impairment Index
Luria-Nebraska Neuropsychological Battery

malingering
neuropsychology
perseverate
phrenology
premorbid
pseudodementia
spatial neglect
Stroop effect
Wernicke, Carl

Exercises

1. Read the original writings of *Paul Broca* at the Classics in the History of Psychology website developed by Christopher D. Green of York University, Toronto, Ontario, at http://psychclassics.yorku.ca/.

2. Explore the presence of clinical neuropsychology online. A good starting point is Neuropsychology Central at http://www.neuropsychologycentral.com/. Using a search engine, enter neuropsychology as a search term.

3. Learn more about that unfortunate railroad worker, *Phineas Gage.* Visit the Phineas Gage homepage at http://www.deakin.edu.au/hbs/GAGEPAGE/.

4. Use the following WAIS-III subtest scores to determine the patient's areas of strength and weakness. These are all age-corrected

scores. Calculate the average for the verbal subtests. Circle those subtests which are either 3 points higher or lower than the average. Repeat the process for the performance subtests.

Verbal Subtests	Performance Subtests
Information = 13	Picture Completion = 8
Digit Span = 7	Picture Arrangement = 11
Arithmetic = 8	Block Design = 13
Vocabulary = 14	Object Assembly = 11
Comprehension = 12	Digit Symbol = 7
Similarities = 12	
Average = _____	Average = _____

5. Try these measures of *mental control*. Count backward from 100 by 3s. Spell the word "chocolate" backward. Recite the months of the year backward, starting with December.

6. Test your *verbal fluency*. See how many words you can write down in 60 seconds that begin with the letter M. Now L. Now D. Try *category fluency* now. Write down types of vegetables. Now animals. Now colors. Which is easier, letters or categories? Why?

7. Access Buros' *Mental Measurements Yearbook* website at http://www.unl.edu/buros/. Enter as keywords each of the *cognitive domains* assessed by a flexible battery (see Table 10.4). Read more about the tests and determine if they would appropriately measure that cognitive ability.

8. Test your *memory*. Name the last five presidents of the United States in reverse order, starting with the current president. Name all 50 states. Without looking, draw a dollar bill.

9. Using the tests discussed for each cognitive domain (Table 10.4), predict how someone with *attention deficit disorder* would perform. On which tests would he do the worst? Which tests would be unaffected?

10. Create questions that would assess a person's *judgment* or *problem solving*, both types of *executive functions*. For example, "What would you do if the water was shut off to your house and you needed to brush your teeth?" See what solutions your friends can offer to these problems.

CHAPTER 11

Achievement Tests

Objectives

1. Use the ability–achievement continuum to distinguish between tests relying on more or less specific training.

2. Outline a typical school testing program.

3. Define the accountability and standards movements.

4. List the major categories of achievement tests.

5. For each of these categories, give one or two examples of actual tests.

6. List typical uses of tests in each category.

7. Identify common features of tests in each category.

Note: for objectives 4–7, it may be helpful to construct a matrix like this:

Category	Examples	Typical Uses	Common Features

Introduction

Achievement testing encompasses a vast and diverse array of tests. In terms of the sheer quantity of testing, achievement tests swamp all other types of tests combined. This is particularly true if we include the nearly infinite number of "teacher-made" tests and textbook-embedded assessments administered every day, at every level of education, in every corner of the globe. But the generalization holds true even if we exclude teacher-made tests and limit the count to more formal, standardized tests. To help organize this vast array of material, it will be useful to begin our coverage of achievement tests with an orientation and overview. First, we distinguish between ability and achievement tests. Then, we consider the role psychologists play in the world of achievement testing. Next, we provide a classification scheme for achievement tests. We use this scheme to organize the remainder of the chapter. Finally, to provide a proper context for some of the tests we consider, we describe a typical school testing program and the accountability movement in education.

The Ability-Achievement Continuum

A distinction is usually made between ability tests and achievement tests. We treated ability tests in previous chapters. Although the separation of ability tests and achievement tests into different chapters is customary and convenient, it is best to think of these tests as falling along a continuum rather than as rigidly distinct compartments. Such a continuum is depicted in Figure 11.1. The **ability–achievement continuum** represents the extent to which *specific training* influences test performance. At the extreme right of the continuum are tests that are highly dependent on specific training. For example, knowledge of Excel software, Civil War battles, accounting procedures, local zoning ordinances, or ability to ride a bicycle, hit a baseball, or sail a boat: All these are dependent on specific training. At the extreme left of the continuum are abilities thought to be highly generalized, for example, detecting number patterns, working anagrams, or simply knowing the meaning of many words. These latter abilities certainly develop as the result of some experiences, but not highly specific ones.

Note that some abilities fall in the middle of the continuum. Arithmetic problem solving is partly dependent on specific training with the number facts used in the

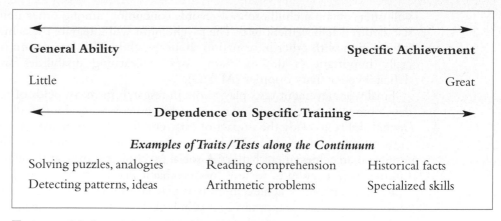

FIGURE 11.1 The ability-achievement continuum.

problem and partly dependent on the more general ability to analyze what must be done with the given numbers. Reading comprehension is partly dependent on word analysis skills and partly dependent on ability to decipher the most important ideas in a passage. It will be useful to keep this continuum in mind as we consider the broad range of achievement tests treated in this chapter.

The Psychologist's Interface with Achievement Tests

Mental ability tests, especially of the individually administered variety, and personality tests, both objective and projective, are the stock-in-trade of the psychologist. Achievement tests are traditionally identified more with the field of education than psychology. However, psychologists interface with the world of achievement testing in a number of important ways. Let us briefly review these before beginning formal treatment of this category of tests.

First, because of their special training in psychometrics, psychologists frequently play an important role in the development of achievement tests. Test development usually requires expertise in the content area covered by the tests as well as in the principles of test construction. Educators or other professionals usually provide the content expertise, psychologists the test construction expertise.

Second, several subfields of psychology have their principal applications in school settings. Most prominent among these subfields are school psychology and counseling. Persons in these professions will frequently work with achievement test results. This work will typically focus on individuals. However, because of their training in testing methodology and interpretation, school psychologists and counselors often serve on test committees that select achievement tests, make reports of school district results to school boards, and perform other such duties.

Third, many psychologists with no direct involvement in schools will frequently receive reports of achievement test results. For example, a child clinical psychologist will often obtain a child's school records containing, among other items, results of standardized achievement tests. The psychologist will integrate the achievement test information with other information about the child. This integration may be especially important in dealing with cases of learning disabilities and attention deficit/hyperactivity disorder (ADHD).

Finally, achievement tests play a role in research in many fields of psychology. A developmental psychologist may use achievement tests, along with measures of mental ability, to study the impact of early childhood experiences. A neuropsychologist may study the relationship between certain brain functions and the pattern of results on an achievement battery. A social psychologist may study achievement test summaries in relation to socioeconomic characteristics for entire nations.

In summary, while achievement tests play an important role in the field of education, they are also important in psychology. The psychologist needs to be familiar with the development of achievement tests, their typical structure, and the types of scores reported for them.

A Broad Classification of Achievement Tests

For purposes of this chapter, we classify achievement tests into six broad categories as shown in Table 11.1. This classification is one of practical convenience rather than theoretical elegance. In practice, the boundaries between these categories are permeable. The first category includes achievement batteries widely used in elementary and secondary school testing programs. The second category includes single-area achievement tests used primarily in secondary and postsecondary educational programs and in job-related contexts. The third category includes achievement tests custom-made for state, national, and international testing programs. The fourth category includes the numerous certification and licensing exams used by professional organizations. The fifth category includes individually administered achievement tests, ordinarily used in conjunction with mental ability tests, in diagnosing student problems; these are sometimes called psychoeducational batteries. For each of these types of tests, we identify examples, typical uses, and common characteristics.

We do *not* treat the large category of teacher-made tests, either those prepared by classroom teachers or those used for training programs in industry and the military. Were this a textbook aimed principally at educators, we would, at this point, spend a good bit of time exploring guidelines for the development and application of tests for classroom use, grading procedures, and related issues. However, we are quite deliberately not taking up these topics. For treatment of these topics, see such sources as Hogan (2007) and Linn and Miller (2005).

TABLE 11.1   *A Broad Classification of Achievement Tests*

Achievement Test Batteries	Single-Area Achievement Tests
Certification, licensing exams	State, national, international tests
Psychoeducational batteries	Teacher-made tests

TABLE 11.2 *A Typical School Testing Program*

Type of Test Grade:	K	1	2	3	4	5	6	7	8	9	10	11	12
Achievement Battery			x				x				x		
Group Ability Test		x			x					x			
State Testing Program				x	x	x	x	x	x			x	
Vocational Interest Inventory									x				
College Admissions Tests												x	x
Other Tests-Selected Cases	x	x	x	x	x	x	x	x	x	x	x	x	x

A Typical School Testing Program

Many of the tests introduced in this chapter appear in a school's testing program. To place the tests in their context, it will be helpful to outline a typical school testing program (see Table 11.2). A typical school administers an achievement battery, our first major category of achievement tests, in several grades, often in every other grade. In some of these grades, the school also utilizes a group–administered mental ability test, such as those described in Chapter 9. In addition, states require that public schools administer a state-sponsored test in several grades. This type of state testing has increased substantially under the No Child Left Behind Act adopted as federal law in 2002. The school testing program usually includes a vocational interest test in the junior high grades. We consider these tests in Chapter 14. Although not formally part of the school testing program, many students take college admissions tests in grades 11 and 12. Finally, subgroups of students take many additional tests administered, for example, by school psychologists or other specialists in connection with remedial programs, learning disability evaluations, selection for gifted programs, and so on.

The Accountability Movement and Standards-Based Education

Treatment of achievement tests would not be complete without some mention of the accountability movement and standards-based education. These movements have had profound influences on how achievement tests are developed, used, and interpreted. In educational circles, **accountability** refers to the fact that schools are responsible—accountable—for their product. The product is student learning. Student learning is often, though not exclusively, indicated by performance on achievement tests. Hence, these tests are an important element in any discussion of accountability. When a legislator or newspaper editor calls for increased accountability, what this often means operationally is giving more tests and more critical attention to test results.

The origin of the educational accountability movement in the United States can be traced roughly to the 1960s. Several events or trends formed the foundation for the movement. Let us identify three of these factors. First, as the decade of the 1950s came to a close, the United States was shocked by *Sputnik:* Russia's (then the Union of Soviet Socialist Republics: USSR) inaugural orbital space flight, catching the U.S. scientific community flatfooted and the U.S. public stunned. In the twinkling of an eye, the assumption that U.S. science, technology, and education were the best in the world was shattered. The ensuing calls for educational reform were deafening. In the two-superpower political climate of the day, it was literally a matter of life and death. A second factor was a dramatic increase in the funding of education. Dollars (adjusted for inflation) per student in the elementary and secondary schools approximately tripled from the early 1950s to the early 1970s; see National Center for Education Statistics (2001) for exact figures. People—taxpayers and legislators—wanted to know what they were getting for their money. Third, in 1964 the U.S. Congress passed the Elementary and Secondary Education Act **(ESEA)** providing federal funding on a greatly expanded scale for a wide variety of educational efforts. Many parts of this legislation stipulated that the educational initiatives needed to be evaluated. Educators initiating programs under ESEA had to be accountable for the success of the programs. The evaluation usually involved standardized tests. The *No Child Left Behind Act*, arguably the most important force in the public schools today, is technically a revision of ESEA. Another federal law, the *Individuals with Disabilities in Education Act of 2004* (see Chapter 16), also has substantial implications for the use of tests in educational settings.

The accountability movement, originating in the 1960s, has evolved into what is called **standards-based education.** This approach calls for clear identification of content for students to learn, specification of required levels of performance, and assurance that students have the opportunity to learn the material. All states now have some version of a standards-based approach to education. Achievement tests are used to determine whether the standards have been met. Cizek (2001b) provides an excellent summary of the development of the standards movement. Thurlow and Ysseldyke (2001) trace the legislative base for the movement.

In today's educational landscape, standardized achievement tests play a significant role. In some states, students need to attain a certain score on a state-prepared or commercially published test to receive a regular high school diploma or to be promoted to the next grade. In some colleges, students need to demonstrate proficiency on a collegewide test before proceeding to upper level courses. Entrance into certain professions depends on successful performance on tests even after completion of a prescribed educational program. These are all examples of **high-stakes tests:** ones in which the outcome has very substantial, immediate consequences for an individual. Test results for an entire school building or district may also have significant implications for school administrators. In this case, interestingly, the test may not be high-stakes for the people taking the test (the students), but it is high-stakes for someone else (the school principal or superintendent).

The accountability movement is a powerful force in modern American education. The public wants proof that students are learning. Achievement tests of one sort or another almost inevitably enter this picture. For a useful review of the place of testing in the accountability movement, see Linn (2000). We have traced here some of the immediate roots of the accountability movement, evolving into the current standards-based education. As with most such movements, one can find earlier precedents. For interesting examples of calls for accountability in earlier days, see Jaeger (1993). Although accountability and the standards-based approach to education are very influential today, they are not without their critics. One of the principal objections is that these forces have led to an unhealthy narrowing of the school curriculum. See Cizek (2001a) for a useful summary of this and other objections.

Achievement Batteries

We consider first the standardized achievement batteries used in elementary and secondary schools. The term **battery** in this context means a coordinated series of tests covering different content areas and multiple grade levels. For many of the types of tests included in this book, there are innumerable examples. However, this is not the case for the major standardized achievement batteries treated in this section. There are five major achievement test batteries in use in the United States. Table 11.3 lists these batteries, their publisher, and date of the most recent edition. We have not attempted to list achievement batteries used in other countries.

TRY IT! ....

Visit the website for one of the publishers listed in Table 11.3. What information is emphasized about the achievement battery listed?

....

Stanford Achievement Test

We illustrate the standardized achievement batteries with the *Stanford Achievement Test*, 10th Edition (SAT10). In general, the other batteries listed in Table 11.3 display

TABLE 11.3 *Major Achievement Batteries*

Battery	Publisher (web address)	Current Edition
California Achievement Tests[a]	California Test Bureau (ctb.com)	2000
Comprehensive Test of Basic Skills[a]	California Test Bureau (ctb.com)	1996
Iowa Tests of Basic Skills[b]	Riverside Publishing (riverpub.com)	2001
Metropolitan Achievement Tests	Harcourt Assessment (harcourtassessment.com)	2000
Stanford Achievement Test	Harcourt Assessment (harcourtassessment.com)	2003

[a] California Test Bureau refers to the *Comprehensive Test of Basic Skills* as TerraNova and to *California Achievement Tests* as TerraNova, Second Edition.

[b] Our reference to the *Iowa Tests of Basic Skills* (ITBS) is intended to include the *Iowa Tests of Educational Development* and the *Test of Academic Progress,* both of which are designed for use in grades 9–12 and are scaled to be continuous with the ITBS.

TABLE 11.4 *Stanford 10: Multiple-Choice Scope and Sequence*

Test Levels, Recommended Grade Ranges, Tests, and Administration Times

Test Levels	S1 K	S1 T	S2 K	S2 T	P1 K	P1 T	P2 K	P2 T	P3 K	P3 T	I1 K	I1 T	I2 K	I2 T	I3 K	I3 T	A1 K	A1 T	A2 K	A2 T	T1 K	T1 T	T2 K	T2 T	T3 K	T3 T
Grade Range	K.0–K.5		K.5–1.5		1.5–2.5		2.5–3.5		3.5–4.5		4.5–5.5		5.5–6.5		6.5–7.5		7.5–8.5		8.5–9.9		9.0–9.9		10.0–10.9		11.0–12.9	
Sounds and Letters	40	30	40	25																						
Word Study Skills					30	20	30	20	30	20	30	20														
Word Reading	30	15	30	25	30	25																				
Sentence Reading			30	30	30	30																				
Reading Vocabulary							30	20	30	20	30	20	30	20	30	20	30	20	30	20	30	20	30	20	30	20
Reading Comprehension					40	40	40	40	54	50	54	50	54	50	54	50	54	50	54	50	54	40	54	40	54	40
Total Reading	70	45	100	80	130	115	100	80	114	90	114	90	84	70	84	70	84	70	84	70	84	60	84	60	84	60
Mathematics	40	30	40	30																	50	50	50	50	50	50
Mathematics Problem Solving					42	50	44	50	46	50	48	50	48	50	48	50	48	50	48	50						
Mathematics Procedures					30	30	30	30	30	30	32	30	32	30	32	30	32	30	32	30						
Total Mathematics					72	80	74	80	76	80	80	80	80	80	80	80	80	80	80	80						
Language					40	40	48	45	48	45	48	45	48	45	48	45	48	45	48	45	48	40	48	40	48	40
Spelling					36	30	36	30	38	35	40	35	40	35	40	35	40	35	40	35	40	30	40	30	40	30
Listening to Words and Stories	40	30	40	30																						
Listening					40	30	40	30	40	30	40	30	40	30	40	30	40	30	40	30						
Environment	40	30	40	30	40	30	40	30																		
Science									40	25	40	25	40	25	40	25	40	25	40	25	40	25	40	25	40	25
Social Science									40	25	40	25	40	25	40	25	40	25	40	25	40	25	40	25	40	25
Basic Battery	150	105	180	140	318	295	298	265	316	280	322	280	292	260	292	260	292	260	292	260	222	180	222	180	222	180
Complete Battery	190	135	220	170	358	325	338	295	396	330	402	330	372	310	372	310	372	310	372	310	302	230	302	230	302	230
Total Testing Time	2 hrs.	15 min.	2 hrs.	50 min.	5 hrs.	25 min.	4 hrs.	55 min.	5 hrs.	30 min.	5 hrs.	30 min.	5 hrs.	10 min.	5 hrs.	10 min.	5 hrs.	10 min.	5 hrs.	10 min.	3 hrs.	50 min.	3 hrs.	50 min.	3hrs.	50 min.
Language Form D					40	40	40	40	45	45	48	45	48	45	48	45	48	45	48	45	48	40	48	40	48	40

K = No. of Items

T = Time in Minutes

(Normed under untimed conditions; times given are for planning purposes only.)

the major features of SAT10 as described later. As is true for all these batteries, SAT10 is actually a vast system of measures rather than a single test, as will become obvious in our presentation. It is also the case that new editions of these batteries tend to appear about every five or six years. SAT10 encompasses two levels of the *Stanford Early School Achievement Test* (SESAT 1 and 2), the main Stanford series, and three levels of the *Test of Academic Skills* (TASK 1, 2, and 3). The tests and levels included within this system are outlined in Table 11.4.

Review of Table 11.4 reveals several features of SAT10 that are typical for the major standardized achievement batteries. Note first that there are different levels of the test designed for different grades. For example, Level P2 (Primary 2) is designed for use in grades 2.5–3.5, that is, from the middle of grade 2 to the middle of grade 3. This use of multiple levels was also true for some of the group-administered mental ability tests considered in Chapter 9. Each level contains a host of specific tests. It is this feature that gives rise to the term *battery*. The specific subtests come and go at different levels (moving from left to right across the table). For example, Sounds and Letters appears at the two lowest levels, but not thereafter. Separate tests in Science and Social Studies do not appear until the Primary 3 level. Despite this come-and-go phenomenon, there is a large degree of continuity flowing through the series. For example, some measures of reading and mathematics occur at all levels. All levels also have Basic Battery and Complete Battery scores. A typical subtest contains about 40 items and requires about 25 minutes administration time. Subtests are aggregated into area totals (e.g., reading or mathematics) that typically have 75 to 100 items. Notice that the ratio of number of items to number of minutes of administration time tends to be in the range of 2:1 to 1:1.

Although not noted in Table 11.4, SAT10 has a Complete Battery and an Abbreviated Battery. The Abbreviated Battery has fewer subtests and these subtests are generally shorter than those in the Complete Battery. There is also a writing test, calling for composing a story or essay and scored by the holistic or analytic method.

SAT10 offers almost every type of derived score we covered in Chapter 3. It includes percentile ranks, stanines, scaled scores, grade equivalents, and normal curve equivalents. Percentile ranks and stanines are offered for both individual scores and group averages. There are also ability/achievement comparisons, performance categories (below average, average, above average) on clusters of related items, and p-values for individual items. Finally, there are "performance standards," criterion-referenced judgments about the adequacy of test performance. Reporting categories are Advanced, Proficient, Basic, and Below Basic.

SAT10 includes a wealth of computer-generated scoring reports. Figure 11.2 shows one of the standard, popular reports for an individual student. Notice that the report provides several types of normed scores, presents graphs that incorporate the notion of a percentile band (see p. 141), and includes results from a group-administered ability test (*Otis-Lennon School Ability Test*), along with an ability-achievement comparison.

SAT10 research programs included approximately 170,000 students in the item tryout program; 250,000 students from 650 school districts in the spring standardization program; 110,000 students in the fall standardization program; and 85,000 students in different equating programs. Extraordinary effort was expended to ensure representativeness of these samples in terms of racial/ethnic distribution,

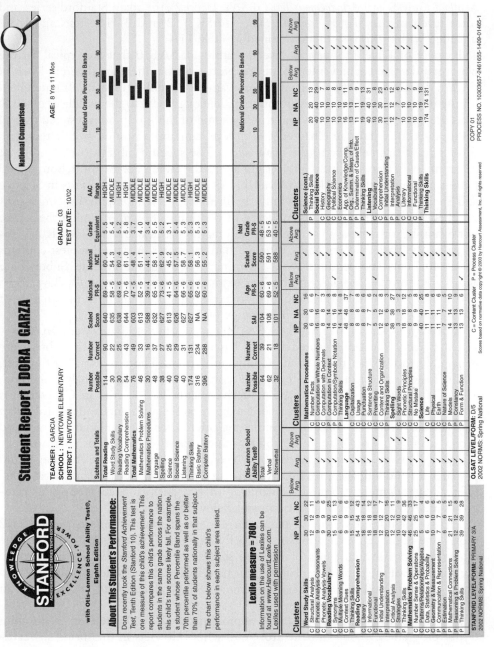

FIGURE 11.2   Sample score report for SAT10.

Source: Stanford Achievement Test, Tenth Edition, sample student report. Copyright © 2003 by Harcourt Assessment, Inc. Reproduced by permission. All rights reserved.

TABLE 11.5   *Reliability Data for SAT10 Tests in Primary 3 (P3) Battery*

Test	No.Items	KR-20	Alt.Form
Total Reading	114	.96	.90
Word Study Skills	30	.85	.82
Reading Vocabulary	30	.87	.82
Reading Comprehension	54	.93	.83
Total Mathematics	76	.94	.90
Mathematics: Problem Solving	46	.91	.85
Mathematics: Procedures	30	.90	.83
Language	48	.91	.86
Spelling	38	.88	.80
Science	40	.86	.80
Social Science	40	.89	.79
Listening	40	.84	.75

Source: Adapted from *Stanford Achievement Test (10th ed.), Spring Technical Data Report,* Tables C-4 and E-3.

socioeconomic status, geographic region, and type of school control (public/non-public). The Technical Manual carefully describes the nature of these research programs and characteristics of participants.

Table 11.5 presents reliability data for major scores for one of the SAT10 batteries. Both internal consistency (KR-20, for Form S) and alternate form (Forms S and T) reliabilities are given. As typically happens with these types of tests, alternate form reliability averages about .05–.08 less than internal consistency reliability. The data illustrate the usual relationship between number of test items and level of reliability. When the number of items is above 60, internal consistency reliability tends to be around .95. When the number of items is in the 30–40 range, internal consistency reliability tends to be in the .85–.90 range. When the number of items drops to under 10, as is the case for cluster scores given in some reports, reliabilities are generally very low. As noted in Chapter 4, beware of short tests.

Typical Uses and Special Features

Achievement batteries are used for a great variety of purposes. Sometimes the diversity of purposes becomes problematic, as these different purposes are not always entirely compatible. The original intent for these tests was to monitor the progress of individual students in the major areas of the school curriculum, with the teacher being the primary recipient of the test information. This is still a major purpose and probably the single most common application of these tests. However, other uses have also become widespread. School buildings and school districts, for example, now use summaries of test scores for groups of students to evaluate the curriculum. In some instances, these summaries are also employed to evaluate the effectiveness of school personnel: teachers, principals, and superintendents. Such usage, of course, is very different from the originally intended purpose.

Scores from achievement batteries are now routinely reported to parents. Furthermore, group summaries are reported to school boards and local communities as measures of school effectiveness. Finally, achievement batteries (or parts of them) are employed in many research projects as dependent variables. For example, the Stanford reading and mathematics test results for the primary grades might be used as measures of the effect of participation in a day care program. These diverse uses put extraordinary strain on the developmental requirements and interpretive materials for these tests.

Materials from the publishers of the achievement batteries understandably emphasize their unique characteristics. However, even casual observation reveals that the similarities among these batteries far outnumber the dissimilarities. Let us identify some of these common features.

First, although one of these batteries may be referred to as "a" test, for example, the Stanford test or the Iowa test, each is actually *a system of many interrelated tests.* There are a dozen or more separate tests at each level, multiple levels, and multiple forms. Increasingly, there are long versions and short versions, multiple-choice and open-ended versions, and editions in different languages or other such variations. Furthermore, there may be item banks, customized versions, and secure editions for the series. The modern versions of these batteries actually consist of well over a hundred identifiably separate tests. However, all these tests are related to one another, not just in name but also in terms of developmental procedures, normative structures, and interpretive systems.

Second, quite apart from the number of identifiably separate tests, the array of *supplementary materials* and scoring reports for these batteries is staggering. There may be separate interpretive booklets for students, parents, teachers, and school administrators. There are numerous options for computer-generated scoring reports. There are practice tests, locator tests, detailed lists of objectives, and a host of other ancillary materials.

Third, the *norming procedures and other research programs* for these achievement batteries are, in general, exemplary. They employ the latest, most sophisticated methodologies. Samples are ordinarily well in excess of what is required for statistical stability. Extraordinary measures are taken to ensure representativeness by gender, race, ethnic group, geographic region, socioeconomic status, and other demographic characteristics. The technical manuals for these batteries are exhaustive.

Fourth, these achievement batteries have long been criticized for their exclusive reliance on multiple-choice methodology. This is no longer true. All the major achievement batteries now employ *methods of assessment in addition to multiple-choice items.* For example, all now have some form of free-writing exercise for the evaluation of the quality of writing. Some of the major batteries offer extensive arrays of open-ended and performance measures. There is still some question about the extent to which these forms of assessment will be used since they are considerably more expensive than multiple-choice tests, especially with respect to scoring costs. There are also significant other questions about some of these alternative methods.

Fifth, all the achievement batteries depend heavily on the *same sources of information for their content.* Included within these sources are (a) statements of curricular goals from professional organizations such as the National Council of Teachers of Mathematics (NCTM), the National Council of Teachers of English (NCTE), and similar organizations; (b) major textbook series; (c) outlines prepared by organizations such as the National Assessment of Educational Progress (see later in this chapter); and (d) content standards from state departments of education, the more populous states being particularly influential in this regard. In establishing the content for these tests, for good or ill, you will not find "mavericks" striking out in new directions.

Achievement Batteries at the College Level

There are now a number of batteries designed for use at the college level. These batteries concentrate on general education outcomes of a college degree program, including such areas as development of writing skill, computer and information literacy, and acquiring at least some exposure to the humanities, natural sciences, and social sciences. This is in contrast to the major field of study (e.g., biology, psychology, nursing, or accounting) that might be addressed by some of the tests we cover later under single-area achievement tests or licensing and certifying exams.

Table 11.6 lists the main examples of college-level achievement batteries. These batteries are widely discussed but not widely used at the college level. However, their use has increased in recent years as the accountability movement has extended its reach to the college level. Interestingly, the essay test in MAAP is scored strictly by computer (see the description of automated scoring in Chapter 6).

TABLE 11.6   *Examples of College-Level Achievement Batteries*

Title	Publisher
Collegiate Assessment of Academic Proficiency (CAAP)	ACT, Inc.
Measure of Academic Proficiency and Progress (MAAP)[a]	ETS

[a] MAAP replaces the *Academic Profile* (AP) as of 2006.

Single-Area Achievement Tests

There are a wide variety of achievement tests that cover a single content domain. These tests are generally designed for use in high school or college, often at the end of a course or an entire program of study, for example, a college major or vocational/technical training program. Such tests are also available as occupational competency tests. In the classification scheme we have adopted in this chapter, we exclude from this category the *parts* of achievement batteries (e.g., the mathematics test from *Stanford Achievement Test*) that could be used as a stand-alone test. We also exclude occupation-related tests that lead to certification or licensing. Obviously, both exclusions could fit in the category of single-area achievement tests, but we treat these tests elsewhere in the chapter.

TRY IT! ....

To illustrate the vast number of tests in the category of single-area achievement tests, go to the website for the ETS Test Collection (http://sydneyplus.ets.org). Enter the name of a subject field such as biology, psychology, Spanish, or mathematics. Scan the list of results. Note that, in addition to achievement tests related to the area, you will probably find measures of attitude toward the area.

....

Examples

Let us consider several examples to illustrate this huge category of tests. The first example is the *Major Field Test in Psychology* (MFT-P, Form 3WMF). This is one of a series of tests designed to measure student learning in the major field of study in college. Other Major Field Tests are available in such areas as chemistry, economics, and history. According to the test manual (Educational Testing Service, 2005b, p. 1), "The content specifications for the Major Field Tests reflect the basic knowledge and understanding gained in the undergraduate curriculum. They have been designed to assess the mastery of concepts, principles, and knowledge expected of students at the conclusion of a major in specific subject areas." The tests were originally designed to be shorter and less difficult versions of the corresponding Graduate Record Examinations (GRE) Subject tests. The tests can be taken online or in paper-and-pencil format; the online version is not a computer-adaptive test but simply presents the test electronically.

The MFT-P consists of 140 multiple-choice items administered in two sittings. For each examinee, the test yields a total score and four subscores, as listed in Table 11.7. The table also gives the percentage of items in the subtests and reliability data. In addition, "assessment indicators" in six areas are provided for groups of examinees. These are based on relatively small clusters of items that clearly would not yield reliable scores for individuals.

TABLE 11.7   *Outline of Scores for the Major Field Test in Psychology II*

Individual Scores	Items	Reliability[a]
1. Learning and cognition	31	.74
2. Perception, sensory, physiology, comparative, ethology	29	.66
3. Clinical, abnormal, personality	24	.69
4. Developmental and social	31	.74
Total	140[b]	.92

[a] KR–20 reliability data based on seniors, Table 18, ETS (2005b).

[b] The numbers of items for the subscores do not sum to 140 since there are some items that do not enter into any of the four subscores, although they do enter the total score.

The manual provides percentile norms based on individuals and on institutional averages. (For the distinction between these two types of percentiles, see p. 100.) Norms are derived from whatever schools have used the test in the most recent three-year period. The manual emphasizes that these are user-norms rather than nationally representative norms. The 2000 norms are based on 8,200 seniors and 210 institutions.

Tests developed by the *National Occupational Competency Testing Institute* **(NOCTI)** provide a plethora of additional examples of single-area achievement tests. NOCTI has over 150 tests of occupational competency for entry level and experienced workers in such fields as die making, appliance repair, cosmetology, and computer programming. A typical NOCTI test has about 180 multiple-choice items and a three-hour administration time. Some of the tests also have a performance component. Each test is based on a detailed content outline of the skills and knowledge considered important for the occupation. Each test has "user-norms" based on all examinees who took the test in the recent past. For some NOCTI tests this number is only a few hundred cases, for other tests several thousand cases.

TRY IT!

Check NOCTI's website (NOCTI.ORG) to see the array of tests. Notice the content specifications listed for each test. These specifications relate to content validity.

A final example of a single-area achievement test is the STAR Math test. This is a **computer-adaptive test** for use in grades 1–12. The item pool consists of approximately 2,400 multiple-choice items ranging from simple addition problems to high school algebra and geometry problems. An individual student completes only 24 items, with items selected by a computerized branching routine. The initial item is selected according to the student's grade. Thereafter, a correct answer branches to a more difficult item, while an incorrect answer branches to an easier item. In the end, it is expected that the student's placement will be accurately determined. National normative data for STAR Math yield grade equivalents, NCEs, and percentile ranks. A computer-generated narrative report provides a criterion-referenced instructional placement recommendation. The single score on the test has within-grade alternate form reliabilities ranging from .72 to .80 with a median of .74 and split-half reliabilities ranging from .78 to .88 with a median of .85 (Renaissance Learning, 2003). An increasing number of computer-adaptive tests like the STAR Math are becoming available for use in schools.

TRY IT!

To see examples of test items and score reports for STAR Math, visit this website: RENLEARN.COM/STARMATH

Typical Uses and Special Features

Single-area achievement tests have two typical uses. First, they are used to determine an individual's performance in a highly focused area such as a body of knowledge or skill. Second, they may be used to evaluate the adequacy of an instructional program. In this second use, it is assumed not only that the test is content valid, but also that individuals are making a reasonable effort to acquire the knowledge or skill tested.

What generalizations can we develop about single-area achievement tests? There is such a vast array of these tests that developing generalizations is somewhat hazardous. However, at least if we limit our purview to typical examples offered by major publishers, we can discern some common characteristics.

Nearly all tests in this category are group-administered, paper-and-pencil, multiple-choice tests.[1] Some occupationally related tests also have a performance component. Test length tends to be in the range of about 50 to 200 items, with many of the tests having over 100 items. Computer-adaptive tests have large item pools, but examinees actually complete only a relatively small number of items. Most of the tests in this category emphasize use of a single, total score, while still giving a few subscores. The total scores tend to be highly reliable—usually .90 or higher. This is not surprising. People's level of knowledge of a well-defined body of information, concepts, and skills is a pretty stable phenomenon when measured with a large sample of items. Reliability of subscores on these tests is almost entirely a function of the number of items in the subtest. Of course, the test manual should report reliability data for subscores as well as the total score. As a general rule, one should be wary of the reliability of any score based on fewer than about 20 items.

To indicate validity, tests in this category depend almost exclusively on content validity. Test content is matched with a course of study, whether an individual course or an entire program, or with a systematic job description. There are occasional attempts to gather other types of validity evidence for these tests, but content validity predominates. Because the contents of programs of study or job specifications change, these tests tend to be updated on a regular basis. It is unusual to find one of these tests in practical use that is more than 10 years old.

Licensing and Certification Tests

We consider here tests used for purposes of licensing and certification. There are numerous tests in this category. We have sometimes been described as a "credentialed society." Tests play a prominent, though certainly not exclusive, role in this process. Educational requirements also play an important role. Sometimes completion of the educational requirements is sufficient. However, it is often the case that a person must pass some type of examination before obtaining a license or certification. Preparation, administration, and interpretation of scores on these examinations generally follow the principles outlined in earlier sections of this book. We group

---

[1] Clear exceptions to this pattern are individually administered reading tests, used primarily to aid in diagnosing reading problems at the elementary school level.

licensing and certification exams together here because they tend to be very similar in purpose, structure, development, and usage. However, there is a technical distinction between licensing and certification. See Schmitt (1995) for an excellent description of the distinction and a general orientation to licensure testing. **Licensing** involves a legal grant by a government agency to practice. Most licensing is controlled by states, although a few licenses are granted by the federal government. The principal concern in licensing is determination that the minimal level of knowledge and/or skill is present to protect the public. **Certification** involves a statement that a level of proficiency has been attained, but it does not necessarily imply a right to do anything. Certification may aim at minimal level or a higher level of knowledge/skill, depending on the particular purpose.

Examples

The examination taken to become licensed as a physical therapist provides an example. The National Physical Therapy Examination is controlled by the Federation of State Boards of Physical Therapy (cf. fsbpt.org). Actual administration is handled through the national network of Thomson Prometric testing centers (see www.prometric.com).

The exam consists of 250 multiple-choice items administered in a four-hour period. Administration is by computer, although not in a computer-adaptive mode. That is, the computer presents all 250 items in succession to the examinee rather than selecting items based on the examinee's responses to previous items. Test content follows a **test blueprint** or content outline that is readily available to candidates for the test (see the fsbpt.org web site for the content outline). Raw scores on the test are converted to standard scores. The Federation of State Boards of Physical Therapy has established a single standard score as a passing score adopted by all states. This physical therapy exam is fairly typical of licensing and certification tests.

A second example is the examination for a Private Pilot Certificate. This exam is administered by the Federal Aviation Administration (FAA), which is responsible for licensing all U.S. pilots. The exam consists of three parts: a written exam containing 60 multiple-choice questions, an oral exam, and a flight exam. The examinee must also have a total of 40 hours of flight instruction and solo flight time. A person must pass all parts of the exam to receive pilot certification. We might note that some of the NOCTI exams mentioned above are also used by professional organizations for certification purposes.

Typical Uses and Special Features

Little needs to be said to describe typical uses of licensing and certifying tests. They are used to document, in a very official manner, the competency of examinees in relevant skills and knowledge. However, there is a secondary use when examinees are products of a clearly identifiable educational program. In such cases, the administrators of the program use results of the test as a measure of the program's adequacy. We should note that various types of professional associations generally govern the use of tests in this category, but these associations often contract with professional testing organizations for preparation of the tests.

The distinctive features of licensing and certifying tests arise from the crucial consequences they have for examinees. First, in order to yield reliable scores, these tests tend to be quite lengthy. Tests having several hundred items and requiring several hours for administration are common. As a result, total scores on these tests tend to be highly reliable, usually in the neighborhood of .95. Second, the tests usually have very clear, explicit content outlines. Examinees usually have access to these outlines well in advance of the test. Third, extraordinary security surrounds these tests. They may be administered only once or a few times each year at carefully controlled testing sites. Furthermore, to protect the security of test content, test items are changed frequently. For some types of testing, it may be a virtue to use exactly the same test items repeatedly. It would be very imprudent to use exactly the same items repeatedly for a certification exam. Fourth, both test developers and test-takers, understandably, have a preoccupation with cutoff scores and how these are derived. Most frequently, a large element of judgment is involved in setting the cutoff scores, although the judgments are informed by examinees' actual performance.

A Primer on Establishing Cutoff Scores

We noted above the crucial role that cutoff scores play for certification and licensing exams. The topic is also important for competency tests that occur in state testing programs. In these cases, a student must obtain a certain score to satisfy a requirement for graduation or promotion. We alluded to such use in our description of a typical school testing program as well as under state testing programs. In addition, many tests offer some criterion-referenced interpretation translating test performance into categories such as basic, proficient, and advanced, or some similar scheme. In all these cases, there is the question of how one determines the **cutoff score:** the point that separates passing from failing, competent from incompetent, or one level of proficiency from other levels. Much attention has been devoted to this question in the psychometric literature. *Standard setting* is the official tag usually applied to the topic, although it also goes under the term cutoff scores or cut-scores. For detailed treatment of this topic, see Cizek (2001b), Impara (1995), and the series of articles edited by Impara and Plake (1995) in the Special Issue on Standard Setting for Complex Performance Tasks in the journal *Applied Measurement in Education.*

Approaches to the problem of establishing cutoff scores fall into two major categories: norm-referenced and criterion-referenced. In the first approach, the cutoff score is established by reference to some point in a set of norms. For example, "competent" may be defined as being in the top 25%, that is, at or above the 75th percentile on the test's norms; or as performing at a grade equivalent of at least 8.0. Such an approach is common for employment testing. For example, the top ten candidates are invited for interviews. This approach has an appealing simplicity. Furthermore, the fact that it is based on actual test performance has merit. In some highly competitive situations, this may be the only viable approach.

On the other hand, a strictly norm-referenced approach clearly has shortcomings in some contexts. Consider the case of a minimum competency test. It may be that everyone has reached the required level of competency. There is no reason why anyone should be failed, even the bottom 10% of examinees. Or it could be that no one has reached the required level of competency. These are criterion-referenced judgments. We would like to have a set of procedures for examining the test content and deciding how well an examinee needs to perform to be declared competent, passing, or acceptable. Numerous methods have been proposed to help formulate such judgments. Zieky (2001), Hambelton (2001), Cizek (2001b), and Cizek, Bunch, and Koons (2004) provide useful summaries of the methods. See Chinn and Hertz (2002) for an example of practical application to certification of marriage and family therapists. Recent years have witnessed a proliferation of methods for establishing cutoff scores, especially in connection with the national and state testing programs described in the next section. Much research is currently directed at the consequences of applying these various methods. Probably the most popular method is Angoff's method or modifications of it. Essentially, the procedure involves imagining a "minimally competent person," making a judgment *for each test item* about the probability that this person will get the item right, then summing these probabilities across all items. The sum will be the cutoff score, that is, the score obtained by the minimally competent person. The procedure can also be used by imagining other persons, for example, a "highly competent" person.

In practice, the two approaches usually work in some combination. In the empirical, norm-referenced approach, some person or group must make a judgment that the 75th percentile, rather than the 60th or 90th percentile, is appropriate. Thus, although the cutoff score is empirically defined, a judgment determines exactly what point is selected. In the judgmental, criterion-referenced approach, before a final judgment is made, it is nearly always the case that the judges observe the empirical results of testing. Often, original judgments are modified in the light of these empirical results.

State, National, and International Achievement Tests

We include in this category those achievement tests that are under the control of or sponsored by a governmental or quasigovernmental body. While this is a convenient classification from some viewpoints, the organization is not entirely satisfactory, as will become apparent as our description unfolds.

State Testing Programs

Although some states have had statewide testing program for many years, the recent No Child Left Behind **(NCLB)** Act dictated that all states have such programs (if they wished to receive certain critical federal funds). The tests differ in each state. However, they have some common features. For example, all cover language arts and mathematics in each of grades 3–8 and at least one grade in the 9–12 range.

Testing of science begins in selected grades in 2007. NCLB dictates the use of criterion-referenced cutoff scores to define "proficiency." And the law dictates use of certain reporting categories. The exact content of the tests differs for each state. Each state defines its own content and exactly how it will test achievement in that content. Each state also defines its own proficiency levels. These state tests have exceptional influence on the conduct of education at the elementary and secondary levels in the United States.

However, because each state determines content and method of testing, it is difficult to summarize this category of tests. In addition, states are continually varying their approaches, and some aspects of the NCLB, which is at the root of these programs, are also fluid. Perhaps it is most useful to point to sources of information about the current status of these state programs. There are several very useful sources for this purpose. The Council of Chief State School Officers (CCSSO; see www.ccsso.org) regularly summarizes the current status of state testing programs. A project known as Align to Achieve (www.aligntoachieve.org) and the Midcontinent Research for Education and Learning (McRel; www.mcrel.org) provide convenient access to the various state websites that describe state testing programs.

A National Testing Program: NAEP

Many tests, such as the SAT, ACT, OLSAT, WAIS, and the Stanford series, may legitimately be called "national" tests. But there is one testing enterprise that merits this appellation in a special way. This is the *National Assessment of Educational Progress* (**NAEP**), which is not a single test but a federally funded testing project. NAEP was formulated in the 1960s specifically to provide a set of benchmarks regarding the educational attainments of Americans. In its earliest years, it included both students in school and out-of-school adult samples. In more recent years, it has been confined entirely to in-school samples, specifically in grades 4, 8, and 12. Each testing phase concentrates on just one or two curricular areas such as reading, mathematics, writing, or geography. For example, NAEP covered civics in 2006 and will do so again in 2010 and 2014. Currently, NAEP covers reading and mathematics each odd-numbered year. Special efforts are made to secure representative samples of students for nationwide and, in some instances, state-level reporting. Reports also give results by gender and ethnic groups. NAEP does not report scores for individual students. It includes both multiple-choice (selected-response) and open-ended (constructed-response) test items. Some of its open-ended items have become models for other testing efforts that refer to the use of "NAEP-like" items. NAEP reports sometimes refer to themselves, perhaps somewhat pretentiously, as the "nation's report card," a term incorporated into its website within the National Center for Education Statistics site: (nces.ed.gov/nationsreportcard). More recently, the National Assessment of Adult Literacy (NAAL) has supplemented the NAEP results (which are limited to in-school students) with measures of English language literacy and health literacy among adults.

TRY IT! ....

Access the NAEP website (nces.ed.gov/nationsreportcard). Then access sample items for one of the curricular areas assessed. What kind of items do you find? Also, note the methods used for reporting results for national samples and for subgroups.

....

International Testing Programs: TIMSS and PISA

From rather obscure beginnings in 1964, the project currently known as Trends in International Science and Mathematics **(TIMSS)** began testing students in 30 to 40 countries, mostly in the more developed economies. The testing was concentrated on science and mathematics and on students in grades 4 and 8 (or comparable levels). With increased calls in the United States to be "first in the world" or to "meet world-class standards," TIMSS results, at first largely ignored in the United States, have garnered considerable public attention. Like NAEP, TIMSS does not report results for individual students; rather, it yields group summaries, in this case average scores for entire countries. More recently, the Program for International Student Assessment (PISA) has targeted 15-year-olds in numerous countries in reading, mathematics, and science.

Each of the national and international testing programs identified here has an excellent website that provides detailed reports of results, illustrative items, descriptions of sampling plans, and so on. In addition, the National Center for Education Statistics reports many of the key results from these projects in an annual publication called *The Condition of Education*, which is also web accessible. All of the relevant websites are listed in Key Points Summary 11.1.

Key Points Summary 11.1

Major National and International Assessment Programs

- NAEP   www.nces.ed/gov/nationsreportcard
- TIMSS   www.nces.ed.gov/timss or www.timss.org
- PISA   www.nces.ed.gov/surveys/pisa
- NAAL   www.nces.ed.gov/naal
- Condition of Education   www.nces.ed.gov/programs/coe

Special Features

The state testing programs are too diverse to warrant any generalizations about their common features. However, the national and international testing efforts do share some distinctive characteristics. First, the emphasis for these programs is on group performance. Second, each wave of testing typically addresses a single area, for example, reading or mathematics. Even when two areas are covered within a single year, they are treated as largely independent projects. In contrast, an achievement battery yields scores in a dozen different areas for each student. Third, the national and international testing programs concentrate on a small number of grade or age cohorts. Finally, these programs attempt to collect extensive information about educational practices (e.g., amount of homework, instructional time, etc.) that might help to interpret test results.

Individually Administered Achievement Tests

All the achievement tests introduced thus far in this chapter are group administered. However, there are some achievement tests deliberately designed for individual administration in much the same manner as the individually administered ability tests covered in Chapter 8.

Examples

We illustrate individually administered achievement tests with two examples. First, there is the *Wechsler Individual Achievement Test,* 2nd Edition (WIAT-II). It includes subtests for Oral Language, Listening Comprehension, Written Expression, Spelling, Word Reading, Pseudoword Decoding, Reading Comprehension, Numerical Operations, and Mathematics Reasoning. In addition, for a brief assessment, three subtests may be used to yield a Screener Composite score. The first edition was designed for use with children in the age range 5–19 years, but the second edition has expanded age coverage to include ages 4 through adults, including norms for college students. A principal goal of the WIAT is to investigate ability-achievement discrepancies. For this purpose, the WIAT is linked to all three of the Wechsler intelligence scales (WPPSI, WISC, and WAIS).

Administration of the WIAT is similar to that for the WISC. The examiner is seated across from the examinee, with stimulus booklet laid out on a table. The examiner establishes rapport and proceeds through the administration in what seems like a conversational tone, but is actually a well-practiced presentation of the standardized directions. The examiner must be thoroughly trained in the use of the WIAT to ensure valid administration. As with WISC there are starting points, discontinue rules, and scoring rubrics to be applied as the test proceeds. Typical administration time is about 50 minutes; as usual, administration time is usually less for younger examinees, more for older examinees.

Norms for the WIAT are based on carefully selected samples spread across the test's target age range. Raw scores on the WIAT can be translated into standard scores ($M = 100$, $SD = 15$), age or grade equivalents, percentile ranks, stanines, and NCEs. Most important, the WIAT norms are cross-referenced to norms on the various Wechsler intelligence scales (see Chapter 8, pp. 296–309). This cross-referencing provides the basis for examining ability-achievement discrepancies. The manual provides a balanced discussion of the problems involved in examining these discrepancies. The manual also provides tables giving the magnitude of differences between various pairs of scores required to reach certain significance levels. (Recall the concept of the standard error of differences from Chapter 4.) For useful reviews of the first edition of the WIAT, see Ackerman (1998) and Ferrara (1998).

A second example of tests in this category is the third edition of the *Woodcock-Johnson* (WJ III; Woodcock, McGrew & Mather, 2001). In its previous editions, the test was known as the *Woodcock-Johnson Psychoeducational Battery*. The WJ III is actually a system of two tests: the *Woodcock-Johnson Tests of Cognitive Ability* (WJ III Cog) and the *Woodcock-Johnson Tests of Achievement* (WJ III Ach). Figure 11.3 outlines the tests in WJ III Ach. The cognitive battery, based on Cattell's theory of **fluid** and **crystallized intelligence** (see pp. 265–266 for a review of this theory),[2] has 10 tests in a Standard battery and an additional 10 tests in an Extended battery. The achievement battery has 12 tests in the Standard battery and allows for up to 10 additional tests in the Extended battery. In all the WJ III system has 42 tests and numerous composites derived from combinations of these tests, making for a dizzying array of information. Test interpretation, as with the WIAT, depends heavily on contrasting performance levels among this multiplicity of tests. The WJ III is normed for ages 2–90 on samples considered representative of the national population for those ages. For reviews of the previous edition (WJ-R), see Cummings (1995), Lee and Stefany (1995), and Webster (1994).

Typical Uses and Special Features

In typical applications of these individually administered achievement tests, there is an interest in diagnosing discrepancies among various achievement levels or between achievement and mental ability. Hence, these tests usually entail joint administration with some measure of mental ability. Determination of specific learning disabilities is a frequent objective of such analyses. Because of the special emphases of tests in this category, these tests are sometimes referred to as **psychoeducational batteries.** Many of the applications of these individually administered achievement tests are tied closely to federal and state laws regarding identification and treatment of various disabilities. We examine these laws in Chapter 16.

Obviously, the most distinctive feature of tests in this category is the fact that they are individually administered. Perhaps more important, their purpose is somewhat different than that of the typical group-administered achievement test in at least three ways. First, while group summaries are important for nearly all the group-administered tests, group summaries are largely irrelevant for the individually

---

[2] WJ III materials refer to the theory as the Cattell-Horn-Carroll or CHC theory.

CURRICULAR AREA	STANDARD BATTERY— FORM A OR B	EXTENDED BATTERY— FORM A OR B
Reading		
Basic Reading Skills	Test 1: Letter-Word Identification	Test 13: Word Attack
Reading Fluency	Test 2: Reading Fluency 📖 🕐	
Reading Comprehension	Test 9: Passage Comprehension	Test 17: Reading Vocabulary
Oral Language		
Oral Expression	Test 3: Story Recall 🎧	Test 14: Picture Vocabulary
Listening Comprehension	Test 4: Understanding Directions 🎧	Test 15: Oral Comprehension 🎧
Mathematics		
Math Calculation Skills*	Test 5: Calculation 📖	
Math Fluency	Test 6: Math Fluency 📖 🕐	
Math Reasoning	Test 10: Applied Problems	Test 18: Quantitative Concepts
Written Language		
Basic Writing Skills	Test 7: Spelling 📖	Test 16: Editing
Writing Fluency	Test 8: Writing Fluency 📖 🕐	
Written Expression**	Test 11: Writing Samples 📖	
Academic Knowledge		
		Test 19: Academic Knowledge
Supplemental		
	Test 12: Story Recall—Delayed	Test 20: Spelling of Sounds 📖 🎧
	Handwriting Legibility Scale	Test 21: Sound Awareness 🎧
	Writing Evaluation Scale	Test 22: Punctuation & Capitalization 📖

📖 = test in the Subject Response Booklet

🕐 = timed test

🎧 = audio-recorded test

  *Tests 5 and 6

  **Tests 8 and 11

FIGURE 11.3 Outline of tests in *Woodcock-Johnson III Achievement Battery*.

Source: Woodcock-Johnson® III Tests of Achievement Examiner's Manual (p. 3), with permission of the publisher. Copyright © 2001 by The Riverside Publishing Company. All rights reserved. No part of the tests may be reproduced or transmitted in any form or by any means, electronic or mechanical, including photocopying and recording or by any information storage or retrieval system without the prior written permission of The Riverside Publishing Company unless such copying is expressly permitted by federal copyright law. Address inquiries to Contracts and Permissions Department, The Riverside Publishing Company, 425 Spring Lake Drive, Itasca, Illinois 60143-2079.

administered tests, except possibly in some research projects. Second, the focus of attention for group-administered tests is often the curriculum or program of study as much as it is the individual examinee. In fact, as noted, individual scores may not even be reported in some circumstances for group-administered tests. Curriculum evaluation is not an issue for individually administered tests. Finally, individually administered achievement tests focus intensively on analysis of intra-individual differences in performance among different achievement areas and between achievement and mental ability. This type of analysis occurs for some group-administered tests, but even when it does occur, it is typically less crucial than for the individually administered achievement test. An exception to these generalizations is the *Wide Range Achievement Test* (WRAT) that is used almost exclusively as a quick screening device.

Some Nagging Questions about Achievement Tests

As noted at the beginning of this chapter, achievement tests are easily the most widely used of all standardized tests. They have played an important role in the historical development of the entire field of testing. They have been subjected to an enormous amount of psychometric research and have evolved as a result of this research. The research has illuminated the use of these tests and guided improvement in their construction. Nevertheless, there are some nagging questions to which we call attention here, without pretending to provide definitive answers.

First, there is something not entirely satisfying about the notion of content validity. To be sure, there is strong consensus that content validity is the key approach to demonstrating the validity of an achievement test. However, this demonstration is always fundamentally a judgment that is not susceptible to any empirical validation. Most useful developments within psychometrics have required empirical demonstration. Content validity sometimes seems like a dead end. There is a judgment that a test has good or poor content validity, but where do you go from there? Is there no other way to approach the issue of the test's validity? It may be that we can do no better than these judgments about content validity. The problem of providing additional evidence regarding validity is exacerbated by the frequent revisions of test content. For example, new editions of the major achievement batteries appear about every six years. State, national, and international testing programs undergo continual change. It is, of course, an admirable goal to keep content current. But this also means that it is very difficult to collect long-term information.

A second issue relates to the ability-achievement distinction introduced at the beginning of the chapter. The formulation presented there seems to make sense. However, let us not accept it too glibly. First, we note that many test items could appear with equally good rationale in either an achievement test or an ability test. Second, we note the extremely high correlation between ability test scores and achievement test scores. In factor analyses involving both achievement and ability tests, one is often hard-pressed to find any factorial difference between the tests. Is there really a difference between these constructs: ability and achievement? Of course, this is not a question exclusively about achievement tests. It is also a question about ability tests.

Third, there is the question about examinee motivation. This is not a serious question when the examinee has something at stake such as in a licensing exam or

---

Key Points Summary 11.2

*Some Nagging Questions About
Achievement Tests*

- How satisfying is content validity?
- How meaningful is the ability-achievement continuum?
- What about examinee motivation?
- How to resolve the testing time-diagnostic information conflict?
- Do constructed-response and selected-response items measure equivalently?

---

an achievement test that will be used to award a grade. In the individually administered test, the examiner has the opportunity to judge the examinee's motivational level. But what about the typical school testing program, a state-mandated test, or a NAEP assessment? We assume that students are making a reasonable effort on the test, but in many instances this would seem to be a tenuous assumption, especially in the middle and high school grades. This may not be a problem, but we do not seem to know much about it.

Fourth, there is a seemingly eternal conflict between users' desire to minimize testing time and maximize diagnostic information. Users would like to have a 15-item test that tells everything about a student's strengths and weaknesses. Unfortunately, these desires are largely incompatible. If you want a short test, you will not get much diagnostic information. If you want diagnostic information, you will need a long test. Computer-adaptive testing may help to alleviate the conflict somewhat, but the basic conflict will always haunt us.

Finally, there is the question about the difference between what is measured by constructed-response and selected-response items. The belief that constructed-response items measure something different, especially something deeper and more meaningful, than selected-response items is widely held, although most tests continue to rely primarily on selected-response items. Even sophisticated psychometric experts are sometimes inconsistent on the subject. They claim, on the one hand, to enhance or enrich their tests with constructed-response items, then, on the other hand, blithely combine the results with multiple-choice items using procedures that assume that all the items are measuring the same construct. This same issue arises in other areas of testing, but it seems particularly acute in the realm of achievement testing. Perhaps the next few years of research will bring some sense to this area of testing. Perhaps not.

Summary

1. Achievement tests are, by far, the most widely used standardized tests. We identified six major categories of achievement tests.
2. Psychologists play several important roles in the world of achievement testing. They provide expertise in test development. Several subspecialities work in schools, where achievement testing is prominent.
3. Most elementary and secondary schools have a school testing program that incorporates a variety of tests and serves a variety of purposes.
4. The accountability movement and the standards-based approach to education have significantly influenced how achievement tests are developed and utilized.
5. Achievement test batteries used in elementary and secondary schools are complex, sophisticated systems comprising many tests and covering many grade levels.
6. Single-area achievement tests are used mostly for end-of-course or end-of-program evaluations.
7. Certification and licensing exams are usually lengthy, highly secure tests used for documenting proficiency.
8. Both norm-referenced and criterion-referenced procedures have evolved for establishing cut-off scores on achievement tests.
9. Nearly all states have legally mandated achievement testing programs for elementary and secondary schools. The programs vary widely in structure.
10. National and international testing programs concentrate on group summaries of performance for carefully selected samples.
11. Individually administered achievement tests, often administered with ability tests, help detect discrepancies between ability and achievement or among achievement areas.
12. We identified several recurring questions about development, use, and interpretation of achievement tests.

Key Terms

ability-achievement
  continuum
accountability
battery
certification
computer-adaptive
  testing
crystallized intelligence

cutoff score
ESEA
fluid intelligence
high-stakes tests
licensing
NAEP
NCLB
NOCTI

psychoeducational
  battery
standards-based
  education
test blueprint
TIMSS

Exercises

1. Think about your own educational history. What standardized achievement tests do you recall taking? What do you remember about these tests?

2. For one of the publishers listed in Table 11.3, access the website. What does the publisher emphasize about the achievement battery?

3. To make sure you can use the information in Table 11.4, answer these questions:
   - What are the names of the math tests at the Primary 3 (P3) level?
   - How many items are in the Intermediate 2 (I2) Complete Battery?
   - What is the administration time for the Advanced 1 (A1) Science test?
   - What test level is recommended for the beginning of grade 2?

4. To make sure you can use the information in Figure 11.2, answer these questions:
   - What was the student's stanine score for Vocabulary?
   - What was the student's grade equivalent (GE) for Reading Comprehension?
   - What was the number of items (No. of Items) for the Spelling Test?

5. Using the ETS Test Collection (http://sydneyplus.ets.org) website, find examples of single-area achievement tests.

6. Access the NOCTI.ORG website. Pick an occupational field of interest to you. Find the content outline for the test in that area.

7. Access the website for the Council of Chief State School Officers: http://www.ccsso.org. The site contains a wealth of information about state accountability systems. Try to find information about the testing program for your home state.

8. Access the NAEP website; NCES.ED.GOV/NATIONSREPORTCARD; or find a hard copy of a NAEP report. What group comparisons are made? What trends over time are reported?

9. For a school system familiar to you, such as the one you attended or where a family member works, consult with a school principal or school psychologist and construct a chart like Table 11.2. Fill in the exact names of the tests used in the school.

CHAPTER 12

Objective Personality Tests

Objectives

1. Define what is meant by an objective personality test.

2. Identify typical uses of personality tests.

3. Describe the problems of response sets and faking and the methods used to deal with these problems.

4. Describe the four approaches to personality test development and their respective advantages and disadvantages.

5. Compare the common characteristics of comprehensive and specific domain personality inventories.

6. Describe the major features of at least two personality inventories.

Introduction

We begin our treatment of the broad area of tests of personality, interests, and attitudes by considering objective personality tests. There is a dizzying array of these tests. It will be helpful to start with some definitions and classifications of the tests that fall into this category. By way of anticipation, we note that later parts of this chapter deal with tests related primarily to normal personality traits, such as extroversion and self-concept. The next chapter (13) deals with abnormal, pathological, or disabling conditions, such as depression and paranoia. The separation should be helpful, though not ironclad. Much of what is covered in the next few sections applies to tests in both categories, thereby serving as an introduction to both this and the next chapter.

In references to **objective personality tests,** the word "objective" has a very special meaning. It means that the test items can be scored objectively. Scoring does not involve any judgment and hence does not require professional training. A clerk or machine can score an objective personality test. In practice, this means that the test responses are multiple-choice in nature. Recall from Chapter 6 that the more technical term for such items is selected-response. The examinee selects a response from a fixed set of alternatives. Table 12.1 shows examples of typical formats for items in objective personality tests. These are just examples, not an exhaustive list of response formats for this type of test.

Although the nature of the response format is the defining characteristic for objective personality tests, they also have a second characteristic: the nature of the test item stems. Typically, the item stems consist of simple, one-sentence statements. Table 12.2 shows examples of such statements. Some items might be as short as one word. For example, there may be a list of adjectives (friendly, prompt, lazy, etc.), and examinees mark those that best describe themselves. Rarely are the item stems in an objective personality test more than a single sentence.

We contrast objective personality tests with *projective* personality measures. (One would expect *objective* tests to be contrasted with "subjective" tests, but this is not the case.) We treat projective tests in Chapter 14. Projective measures use a constructed-response or free-response format. This format requires some judgment in scoring. Thus, the scoring method is the crucial distinction between objective and projective tests, although the item stems or stimuli also usually differ.

We encounter several other terms in this field. First, an objective personality test is often called an **inventory.** We meet this rather odd designation only in the area of

---

TABLE 12.1 *Response Formats Commonly Used in Objective Personality Tests*

True—False

Agree—Disagree

True—False—Uncertain

Strongly Agree—Agree—Uncertain/Neutral—Disagree—Strongly Disagree

Choosing between two statements, for example: Mark the one that best describes you.

A. I like most people.   B. I usually work very hard.

TABLE 12.2	*Types of Statements That Might Appear in Objective Personality Tests*

1. I like most people.
2. I rarely lose my temper.
3. Most people work hard.
4. I sometimes hear voices.
5. The weather here is usually awful.
6. I get mad easily.
7. Most children are bad.
8. Newspapers are full of lies.
9. You can't count on most people for an honest job.
10. Life is a bag of problems.
11. Strange things happen in my head.
12. I have close friends in most cities.
13. I usually get things done on time.

personality and vocational interest testing. The term simply means a test. Consistent with practice in the field, we use the terms *test* and *inventory* interchangeably in this chapter. Second, we note that some sources use the term **structured test** instead of *objective* to characterize the tests treated in this chapter. We prefer the term *objective* to *structured*, but it is not worth quibbling about which is the better term.

Uses of Objective Personality Tests

There are four primary uses of objective personality tests (see Key Points Summary 12.1). *First* and foremost, *clinical* psychologists use them to provide a standardized assessment of personality traits and characteristics. Such clinical usage motivated the development of many of the most widely used personality tests. For example, it is common to use one or more of these tests early in the evaluation of a client. One of the tests may also be used later in the treatment process to document changes in the individual. Of course, clinical psychologists also gather

Key Points Summary 12.1

The Major Uses of Objective Personality Tests

- Clinical
- Counseling
- Personnel Selection
- Research

information from other sources, including interviews, medical records, school and/or work records, interviews with family members, and other types of tests, especially mental ability tests.

We can include **forensic** use as a subcategory under clinical use. Forensic use refers to any use related to legal proceedings. For example, a judge may ask for a personality evaluation of a defendant in a criminal case or of parents in a child custody case. See Chapter 16, pp. 613–615 for further description of forensic usage. Another subcategory under the clinical topic is *neuropsychological* assessment. We treated this topic in more detail in Chapter 10. Recall that, though focusing on cognitive functions, neuropsychological assessment usually includes some assessment of personality, most frequently by means of an objective personality inventory.

A *second* use of objective personality tests is for *counseling* purposes. For example, when working with a couple in a marital counseling context, it may be helpful to have personality profiles for the husband and wife. When working with a college student experiencing unusual (but not pathological) stress, the college counselor may use a personality inventory.

Third, personality tests are sometimes used for *personnel selection.* Of course, tests of ability and achievement are very often employed for this purpose. However, for some jobs, personality tests are also used. The focus may be on identifying individuals with personality traits predictive of success in a certain occupation. Or the focus may be on identifying individuals who may be "problem" employees, for example, as indicated by integrity tests (see pp. 583–619 for separate discussion of this topic).

Fourth, objective personality tests are widely used for *research* about the human personality. In fact, many of these tests were developed primarily to investigate personality constructs rather than for applied usage. Research use of personality tests falls into three broad categories. First, the tests are used for basic research about the nature and structure of personality itself. This usage goes hand-in-hand with the development of personality theories. Second, there is an enormous amount of research related to the clinical application of these tests. This research usually relates to the validity and reliability of the tests for different types of populations. For example, how do depressed individuals or substance abusers perform on a particular test? Third, personality tests are employed in a diverse array of studies to determine how personality characteristics relate to other variables. For example, do personality variables help to predict success in school? Do personality variables relate to the ability to learn nonsense syllables? What are the personality characteristics of highly creative artists or of high-tech entrepreneurs? Investigating personality correlates of a variety of other variables is a matter of limitless fascination.

A Functional Classification of Objective Personality Tests

To help us deal with the staggering array of objective personality tests, it will be helpful to introduce a classification system. The system we use is a functional one, emphasizing distinctions that arise in practice, rather than one of great theoretical

TABLE 12.3 *A Functional Classification of Objective Personality Test[a]*

Orientation	Scope of Coverage	
	Comprehensive	Specific Domain
Normal	Edwards Personal Preference Schedule	Piers-Harris Children's Self-Concept Scale
	Sixteen Personality Factor Inventory	Rotter Locus of Control Scale
	NEO Personality Inventory	Bem Sex Role Inventory
Abnormal	MMPI-2	Beck Depression Inventory
	Millon Clinical Multiaxial Inventory-III	State-Trait Anxiety Inventory
	Personality Assessment Inventory	Suicidal Ideation Questionnaire

[a] Thanks to John C. Norcross for suggesting this classification scheme.

elegance. Table 12.3 shows our two-dimensional classification system. For each category in the 2×2 array, the figure includes examples of tests. Some of these examples are described in more detail later in the chapter.

Along the left side of Table 12.3, we distinguish between tests that orient themselves toward either the normal or abnormal personality. Some objective personality tests are designed primarily to deal with *abnormal characteristics, pathologies, and problems.* These tests are the stock-in-trade of the clinical psychologist. Tests in this category often represent the name of the abnormality being measured (e.g., anxiety, depression, etc.) in the title of the test or in the name of scales within the test. Other tests are designed to measure personality traits in the *normal population.* These tests may be used by counseling psychologists and for research on a wide variety of issues related to personality variables in everyday life. The titles of these tests are usually nondescript, while the names of scales within the tests reference typical personality traits or constructs, for example, extroversion or self-concept. This distinction between the normal and the abnormal is precisely the basis for separating this chapter from the next, particularly in the examples of tests covered.

Along the top of Table 12.3, we distinguish between those tests that attempt to provide very broad coverage and those that have a narrow focus. Those providing very broad coverage we call **comprehensive inventories.** Those with a narrow focus we call **specific domain** tests. This distinction is worth pursuing in some detail.

TRY IT! ....

Classify each of these tests in the system given in Table 12.3.

Tennessee Self-Concept Scale

Basic Personality Inventory

Drug-Abuse Screening Test

Comprehensive Inventories: Common Characteristics

Table 12.4 lists some of the widely used comprehensive personality inventories. Review of typical entries in this category reveals that they share certain common characteristics, beyond the fact that they attempt to be relatively comprehensive and use a selected-response format. Before we examine some of these inventories in detail, it will be helpful to identify these characteristics. Then we will review common characteristics of the entries in the specific domain category. Of course, within each category, we will observe some exceptions to the list of common characteristics, but the lists should be helpful anyway.

1. The **comprehensive inventories** tend to have a *large number of items,* usually at least 200 and ranging up to 600 items. That is a lot of test items! See Table 12.4 for the number of items in some of the more popular comprehensive inventories.

2. Because the item stems are short and responses are multiple-choice, examinees typically complete these inventories in *30 to 60 minutes,* despite the large number of items, although some of the longer inventories may require 90 minutes. In contrast to tests in the ability-achievement domain, these personality inventories do not have time limits. However, examinees are usually encouraged to answer the items quickly rather than laboring over them.

3. Tests in this category tend to yield *many scores.* A typical entry reports 15 to 20 scores. Even when one of these tests concentrates on a specific number of traits, the test often yields additional scores. For example, the *NEO PI-R* is considered one of the best examples of a measure of the "Big Five" personality traits. Indeed, it does

TABLE 12.4   *Examples of Comprehensive Objective Personality Tests*

Test	Publisher	Date	Items
Edwards Personal Preference Schedule (EPPS)	Psychological Corporation	1953	225
California Psychological Inventory (CPI)	Consulting Psychologists Press	1987	462
Minnesota Multiphasic Personality Inventory-2 (MMPI-2)	University of Minnesota	1989	567
Myers-Briggs Type Indicator (MBTI)	Consulting Psychologists Press	2003	93–290[a]
NEO PI-R	Psychological Assessment Resources	1992	243
Sixteen Personality Factor Inventory (16PF, 5th ed.)	Institute for Personality and Ability Testing	1994	185
Millon Clinical Multiaxial Inventory-III (MCMI-III)	NCS Assessments	1994	175
Personality Research Form (PRF)	Research Psychologists Press	1989	300–440[b]
Personality Assessment Inventory	Psychological Assessment Resources	1991	344

[a] The various forms of the MBTI range from 93 to 290 items.

[b] There are six forms of the PRF, with number of items varying from 300 to 440 in different forms.

yield a score for each of these Big Five traits. But it also yields 30 "facet" scores for a total of 35 scores. The 16PF, as implied by its title, yields scores for each of 16 traits. But it also has 5 scores, based on combinations of the 16 main scores, corresponding roughly to the Big Five personality traits, plus 3 response tendency scores, for a grand total of 24 scores.

In some instances, it is difficult to state exactly how many scores one of these inventories yields because, in addition to the "regular" scores originally intended, subsequent studies have identified other subsets of items that yield new scores. The classic example of this phenomenon is the MMPI/MMPI-2. Investigators continue to find items that differentiate one group of people from another, then combine these items into a new scale.

The multiplicity of scores for the comprehensive inventories gives rise to an important consideration that will affect our evaluation of the tests. Although the full inventory has many items, as noted, individual scales often do not have very many items. This limits the reliability of many of these individual scales. One sometimes reads that personality tests are not as reliable as ability and achievement tests. In at least some instances, this generalization arises because the personality scales are based on relatively few items.

In the domain of ability and achievement tests, it is common to report a total score in addition to a number of subscores. It is interesting to note that this is not the case in the personality domain. None of these inventories combines all of its subscores into a single, total score. Apparently, psychologists do not think there is a personality "g."

4. A fourth characteristic of the comprehensive inventories is that they have *many applications.* They are used in many different contexts, for a variety of purposes, by many kinds of psychologists. They are also used in an enormous variety of research projects to advance our understanding of the human personality and to identify group differences in clinical conditions.

TRY IT!

To see the variety of research projects employing the comprehensive personality inventories, enter the name of any *one* of the inventories listed in Table 12.4 as key words in any library electronic database. PsychInfo would be ideal. To avoid getting an overwhelming number of references, limit the search to a five-year period.

5. Comprehensive inventories developed in recent years typically make a deliberate effort to provide well-defined, *nationally representative norm groups.* This was not the case for earlier versions of tests in this category (and still is not true for some comprehensive inventories that have not been revised recently). Although the tests were used in a national context, their norms were often notoriously parochial and unrepresentative. Improvements in this regard for the comprehensive inventories might be counted as one of the signal contributions of the psychometric tradition of conducting reviews of tests. We often lament the lack of progress resulting from the reviewing process, but better norms for comprehensive personality inventories provide at least one bright spot in this picture. A crasser view would attribute the change to commercial competitive pressures rather than responsiveness to professional critiques.

6. A final, emerging characteristic of these comprehensive inventories, at least for those with recent editions, is the provision of *narrative reports.* Tests such as the MMPI-2, the NEO PI-R, the 16PF, and the Millon have extensive narratives that incorporate interpretations based on validity studies as well as normative comparisons. The production of such narrative reports is now being wedded to electronic transmission of responses. An examinee can enter responses to the personality inventory online to the publisher's computer, and moments later the clinician can have in hand an extensive narrative interpretation of the examinee's profile of test scores. This is an important new development in the world of testing.

Specific Domain Tests: Common Characteristics

Table 12.5 provides examples of some of the numerous specific domain tests. In general, the characteristics of the **specific domain tests** are the opposite of those for the comprehensive tests. However, there are some exceptions to this generalization. The specific domain tests exhibit the following characteristics.

1. They have relatively *few items.* It is not unusual for one of these tests to have fewer than 30 items. It is rare for one of them to have as many as 100 items. Despite their brevity, these tests often have excellent internal consistency reliability, precisely because they focus on one narrow domain.

2. Corresponding to their small number of items, these tests can be *completed quickly,* often requiring only 10 to 15 minutes.

TABLE 12.5   *Examples of Specific Domain Objective Personality Tests*

Test	Publisher	Date	Items
Beck Depression Inventory-II	Psychological Corporation	1996	21
Beck Scale for Suicide Ideation	Psychological Corporation	1991	21
Bem Sex Role Inventory	Mind Garden	1978	60
Children's Depression Inventory	NCS Assessments	1992	27
Coopersmith Self Esteem Inventory	Consulting Psychologists Press	1981	25
Eating Disorder Inventory—3	Psychological Assessment Resources	2004	91
Fear Survey Schedule	Educational & Industrial Testing Service	1969	108
Hamilton Depression Inventory	Psychological Assessment Resources	1995	23
Piers-Harris Children's Self-Concept Scale-2	Psychological Assessment Resources	2002	60
State-Trait Anxiety Inventory	Mind Garden	1983	40
Suicidal Ideation Questionnaire	Psychological Assessment Resources	1987	30
Tennessee Self-Concept Scale	Western Psychological Services	1996	(Adult) 83 (Child) 76

3. Specific domain tests usually have *few scores,* often only one score. When they have more than one score, the different scores have a close conceptual relationship. For example, there may be separate scores for several facets of self-concept or several areas of depression. Whereas the different scores on comprehensive tests are never summed into a total score, the different scores on a specific domain test, because they are closely related, may be summed into a total score.

4. Specific domain tests do not have a wide range of applications. They usually have very *targeted audiences and uses.* Self-concept measures may be an exception to this observation.

5. Specific domain tests typically have very *limited norm groups.* In some instances, no norms are presented. In other instances, the norm groups are nearly pure examples of "convenience norms" (see Chapter 6 for a discussion of this type of norm group). That is, the norms are based on one or more readily available groups, with little or no attempt to reference the groups to some general population.

6. Finally, the *scoring and the score reports tend to be very simple* for specific domain tests. The tests are not difficult to score, and since they have few scores, complicated interpretive schemes are not needed.

Before leaving the distinction between comprehensive and specific domain tests, we should comment on circumstances of their practical application. The comprehensive inventories tend to be used when the psychologist needs to investigate many possibilities for an individual. When we do not know what an individual's problem may be or when we need to study many facets of personality, then a comprehensive battery is appropriate. However, if we have a fairly clear idea of where to focus, then a specific domain test is more appropriate. The trade-off is between breadth of information and time (and expense). The comprehensive test provides more information but requires more time. The specific domain test is short and simple, yet it offers a narrower band of information. (See Table 12.6.)

TABLE 12.6 *Summary of Main Differences between Comprehensive and Specific Domain Tests of Personality*

Characteristic	Comprehensive	Specific Domain
Number of items	Many; usually several hundred	Few; usually 20–80
Administration time	Averages 45 minutes, may be more	Usually 10–15 minutes
Number of scores	Many	Few, often only one
Range of applications	Wide	Narrow
Norm groups	Good representativeness[a]	Very limited
Reports	Elaborate; often narrative[a]	Simple

[a] This description only applies to recently developed or revised comprehensive inventories.

The Special Problems of Response Sets and Faking

Objective personality tests—both those aimed at normal traits and those aimed at abnormal conditions—are plagued by the problems of response sets and faking. A **response set** is a person's tendency, either conscious or unconscious, to respond to items in a certain way, independent of the person's true feeling about the item. Other terms commonly encountered in the literature on this topic are **response distortion** (a person's true feelings are distorted in some way by the response set) and **impression management** (a person tries to create a certain impression by the responses given). A similar concept is that of **response styles.** Common response styles are the tendency to respond in socially desirable ways, to agree with statements, or to disagree with statements. **Socially desirable responses** are responses generally approved by society, for example, being friendly and industrious. The tendency to agree, also known as the acquiescence or yea-sayer tendency, means the respondent may agree with almost any statement, whereas the tendency to disagree (the nay-sayer tendency) means the respondent is inclined to disagree with almost any statement.

These tendencies themselves might be considered personality characteristics that merit measurement in their own right. In fact, some tests do yield separate scores for these response sets. However, they create a problem when they interfere with the measurement of other personality traits. Consider the trait of "friendliness." People vary on this trait from being very friendly to very unfriendly. Generally, we consider it socially desirable to be friendly. If a person responds to items in a friendliness scale in a "friendly" direction because that direction is viewed as socially desirable when, in fact, the person is not very friendly, then we have a problem. If the person responds in a friendly direction because he or she really is friendly, quite apart from the fact that the responses are socially desirable, that is what we want to happen. The trick is to disentangle the friendliness variable from the social desirability variable. As we will see, personality tests have adopted a variety of strategies to deal with this and other response tendencies.

Faking is a deliberate attempt to create a favorable or unfavorable impression. (The fancier term is *dissimulation.*) **Faking good** means to create a favorable impression. **Faking bad** means to create an unfavorable impression; this is sometimes called **malingering.** In many circumstances, the examinee has no motivation to fake. He or she may be quite content to present an honest portrayal. However, in other circumstances, there may be considerable motivation to convey an especially favorable or unfavorable impression. For example, a person applying for a job as a salesperson may wish to appear as an extroverted go-getter. A person on trial for murder may wish to portray an image as an unstable, even delusional, person for a defense of diminished culpability. Of course, the applicant for the sales job may really be an extroverted go-getter, and the defendant in the murder trial may really be delusional. As with the social desirability issue discussed earlier, the trick is to disentangle faking from real personality characteristics.

Strategies for Dealing with Response Sets and Faking

Psychologists have devised a variety of strategies to detect and/or reduce the influences of response sets and faking on personality test scores. It is essential to understand these strategies since they will be referenced frequently both in our treatment of specific tests later in this chapter and in your review of manuals for personality tests. Most of the strategies fall into one of four main categories (see Key Points Summary 12.2.)

The first category includes references to **extreme empirical frequencies** for normal groups. A "normal" group here means a representative sample from the population having no more than the usual number of individuals with personality deviations; members of this group have no particular motivation to give anything other than honest answers. The actual frequency of responses to items is determined for such a group. It may turn out that virtually no one in the group says that they "like most people" or that they have "close friends in most cities." Hence, when an examinee marks "True" for one of these items, we suspect he or she may be "faking good" or may be overly influenced by a social desirability tendency. It may be that virtually no one, perhaps even among disturbed persons, indicates that "newspapers are full of lies." A person who marks such an item as "True" might be suspected of "faking bad." Of course, conclusions about faking are not based on responses to just one or two items. An inventory may contain a dozen or more such items, yielding a score for suspected faking.

The second strategy determines **response consistency** to similar items. In Table 12.2, items 2 and 6 and items 3 and 9 form such pairs of similar items, although the wording is in opposite directions within each pair. To be sure, there are slight differences in shades of meaning for the items within each pair, but the similarities in meaning are much greater than the differences. We would expect the person marking "T" for item 2 to mark "F" for item 6. So, too, for responses to items 3 and 9. Furthermore, we could empirically demonstrate a very high correlation for responses to these item pairs. What would we make of an examinee who marked

"T" for both items 2 and 6, and for both items 3 and 9? We may have an extreme yea-sayer. If all the responses are "F's" we may have an extreme nay-sayer. If both responses are "T" on some pairs and both are "F" on other pairs, the examinee may be responding at random. By determining the consistency of responses on, say, 15 pairs of similar items, we can get a consistency score. We may determine that in our normal group of respondents most people are consistent on all 15 pairs and very few are inconsistent on more than 2 of the 15 pairs. Hence, scores of 3 or more may lead us to question the validity of other scores on the inventory.

TRY IT!

Which person seems to show *inconsistent* responses to these two test items? Responses are T = True, F = False.

Item	Person A	B	C
I get along with most people.	T	F	F
I dislike most people I meet.	F	T	F

A third strategy deals with the yea-saying and nay-saying response tendencies by *balancing* the *directionality* of items. Suppose we are measuring the trait of "friendliness." We might start by writing items like the first two in Table 12.7. A "True" response to these items counts in the "friendly" direction. However, if all items in the scale have this directionality, that is, a True response indicates friendliness, *and* an examinee has a yea-saying tendency, then measurement of friendliness will be entangled with the yea-saying response tendency. To help control for this, we include items like 3 and 4 in Table 12.7. For these items, a "False" response would be scored in the friendly direction. Thus, a maximum friendliness score results from responses of T, T, F, and F to these four items, respectively. It is not difficult to see how the same reasoning applies to controlling a nay-saying response tendency.

Many personality inventories attempt to have some balance, although not always an exact balance, in the directionality of items for a trait. An inelegant attempt to

TABLE 12.7   *Example of Balancing the Directionality of Items*

Item	Responses in Direction of Friendliness True (T)	False (F)
1. I enjoy being with friends.	T	
2. I often go places with friends.	T	
3. Friends are more trouble than they're worth.		F
4. I have very few friends.		F

Source: From the Edwards Personal Preference Schedule (Edwards, 1959). With permission of the Allen L. Edwards Living Trust.

introduce balance just inserts "not" in the stem for some items. This often leads to a linguistically awkward situation in which the examinee must use a double negative to express a positive feeling. For example, concerning the items in Table 12.7, an item such as "I do not have many friends" requires a "False" response to indicate friendliness, a clumsy solution.

A fourth strategy, devised mainly to deal with the social desirability variable, requires examinees to *choose between statements matched* on social desirability. This matching is determined empirically by having judges rate the social desirability of responding in a certain direction on each item. Then items with similar levels of social desirability are placed in pairs (or triads). The examinee is asked to choose the one statement that is most descriptive of herself. Since statements in the pair are approximately equal in social desirability, her choice should be determined by her personality rather than by the tendency to give a socially desirable response. Matching can be on some variable other than social desirability, but this technique is usually employed to control for social desirability.

Consider the pairs of statements in Table 12.8. Suppose we have determined empirically that the pairs of statements are matched on social desirability. Suppose further that statement 1A is scored on a "conscientiousness" scale; statements 1B and 2A (with scoring reversed) are scored on a "sociability" scale; and 2B is scored on a "personal control" scale. Since the pairs are matched on social desirability, examinees' choices should be determined by their status on conscientiousness, sociability, and personal control rather than by a tendency to respond in a socially desirable (or undesirable) direction.

TRY IT!

The task is to rate the items in Table 12.2 on social desirability. Use a 10-point scale, with 10 as most desirable and 1 least desirable. Which two items would you rate near 10? Which two items would you rate near 1?

Ratings near 10:   Items _____ and _____

Ratings near 1:   Items _____ and _____

Compare your ratings with ratings made by someone else.

After we have determined a score for a response tendency or faking, there are two main methods for using this information. First, the response tendency score (e.g., yea-saying) may lead to adjustments in scores for the personality traits that are of primary interest. Second, the score for a response tendency may lead to

TABLE 12.8   *Choosing Between Statements Matched on Social Desirability*

Directions: In each pair, pick the statement (A or B) that *best* describes you.

1A. I usually work hard.   1B. I like most people I meet.
2A. I often feel uneasy in crowds.   2B. I lose my temper frequently.

invalidating all the other scores or, at least, raising serious question about the validity of the other scores. For example, if there are too many inconsistent responses, we may assume that the examinee was responding at random, carelessly, or incoherently so that none of the scores are useful indicators of personality traits.

Scores for consistency and various response tendencies are often called *validity indexes* on objective personality tests. The term is unfortunate because it does not mean the same thing as test validity treated in Chapter 5. In general, test validity refers to the extent to which the test is measuring what it purports to measure. Validity indexes on personality tests refer to whether the examinee's responses are suspect, not whether the test is measuring what it purports to measure.

Major Approaches to Personality Test Development

Four principal methods have been employed in developing objective personality tests (see Key Points Summary 12.3). More so than for other types of tests, the method of development provides a framework for understanding these tests. Hence, before describing specific personality tests, we outline these major approaches to test development and describe the advantages and disadvantages of each approach. We should be aware at the outset that most tests today use some combination of these methods.

Content Method

The content method, also known as the logical or rational method, develops test items and scales based on simple, straightforward understanding of what we want to measure. It might be called the commonsense approach to test development. For example, if we want to measure extroversion, then we ask a set of questions about relating to people. If we want to know whether a person has a tendency toward hypochondriasis (excessive concern for personal health), then we ask questions

---

Key Points Summary 12.3

Major Approaches to Developing Objective Personality Tests

- Content
- Criterion-keying
- Factor Analysis
- Theory

about fear of germs, thoughts about illness, and so on. The content approach approximates a written form of what might be covered in an interview.

This approach was the basis for the development of the first widely used personality test, the *Woodworth Personal Data Sheet*. As indicated in Chapter 1, the Woodworth put in written form the questions a clinician might routinely ask in a personal interview. However, by putting the questions in written form, the test could be administered to groups, thus saving time and expense.

TRY IT!

Use the content approach to develop items for a test measuring "sociability." For this scale, very sociable persons score high, unsociable persons score low. The first two items are given. Each item calls for a simple "Yes" or "No" response. Add another item.

	Yes	No
1. I enjoy being in a crowd.	O	O
2. Meeting new people is difficult for me.	O	O
3. _____	O	O

Advantages and Disadvantages

The content approach has the obvious advantage of simplicity. Furthermore, given a reasonable understanding of the construct to be measured, it is usually easy to generate items using this approach. The approach also has good face validity. The major drawback of the content approach is that responses are subject to distortion through response styles and either conscious or unconscious efforts to fake good or fake bad. In fact, recognition of this disadvantage led to development of other approaches to construction of personality tests.

In contemporary practice, a pure content approach is not used very much for comprehensive inventories. However, the content approach is still the primary approach employed for specific domain tests, although the approach is nearly always supplemented with other information supporting the validity of the test.

Criterion-Keying Approach

In the **criterion-keying** approach, items are selected for a personality scale strictly in terms of the their ability to discriminate between two well-defined groups of examinees. "Discriminate" here is used in the sense of item discrimination as described in Chapter 6 (see pp. 228–230). Typically, one of the groups consists of "normal" individuals, that is, persons identified as *not* having any pathological condition, or as a representative sample of the general population in which the incidence of any pathological condition would be low. The other group, typically, is a clinically defined group clearly identified as having a certain condition. This is the "criterion" group referenced in the name of this technique. The technique is also known as the empirical keying approach since it depends entirely on empirical definition of each scale.

Consider the following example (based on fictitious data). We wish to develop a personality test that will help identify depressed individuals. We administer the items in Table 12.9 to a group of 50 persons clearly identified as depressed in a series of in-depth interviews with three psychologists. We also administer the items to 50 well-adjusted, nondepressed individuals. Results of this study are summarized in Table 12.9.

TABLE 12.9   *Illustrative (but Fictitious) Data for Criterion-keying Approach to Item Selection*

Item (Mark True or False to each item)	%D	%N	Disc. Index	Selected
1. I'm content with my job.	.67	.78	.11	
2. I feel uncomfortable around people.	.20	.18	.02	
3. Most people are happy.	.34	.67	.33	★
4. My favorite color is green.	.31	.11	.20	★
5. A lot of things bother me.	.21	.18	.03	
6. I'm unhappy much of the time.	.50	.10	.40	★
7. Most people are trustworthy.	.78	.76	−.02	
8. I get sick frequently.	.32	.15	.17	★

%D = Percentage of respondents in Depressed group marking True.

%N = Percentage of respondents in Normal group marking True.

Disc. Index = Discrimination Index (%D − %N).

Selected (★) = Item selected for inclusion in the Depression Scale.

In this example, we would select items 3, 4, 6, and 8 for our Depression Scale. Scoring of some items is reversed so that all responses are "going in the same direction." Low scores on our scale indicate depression, although we could obviously reverse the scoring for the entire scale so that high scores indicated depression. There are a number of surprises in the data. We might think that item 1 would go in the depression scale. If we used the content approach previously described, this item probably would go in the depression scale. From this content perspective, item 5 might also be selected. However, empirically, neither item 1 nor item 5 discriminates adequately between the depressed and normal groups, so these items are not selected for our scale. Items 3 and 6 are selected for the scale, and this is no surprise. One can understand why depressed individuals would respond differently than normal individuals to these items. However, item 4 is a surprise. Why would "favorite color" differentiate between depressed and normal people? Here is the essence of the criterion-keying approach: It is immaterial why this item differentiates. The fact is that it does differentiate; therefore it is a good item for the depression scale. We may or may not understand why item 8 differentiates, but it does and, therefore, it is also selected.

The criterion-keying approach was pioneered in the original development of the MMPI and the *Strong Interest Inventory,* two tests we will examine in more detail later in this book. In Strong's work the groups were defined by occupational classification (e.g., social worker, plumber). The methodology works whenever we can clearly define groups. The methodology is now well entrenched in psychometrics. Hence, it is essential that the student of psychological testing understand it.

Advantages and Disadvantages

Criterion-keying has proven to be an enormously fruitful approach to test development. It focuses our attention on exactly what a test is doing or on what we want the test to do. Its raw empiricism is a useful antidote to the fanciful notions that often run amok in the world of personality theorizing. Its directness and simplicity of application encourage new research applications. These are all positive features.

The criterion-keying approach has three principal drawbacks. First, its extreme atheoretical orientation limits the generalizability of score interpretation. Suppose we have shown that a set of items differentiates depressed from nondepressed people. What else can we do with the score? There is nothing in the criterion-keying methodology that suggests any other interpretations. Does the score relate to any general personality traits? No. Does the score suggest anything about general characteristics of depression? No. At least not obviously so. Does the score provide any hints about treatment? No. Thus, other than to aid in classification, the criterion-keying approach is rather barren.

Second, the criterion-keying approach is applicable only when we have some well-defined criterion groups. We have such groups for commonly used diagnostic categories, such as depressed, paranoid, obsessive, and so on. We may be able to create such groups for a construct like "adjustment," identifying by nomination some people who seem particularly well adjusted and others who are not very well adjusted. The classifications here may not be so comfortable as in the case of the clinical groups just mentioned. For other personality traits, we may feel distinctly uncomfortable identifying criterion groups. Examples of such traits might include locus of control, self-esteem, and ego strength. Thus, the criterion-keying approach does not seem to be equally applicable across the spectrum of personality traits and characteristics of interest to us.

The third point to be made about the criterion-keying approach is really a caution about interpretation rather than a limitation of the method itself. The approach emphasizes differentiation between groups. The typical description of the method, such as that presented earlier, emphasizes how this differentiation is maximized. One might easily get the impression that use of the criterion-keying approach leads to clear separation of groups, for example, into depressed and nondepressed individuals, separated by a clearly defined cut-score. However, this is not the case. The general rule is overlap in the distributions of scores for the two groups rather than clear separation. In test interpretation, one needs to be aware of how much overlap there is in these distributions. (See the discussion of Contrasted Groups in Chapter 5 for more detailed treatment of this topic.)

Factor Analysis

Recall the explanation of **factor analysis** from Chapter 5. The basic purpose is to identify the dimensions (factors) underlying a large number of observations. The identification of underlying dimensions occurs by examining the interrelationships (correlations) among all the observations. In the realm of ability tests, the process often involves studying the correlations among many tests. For personality tests, the process ordinarily involves examining the correlations among many test *items*. One begins with a large pool of items, like those shown in Table 12.2. These items are administered to a representative sample of people. The test developer determines the correlations among responses, then applies factor analytic methodology. Finally, the test developer interprets the results, usually giving a pithy name to each factor and describing the meaning of the underlying dimensions.

Advantages and Disadvantages

There are likely some basic dimensions to the human personality. Factor analysis is the primary methodology for helping to identify these dimensions. Thus, its principal advantage is bringing order to an undifferentiated mass of items and responses. In doing so, it clarifies our thinking about the human personality by identifying "what goes with what." Based on everyday observation, we can debate endlessly about whether two notions represent the same or different personality characteristics. Factor analysis provides an empirical method for answering such questions. For this reason, the factor analytic approach has generated an enormous amount of research. One can hardly get through an issue of a journal related to personality assessment without encountering a factor analysis of some personality test.

The factor analytic approach to personality test development has three principal drawbacks. First, the final results depend critically on the content of the initial pool of items. If you do not include any items tapping dimension X, then your factor analysis will not identify this dimension. Thus, the rationale for generating the initial pool of items is crucial.

Second, there are endless—and often passionate—debates among factor analysis experts about the appropriateness of different methodologies. What type of correlation coefficients can or should be used? What factor extraction methods and what rotation procedures are appropriate? Treating the details of any of these arguments would take us too far afield. However, the frequency and intensity of these debates prompt us to be cautious about facile acceptance of any single application of factor analysis.

Third, the initial description of factor analysis suggests that it might yield a reasonably definitive set of factors. However, actual practice reveals a different picture. Final results of factor analytic work could be described as fluid rather than definitive. For example, the *NEO Personality Inventory* (see later) purports to measure the Big Five personality traits. But in addition to 5 scores corresponding to the Big Five factors, the test also yields 30 "facet" scores. One is left wondering: Are there 5 or 30 basic dimensions? The *Sixteen Personality Factor Inventory* (16 PF) identifies 16 basic dimensions for the human personality, but it also yields 5 scores corresponding to the Big Five traits. Again, one is left wondering: Are there 16 or 5 basic dimensions? Postulating some type of hierarchy among factors provides a way out of this difficulty. Such an approach has been well developed in the ability domain, as we saw in Chapter 7 for theories of intelligence. The approach also has relevance in the personality domain.

Theory-Driven Approach

The fourth approach to development of personality tests depends on reference to some personality theory. The test developer adopts a particular theory about the human personality, then builds test items to reflect this theory. The theory might say there are four dominant traits or six main types of people. Then there should be items relating to each of these traits or types. The theory might be a grand one, attempting to describe the full scope of the human personality, or a more restricted theory, attempting to describe only one aspect of personality.

Advantages and Disadvantages

The principal advantage of the theoretical approach is that it provides an operational definition of the theory. This operational definition should lead to further research about that theory. That research, in turn, may lead to further development of the test. In the best of circumstances, the interaction of test development and theory construction leads to continuing refinements of both test and theory. A good theory is a very powerful device. A good test of a good theory can have great utility.

There are two main drawbacks to the theoretical approach to personality test development. First, the test's utility is generally limited by the theory's validity. If the theory is not very adequate, then even a test that is a good representation of the theory is not likely to be very useful. Second, there is always concern about how well the test reflects the theory, even if the theory is a good one. It is not easy to demonstrate that a particular test is, in fact, a valid reflection of a particular theory. It is perhaps for this reason that the theoretical approach has not been as widely used for personality test development as one might expect it to be.

Combined Approaches

As noted at the beginning of this section, understanding the method used to develop a test aids our understanding of how the test might be used. Each test has a primary approach to test development. This primary approach gives the test a certain flavor. However, in practice, nearly all tests employ multiple approaches at some stage of test development. This will become more evident when we consider specific examples of tests later in the chapter, but we note a few examples of these multiple approaches here.

First, at least to some extent, all personality tests begin with some version of the content approach. To construct an initial list of items for the test, the test developers begin with common understandings of personality traits, characteristics, and pathologies. Even in the criterion-keying approach, in which the content of items is immaterial, test developers begin with items that seem to relate to personality characteristics. Thus, to some extent, everyone uses a content approach. Second, in a related vein, even when a test is not intended as a direct measure of some theory, the test developer's understanding of personality theories will suggest certain types of items and scales. Thus, at least to some extent, everyone uses a theoretical approach.

Third, regardless of the primary approach used in test development, it is almost inevitable that someone will conduct a factor analysis of the test items. The test authors might do this, with results reported in the test manual. Alternatively, other investigators may do it after the test is published, with results reported in journal articles. Finally, criterion-keying of items, to demonstrate differentiation of two or more groups, is commonly applied to personality tests after they are published. This may result in suggesting additional scales for the tests, especially for the comprehensive personality tests with their multiplicity of items. Thus, both factor analysis and criterion-keying are frequently applied to personality tests even when these methods were not the primary vehicles for test development.

Examples of Comprehensive Inventories

In the following sections, we examine examples of objective personality tests, first some of the comprehensive inventories, then some of the specific domain tests. We select examples that illustrate some of the points covered in earlier parts of the chapter. We do not attempt to provide an exhaustive list of all objective personality tests. There are far too many to do that. Furthermore, there are already good sources of information for such lists. See the sources of information presented in Chapter 2. For lists of the most widely used tests, see Camara, Nathan, and Puente (1998, 2000) and Piotrowski (1999). In addition, we are not attempting a complete review of the tests we present. Rather, we present an overview of the general nature of the tests. Consult Buros' *Mental Measurements Yearbook* and *Test Critiques* for such reviews.

The Edwards Personal Preference Schedule (EPPS): An Example of a Theory-Based Test

The *Edwards Personal Preference Schedule* (**EPPS**; Edwards, 1959) illustrates an objective personality inventory whose structure originates with a theory of personality. The theory is that of Henry Murray et al. (1938). Murray's actual 1938 study, though informed by his extensive experience, provided a remarkably thin base—a study of 50 (only 50) men (only men) at Harvard (only Harvard). However, the publication has had amazing influence. Apparently, the theory struck a resonant chord with many psychologists. At the heart of the theory is the notion that, whereas people have basic biological needs (Murray identifies 12 such "viscerogenic" needs), people also have basic psychological needs. It is difficult to discern a single, definitive list of these psychological needs in the original work, but there were at least 20. For example, Engler (1999) gives 20 needs, Carver and Scheier

TABLE 12.10   *Examples of Scores on the Edwards Personal Preference Schedule*

Scale	Brief Description
1. Achievement	Need to strive, do one's best
2. Deference	Need to get suggestions from others, to conform
3. Order	Need to be neat, organized
4. Exhibition	Need to attract attention, to be noticed

(1996) give 27 needs. Some of the more widely recognized needs are Achievement—the need to succeed—and Affiliation—the need to have friendships and other comfortable relationships. Edwards set out to measure 15 of these needs. Table 12.10 gives examples. Ordinarily when a test takes its structure from a particular theory, the test manual makes an effort to explain the theory and demonstrate how the test reflects that theory. This is not the case with the EPPS. After brief acknowledgment that the test purports to measure variables in Murray's list, there is no further mention of the theory. Nor is there any explanation as to why only 15 needs were selected; nor is any attempt made to demonstrate that the items fairly represent each need.

The EPPS manual expresses great concern about the influence of social desirability on responses. To deal with this influence, the test employs a forced-choice methodology for its items. Thus, the EPPS provides an excellent example of the consequences of using the forced-choice item format. We will return to this topic.

The EPPS consists of 225 *pairs* of statements, most of which begin with "I feel..." or "I like..." Each statement represents one of the 15 needs. Each need is paired with each other need yielding 14 pairs for each of 15 needs; then there are two sets of such pairs for all 15 needs. Thus, an examinee who *always* chooses the statement representing, say, Achievement receives a raw score of 28 on Achievement. An examinee who never chooses an Affiliation statement receives a raw score of 0 on Affiliation. Table 12.11 shows an example of an EPPS item. Statement A represents the Affiliation need; statement B represents the Achievement need.

The forced-choice methodology yields **ipsative scores.** If you go up in one area (need), you necessarily go down in another area. You cannot be high on all the scales; you cannot be low on all the scales. The *average* score across all scales will be the same for everyone. If your highest score is Affiliation, this means it is higher than any other area for you. It does not mean that you are high on Affiliation in any absolute sense; nor does it mean you are higher than other people on Affiliation, although you may

TABLE 12.11   *Sample item from the EPPS*

76	A. I like to be loyal to my friends.
	B. I like to do my very best in whatever I undertake.

Source: From the *Edwards Personal Preference Schedule* (Edwards, 1959). With permission of the Allen L. Edwards Living Trust.

be. If your lowest score is Achievement, this does not necessarily mean you are low in Achievement in any absolute sense; it only means you are lower in Achievement than in other areas. Interpretation of such ipsative scores requires some mental gymnastics. This is especially true when the ipsative raw scores are translated into norms, which the EPPS does allow. Figure 12.1 shows a profile of scores on the EPPS for an adult woman. Notice the pattern of scores for Order (ord) and Exhibition (exh). Both have raw scores of 14, placing these needs in the middle of Mona's range of needs on the 15 scales. However, this level of raw score (14) places her at the 38th percentile on Order and at the 78th percentile on Exhibition.

The EPPS provides two norm groups, with separate norms by gender within each group. The first group consists of approximately 1,500 college students with roughly equal representation by gender. Selection of this group appears to have been ad hoc in the extreme. No specific information is given about individuals in the group other than their age distribution and the fact that they were college students. No inferences can be drawn about what population this group might represent. The second group consists of approximately 9,000 adults, again about equally divided by gender, who participated in a national consumer purchase panel. Description of this norm group by age, income, education, city size, and region is

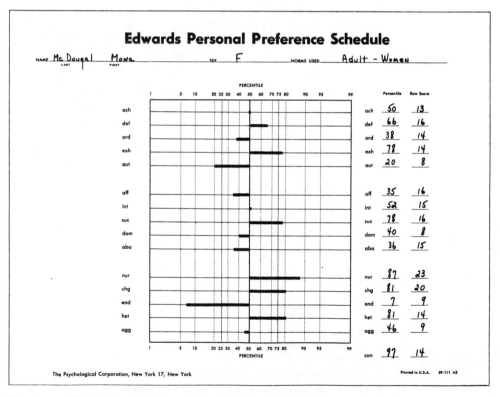

FIGURE 12.1 Sample score profile for the EPPS.

Source: From the *Edwards Personal Preference Schedule* (Edwards, 1959, p. 17). With permission of the Allen L. Edwards Living Trust.

available. Except for the fact that this information is provided elsewhere rather than in the test manual, this is one of the best extant examples of an attempt to get a nationally representative set of norms for a personality test. By now, however, one must question the usefulness of any norms developed nearly 50 years ago.

In addition to providing scores on the 15 needs variables, the EPPS yields scores for Consistency and Profile Stability. The Consistency score is based on 15 pairs of items that are repeated exactly in the test. The typical (median) individual is consistent on at least 12 of the pairs. The EPPS manual suggests that a Consistency score of 9 (only about 2% of the college norm sample scored less than 9) leads to questioning the validity of the entire test. This is a good example of a validity score for an objective personality test.

The Profile Stability score is cleverly determined by the way the answers are recorded on the answer sheet. Half of the responses for each variable are in a row and half are in a column. Profile Stability is determined by correlating the row and column scores.

Reliability for the EPPS scales is moderate. Internal consistency (split-half) reliabilities, based on the full college sample, range from .60 to .87, with a median of .78. Test-retest reliabilities, determined for only 89 cases from the college sample, with a one-week interval, range from .74 to .88, with a median of .83. (It is unusual for test-retest reliability to exceed internal consistency reliability, but in this instance the result may be due to the differences in samples used for determining the two types of reliability.) Validity evidence for the EPPS as presented in the manual is poor. It reports inconclusive correlations of EPPS scores and self-reports on the corresponding variables. It also reports inconclusive correlations between EPPS scales and scales on other tests. The EPPS is a prime example of a test with a promising start but inadequate follow-up and revision. Perhaps for this reason, the EPPS has faded in use. However, it merits inclusion here because it nicely illustrates a test's origin in a theory and the use of an ipsative approach to measurement.

The NEO Personality Inventory-Revised: An Example of a Factor Analytic Test

Psychologists have a long tradition of applying factor analysis to the personality domain. Among the pioneers of this tradition are Guilford (1959a), Cattell (1966), and Eysenck (1970), all of whom have produced factor analytically based tests of personality. In addition, even those tests developed from another perspective, for example, the MMPI or EPPS, have frequently been subjected to factor analysis. Arising out of all this research is the "Big Five" or "five-factor" theory of personality. In a widely cited article in the 1990 *Annual Review of Psychology,* Digman (1990, p. 418) refers to the Big Five theory as "a rapid convergence of views regarding the structure of the concepts of personality ... [and] ... a theoretical structure of surprising generality." Wiggins and Trapnell (1997) refer to the five-factor model as "venerable" and representing a "working consensus" in the field of personality theory. Quite simply, the theory says that, considering all the factor analytic research, it appears that there are five basic factors or dimensions in the human personality. This is a "theory" only in the weakest sense. A theory should have explanatory power, show the dynamic relationships among constructs, and allow for predictions. The five-factor theory does none of these. It is purely descriptive. It says the research typically identifies five personality factors. Hence, it is sometimes called a model rather than a theory. Nevertheless, in the long, arduous, controversial study of personality, this generalization about the Big Five represents a significant milestone.

Exact names for the five factors vary somewhat from one author to another. A commonly used system applies these names: Openness, Conscientiousness, Extraversion, Agreeableness, and Neuroticism. These names yield the oft-cited acronym OCEAN. (We might note that, with a different order but remaining in the aquatic mode, CANOE would do as well.)

The *NEO Personality Inventory—Revised* (**NEO PI**; Costa & McCrea, 1992) is considered one of the premier tests for the Big Five personality factors. Hence, we use it as our main example of the factor analytic approach to personality test development. The "NEO" tag applies to three related instruments. First, there is the NEO PI-R Form S, a 240-item self-rating instrument (i.e., the examinee rates him/herself). Second, there is the NEO PI-R Form R consisting of the same 240 items, but reworded in the third person, to be used by another person (e.g., a spouse) to rate the individual. (The "R" in NEO PI-R stands for "revised" and should not be confused with the "R" in Form R.) Third, there is the *NEO Five Factor Inventory* (NEO FFI), a short, 60-item version of the NEO PI. Our comments here are limited to the NEO PI Form S, the most widely used of the three instruments. The "NEO" title references just three of the Big Five personality factors since an earlier version of the test represented only these three factors. However, the current, revised edition—the one covered here—gives equal representation to all five factors.

The item stems in the NEO PI are similar to the generic items in Table 12.2. Examinees respond on a five-point scale: Strongly Agree, Agree, Neutral, Disagree, or Strongly Disagree. The test yields *five domain* scores, corresponding to the Big Five personality traits. Each domain contains *six facet* scores, these representing more specific manifestations of the domains. With five domains and six facets per domain, the test has a total of 30 facet scores. Each facet is measured by eight items, leading to the total of 240 items (8 × 30). Table 12.12 shows the names of the domains and facets in the NEO PI. For each facet, the test manual provides a brief description, usually with a contrast between high and low scorers. Table 12.13 shows the manual's description for the Assertiveness facet within the Extraversion domain.

The NEO PI does not have any formal validity indexes. Examinees are asked at the end of the inventory whether they have answered all the questions and done so honestly. Obviously, if an examinee indicates that he or she did not respond honestly, the validity of the test is questionable. The manual also recommends visual inspection of the answer document to determine pattern-marking (e.g., ten "Strongly Agree" responses in succession) that may indicate insincere responding. And, the manual recommends counting the number of Agree and Strongly Agree responses to detect possible yea-saying (high count) or nay-saying (low count) response tendencies. However, no norms are given for this count.

Raw scores for the domain and facet scores convert to T-scores and percentiles. Norms are provided for adults (ages 21 and up) and for college-age individuals (ages 17–20). For both groups, norms are presented for men and women separately as well as combined. The adult norms come from 500 men and 500 women drawn from three studies to match the U.S. population in terms of age and race (white,

TABLE 12.12   *List of Domain and Facet Scores in the NEO PI*

Neuroticism	**Extraversion**
N1: Anxiety	E1: Warmth
N2: Angry Hostility	E2: Gregariousness
N3: Depression	E3: Assertiveness
N4: Self-Consciousness	E4: Activity
N5: Impulsiveness	E5: Excitement-Seeking
N6: Vulnerability	E6: Positive Emotions
Openness	**Agreeableness**
O1: Fantasy	A1: Trust
O2: Aesthetics	A2: Straightforwardness
O3: Feelings	A3: Altruism
O4: Actions	A4: Compliance
O5: Ideas	A5: Modesty
O6: Values	A6: Tender-Mindedness
Conscientiousness	
C1: Competence	
C2: Order	
C3: Dutifulness	
C4: Achievement Striving	
C5: Self-Discipline	
C6: Deliberation	

Source: Reproduced by special permission of the Publisher, Psychological Assessment Resources, Inc., 16204 North Florida Avenue, Lutz, Florida 33549, from the Revised NEO Personality Inventory, by Paul T. Costa, Jr., Ph.D. and Robert R. McCrae, Ph.D. Copyright © 1978, 1985, 1989, 1992 by PAR, Inc. Further reproduction is prohibited without permission of PAR, Inc.

black, other). Data are not provided on the socioeconomic or educational level of these individuals. The college-age norms are based on cases from two sites, one in Canada, the other in the southeastern United States. Few details are given about the characteristics of these samples. When machine-scored, the NEO PI-R yields an extensive narrative report. Table 12.14 contains excerpts from a sample narrative report. Statements in the report depend partly on simple translation of normative comparisons into words and partly on implications of research studies with the test.

TABLE 12.13   *Description of the Assertiveness Facet in the Extraversion Domain of the NEO PI*

E3: Assertiveness. High scorers on this scale are dominant, forceful, and socially ascendant. They speak without hesitation and often become group leaders. Low scorers prefer to keep in the background and let others do the talking.

Source: Reproduced by special permission of the Publisher, Psychological Assessment Resources, Inc., 16204 North Florida Avenue, Lutz, Florida 33549, from the Revised NEO Personality Inventory, by Paul T. Costa, Jr., Ph.D. and Robert R. McCrae, Ph.D. Copyright © 1978, 1985, 1989, 1992 by PAR, Inc. Further reproduction is prohibited without permission of PAR, Inc.

TABLE 12.14   *Excerpts from a Typical NEO PI-R Narrative Report*

Global Description of Personality: The Five Factors

The most distinctive feature of this individual's personality is his standing on the factor of Neuroticism. Individuals scoring in this range are prone to experience a high level of negative emotion and frequent episodes of psychological distress. They are moody, overly sensitive, and dissatisfied with many aspects of their lives.

· · ·

This person is very high in Conscientiousness. Men who score in this range lead very well-ordered lives, striving to meet their goals in a planful and deliberate manner. ... Raters describe such people as careful, reliable, hardworking, and persevering.

· · ·

Finally, this individual scores in the average range in Agreeableness. People who score in this range are about as good-natured as the average person. They can be sympathetic but can also be firm.

Detailed Interpretation: Facets of N, E, O, A, and C

Openness

In experiential style, this person is generally open. He has a vivid imagination and an active fantasy life... He is interested in intellectual challenges and in unusual ideas and perspectives and he is generally liberal in his social, political, and moral beliefs.

Personality Correlates: Some Possible Implications

Coping and Defenses

In coping with the stresses of everyday life, this individual is likely to react with ineffective responses, such as hostile reactions toward others, self-blame, or escapist fantasies. ... In addition, he is somewhat less likely to use positive thinking and direct action in dealing with problems.

Source: Reproduced by special permission of the Publisher, Psychological Assessment Resources, Inc., 16204 North Florida Avenue, Lutz, Florida 33549, from the Revised NEO Personality Inventory, by Paul T. Costa, Jr., Ph.D. and Robert R. McCrae, Ph.D. Copyright © 1978, 1985, 1989, 1992 by PAR, Inc. Further reproduction is prohibited without permission of PAR, Inc.

Internal consistency measures (alpha coefficients) for the domain scores, for a sample of 1,539 adults, are adequate, ranging from .86 to .92, with a median of .89. Alpha coefficients for the 30 facet scores are generally low, ranging from .56 to .81, with a median of .71. Internal consistency measures are not reported for the college-age sample. The test manual does not report test-retest reliability data for the NEO PI for either adult or college samples; some test-retest data are referenced for the predecessor instrument.

Validity data consist primarily of a number of factor analyses and a host of studies correlating NEO PI scores with scores on other personality tests. Most of the correlations are with domain scores, although some involve facet scores. The hundreds of correlations with numerous other tests illustrate how difficult it is to develop simple generalizations about the validity of one of the comprehensive personality inventories. For reviews of the NEO PI, see Botwin (1995), Juni (1995), and Tinsley (1994).

Specific Domain Tests

We next examine specific domain measures. Before considering this section, the reader might wish to review the general characteristics of these measures as summarized in Table 12.6. There are literally thousands of these specific domain measures. We will examine one specific test, then discuss an emerging area where such specific domain tests are commonly used.

Piers-Harris Children's Self-Concept Scale

Self-concept is a construct of wide concern to psychologists. Numerous tests have been developed to measure this construct. Byrne (1996) identified 82 self-concept measures, culled the list according to several criteria, and then provided reviews of 24 measures she felt "will offer some assurance that [the] instrument is psychometrically sound" (p. 67). As noted in Chapter 2, Byrne's work is an excellent survey of many self-concept measures.

We describe here the *Piers-Harris Children's Self-Concept Scale, Second Edition* (Piers & Herzberg, 2002). Subtitled "The way I feel about myself," the test is usually known simply as the **Piers-Harris** 2, although the unwieldy PHCSCS is also sometimes encountered. Of the numerous extant measures of self-concept, it is perhaps the most widely used of all. At least in its first edition (Piers, 1996), it ranked among the more widely used measures in such fields as school psychology (Archer et al., 1991; Kennedy et al., 1994; Piotrowski, 1999).

Piers-Harris 2 is a 60-item self-report measure targeted for children and adolescents aged 7 to 18 years. Examinees respond to statements about themselves in a simple Yes-No format. See Table 12.15 for two sample statements. Approximately half of the items are worded so that a Yes response indicates positive self-concept (e.g., item 18 in Table 12.15); the other half are worded so that No indicates positive self-concept (e.g., item 29). This arrangement provides an example of balancing the directionality of items to control for yea-saying and nay-saying response tendencies.

The Piers-Harris 2 yields a total score and six "domain" scores derived from factor analysis of the items. Table 12.16 shows the names of the domains and the number of items per domain. Many of the items appear in more than one domain, some in as many as three clusters. This is very odd given the factor analytic origin of the domains.

TABLE 12.15 *Sample Items from the Piers-Harris*

	Yes	No
18. I am good in my schoolwork.	Y	N
29. I worry a lot.	Y	N

TABLE 12.16 *Scores for the Piers-Harris*

Domain	No. of Items
Behavior Adjustment (BEH)	14
Intellectual and School Status (INT)	16
Physical Appearance and Attributes (PHY)	11
Freedom from Anxiety (FRE)	14
Popularity (POP)	12
Happiness and Satisfaction (HAP)	10
Total	60[a]
Inconsistency Index	15
Response Bias Index	(all items)

[a]The total number of items is less than the sum of the number of items within domains because some items appear in more than one domain.

An Inconsistency Index is derived by comparing responses on 15 pairs of conceptually and empirically related items. A Response Bias Index is based on a simple count of all "Yes" responses, thus ranging from 0 to 60. A low score may indicate a nay-saying tendency, and a high score may indicate a yea-saying tendency. The Piers-Harris manual suggests cutoff scores for identifying inconsistent response patterns and yea-saying or nay-saying tendencies; these indexes are also plotted as continuous variables on the score profiles. These are excellent examples of validity indexes for a specific domain test. There is no validity index for the social desirability variable. The manual simply notes the importance of taking this variable into account when interpreting scores.

Raw scores on the Piers-Harris—the two validity indexes, the six domain scores, and the total score—are plotted on a profile showing (normalized) T-scores and percentiles. Norms are based on a sample of 1,387 children showing reasonable representation of the U.S. population by sex, racial/ethnic background, geographic region, and household education level. The norm sample for Piers-Harris 2 is a major improvement over the norm sample for the first edition; that sample was confined to only one rural school system.

The score profile may be plotted by hand. The test publisher also produces three narrative reports when the test is machine-scored. The most detailed of these, the Individual Report, yields interpretive comments for each of the scores listed in Table 12.16. For a specific domain test, the Piers-Harris 2 narrative reports are unusually extensive.

Internal consistency (alpha) reliability of the Piers-Harris 2, based on the standardization sample, averages about .90 for the total score and .78 for the domain scores, with a few indexes dipping to the lower .70s and even .60s within certain age groups. No test-retest reliability data are presented for Piers-Harris 2; test-retest data for the first edition are limited almost entirely to total scores. This is a significant technical deficiency in the manual.

Validity information presented in the manual consists primarily of correlations with teacher and peer ratings, correlations with a host of other tests, contrasts between groups presumed to be high and low in self-concept, and consideration of the factor structure of the test. The factor analytic studies evoke some interesting questions. The median intercorrelation among domains is .64, with some correlations reaching into the .80s. These are high correlations for domains purported to be relatively independent. To some extent, these relatively high intercorrelations follow from the fact that some items appear in more than one scale. Oswald's (2005) review of Piers-Harris 2 raised such questions about the factor structure of the test. More broadly, however, one must face the question of whether self-concept has a hierarchical structure, much like the hierarchies in intelligence (see Chapter 7). Marsh has argued, vigorously, that the correlations between different facets of self-concept are so low that it is not legitimate to produce a "total self-concept" score (see Marsh, Parada, & Ayotte, 2004).

Here is the crux of the argument: If several subscores are very highly correlated, then it appears that there is only one underlying trait (in this case, general self-concept) and separate subscores should not be provided. On the other hand, if several subscores have very low correlations, then it makes no sense to sum them into a total score. They should be left separate. For example, what sense does it make to give a "total score" for height, IQ, and speed in the 100-meter dash (three traits with nearly zero correlation)? The argument provides a good example of how sound theory, based on psychometric research, can and should inform practical test usage.

Piers-Harris-2, the edition described here, differs from the first edition just slightly in structure. The second edition has fewer items (60 vs. 80) but covers the same basic areas. The areas are now called domains rather than clusters, and domain names are adjusted slightly. The greatest difference from the first to the second edition is in the normative base, as noted earlier. For reviews of the first edition, see Cosden (1984), Epstein (1985), and Jeske (1985). For reviews of the second edition, see Kelley (2005) and Oswald (2005).

Measures within Positive Psychology

The current chapter concentrates on measures within the normal range of personality traits, separating these from measures of clinical conditions, to be covered in the next chapter. The contrast is perhaps starkest when we consider measures within positive psychology.

The measures considered in the next chapter focus on problematic behavior and cognitive states: depression, anxiety, obsessions, and so on. This is understandable because these are the "stuff" of clinical work. However, the recent development of **positive psychology** calls our attention to the other side of human beings. As if suggesting that twenty-first century psychology might deal more satisfactorily with this other side, the January 2000 issue of the *American Psychologist*, the flagship journal of the American Psychological Association, featured a Special Issue on Happiness, Excellence, and Optimal Human Functioning. As the lead article by Seligman and Csikszmenthalyi (2000) noted: "The exclusive focus on pathology that has dominated so much of our discipline results in a model of the human being lacking the positive features that make life worth living" (p. 5). Included within the scope of this burgeoning field are constructs such as hope, bravery, prudence, vitality, wisdom, optimism, humor, spirituality, and a host of others, in addition to the pervasive notion of happiness. Peterson and Seligman

(2004) provided a preliminary taxonomy of constructs within the field, subtitling the introduction as a "manual of the sanities" (p. 13). The taxonomy has 6 major categories and 24 subcategories.

Newly emerging fields often leave measurement until later, preferring to concentrate initial energies on descriptions of relevant constructs and their possible interrelationships. To the credit of those active in the field of positive psychology, they have not delayed the measurement work. Rather, their work is shot through with attempts to provide operational definitions of their constructs with specific tests. For example, each chapter in the volume edited by Lopez and Snyder (2003) considers various measures for a host of positive psychological constructs, including, for example, gratitude, empathy, and sense of humor. In addition, each chapter in Peterson and Seligman's (2004) taxonomy concentrates on describing a construct but also addresses measures for each construct.

TABLE 12.17 *Examples of Positive Psychology Traits*

Optimism	Hope	Self-efficacy
Gratitude	Forgiveness	Empathy
Self-esteem	Wisdom	Subjective well-being
Bravery	Prudence	Humility

Readers interested in further exploration of these measures of positive psychological constructs should consult the books by Lopez and Snyder (2003) and Peterson and Seligman (2003). For the present, we content ourselves with three generalizations about these measures. First, as is the case for the popular measures we examine (e.g., NEO-PI, MMPI-2), most of the measures of positive psychology constructs are of the *self-report variety*, using simple statements as items and Likert-type response formats. Refer to the response formats in Table 12.1 and the statements in Table 12.2. Use the same types of response formats and substitute appropriate statements for the relevant construct. This is what you find in the typical measure of positive psychological constructs. There are, of course, some exceptions.

The second generalization relates to the types of *psychometric research* conducted with these measures. The issues are the same as for all other measures: internal consistency and test-retest reliability; validation by factor analysis, examination of expected group differences, and studies of convergent and discriminant validity; and, of course, the ever-present concern for representativeness of normative data.

TRY IT! ....

Consider the traits identified in Table 12.17. These are just examples, not an exhaustive listing. Can you add any to the list?

....

Third, while some measures of personality attempt to cover many different areas, for example, the multiplicity of scores obtained from NEO-PI or MMPI-2, measures in positive psychology tend to concentrate on only one construct at a time or a few closely related constructs. There are *no comprehensive inventories* in positive psychology—at least not yet. The Peterson-Seligman taxonomy may provide a basis for a change in this circumstance.

An Example: Subjective Well-Being

Overall, how satisfied are you with life? Respond on a scale from 1 to 10, where 1 is very dissatisfied and 10 is very satisfied.

How happy are you? Respond on a scale from 1 (very unhappy) to 5 (very happy).

Mark the face that shows how you most often feel.

These items illustrate approaches to measuring the global concept of subjective well-being (SWB). Although positive psychology is relatively new as an identifiable field, SWB has been studied for many years, but it fits nicely within this emerging field. Measurement of SWB presents some very interesting challenges and results.

In terms of overall structure, SWB follows a pattern very similar to the hierarchical model of mental ability examined in Chapter 7. At the lowest level, there are many specific feelings and personal assessments. For example, how do you feel about this school subject versus that school subject? How do you feel on Friday afternoon versus Monday morning? These highly specific assessments aggregate into several intermediate levels. Keyes and Magyar-Moe (2003) outlined several of the extant systems. One system distinguishes between psychological well-being and social well-being. Each of these categories is further subdivided. For example, psychological well-being encompasses such areas as self-acceptance, purpose in life, and personal growth. Another system distinguishes among psychological, social, and emotional well-being, each with several subcategories. Power (2003) summarized the system used in the World Health Organization's Quality of Life study. This system had four domains (physical, psychological, social, and environmental), each with several facets. Multidimensional measurement instruments exist for each of these systems.

Just as the hierarchical model for mental ability had "g" at its apex, the various systems just described seem to amount to a global SWB. This global SWB is assessed with the very simple types of statements and response scales presented at the beginning of this section. An enormous amount of research, including many cross-cultural studies, has been completed with these simple measures. For summaries of the use of these global measures and their correlations with a wide variety of real-world behaviors, see Diener (2000; see also Diener, 1984; Ryan & Deci, 2001), Myers (2000), and Seligman et al. (2005).

Trends in the Development and Use of Objective Personality Tests

What conclusions might be drawn from our survey of objective personality tests? And what might we project for the future of this category of tests? We offer the following points in answer to these questions (see Key Points Summary 12.4).

1. We note that new objective personality tests are being developed at an astonishing rate. New instruments appear in virtually every issue of journals such as *Psychological Assessment* or the *Journal of Personality Assessment*. Refinements in existing instruments continually appear, too. Commercial publishers are churning out new personality tests and revisions of old tests at a dizzying pace. One concludes that the field of objective personality testing is in a robust state of health. Psychologists apparently see a real need for these types of tools. Incidentally, this rapid rate of development reinforces the need to be familiar with the sources of information treated in Chapter 2.

2. Methods for developing objective personality tests have matured. We have come a long way from the first, crude attempts to measure personality traits and detect pathological conditions with objectively scored inventories. Specifically, the potential influences of response sets and faking are widely recognized, and methods for dealing with these influences are readily applied in the test development process. Furthermore, we realize the need to demonstrate test validity empirically rather than rely on hunches about what a test is measuring. Use of criterion-keying and research on group differences are primary methods used for such demonstration.

Key Points Summary 12.4

Trends for Objective Personality Tests

- Many New Tests Being Published
- Methods of Development Have Matured
- Managed Care Emphasizes Convenience and Lower Cost
- Production of Narrative Reports Now Common

3. One of the classical contrasts in considering the relative merits of different types of tests is between objective personality tests and projective techniques, a category we take up in Chapter 14. The contrast is usually made in terms of reliability and validity. However, with the emergence of managed care approaches to cost containment in the delivery of health services, the lower cost of objective personality tests, in comparison with projective tests, has increasing relevance (Piotrowski, 1999). Although an examinee may devote about the same amount of time to taking either a projective or objective test, there is a substantial difference in clinician's time. It may take an hour for the clinician to administer a projective test and another hour to score it. For an objective personality test, the examinee can record answers on a keyboard, responses are conveyed by telephone lines to a remote computer, and in a matter of seconds, the clinician has a complete report of scores—with essentially no time expended by the clinician. This matter of convenience and cost-saving is likely to have a significant influence on the relative use of objective and projective tests. Specifically, the managed care environment favors objective over projective tests. Within objective tests, managed care favors the shorter specific domain tests over the comprehensive inventories.

4. Narrative reports of performance on objective personality tests are now common. It is important for the student to recognize the advantages and potential drawbacks of such reports. On the plus side, they can provide enhanced interpretability for both the psychologist and the client. On the other hand, one needs to approach these reports with due caution. They can sound terribly definitive. One needs to remember that they are based on fallible (less than perfectly reliable) scores and that they normally do not incorporate information from outside the test itself. Ultimate responsibility for interpretation of the test rests with the psychologist using the test, not with the computer program generating the report.

Summary

1. The defining characteristic of an objective personality inventory is its use of a selected-response format. Also, it typically has short statements for item stems.

2. Objective personality tests find practical application in a wide variety of areas, including counseling, personnel, and research work.

3. Objective personality tests can be conveniently classified into comprehensive inventories and specific domain tests. Within each of these categories, some tests focus on normal personality traits while others focus on abnormal characteristics, especially pathological conditions.

4. Response sets and faking may influence responses to objective personality tests. Four principal methods are used to control for or mitigate the influence of these factors: checking extreme empirical frequencies, checking consistency of response on similar items, balancing directionality of items, and using forced-choice item types.

5. There are four major approaches to development of objective personality tests: content, theoretical, factor analysis, and criterion-keying. Each has its distinctive advantages and disadvantages. In practice, some combination of these approaches is ordinarily employed.

6. These tests illustrated the comprehensive inventories: the *Edwards Personal Preference Schedule* as an example of the theory-driven approach and the NEO PI as an example of the factor analytic approach.

7. Illustrating specific domain tests were the *Pier-Harris Children's Self Concept Scale* and the host of scales used within the emerging field of positive psychology, including both simple and multidimensional measures of subjective well-being.

8. We noted certain trends in the current use of objective personality tests and speculated about their future in applied fields of psychology. An astonishing number of new tests continues to appear in this category. Test development is now more sophisticated. Narrative reports are now widely employed.

Key Terms

comprehensive inventory
criterion-keying
EPPS
extreme empirical frequency
factor analysis
faking bad
faking good

forensic
impression management
inventory
ipsative scores
malingering
NEO PI
objective personality test
Piers–Harris
positive psychology

response consistency
response distortion
response set
response style
socially desirable responses
specific domain test
structured test

Exercises

1. Access the ETS Test Collection (http://sydneyplus.ets.org). As the key word, enter the name of any personality trait. Pick a trait of particular interest to you. Examples of traits are anxiety, depression, extroversion, and self-concept. See what tests are listed. Try to classify some of the entries in the organizational scheme used in Table 12.3.

2. Several personality inventories have their origin in systematic study of the adjectives we use to describe personality characteristics. Try this approach yourself. List 20 adjectives that depict personality. It may be helpful to think of how you would describe people you know. Compare your list with the lists developed by other students.

3. Recall that a potential weakness of the factor analytic approach to test development is that if you do not include items about a certain trait in the original pool of items, then you will not identify that trait in your factor analysis. Examine the items in Table 12.2. What personality traits do not seem to be represented in these items? (If you completed Exercise 2, some of your adjectives may suggest traits that may be overlooked in Table 12.2.)

4. Access the website for the publisher of one of the comprehensive inventories listed in Table 12.4. Then locate information about the inventory. What characteristics of the test does the publisher's website emphasize? See Appendix C for publishers' websites.

5. Here are examinee responses to four items that might appear in a personality inventory. Which responses seem to be inconsistent? Responses are T = True, F = False.

Item	Examinee	A	B	C
1. I like most people.		T	F	T
2. I usually work hard.		F	F	F
3. Many people are a nuisance.		F	T	F
4. I'm basically lazy.		T	T	F

Inconsistent responses: Examinee _____ on items _____ and _____.

6. Suppose you were trying to "fake good" to create a favorable impression. How would you respond to the items in Exercise 5? Responses are T = True or F = False.

7. Here are a person's T-scores on the five domain scores for the *NEO PI-R*. Write three sentences describing this person without using the names of the domain scales.

Domain:	Neuroticism	Extraversion	Openness	Conscientiousness	Agreeableness
T-score:	60	45	40	65	45

CHAPTER 13

Clinical Instruments and Methods

Objectives

1. Identify similarities and differences between tests of normal personality traits and clinical instruments.

2. Contrast structured and unstructured clinical interviewing techniques.

3. Describe major features of comprehensive clinical instruments, for example, SCID, SCL-R-90, MMPI-2, and Millon instruments.

4. Describe major features of specific domain clinical instruments, for example, BDI-II, EDI-3, and STAI.

5. Outline the approach used for behavior rating scales.

6. Describe the basic notion for behavioral assessment techniques and give examples of specific applications.

7. Discuss trends in the development and use of clinical instruments.

Introduction

This chapter treats a variety of tests and techniques used in clinical settings. Such settings include hospitals, private practice, counseling centers, and psychological clinics in schools. The tests and techniques covered here have some similarities to the tests of normal personality traits covered in the previous chapter, but they also have some differences (see Key Points Summary 13.1). Let us outline these similarities and differences.

Perhaps the most obvious *similarities* between the two categories lie in the nature of the test items and response formats. Recall the description of these two characteristics from the previous chapter. The tests tend to use very simple statements as test items, for example, "I am often sad." And the tests tend to use very simple response formats, for example, "Yes-No" or "Agree-Unsure-Disagree." A second similarity, introduced in the previous chapter, is that the two categories are conveniently subdivided into comprehensive instruments and specific domain instruments. We use this organizational scheme in this chapter. The comprehensive clinical instruments attempt to survey all potential areas of difficulty, thus yielding numerous scores. The specific domain instruments concentrate on just one area, for example, depression or eating disorders, yielding just one or a few closely related scores. Tests in both categories have used similar strategies for development, although criterion-keying has been more important for the clinical instruments. Tests in both categories also share the concern about response sets and faking.

There are several *differences* between the categories of tests treated in this and the last chapter. The most obvious is their respective orientations. Tests in the last chapter relate primarily to the normal range of personality traits. Tests and other assessment techniques treated in the present chapter relate primarily to psychopathology or at least to some personal difficulty. There are also some less obvious differences between the two categories. The clinical instruments are almost always administered on an individual basis, specifically in a clinical setting. Tests covered in the previous chapter are often administered in group settings. The manuals for clinical instruments emphasize use of the results for diagnosis, treatment planning, and follow-up evaluation. One does not find such discussions in manuals for tests like the NEO PI-R.

Although we treat tests of normal personality traits and clinical instruments as separate categories, it must be admitted that there is some overlap in the categories. For example, the *Piers-Harris Children's Self-Concept Scale*, covered in the last chapter, might be used to screen for students with very low self-concept, thus suggesting the need for further evaluation. At the same time, the *Eating Disorder Inventory*, covered in the present chapter, has its own self-esteem scale, with items very similar to those found in the Piers-Harris. Thus, the distinction we use in these two chapters is not ironclad.

Finally, we note that the tests covered in the next chapter, projective techniques, are used almost exclusively as clinical instruments. However, they are distinctly different in structure from the instruments covered in the present chapter, thus warranting separate coverage.

> **Key Points Summary 13.1**
>
> *Comparing Tests in Chapters 12 and 13*
>
> **Similarities**
>   Nature of Items and Response Formats
>   Subdivisions for Comprehensive and Specific Domain Tests
>   Strategies for Development
>   Concern for Response Sets, Faking
>
> **Differences**
>   Orientation
>   Settings for Administration
>   Diagnosis, Treatment Planning, Follow-up

The Clinical Interview as Assessment Technique

When introducing various tests throughout this book, we have frequently referred to the test's ranking in surveys of test usage. Such surveys have guided our selection of which tests to describe. In accord with the book's emphasis on being practical, we have concentrated on the most widely used tests. When "interview" is included in these surveys, it always ranks first (see, for example, Culross & Nelson, 1997; Watkins, Campbell, Nieberding, & Hallmark, 1995). Of course, including "interview" as if it were a specific test, like the WAIS or MMPI, is a bit misleading. It's like asking: Do you ever get biographical information, such as age and sex, for your clients? Well, of course. But that's not a test. So, too, the interview is not a single, specific test; thus, it cannot be directly compared with other specific tests. Nevertheless, the survey results remind us that the clinical interview is almost universally used. And it also reminds us that we need to ask the same questions about the interview as we ask about any test. Is it reliable? Is it valid? Is it fair? Is it cost effective?

Research on what might be called the traditional interview has yielded distressingly pessimistic answers to these questions. That is, the traditional interview is not very reliable; it has limited validity; it opens itself to the operation of biases; it is not very cost effective. For useful summary of the research on these questions, see Groth-Marnat (2003). Concern about the technical adequacy of the traditional clinical interview, augmented by the demands of managed care, has led to the development of the **structured clinical interview**, the main topic of this section.

Unstructured, Semistructured, and Structured Interviews

It is customary in the world of clinical interviews to distinguish among unstructured, semistructured, and structured interviews. The *unstructured interview*, sometimes called the "traditional" interview, follows no particular pattern and varies from one client to another as well as from one clinician to another. This does not mean that the interview is thoughtless or slapdash. At the other extreme, the structured clinical interview aims to cover the same topics, with the same questions, with every client. It aspires to be both comprehensive and consistent. Included within the consistency are both the questions and the response coding. Furthermore, there is a specific record of responses, not just a general impression or recollection. The *semistructured approach*, as you might guess, falls between the unstructured and structured approaches. It has some standard questions, but it is partly tailored to the individual client.

The three approaches fall along a continuum rather than being discrete categories, ranging from complete uniqueness to unswerving sameness. As we shall see, even the structured approach typically has some elements of customization. For example, if a client is evidently lucid but presents with complaints of dysphoria, it does not make much sense to spend a great deal of time inquiring about hallucinations, even if such queries are part of a full structured interview inventory.

The DSM

One cannot understand most of the contemporary structured interviews without reference to the *Diagnostic and Statistical Manual of Mental Disorders, 4th Edition, Text Revision* (**DSM-IV**; American Psychiatric Association, 2000). It would certainly take us far afield from our main concerns to provide a reasonable description of DSM-IV. However, we must note the following features of this crucial source. First, it is the common standard for diagnostic labels in contemporary clinical practice. Thus, it has assumed enormous importance for communicating among professionals. It has also become essential for most reimbursement purposes. Second, the main outcome in using DSM-IV is arrival at a diagnostic category, essentially a label, for example, 309.21 Separation Anxiety Disorder. Thus, it results in a nominal classification, although some categories have subdivisions for varying levels of severity. Third, it is symptom oriented. The clinician's key task is identifying symptoms that DSM-IV lists for a condition. These three features provide the basis for most structured clinical interviews: determine symptoms, leading to classification in DSM-IV.

Structured Clinical Interview for DSM-IV Axis I Disorders

The *Structured Clinical Interview for DSM-IV Axis I Disorders* (**SCID-I**; First, Spitzer, Gibbon, & Williams, 1997) is the most widely referenced of the structural clinical interviews. Stewart and Williamson (2004) stated that "The SCID is the 'gold standard' for valid and objective diagnosis of comorbid psychiatric disorders" (p. 186). Interestingly, the SCID User's Guide also used the term *gold standard* but did so in a negative way, noting that "Unfortunately, a gold standard for psychiatric diagnosis remains elusive" (First et al., 1997, p. 46). Thus, we are apparently in the awkward position of having a gold standard that is not tied to any gold. That is, to the extent that the DSM system is defective or ambiguous, an instrument specifically aligned

TABLE 13.1 *List of Modules in SCID-I-Clinical Version*

A.	Mood Disorders	D.	Mood Disorders
B.	Psychotic Symptoms	E.	Substance Abuse Disorders
C.	Psychotic Disorders	F.	Anxiety and Other Disorders

with that system will almost certainly have problems. Nevertheless, we provide here a brief description of SCID.

Before doing so, however, a few words about the "lingo" of structured clinical interviews will be helpful. Although the instrument we describe is called the "structured clinical interview," many such instruments incorporate the term *structured clinical interview* into their titles. See Rogers (2001) for excellent descriptions of a dozen such instruments. Furthermore, even for the instrument described here, there are several versions. For example, SCID-I has a Clinical Version and a longer Research Version. There is a SCID based on DSM-III and another based on DSM-IV. There is a SCID for Axis I Disorders and another for Axis II Disorders. Finally, in practice, a clinician using SCID (any of them or any of the other structured clinical interviews) ordinarily applies only part of the instrument. Thus, reference to use of the structured clinical interview or even to SCID has ambiguous meaning.

Here is how SCID-I-CV works:

- There is an Administration Booklet, containing questions and directions for proceeding, and a Scoresheet for recording and coding responses. The interviewer has both open at once.

- After recording basic identifying information, start with one of the major DSM categories, for example, Mood Disorders or whatever seems most appropriate. These categories correspond to SCID modules, as listed in Table 13.1.

- Ask questions about symptoms, as indicated in the Administration Booklet.

- Record responses, but also code responses, indicating presence (+), absence (−), or inadequate information (?) for each response.

- Follow the "skip out" rules (see below).

- When the interview has been concluded, complete the Diagnostic Summary. This summary relates responses to DSM category numbers and labels.

The "absence" code applies not only to complete absence of the symptom but also to what are called "subthreshold" levels—that is, something not up to the level indicated as clinically significant in the DSM. The "skip-out" rules direct the interviewer to discontinue asking questions in a particular category when it becomes apparent that it is not fruitful to continue pursuing that category. These rules function like the "stop" rules in individually administered intelligence tests. In a typical application, where only one or a few modules are used, completing the SCID requires about one hour. Completing all modules, usually done only in research applications, may require three hours.

SCID attempts to strike a middle course between complete, rigid standardization and the traditional unstructured interview, although clearly coming down more on the standardized side. For example, on the list of Dos and Don'ts in the User's Guide one finds: "Do stick to the initial questions, as they are written, except for minor modifications" and "Don't make up your own initial questions because you feel that you have a better way of getting the same information." On the other hand, "Do use your own judgment about a symptom, considering all the information available" and "Don't focus only on getting an answer to the SCID-CV question" (First et al., 1997, pp. 12–13).

Finally, it should be emphasized that the clinical interview is not intended to be the only source of information about a client. It may be supplemented by a variety of tests, such as those covered elsewhere in this book, for example, MMPI-2, BDI-II, or some of the neuropsychological tests. Information may also be garnered from family members. In some circumstances, a physical exam will be in order.

The Employment Interview: A Sidebar

We have concentrated on the clinical interview. It is typically conducted by a clinical psychologist, psychiatrist, social worker, or other professional upon a client's initial visit. The principal goal is diagnosis, followed by treatment planning. However, virtually everything said earlier about the clinical interview applies equally well to the employment interview, except that the goal is employee selection rather than diagnosis. Specifically, research on the employment interview shows that the typical interview has notoriously low reliability and validity. And, just as for the clinical interview, the proposed remedy is a structured interview. For reviews of research on employment interviews, see Herriot (1989), Posthuma, Morgeson, and Campion (2002), and Taylor and O'Driscoll (1995). Edenborough (2002) covers a variety of approaches to employment interviewing, including structured interviews, as well as sketching an interesting history of interviewing. Taylor and O'Driscoll (1995) provide a thorough description of the "nuts and bolts" of the structured approach to employment interviewing. Paralleling the specificity and relevance criteria used in the structured clinical interview, the structured employment interview emphasizes (a) asking the same questions of all candidates, (b) coding responses, and (c) concentrating on areas directly relevant to the job.

Finally, we should note that the employment interview, like the clinical interview, does not stand alone. Information garnered from the interview complements information from other sources, including formal tests. Relevant tests include an assortment of specialized aptitude tests directly related to particular job skills and tests of general mental ability. In fact, use of such tests seems to be making somewhat of a comeback.

TRY IT!

Suppose you were constructing a structured interview for hiring college teachers. What questions would you ask of all applicants? Make sure the questions relate directly to the skills required for the position.

Examples of Comprehensive Self-Report Inventories

As we did in the previous chapter, we present examples of both comprehensive and specific domain instruments with a clinical orientation. The structured interviews just covered were typically comprehensive but were distinguished by their interview nature. What we cover next are strictly self-report in nature.

The Minnesota Multiphasic Personality Inventory (MMPI)

An easy selection—one might say the required selection—for an example of a comprehensive, self-report clinical instrument is the *Minnesota Multiphasic Personality Inventory* (**MMPI**), known in its current, second edition as MMPI-2. Weighing in at a hefty 567 items, the MMPI-2 requires 60 to 90 minutes to complete and may take as much as two hours for examinees with low reading levels or high distractibility levels. This instrument is on nearly everyone's list of most frequently used, most widely researched, and most often referenced tests. For example, it is the single most frequently used test by neuropsychologists and second most frequently used by clinical psychologists (Camara et al., 2000). It has been used in over 10,000 published research studies. Quite apart from the frequency of its use, the MMPI was a pioneer in the development of validity indexes and the criterion-keying approach to test development. Hence, it is an exceptionally fruitful source of study for the student of psychometrics.

Use of the MMPI is practically a subculture within psychology. It has its own language, customs, and rituals. To one initiated into the subculture, it is rich in tradition and meaning. For example, an examinee might be characterized as a "24 code type with elevated F scale." This brief description speaks volumes to the clinician thoroughly familiar with the MMPI. To the uninitiated, it can be baffling. The latter characterization of a person is gibberish to one not familiar with the inner workings of the MMPI. In the short space available to us here, we can only present the highlights of the test's structure, usage, and research base. For details, the interested reader is urged to consult Graham (2000), Newmark and McCord (1996), the standard reviews (Archer, 1992; Duckworth & Levitt, 1994; Nichols, 1992), and, of course, the MMPI-2 manuals (Butcher, 1993; Butcher, Dahlstrom, Graham, Tellegen, & Kaemmer, 1989).

The First Edition

The MMPI was first published in 1942; the revised edition, MMPI-2, appeared in 1989. Our principal interest is in the current edition, MMPI-2. However, the MMPI is one of the great psychometric sagas, so we should spend some time describing the first edition and the context for its development.

At the time of its development, the 1930s, personality assessment was dominated by content-based inventories. These tests were plagued by problems of response sets and faking. Furthermore, the meaning of their scores, especially for clinical usage was being questioned. Putting aside problems of response sets, what did the scores tell the clinician? Of course, meaningfulness to the clinician was defined to a significant extent by what the clinician was trying to do. At that time, a principal concern was accurate diagnosis of psychological disorders, resulting in application of the correct diagnostic label (in the then-current terminology) to a case. The original MMPI had two key features. First, validity indexes were explicitly used. These are described later along with other MMPI scores. Second, the test used criterion-keying to develop nine clinical scales; one other scale was subsequently added to bring the number of clinical scales to ten. Items for each scale (except Social Introversion, Si) were selected by contrasting responses of cases clearly diagnosed in that category with a group of "normals." The normals were 724 hospital visitors. Item selection for the clinical scales also underwent cross-validation. All of this research (again, except for the Si scale) was conducted at the University of Minnesota hospital. The normals served as the basis for T-score and percentile norms on the MMPI. The test was consistently criticized for this restricted normative base: a relatively small group of individuals, all from one state, nearly all white, primarily rural, and obviously limited to the late 1930s. The tenth scale (labeled 0 rather than 10) was developed later at the University of Wisconsin.

The MMPI rapidly became the clinician's preferred instrument for objective personality assessment. It was widely used not only in practice but for research. As the research base grew, interpretability of scores was enhanced. In fact, the MMPI is probably the best single example of how the practical utility of a psychological test increases through research after its publication.

TRY IT!

To appreciate the extent of use of the test in research, enter MMPI-2 as keywords in an electronic database such as PsycInfo or ERIC. It may be best to restrict the search to just a few years. Examine the selection of studies. Determine how the test is used.

The 1989 Revision

Given the widespread use and substantial research base for the original MMPI, revision was approached with some trepidation. Actually, revisions were quite modest. Most of the research on comparability of the first and second editions suggests a reasonably seamless transition (Graham, 2000). There were five main types of revision.

First, a few items were revised or replaced, especially items with obsolete or gender-specific references. Second, clinical scales were now referenced by number (1, 2, 3, …) rather than by diagnostic category. This change partly reflects a change in diagnostic terminology. Perhaps more important, research results have greatly expanded the interpretive framework for the scales, going well beyond particular diagnostic labels. For example, a scale originally labeled with a diagnostic category may now be known to indicate three basic personality traits, some of which have no obvious connection to the original diagnostic label. Third, entirely new norms were developed. The restandardization is described next. Fourth, several new validity indexes were added. Finally, the T-score to signal high scores was lowered from 70 to 65.

Scores

The MMPI-2 is a veritable cornucopia of scores. Usually, we can say definitively that a test yields, say, 5 or 12 scores. It is difficult to state exactly how many scores the MMPI-2 yields. Let us try to sort through at least the major categories of scores for this test. We can divide MMPI-2 scores into six major categories (see Key Points Summary 13.2).

First, there are validity indexes. Among these are four traditional indexes that appeared in the original MMPI and are carried forward to MMPI-2. Then there are three new indexes created for MMPI-2. A large research base exists for the traditional indexes and they are routinely reported on the MMPI-2 Basic Profile (see Figure 13.1). The research base for the new validity indexes is thin, but growing.

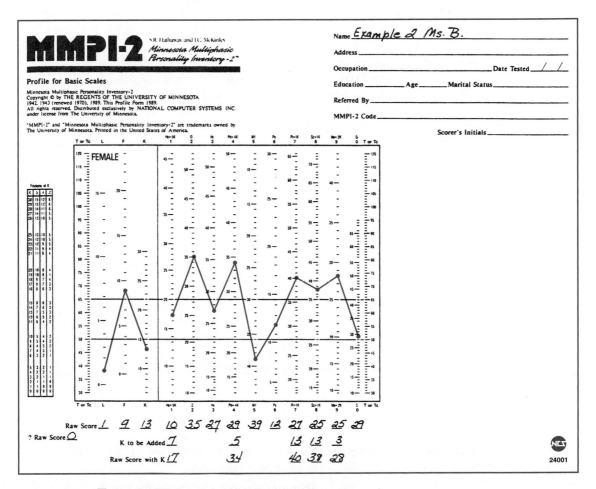

FIGURE 13.1 Sample MMPI-2 basic profile.

Source: MMPI-2 (Minnesota Multiphasic Personality Inventory-2) Manual for administration and scoring, (p. 35). Copyright © 1942, 1943, 1951, 1967 (renewed 1970), 1989 by the Regents of the University of Minnesota. All rights reserved. Used by permission of the University of Minnesota Press. "Minnesota Multiphasic Personality Inventory-2" and "MMPI-2" are trademarks owned by the Regents of the University of Minnesota.

Key Points Summary 13.2

Major Categories of MMPI-2 Scores

- Validity Indexes
- Clinical Scales
- Content Scales
- Supplementary Scales
- Critical Items
- Code Types

Scores on these indexes are not routinely reported on the MMPI-2 Basic Profile. Table 13.2 provides a brief description of each of the validity indexes.

There is good reason to begin the description of MMPI-2 scores with consideration of the validity indexes. In practice, interpretation of all MMPI-2 scores starts with examination of the validity indexes. If one or more of the validity indexes is grossly atypical, then the other scores may not be interpreted at all. We may conclude

TABLE 13.2 *MMPI-2 Validity Indexes*

Abbreviation	Name	Items	Brief Description
Traditional Indexes			
?	Cannot Say	All	A simple count of the number of omitted or double-marked items.
L	Lie	15	Responses may indicate tendency to create favorable impression or fake good.
F	Infrequency	60	Items with low endorsement rates. Responses may indicate attempt to fake bad.
K	Correction	30	Responses may indicate a fake-good response tendency, but at more subtle level than indicated by L-scale items.
New Indexes			
TRIN	True Response Inconsistency	23 pairs	Number of true (or false) responses on pairs of items opposite in content.
			True (or false) to both items in the pair is inconsistent.
VRIN	Variable Response Inconsistency	67 pairs	Number of inconsistent responses to pairs that may be either similar or opposite in content.
F_B	Back F	40	F-type items that occur later in the test. Help determine if later response patterns are similar to earlier patterns.

that the examinee was responding at random or trying so hard to fake a good or bad impression that the entire test is useless. In less serious cases, the validity indexes may suggest that exceptional caution is required when interpreting scores.

Special mention should be made of the K (correction) score. It is not only a score by itself but also leads to modification of several clinical scale scores. In Figure 13.1, notice the entry at the bottom of the profile:"K to be Added." Then notice the narrow table labeled "Fraction of K" to the left of the profile. Finally, notice the labels for the clinical scales at the bottom of the profile. Some of the scale abbreviations reference K. For example, the first scale (Hs, 1) is labeled Hs + .5K. This means that .5 × K-score is to be added to the original Hs score. Scales 7, 8, and 9 also have "K corrections." In effect, the test authors are saying: We are going to inflate your reported level of deviance by an amount proportional to your effort to "fake good" in order to get a more accurate indicator of your real level of deviance. The authors concluded that such compensatory scoring was warranted for only certain scales.

Interpretation of the validity indexes is not as simple as it may first appear. For example, an elevated F-score, rather than indicating an effort to fake bad, may indicate severe pathology or a "cry for help." A high F_B score, based on items in approximately the last one-third of the test, may indicate that the examinee's attention wavered or even became hostile late in the testing session. However, it may not invalidate the clinical scales because their items are predominantly in the first two-thirds of the test.

The *clinical scales* constitute the second major category of scores. They are the most distinctive scales in the MMPI-2 and the ones that give the test its special flavor. Table 13.3 lists the 10 clinical scales. Their criterion-keyed origin was described earlier. In various contexts, one of these scales may be referred to by its number, its original name, or the abbreviation for that name. The number of items varies widely from one scale to another, ranging from 32 to 78 with a median of 49. There is some overlap in items between scales—that is, a particular item may appear in more than one scale. The clinical scales and traditional validity indexes constitute what are called the *basic scales* for the MMPI-2. These are the scales profiled in Figure 13.1.

The third category of scores consists of the *content scales.* Although the MMPI is best known for its criterion-keying approach to scale development, the content scales were developed by rational analysis of the items. Clinical experts examined the items and

TABLE 13.3 *MMPI-2 Clinical Scales*

Number	Original Name	Abbreviation	Number of Items
1	Hypochondriasis	Hs	32
2	Depression	D	57
3	Hysteria	Hy	60
4	Psychopathic Deviate	Pd	50
5	Masculinity-femininity	Mf	56
6	Paranoia	Pa	40
7	Psychasthenia	Pt	48
8	Schizophrenia	Sc	78
9	Hypomania	Ma	46
0	Social Introversion	Si	69

grouped together those that seemed to measure the same construct. These groups of items were further refined by examining item-total correlations to improve scale homogeneity. Butcher et al. (1989) identify 15 content scales: anxiety, fears, obsessiveness, depression, health concerns, bizarre mentation, anger, cynicism, antisocial practices, Type A, low self-esteem, social discomfort, family problems, work interference, and negative treatment indicators. Number of items per scale ranges from 16 to 33, with a median of 24 items. Thus, the content scales are considerably shorter, on average, than the clinical scales. T-scores for the content scales are regularly profiled in MMPI-2 score reports, although they appear on a different profile than the basic scales.

TRY IT! ....

Examine the items in Table 12.2. Identify subgroups of items that you think relate to the same construct or content domain.

....

The fourth category of MMPI-2 scores consists of a daunting list of *supplementary scales,* so many perhaps that there may not be a definitive count. Some of these have been constructed by criterion-keying for additional groups (e.g., alcoholics vs. normals). Other scales have arisen from rational analysis, similar to the content scales. Still others have resulted from factor analysis of the MMPI-2 item pool. Some of the supplementary scales have been widely researched and are incorporated into MMPI-2 reports, although often just tentatively so. Other supplementary scales have not been well researched, hence are not routinely reported. We will not describe or list any of the vast number of supplementary scales. However, the reader should be aware of their existence.

The fifth category of scores consists of what are called *critical items.* These "scores" are literally just reports of responses to individual items. However, the items are those that appear to have special significance. For example, suppose a test contained the item: I often feel like slitting my wrists. Regardless of how responses to this item contribute to a total score, a response of True will catch your attention. You will want to explore that response with the client. There are several lists of critical items, generally identified by the name(s) of the persons who developed the list. As with the supplementary scales, we will not catalog these lists, but the reader should be aware that critical items constitute a reporting category.

The sixth and last category consists of *code types.* Since code types are a mechanism for reporting as well as a category of scores, they are described in the next section.

Norms and Reports

MMPI-2 norms are based on 1,138 men and 1,462 women, a total of 2,600 cases, drawn from six states, several military bases, and one Indian reservation. The test manual presents detailed analysis of the norm sample in terms of age, marital status, race, income, education, and occupation. The norm sample is reasonably representative of the U.S. adult population in terms of most characteristics, but overrepresented at higher educational and professional occupational levels. Raw scores convert to T-scores and percentiles. T-scores are the typical reporting medium, as illustrated in the sample profile in Figure 13.1. Percentiles are gender-specific. MMPI-2 norms constitute a major improvement over the original MMPI norms.

There are three major methods for reporting MMPI-2 scores: profiles, narratives, and code types. First, the profile (see Figure 13.1) is a common reporting mechanism. One profile form reports the traditional validity indexes and clinical scales. A similarly configured profile is used for the content scales.

A second method for reporting MMPI-2 results is the narrative report. There are actually several types of narrative reports, developed and issued by different vendors. We confine our remarks to *The Minnesota Report: Adult Clinical System—Revised* (Butcher, 1993) that might be called the official report since the MMPI-2 publisher sponsors the report. This extensive report—often 15 pages long—incorporates profiles for the validity indexes, clinical scales, content and some supplementary scales, and responses to critical items. The narrative portion of the report comments on such matters as profile validity, symptomatic patterns, and treatment considerations, among other topics. Table 13.4 presents excerpts of statements from one report.

Code Types

The third major method for reporting MMPI-2 scores is **code types.** This type of report is relatively unique to this instrument. It is essentially a new type of norm score, hence requires some introduction. A key interpretive idea with the MMPI is

TABLE 13.4 *Excerpts from a Typical MMPI-2 Narrative Report*

PROFILE VALIDITY
The client omitted 7 items on the MMPI-2. Although this is not enough to invalidate the resulting MMPI-2 clinical profile, some of his scale scores may be lower than expected because of these omissions...

SYMPTOMATIC PATTERNS
Individuals with this MMPI-2 clinical profile tend to exhibit a pattern of chronic psychological maladjustment. The client is probably experiencing severe personality deterioration and is likely to have problems with intense anxiety, somatic distress, agitation, and anger. He may also have many problems caused by general ineffectiveness in dealing with life.

INTERPERSONAL RELATIONS
His interpersonal relationships are probably disturbed, and he tends to manipulate others by developing physical symptoms.

DIAGNOSTIC CONSIDERATIONS
Probable diagnosis is Schizophrenic Disorder or Severe Somatization Disorder.

TREATMENT CONSIDERATIONS
Individuals with this MMPI-2 clinical profile tend to be experiencing unexplainable and bizarre physical symptoms. They tend to be quite eccentric and have unusual thinking about their bodily processes...
Examination of item content reveals a considerable number of problems with his home life. He feels extremely unhappy and alienated from his family.

Source: Adapted from MMPI-2TM (Minnesota Multiphasic Personality Inventory-2 TM) User's guide for the Minnesota report: Adult clinical system-Revised (pp. 45–47). Copyright © 1989, 1993 by the Regents of the University of Minnesota. All rights reserved. Used by permission of the University of Minnesota Press. "Minnesota Multiphasic Personality Inventory-2" and "MMPI-2" are trademarks owned by the Regents of the University of Minnesota.

TABLE 13.5   *Illustration of Code Typing to Identify Highest Scores in a Profile*

Test	A	B	C	D				
		T-Scores				**Scores in Order**		
Sue	60	55	80	75	C	D	A	B
Bill	55	45	65	60	C	D	A	B
Anne	85	90	80	75	B	A	C	D

examination of peaks in the profile of scores. Regardless of whether the highest scores are extremely high or just moderately high, special meaning is attached to what scores are the highest in the profile. Consider the simplified example in Table 13.5. On tests A, B, C, and D, Sue and Bill have quite different levels of score. However, when their scores are ranked in order, within their own score profiles, the order of scores is the same. They both show "peaks" at C and D. In the MMPI-2 scheme, they would be referred to as a CD code type. On tests C and D, Anne has the same scores as Sue. However, Anne is a different code type because her highest scores are on tests A and B.

MMPI-2 code types utilize the clinical scale numbers and the letter designations for the traditional L, F, and K validity indexes (see Tables 13.2 and 13.3). Scale numbers are ordered from highest to lowest T-scores, going left to right, followed by ordering of the validity indexes. Symbols (such as ! and ⋆) are used after scale number to indicate absolute level of score elevation. For the complete set of rules for coding, see Butcher et al. (1989) or Graham (2000). In actual practice, greatest attention is devoted to the two highest scores. This is called a two-point code type, for example a 2-4 or 4-2 code type. The two highest scores are usually considered interchangeable, so 2-4 and 4-2 are considered the same code type, not two different code types. There is also a three-point code type but the two-point system has been most widely used.

TRY IT! ....

What is the two-point code type for the MMPI-2 profile shown in Figure 13.1? Be sure to use the T-scores, not the Raw Scores to determine the code type.

....

A substantial amount of research has been conducted to determine characteristics of persons with certain code types. For example, Graham (2000, pp. 95–96) reports that 24/42 code types "appear to be angry, hostile, resentful, critical, and argumentative … [and] … the prognosis for traditional psychotherapy is not good." Knowing the research on code types can provide an important interpretive framework for the clinician.

Reliability and Validity

Table 13.6 summarizes reliability data from the MMPI-2 manual (Butcher et al., 1989). The data include ranges and median coefficients for internal consistency and

TABLE 13.6   *Summary of Reliability Data for MMPI-2 Scores*

	Alpha		Test-Retest	
Scales	Median	Range	Median	Range
Validity	.64	.57–.73	.80	.69–.84
Clinical	.62	.34–.87	.82	.58–.92
Content	.86	.67–.86	.85	.78–.91

test-retest reliability. The manual presents all data separately by gender. The summary presented here pools the data for males and females. Additional data are given in the manual for some supplementary scales, but these data are not included in our summary.

The data in Table 13.6 suggest several conclusions. First, internal consistency of the validity indexes and clinical scales is generally weak, with some of these scales having extremely low internal consistency reliability. This is perhaps understandable for the clinical scales given the method of their development. It is, nonetheless, disconcerting. Test-retest reliability is noticeably better for both the validity and clinical scales. The median figures are tolerable, although some scales in the low portion of the range are still weak. Internal consistency reliabilities for most of the content scales are adequate. This, too, is understandable, given that item homogeneity was one of the criteria used in developing these scales. Most of the content scales also have adequate, although not exceptionally high, test-retest reliability. Note that the reliability data are more favorable for the content scales than for the clinical scales even though the content scales are generally much shorter than the clinical scales. The median number of items per scale is 24 for content scales and 49 for clinical scales. One sometimes hears the opinion that it is the nature of personality variables that prevents personality tests from having very high reliabilities. This is not necessarily true, as will be illustrated with some of the specific domain tests treated in the next section. What limits reliability, for the most part, is how the tests are constructed.

Validity data for the MMPI-2 are simply too extensive and complex to allow for a useful summary in a short space. One needs to consult the original manuals and the research literature to make any sense of this vast array of information. We do, however, wish to point out that factor analytic studies suggest that the MMPI-2 measures only about four underlying dimensions. The two most well defined of these dimensions are psychotic mentation and neurotic tendencies (Butcher et al., 1989; Graham, 2000). For reviews of the MMPI-2, see Archer (1992), Duckworth and Levitt (1994), and Nichols (1992).

The Millon Clinical Multiaxial Inventory (MCMI) and the Millon Family

Theodore Millon is the principal author of a family of objective personality tests. Table 13.7 lists current members of the family. Some of the entries in this table are

TABLE 13.7   *The Millon Family of Inventories*

Inventory	Acronym	Publication Date
Millon Clinical Multiaxial Inventory	MCMI	1976
Millon Clinical Multiaxial Inventory—II	MCMI-II	1987
Millon Clinical Multiaxial Inventory—III	MCM-III	1994
Millon Adolescent Personality Inventory	MAPI	1982
Millon Adolescent Clinical Inventory	MACI	1993
Millon Behavioral Health Inventory	MBHI	1974
Millon Behavioral Medicine Diagnostic	MBMD	2001
Millon Index of Personality Styles	MIPS	1994
Millon Pre-Adolescent Clinical Inventory	M-PACI	2005

revisions of other entries, sometimes with a change in edition number (e.g., I, II) but other times with an entirely new test title. Thus, reference to "the Millon" can be quite confusing. However, the most widely used member of the family is the *Millon Clinical Multiaxial Inventory* **(MCMI)**. Reference to "the Millon" is usually to this instrument, although there is still some ambiguity since it is available in three editions (I, II, and III). According to Camara et al. (2000), the MCMI is now the tenth most widely used instrument by clinical psychologists (the MMPI is second, while WAIS is first).

The MCMI fits in our classification scheme (Table 12.3) as a comprehensive inventory with an orientation toward the abnormal. This is the same quadrant as for the MMPI. In fact, the MCMI has emerged as a main competitor to the MMPI. Like the MMPI, the MCMI has a virtual subculture surrounding it. Use of the MCMI requires careful study of specialized terminology, novel procedures, and underlying assumptions. In this chapter, we hit just the highlights for the MCMI.

The MCMI is a good example of a combined approach to development of a clinical inventory. There are three threads running through its development. First, it begins with an orientation around Millon's theory of personality. Items were originally prepared to reflect aspects of this theory. Since its first publication (Millon, 1969), the theory has undergone various elaborations and restatements. Sometimes called a biosocial-learning theory, it postulates three basic polarities in the human personality: pleasure-pain, self-other, and active-passive. The theory also postulates a continuum of the normal and abnormal personality, with severe personality disorders being extreme expressions of the polarities. Millon (1981) identified eight basic personality patterns, then added three more severe variants of these basic patterns. The three polarities, eight patterns, and their variants surface in various ways in the scales for the MCMI, although changes have occurred from one edition of the test to another. Development of the MCMI has also utilized clinicians' ratings of the items in terms of appropriate content categories. Finally, items were subjected to standard item analysis to improve scale homogeneity. Researchers other than Millon have also completed factor analysis of the MCMI items.

The MCMI has three distinctive features. First, and probably most important for its growth in popularity in recent years, it makes an explicit attempt to align its scores with the Diagnostic and Statistical Manual (DSM) of the American Psychiatric

Association. As noted earlier, the DSM in its various editions has provided the main diagnostic system and terminology for mental disorders throughout the mental health field. In its current edition (DSM-IV, American Psychiatric Association, 2000), the DSM uses six axes for classification: hence, it is multiaxial. The MCMI attempts to reflect these axes, especially axis I (clinical disorders) and axis II (personality disorders). Since the DSM is the official classification system, to the extent that the MCMI (or any test) relates to the DSM, the test will be attractive to practitioners.

Second, the MCMI is much shorter than the leading test in the field, the MMPI. Whereas the MMPI-2 has 567 items and requires about 60 minutes to complete, the MCMI-III has only 175 items and requires about 25 minutes to complete. From the 175 true-false items, the MCMI-III yields 26 scores. Recently, the Millon has added 42 new scores called "Grossman Facet Scales," which are sort of subscores under the other scores. Including these additions, there are a rather astonishing 70-some scores coming from the 175 true-false items in the MCMI-III. Third, the MCMI employs "base rate" scores. These scores take into account, when flagging problem areas, the base rate for types of psychological problems in the population. For example, condition X is more prevalent (has a higher base rate) than condition Y. Thus, a scale for condition X should flag more problem cases than a scale for condition Y. In contrast, on most tests, a high or problem score is usually defined in a strictly normative sense; for example, a T-score of 70 or greater may be considered problematic, regardless of differing base rates in the population. These base rate scores are a very interesting development.

Table 13.8 summarizes the major categories of scores on the MCMI-III and gives examples of some scales within each category. Anyone familiar with the DSM will recognize the attempted alignment with DSM terminology. The Modifying Indices are types of validity indices for the MCMI-III.

TRY IT! ....

To see an example of an MCMI-III report, go to:
http://www.pearsonassessments.com/reports/mcmi3profile.pdf
How does this report compare with the MMPI report in Figure 13.1?

....

TABLE 13.8 *Major Categories of Scores and Examples of Scales on MCMI-III*

Category	Example Scales
Personality Disorder Scales	
Moderate	Histrionic, Antisocial, Compulsive
Severe	Borderline, Paranoid
Clinical Syndromes	
Moderate	Anxiety, Bipolar: Manic, Alcohol Dependence
Severe	Thought Disorder, Delusional Disorder
Modifying Indices	Disclosure, Desirability
Grossman Facet Scales	42 subscores under Disorder and Clinical scales

The advantages and disadvantages of the MCMI have been hotly contested. The reader should consult the reviews of the MCMI, cited later, for thorough treatment of the relevant issues. Here, we briefly identify two main lines of argument. First, as noted earlier, the MCMI is quite brief for a comprehensive inventory, but it still yields many scores. Practitioners find this brevity very attractive. However, the combination of brevity and multiplicity of scores is attained by using the same items in different scales. Partly as a result of this feature, some of the scales are so highly inter-correlated that it is difficult to justify giving them different names. It's like having separate events at a track meet for the 100-yard dash and the 100-meter dash. Why bother? In its various editions, the MCMI has struggled with this issue. Second, as also noted previously, the attempt to align MCMI scales with the DSM has been very attractive to clinicians. However, there is a price to pay, in two respects. First, the DSM itself is not perfect. To the extent one is successful in aligning a test with it, the test itself will be imperfect. Second, the DSM changes. It is now in its fourth edition. MCMI-II tried to match DSM-III. Then along came DSM-IV. MCMI had to be revised: thus, MCMI-III. Recall from our description of the MMPI the concern about generalizing from the original MMPI to MMPI-2. Numerous studies labored over this matter. The MCMI has undergone two rather substantial revisions in the relatively short time it has been available. This causes significant strain in generalizing from earlier studies to the current edition. In modern Western society, we tend to like rapid developments and "brand new" products. In the case of test development, sometimes we need to slow down in order to let research inform us properly.

All the Millon inventories listed in Table 13.7 have a common flavor and approach. They are rooted in Millon's biosocial-learning theory with its three polarities, although drawing on this theory to varying degrees. They all combine theoretical and empirical approaches to test development. They also feature extensive narrative reports and other supplementary materials. With one exception, they are designed mainly for use with clinical groups, have norms based on clinical groups, and incorporate some type of base rate reporting. However, beyond the MCMI described above, they have unique purposes and target groups.

Recent editions of Buros MMY contain particularly useful reviews of the MCMI-III (Choca, 2001; Hess, 1998; Retzlaff, 1998; Widiger, 2001). Groth-Marnat (2003) gives a thorough description of the development, research, and interpretive scheme for the MCMI-III. The overview by Millon and Davis (1996) is a useful review of the rationale for the test. Millon's (1997) edited collection and Strack (2002) provide useful information about all the Millon inventories.

Symptom Checklist-90-R

Symptom Checklist-90-R (**SCL-90-R**; Derogatis, 1994) is one of the classic instruments for a quick, self-report survey of a diverse array of dysfunctional states. This is a good instrument to examine because numerous other measures follow a similar pattern—and their number seems to be increasing exponentially each year. The intended target group for SCL-90-R is persons 13 years or older. As suggested by its title, it contains 90 items. Each item identifies a symptom such as a feeling (many of the items actually begin with the word "feeling"), thought pattern, or behavior expressed as a word or phrase. Responses are given on a five-point scale: 0 = Not at all, 1 = A little bit, 2 = Moderately, 3 = Quite a bit, 4 = Extremely. Typical administration time is about 15 minutes. Clients use "the past 7 days including today" as the time frame for their ratings.

TRY IT!

Using the SCL-90-R response scale, make up two items that you think might indicate psychological problems. One item is given. Add two more. Make the items brief.

	Not at all	A little bit	Moderately	Quite a bit	Extremely
	0	1	2	3	4
Afraid of meeting people	0	1	2	3	4
_____	0	1	2	3	4
_____	0	1	2	3	4

The SCL-90-R is a lineal descendant of the *Woodworth Personal Data Sheet*. Recall our discussion of this instrument in the history of testing. It was devised as a substitute for a personal interview in screening U.S. military recruits in Word War I. A personal interview was simply too time consuming, but Woodworth felt that much crucial information could be obtained with a simple paper-and-pencil form. Woodworth's scale became widely used but lost favor because of concern about response distortion. The MMPI gained in popularity partly by its explicit use of validity scales to check for possible response distortion, as described earlier. The SCL-90-R uses the same basic rationale as the Woodworth. That is, it gathers initial information with a simple paper-and-pencil form covering a broad array of symptoms. Then, follow-up is conducted as needed. For example, you can determine (with no investment of a clinician's time) that a person has marked "4 (Extremely)" for five items related to anxiety and perhaps to no other items. That certainly suggests that the clinician should begin to investigate anxiety (and not phobias or several other possible avenues). Of course, completing a diagnosis goes well beyond looking at the scores on one inventory. But the scores, easily obtained, give you some place to start.

The SCL-90-R yields 12 scores. Nine are called primary symptom dimensions and three are global indices. The titles, numbers of items, and brief descriptions of the *nine primary symptom dimensions* are:

• Somatization (12)—bodily dysfunctions
• Obsessive-compulsive (10)—recurrent thoughts, actions
• Interpersonal Sensitivity (9)—feelings of inadequacy, inferiority
• Depression (13)—gloom and doom
• Anxiety (10)—tension, panic
• Hostility (6)—anger, aggression, resentment
• Phobic (7)—unwarranted fears

- Paranoid Ideation (6)—excessive suspiciousness
- Psychoticism (10)—withdrawal, isolation, hallucination

The perceptive reader will note that the number of items in these scales comes to 83. The other seven items are simply called "additional items," covering a miscellany of symptoms such as problems of eating and sleeping but forming no coherent category.

The 90 items yield the following *three Global Indexes*:

- Global Severity Index (GSI)—sum of responses to all 90 items.
- Positive Symptom Distress Index (PSDI)—sum of responses divided by the number of nonzero responses, taken as an indicator of "average distress."
- Positive Symptom Total (PST)—number of nonzero responses, taken as a measure of symptom breadth.

The manual notes that the Global Severity Index is the "best single indicator of the current level or depth of the disorder [and] should be used in most instances where a single summary measure is called for" (Derogatis, 1994, pp. 12–13).

The SCL-90-R uses normalized T-scores for norms. The manual recommends that a T-score of 63 serve as the cutoff to identify a case as a "positive risk." (Refer to Chapter 3 for a refresher on T-scores. Note that according to Table 3.1, a T-score of 63 corresponds to the 90th percentile.) Rather than having a single set of T-scores, the manual provides separate T-score norms based on the following groups: psychiatric outpatients, psychiatric inpatients, nonpatients (adult), and adolescent nonpatients. Each of these groups is further subdivided into male and female norms, for a total of eight different normative groups. Thus, the clinician can select the most appropriate basis (that is, norm) for interpreting a client's scores. It may even be appropriate to consider the results from more than one norm group. For example, a raw score of 1.11 on Somatization corresponds to a T-score of 63 for nonpatient females, thus at the borderline for flagging a problem; that same raw score corresponds to a T-score of 52 for psychiatric inpatients, thus in the normal range for this group. All of the norm groups are of the convenience type (see Chapter 3); it is difficult to judge to what extent they might be representative of some wider populations, although the manual makes a reasonable effort to describe the groups.

Scores on the SCL-90-R appear to have reasonable internal consistency reliability, generally in the mid-.80s. Test-retest stability ranges from .68 to .90, with a median of .80 and most values between .75 and .85. There is certainly room for caution about the stability of a few of the scales.

One crucial question about the validity of the SCL-90-R is the independence of the nine symptom clusters. The manual makes the case that the nine scales are reasonably independent in a factorial sense. Other sources suggest that there may be only one or two underlying dimensions of psychopathology, a factorially based criticism also directed at the MMPI.

Examples of Specific Domain Tests

Next we identify several examples of specific domain measures. Before reading about these examples, the reader may wish to review the common characteristics of these measures as summarized in Table 12.6. There are literally thousands of specific domain measures in use. The examples we treat here are among the more widely used tests.

The Beck Depression Inventory (BDI)

The *Beck Depression Inventory*—Second Edition (**BDI-II**; Beck, Steer, & Brown, 1996) is an excellent example of a specific domain test. Camara et al. (1998, 2000) report that among tests used for personality and psychopathological assessment, the BDI-II ranks sixth for clinical psychologists and second (behind only the MMPI) for neuropsychologists.

According to the manual (Beck et al., 1996, p. 1), the BDI-II is a "self-report instrument for measuring the severity of depression in adults and adolescents." Consisting of a mere 21 items, the test can be completed in 5 to 10 minutes. The test manual itself is a compact 38 pages. Each item calls for response on a 4-point (0–3) graded scale, ranging roughly from "not a problem" to "major problem." Item stems are the essence of simplicity: Single words or phrases describe some depressive symptom. Table 13.9 shows an item similar to those in the BDI-II.

Summing responses on the 0–3 scales over 21 items yields a raw score range of 0–63. To describe degree of depression, the manual (page 11) suggests these labels for various score ranges:

0–13	Minimal
14–19	Mild
20–28	Moderate
29–53	Severe

The cut-points for these descriptions were derived empirically to distinguish optimally among several clinically evaluated groups. Score interpretation depends on these classifications; no traditional norms (e.g., percentiles or standard scores) are given in the manual.

The manual presents reliability and validity data based on a sample of 500 outpatients clinically diagnosed according to DSM criteria at four sites, as well as on a sample of 120 students from one Canadian college. The BDI-II manual reports alpha coefficients of .92 for the outpatient sample and .93 for the college sample. Test-retest reliability of .93 is reported for a subsample of 26 cases from the outpatient group, with a retest interval of one week.

TABLE 13.9 *Item Like Those in the BDI-II*

Mark the statement that best shows how you felt in the past two weeks.

Worry

0. I am not especially worried.
1. I worry quite often.
2. I worry about almost everything.
3. I worry so much it hurts.

Regarding validity, the BDI-II manual reports correlations with a variety of other tests, arguing for both convergent and discriminant validity. It attempts to show, in the case of discriminant validity, that the test is not primarily a measure of anxiety. A factor analysis suggests that the BDI-II items tap two dimensions, one labeled Somatic-Affective, the other labeled Cognitive.

An interesting feature of the BDI-II is the fact that the manual gives item characteristic curves (ICC's) for *each response* to each item. These ICCs do not enter formally into score interpretation, but they help the user understand how each item and even each response functions within the context of the total score. For reviews of the BDI-II, see Arbisi (2001) and Farmer (2001).

The Eating Disorder Inventory (EDI)

The *Eating Disorder Inventory-3* (**EDI-3**; Garner, 2004) provides another excellent example of a specific domain instrument with clinical application. Like the BDI-II, the EDI-3 focuses on a specific problem area. Unlike the BDI-II, the EDI-3, as we shall see below, provides several scores rather than just one. In this way—that is, providing several scores within a relatively restricted domain—the EDI-3 is like the Piers-Harris. The second edition of this test, EDI-2, has been the most widely used measure for eating disorders. We presume that the EDI-3 will maintain that frontrunning status. However, the transition to the new edition will not be a simple matter for users because the new edition is considerably more complex than its predecessor.

TABLE 13.10 *Structure of the Eating Disorder Inventory-3*

Composite	Scale	Number Items
Eating Disorder Risk	Drive for Thinness	7
	Bulimia	8
	Body Dissatisfaction	10
Ineffectiveness	Low Self-Esteem	6
	Personal Alienation	7
Interpersonal Problems	Interpersonal Insecurity	7
	Interpersonal Alienation	7
Affective Problems	Interoceptive Deficits	9
	Emotional Dysregulation	8
Overcontrol	Perfectionism	6
	Asceticism	7
General Psychological Maladjustment	8 scales above plus	(57)
	Maturity Fears	8

Response Style Indicators

Inconsistency	10 pairs of items
Infrequency	10 items
Negative Impression	All items (except 71)

The EDI-3 is a self-report form "aimed at the measurement of psychological traits or symptom clusters relevant to the development and maintenance of eating disorders" (Garner, 2004, p. 4). The test manual distinguishes between scales directly relevant to eating disorders and those scales related to more general psychological traits that predispose to eating disorders. This bifurcation is an important characteristic of the EDI-3.

The test consists of 91 items; oddly, one item (71) is not scored. Table 13.10 lists the names of the scales and number of items for each, as well as the composite scores and Response Style Indicators for EDI-3. Both the composite scores and the response style indicators are new to EDI-3; they did not exist in EDI-2. Composites are sums of T-scores for their included scales, with sums then converted to their own T-scores. The response style indicators are classic examples of "validity indexes" such as those encountered earlier for the MMPI-2. No items overlap between subscales on the EDI-3.

Scales in the Eating Disorder Risk composite relate directly to eating disorders. All other scales relate to more general traits. The manual refers to these latter as the Psychological Scales. Note that the Psychological Scales have several composites and that all of these scales sum to the General Psychological Maladjustment Scale.

Table 13.11 shows a sample item from the EDI. This item fits in the Body Dissatisfaction scale. It occurred in EDI-2 and continues in EDI-3. Responses are made on a six-point scale ranging from "Always" to "Never." For most items, a response in the direction of high frequency is "symptomatic." For these items, the scoring is: Always = 4, Usually = 3, Often = 2, Sometimes = 1, and the other responses (Rarely, Never) = 0. For about one-third of the items, a low frequency response is symptomatic; thus item score weights are reversed for these items. Scores within scales are sums of these response values. The item response values are somewhat different than in EDI-2.

The EDI-3 manual provides T-score and percentile rank norms for three different groups: U.S. Adult clinical sample (N = 983), International Clinical sample (N = 662), and U.S. Adolescent Clinical sample (N = 335). Each of these clinical samples contained cases of anorexia nervosa–restricting type, anorexia nervosa–binging/purging type, bulimia nervosa, and eating disorder not otherwise specified. These four categories correspond to DSM-IV categories for eating disorders. All cases in these norm groups were females. Both U.S. normative groups were drawn from five states, with the great majority of cases coming from Midwestern states. The International samples came from Australia, Canada, Italy, and the Netherlands.

TABLE 13.11 *Sample Item from the Eating Disorder Inventory*

45. I think my hips are too big.	A U O S R N
(A = Always U = Usually O = Often S = Sometimes R = Rarely N = Never)	

Source: Reproduced by special permission of the Publisher, Psychological Assessment Resources, Inc., 16204 North Florida Avenue, Lutz, Florida 33549, from The Eating Disorder Inventory-3, by David M. Garner, Ph.D., Copyright © 1984, 1991, 2004 by PAR, Inc. Further reproduction is prohibited without prior permission from PAR, Inc.

The samples are good illustrations of convenience norm groups, but the EDI-3 groups are far more extensive than the norm groups for EDI-2, all of which came only from Toronto, Canada. The manual refers to female nonclinical samples (also called the "female controls"), but little information is given about the nature of these groups. Finally, means and standard deviations are provided for both clinical and nonclinical males, but complete normative tables are not provided for these groups. In fact, these data are presented in the manual's section on validity rather than norms.

Raw scores on the scales are plotted on a profile form that displays, with shaded areas, the range from 25th to 67th percentiles for the clinical and nonclinical normative groups. Figure 13.2 shows such a profile. Notice that scores for this case rather clearly fall into the clinical group's range, except for the score in Body Dissatisfaction, which is more in the nonclinical group range. Notice also the extreme elevation for the Bulimia and Emotional Dysregulation scales. This is an unusual but interesting method for reporting test scores.

TRY IT! ....

Examine the EDI-3 profile in Figure 13.2. Compare the darker and lighter shaded areas. Which scales appear to give the most separation between Clinical and Control norm groups? Which scales show the least separation between the two groups?

....

The EDI-3 manual reports internal consistency (alpha) reliabilities for the three clinical norm groups described earlier. In addition, the manual reports alpha and test-retest reliabilities from a variety of other sources. Most of the reliability coefficients are in the range of .80 to .95, although a few fall into the .60s for selected subscales with some samples. Most of the alpha reliabilities are excellent. Test-retest reliabilities are also high, although only one study based on 34 cases is provided for these data. The manual also presents a wide array of validity information. It includes correlations with a host of other tests, extensive factor analytic work, especially related to the new structure of the test, and contrasted group studies. As usual, it is a daunting task to sort through and make sense of the hundreds of correlations presented to make the case for the test's validity.

Development of the EDI-3 presents a classic example of multiple approaches to test development. First, a pool of items was developed by clinicians familiar with eating disorders: the content approach. Next, these items were subjected to criterion-keying by contrasting item responses of an eating disorder group and a nonpatient group. Furthermore, item-subscale correlations were determined to help ensure subscale homogeneity. This is essentially similar to a factor analytic approach; in fact, factor analysis was subsequently conducted to confirm the relative independence of the subscales and the coherence of composites.

Complementing the main form of the test is a Symptom Checklist (EDI-3 SC) that inquires about such matters as dieting, exercise, and (for females only) menstrual history. New with the third edition is the EDI-3 Referral Form. This is essentially a short form, consisting of 25 items from the main test, and is intended as

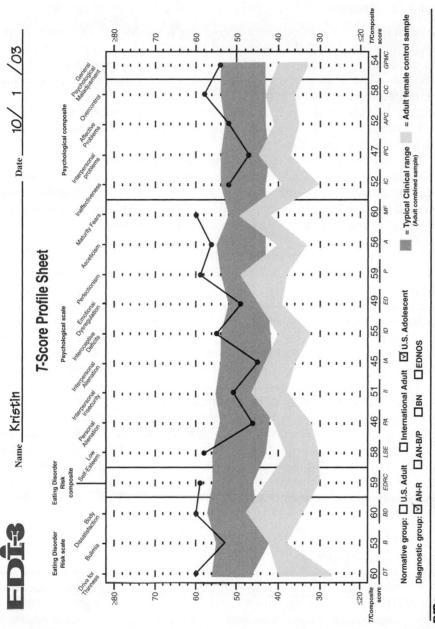

FIGURE 13.2 Sample Profile for the EDI-3.

Source: Reproduced by special permission of the Publisher, Psychological Assessment Resources, Inc., 16204 North Florida Avenue, Lutz, Florida 33549, from The Eating Disorder Inventory–3, by David M. Garner, Ph.D, Copyright © 1984, 1991, 2004 by PAR, Inc. Further reproduction is prohibited without prior permission from PAR, Inc.

a quick screening device to detect cases warranting more detailed assessment with the full EDI-3.

State-Trait Anxiety Inventory

Our final example of a specific domain instrument is the *State-Trait Anxiety Inventory* (**STAI**; Spielberger, 1983). Piotrowski and Lubin (1990) report that the STAI is easily the most widely used instrument for the assessment of anxiety by health psychologists. The STAI is also one of the most widely cited tests in the professional literature related to all types of tests (Plake & Impara, 1999). As indicated by the test's title, the STAI attempts to distinguish between state anxiety (S-anxiety)—a temporary, transitory condition—and trait anxiety (T-anxiety)—a more permanent, enduring personality characteristic.

The STAI uses 20 items on one side of the test form to measure S-anxiety and another 20 items on the other side of the form to measure T-anxiety. The items are highly similar, although item analysis data used for item selection identified some differentiation in the nature of the items. Table 13.12 shows sample items from the S-anxiety (item 6) and T-anxiety (item 32) scales. The table also shows the response formats for the items.

The crucial difference between the two sets of items is in the directions for responding. For the S-anxiety items, examinees respond in terms of "how you feel *right now*, that is, *at this moment*." For T-anxiety items, examinees respond in terms of "how you *generally* feel." The manual notes that for the S-anxiety items, examinees can be asked to respond in terms of a particular situation other than "right now," for example, how they feel just before an exam. Item responses are scored 1–4, then summed to yield a total score for each scale. For most items, a high frequency response indicates anxiety, but for some items a low frequency response indicates anxiety; hence item response weights are reversed for these items. Total scores on each scale can range from 20 (low anxiety) to 80 (high anxiety). Average scores for high school students, college students, and working adults tend to be in the 35–40 range. The STAI does not use any validity indexes. Rather, the manual simply suggests that the administrator establish rapport with examinees and emphasize the importance of responding honestly. The manual also suggests that if the circumstances are such that less than forthright responses might be expected, then the STAI should be supplemented with a test that does have validity indexes.

TABLE 13.12   *Sample Items from the STAI*

	Not at All	Somewhat	Moderately	Very Much So
6. I feel upset.	[1]	[2]	[3]	[4]
	Almost Never	Sometimes	Often	Almost Always
32. I lack self-confidence.	[1]	[2]	[3]	[4]

Source: Reproduced by special permission of the Publisher, Mind Garden, Inc., Menlo Park, CA, USA www.mindgarden.com from the State-Trait Anxiety Inventory by Charles D. Spielberger. Copyright © 1983 by Charles D. Spielberger. All rights reserved. Further reproduction is prohibited without the Publisher's written consent.

The STAI is designed for use with high school students, college students, and adults. There is also a *State-Trait Anxiety Scale for Children* (STAI-C; Spielberger, 1973); we do not include that test in our comments here. Norms—percentile ranks and T-scores—are provided for a variety of convenience samples, including high school students, college students, military recruits, normal adults, neuropsychiatric patients, general medical and surgical patients, and prison inmates. The labeling of the STAI norms offers an excellent example of the need to be alert to spotting norms based on convenience samples. For example, the norms for "college students" are based entirely on students in an introductory psychology course at one institution. The norms for "normal adults" are based entirely on employees in one federal agency.

Development of the STAI is an interesting case of how an instrument evolves through a series of refinements based primarily on item analysis procedures. Each stage of analysis leads to adjustments in pursuit of the test's purpose, in this case to distinguish between state and trait anxiety. Internal consistency (alpha) reliability for the S-anxiety and T-anxiety scales for a variety of samples averages .90 or better. This is not surprising since the developmental research for the test involved exceptional efforts to ensure high item-test correlations. The STAI provides a good case study of how it is possible to obtain high internal consistency reliability by testing a well-defined construct and using appropriate item analysis procedures.

Consideration of test-retest reliability for the STAI presents an unusual case. One would hope for high test-retest reliability for the T-anxiety scale. However, if S-anxiety really is a transitory phenomenon, one would not expect it to have high test-retest reliability. Indeed, this is what tends to happen. For a variety of samples, test-retest reliabilities for T-anxiety tend to be about .75, whereas for S-anxiety test-retest reliabilities tend to be about .30. Ordinarily, a test-retest reliability of .30 would be a shocking, psychometric disaster. However, given the rationale for the S-anxiety measure, this level of test-retest reliability seems understandable, perhaps even desirable.

Validity data for the STAI fall into four major categories. First, there are correlations with other tests, especially those purporting to measure anxiety. Second, there are group contrasts, especially for groups in which it could be argued that there should be different patterns for S- and T-anxiety scores. Third, there are studies of the effects of temporary stressors, especially to show that S-anxiety scores elevate while T-anxiety scores remain stable in such situations. Finally, there are factor analytic studies designed to show separation of the S- and T-anxiety items. It is hardly surprising that some researchers doubt the validity of separating state and trait anxiety. Hence, the STAI manual goes to considerable length in addressing this issue. For reviews of the STAI, see Chaplin (1984), Dreger (1978), and Katin (1978).

Behavior Rating Scales

We turn now to a group of clinical instruments that merit their own category. **Behavior rating scales (BRSs)** have become widely used for determining such conditions as attention disorders, hyperactivity, depression, and assorted emotional

TABLE 13.13   *Examples of Items and Ratings Typical of Behavior Rating Scales*

This child ...	0 Never	1 Sometimes	2 Often	3 Always
1. Hits other kids	0	1	2	3
2. Fidgets	0	1	2	3
3. Does sloppy work	0	1	2	3
4. Cries	0	1	2	3
5. Screams at others	0	1	2	3
6. Completes work late	0	1	2	3
7. Makes strange noises	0	1	2	3
8. Squirms when seated	0	1	2	3

problems. The BRS has two essential features. First, someone other than the person being evaluated completes the rating. Typically, the "someone else" is a teacher, parent, or other caregiver. In this way, a BRS is much like the adaptive behavior scales discussed in connection with mental retardation in Chapter 8. The only difference is that the adaptive scale aims at functional skills such as eating and simple consumer skills, whereas the BRS aims at problem behaviors, such as hyperactivity.

The second essential feature is that the BRS, as suggested by the title, lists specific behaviors. This is also similar to the adaptive behavior scale. The person completing the form indicates the frequency of observing the behavior. The behavioral descriptors are usually short: one to three words. Table 13.13 shows typical descriptors that might appear in a BRS. Notice that the items try to concentrate on specific, observable behaviors. In contrast, self-report inventories, such as the BDI and EDI, often concentrate on feelings or perceptions. The BRS ratings are made on 3–5 points scales, typically ranging from "Never–Always" or "Definitely Not True–Definitely True." The right-hand part of Table 13.13 shows such a rating scheme.

It is convenient to consider two broad groups of BRSs. The first group includes several multi-score systems. These systems attempt to cover a multitude of conditions, typically yielding a dozen or more scores. The second group includes instruments that target just one area. Let us briefly describe examples from each category.

Multi-score Systems

There are three widely used multi-score behavior rating scales (see Table 13.14). Additional multi-score systems may be used, but these three get most of the action. We sketch here the common features of these scales rather than giving detailed descriptions of any one of them. For detailed treatment of any of these scales, see Ramsay, Reynolds, and Kamphaus (2002) and Andrews, Saklofske, and Janzen (2001). Also see the manuals for the separate scales (Conners, 2001; Achenbach,1991; and Reynolds & Kamphaus, 2004).

TABLE 13.14 *The Three Widely Used Multi-Score Behavior Rating Scales*

Title	Acronym
Behavior Assessment System for Children	BASC
Child Behavior Checklist	CBCL
Conners' Rating Scale	CRS

Each of the multi-score systems is actually a collection of several instruments. Typically, the system has separate scales to be completed by parents, teachers, and the child. The children's forms are actually like the self-report instruments described earlier. That is, the child is describing himself or herself. The parent and teacher forms call for rating the child's behavior. In addition, some of these multi-score systems have long forms and short forms, as well as levels for younger and older children. Thus, reference to using "the Conners" or "the BASC" can be ambiguous. It could mean a parent's long form or short form, a teacher's long form or short form, or a child self-report. We need to be careful about such references.

The most important feature of the multi-score systems is their attempt to cover many problem areas. Some of the forms yield several dozen scores. Table 13.15 lists areas commonly covered by these multi-score systems. Of course, each system has its own unique set of scores, but, the areas listed in the table give the flavor of these multi-score systems.

TABLE 13.15 *Examples of Areas Covered in Multi-Score Behavior Rating Scales*

Aggression	Anger
Anxiety	Depression
Hyperactivity	Inattention
Opposition	Withdrawal

Single-area Scales

There are numerous single-area behavior rating scales; their items and response scales are of the same type as those listed in Table 13.13. However, as suggested by the title "single-area," they concentrate on just one problem area—for example, inattention. Thus, they tend to be much shorter than the multi-score systems. Whereas a multi-score instrument may have about 100 items, a single-area scale may have only 20 items. Although each of these single-area scales concentrates on just one area, the scale may actually yield several scores. However, the scores are closely related, for example, covering different aspects of hyperactivity or depression. Like the multi-score systems, the single-area scales are typically completed by a teacher, parent, or other caregiver.

Among the most widely used single-area scales are the *ADHD Rating Scale IV* (DuPaul, Power, Anastopoulos, & Reid, 1998) and the *ADHD Symptom Checklist—4* (Gadow & Sprafkin, 1997). As suggested by their titles, these scales focus on attention deficit/hyperactivity disorder. Each requires only about 10 minutes to complete. The types of items are like those in Table 13.13 but are limited to behaviors in the ADHD syndrome. For useful, brief descriptions of single-area behavior rating scales, see Volpe and DuPaul (2001).

Behavior rating scales, both multi-score systems and single-area scales, are now widely used in educational settings. They help identify children with special problems, quantify the extent of the problem, and serve as a follow-up measure to show progress in alleviating the problem.

Behavioral Assessment

Behavioral assessment is not a specific test. Nor is it a particular method such as multiple-choice items or projective techniques. Rather, behavioral assessment represents a general approach or even a philosophy about gathering information for important human characteristics. The "behavioral assessment argument" goes like this. If we want information about depression, phobias, or anxiety, why ask a series of test questions that provide only indirect information about these characteristics? Why not observe the characteristics directly? For example, observe instances of depressed behavior. Observe phobic behavior. Observe instances of anxiety in a social setting. Proponents of behavioral assessment contrast it with *traditional assessment*, which in this context means assessment with tests, such as the MMPI-2, the NEO PI-R, or the Rorschach. The behavioral assessment theory has three main principles. First, think of overt behaviors rather than underlying traits. Second, to measure a particular kind of behavior, get as close to that behavior as possible. Also, note the immediate antecedents and consequences of the behavior—what comes just before and after the behavior. Third, try to relate the measurement as much as possible to what you want to do with the information. For example, if you measure something to remedy a problem, tie the measurement to the method for remediation. The first two principles are the most important ones from a theoretical perspective. The third principle is most important from a practical perspective. It is particularly apt for clinical uses of measurement. Behavioral assessment has great intuitive appeal, perhaps deceptively so.

Behavioral assessment traces its roots to two streams of thought within psychology. First, it was a reaction against psychodynamic theories, with their emphasis on remote roots of problems. For example, the psychodynamic clinician would look for the roots of a phobia in the person's childhood. Reacting against this theory, clinicians began to think perhaps one could eliminate the phobia without delving into childhood. Simultaneously, there was growing impatience with the highly generalized traits measured by some paper-and-pencil tests and by projective techniques. These were some of the same concerns as expressed earlier that led to environmental assessment. For example, Mischel's (e.g., 1968) theories were as important to behavioral assessment as to environmental assessment. Second, behavioral assessment

> **Key Points Summary 13.3**
>
> *Major Categories of Behavioral Assessment Techniques*
>
> - Direct/Naturalistic Observation
> - Analogue Behavioral Observation
>   Situational Tests
>   Role-Playing
> - Behavioral Interviewing
> - Self-Monitoring and Self-Report
> - Cognitive-Behavioral Assessment
> - Physiological Measures

developed in conjunction with behavior therapy. This was part of the behaviorist revolution in clinical psychology. It was a matter of bringing the learning theories of Pavlov and Skinner to bear on clinical problems. Extinguish the phobia using Pavlovian principles. Or substitute an alternative response using Skinnerian principles. Using these concepts and techniques for therapy called for different kinds of measures. The clinician needed measures of physiological reactions and counts of specific behaviors, not reflections about an inkblot. To get the flavor of the early writings on behavioral assessment, see Goldfried and Kent (1972) and Goldfried (1976). To see the change in perspective over the years, see the treatment of behavioral assessment in Phares and Trull (1997).

Behavioral assessment seeks to be highly specific to the particular circumstances of each case. Therefore, we do not encounter widely used tests in this area. Rather, we have categories of techniques. The techniques within each category must be tailored to specific cases. In this section, we list the major categories (see Key Points Summary 13.3) and briefly illustrate an application within each. Some of the categories are quite distinctive while others shade off into one another.

Direct or Naturalistic Observation

Direct or naturalistic observation might be called the flagship technique for behavioral assessment. It calls for observing the behavior in the environment in which it naturally occurs. Consider the case of a child manifesting aggressive behavior in school. We might have an observer in a classroom noting the frequency, type, duration, and intensity of aggressive behaviors manifested by a child. The school psychologist might use this as baseline information to mark progress in dealing with the case. The psychologist might design a series of reinforcements, both negative and positive, to reduce the target behaviors. Or consider the case of a person petrified by large crowds. We might observe the person as she approaches a crowded area and record exact behaviors while in the situation. After applying some treatment, we might again observe the person in a social setting to see if behavioral change has occurred.

Analogue Behavioral Observation

Direct observation, while appealing, obviously has its drawbacks. It is usually very inconvenient and expensive. Furthermore, we may not know when certain types of behavior will occur. For example, a person may suffer from panic attacks once every two weeks. That can wreak havoc with the person's life, but we do not know exactly when the next attack will occur. A married couple may quarrel once a month, thus threatening the marriage. But we do not know when to watch for the next outburst. **Analogue behavioral observation** attempts to simulate direct observation. Haynes (2001) defined it this way: "Analogue behavioral observation involves the observation of clients (e.g., individual children and adults, families, couples) in an environment that is designed to increase the chance that the assessor can observe clinically important behavior and interactions" (p. 3). We subsume under this category **situational tests** and **role-playing.** A situational test involves placing the person in a situation that approximates one for which we would like to make a prediction. For example, suppose we want to predict how well a person will function in a job that requires working with other people. Of course, we could try to predict this from, say, MMPI scores. The behavioral assessment approach would be to place the person in a simulated committee meeting and see how the person behaves. We might even have confederates in the meeting who deliberately try to provoke the person or get the meeting off track. Then, people within the meeting or external observers could rate the person's functioning within the meeting. The **leaderless group discussion** is one application of this method. Here, the group has a topic to discuss, but there is no one in charge. The situation allows us to observe how a person reacts in that situation. We might be particularly interested in determining whether the person we are assessing asserts some leadership.

In role-playing, as suggested by the name, we ask the person to assume some role. For example, in an assertiveness training program, we might ask the person to be firm and take a stand on some issue in a group setting. We can observe how the person fares with this task, subsequently analyze the experience with the person, and then repeat it to see if progress has been made. Notice that we are not delving into the person's unconscious. We're just trying to assess behavior directly and change it.

Behavioral Interviewing

Interviewing might be a surprise entry in a list of behavioral assessment techniques. In fact, it never occurred in early lists. It is now a standard entry. However, the behavioral interview is quite different from what you may think of as an interview. In the behavioral interview, in accordance with the behavioral assessment principles outlined earlier, the interviewer concentrates on details of specific behaviors. Consider the case of a person who has trouble controlling his or her temper. The interviewer may ask for a specific instance. So, you exploded at your roommate. When did this happen? Was anyone else present? What did your roommate do? What were you doing just before you exploded? How long did the outburst last? And so on. A similarly detailed list of questions might be directed to the panic attack victim. Where were you? What were you doing just before the attack? What time of day was it? And so on. Essentially, the interviewer is trying to approximate direct observation.

Self-Monitoring and Self-Report

Another way to approximate direct observation is to have the person make careful records of behavior. Cone (1999) defines **self-monitoring** as "the act of systematically observing and recording aspects of one's own behavior and internal and external environmental events thought to be functionally related to that behavior" (p. 411), Clinicians clearly use self-monitoring techniques on a routine basis (Korotitsch & Nelson-Gray, 1999). The records might be counts (how many cigarettes smoked in a day) or categories of activities. An interesting example using categories involves the **experience sampling method** (Csikzentmihalyi & Larson, 1987). A person has a list of activity categories. At random times during the day, the person is "beeped." The person records what he or she is doing at that moment. This could be used, for example, with a student to determine how much time the student actually spends in study. With the cigarette count, the goal is to reduce the count. The person might also record what the circumstances were for each light-up. This might help determine what tends to cause an increase in smoking. With the studying activity, the goal is to increase the activity. By noting alternative activities, the student will know what he was doing other than studying. Watching TV or "hanging out with friends" might be the culprit.

Most listings of behavioral assessment techniques include self-report. This comes dangerously close to being a traditional assessment method, such as those reviewed in Chapter 12. In fact, it does demonstrate that behavioral and traditional assessment methods fall along a continuum rather than being entirely different. In the context of behavioral assessment, self-report requires very detailed reporting of behaviors, their antecedents, and circumstances.

Cognitive-Behavioral Assessment

In *cognitive-behavioral assessment* a person's thoughts are treated as behaviors. The basic notion is that the problem is how a person thinks about a situation. If there is a problem, it is probably about these thoughts, not about some external behavior. Fears, low self-esteem, depression: all are matters of a person's thoughts. The remedy is to change the thoughts. So, we want to get the thoughts out in the open. As with the other behavioral assessment techniques, the trick is to be highly specific. One method is the **talk-aloud technique.** The person imagines herself in a phobic situation and verbalizes all her thoughts. A type of behavioral interview may also be used to elicit these thoughts. This may sound very similar to a traditional psychoanalytic interview. The principal difference is in the orientation. The orientation in the cognitive-behavioral setting is toward the here-and-now, rather than to the distant past. The orientation is also toward changing the thought patterns, more or less immediately, rather than toward understanding unconscious processes. For detailed discussion of this method, see Glass and Arnkoff (1997).

Physiological Measures

Physiological measures provide one of the best examples of behavioral assessments. They are a pure behaviorist's delight. According to the pure behaviorist, fear is just a bundle of physiological reactions. So, too, is anxiety. So is love! Hence, if you want to measure fear or anxiety, measure physiological reactions. Consider, for example, a fear of public speaking. This fear comprises an elevated heart rate, increased electro-dermal conduction, constricted pupils, and so on. To deal with this fear, we need to establish a base rate on these measures, use techniques to modify the physiological reactions, and then measure them again. If we are successful, heart rate and conduction go down, the pupils no longer constrict, and so on. Therefore, the fear is gone. We might use biofeedback techniques, along with cognitive-behavioral think-aloud techniques, to accomplish the physiological changes. Notice in this example the interplay of the assessment and the treatment.

Concluding Comments on Behavioral Assessment Methods

Much of the early writing on behavioral assessment, as well as some contemporary work, was excessively optimistic and even naïve. It essentially said: Measure behavior directly and you won't have to worry about matters of reliability and validity. Further, it gave the impression that behavioral assessment was simple. However, it soon became apparent that these measures were often *not* simple and that matters of reliability and validity *were* very important. Behavioral assessment can be very time-consuming and cumbersome.

Proponents of behavioral assessment now realize that their techniques must answer the same questions as traditional measures do. There are the questions of reliability, validity, norms, as well as efficiency and convenience. Current developments within the area show a healthy regard for these concerns, as indicated by the recent Special Issues of *Psychological Assessment* on self-monitoring (Cone, 1999) and analogue behavioral observation (Haynes, 2001).

Trends in the Development and Use of Clinical Instruments

We suggest four major trends in the development and application of the kinds of clinical instruments described in this chapter (see Key Points Summary 13.4). Some of these trends are the same or, at least, similar to trends observed for personality tests in the last chapter. Other trends are distinctly different.

The first trend relates to the increasing dominance of the DSM-IV. Today, nearly all clinical instruments attempt to link results to DSM-IV categories. In fact, some clinical instruments use DSM-IV categories as a starting point. This trend is so obvious and overwhelming that it is easy to overlook.

> **Key Points Summary 13.4**
>
> *Trends in Development and Use of Clinical Instruments*
>
> - Influence of DSM-IV
> - Emphasis on Treatment Planning and Follow-up Evaluation
> - Use of Briefer Instruments
> - Growth in Number of Instruments

Second, although these clinical instruments have a primary orientation toward diagnosis (specifically into DSM-IV categories), there is increasing emphasis on treatment planning and follow-up evaluation. That is, results should not only tell me what's wrong (diagnosis), but also what I should do about it (treatment). During the course of treatment, I should readminister the instrument to see if progress is being made.

Third, a trend toward use of briefer instruments has emerged. To be sure, longer instruments, especially the MMPI-2, are still widely used. However, two forces seem to be encouraging the use of briefer instruments. The first is managed care, with its emphasis on time efficiency (read dollar savings). The second, mentioned in the previous point, is the desire for follow-up evaluation. It is not hard to give (or take) something like the BDI-II several times over a few months. But the MMPI-2 several times?

Finally, as observed for tests of normal personality traits, we are witnessing a veritable explosion in the publication of new (or revised) clinical instruments. This is especially apparent for brief instruments. While it is not child's play to develop and publish a 20-item test focused on one problem area, it is not a gargantuan task. In contrast, development of an MMPI-2 or MCMI requires Herculean effort and resources. This growth in number of new instruments emphasizes the need for professionals to know the fundamental principles applicable to test evaluation, that is, the principles of reliability, validity, and norms.

Summary

1. This chapter examines clinical instruments and methods directed primarily at the identification of psychological disorders. The instruments and methods are similar in some ways and different in other ways from the inventories described in the previous chapter. The similarities include the nature of the items and response formats, the convenient subdivisions for comprehensive and specific domain tests, the strategies for development, and the concern for response sets and faking. The differences center around the general orientation for use,

settings for administration, and concern for diagnosis, treatment planning, and follow-up.

2.   Some type of clinical interview is almost universally used. The traditional, unstructured interview is fraught with technical inadequacies. Structured clinical interviews attempt to alleviate these problems. The most well-known example is the *Structured Clinical Interview for DSM-IV Axis I Disorders* (SCID-I). It attempts to use a careful sequence of standardized questions leading to a DSM diagnostic category. We noted, parenthetically, that much of what was said about the clinical interview applies equally well to the employment interview.

3.   The MMPI-2 is the most widely used self-report instrument for clinical evaluation. Its origin, structure, scores, use in research, and even its vocabulary are legendary in the clinical field. It provides a premier example of criterion-keying in test development, although its current array of scores goes well beyond those arising from criterion keying. It also illustrates very clear application of "validity indexes" and "code types" in the reporting process.

4.   Several other inventories aim to provide comprehensive examination of disorders. First, there is the Millon "family" of inventories, the most widely used being the MCMI-III. It attempts careful articulation with DSM-IV. SCL-90-R is one of the briefer comprehensive inventories; it yields nine primary scores and three global indexes.

5.   We examined three specific domain instruments, each targeting a specific area of psychological problems. The *Beck Depression Inventory* (BDI-II), the most widely used index for symptoms of depression, is a surprisingly brief instrument—just 21 items. The *Eating Disorder Inventory* (EDI-III) attempts to provide information about such disorders as anorexia and bulimia, but also about psychological conditions that may exacerbate or lead to eating disorders. The *State-Trait Anxiety Inventory* (STAI) attempts to distinguish between temporary and more lasting anxiety dispositions.

6.   Behavior rating scales are noticeably different from the other instruments described in this chapter. They are completed by someone other than the person being evaluated, for example, by a parent, caregiver, or teacher. However, as was true for the self-report inventories, the behavior rating scales can be conveniently divided into comprehensive and specific domain instruments.

7.   Behavioral assessment techniques include several methods that attempt to examine behavior more directly than is the case with self-report inventories. We identified the following examples of these techniques: direct or naturalistic observation, analogue behavioral observation, behavioral interviewing, self-monitoring, cognitive-behavioral assessment, and physiological measures. Although such techniques aspire to be more direct measures than are self-report inventories, they must still demonstrate reliability and validity, as well as deal with matters of practicality.

8.   We identified four trends for the clinical instruments described in this chapter. DSM-IV has exerted great influence on the development and structure of these instruments. There is substantial emphasis on treatment planning and follow-up evaluation, partly as a result of the demands of managed care. Perhaps also resulting from those demands, we are seeing increased use of briefer

instruments. Finally, we noted the very great increase in the number of clinical instruments now being developed.

Key Terms

analogue behavioral
  observation
BDI
behavior rating scale
  (BRS)
code type
DSM-IV
EDI

experience sampling
  method
leaderless group
  discussion
MCMI
MMPI
role-playing
SCID

SCL-90-R
self-monitoring
situational test
STAI
structured clinical
  interview
talk-aloud technique

Exercises

1. Here is a set of MMPI-2 T-scores. What is the person's two-point code type?

Scale:	1	2	3	4	5	6	7	8	9	0
T-score:	45	65	50	75	52	48	63	59	48	52

2. Look at the sample of items in Table 13.13, that is, items that might appear in a behavior rating scale. Add five more items to the list. Make sure the items cover specific behaviors, especially behaviors that might be problematic.

3. To access sample reports for MMPI-2 and MCMI-III, go to this website: http://www.pearsonassessments.com/reports/. Examine some reports for each inventory. What do you conclude about the nature of these reports?

4. Look at the item in Table 13.9. What other items, using this same type of format, would you expect to find in a list of symptoms for depression. Make a list of three such items. Then, if you have access to the BDI-II test booklet, check your items against the items actually included.

5. Here is an example of applying behavioral assessment methodology. Identify a topic you find mildly anxiety-inducing, such as public speaking or taking a final exam. Imagine yourself in the situation. Record your exact thoughts. List events immediately preceding the situation. Try to be as specific as possible.

6. Use the ETS Test Collection site (http://sydneyplus.ets.com). Enter as key word(s) a psychological disorder, such as paranoia, anxiety, or depression. How many entries do you get? Can you tell anything about the quality of the tests/inventories from what you get?

Chapter 14

Projective Techniques

Objectives

1. Identify the major characteristics of projective techniques.

2. Describe the projective hypothesis.

3. Identify the major uses of projective techniques and the most frequently used projectives.

4. Outline major features of the Rorschach, including Exner's Comprehensive System.

5. Outline major features of the Thematic Apperception Test.

6. Outline major features of sentence completion and human figure drawing techniques.

7. Discuss factors affecting future use of projective techniques.

Projective techniques constitute one of the most fascinating topics not only in psychological testing but in all of psychology. They are among the most easily recognized symbols of psychology in contemporary society. Who has not encountered reference to an inkblot in a movie, a novel, or a cartoon? Projective techniques are also among the most controversial psychometric topics. To some, they are vilified as nonsense, psuedoscience, something to be consigned to the psychological scrap heap, along with phrenology. To others, they are a rich source of insight, beside which the Yes–No answers to an objective personality inventory are trivial, even demeaning. For good examples of the controversy surrounding projective techniques, see Lilienfeld, Wood, and Garb (2000) and the two Special Sections on the Rorschach in *Psychological Assessment* (Meyer, 1999, 2001). Although the Special Sections concentrate on the Rorschach, many of the arguments—pro and con—generalize to other projective techniques. In this chapter, we explore this intriguing category of tests. We examine the rationale for these techniques, describe their uses, and present examples of the more frequently used methods. We conclude by suggesting some future trends for projective techniques.

FIGURE 14.1 Projective stimuli, occurring in the strangest places, evoke different responses from different people.

Source: Reprinted with permission of offthemark.com, Atlantic Feature Syndicate.

General Characteristics of Projective Techniques and the Projective Hypothesis

Projective techniques have two key features. First, the test items are typically somewhat **ambiguous stimuli.** It is not immediately clear what the test stimulus means. This is in contrast to the items in objective personality tests (e.g., I often feel sad) for which the meaning is reasonably clear (although some might argue that the word "often" is open to interpretation). The second key feature of projective techniques is that they use a *constructed-response format*, also known as a free-response format. This is in contrast to objective personality tests, which use a selected-response format. As we have noted in several places throughout this book, use of constructed-response format creates special challenges for scoring the responses.

The rationale underlying projective techniques is often called the **projective hypothesis.** *If the stimulus for a response is ambiguous, then the response itself will be determined by the examinee's personality dynamics.* Little in the nature of the projective test's stimulus dictates what a reasonable response would be. How, then, does the examinee formulate a response? According to the projective hypothesis, the response will be formulated in terms of the person's desires, fantasies, inclinations, fears, motives, and so on. Thus, it is thought, the projective test is an ideal way of uncovering deep-seated, perhaps unconscious, personality characteristics. The projective test may probe deeply, whereas the objective personality test only touches surface features of the personality—or so the hypothesis goes.

Although it is not part of the projective hypothesis, a psychoanalytic approach to personality exploration is often allied to the hypothesis. Many proponents of projective techniques have come from the psychoanalytic tradition. However, one can advocate the projective hypothesis from other perspectives, too. For example, some version of a gestalt approach, emphasizing the interaction of personality and perception, may be sympathetic to the projective hypothesis.

Uses of Projective Techniques

There are *two principal uses* for projective techniques. First, they are used for the *assessment of individual cases* in clinical, counseling, and school psychology. Second, they are used for *research*. Let us first consider the applied use. According to surveys of psychologists' uses of tests, projective tests receive high rankings with remarkable regularity. Consider these findings. In a survey of psychologists who work with adolescents, Archer, Maruish, Imhof, and Piotrowski (1991) found that 7 of the 10 most frequently used tests were projective techniques. Surveying school psychologists, Kennedy, Faust, Willis, and Piotrowski (1994) found that 6 of the top 10 tests were projective techniques. According to Watkins, Campbell, Nieberding, and Hallmark (1995), among clinical psychologists, 5 of the 7 most frequently used tests are projective techniques. These patterns have been true over a long period of time (Lubin, Larsen, & Matarazzo, 1984) and across a variety of settings (Lubin, Larsen, Matarazzo, & Seever,

TABLE 14.1   *The Eight Widely Used Projective Techniques*

Rorschach Inkblot Test	Sentence Completion Tests
Thematic Apperception Test (TAT)	Human Figure Drawings
Children's Apperception Test (CAT)	House-Tree-Person Test (HTP)
Bender Visual–Motor Gestalt Test	Kinetic Family Drawing Test (KFD)

1985). Even in the face of psychologists' predictions that usage of projective techniques will decline (Piotrowski & Keller, 1984), the most recent surveys show that projectives continue to be widely used (Camara, Nathan, & Puente, 2000).

It will be useful at this point to identify exactly which projective techniques receive high rankings. The following eight "tests" regularly appear high in the rankings: the Rorschach Inkblot Test, the Thematic Apperception Test (TAT), the Children's Apperception Test (CAT), sentence completion tests, human figure drawings, the Bender Visual–Motor Gestalt Test (Bender), the House-Tree-Person (HTP) test, and the Kinetic Family Drawing (KFD) test (see Table 14.1). In fact, virtually no other projective techniques receive high rankings in any of the surveys, although there are many other projective tests.

While not gainsaying the widespread use of projective techniques, there are a number of peculiar features of these tests that probably lead to inflating their position in the rankings of test usage. Consideration of these features actually provides an excellent introduction to the entire field of projective techniques. Hence, we will spend some time exploring these peculiar features. First, psychologists often use a projective technique only in a very informal way. (We expand on this point later.) They may not even score it in any formal sense. They may use only part of the stimulus materials. Some of the test materials may serve an **ice–breaker** function, almost part of a conversation in a clinical interview. This is hardly the concept of a psychological test applied to other types of tests. Most surveys of test usage do not make any distinctions regarding these matters. However, some surveys do make distinctions, and these are revealing. For example, Kennedy et al. (1994) asked respondents to indicate reasons for use of the test. In a significant number of instances, respondents said that a projective test was used as an "ice-breaker." Many respondents also indicated that they did not use "standardized" scoring procedures with the projective tests. For some projectives, a majority of respondents reported use of a "personalized" scoring system, and some reported using no scoring system. In contrast, for objective measures, very few of the respondents reported using the test as an ice-breaker or using anything other than the standardized method of scoring the test. Hence, when asked only whether a particular test is used, a respondent will likely answer "Yes" even if the test is used only informally.

Second, most of the projective techniques have a variety of scoring systems. We explore this point in more detail when we take up several of the projective techniques later in the chapter. Since the scoring system is actually part of the test, each scoring system should be represented as a different test; hence each system should be represented separately in the survey. Someone who is using the Klopfer system to score the Rorschach cards is not using the same test as someone who is using the Exner system to score the Rorschach. Nevertheless, the way most test-usage surveys are conducted, anyone using any system for the Rorschach contributes to the high ranking for the single Rorschach entry on the survey form. The most extreme examples of this phenomenon are the sentence completion and human figure drawing categories. These are not specific tests. There are actually dozens of specific sentence completion tests. In many of the surveys, they are all grouped in one generic category: sentence completions. It may be that no one of these tests has very wide use. However, when they are grouped into a category, the category achieves a high ranking. Similarly, there are many specific human figure drawing tests. Surveys tend to group them all together in a single category, thus yielding a high ranking.

TRY IT!

To appreciate the variety of sentence completion tests currently available, enter the key words SENTENCE COMPLETION in ETS Test Collection (sydneyplus.ets.org). Observe the variety of resulting entries.

Finally, we note that projective techniques are ordinarily used in the assessment of personality variables. However, in some cases they are used for quite other purposes, but even when employed for these other purposes, they still contribute to the high rankings of projectives in comparison with other tests. The best example of this difficulty is the *Bender Visual Motor Gestalt Test,* usually referred to simply as the Bender. Some surveys explicitly classify the Bender as a projective technique (e.g., Piotrowski & Keller, 1984; Watkins et al., 1988), presumably because it is often used to assess personality. However, in some circumstances, the Bender serves primarily as a neuropsychological examination to aid in the detection of brain dysfunction. This bifurcated usage is illustrated in the report by Camara et al. (1998) in which the Bender is highly ranked for *both* personality assessment and neuropsychological assessment. In a similar vein, we note that the most popular form of the human figure drawings test was designed originally to measure intelligence, with a specific point scoring system for this purpose, although today it is used primarily as a projective measure of personality. Thus, the multifaceted use of some of these tests also contributes to the high rankings of projective techniques.

In addition to their use for applied clinical work, projective techniques are widely used for *research.* The research falls into two major categories. First, there is an enormous amount of research on the psychometric characteristics of the projective measures themselves. This research examines the reliability and validity of the techniques and does so with a wide variety of groups. Second, projective techniques are often used as a criterion variable. In this usage, it is assumed that the projective technique possesses acceptable reliability and validity. Then it is used to define variables in the realm of personality or intellectual functioning.

Indicators for the Use of Projectives

For applied work, there are circumstances that may lead a psychologist to prefer use of a projective test to an objective personality test or, at least, to include a projective test in a battery of tests administered to a client. First, most projectives do not require reading. Objective personality inventories typically require reading (although some make provision for reading the items to the examinee). Thus, if the examinee cannot read or reads only at a very low level, a projective test may be desired. Second, although projective tests are susceptible to faking (either good or bad), they are probably more difficult to fake than objective personality inventories. Thus, if it is suspected that the examinee may have strong motivation to fake, a projective test may be preferred. Third, many projective techniques allow for development of an exceptionally broad range of hypotheses about personality dynamics. Thus, if the psychologist has little initial basis for judging a client's difficulty, a projective test may be beneficial.

Administration and Scoring of Projective Techniques: A Forewarning

When a psychologist says that she used the WISC-IV, it is safe to assume that the test was administered according to standard procedures, that the entire test was completed, and that it was scored according to the criteria specified in the WISC manual. If a psychologist is interpreting an MMPI profile, it is safe to assume that the test was scored in the usual manner; in fact, the test was probably scored with a computer program licensed from the test publisher. In contrast, when we hear that a Rorschach or TAT has been administered, we can assume little about what that means. Since directions for administering projective techniques are usually simple, it is likely that a fair approximation of the ordinary directions was used. However, in some instances, not all the stimulus materials are used. For example, of the 20 TAT cards or the 10 Rorschach cards only a few may have been used. Scoring presents a much more varied picture.

Examination of the research literature and descriptions of clinical practice reveal three general approaches to scoring projective techniques (see Key Points Summary 14.1). These three approaches are probably points along a continuum in actual practice. The first approach involves *formal scoring* according to established rules. We can call this the quantitative or psychometric approach. It is the same approach as used in scoring a WISC. It yields specific scores that may be related to norms and are subject to ordinary studies of reliability and validity. At the other extreme, there is the *informal* use that involves no scoring and no definite conclusions.

Key Points Summary 14.1

Three General Approaches to Scoring Projective Tests

1. Formal
2. Informal
3. Holistic/Impressionistic

The projective stimuli are used in much the same way as elements in an interview. In this approach, presenting a few Rorschach cards is roughly equivalent to asking "How are you doing today?" Such usage aims to develop hypotheses that will be pursued more specifically in subsequent work. Hence, this usage is often called hypothesis-generation. For example, the outcome of this informal use may simply be to suggest the need for a specific measure of depression or the need to discuss family relationships. The third approach to scoring a projective technique involves reaching some conclusion, for example, a diagnostic classification based on the *overall impression* given by the examinee's responses rather than through an analysis of specific scores. For example, the clinician administers the Rorschach or Draw-A-Person test in a standardized manner. The formal scoring systems are not applied. However, based on the holistic impression given by the responses, the clinician concludes that the examinee is schizophrenic. This approach is often called holistic or impressionistic scoring.

We will see reference to these different methods of scoring as we examine specific projective techniques in the next several sections. One should also be alert to these different methods when reading journal articles or clinical reports that employ projective techniques.

The Rorschach Inkblot Test

The Rorschach Inkblot Test, also known as the Rorschach Inkblot Method or Rorschach Inkblot Technique, is easily the most widely used projective technique. Quite apart from its specific characteristics, it illustrates many of the problems to be faced by any projective technique. For both reasons, we will spend more time on the **Rorschach** than on other projective techniques covered in this chapter.

The Materials

A variety of techniques employ inkblots as stimulus materials. Clearly the most famous and most widely used are the ones identified with Hermann Rorschach, a Swiss psychiatrist who experimented with a set of inkblots in the early 1900s. Rorschach died at the age of 38, just shortly after his first and only major publication about his work with the inkblots. Rorschach's insightful work was clearly in a preliminary stage when he died. His set of inkblots served as the basis for most of the subsequent work with the inkblot technique. Hence, our presentation concentrates on these Rorschach inkblots.

TRY IT!

Nearly all psychometric novices misspell "Rorschach." Although it does not agree very well with the pronunciation of the name (Roar-schock), you might think of the spelling this way: Rors–ch·a·ch. Getting it right is a sign (albeit a small one) of professional maturity.

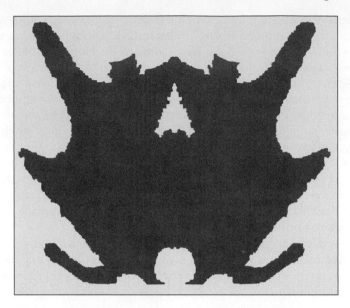

FIGURE 14.2 An inkblot similar to the achromatic Rorschach blots.

Recent surveys of test usage regularly rank the Rorschach among the most frequently used tests (see, e.g., Camara et al., 2000; Frauenhafer et al., 1998). Craig and Horowitz (1990) asked directors of clinical practicum sites to identify tests for which graduate students in clinical psychology should receive training. The Rorschach ranked first in response to this question.

The Rorschach inkblots consist of 10 bilaterally symmetrical blots. (Actually, a few of the cards have very slight asymmetries.) Figure 14.2 shows a blot similar to the first several Rorschach blots. Each blot appears on a rigid piece of cardboard, approximately 6 × 9 inches: about the size of the cover on this book, although not quite as thick. The cards are numbered I, II … X on the back, in the upper right corner. The numbering gives the standard order for presentation of the cards. The placement of the card number allows the cards to be presented to the examinee in a standard orientation. A rather smallish reproduction of Hermann Rorschach's signature also adorns the back of each card in some printings. The Roman numerals on the cards are especially important because the literature on the Rorschach is replete with references to typical or atypical responses to certain cards identified by these numerals. For example, an author may say "the client's response of 'two birds in flight' to Card III is very unusual." The psychologist experienced with the Rorschach can relate to such a statement.

Most simulations of Rorschach inkblots show a solid black blot on a white background, probably because this is very easy to reproduce. Actually, none of the blots are solid black; some have no black in them at all. Five cards (I, IV, V, VI, and VII) are entirely achromatic, containing various shades of gray and some solid black portions. Two cards (II and III) are mostly black and gray but with some blotches of red. The last three cards are entirely chromatic. Two cards (VIII and IX) are muted pastel combinations of pink, green, and orange. The last card (X) is a profusion of pink, blue, yellow, and green.

TRY IT! ....

Actually, *don't try it.* When reading about the various projective techniques presented in this chapter, you may have a nearly irresistible desire to try out projective stimuli on friends and acquaintances and to interpret their personalities based on the responses. Don't do it! It takes advanced training to use these techniques. As a student of psychological testing, you have a special responsibility. A student of biology or history can "fool around" with these techniques harmlessly because no reasonable person would take these students' interpretations seriously. However, if someone knows that you are studying psychological testing, they may believe that you are qualified to make such interpretations. You're not—not until you have studied these procedures far more than you will do in this chapter. As in other chapters, we have a variety of TRY IT exercises sprinkled throughout the text, as well as exercises at the end of the chapter. However, *none* of them asks you to solicit other people's responses to projective stimuli or to analyze other people's personalities.

....

Administration and Scoring

Hermann Rorschach's 1921 book, *Psychodiagnostik,* did not give a standard set of directions for either administering or scoring the 10 inkblots. Following Rorschach's untimely death in 1922, over a period of several decades, a number of American psychologists developed *systems,* that is, directions for administering and scoring, for Rorschach's inkblots. There were five such systems, each identified in the literature with the name of the system's principal architect. The systems included those of Beck (1937), Klopfer (1937; Klopfer & Kelley, 1942), Hertz (1943, 1948), Rapaport (Rapaport, Gill, & Schafer, 1946), and Piotrowski (1937, 1957). Notice that the earliest references for all these systems sprouted in the relatively restricted time period 1937–1946. There was also the Holtzman Inkblot Technique (Holtzman, 1961). Notice that the word "Rorschach" does not appear in the title. This was quite deliberate on Holtzman's part. He wanted to use inkblots but in a quite different way from any of the other Rorschach systems. For example, he allowed only one response to each inkblot. Nevertheless, the Holtzman technique is often lumped together with the other Rorschach systems. Aiken (1999) provides brief but interesting historical sketches for the origins of these systems. Each of these systems gained some currency but none became the industry standard. In fact, having all these partially overlapping yet partially conflicting systems led to confusion. Recall our treatment of the *Wechsler Intelligence Scale for Children* in Chapter 8. Imagine that there were several different sets of directions for administering this test, different ways of scoring responses, and different score profiles for it.

The result would be chaos. That is the situation that prevailed for many years with the Rorschach.

Another American psychologist, John Exner, Jr. (Exner, 2003), produced what is called the **Comprehensive System** for administering and scoring the Rorschach inkblots.[1] Exner attempted to incorporate the best, most defensible, and apparently most fruitful features of all five systems into his Comprehensive System. This system has become the industry standard in recent years. Hiller et al. (1999) referred to the "almost universal adoption of the Exner Comprehensive Sytem for the Rorschach" (p. 292). Hilsenroth and Handler (1995) reported that 75% of graduate students in their study were taught the Exner system for using the Rorschach. This is the system we will describe. However, the reader should be aware that when searching the literature, any one of several alternative systems might be encountered in a particular study. Recall also that, in practice, a psychologist may use a "personalized" system or no system at all.

Procedures for administering the Rorschach in the framework of Exner's Comprehensive System are simple. Administration proceeds in two phases: the response phase (also known as the association or free association phase) and the inquiry phase. In the **response phase,** the Card is handed to the examinee and the examiner asks "What might this be?" If the examinee seeks guidance on how to respond or what is permitted (e.g., turning the card), the examiner is nondirective, using answers such as "It's up to you" or "However you like." If the examinee is overly brief, for example, giving only one-word responses (e.g., "a butterfly"), the examiner encourages fuller responses. For example, the examiner may say, "Most people see more than one thing." Each of the 10 blots in turn is presented with these simple instructions. The examiner is seated next to the examinee side-by-side. The Rorschach card is handed to the examinee.

While the examinee responds to a blot, the examiner records what is being said, as well as noting emotional tonality. Exner emphasizes that responses should be recorded *verbatim*. Response time is also noted. This record will be important not only for subsequent scoring of responses but also for use in the inquiry phase.

In the **inquiry phase,** each of the 10 blots is again presented to the examinee. Now the examiner, using notes from the response phase, asks the examinee to explain and elaborate on answers given in the response phase. The examiner may ask "Show me where you saw the____." Of course, the examiner is also recording the examinee's responses (verbatim) in this second phase. Exner emphasizes that the purpose of the inquiry phase is to aid in coding the responses obtained in the response phase, not to elicit completely new responses.

The record of responses is called the **protocol.** This term is used throughout the literature on most projective techniques. The term is occasionally applied outside

---

[1]We refer here to the fourth edition of Exner's classic book: *The Rorschach: A Comprehensive System: Vol. 1: Basic Foundations and Principles of Interpretation.* The first edition, where the system was first presented, appeared in 1974, the second in 1986, and the third in 1993. Volume 2 (on "advanced interpretations") and Volume 3 (on usage with children and adolescents) appeared in various editions from 1978 to 2005. A thorough treatment of Exner's work requires consulting all these volumes. See also Weiner (2003).

the field of projectives—for example, the protocol of MMPI responses—but, for the most part, it is peculiar to projective methods.

Administration of the Rorschach is exceedingly simple. However, the scoring is decidedly not. In fact, the scoring, officially called **coding** the responses, is very elaborate and detailed. We sketch here just the broad outlines of the Comprehensive System's coding scheme. Consider the following responses to an imaginary blot:

Response phase: I see here what looks like a dead animal, a road-kill kind of thing. And I guess this red is blood, so it must have happened recently. Over on the side here, it looks like something flowing, maybe a puddle running off the road.

Inquiry phase: Here (pointing to the central part of the blot) is the dead animal and here is the blood squirting out. Over here (touching peripheral part of blot) is the water flowing off to the side of the road, probably into a gutter on the side of the road.

What does the psychologist do with these responses? The most important point to understand is that the psychologist does not immediately leap to conclusions based on these responses. The popular image of interpreting Rorschach responses may be a freewheeling approach sprinkled with sudden flashes of insight into the depths of a person's psyche. In practice, however, interpretation, in Exner's Comprehensive System, is based on a very empirical, norm-referenced approach, following a detailed coding procedure. The responses listed previously and responses to each of the other blots are carefully coded. Then certain summations, percentages, and ratios of coded responses are determined. Finally, these summations and ratios are referenced to norms, based on the responses of nonpatient and patient samples. In this sense, interpreting responses to the Rorschach inkblots resembles the criterion-keying procedure we encountered with the MMPI. For example, it may be that a "road-kill" in the central part of this blot is quite common in nonpatient groups. On the other hand, it may be that seeing water flowing from the edge of the blot is not common among nonpatient groups, but is a frequent response of persons suffering unusual familial stress. How would we know that? This is the sort of result that comes from conducting numerous studies of how well-defined groups actually respond to the inkblots. From the single "road-kill" response, we conclude nothing. All the responses must be coded. If the examinee sees dead, squashed animals in most of the cards, that may mean something.

The Coding System

We provide here the broad outline and selected details of the Comprehensive System's coding process. In describing the MMPI-2 in the preceding chapter, we noted that the test has a language all its own. This is even truer of the Rorschach, as will become amply clear when we introduce the coding system. We note, first, that although it is not treated as a coding category, the total number of responses *(R)* is the initial fact determined for the Rorschach protocol. Exner (2003) emphasizes that at least 14 responses should be present for the protocol to be considered

TABLE 14.2. *Examples of Scores in Exner's Comprehensive System*

Primary Categories

Location   Contents
Developmental Quality   Populars
Determinants   Special Scores
Form Quality

Ratios, Percentages, Derivations

Ideation   Processing
Affect   Interpersonal
Mediation   Self-perception

Constellations

Depression Index
Perceptual Thinking Index
Coping Deficit Index
Hypervigilance Index

interpretable. Table 14.2 lists examples of the major coding categories in the Exner system. These are not complete lists, and the lists have changed somewhat over time. At the top of the table, we list primary coding categories.[2] For the most part, these scores are simple counts of responses within codes (example codes are described next). Next, we list ratios, percentages, and derivations. These are transformations of counts in the primary categories. Finally, there are constellations. In general, a constellation is a yes/no indicator (e.g., positive for depression) if a certain number of conditions are met, the conditions arising from items entered in the primary coding categories or in the ratios, percentages, and derivations. It is evident that the coding system is complex and gives rise to a great many scores. We will illustrate a few of the codes and derivations to give the flavor of the system.

The simplest of all the codes, the **location codes,** indicate the part of the card the examinee references. Table 14.3 shows the location codes.

Notice these two features of the location codes. First, one might surmise that the codes would refer to particular locations on the card (e.g., upper left, center, etc.), but they do not. The main distinction in the location codes is whether the response is to the whole blot or just part of it. Second, notice that the distinction between D and Dd is purely empirical. For example, considering the blot in Figure 14.2, if many people refer to the upward extensions, then such a response is coded D. If only a few people reference these extensions, the response is coded Dd. There is no theory involved. How are "many people" (D) or "few people" (Dd) defined? In Exner's system, a detail referenced by *fewer than 5%* of respondents is considered

---

[2] Usage of the term *primary* for these categories is ours, not Exner's. We use this term strictly for pedagogical purposes.

TABLE 14.3   *The Location Codes in the Comprehensive System for the Rorschach*

Symbol	Definition	Criterion
W	Whole response	Where the entire blot is used in the response. All portions must be used.
D	Common detail	A frequently identified area of the blot
Dd	Unusual detail	An infrequently identified area of the blot
S	Space	A white space area is used in the response (scored only with another location symbol as in WS, DS, or DdS)

Source: From Exner, J. E. The Rorschach: A comprehensive system. Volume 1: Basic foundations (4th ed.), p. 77. Copyright © 2003. Reprinted with permission of John Wiley & Sons, Inc.

uncommon. One determines the frequency of various responses by reference to norm tables in Exner's first volume.

TRY IT!

Refer to the response given on pages 528–529 to the blot in Figure 14.2. How would you apply the location codes? Notice first that there are actually two responses ($R = 2$) given by the client.

Codes for determinants are the most complex and extensive of all the codes. There are 9 major categories and 24 subcategories for determinants. Table 14.4 lists the codes for one major category and its subcategories to illustrate these types of codes. Note how specific the instructions are for use of the codes. In general, **determinants** indicate what features of the blot influenced or determined the examinee's responses. For example, to what extent was a response determined by perceived color, movement, animal or human figures, and so on for the other subcategories?

Popular responses are those occurring in at least one-third of the responses to a card in the norm group. This is strictly a norm-referenced coding. The 15 categories of **Special Scores** include such areas as Morbid (MOR; references to death, killing, etc.), Aggressive (Ag; fighting, attacking, etc.), and Cooperative Movement (COP) responses. These codes identify unusual features of responses. They apply only when such unusual features are present and are in addition to the more standard, universally applied codes such as location and determinants.

As indicated earlier, scores in the ratios, percentages, and derivations category arise from combinations of scores in the primary codes. Some of these are very simple, for example, the percentage of responses that are "popular." Others are more complicated, for example, adding several codes with special weights applied to some of the codes.

TABLE 14.4 *Examples of Categories for Coding Determinants in the Comprehensive System for the Rorschach*

Category	Symbol	Criteria
Movement	M	*Human movement response.* Used for responses involving the kinesthetic activity of a human, or of an animal or fictional character in human-like activity.
	FM	*Animal movement response.* Used for responses involving a kinesthetic activity of an animal. The movement perceived must be congruent to the species identified in the content. Animals reported in movement not common to their species should be coded M.
	m	*Inanimate movement response.* Used for responses involving the movement of inanimate, inorganic, or insensate objects.

Source: From Exner, J. E. The Rorschach: A comprehensive system. Volume 1: Basic foundations (4th ed.), p. 87. Copyright © 2003. Reprinted with permission of John Wiley & Sons, Inc.

Sequence of Scores and Structural Summary

The codes previously described are summarized in the Sequence of Scores and Structural Summary. The Sequence of Scores simply lists each card number, response number, and codes for each response. It is important for computer entry of data and for research purposes. It has some potential for interpretation, but it is not a major interpretive vehicle.

The **Structural Summary** is the primary source document for interpretation. It contains summaries of all the codes plus a section of ratios, percentages, and derivations that are derived from the codes. For example, one entry shows the ratio of W:M—that is, the ratio of Whole responses from the location codes to human Movement responses from the determinants codes. The Structural Summary is essentially uninterpretable to anyone without advanced training in Exner's Comprehensive System. Computer-generated narrative reports, similar to those we have examined for the MMPI-2 and several other tests, are now available for the Rorschach.

Although Exner's Comprehensive System emphasizes establishing empirical relationships between personal characteristics and specific codes (and derivatives from them), there are some general themes. For example, "form" responses are particularly relevant for investigating ideation; "color" responses relate more to emotional states.

Evaluation of the Rorschach

The research literature on the Rorschach is so vast that it nearly defies summary. Reading even a sampling of the research is almost like taking a Rorschach: What you see in it may be determined more by personal predispositions than by what is actually there! On the one hand, one can find outright condemnations of the

Rorschach. For example, Hunsley and Bailey (1999) concluded "there is currently no scientific basis for justifying the use of Rorschach scales in psychological assessments" (p. 266). See also Dawes (1994) and Lilienfeld et al. (2000) for unsympathetic treatment of the Rorschach and, in general, all projective techniques. On the other hand, Weiner (2001) retorted that "Hunsley and Bailey's sweeping indictment of Rorschach assessment as failing to meet professional standards of practice, ignoring as it does abundant evidence to the contrary, is without merit" (p. 428). Viglione (1999) concluded: "The evidence reveals that many Rorschach variables are efficient tools for clinical, forensic, and educational applications" (p. 251). Viglione and Hilsenroth (2001) stated that "a large body of empirical evidence supports the reliability, validity, and utility of the Rorschach. This same evidence reveals that the recent criticisms of the Rorschach are largely without merit" (p. 452). Based on meta-analysis comparing validity coefficients for 31 MMPI studies and 34 Rorschach studies, Hiller et al. (1999) concluded that the validity data were approximately equal for these two well-known instruments, although validity coefficients were, on average, very modest for both tests. Atkinson (1986) and Parker, Hanson, and Hunsley (1988) also concluded that the Rorschach was approximately equivalent to the MMPI in validity. Needless to say, the debate over the Rorschach is vigorous.

For further review of the Rorschach, consult the following sources. Groth-Marnat (2003) provides a thorough, chapter-length review of research on the Rorschach, with an excellent chronology of the various phases in development of the test. Erdberg (1996) gives a generally sympathetic review, along with an exposition of clinical applications of the test. Dana (1978) presents the Buros MMY review. In *Test Critiques,* Lerner and Lerner (1985) note the "significant resurgence of the use of the Rorschach Inkblot Test" (p. 523); they related this resurgence to recent developments in personality theories.

How do we make sense out of all these conflicting conclusions? To provide perspective, we note that, just as for any test, one must concentrate on specific scores, not the test as a general technique. With that in mind, we venture the following generalizations. First, application of the Exner system clearly results in generating reliable scores for many, though not all, variables. For example, see Tables 11.3 and 11.4 in Exner (2003, pp. 179–180). Application of "personalized" systems leaves us with no conclusion. Second, validity data vary enormously. Hiller et al. (1999), Viglione (1999), Atkinson (1986), Parker et al. (1998), and Atkinson et al. (1986) have certainly identified numerous studies that showed significant validity for a variety of Rorschach scores. There are also numerous studies that have come up empty-handed when attempting to demonstrate Rorschach validity. Overall, we conclude that when the test is administered and scored in a standardized manner, it certainly can produce some respectable validity evidence. One crucial question is raised by Dawes (1994): Does the Rorschach have any *incremental validity*? Recall our discussion of the concept of incremental validity on pages 182–183. In a related vein, we need to ask whether the time and expense of administering and scoring the Rorschach is worth it. Does it add significantly to the information one can get from an easily administered MMPI or even a simple 10-minute conversation with a client? Of course, this is a crucial question for any test, but it is particularly relevant for the Rorschach because of the time and cost involved in use of this test.

Thematic Apperception Test (TAT)

The Thematic Apperception Test (**TAT**; Murray, 1943) is the second most widely used projective technique, according to several surveys of test usage (Camara et al., 2000; Piotrowski & Keller, 1984, 1989; Wade & Baker, 1977). It has ranked as a "top ten" test over a long period of time (Lubin, Larsen, & Matarazzo, 1984). In terms of importance for training of counseling psychologists, the TAT outranked the Rorschach in the projective category. However, there is some evidence that its use has slipped in recent years (Dana, 1996).

The TAT consists of 30 cards, 29 of which contain a picture and one of which is entirely blank. Each card is 9 × 12 inches in dimension; the picture covers only about two-thirds of the card. Figure 14.3 shows an actual TAT card (reduced in size). The pictures were deliberately selected to be ambiguous, although obviously not as ambiguous as an inkblot.

Not all TAT cards are intended for use with all examinees. The intended use differs for boys, girls, men, and women. Eleven cards, including the blank, are intended for all examinees, seven are for boys and men only, seven for girls and women only, and one card each for other subsets, for example, women only. A code on the back of the card identifies the intended target group, for example, 12BG is card 12 aimed at boys and girls, while card 12M is aimed at adult men.

FIGURE 14.3   Example of TAT card: Card 12F.

Source: Reprinted by permission of the publishers from Henry A. Murray, THEMATIC APPERCEPTION TEST, 12F, Cambridge, Mass.: Harvard University Press, Copyright © 1943 by the President and Fellows of Harvard College, Copyright © 1971 by Henry A. Murray.

Twelve TAT cards depict one person, eleven have two people, five have more than two people, and two have no people. Most of the pictures have a shadowy, some would say gloomy, appearance. (One must be careful in characterizing the pictures lest the description be taken as a projective response!)

The TAT originated in the work of Henry Murray (Murray et al., 1938), who postulated a set of psychological needs (affiliation, autonomy, aggression, etc.) and presses (environmental forces). Murray believed that responses to the ambiguous TAT pictures would help to reveal a person's dominant needs and presses.

The original directions for administering the TAT were as follows (Murray et al., 1938, p. 532):

> The subject [is] seated in a comfortable chair with his back to the experimenter and the following directions [are] read to him:

> This is a test of your creative imagination. I shall show you a picture and I want you to make up a plot or story for which it might be used as an illustration. What is the relation of the individuals in the picture? What has happened to them? What are their present thoughts and feelings? What will be the outcome? Do your very best. Since I am asking you to indulge your literary imagination you may make your story as long and as detailed as you wish.

In Murray's original scheme, each examinee would respond to 20 cards. The average response time to a card was 5 minutes, thus requiring about 100 minutes or almost two hours, to be divided into two testing sessions.

Administrative arrangements for the TAT are, unfortunately, quite varied in practice. First, while a full administration calls for use of 20 cards requiring two one-hour testing periods, almost no one now uses a full set of 20 cards with an individual examinee. Hence, comparing results across examinees is difficult. Second, exact instructions may vary from one examiner to another. It appears that most examiners use an approximation of Murray's instructions given earlier, but there is still considerable variety in practice. Many users find the statement that this is a test of creative imagination to be deceptive and, therefore, do not use that part of the directions. In nearly all situations, the examiner asks for a story that tells what is happening, what leads up to this, and what might happen next. If necessary, examinees are encouraged to identify the thoughts and feelings involved in the picture. As with the Rorschach, more rather than less is desired in the response. Finally, we note that whereas Exner's Comprehensive System has emerged as the industry standard for administration and scoring the Rorschach, no comparable system has emerged for the TAT.

The most influential contemporary work on the TAT is that of Leopold Bellak. His book, now in its sixth edition (Bellak & Abrams, 1997), serves as the "real" TAT manual for many users. Bellak has tried to do for the TAT what Exner did for the Rorschach: systematize the administration and scoring; and conduct the necessary psychometric research. Bellak recommends the use of exactly 10 cards (1, 2, 3BM, 4, 6BM, 7GF, 8BM, 9GF, 10, and 13MF). The Bellak Scoring System has specific scoring categories, including such variables as main theme, main hero, and main needs and drives of the hero. These specific categories are in contrast to a purely impressionistic use of responses to the cards. Bellak's approach has a distinctly psychoanalytic flavor. At the same time, this work unabashedly espouses a hard-nosed psychometric attack on matters of reliability, validity, and norms. Bellak's benchmark book also treats two spinoffs from the TAT: the *Children's Apperception Test* (CAT) and the *Senior Apperception Test* (SAT). Anyone with serious interest in the TAT should consult Bellak's work.

TAT responses may be written rather than spoken. Oral responses are the norm for clinical usage. Written responses are sometimes encountered for research purposes. Written responses have the obvious advantage of allowing for group administration and use of larger samples for research. However, there are systematic differences between oral and written responses (see, e.g., Dana, 1996).

What does research say about the psychometric characteristics of the TAT? Due to the diversity of administrative and scoring procedures for the TAT, it is considerably more difficult to develop generalizations for the TAT than for the Rorschach or the RISB (covered in the next section). Researchers have established respectable reliability and validity when using the TAT for well-defined constructs. The work of McClelland and Atkinson with the constructs of achievement motivation and affiliation illustrate this generalization (see Atkinson, 1958; McClelland, 1985; McClelland, Atkinson, Clark, & Lowell, 1953; Spangler, 1992). However, these results have been attained mostly in settings atypical of ordinary clinical practice, which is the primary application site for the TAT. Overall, reviewers have not been kind to the TAT. Although noting that the TAT is a potentially rich source of information, nearly everyone decries the lack of standardization in administration and scoring.

What do we learn from our examination of the TAT? First, obtaining responses to ambiguous pictures has proved to be a very popular device with psychologists. There is, apparently, a deep-seated feeling that such a technique allows the projective hypothesis to operate. The popularity of the TAT over a long period of time is quite remarkable. Second, we observe that usage of the TAT seems to be waning. Why? Almost certainly the decline is attributable to the lack of a systematic scoring system (Dana, 1996). Psychologists have paid increasing attention to the need for solid reliability, validity, and normative information about tests. In the absence of a dominant, clearly defined scoring system, it is difficult to accumulate the reliability, validity, and normative data required for contemporary test usage. Lacking standardization, it will probably continue to move toward the periphery of the world of testing, not quickly, but inexorably. For reviews of the TAT, see Ryan (1985), Swartz (1978), Dana (1996), and Groth-Marnat (2003). Dana's and Groth-Marnat's treatments are especially complete and informative regarding contemporary usage of the TAT. Smith's (1992) selections provide a useful summary of research for the TAT and TAT-like procedures. Gieser and Stein (1999) give a useful collection, especially for historical perspective on the TAT. Of course, Bellak and Abrams (1997) should also be consulted.

Rotter Incomplete Sentences Blank (RISB)

As noted earlier in this chapter, there are many specific examples of incomplete sentence tests. A recent check with the ERIC Test Locator and the ETS Test Collection Database revealed over 30 such tests. One of these stands out from the others in terms of frequency of use, the extent of its research base, and general reputation: the *Rotter Incomplete Sentences Blank,* Second Edition (**RISB**; Rotter, Lah, & Rafferty, 1992). The current edition differs minimally from the first edition (Rotter & Rafferty, 1950) in terms of purpose, structure, and sentence stems. However, the test manual has been thoroughly updated, especially by summarizing the vast amount of research conducted with the RISB over the 40 years between editions. The revised manual also includes improved scoring guides and new norms.

There are three forms of the RISB: high school, college, and adult. (The RISB uses the term *form* to refer to different levels of the test rather than in the sense of alternate, roughly equivalent forms.) The college form was the original form and is the one on which the most research has been conducted. The high school and adult forms differ from the college form only in a few item stems. We will return to this matter of the forms later. In the meantime, unless otherwise noted, we discuss the college form.

The RISB consists of 40 incomplete sentences or *stems.* The stems are typically only two words in length, sometimes only one word, with a few garrulous four- or five-word stems. Table 14.5 shows two item stems from the RISB. As shown here, the test sheet provides only one line for the examinee's response to each item stem. The entire set of items, including space for responses, fits on the front and back of one sheet of $8\frac{1}{2} \times 11''$ paper. Directions are very simple. The examinee is asked to express "your real feelings" in a complete sentence for each item. The examinee usually completes the form in 20 to 25 minutes.

TABLE 14.5   *Sample Items from the RISB*

5. I regret _____
10. People _____

Source: Rotter, J. B., Lah, M. I., & Rafferty, J. E. Manual: Rotter Incomplete Sentences Blank, 2nd Ed. Copyright © 1992 by Harcourt Assessment, Inc. Reproduced by permission. All rights reserved.

The RISB differs from other frequently used projective techniques, for example, the Rorschach and TAT, in two important ways. First, the physical arrangement of the test encourages a concise response to each item. It is conceivable that an examinee could ramble on when completing a sentence, but this is unlikely to happen. In contrast, examinees are encouraged to be expansive when responding to the Rorschach or TAT.

Second, the RISB purports to measure only one construct: *adjustment* (or, its polar opposite, maladjustment). Consistent with that unitary purpose, the RISB yields only one score: the Overall Adjustment Score. The test manual defines adjustment as:

> the relative freedom from prolonged unhappy/dysphoric states (emotions) of the individual, the ability to cope with frustration, the ability to initiate and maintain constructive activity, and the ability to establish and maintain satisfying interpersonal relationships. (Rotter et al., 1992, p. 4)

Maladjustment, of course, is defined as the opposite of these characteristics.

Each item in the RISB is scored for signs of adjustment/maladjustment on a 7-point scale (0–6). On this scale, 6 indicates the most severe maladjustment, 0 indicates a very positive, healthy response, and 3 represents a "neutral" response, signifying neither good nor poor adjustment. The sum of item scores is prorated for omitted responses. Scores on individual items are added to yield the Overall Adjustment Score, which can range from 0 (very well adjusted) to 240 (extremely maladjusted, i.e., scored 6 on each item). In the norm groups, most Overall Adjustment Scores fall in the range from about 100 to 170. Note that "neutral" responses to all items would yield a total score of $3 \times 40 = 120$. The mean score for the norm groups (see later) is about 130.

TRY IT!

For each of the two item stems in Table 14.5, write completions that you believe indicate a moderate degree of adjustment—a score of 2 on the 7-point scale. Then write completions you believe indicate a moderate degree of maladjustment—score of 5 on the 7-point scale.

The RISB manual provides detailed guidelines for scoring items. It gives the general rationale for scoring, sample responses for each scoring weight on each item (separately for men and women), and an appendix with six practice-scoring cases. With respect to scoring, the RISB manual is reminiscent of the manuals for individual intelligence tests like the Wechsler scales.

The RISB manual summarizes numerous studies of the reliability and validity of the Overall Adjustment Score. Inter-scorer reliability, of course, as with other projective measures, is a matter of special concern. Several studies reported in the manual document that, indeed, the test has good inter-scorer reliability, averaging around .90. Internal consistency reliability (split-half and Cronbach's alpha) average around .80. Retest reliability coefficients are quite variable, depending on the test-retest interval. For intervals of 1–2 weeks, the coefficients approximate the internal consistency reliabilities. For intervals of several months to several years, the coefficients plummet to an average of around .50. The situation reminds us of the reliability for the *State-Trait Anxiety Inventory* (see Chapter 13). It appears that adjustment, as measured by the RISB, is a reasonably stable *state*, but not a very stable *trait*. The RISB manual contains a forthright discussion of this matter.

A host of validity studies have been conducted with the RISB. The manual presents a comprehensive review of these studies. They include investigations involving contrasts between known groups; correlations with other measures of adjustment, anxiety, and other personality constructs; factor analyses; and relationships with intelligence and achievement. In general, the validity studies support the proposition that the RISB measures the construct of adjustment, although, as is typical with psychological tests, the evidence from any one study is not definitive. The strength of the RISB manual is that it presents many studies, thereby giving the user an appropriate context for drawing conclusions.

As an outgrowth of one of the contrasted group validity studies reported in the manual, a cutoff score of 145 is suggested for identifying maladjusted cases. However, the basis for the contrast—self-referrals to a counseling center versus a general college sample—is not a strong one. This suggested cutoff score is approximately one standard deviation above the mean score for the norm groups.

The RISB manual presents gender-specific norms based on 110 females and 186 males from three studies conducted with different samples from 1977 to 1989. The manual gives little information about the nature of these samples. Furthermore, no norms are given for the high school or adult forms of the test. For a test as widely used as the RISB, we would expect more: both numbers of cases and information about the cases in the norm groups. The manual does provide means and standard deviations for a host of published studies, but this is not an adequate substitute for a decent set of norms. Even the norms that are given are simply cumulative percentages for 5-point intervals of Overall Adjustment Scores. The manual recommends developing local norms. That is a useful practice only if the definition of adjustment/maladjustment differs substantially from one local population to another, a dubious proposition.

One of the peculiar features of the RISB as a projective technique is that it steadfastly purports to measure *only one variable: adjustment*. Most projective techniques purport to measure a multitude of variables. Can the RISB be used to measure anything other than adjustment? People have certainly tried to do so. The RISB manual identifies 15 studies that have attempted to use the test to measure dozens of other variables (e.g., death anxiety, dependency, hostility, etc.). The RISB manual takes an arm's-length approach to these studies, neither decrying nor endorsing the efforts to measure other variables, but simply noting that the efforts have been made.

What do we learn from examining the RISB? There are, at least, the following lessons. First, it is clear that one can develop quite specific scoring criteria for a projective stimulus. Second, good inter-rater reliability can be achieved with these criteria. The first two generalizations are certainly similar to lessons learned from our examination of Exner's work with the Rorschach. Third, to accomplish the two latter objectives, it is important to have a construct clearly in mind. In the case of the RISB, the construct is adjustment/maladjustment. Fourth, this trait (adjustment), as measured by the RISB, appears to be stable over short periods of time, but not very stable over periods exceeding a few months. The trait is not completely unstable, like a sand castle in high tide, but it does not evidence the long-term stability of such human traits as verbal intelligence. Finally, we observe the need for well-established norms and cutoff score(s) for a test like this.

For reviews of the RISB, Second Edition, see Boyle (1995) and McLellan (1995). Cosden (1985) reviews the RISB, First Edition. Oddly, despite the widespread use of sentence completion techniques, two of the best reference works on widely used tests (Groth-Marnat, 2003; Newmark, 1996) do not include chapters on either the RISB or sentence completion techniques in general.

Human Figure Drawings

Perhaps more so than for any other area of testing, the area of human figure drawings is populated by initials—sometimes in a very confusing manner (see Table 14.6). At the most specific level, we have **HTP** (or H-T-P) for the House-Tree-Person Test and **KFD** for the Kinetic Family Drawing Test. Each is briefly described. These tags usually do not present any identity problems. Then there is the **DAP** (or D-A-P) standing for the Draw-A-Person Test. This is often ambiguous. The initials may represent a specific test, or they may cover all the tests that call for drawing individual persons. In this usage, DAP includes the Draw-A-Man Test—the forerunner of all these tests—that, interestingly, never seems to be abbreviated as DAM! Finally, we encounter **HFD,** standing for human figure drawings. Sometimes this designation includes all projective drawings that include humans, thus encompassing DAP, HTP, KFD, and several other variations. At other times, HFD is equivalent to the generic DAP, that is, including all drawings of individual people. Still other times HFD references a specific Draw-A-Person Test.

Human figure drawings regularly appear near the top of any ranking of test usage. Before commenting further on the frequency of the use of this projective technique, we should reiterate a point made earlier. There are a variety of specific tests that involve drawing human figures. Such drawings constitute a general technique, not a specific test. However, many surveys of test usage group all the specific approaches under the single title "human figure drawings" or "draw a person," thus obscuring exactly what tests are used. Furthermore, psychologists employ human figure drawings for an exceptionally wide range of purposes, including assessment of personality, intelligence, and neuropsychological dysfunction. These factors complicate our understanding of ordinary use of human figure drawings.

With the latter cautions in mind, we note the following results for human figure drawings in surveys of test usage. In surveys of clinical, counseling, and school psychologists, human figure drawings are identified as among the most frequently used tests (see Archer et al., 1991; Camara et al., 2000; Hutton et al., 1992; Kennedy et al., 1994; Piotrowski & Keller, 1984). When the tests are separately identified, the DAP is usually the most widely used, followed closely by the HTP. The DAP usually follows the Rorschach and TAT (and sometimes sentence completions) in frequency of use among the projective tests, although in some instances the DAP even outranks these two stalwarts.

TABLE 14.6 *Common Abbreviations Used with Projective Drawings*

HFD	Human Figure Drawings
DAP or D-A-P	Draw-A-Person
HTP or H-T-P	House-Tree-Person Test
KFD	Kinetic Family Drawing Test

TRY IT! ....

To gain an appreciation of the variety of specific tests involving human figure drawings, enter the key words "Draw A Person" in the ETS Test Collection (sydneyplus.ets.org) or in a literature database such as PsycInfo. Note the number of different tests that these key words retrieve.

....

The first widely used human figure drawing test was Florence Goodenough's (1926) Draw-A-Man Test. This test was intended as a nonverbal measure of intelligence. Through its successors (Harris, 1963; Naglieri, 1988), this methodology still experiences use for the measurement of intelligence. However, not long after introduction of the Draw-A-Man Test, various psychologists began using the test as a projective measure of personality. The most famous and systematic of the efforts to use human figure drawings as a projective personality test was that of Machover (1949). For another example of the attempt to use human figure drawings as a personality measure, see Naglieri, McNeish, and Bardos (1991).

Directions for administering the DAP vary widely, but usually contain the following key elements. The person is given a blank $8\frac{1}{2} \times 11$ inch sheet of paper and a pencil with eraser. The person is asked to draw a person; sometimes the directions are to "draw a picture of yourself," sometimes simply "draw a picture of a person." After completing the first picture, the examinee is asked to "draw a person of the opposite sex." The drawings are usually completed in 5 to 10 minutes. The examiner may follow up with questions about features of the drawings.

There are a variety of systems for scoring human figure drawings. None of them holds a dominant position. Arguably the most influential historical work on human figure drawings is that of Machover (1949). Statements from Machover's work have become part of the lore surrounding the use of human figure drawings. Table 14.7 contains a sampling of typical statements from Machover, many of which filtered into other works. Characterizations such as those given in Table 14.7 are given for

TABLE 14.7 *Sample Statements from Machover (1949) on Human Figure Drawings*

"Disproportionately large heads will often be given by individuals suffering from organic brain disease, those who have been subjected to brain surgery, and those who have been preoccupied with headaches or other special brain sensitivity." (p. 37)

"The subject who deliberately omits facial features in a drawing, showing careful and often aggressive delineation of contour and detail of other parts of the figure, is one who is evasive about the frictional character of his interpersonal relationships." (p. 40)

"Since the mouth is often the source of sensual and erotic satisfaction, it features prominently in the drawings of individuals with sexual difficulties." (p. 43)

"The long and often thin neck, resulting in a striking separation between the body and the head, is most often seen in the schizoid, or even schizophrenic individual." (pp. 57–58)

virtually every body detail. The facile generalizations, unsupported by any cited research, abound in the work. Adopted by persons insufficiently sensitive to the need for empirical verification, the statements have been taken as fact rather than as hypotheses to be explored. When treated as hypotheses and tested, the results have been disappointing, to say the least. Groth-Marnat (1999) referred laconically to the "largely unencouraging empirical research" (p. 506) of projective drawings.

Several authors have attempted to establish psychometrically sound approaches to HFD procedures. A good example is *Draw-a-Person: Screening Procedure for Emotional Disturbance* (DAP: SPED; Naglieri et al., 1991). The general result seems to be modest success. See Cosden (1995) and Morrison (1995) for reviews of the DAP: SPED. Some degree of reliability can be achieved. Validity seems to be largely limited to a moderate effect size for identifying overall maladjustment; more refined distinctions remain elusive.

Two popular offshoots of the draw-a-person technique are the *House-Tree-Person* (HTP; Buck, 1948, 1966) and the *Kinetic Family Drawing* (KFD: Burns & Kaufman, 1970, 1972). Both are intended primarily for use with children. In both cases, the theory is that the child is more likely to reveal unique, perhaps unconscious, elements of personality with these drawings than with the drawings of just individuals. In the HTP, as suggested by the title, the child draws a tree, a house, and a person. In the KFD, the child draws a picture of a family "doing something." (Kinetic, from the Greek word *kinetikos,* means related to motion or energy.) An alternate version asks the child to draw something happening in school.

Hope springs eternal regarding the potential of HFDs for revealing hidden aspects of the human personality. In a largely sympathetic, even proactive, review of various HFD procedures, Handler (1996) opines that, although research to date has been disappointing, perhaps researchers have not conducted the right kind of studies. Groth-Marnat (1999), in a largely unsympathetic review, notes that "explanations need to be provided for the continued popularity of projective drawings"(p. 506). He adds that at least the techniques seem fruitful sources of hypotheses.

The Future of Projective Techniques

As evidenced by the various surveys of test usage referenced throughout this chapter, projective techniques are well entrenched in the practice of psychology. What about the future? Will projectives continue to be widely used? Will there be any changes in how they are used? The answers to these questions are not entirely clear, but we can at least identify *three factors* relevant to answering the questions (see Key Points Summary 14.2).

Training of Psychologists

The first factor relates to *training of psychologists,* especially in such areas as clinical, counseling, and school psychology. It is clear that psychologists continue to be trained in the use of projective techniques. Apparently, those responsible for such training think it is important to be proficient with these techniques. Belter and Piotrowski (2001) surveyed APA-approved doctoral programs in clinical psychology regarding tests covered in required courses. They found that two of the five tests identified by over half of the programs were projective techniques (the Rorschach and TAT). Clemence and Handler (2001) surveyed directors of internship training sites to identify assessment techniques the directors wanted interns to be familiar with. Five of the top ten nominations were projective techniques. (All five are listed in Table 14.1 at the beginning of this chapter.) Furthermore, newly trained psychologists are likely to use in practice those tests employed in their training. Adding these factors to the inertia built into any field of practice leads to the conclusion that projective techniques will continue to play a prominent role in psychological assessment in the near future. For additional practices and recommendations regarding training of psychologists in the use of projective techniques, see Craig and Horowitz (1990), Culross and Nelson (1997), Hilsenroth and Handler (1995), Marlowe, Wetzler, and Gibbings (1992), Piotrowski and Keller (1984), and Watkins, Campbell, and McGregor (1988).

Emergence of Managed Care

Second, the *emergence of managed care* in health delivery influences test usage (see Acklin, 1996; Ben-Porath, 1997; Piotrowski, 1999). This trend may have special implications for the use of projective techniques. The emphasis in managed care is on specific diagnosis and immediate treatment rather than on more global evaluation and long-term outcomes. As Nietzel, Bernstein, and Milich (1998) succinctly note, "Today, many clinicians are asked to limit their assessments to initial screening of patients, rapid measurement of symptoms, differential diagnosis of disorders, and recommendations for treatment" (p. 100). Projective techniques seem to be particularly suited to in-depth, exploratory analyses, linked naturally with more holistic, systemic treatment. Moreover, projective techniques are inherently more expensive than objective personality tests. Consider this comparison. Client A comes to the clinic. A paraprofessional hands the client an objective personality test, briefly explains the purpose of the test and procedures for answering the questions using a keyboard. The client keys in the answers. Three minutes after the client finishes, the clinical psychologist receives a computer-generated report containing a score profile and interpretive commentary. The psychologist reviews the report for 10 minutes and, with a wealth of information in hand, is ready to interview the client. Client B comes to the clinic. The clinical psychologist takes about an hour to administer a projective test, say the Rorschach. The psychologist then takes another hour to score (code) the responses. Finally, the psychologist spends another half-hour interpreting the scores, before actually interviewing Client B. Professional time invested: for Client A—10 minutes, for Client B—150 minutes. Facing this differential, there must be a very strong rationale to justify use of the projective technique. In fact, where cost is a concern, this differential does seem to be leading to decreased use of projective techniques.

Key Points Summary 14.2

Factors Influencing the Future Use of Projective Techniques

- Training of Psychologists
- Influence of Managed Care
- Demand for Objective Scoring, Norms, and Psychometric Quality

---

Objective Scoring, Norm-referenced Interpretation, and Psychometric Quality

Third, when projective techniques are used in a formal way, it seems clear that the trend is toward more *objective scoring, norm-referenced interpretation, and psychometric quality.* The clearest example of this trend is the way in which Exner's Comprehensive System has influenced use of the Rorschach. As noted earlier, this system is now the industry standard, although it is not the only system in use (Hiller, Rosenthal, Bornstein, Berry, & Brunell-Neulieb, 1999; Hilsenroth & Handler, 1995; Piotrowski, 1996). Emergence of Exner's system has, in general, sensitized users of projective techniques to the need for standardized directions, systematic coding, adequate reliability, and demonstrated validity. Use of the TAT, increasingly criticized because of its lack of standardized administration and scoring, seems to be waning (Dana, 1996). However, as noted earlier, Bellak's work may have a salutary effect on TAT usage. More recently developed projective techniques, as well as new developments for older techniques, routinely report data on norms, inter-rater reliability, concurrent validity, and other psychometric issues. In the past, it was not unusual to hear claims that these issues were irrelevant for projective techniques. Virtually no one makes such claims today. However, it does seem likely that the informal, exploratory use of these techniques will continue to represent a significant part of their total usage.

Summary

1. Projective techniques use relatively ambiguous stimuli and a constructed-response format.
2. According to the projective hypothesis, responses to the ambiguous stimuli will be determined primarily by deep-seated, perhaps unconscious, personality traits, motives, and drives. The projective hypothesis is often associated with a psychoanalytic approach to personality exploration, although the association is not a necessary connection.
3. Projective techniques are very widely used in clinical practice. They are also used for research about personality.

4. Describing uses of projective techniques is complicated by the fact that they are administered and scored in a variety of ways by different users.

5. The Rorschach Inkblot Test is the most widely used projective technique and one of the most widely used of all psychological tests. It consists of 10 cards, each containing a bilaterally symmetrical inkblot. Examinees respond to the simple question: What might this be?

6. For many years, there were five competing systems for administering and scoring the Rorschach, leading to confusion and conflicting results. More recently, Exner's Comprehensive System has become the industry standard for the Rorschach. Exner's work has led to a resurgence of interest in the Rorschach.

7. The *Thematic Apperception Test* (TAT) is the second most widely used projective technique. It consists of 30 black-and-white photos (including one blank card). Various combinations of 20 of the 30 cards constitute the classic administration, although practitioners ordinarily use smaller numbers of cards. Examinees tell a story about each picture. Variations in procedures for administration and scoring the TAT limit our ability to develop generalizations about its reliability and validity.

8. The *Rotter Incomplete Sentence Blank* (RISB) is the most widely used of the numerous sentence completion tests. It consists of 40 sentence stems for which the examinee supplies written completions. The RISB attempts to measure general adjustment. It does so with a very standardized set of directions and scoring rubrics.

9. A variety of human figure drawing (HFD) tests are popular clinical tools. Some version of a Draw-A-Person (DAP) Test is the most widely used. The technique has been plagued by unsupported claims for the validity of highly specific signs in the drawings. In general, psychometric properties of HFDs have not been encouraging. Nevertheless, they do serve to generate hypotheses for follow-up exploration.

10. Projective techniques, no doubt, will continue to be a staple in psychologists' practice. However, the pressures of managed care may lead to some reduction in their use. For formal use, the field seems to be moving in the direction of more standardized administration and scoring procedures; and there are higher expectations for reliability and validity evidence.

Key Terms

ambiguous stimuli	ice-breaker	response phase
coding	inquiry phase	RISB
Comprehensive System	KFD	Rorschach
DAP	location codes	Special Scores
determinants	populars	Structural Summary
HFD	projective hypothesis	TAT
HTP	protocol	

Exercises

1. It is a rite of passage for the novice psychometrician to prepare his or her own inkblots. But it is not as easy as it sounds. At first, you think: Just pour some ink on a piece of paper and fold it over. However, it's not that simple. For starters, while ink was once readily available—before ballpoint pens, typewriters, then PCs—it is not readily available these days. We suggest you try children's finger paints. Coffee, soda, and similar liquids do not have adequate consistency; they just absorb into the paper. Finger paints have the right kind of consistency for making your inkblots. Be sure to use washable paint, because this exercise can get messy. Try some with black paint and some with a few pastel colors. Construction paper works better than regular typing paper. An $8\frac{1}{2} \times 11''$ piece of paper sliced to $8\frac{1}{2} \times 5\frac{1}{2}''$ gives a good approximation to the actual size of a Rorschach card.

   Do *not* put a blob of paint in the middle of the sheet, then fold it. That just does not work very well. Before putting paint on the sheet, fold the sheet in half, then unfold it. Then put a blot of paint near the fold but on only one side of it. Then fold the sheet over and smooth it out. Try this procedure with several sheets, experimenting with different numbers of blobs of paint. Also, try the procedure with a few different colors for different blobs. Some of your productions will appear to be potentially useful, others will not. Rorschach tried many different blots, not just the 10 in use now.

2. To illustrate the varied uses of projective techniques, select an electronic database such as PsycInfo or the ETS Test Collection. Do a search with the key words "Rorschach" or "Thematic Apperception Test." Note the variety of resulting reports. Can you determine from titles of the reports whether they deal primarily with the test's psychometric properties or with use of the test as a criterion variable? Note that some reports may simply discuss the test rather than using it in a research project.

3. Suppose you wish to use the RISB to measure *depression*. For each of the two item stems in Table 14.5, write a one-sentence completion that you think indicates a *moderate* degree of depression and another completion indicating *severe* depression.

4. Access this website for Psychological Assessment Resources: www.parinc.com. Here you will find a series of reports for the Rorschach protocol, including a Sequence of Scores, a Structural Summary, and computer-generated narrative reports. The site is updated frequently, so you may have to do a little searching to find the reports. At present, these are exact URLs, but be alert for updates:

   - http://www3.parinc.com/uploads/samplerpts/RIAP5SS.pdf
   - http://www3.parinc.com/uploads/samplerpts/RIAP5StrucSum.pdf
   - http://www3.parinc.com/uploads/samplerpts/RIAP5IR.pdf
   - http://www3.parinc.com/uploads/samplerpts/RIAP5FE.pdf

   Can you decipher the location codes in the Structural Summary? Most of the codes will not be understandable to the novice. However, the narrative reports should be understandable. Can you spot the norm-referenced statements built into the reports?

5. How would you design a study to test the first generalization noted in Table 14.7?

6. Use what you know about the relationship of the mean and standard deviation to percentiles to estimate what percent of the norm group would be above the suggested cutoff score on the RISB. The mean is approximately 130 and standard deviation approximately 17. Assuming the distribution of scores is approximately normal (which it is), what percent of the cases are above the cutoff score of 145? If necessary, refresh your knowledge of these matters by reference to Table 3.1 and Figure 3.11 in Chapter 3.

CHAPTER 15

Interests and Attitudes

Objectives

1. Describe the main difference between measures of personality and measures of interests and attitudes.

2. Compare the two traditional approaches to career assessment in terms of origin of the scales and item format.

3. Outline the Holland hexagon and place the six codes on its vertexes.

4. List the main features of the *Strong Interest Inventory*.

5. List the main features of the *Kuder Career Search*.

6. Outline the main features of the *Self-Directed Search*.

7. List four main generalizations about career interest assessment.

8. Describe the basic approaches to attitude measurement in the Likert, Thurstone, and Guttman procedures.

9. Identify the essential difference between attitude measurement and public opinion polling.

Introduction

The three previous chapters reviewed tests that aimed at a broad assessment of the human personality or at one narrowly defined characteristic such as depression. Continuing our exploration of the noncognitive domain, we now examine tests of interests and attitudes. The distinction between tests treated in this chapter and "personality" tests is quite common. However, as we will see, the distinction is not ironclad. The most important difference is in the purposes for use of the tests rather than in the nature of the tests themselves. Furthermore, the distinction between the terms *interests*, *attitudes*, and *personality* is blurry, depending again more on purpose than on anything else. Some of the tests of "interests" originate with a theory of personality. Nevertheless, the distinctions among these terms (personality, attitudes, etc.) are common within the field, and we will find that they provide a convenient grouping of tests.

When psychologists refer to "interest" testing, they usually mean career interests or vocational interests (we use the two latter terms interchangeably). This is a large, applied area of testing, especially for counselors. The chapter begins with treatment of this large area.

Orientation to Career Interest Testing

Treatment of career interest testing requires some special orientation. There are two dominant names in this field and two primary approaches to test development. Associated with these names and approaches are a series of tests that have largely defined the field of vocational interest testing. We will examine the most recent versions of these tests later. A preliminary orientation will facilitate the later review of these tests.

Strong and Kuder

The two dominant names in this field are **Edward K. Strong, Jr.,** and **G. Fredric Kuder.** Because their names are encountered so frequently, it is worthwhile to give a thumbnail sketch of each man.

Strong began his work on vocational interest measurement in the 1920s while teaching at Carnegie Institute of Technology, now Carnegie Mellon University, in Pittsburgh. He soon moved to Stanford University where he completed most of his work. The first edition of Strong's test appeared in 1927. Recall from Chapter 1 that this period was the heyday of early test development efforts. It was the same era that saw the first Otis intelligence tests, the first standardized achievement batteries, the Rorschach, and a host of other "firsts" in the world of testing. At that time, Strong was almost the only person doing significant work on the measurement of vocational interests. Later in his life and continuing after his death in 1964, Strong had several collaborators. Their names sometimes appear as co-authors on Strong's test, but the Strong name appears on all editions of his test to date.

G. Fredric Kuder split his interests between vocational interest measurement and test theory. Recall the Kuder-Richardson reliability formulas (especially KR 20 and KR 21) from Chapter 4. Kuder was also the founding editor of *Educational and Psychological Measurement,* a journal we mentioned as a key publication in the history of testing. Kuder's work on vocational interest measurement began in the 1930s, leading to the publication of his first test in 1939. Since that time, he has contributed prolifically to this field.

For a useful review of the historical development of the Strong inventory, see Donnay (1997). For the history of the Kuder inventories, see Zytowski (1992). For a summary of the entire field of career interest assessment, see Betsworth and Fouad (1997). For a comprehensive list of instruments in the field with evaluative comments, consult *A Counselor's Guide to Career Assessment Instruments* by Kapes and Whitfield (2002).

Traditional Approaches

Vocational interest measures differ in two main ways. The literature of the field is replete with references to these differences and, hence, it will be helpful to review them. The first difference relates to the *origin of scales or scores* on the tests. One approach uses an empirical, criterion-keying basis for development of scales. Recall the essence of the criterion-keying approach. We described it in Chapter 6 and in Chapter 13 in connection with the MMPI. The procedure involves determining which items differentiate between well-defined groups. The exact nature of the items and the reasons for the differentiation are immaterial. Of course, the content of the items will generally be about interests and job-related activities, but that is not necessarily true. For purposes of vocational interest testing, the groups are occupational groups, for example, elementary school teachers, accountants, and so on. We obtain sets of items that differentiate each of these groups from the general population. The items that differentiate members of an occupational group from the general population constitute a scale for that occupation. From a practical viewpoint, with criterion-keyed results in hand, here is what the counselor will say to a client. "Your interests are quite similar to the interests of accountants. You might want to consider that field."

Strong's original test used the criterion-keying approach. Recall that the MMPI used the same approach, except that the groups were clinical groups (depressed, paranoid, etc.) rather than occupational groups. Although the MMPI may be the

> ## Key Points Summary 15.1
> ### *Traditional Differences in Approaches to Career Interest Measurement*
>
> - Origin of Scales: Criterion-keying versus Broad Areas
> - Item Format: Absolute versus Relative Level of Interest

more famous example of criterion-keying, Strong's use of the technique predated the MMPI usage. Strong was the real pioneer for criterion-keying as a method for test development.

The second approach to scale development aims to produce scales corresponding to broad areas of interest. For example, the areas might be artistic, persuasive, or scientific. Each broad area can be related to occupations. For example, a high score in the persuasive area may suggest work in sales; a high score in the artistic area may suggest graphic arts, interior design, and related fields. Kuder's original tests used this approach to scale development.

A second difference in approach relates to use of *absolute versus relative types of scores.* We discussed this difference in Chapter 12. The difference arises from the response format used for items. The difference corresponds to an absolute versus relative interpretation of levels of interest. Consider the examples in Table 15.1. In

TABLE 15.1 *Types of Items Used for Measuring Interests: Absolute versus Relative Levels of Interest*

Absolute Level

Rate the extent to which you like each of these activities:

	Dislike	Neutral	Like
Dissecting frogs	O	O	O
Analyzing data	O	O	O
Selling magazines	O	O	O

Relative Level

Among these three activities, mark M for the one you like the Most and mark L for the one you like the Least. Make no mark for the other activity.

Dissecting frogs	[M]	[L]
Analyzing data	[M]	[L]
Selling magazines	[M]	[L]

the "absolute" format, you could like all the items or dislike all of them. In the "relative" format, you can prefer only one item and you must reject one item.

Uses of Career Interest Tests

Career interest inventories are widely used, especially in the field of counseling. In surveys of tests used by counselors, career interest inventories, especially the three we describe later in this chapter, regularly rank near the top of the lists (Bubenzer, Zimpfer, & Mahrle, 1990; Frauenhoffer et al., 1998; Watkins, Campbell, & McGregor, 1988; Watkins, Campbell, and Nieberding, 1994; Watkins et al., 1995). Most of the usage occurs in the school context, first in the grade 9–12 range, then at the college level. There is also some use related to midlife career changes. Even among clinical psychologists, some career interest inventories experience significant usage (Camara, Nathan, & Puente, 1998).

A Forewarning on Names

The world of vocational interest testing is like a hall of mirrors when it comes to test names. This is particularly true for tests associated with the two leading names in the field: Strong and Kuder. Sometimes the test name changes from one edition of the test to another; sometimes it does not. For example, the *Strong Interest Inventory* (**SII**) is the newer edition of the *Strong-Campbell Interest Inventory* (SCII). The SCII was the newer edition of the *Strong Vocational Interest Blank* (SVIB). Two different editions of the SII are sometimes distinguished only by a

"When I grow up, I don't know whether
to be a stunt man or train driver."

Source: From catoonstock.com. Reproduced by permission.

form designation: T325 and T317. The SII has now evolved into the *New Revised Strong Interest Inventory Assessment* (Donnay et al., 2005), referred to in some of the publisher's advertising and manuals simply as the *Strong Interest Inventory* or even more simply as the *Strong*, thus confirming our earlier observation about potential confusion among editions of tests.

Over on the Kuder side, the *Kuder Preference Record—Vocational* eventually turned into the *Kuder Occupational Interest Survey* (KOIS) and then into the *Kuder Career Search with Person Match*. There was at one time also a *Kuder Preference Record—Personal* that was intended more as a personality measure. There is also a *Kuder General Interest Survey,* published between two editions of the KOIS and using, in part, KOIS items. Reference to "the Kuder" or "the Strong" is often ambiguous. Even in the professional literature, it is not uncommon to find reference to one title (or set of initials) when, in fact, a different edition of the test was used. For most widely used tests, it is customary to refer to a specific edition of a test, for example, WAIS-III, MMPI-2, or Stanford 10th edition. This salutary practice does not extend to vocational interest measures. In fact, it often seems that there is an attempt to obscure differences between editions. For example, the *Strong Interest Inventory* manual often refers simply to research on "the Strong," regardless of whether the research was conducted with the SVIB, SCII, SII T325, or SII T317. To help the student deal with the situation, Table 15.2 gives the genealogy of the Strong and Kuder tests.

Further complicating the matter is the fact that **John Holland** has both his own vocational interest test *and* an interpretive scheme for vocational interests (see Holland's hexagon in the next section). Other authors have adopted the Holland interpretive scheme. The novice in the field might think that reference to Holland's

TABLE 15.2   *Genealogy of the Strong and Kuder Tests*

Strong

Strong Vocational Interest Blank (SVIB)—Men	1927
Strong Vocational Interest Blank (SVIB)—Women	1933
Strong-Campbell Interest Inventory (SCII)	
(merged men's and women's forms)	1974, 1981
Strong Interest Inventory (SII). Form T325	1985
Strong Interest Inventory (SII). Form T317	1994
New Revised Strong Interest Inventory Assessment	2004

Kuder

Kuder Preference Record—Vocational	1934
Kuder General Interest Survey (KGIS), Form E	1963
Kuder Occupational Interest Survey (KOIS), Form D	1966
Kuder Occupational Interest Survey (KOIS), Form DD	
(same items as Form D, new score reports)	1985
Kuder Career Search with Person Match (KCS)	1999

work implies Holland's test, but often it does not. Rather, it references use of Holland's interpretive scheme in someone else's test, especially the Strong. This is all very disconcerting to the student new to the field. However, that's the way the field currently exists.

Holland Themes and the RIASEC Codes

John Holland (1959, 1966, 1997) developed a theory about vocational choice that has provided a popular method for reporting career interest scores. According to this theory, career interests can be organized around six major themes or types. Table 15.3 summarizes the six types. The themes are similar to factors or dimensions that we have encountered in other contexts. However, the themes are not equally independent of one another; some are more closely related than others.

TABLE 15.3   *The Six Personality Types in Holland's System*

The **Realistic** type likes realistic jobs such as automobile mechanic, aircraft controller, surveyor, farmer, electrician. Has mechanical abilities but may lack social skills. Is described as:

Asocial	Inflexible	Practical
Conforming	Materialistic	Self-effacing
Frank	Natural	Thrifty
Genuine	Normal	Uninsightful
Hardheaded	Persistent	Uninvolved

The **Investigative** type likes investigative jobs such as biologist, chemist, physicist, anthropologist, geologist, medical technologist. Has mathematical and scientific ability but often lacks leadership ability. Is described as:

Analytical	Independent	Rational
Cautious	Intellectual	Reserved
Complex	Introspective	Retiring
Critical	Pessimistic	Unassuming
Curious	Precise	Unpopular

The **Artistic** type likes artistic jobs such as composer, musician, stage director, writer, interior decorator, actor/actress. Has artistic abilities—writing, musical, or artistic—but often lacks clerical skills. Is described as:

Complicated	Imaginative	Intuitive
Disorderly	Impractical	Nonconforming
Emotional	Impulsive	Open
Expressive	Independent	Original
Idealistic	Introspective	Sensitive

(continued)

TABLE 15.3   *(continued)*

The **Social** type likes social jobs such as teacher, religious worker, counselor, clinical psychologist, psychiatric case worker, speech therapist. Has social skills and talents but often lacks mechanical and scientific ability. Is described as:

Ascendant	Helpful	Responsible
Cooperative	Idealistic	Sociable
Empathic	Kind	Tactful
Friendly	Patient	Understanding
Generous	Persuasive	Warm

The **Enterprising** type likes enterprising jobs such as salesperson, manager, business executive, television producer, sports promoter, buyer. Has leadership and speaking abilities but often lacks scientific ability. Is described as:

Acquisitive	Energetic	Optimistic
Adventurous	Excitement-seeking	Self-confident
Agreeable	Exhibitionistic	Sociable
Ambitious	Extroverted	Talkative
Domineering	Flirtatious	

The **Conventional** type likes conventional jobs such as bookkeeper, stenographer, financial analyst banker, cost estimator, tax expert. Has clerical and arithmetic ability but often lacks artistic abilities. Is described as:

Careful	Inflexible	Persistent
Conforming	Inhibited	Practical
Conscientious	Methodical	Prudish
Defensive	Obedient	Thrifty
Efficient	Orderly	Unimaginative

Source: Reproduced by special permission of the Publisher, Psychological Assessment Resources, Inc., 16204 North Florida Avenue, Lutz, Florida 33549, from the Self-Directed Search Professional User's Guide by John L. Holland, Ph.D., Amy B. Powell, Ph.D., and Barbara A. Fritzsche, Ph.D. Copyright © 1985, 1987, 1994, 1997 by PAR, Inc. Further reproduction is prohibited without permission of PAR, Inc.

Key Points Summary 15.2

The Three Major Career Interest Inventories

1. Strong Interest Inventory
2. Kuder Career Search
3. Self-Directed Search (SDS)

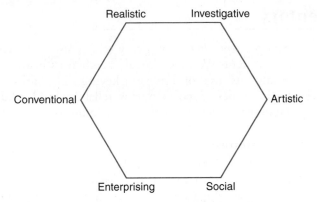

FIGURE 15.1   The Holland hexagon.

Source: Reproduced by special permission of the Publisher, Psychological Assessment Resources, Inc., 16204 North Florida Avenue, Lutz, Florida 33549, from the Self-Directed Search Professional User's Guide by John L. Holland, Ph.D., Amy B. Powell, Ph.D., and Barbara A. Fritzsche, Ph.D. Copyright © 1985, 1987, 1994, 1997 by PAR, Inc. Further reproduction is prohibited without permission of PAR, Inc.

The degrees of relationship can be depicted by a hexagon, as shown in Figure 15.1. The vertexes of the hexagon represent the six themes or types. Placement of the themes relative to one another represents their degree of relationship. Adjacent themes have moderately high correlations. Diagonally opposite themes have low correlations. Notice the initials of the themes, going in clockwise order from the upper left vertex: **RIASEC.** This acronym signals that a Holland-type scheme is being used to report scores. It also gives rise to a coding system reminiscent of the MMPI-2 codes (see pp. 493–494 in Chapter 13). Specifically, we might report the two highest RIASEC codes for an individual. For example, a person's code type might be SA (highest scores on Social and Artistic) or ES (highest scores on Enterprising and Social). The Holland themes have struck a resonant chord with counselors and other users of career assessment instruments. Hence, one encounters reference to Holland themes, the Holland hexagon, RIASEC codes, or simply RIASEC in a variety of contexts within the world of career assessment. We will encounter the RIASEC codes in our treatment of both the Strong and Kuder tests. Later, we will treat Holland's inventory, the *Self-Directed Search,* which obviously also uses the RIASEC scheme.

TRY IT!

We will encounter the RIASEC coding scheme frequently in the next three sections. Memorize it. Get both the names and the order of the codes correct. Without looking at Figure 15.1, fill in the labels for the vertexes in the Holland hexagon, starting with R.

R

Strong Interest Inventory

As noted earlier, the *Strong Interest Inventory* is very widely used. Hence, it is a good candidate for detailed treatment. We have already sketched its history and some of its key features, especially its use of criterion-keying. The following sections describe the types of items, types of scores, norms, reliability, and validity information for the Strong. We describe here the new revised edition.

Structure and Types of Items

The new Strong (Donnay et al., 2005) contains 291 items in six categories, as outlined in Table 15.4. In general, you respond to a series of simple descriptors (e.g., gardening, analyzing data) by marking your degree of liking for each item. The new Strong uses a five-point response scale, whereas all previous versions used a three-point scale (Like, Indifferent, Dislike). The directions say, "Do not spend too much time thinking about each [item]. Rely on your first impression." The SII takes 35 to 40 minutes to complete. It is intended for high school and college students, as well as adults.

Types of Scores

The SII yields five types of scores, as listed in Table 15.5. The total number of separate scores is over 200, so it is helpful to look at the scores by type. Study this table carefully. Later sections will make frequent reference to these types of scores.

TABLE 15.4 *Summary of the Structure of the New Revised Strong Interest Inventory Assessment*

Category	Items	Examples[a]	Response Scale[b]				
Occupations	107	Physical therapist	[SL]	[L]	[I]	[D]	[SD]
		Talk show host	[SL]	[L]	[I]	[D]	[SD]
Subject Areas	46	Communications	[SL]	[L]	[I]	[D]	[SD]
		Exercise science	[SL]	[L]	[I]	[D]	[SD]
Activities	85	Analyzing data	[SL]	[L]	[I]	[D]	[SD]
		Helping the elderly	[SL]	[L]	[I]	[D]	[SD]
Leisure Activities	28	Gardening	[SL]	[L]	[I]	[D]	[SD]
		Traveling	[SL]	[L]	[I]	[D]	[SD]
People	16	Political leaders	[SL]	[L]	[I]	[D]	[SD]
		Elderly	[SL]	[L]	[I]	[D]	[SD]
Your Characteristics	9	Am very organized	[SL]	[L]	[D]	[U]	[SU]
		Have high drive	[SL]	[L]	[D]	[U]	[SU]
Total	291						

[a] These are not actual items from the Strong. They are meant to illustrate the types of items in each category.
[b] SL = Strongly Like, L = Like, I = Indifferent, D = Dislike, SD = Strongly Dislike

The response scale changes for the Your Characteristics category, ranging from Strongly Like me to Strongly Unlike me.

TABLE 15.5   *Types of Scores Yielded by the Strong Interest Inventory*

1. General Occupational Themes (GOTs)   6 scores
   Based on the Holland hexagon. Scores are Realistic, Investigative, Artistic, Social, Enterprising, and Conventional (RIASEC).

2. Basic Interest Scales (BISs)   30 scores
   Based on factor analysis of items. Scores in such areas as Athletics, Science, Military, Sales.

3. Occupational Scales (OSs)   122 occupations
   The classic Strong scales criterion-keyed to various occupational groups.

4. Personal Style Scales   5 scores
   New in 1994 edition. Scores for Work style, Learning environment, Leadership style, Risk taking, Team orientation.

5. Administrative Indexes   3 summaries
   Total responses. Typicality index. Percentages within response categories.

The General Occupational Themes (GOTs) correspond to the Holland categories described earlier (see Figure 15.1). They represent very broad areas of interest. The Basic Interest Scales (BISs) also represent general interest areas but are somewhat more narrowly defined. For purposes of reporting, BISs are grouped within GOTs. For example, the BISs for law, management, and sales are all grouped under the Enterprising GOT.

The Occupational Scales (OSs) are the traditional criterion-keyed scales for various occupational groups. A high score on one of these scales, say, paralegal or social worker, means that the examinee has interests similar to those of individuals already in that occupation. In previous editions, not all occupations had norms for both men and women, but the current edition supplies norms by gender for all 122 occupations.

The Personal Style Scales, new in the 1994 SII, encompass an odd mixture of five scores related to environmental preferences and ways of relating to people and situations. The Administrative Indexes provide information about whether the inventory was answered sincerely. In the parlance of Chapter 12 on Objective Personality Tests, these are validity indexes. The Total Response Index simply shows the number of items marked (out of 291). Reports are not generated if fewer than 276 items were marked. The Typicality Index is based on 24 item pairs where one would expect similar responses. A warning is printed if inconsistency occurs for 17 or more of these pairs. The Item Response Percentages report simply shows the distribution of responses across the five points in the response scale for all items. Unusually large percentages in any one category suggest special caution when interpreting that protocol. For example, what would you make of the fact that an examinee gave "indifferent" responses to 75% of the items?

TRY IT! ....

Try to think up two additional items for each category in Table 15.4. Pick one for
which you would respond "Like" and one for which you would respond "Dislike."

....

Norms

Description of the norm groups for the Strong requires careful explanation (see
Figure 15.2 for additional clarification). First, there is the General Representative
Sample (GRS), composed of 2,250 cases, equally divided by gender. The GRS
served as the basis for developing a standard score system with $M = 50$ and $SD =$
10. This is the familiar T-score system, widely used with other tests. These standard
scores apply to the GOT and BIS scales.

However, separate standard score systems (but again with $M = 50$ and $SD = 10$)
were developed for the Occupational Scales. Obviously, norms for the Occupational Scales derive from samples within each occupation. These samples go beyond
the cases in the General Representative Sample described earlier. A considerable
variety of methods were used to recruit participants for these norm groups. In general, persons within each occupational norm group had to (a) perform the main
duties of the job, (b) have at least three years of experience in the job, and (c) express
satisfaction with the job. The Strong manual candidly admits the difficulty in securing adequate samples and the potential bias introduced by the entirely voluntary
(and somewhat irksome) nature of participation. Perhaps more importantly, it must
be noted that some of these samples were drawn from databases stretching back into
the 1970s, with somewhat over half after 1990. Also, the occupational norm groups
vary considerably in size, from under 100 to over 1,000, with the typical group
being in the range of 200 to 400.

Thus, several separate standard score systems are in operation. In addition, all
percentile scales (for GOTs, BISs, and OSs) are separate by gender. For example, a
standard score of 50 on the Realistic GOT shows that a person is perfectly average
in comparison to the general population. A standard score of 50 on the Accountant
OS shows that a person is exactly average for accountants, who are very different

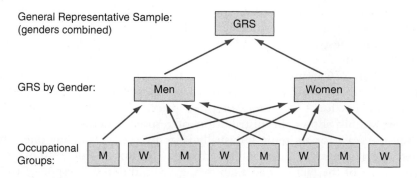

FIGURE 15.2 Outline of the norm groups for the Strong.

General Occupational Themes (GOTs) — Really the 6 RIASEC areas
  Rank ordering of the RIASEC areas.
  Three highest areas yields theme code (e.g., CEA).

Basic Interest Scales — 30 areas
  Rank ordering, with emphasis on 5 highest areas.

Occupational Scales — 122 occupations
  Rank ordering, with emphasis on 10 highest occupations.

Personal Style Scales
  Simple percentile plot of all 5 scales.

Administrative Indexes
  Simple summary; no normative comparisons.

Note: Standard scores supplied for all scales. Percentiles for rankings are always within gender.

FIGURE 15.3   Outline of the structure of a Strong Interest Inventory report.

from the general population in many ways. A standard score of 50 on the Accountant OS will place a woman at a much higher percentile (on the women's norms) than it will place a man (on the men's norms). Figure 15.3 outlines the structure of a *Strong Interest Inventory* report.

All together, a host of different normative structures undergird the total array of Strong scores. This emphasizes the need for technical expertise regarding such matters when one is attempting to interpret the results. This caution applies to nearly all career interest inventories, not just to the Strong.

TRY IT! ....

To see an example of an actual 14-page Strong report, go to:
www.cpp.com/samplereports; then click on one of the Strong profiles.

....

Reliability

The Strong manual reports extensive reliability data for all scales except the Administrative Indexes. Internal consistency (Cronbach's alpha) is reported for GOTs and BISs based on the General Representative Sample. The median alpha for GOTs is .92, and none of the scales fall below .90. The median alpha for the 30 BISs is .87, with none below .80. The median alpha coefficient for the Personal Style scales is .86. Oddly, alpha coefficients are not reported for the OSs.

Test-retest reliability for several different groups is reported for all scores, again with the exception of the Administrative Indexes. For GOTs, almost all test-retest reliabilities are in the mid-.80s, with none below .80. For BISs, too, most test-retest reliabilites are in the mid-.80s, with none falling into the low .70s. Test-retest reliabilities of the Personal Style scales are generally in the mid-.80s. It is curious that no reliability data are given for the Administrative Indexes.

What do we conclude about all this reliability information for the SII? First, it is apparent that career interests are remarkably stable. This is certainly comforting to counselors and others who need to rely on this information. Second, in the few instances in which the reliability data are only marginally acceptable, for example, falling into the .70s, the problem is almost invariably the brevity of the scale. Recall the general principle that reliability is heavily dependent on the number of items in a scale. Some of the SII scales, especially among the BISs, have as few as five or six items. Third, we note with chagrin the absence of reliability data for the Administrative Indexes. Reliability data should be reported for any information one is expected to interpret, even if expressed in some form other than a conventional score.

Validity

How does one demonstrate the validity of a career interest measure? Is there a criterion to be predicted? Is there a conceptual trait to be documented? These questions do not admit of simple answers. There are two common methods for demonstrating the validity of a career interest measure and a host of ancillary methods. The first common method is to show that test results differentiate between existing occupational groups in predictable directions. For example, if there is a "teacher" scale on the interest inventory, then people who are currently in the teaching profession should score high on this scale; they should score higher on this scale than on any other scale; and they should score higher on this scale than any other occupational group does. The second common method for demonstrating the validity of a career interest measure is to show that scores are predictive of the occupation (or college major) that people ultimately select. For example, it should be the case that people who score highly on the "teacher" scale tend to become teachers rather than, say, salespersons. Conversely, people who score highly on the "sales" scale tend to become salespersons rather than, say, research scientists.

The Strong manual contains a plethora of studies along the lines just described. In fact, among the widely used career interest inventories, the Strong clearly presents the most validity information. Considering the historical importance of the criterion-keying for occupational scales in the Strong, a question of special relevance is the extent to which these scales differentiate people in the occupation from the general population. The Strong manual, understandably, devotes considerable attention to this comparison. For purposes of statistical analysis, the question becomes a matter of effect size in a group comparison: exactly the situation we described for the group contrast approach in discussing validation procedures in Chapter 5. We reintroduce the relevant figure from that chapter, relabeling the contrast groups, in Figure 15.4. Cohen's $d = (M_1 - M_2)/SD$ describes the degree

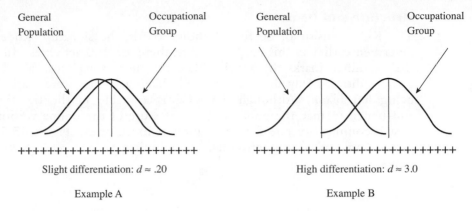

FIGURE 15.4 Describing degree of differentiation for Strong Occupational Scales.

of differentiation.[1] Using this method, the median *d* for OSs is 1.51, which is about halfway between the two examples in Figure 15.4. The *d* statistics range from about 1.00 to 2.64, all respectable, but a considerable range.

The Strong manual reports numerous studies showing that persons with high scores on a particular scale tend to ultimately enter occupations consistent with that score. In a method used in several studies, persons with scale scores of 45 or higher on a scale were followed for 3 to 18 years in order to determine their occupation. In nearly half of the cases, the persons were, in fact, employed in a field consistent with their Strong scores. Of course, this means that about half of the people did not go into a field consistent with their scores. The Strong manual also contains substantial information about correlations among the scales. This information is generally supportive of the construct validity of the test.

A major problem with interpretation of much of the validity information for the Strong is that many of the studies were conducted with earlier versions of the test. The Strong manual continually asserts that studies with earlier versions should be applicable to the latest version. However, it takes somewhat of an act of faith to accept these assertions.

Kuder Career Search (KCS)

The *Kuder Career Search* (**KCS**) *with Person Match* is the latest (Zytowski, 2005) in the long line of Kuder instruments (for a genealogy, see Table 15.2). It replaces the *Kuder Occupational Interest Survey* (KOIS) and uses many of the items and concepts from that predecessor. The publisher markets the KCS as part of the Kuder Career Planning System, which includes an electronic career portfolio, a database management system, and several other elements. Here we treat only the KCS.

---

[1]The Strong manual also uses Tilton's Q index, which is almost perfectly correlated with Cohen's *d*.

Structure and Items

The KCS consists of 60 forced-choice triads, the signature Kuder approach described earlier in this chapter. Thus, there are 180 activities. In each triad, the examinee marks the activity liked the most, next most, and least. (In all earlier editions, only the most and least liked activities were marked, the third being left blank). Although the KCS is available in the traditional paper-and-pencil format, the publisher promotes use of the online version, which is now a common avenue for career interest inventories. Figure 15.5 provides a "screenshot" of what a person taking the online version sees. Notice the triad items.

TRY IT! ....

To get a feel for the Kuder forced-choice format, mark your answers to the items in Figure 15.5.

....

Scores

The KCS uses two types of scores and an innovative method of reporting. The first type of score is a set of 10 Activity Preference Scales (Vocational Interest Estimates or VIEs in the KOIS). These are intended as relatively homogeneous scales representing major dimensions of interests—very similar to the Strong Basic Interest Scales. The Activity Preference Scales include:

Outdoor	Mechanical	Science	Art	Music
Literary	Social Service	Persuasive	Clerical	Computational

Rather oddly, scores on these scales are reported only for the paper-and-pencil version of the test, not the online version. However, they do enter into the third type of report described later.

The second type of score is a set of six Career Clusters, including:

Outdoor/Mechanical	Science/Technical	Art/Communication
Social/Personal Services	Sales/Management	Business Operations

Not coincidentally, these six career clusters line up with the RIASEC codes.

The third method of reporting, the root of the name for the new instrument, involves matching the person completing the KCS with a number of people already in the workforce who have similar profiles. The profiles are constructed based on the 10 Activity Preference Scales. The person gets a list of people with similar profiles, along with descriptions of these people and their work activities. Figure 15.6 shows part of the report generated from the online version of the KCS. Notice that the report begins with a profile of Career Clusters in rank order. Then the report lists seven persons for the highest Career Cluster and even for the second highest. Clicking on a person (say, Person Match 2) brings up a description of that person's job. The description is based on questionnaires

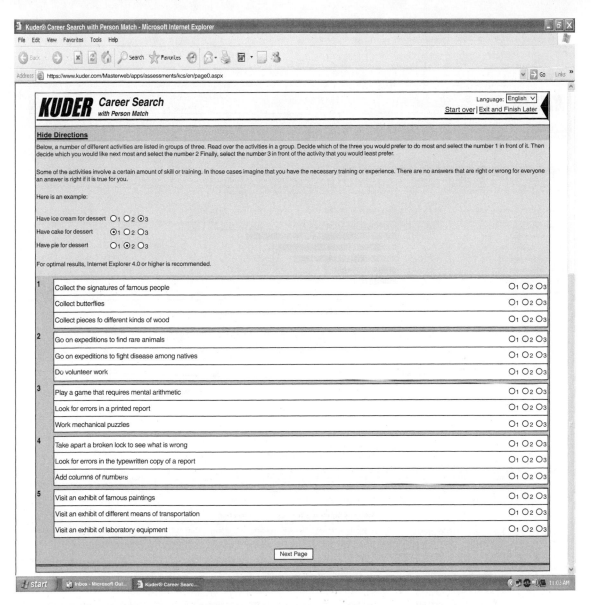

FIGURE 15.5   Screenshot of Kuder Career Search (first page) online version.

Source: Reproduced with permission of National Career Assessment Services, Inc. All rights reserved.

completed by 2,000 persons (the Person Match pool), with responses then edited to represent a mini-interview. The methodology provides an interesting twist to psychologists' continuing pursuit of interpreting test information—time will tell how successfully done.

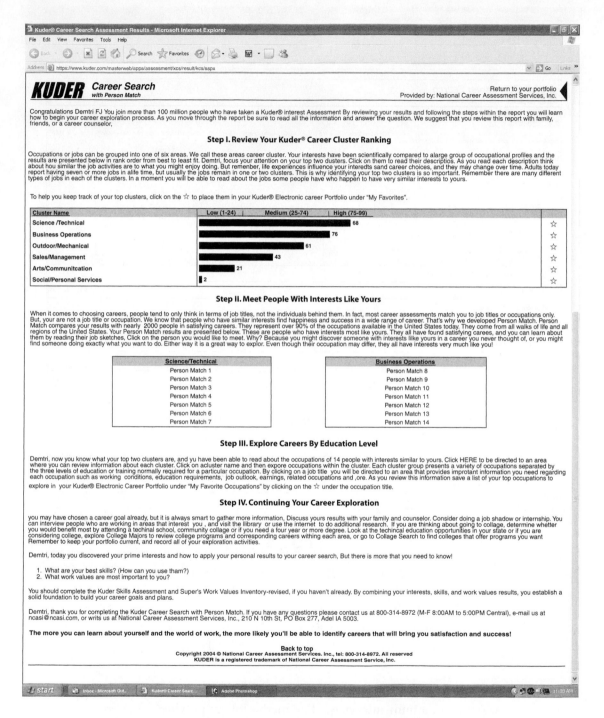

FIGURE 15.6 Part of Kuder Career Search online report.

Source: Reproduced with permission of National Career Assessment Services, Inc. All rights reserved.

Reliability and Validity

The KCS manual provides surprisingly sparse reliability data. For example, KR–20 reliabilities are reported for a sample of only 146 adults, not further described, and only for the Activity Preference Scales. These reliabilities range from .70 to .80, with a median of .73: puzzlingly low. The manual also reports correlations between Career Cluster scores versus Strong Interest Inventory scores and Self-Directed Search scores (described next) based on only 77 college students, not further described. The correlations range from .12 to .57, with a median of .50, again puzzlingly low. One hopes the professional literature will add to the array of data on the KCS.

Self-Directed Search (SDS)

The Self-Directed Search (**SDS**) advertises itself as the most widely used career interest inventory. According to some sources (e.g., Watkins, Campbell, & Nieberding, 1994), it is second to the SII in use among counseling psychologists. The SDS may, in fact, outrank the SII because the SDS can be taken independent of a counselor. Whether first or second in rank, the SDS is clearly a very popular instrument. Its extent of use comes as a bit of a surprise because it does not have the distinguished history, elaborate reports, and other such characteristics of the Strong and Kuder inventories. In fact, a sort of lowbrow informality seems to be part of the attractiveness of the SDS. The SDS manual emphasizes that the inventory is self-administered, self-scoring, and self-interpreted. As if almost eschewing the technical sophistication, multiplicity of scores, and computer processing of the Strong and Kuder inventories, to say nothing of their fabled histories, the SDS aims at simplicity. This simplicity appears to explain its relatively rapid rise in popularity.

The SDS first appeared in 1971. New editions appeared in 1977, 1985, and 1994. There are several forms of the current edition, designed mainly for different age groups. We concentrate here on Form R of the 1994 edition, intended for high school, college, and adult groups. This is the most widely used and researched form.

The SDS originates with John Holland's RIASEC scheme (Holland, 1959, 1966, 1997). Review Figure 15.1 for the codes in this scheme. According to Holland's theory, there are six basic personality types. Furthermore, there are these six types of work environments. Career satisfaction should result when there is a good match between personality type and work environment. Recall that the Strong and Kuder inventories incorporate the RIASEC codes, whereas the entire SDS is based on the RIASEC system.

Holland's first, formal statement of the six types was in his 1959 article, although he had published an attitude measure, the *Holland Vocational Preference Inventory,* as early as 1953. The 1959 article did not employ the hexagonal order (RIASEC) and the original terms were motoric, intellectual, supportive, conforming, persuasive, and esthetic. He elaborated the 1959 article in a 1966 book; the most recent comprehensive statement is in a 1997 book. The student interested in career assessment research would be well served to read Appendix E of this 1997 book on "Research Suggestions for Students."

TABLE 15.6   *Organization of the Self-Directed Search (SDS)*

Part	Number Items per RIASEC Area	Response	Nature of Items
Activities	11	Like/Dislike	Activities you might like to do
Competencies	11	Yes/No	Things you can do well
Occupations	14	Yes/No	Occupations that interest you
Self-estimates	2	7-point scale	Self-rating of ability
		(7 = high, 1 = low)	

Structure and Items

The SDS consists of 228 items and requires about 30 minutes to complete. The items appear in four major parts. Within each part, items are grouped according to RIASEC code. Table 15.6 shows the parts, number of items per part, response format, and nature of the items. Scoring simply involves adding the number of Yes's, Like's, and self-estimates within each area across the four parts. This yields six raw scores referred to as Summary Scale Scores, one for each RIASEC area. The maximum possible score in each area is 50 (11 "Like's" on Activities in an area, 11 "Yes's" on Competencies, 14 "Yes's" on Occupations, and two "7's" on Self-estimates). The minimum score for an area is zero. After adding the scores, the person determines the three highest raw scores. This yields the person's three-letter RIASEC code.

A fifth part of the SDS, Occupational Daydreams, is not formally scored but may be useful when interpreting results. In this part, the person is asked to "List the careers you have daydreamed about as well as those you have discussed with others." The person also finds the RIASEC codes corresponding to these occupations.

An essential supplement to the SDS summary of scores—the RIASEC 3-letter code—is *The Occupations Finder*. This brief, 16-page booklet lists hundreds of occupational titles by RIASEC code. Accompanying each occupational title are the official key for that entry in the *Dictionary of Occupational Titles* (DOT; U.S. Department of Labor, 1991) and an indicator of the educational level required for that occupation. The DOT lists over 10,000 job titles. It is widely used in the career counseling field. The SDS educational level is described within a 6-point system, ranging from "advanced degree" to "no special training." Table 15.7 shows sample entries from *The Occupations Finder* for one of the RIASEC codes. There are actually 37 occupational titles listed for the SEC code.

Norms

Interpretation of SDS scores depends mostly on the Summary Score Scales, which are raw scores, translated into RIASEC codes. Thus, the SDS provides a criterion-referenced approach to interpretation, although elements of a normative approach were incorporated into the item selection procedures. Norms are not an important part of the interpretive scheme. Nevertheless, the SDS manual

TABLE 15.7 *Sample Entries from The Occupations Finder for the SEC Code*

Code SEC	DOT	ED
Library Director	(100.117–010)	6
...		
City Manager	(188.117–114)	5
...		
Camp Counselor	(159.124–010)	4
...		
Security Guard	(372.667–034)	3

Source: Adapted from Holland (1994).

provides percentile rank norms separately for high school, college, and adult samples, further broken down by gender within each group. Table 15.8 summarizes sample sizes for each group. The manual presents little information about the procedures for selecting individuals for the norm groups. Hence, it is best to view the norm groups as convenience samples, with all the limitations implied by that sampling procedure.

Reliability and Validity

The SDS manual presents internal consistency reliabilities (KR-20), based on the norm samples previously described, for the Activities, Competencies, and Occupations scales, as well as the Summary Scale Scores. Reliabilities for the Activities, Competencies, and Occupations scales are of little interest, since it appears that these scales are never interpreted separately from the Summary Score Scales. Internal consistency reliabilities for the Summary Score Scales are all in the low .90's (.90–.94). Test-retest reliabilities, based on very limited samples ($n = 73$) tested over 4 to 12 weeks, ranged from .76 to .89. More information on the temporal stability of the SDS is clearly needed.

The SDS manual approaches validity from several angles. As is typical for career interest inventories, validity information for the SDS tends to be an amalgam of data from successive editions of the test. First, it attempts to show that the scales are reasonably independent of one another and consistent with the Holland hexagonal model (Figure 15.1). Second, as with other career interest

TABLE 15.8 *Numbers of Cases by Group for SDS Norms*

Gender	Age Group		
	High School	College	Adult
Male	344	399	251
Female	475	713	405

inventories, there are numerous studies of "hit rates," showing the extent to which SDS scores are consistent with such criteria as college major or actual occupation. Finally, there are many studies of the correlation between SDS scores and a host of personality tests, such as the NEO PI-R (see pp. 467–473). Interest in relationships with personality tests is somewhat unusual for a career assessment inventory. However, this interest is consistent with the SDS philosophy that career choice is a matter of matching personality type with type of job environment.

The SDS manual contains an innovative chapter on "Effects and Outcomes." In the terminology we introduced earlier, we would call this "consequential validity," although the SDS manual does not use this term. The chapter reports studies of whether use of the SDS makes any difference in people's lives. The manual (Holland, Fritzsche, & Powell, 1997) notes, "Unless this experience [taking, scoring, and interpreting the SDS] makes a difference, high levels of reliability and validity are of no practical use" (p. 57). For example, does taking the SDS lead to a sense of greater clarity about vocational choice? Does it lead to considering more career options? How does taking it on one's own compare with having a session with a career counselor? Results of these "effects and outcomes" studies are generally, though not universally, favorable for the SDS. More important for our purposes in this book, the SDS chapter points a salutary direction for other test manuals.

TRY IT! ....

Without actually taking the SDS, try to rank yourself in the RIASEC codes (1 is high, 6 is low).

Area	**R**ealistic	**I**nvestigative	**A**rtistic	**S**ocial	**E**nterprising	**C**onventional
Rank	_____	_____	_____	_____	_____	_____

Based on this ranking, what is your three-letter code? _____

....

Some Generalizations about Career Interest Measures

What generalizations might we develop about career interest measures, at least based on our examination of three widely used measures? Several observations suggest themselves.

1. People's career-related interest patterns do seem to be *quite reliable,* at least from middle adolescence onward, as measured by these tests. This is true in terms of both internal consistency and temporal stability. However, the reliabilities are not perfect and in a few instances are really quite low. The formal reports of test scores in the career interest field tend to mention these facts about reliability less than is the case in other areas of testing. For example, the standard error of

measurements for scores, though reported in the technical manuals, are not ordinarily incorporated into the score reports.

2.   Particularly if we use ultimate career choice as the criterion, it appears that career interest measures do have a *respectable degree of validity.* Occupational groups do tend to differ in their interest patterns, and people tend to enter occupations consistent with their own interests. However, a note of caution is in order. All of the test manuals and other research reports, understandably, tend to emphasize average differences between occupational groups, while obscuring overlap in distributions. Furthermore, the reports emphasize that correspondence between test scores and occupational entry is well above chance levels, while often failing to call attention to the substantial number of instances when there is lack of correspondence.

3.   Career interest measures are remarkably *devoid of references to more modern psychometric techniques.* Even in the most recent manuals for the widely used inventories there is little or no reference to such topics as item response theory, differential item functioning, generalizability coefficients, consequential validity, and so on. To be sure, some of these concepts are highly relevant to career-interest inventories, and the manuals tangentially touch on the topics. However, the formal use of the techniques and terminology of modern psychometrics seems to have passed by the field of career-interest assessment, or vice versa.

4.   *Reviewers of career-interest inventories almost uniformly express overall satisfaction with the utility of the instruments, even after noting some serious deficiencies in the technical quality of the instruments.* This is a curious result. In other realms of testing, it is not unusual for reviewers to render quite severe judgments about tests that actually meet higher technical standards than do the widely used career-interest inventories. Perhaps the kinder, gentler tone is because the career-interest inventories virtually never become "high-stakes" tests. Results help test-takers explore and discuss options, but they do not prevent entry into an occupation, as, for example, a licensing exam might.

5.   Increasingly, career interest inventories are being *completed online*, with results provided immediately to the user. Publishers of all three of the inventories examined in this chapter vigorously promote such online usage. This mode of administration and reporting places a special burden on authors and publishers. Traditional administration was typically in a classroom, with reports going to a counselor who would review reports with students (or other clients) individually or in a group session. At a minimum, users would know to whom they should go to discuss the results. That is not the case with online administration and reporting. The online reports of results need to be salted with cautions about imperfect reliability and validity, cautions that are not always apparent in the reports.

6.   In his early work, Strong assumed a positive *relationship between interests and ability* to pursue those interests. He soon found this was not true, a finding amply confirmed elsewhere. A person may want to be an artist but just does not have the skill to be successful in that endeavor. Another person may want to be a physician but does not have the ability to complete the requisite

science courses. Hence, from a practical viewpoint, career interest testing must be supplemented with relevant information from the ability domain. Today's typical interest inventory has a companion inventory (or a section within the interest inventory) related to ability. However, these companions or sections rely entirely on self-estimates of abilities. For example, on a scale from 1 to 7, how good are you at math? Considerable attention must be directed at the relationship between these self-estimates and actual measures of abilities. It is not always clear that this has been done.

Key Points Summary 15.3

Generalizations about Career Interest Measures

- Quite Reliable
- Respectable Degree of Validity
- Little Use of Modern Psychometric Techniques
- Reviews Express Overall Satisfaction
- More to Online Completion
- Assessing Ability along with Interest

Attitude Measures

Psychologists love to measure attitudes. This is understandable because our attitudes toward a host of issues seem to color our lives—attitudes toward work, toward other people, toward political parties and issues, and on endlessly: These are important human characteristics. Measurement of attitudes is especially prominent in the field of social psychology. Here are just a few examples:

- What are young children's attitudes toward immigrants?
- Does attitude toward organ donation relate to actually registering for donation?
- How do attitudes toward religion change with age?
- Is attitude toward the elderly a unidimensional trait?

We must first inquire about what distinguishes attitudes from interests or personality traits. It is common to use these terms as if they were distinct. However, their boundaries are fuzzy. In fact, at times, the reference points for these terms are indistinguishable. For example, extroversion may sometimes be thought of as a personality trait and at other times as an attitude. A person's thoughts and feelings about a particular job may be thought of as a vocational interest or as an attitude toward the job. Nevertheless, the measurement of attitudes is usually treated separately from the measurement of personality traits and career interests.

An attitude is usually defined with respect to its object. The object may be a concept (e.g., democracy), a practice (e.g., capital punishment), a group (e.g., Italian-Americans), an institution (e.g., this college), or an individual (e.g., Dr. Cannon). The possibilities are almost unlimited. You can have an attitude toward almost anything. Most researchers think of attitudes as having three components. The first component is cognitive: thoughts about the object, especially conscious, articulated thoughts. The second component is emotional: feelings about the object. The third component is behavioral: actions taken or likely to be taken regarding the object.

Most of our measures of attitudes are of the paper-and-pencil variety. A person answers questions about the object or reacts to statements about the object. The questions or statements about the object are the item stems. Typically, responses are multiple-choice, for example, Agree-Disagree, Yes-No, and so on. Given this format, we conclude that most attitude measures address the cognitive component of attitudes. Some items may ask about the person's feelings (the emotional component) or actions (the behavioral component). However, even for these items, the responses report what the person thinks about his or her feelings and actions rather than being a direct measure of those feelings or actions.

Although most measurement of attitudes involves paper-and-pencil reports, there are other techniques for measuring attitudes. Physiological measures (e.g., galvanic skin response or pupillary dilation) may be particularly useful for investigating the feeling component. Direct observation may yield information about the behavioral component. In this section, we concentrate on the paper-and-pencil measures simply because they are the most widely used.

There are a virtually unlimited number of attitudes. Correspondingly, there are a virtually unlimited number of attitude measures. Shaw and Wright (1967), for example, provide hundreds of specific attitude measures. Two of the lengthiest chapters in the *Directory of Unpublished Experimental Mental Measures* (Goldman & Mitchell, 2003) contain measures of "attitudes" and "values." Robinson, Shaver, and Wrightsman (1991) also supply numerous examples of such measures. A good rule of thumb is: If you can think of an attitude, almost certainly someone has created a scale to measure it. Although there are many attitude measures, no one of them is widely used in the way that the MMPI, SAT, or WISC is widely used. Moreover, most of these measures have rather meager research bases in comparison with most widely used tests. In all the other areas of testing covered in this book, we identified a few tests that were widely used and then described those tests. However, this approach will not work in the area of attitude measures.

What especially distinguishes attitude measures is the *method of scale construction*. The professional literature often refers to one of these methods when describing a specific measure. Hence, it behooves the student to be familiar with some of these methods and what the methods imply about the nature of the scale. There are numerous methods. We will describe three of the more widely cited methods (see Key Points Summary 15.4). The reader may consult the following classic references for descriptions of other methods, as well as for more detailed treatment

> ## Key Points Summary 15.4
> ### Widely Cited Methods of Attitude Scale Construction
>
> - Likert Method of Summated Ratings
> - Thurstone's Method of Equal Appearing Intervals
> - Guttman's Scalogram Analysis

of the three methods we cover here: Edwards (1957), Shaw and Wright (1967), and Torgerson (1958).

Likert Scales

By far the most widely used method for attitude scale construction today is Likert's method (Likert, 1932).[2] In the technical literature, it is often called the **method of summated ratings.** In its purest form, the **Likert** method has the following features. First, start with a large number of item stems expressing some aspect of the attitude toward the target object. The basic notion is that each item gives some information about the person's attitude. Summing all this information defines a holistic attitude toward the target object. Figure 15.7 helps to illustrate the Likert approach.

Second, give responses on the following five-point scale: *Strongly Agree, Agree, Uncertain or Neutral, Disagree, Strongly Disagree.* See Table 15.9 for a sample set of responses. Responses with these verbal labels are usually converted to numerical form. Schemes for assigning numerical values to these responses vary. One common practice is to assign values of 5, 4, 3, 2, and 1, respectively. An alternative is to use +2, +1, 0, −1, and −2, respectively. Third, conduct item analysis to select those items that

TABLE 15.9 *Sample Responses to a 15-item Likert Scale*

Item	1	2	3	4	5	6	7	8	9	10	11	12	13	14	15
Tom	SA	A	A	SA	SA	U	A	SA	A	SA	SA	A	U	A	SA
Dick	A	U	U	D	D	A	A	U	A	D	D	U	D	U	A
Harry	D	SD	SD	SD	SD	U	U	D	D	SD	SD	D	D	SD	D

Tom has a favorable attitude toward the topic: mostly A and SA responses.

Dick has a neutral attitude or mixed feelings: a mixture of U, D, and A responses.

Harry has an unfavorable attitude toward the topic: mostly D and SD responses.

[2] Is it Lie-kert (long i) or Lick-ert (short i)? Most people say Lie-kert. Dr. Likert said Lick-ert.

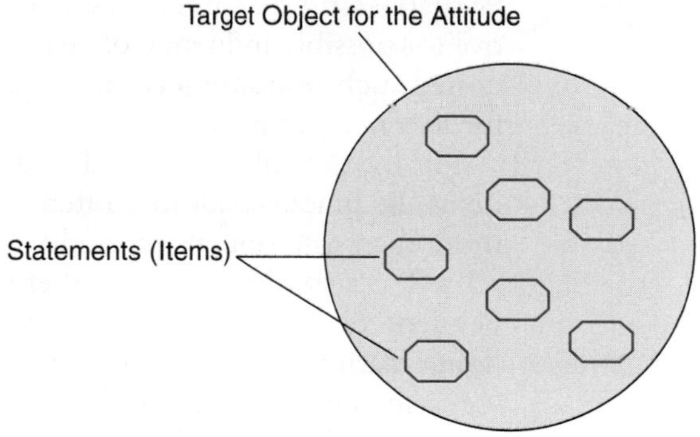

Target Object for the Attitude

Statements (Items)

FIGURE 15.7 Schematic illustration of Likert approach to attitude measurement.

correlate most highly with the total score. (Total score is the sum of numerical values for responses to individual items. Hence the name: method of summated ratings.) Finally, construct a final scale based on results of the item analysis.

TRY IT!

Assign these values to the responses in Table 15.9 for Dick:

$SA = +2$ $A = +1$ $U = 0$ $D = -1$ $SD = -2$

What is Dick's score on the 15 items?

There are several common variations on the latter description of Likert scale construction. First, technically, the Likert methodology calls for a five-point response scale. However, variations on this matter are common. People use 3, 7, 10, 25, 99—any number of response categories and still call it the Likert method. Many studies have addressed the relative advantages of using different numbers of points on the response scale (see, e.g., Cheng, 1994; Johnson & Dixon, 1984; Matell & Jacoby, 1972). Second, labels for the response categories vary widely. As noted earlier, Likert's original method used the Strongly Agree–Strongly Disagree labels. However, other labels are common. Examples (citing just the end points) are: Strongly Approve to Strongly Disapprove, Like Very Much to Dislike Very Much, and Very Frequently to Very Infrequently. The author of the scale may customize the labels to fit the item stems. In fact, in some cases the response labels may vary from one group of items to another within the same attitude scale. For example, the first five items may use the Strongly Agree–Strongly Disagree format, while the next five items use a Strongly Approve–Strongly Disapprove format.

Third, in the simple form of the Likert method, all items have the same **directionality.** For example, a Strongly Agree response always indicates a favorable attitude toward the object. In practice, it is common to reverse the directionality of some items so that one end of the response continuum sometimes corresponds to a favorable attitude, sometimes to an unfavorable attitude. This variation helps to control for possible influence of yea-sayer or nay-sayer response sets. Recall that we discussed such response sets on pages 454–458. Notice the difference in directionality for items in Figure 15.8.

Finally, the Likert method assumes that one attitudinal dimension underlies the items. In practice, authors often factor analyze the item responses to determine if more than one dimension underlies the items. For example, factor analysis of items related to attitudes toward mathematics may reveal that there are two relatively independent dimensions: attitude toward the usefulness of math and attitude toward doing math problems. Thus, the attitude scale will yield two scores. Of course, in this scenario, the total score used for item analysis is based on items within a single factor.

The Likert format for attitude scales is widely used today. For many attitudes it is easy to construct items. The response format is quite flexible. And the research methodology for selecting items and determining internal consistency reliability is quite simple. Therefore, we encounter Likert scales in a wide variety of applications.

Thurstone Scales

A second popular methodology for constructing attitude scales is Thurstone's method. Actually, Thurstone elaborated a variety of methods for measuring attitudes; see Thurstone (1959) and Edwards (1957) for convenient listings. However, reference to the **Thurstone** method for measuring attitudes is usually to the method of **equal appearing intervals** (Thurstone & Chave, 1929). Most contemporary applications of Thurstone's method do not include all his attempts to create a psychophysically sophisticated scale. Here are the core elements of Thurstone methodology in practice today. First, write a large number of statements expressing attitudes toward the target object. Statements should cover all possible shades of opinion (see Figure 15.9). Think of opinions as ranging from very favorable to very unfavorable, from love it to hate it. The response format for all statements is simply Agree-Disagree. In practice, the respondent may simply be asked to mark the statements with which he or she agrees. See Figure 15.10 for an example. Second, have a group of judges sort the statements into 11 categories ranging from most to least

	SA	A	U	D	SD
1. The government is working quite efficiently.	0	0	0	0	0
2. Most government employees are overpaid.	0	0	0	0	0
3. Government programs are essential for society.	0	0	0	0	0
4. Private enterprise should replace most government action.	0	0	0	0	0

Note 1: SA = Strongly Agree, A = Agree, U = Uncertain, D = Disagree, SD = Strongly Disagree

Note 2: Items 2 and 4 would be reversed for purposes of scoring.

FIGURE 15.8 Sample items for a Likert-type scale for measuring attitude toward the government.

favorable. The categories are supposed to be equidistant from one another. Thus, the difference between categories 5 and 6 should be the same as the difference between categories 8 and 9—hence the name, method of equal appearing intervals. Thurstone was quite concerned with these psychological distances. However, one can apply the methodology without obsessing over this point. Third, determine for each statement the average category placement and some measure of variation in category placement. For example, for statement number 23, determine the mean and standard deviation of category placements. Fourth, eliminate statements that have large standard deviations. These are statements for which judges do not show good agreement. Fifth, group together statements with similar average category values, for example, all statements with average values 6.0–6.9. Finally, select a few statements to represent attitudinal positions along the continuum from least to most favorable. Starting with 100–150 statements, the final scale might have 30 statements. Figure 15.9 shows sample statements with their associated scale values. Notice the difference in "favorableness" expressed by these statements. Then notice how these scale values work in the array of items in Figure 15.10.

TRY IT!

Refer to Figure 15.9. Write an item that you think might have a scale value of 7.0. Of course, in practice, your item would have to be rated by a group of judges.

Following Thurstone's initial use of this methodology, many other authors developed Thurstone-type scales. However, the methodology is not widely used today. It appears to require too much effort to conduct the necessary research for Thurstone scaling, particularly in comparison with Likert methodology. However, the basic notions developed by Thurstone have been very influential in the evolution of item response theory.

Mark Agree (A) or Disagree (D) for each item.

Scale Value

1.2	These people are the world's worst group.	A	D
1.4	This group causes quite a few problems.	A	D
5.2	Like most groups, this group is a mixture of good and bad.	A	D
5.4	I have mixed feelings about this group.	A	D
10.2	These people make a very positive contribution to the world.	A	D
10.8	This group is tops at everything.	A	D

FIGURE 15.9 Examples of items from a Thurstone-type scale for measuring attitude toward any group.

	Low, unfavorable scale values																High, favorable scale values		
Item	1	2	3	4	5	6	7	8	9	10	11	12	13	14	15	16	17	18	19	20
Person A	✓	✓	✓	✓	✓	✓		✓												
Person B							✓			✓	✓	✓	✓	✓		✓				
Person C													✓			✓	✓	✓	✓	✓	✓

Person A marks "agree" mostly to items with low scale values.

Person B marks "agree" mostly to items with moderate scale values.

Person C marks "agree" mostly to items with high scale values.

FIGURE 15.10   Schematic illustration of how three people's attitudes are located on a Thurstone scale.

Guttman Scales

The third method of attitude scale construction referenced frequently in the professional literature is the **Guttman** method. Its technical name is **scalogram analysis.** However, it is usually just called Guttman scaling, after its author (Guttman, 1944, 1947; see also Guttman & Suchman, 1947).[3] Although this method receives frequent reference, it is not actually applied in very many instances. Its technical requirements are too stringent. It assumes more consistency, even rigidity, in people's attitudes than actually exists. Hence, illustrations of Guttman scaling often employ trivial, even silly examples. Nevertheless, Guttman scaling is a useful conceptual tool, not only for the measurement of attitudes but also for the measurement of other traits such as intelligence, achievement, depression, and so on.

The basic idea of Guttman scaling is to get a set of items ordered with complete internal consistency. We then locate a person's position within this ordered set of items. Once a person's position is located, if the scale meets the Guttman criteria, we know how the person will respond to *all* items. The "trick" is to find the person's change-point in the items. That change-point completely describes the person's response pattern. The person answers all items on one side of the change-point in one direction and all items on the other side of the change-point in the opposite direction. Consider the responses in Figure 15.11. There are eight attitude items. Persons A, B, and C respond agree (+) or disagree (−) to each item. Each person's response pattern is completely consistent on either side of that person's change-point.

To create a Guttman scale (i.e., do a scalogram analysis), we determine whether the item responses fit a pattern like that in Figure 15.11. If there are many inconsistencies (e.g., + + − + − +), then the items do not form a Guttman scale. An important term in Guttman scaling is **replicability**, sometimes called "rep."

---

[3] Guttman (1947, p. 247) said, "We shall call it the Cornell technique for scalogram analysis." The Cornell tag did not stick.

Items	1	2	3	4	5	6	7	8
Person A	+	+	−	−	−	−	−	−
Person B	+	+	+	+	−	−	−	−
Person C	+	+	+	+	+	+	−	−

FIGURE 15.11   Illustration of responses in a Guttman scale.

Replicability tells the extent to which the pattern of responses *is* entirely consistent. Developers of Guttman scales like to see a "rep" of at least 90%.

In our example, we are applying the notion of Guttman scaling to attitude measurement. The + and − responses correspond to "agree" and "disagree" responses. However, think of the + and − responses as corresponding to "correct" and "incorrect" answers to a mathematics aptitude test. This illustrates how the concept of Guttman scaling can be applied to other areas.

Public Opinion Polls and Consumer Research

At some point, the measurement of attitudes shades off into public opinion polls. What is the crucial distinction? Certainly it is *not in the nature of the questions.* Items in attitude scales could easily appear in public opinion polls and vice versa. The crucial distinction is in the target for the inference to be made from the results. In the case of attitude measures, the primary target is an individual. We want to locate an individual along an attitudinal continuum. In the case of public opinion polls, the target is a group. We are primarily interested in the position of a group of people. For example, we may want to determine what percent of people will vote for a certain candidate, what percent of people favor capital punishment, or what brand of cereal people prefer. Reference to "brand of cereal" reminds us that public opinion polls include the field of consumer research, where our interest is in people's attitude toward some product or service. As with other public opinion polls, consumer research focuses on group results.

Summary

1. Differences between personality tests, covered in the previous chapters, and tests of interests and attitudes depend more on the purpose of testing than on the nature of the tests themselves.
2. Career interest inventories are widely used in psychology, especially in the counseling specialty.
3. Three inventories dominate current usage: the *Strong Interest Inventory,* the *Self-Directed Search,* and the *Kuder Career Search with Person Match.*
4. Traditional approaches to career interest measurement divide along two dimensions: the origin of the scales (criterion keying versus broad areas) and item format (absolute versus relative).

5. The names of Edward K. Strong, Jr., and Frederic Kuder have dominated the field through successive editions of their inventories for over 50 years. In more recent times, the work of John Holland has become prominent.

6. Holland's hexagon, the RIASEC coding scheme, provides a commonly used reporting system for several tests, as well as a theoretical base for the Self-Directed Search instrument.

7. The *New Revised Strong Interest Inventory* (SII) has 291 items in 6 blocks. It yields over 200 scores in five categories, conveyed in a colorful report format. The SII has extensive reliability and validity information collected in many studies over a long period.

8. The *Kuder Career Search with Person Match,* the latest in a long line of Kuder career interest inventories, uses forced-choice items and yields scores on 10 vocational interest areas. Its innovative reporting method matches the examinee with persons already employed in relevant occupations.

9. Aiming for simplicity, the *Self-Directed Search* (SDS) emphasizes that it is self-administered, self-scored, and self-interpreted. Holland's RIASEC codes provide the theoretical base for the SDS structure and reporting format. The codes link to occupations organized by the RIASEC system.

10. We developed four generalizations about the widely used career interest inventories: comments about their reliability, validity, relative lack of use of modern psychometric techniques, and favorableness of reviews.

11. There are thousands of specific attitude measures. No single one is widely used. We described three methods of attitude scale construction: the Likert, Thurstone, and Guttman methods.

12. Public opinion polling uses questions similar to those used in attitude measurement, but the focus of attention in polling is on group results rather than individual results.

Key Terms

directionality	Likert	SDS
equal appearing intervals	method of summated	SII
Guttman	ratings	Strong, Edward K. Jr.
Holland, John	replicability	Thurstone
KCS	RIASEC	
Kuder, G. Fredric	scalogram analysis	

Exercises

1. Look at the report for the Kuder Career Search in Figure 15.6. Suppose this is the profile for a high school senior trying to decide on a college major. What advice might you give this student? What information besides the Strong results should the student consider when choosing a college major?

2. Examine the array of item responses in Table 15.9 for Likert items. Apply what you learned in Chapter 4 about internal consistency reliability. Do the responses show a high degree of internal consistency? Briefly explain.

3. Career interest inventories such as the Strong and Kuder usually provide normative data based on occupational groups and college majors. Some of the normative data may be 40 years old. Do you think interest patterns of occupational groups and college majors remain essentially the same over that period? Try to think of two occupations and two college majors that would remain the same over that time. Think of two of each that might have changed substantially. How would you study the stability of interest patterns over time?

4. Although procedures for performing a Guttman (scalogram) analysis of an attitude measure can be daunting, SPSS allows you to conduct such an analysis easily. In SPSS Version 12.0 (as well as in several other versions), click on Analysis, then Scale, then Reliability Analysis. Then, under Model, click on Guttman. Make up a small data set, such as that in Figure 15.11, but use numerical values rather than +'s and −'s. Apply the Guttman procedure and observe the output.

5. In the section on public opinion polls, we noted that the nature of the questions (items) in public opinion polls is often the same as in attitude measures. To observe this similarity, go to www.gallup.com. Check some of the questions used in any recent Gallup poll. Could these same questions be used for a paper-and-pencil attitude measure?

6. To observe the enormous variety of attitudes investigated by psychologists, do a search in a database such as PsycInfo with the key word "attitude." To avoid getting an overloaded list, limit the search to just one or two years. Simply note the variety of reference points for "attitude." You can also obtain a good idea about the great variety of attitude measures by consulting some of the sources listed in Chapter 2, such as Shaw and Wright (1967) or Robinson, Shaver, and Wrightsman (1991).

7. Imagine you were constructing the *Strong Interest Inventory*. For each of Parts I–III, as shown in Table 15.4, add two items that you think might be useful.

Part	*New items*	
I. Occupations	_____	_____
II. School subjects	_____	_____
III. Activities	_____	_____

8. What special features of the career interest inventories do the publishers emphasize? Go to these websites to find out:

For the Strong: www.cpp.com/samplereports/

For the Kuder: www.ncasi.com

For the SDS: www.self-directed-search.com or www.parinc.com

CHAPTER 16

Ethical and Legal Issues

Objectives

1. Distinguish between ethical and legal considerations.

2. List the main sources of ethical principles for psychologists' use of tests.

3. Identify the primary ethical principles governing psychologists' use of tests.

4. Describe the three-tier system for test user qualifications.

5. Identify the three sources of "laws."

6. Summarize the main provisions of these laws relevant to testing: the Civil Rights Acts, IDEA, ADA, FERPA, the EEOC Guidelines, and the Fourteenth Amendment.

7. Identify important principles addressed in these court cases: *Griggs, Debra P., GI Forum, Larry P., PASE, Crawford,* and *Karraker.*

8. Describe the main forensic applications of tests.

us Law

chapter explores ethical and legal issues in the world of testing. Ethical and legal issues are closely related, but they are not identical. **Ethics** deals with what one should or should not do, according to principles or norms of conduct. The **law** deals with what one must or must not do, according to legal dictates. In many areas, ethics and the law overlap. Laws often develop from our notions of ethical principles. It is both illegal and unethical to murder or steal. However, ethics and the law are not synonymous. Let us consider some examples to illustrate the difference. There may be a local zoning law prohibiting construction of a building within 50 feet of a highway. You build within 49 feet. Illegal? Yes. For your 49-foot setback, you may be fined, imprisoned, or required to move your building. Is the 49-foot setback unethical? Probably not, except insofar as we have an obligation to respect laws in general. In fact, you may have mistakenly thought you were using a 50-foot setback, but measured the distance poorly, in which case your conduct was certainly not unethical—but it is still illegal. However, it is unethical for you to sell the building to someone else without disclosing the zoning violation. You lie to your spouse about your consulting fee income. Unethical? Yes. Illegal? No. You lie to the Internal Revenue Service about your consulting fee income. Unethical? Yes. Illegal? Yes. These simple examples illustrate the difference between ethical and legal issues.

In the next section, we examine ethical principles applied to testing: the should's and ought's (and should not's and ought not's). In the following section, we examine legal matters: the must's and must not's. Considering all of these matters requires a certain degree of maturity in the field. We will find that many ethical principles and laws relate to topics such as reliability, validity, and norms, as treated in earlier chapters. That is why we have reserved consideration of ethical and legal issues until this final chapter.

Ethical Issues

To begin our exploration of ethics applicable to testing, consider these cases.

- Dr. Nina, a school psychologist, will be testing Jim, a troublesome and possibly troubled, 12-year-old, referred by the school principal. Dr. Nina will assess Jim's intelligence, probably with the WISC, and personality characteristics, with several different inventories. Of course, Dr. Nina will also interview Jim, talk with his teachers, and review his school records. Should Dr. Nina tell Jim about the purposes of the testing? Or would it be better to disguise those purposes?

- What should Dr. Nina tell Jim's parents before the testing? What about after the testing? Should Dr. Nina inform the parents fully about the results? Or would they be better off not knowing everything?

- Psychological Test Resources, Inc. (PTR), a publisher of psychological tests, has a well-established instrument for assessing attention deficits. The test manual provides an excellent array of validity and reliability data, as well as up-to-date norms. PTR has just developed a computer-based version of the traditional paper-and-pencil form of the test. What studies should PTR undertake before releasing the new computer-based version?

- Dr. Mark uses the computer-based interpretive report for the MMPI-2 (see p. 493). Whose responsibility is it to ensure that the report is validly interpreted—Dr. Mark's or the people who prepared the report? Who should worry about this?

These few cases illustrate some of the ethical issues involved in the use of psychological tests. Notice the use of the word "should" in these cases. This word signals that ethical principles might be involved. In the following sections, we explore psychologists' efforts to develop principles that might apply to these and other cases.

Background on Professional Ethics

The ethics applicable to testing lie within the more general field of ethics for psychologists. Our main concern is ethics applicable to testing, but these ethics do not exist in a vacuum. Three key documents provide background for contemporary ethical codes in psychology. These three documents developed in the fields of medical practice and research. Nevertheless, they are the origin of basic concepts and even terminology for the psychology-specific codes we will examine.

The first key document is the *Hippocratic Oath*. Hippocrates, often labeled the Father of Medicine, was a Greek physician who practiced around 400 B.C. His oath, taken for centuries by physicians, incorporated the notions of the primacy of the patient's welfare, competence (and the boundaries of competence), and confidentiality. It is the origin of the oft-cited phrase "do no harm." The second key document is the *Nuremberg Code* (see U.S. Government Printing Office, 1949). Shuster (1997) called this code "the most important document in the history of medical research" (p. 1436). The code developed from the Nuremberg trials following World War II. These trials prosecuted various groups of Nazi war criminals. The "Doctors' Trial" dealt with physicians who used concentration camp inmates for medical experimentation. Although the context for the Nuremberg code was experimentation rather than ordinary practice, the code has heavily influenced our thinking about health care practice. Wherever the code refers to "experimentation," substitute the word "practice" (or therapy or testing) and you have essential points in today's ethical codes. The Nuremberg Code has been particularly influential in its insistence on the principle of voluntary consent, an important development over the Hippocratic Oath. The third key document is the *Belmont Report,* issued in 1979 under the sponsorship of the U. S. Department of Health, Education, and Welfare (USHEW; 1979). The Belmont Report states the basic ethical principles governing the use of human subjects in research. Although the report's context was research rather than practice, principles articulated in the report have influenced codes of professional ethics for practitioners. The report identifies three basic ethical principles: respect for persons, beneficence, and justice. We will see these principles in ethical codes for psychologists.

TRY IT! ....

Check this website for the Center for Study of Ethics in the Professions: www.iit.edu/departments/csep. It contains ethical codes for over 850 professional associations, businesses, and so on. Can you find the code of ethics for any organization relevant to psychology? (*Hint:* Check under Index, then Health Fields.) You can also find the Oath of Hippocrates at this site.

....

Ethical codes for a specific profession serve several purposes. The first and most important purpose is to provide guidance. Most professionals conscientiously subscribe to such principles as "do good and avoid evil" and "do no harm." However, within any profession, there are common situations where the most general principles do not provide sufficient guidance. The professional person needs to be sensitized to these situations and reminded about what the best thinking is about appropriate conduct. As part of this sensitizing function, codes of ethics often help deal with conflicting principles, that is, to indicate which of several conflicting principles takes precedence in particular situations.

A second reason for codes of professional ethics is to protect the reputation of the profession. The code of ethics represents a kind of social contract between the profession and society. In this connection, many professional associations have procedures for filing complaints about unethical practices and procedures for adjudicating such complaints. The basis for a complaint is alleged violation of the code of ethics. In this sense, the code is not just a guide to good practice but also a quasi-legal document applicable to members of the association. For a useful treatment of the history and purpose of ethical codes, see Bayles (1989).

Sources of Ethical Principles for Testing

There are two main documents for ethical principles applicable to psychological testing. The first is the *Standards for Educational and Psychological Testing* (AERA, APA, NCME, 1999). Usually called simply "the *Standards,*" we referenced this document extensively in Chapters 3–6. Recall that the *Standards* document is filled with references to what should or should not be done in the construction, administration, and interpretation of tests. These "should's" and "should not's" constitute ethical principles for the profession.

Table 16.1 outlines the *Standards.* Our treatment in Chapters 3–6 drew primarily on Part I of the *Standards:* matters relating to validity, reliability, norms, and test construction. In effect, the test itself is the focus of attention in Part I, which is the longest part of the *Standards.* In Part II, the individual—the examinee—is the reference point. Part II deals with matters such as informed consent, providing results to the individual, and the possible effects of cultural differences. Part III takes up special issues that arise in particular settings, for example, in employment or educational testing. Parts II and III draw heavily on the concepts presented in Part I. For example, Part II discusses the relevance of validity concepts to testing

TABLE 16.1 *Outline of the Standards for Educational and Psychological Tests*

Introduction
Part I. Test Construction, Evaluation, and Documentation
    Validity (24)[a]
    Reliability and Errors of Measurement (20)
    Test Development and Revision (27)
    Scales, Norms, and Score Comparability (21)
    Test Administration, Scoring, and Reporting (16)
    Supporting Documentation for Tests (15)
Part II: Fairness in Testing
    Fairness in Testing and Test Use (12)
    The Rights and Responsibilities of Test Takers (13)
    Testing Individuals of Diverse Linguistic Backgrounds (11)
    Testing Individuals with Disabilities (12)
Part III: Testing Applications
    The Responsibilities of Test Users (24)
    Psychological Testing and Assessment (20)
    Educational Testing and Assessment (19)
    Testing in Employment and Credentialing (17)
    Testing in Program Evaluation and Public Policy (13)

[a] Indicates the number of standards in each section.

persons with disabilities or language differences; Part III treats validity concepts applicable to personnel selection.

The second main source of ethical principles applicable to testing is the American Psychological Association's (APA, 2002) *Ethical Principles of Psychologists and Code of Conduct.* Various sources abbreviate this unwieldy title as the "Ethical Principles" or "Code of Conduct." The document itself uses the term the *Ethics Code,* which we will adopt here. The APA first published an ethics code in 1953. The code has undergone several revisions, the most recent prior to the current version in 1992 (APA, 1992). The 2002 code represents a substantial revision of the 1992 code in organization and terminology, but not in substance. For example, in the 1992 code "competence" was a general principle, whereas it constitutes a section of standards in the 2002 code. Its essence remains the same, although the 2002 code gives more detail on several points.

Table 16.2 gives the outline for the 2002 version of the **APA Ethics Code.** Following the Introduction and Preamble, the code gives five basic principles. Table 16.3 gives the first sentence from each principle to indicate its basic content. The numbered sections of the code contain the "standards." Each of the standards consists of several specific points. We indicate the titles of each point only for Section 9: Assessment because of its obvious relevance to our topic. However, several other sections contain critical points applicable to testing. Of special importance, as we will see, are the sections on competence, human relations, privacy and confidentiality, and record keeping.

TABLE 16.2   *Outline of the APA Ethics Code, 2002 Edition*

Introduction and Applicability
Preamble
General Principles
   A.   Beneficence and Non-Maleficence
   B.   Fidelity and Responsibility
   C.   Integrity
   D.   Justice
   E.   Respect for People's Rights and Dignity
Ethical Standards
   1.   Resolving Ethical Issues
   2.   Competence
   3.   Human Relations
   4.   Privacy and Confidentiality
   5.   Advertising and Other Public Statements
   6.   Record Keeping and Fees
   7.   Education and Training
   8.   Research and Publication
   9.   Assessment
           9.01.   Bases for Assessments
           9.02.   Use of Assessments
           9.03.   Informed Consent in Assessments
           9.04.   Release of Test Data
           9.05.   Test Construction
           9.06.   Interpreting Assessment Results
           9.07.   Assessment by Unqualified Persons
           9.08.   Obsolete Tests and Outdated Test Results
           9.09.   Test Scoring and Interpretation Services
           9.10.   Explaining Assessment Results
           9.11.   Maintaining Test Security
  10.   Therapy

Source: American Psychological Association, 2002.

Other Sources

In addition to the *Standards* and the APA Ethics Code, there are other sources relevant to the ethical use of tests. First, several other professional associations have their own codes of ethics, which include specific reference to test usage. Examples include the American Counseling Association (ACA) and the National Association of School Psychologists (NASP). The ACA Code of Ethics (ACA, 2000) consists of seven sections, with a total of over 150 specific principles. The principles of greatest relevance to testing are in Section E: Evaluation, Assessment, and Interpretation. Other parts, particularly the section on research, also touch on testing. NASP (2000) embeds its Principles for Professional Ethics within a more general document, the NASP Professional Conduct Manual. Within the Principles document, Section

TABLE 16.3 General Principles of the APA Ethics Code

A. *Beneficence and Non-Maleficence.*[1] "Psychologists strive to benefit those with whom they work and take care to do no harm."

B. *Fidelity and Responsibility.* "Psychologists establish relationships of trust with those with whom they work."

C. *Integrity.* "Psychologists seek to promote accuracy, honesty, and truthfulness in the science, teaching, and practice of psychology."

D. *Justice.* "Psychologists recognize that fairness and justice entitle all persons to access to and benefit from the contributions of psychology."

E. *Respect for People's Rights and Dignity.* "Psychologists respect the dignity and worth of all people and the rights of individuals to privacy, confidentiality, and self-determination."

Source: From American Psychological Association (2002), *Ethical Principles of Psychologists and Code of Conduct.*

IV.C: Assessment and Intervention and Section IV.D: Reporting Data and Conference Results are most relevant to testing. As with the ACA code, several other sections of the NASP code also touch on test-related matters. The NASP code, understandably, pays special attention to the role of parents and legal guardians. In general, the APA, ACA, and NASP codes are very similar in structure and highly congruent in substance. They differ primarily in language and context.

In addition to the Ethics Code, the APA periodically issues other policy statements relevant to special aspects of testing. For example, there is an APA statement on computer-based testing and interpretation (APA, 1986) and another on child custody evaluations (APA, 1994). Another example is the APA's Guidelines for Test User Qualifications (Turner, DeMers, Fox, & Reed, 2001), which covers much the same ground as Section 9 of the Ethics Code. Such statements often appear in the *American Psychologist,* APA's flagship journal. Obviously, these statements treat a narrower range of topics than the more general Ethics Code.

TRY IT!

Access the APA Ethics Code at www.apa.org/ethics.
What does the code say in section 9.03 about informed consent?

Recall that the *Standards* is a joint publication of three organizations: American Educational Research Association (AERA), American Psychological Association (APA), and National Council on Measurement in Education (NCME). These

---

[1] Here is a brief vocabulary lesson for these rather large words. Beneficence comes from the Latin *bene,* meaning good, as in benefit or benediction, and *facio,* meaning do, as in factory. Maleficence comes from the Latin *mal,* meaning bad, as in malice or malnutrition, and again *facio,* to do. Hence, the simple translation of "beneficence and non-maleficence" is "do good and do no harm."

same three organizations, plus several other professional associations, sponsored the Joint Committee on Testing Practices (JCTP), which issued a *Code of Fair Testing Practices in Education* (JCTP, 2004, available at www.apa.org/science/fairtestcode.htm). The first version appeared in 1988, and a revised version in 2004. This code provides parallel standards for test developers and test users in four major areas: developing and selecting tests; administering and scoring tests; reporting and interpreting tests; and informing test-takers. The standards aim at consistency with those published by other groups, such as those we have outlined earlier, but are more specific to the educational context. The JCTP is currently developing a set of guidelines for assessment of individuals with disabilities.

Finally, we mention an excellent book, *Ethics in Psychology: Professional Standards and Cases* (Koocher & Keith-Spiegel, 1998) that provides extended treatment of ethical issues, with interesting case examples. Chapter 7, Psychological Assessment: Testing Tribulations, is especially relevant for our topic here. Though based on the 1992 APA code, the commentary by Canter, Bennett, Jones, and Nagy (1994) is also useful; it is especially helpful for historical background on the code.

Generalizations about Ethical Use of Tests

From all these sources we derive the following essential ethical principles applicable to the use of tests. This summary (see Key Points Summary 16.1) does not serve as a substitute for the full text of any of the codes, which the reader is encouraged to consult for further detail. However, this summary covers the main points for an introductory treatment. Our main point of reference is the APA Ethics Code.

Competence

To utilize tests responsibly, the psychologist should develop **competence** in assessment concepts and methodology. The concepts include the basic ideas covered in Chapters 3–6 of this book: norms, reliability, validity, and test construction. The methodology includes the specific procedures applicable to a particular test, such as its administration, scoring, and technical characteristics. Competence with respect to methodology implies conforming to the procedures for administering, scoring, and so on. A person lacking competence in the concepts and methodology of assessment should not use tests.

The competence principle has several subsidiary principles. The psychologist is responsible for continually updating his or her knowledge and skills regarding assessment. The psychologist must recognize the boundaries of competence. (The term *boundaries of competence* is a common one in the ethics literature.) For example, a psychologist may be competent in the use of individual intelligence tests, but not projective techniques. A psychologist may be competent in use of one projective technique (say, Rotter's incomplete sentences), but not in another projective technique (say, Exner's Rorschach system). The psychologist must recognize these boundaries of competence. Finally, the code calls special attention to the need for knowledge regarding diverse populations. The psychologist needs to study and be sensitive to such factors as cultural background and language preference.

Informed Consent

The patient, client, or subject must voluntarily consent to the assessment. The psychologist is responsible for informing the person about the nature and purpose of the assessment. Moreover, the psychologist must provide this information in a form and language understandable to the person. In the case of children or others of limited capacity, consent must be obtained from a parent, legal guardian, or suitable substitute. **Informed consent** entails continuing consent. That is, the person may withdraw consent at any time.

The APA Ethics code includes some exceptions to the informed consent principle. For legally mandated assessment, the psychologist must inform the person about the nature and purpose of assessment, while not requiring the person's consent. There are also instances of implied consent. For example, a person applying for a job gives implied consent. By seeking the job, the person implies willingness to complete the job application process, including any testing. Institutional testing programs, for example, school testing programs, also constitute an exception.

Key Points Summary 16.1

Summary of Ethical Principles Related to Testing

Broadly Applicable Principles:
- Ensuring Competence
- Obtaining Informed Consent
- Providing Knowledge of Results
- Maintaining Confidentiality
- Guarding Test Security

Principles with More Limited Applicability:
- Setting High Standards for Test Development
- Assuming Responsibility for Automated Reporting
- Working to Prevent Unqualified Test Use

Knowledge of Results

The patient, client, or subject has a right to full disclosure of test results. Hence, the psychologist should provide these results and do so in language that is reasonably understandable to the individual. This principle, like the informed consent principle, arises from considering the client as an autonomous, self-determining individual. Also like the informed consent principle, the **knowledge of results** principle has certain exceptions, for example, in employment testing.

Confidentiality

The psychologist should treat test results as confidential information. Release of the test results should only be made to another qualified professional *and* with the consent of the client. Of course, the psychologist must not refer to the test results outside the context and purpose for which the results were obtained.

An important subsidiary principle to **confidentiality** relates to record keeping. The psychologist should maintain assessment results in a secure manner and eventually dispose of them in a manner befitting confidential information with a rational document retention policy. There are exceptions to the confidentiality principle as required by law or court action.

Here is an important point that is not directly related to testing but worthy of mention. The psychologist's general responsibility to maintain confidentiality is waived when grave harm may come to the client or others. For example, if the psychologist learns, through testing or other means, that an individual plans to murder someone or commit suicide, the more general principle of avoiding harm takes precedence over the principle of confidentiality. For details of a landmark case on this point, see *Tarasoff v. University of California* (P.2d 334, 9th Circuit 1976).

Test Security

The psychologist should maintain **test security.** Test materials are held in a secure environment. Test items are not revealed in casual conversations and public media. Exceptions are made for formal training programs and when mandated by law.

The five principles outlined here cover the main points in the ethical codes related to testing. However, there are three additional points with more limited applicability. We consider these now.

Test Construction and Publication

All the other principles outlined here apply to the psychologist using tests. Many psychologists use tests—relatively few develop new tests. Psychologists engaged in test construction and publication have special obligations. They must maintain high standards in developing tests and refrain from making unwarranted claims about the quality of their products. Test developers are expected to have expertise regarding such matters as reliability, validity, and norms; and to apply this expertise in the test development process. After a test is developed, psychologists must provide adequate information about the technical characteristics of the test. In addition, they must exercise due caution in describing the test.

Automated Scoring/Interpretation Systems

Recent years have witnessed a proliferation of automated scoring and interpretive systems for tests, especially the more widely used tests. Computer-generated narrative reports are a good example. We have examined a few of these in earlier chapters. The ethical codes for psychologists express special concern about these automated systems. The essential point is that the psychologist utilizing such systems retains responsibility for proper interpretation of the test results. Responsibility does not transfer to the developer of the system, although, as per the preceding section, the developer has his or her own ethical responsibilities.

Unqualified Persons

The psychologist does not allow or condone the use of tests by unqualified persons. For example, within her practice, the psychologist does not allow a clerical staff member, untrained in testing, to administer the PPVT or WISC to clients. Psychologists also take prudent action when observing that unqualified persons are administering tests even in circumstances beyond the psychologist's immediate control.

Test User Qualifications

The profession of psychology has attempted to control the use of tests by specifying qualifications for the purchase of tests. We usually refer to these attempts under the heading of **test user qualifications.** A more accurate title would be "test purchaser qualifications." It is at least possible, for commercially published tests, to exercise some control at the point of purchase. Once purchased, it is very difficult to control a test's use. One of APA's earliest attempts to construct any type of ethics code related precisely to this point (Eyde et al., 1988). This early effort highlights both the central role testing has played in psychology and the special concern psychologists have long had about proper test usage. As Koocher and Keith-Spiegel (1998) note: "Psychological testing is at the very heart of our professional history" (p. 166).

In Chapter 1, we recounted the history of the *Standards for Educational and Psychological Tests,* a document referenced repeatedly in this book. The 1950 edition of the *Standards* introduced a three-tier system for test user qualifications. Later editions abandoned this system. However, many test publishers found the three-tier system a convenient mechanism for dealing with the nettlesome issue of who could or could not purchase various kinds of tests. Many publishers adopted the system and continue to use it, even though it is no longer in the *Standards.*

The three tiers in this system are as follows:

Level A—Minimal training required. Test administration involves reading simple directions. Covers such tests as educational achievement and job proficiency.

Level B—Some knowledge of technical characteristics of tests required. Covers such tests as group-administered mental ability and interest inventories.

Level C—Requires advanced training in test theory and relevant content areas. Covers individually administered intelligence tests and personality tests.

TRY IT!

How would you classify each of these tests in the three-tier system for test user qualifications:

Stanford Achievement Test _____   WAIS-III _____

Rotter's Incomplete Sentences _____   Strong Interest Inventory _____

Although this three-tier system is widely known, its actual application and enforcement seem to be somewhat uneven (Robertson, 1986). A consortium of professional associations sponsored a project to develop a more sophisticated and databased approach to test user qualifications (Eyde, et al., 1988; Moreland, et al., 1995). The project did develop a more sophisticated approach. However, it is not yet clear whether the effort will have a widespread and lasting impact on the field.

Legal Issues

What do tests have to do with the law? How can the seemingly arcane topics of validity coefficients and norm groups possibly relate to the nitty-gritty matters of the legislature and courtroom? As we will see, quite a bit. Consider the following questions.

- The ABC Widget Company uses the Pennsylvania Screening Test to help select employees. An African-American applicant (who was not hired) files a complaint with the Equal Opportunity Employment Commission that the test was discriminatory. What legal principles apply to this claim?

- A school psychologist uses the WISC-III to determine whether an Asian-American child should be assigned to a special education program. Is this legal?

- In the latter case, the child's parents want to see the test results. Is the psychologist legally bound to give the results to the parents?

- A student claims that he needs extra time to complete a test because of a learning disability. Is the school legally bound to accommodate the request?

- You are a clinical psychologist. A judge asks you to determine whether a person accused of murder is "competent to stand trial." How will you proceed? Will you use any tests?

These are just a few examples of the fascinating ways in which tests interface with the law. In the following sections, we explore this interface. Before we begin, a note of caution. When introducing such tests as the WAIS-III and MMPI-2, we often noted that actual use of these tests required advanced training. Our coverage was merely an introduction and overview. A similar caution applies to our treatment of legal issues. We provide an overview of the laws and their application. However, this overview will not prepare you to present a case in court.

Areas of Application: An Overview

Tests interface with legal issues primarily in four areas (see Key Points Summary 16.2). The first area is use of tests for employment decisions. Employment means hiring, firing, promotion, and related areas. The major concern is with equality of opportunity by race and gender. In practice, hiring has received the greatest attention.

The second area is use of tests in education. There are two main subcategories of activity. The first subcategory is use of tests for placement decisions, particularly for special education programs. The second subcategory relates to certification, for example, for awarding high school diplomas.

For the areas of application in employment and education, there have been two main target groups: racial/ethnic minorities and persons with disabilities. The racial/ethnic minorities, as defined by the U.S. government, are African American, Hispanic, Asian American, and Native American. We will define the category of persons with disabilities below in connection with the Americans with Disabilities Act (ADA).

The third major area of application is in forensic psychology. Forensic psychology deals with the application of psychology, including but certainly not limited to tests, in legal actions. Some psychologists specialize in forensic activities. We use the term here, loosely, to refer to any psychologist's actions when they are performed in court proceedings. The court itself may call on a psychologist to give expert testimony on such matters as mental competence. Alternatively, the psychologist may serve as an expert witness for either the prosecution or defense. For example, in the case of a

---

Key Points Summary 16.2

The Interface of Tests and the Law: Four Major Contexts

1. Employment
2. Education (Placement, Certification)
3. Forensics
4. Mandated Test Programs

head injury sustained in an accident, a neuropsychologist may testify about the extent of damage, drawing heavily on results from a variety of tests. We examined relevant examples in Chapter 10.

The fourth area of application is mandated testing programs, especially state testing programs. We discussed such programs in Chapter 11. There is no need for further treatment here, except to note that these tests are an example of the interface of testing and the law.

Definition of Laws

In ordinary conversation, the word "laws" connotes a written prescription originating with some legislative body. There is a law, in most states, that the speed limit on rural interstate highways is 65 miles per hour. There is a law that one must be 21 years old to purchase alcoholic beverages. However, this common meaning of the word "laws" is not sufficient for our purposes. To discuss the interface of tests and "the law," we need an expanded definition. For our purposes, laws originate from three sources (see Key Points Summary 16.3).

The first type of law is **statutory law or legislation.** This is the common meaning of the term *law*. These laws originate with a legislative body, such as the U.S. Congress, state legislature, or local governing body. Typically, the legislature's action must be endorsed by an executive (e.g., the president or governor) before becoming law. For simplicity we include the U.S. and state constitutions in this category. The second type of law is **administrative law or regulations.** An administrative agency, ordinarily in the executive branch of government, prepares these regulations. Very often, they provide the details on implementing a particular law. Although not passed by a legislature, these regulations usually have the force of law. The third type of law is **case law,** that is, court decisions. Courts interpret the meaning of laws when applied in particular circumstances. A court's decision, once rendered, has the force of law, at least within the jurisdiction of the court. Included within our definition of court decisions are consent decrees and consent orders. In these instances, the court does not render a decision in favor of one of the contesting parties, but in the process of contesting the issue, the parties reach agreement as to how the issue will be resolved.

Key Points Summary 16.3
Three Sources of Laws

1. Statutory Law; Legislation
2. Administrative Law; Regulations
3. Case Law; Court Cases

The force of the law is much the same regardless of its origin: statutory, administrative, or case. That is, all these sources give rise to laws that must be obeyed.

Laws Related to Testing

We outline here the statutory and administrative laws of primary importance in the field of testing. In the following section, we will examine some relevant court decisions (case law). We begin with a primer on terms and sources of information.

Most of the laws relevant to testing are federal in origin. There are a few state laws and even, occasionally, a local law related to testing. Each state also generally has specific laws and regulations designed to implement federal laws within the state's organizational structure. However, we concentrate here on federal laws since they are the dominant forces related to testing.

Reference to laws brings with it a blizzard of numbers and initials. To assist with our review we identify the following special terms and abbreviations:

U.S.C. stands for United States Code. This means a law passed by the U.S. Congress. A number, identifying the general area of law, precedes the initials U.S.C., and a section number follows the initials. For example, 29 U.S.C. § 791 designates part of the Rehabilitation Act described later. (The symbol § is read as "section.")

C.F.R. stands for Code of Federal Regulations. This is administrative law, whereas U.S.C. is statutory law. Numbers preceding and following "C.F.R." identify the particular regulation. For example, 29 C.F.R. 1607 designates the EEOC Uniform Guidelines on Employee Selection Procedures described below.

P.L. stands for Public Law. A specific P.L., for example, P.L. 94–142, has two parts. The first part (94) indicates the congressional year, here the 94th Congress. The second part indicates the numbered law within that congressional year, here the 142nd law passed by the 94th Congress. The P.L. number is unrelated to the U.S.C. number. The P.L. number for some laws, including our example here, P.L. 94–142, becomes the popular method for referencing the law. In other instances, the popular name for a law comes from the law's title, for example, the Civil Rights Act or an acronym such as IDEA: the Individuals with Disabilities Education Act. IDEA is actually a successor to P.L. 94–142. One goes by an acronym, the other by a P.L. number.

We list the major laws related to testing in Figure 16.1 roughly in historical sequence. However, several points must be emphasized about this order. First, many of these laws are under continual revision. This most often occurs by amendment, where the name and number of the law remain the same but amendments are attached. At other times, the revision is so sweeping as to merit a new name and number, but many of the basic ideas for the new law come from the earlier version. Tracing the lineage of a particular law can be very challenging. Second, partly because of these changes, what once was legal may now be illegal and vice versa. Third, among the laws described, there is much cross-referencing. The laws listed in Figure 16.1 form a web or network. They are not isolated, entirely independent entities. For example, one law may indicate that it incorporates a definition from another law. In such a case, in order to interpret the one law, the reader must consult the other

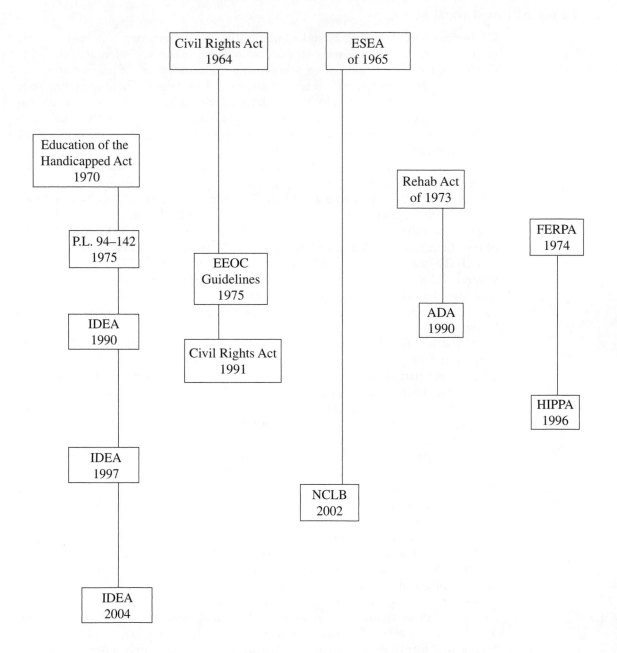

FIGURE 16.1   Major laws related to testing.

law. Here is an important related point: Names change without change in meaning. For example, earlier laws referred to *handicapped,* but more recent laws use the term *disabled* or *persons with disabilities* to identify the same category; see Data Research (1994) as well as the preamble to 42 U.S.C. § 2000 for this particular change. Earlier documents also referred to Negroes, whereas now the term *African Americans* prevails. Fourth, many "laws" have both statutory and administrative versions. One needs to consult both sources for a full understanding of "the law."

For readers interested in pursuing the full text of laws or court cases, the following sources, unfamiliar to most students of psychology, will be helpful. United States laws (U.S.C.s) and regulations (C.F.R.s) are available on general websites. In addition, various government agencies maintain their own websites, including the laws and regulations the agencies oversee. Often, these websites also include ancillary materials such as simplified versions of the laws and training programs related to implementing the laws. For court cases, there are two standard databases: LexisNexis and Westlaw. Each database maintains a comprehensive and cross-referenced list of court decisions. These are essential tools for lawyers. They are very useful sources for psychologists interested in the interface of testing and the law. Most major academic libraries will subscribe to at least one of these databases.

Useful Sources of Information on Laws

For the full text of U.S. laws (codes), go to: http://uscode.house.gov/search/criteria.shtml

For the full text of U.S. regulations, go to: http://www.gpoaccess.gov/cfr/index.html

For court cases as well as laws and regulations, access either of these databases: LexisNexis or Westlaw

What to Watch for

All the laws we review below have much broader scope than just testing. Our special concern will be with the testing implications. As we move through the various laws, be alert for the following points:

1. Some laws require the use of tests and other types of assessments. This is obviously the case with mandated state testing programs. However, it is also true for laws related to persons with disabilities.

2. Some laws require that appropriate validity information be available to justify the use of tests. This is particularly true regarding employment tests, although it also applies to certain uses of educational tests.

3. Laws related to persons with disabilities place heavy emphasis on diagnostic functions. In practice, this usually means using a variety of tests or multi-score tests.

4. Some of the laws make specific reference to accommodations in testing conditions, including the language used for the test. Such accommodations create a special challenge in considering the test as a standardized instrument.

Watching for these points as we examine various laws will help to focus attention on why we are considering these laws. Our later examination of court cases will also focus on some of these issues.

TABLE 16.4 *Section 1 of the Fourteenth Amendment of the U.S. Constitution*

All persons born or naturalized in the United States, and subject to the jurisdiction thereof, are citizens of the United States and of the state wherein they reside. No state shall make or enforce any law which shall abridge the privileges or immunities of citizens of the United States; nor shall any state deprive any person of life, liberty, or property, without **due process** of law; nor deny to any person within its jurisdiction the **equal protection** of the laws. [emphasis added.]

The Fourteenth Amendment

The first law relevant to testing is the **Fourteenth Amendment** to the U.S. Constitution, specifically, Section 1. One part of Section 1 is the "due process" clause. Another part is the "equal protection" clause. Table 16.4 presents Section 1 of the Fourteenth Amendment, with key words marked in boldface. The **equal protection clause** is the most important part for testing. The Fourteenth Amendment was ratified in 1868. Its principal intent was to prevent states (mainly the former Confederate states) from passing laws restricting the rights of former slaves. Who would have thought that a constitutional amendment passed in 1868, in the aftermath of the Civil War, would relate to the use of psychological tests in the year 2007? It does. Here is the key notion: If a test (or anything else) operates to arbitrarily restrict the rights (including opportunities) of some individuals (citizens), then the equal protection clause of the Fourteenth Amendment becomes relevant.[2]

When developing the following laws, the U.S. Congress has frequently referenced the Fourteenth Amendment. Occasionally, Congress has also used two other reference points. The first is the power to regulate interstate commerce, given to Congress in Article I, Section 8(3) of the U.S. Constitution: "To regulate commerce with foreign nations, and among the several states, and with the Indian tribes." The second is controlling purse strings related to federal programs. If a state or other agency does not take certain actions, Congress withholds federal funds from that state or agency. Controlling the purse strings can be an enormously powerful mechanism. However, the Fourteenth Amendment has been the most frequent reference point for these laws and associated court cases.

The Civil Rights Acts of 1964 and 1991

Fast forward from the post–Civil War era to the mid-1960s, the era of the civil rights movement in the United States. The most influential piece of legislation relevant to testing passed in modern times was the **Civil Rights Act** of 1964.

---

[2] The Fifth Amendment also has a "due process" clause. It deals with matters such as double jeopardy, self-incrimination, and other items not relevant to our considerations here.

Specifically, Title VII of this act dealt with employment discrimination. In fact, one popular name of the Civil Rights Act was the *Equal Employment Opportunity Act.* The principal concern was that employers might arrange their employment procedures, including tests, to exclude African Americans. Of course, the resulting laws ultimately covered other minority groups, including women, but the primary target group was African Americans. The Civil Rights Act of 1964 created the Equal Employment Opportunity Commission (EEOC). The EEOC, in turn, created the Uniform Guidelines described later, a prime example of administrative law. Congress passed a major revision of the Civil Rights Act in 1991. Most of the 1964 provisions remained intact. However, there was one major change relevant to testing that we will examine: the use of subgroup norms.

Rehabilitation Act of 1973 and Americans with Disabilities Act of 1990

Two closely related laws are the Rehabilitation Act of 1973 (29 U.S.C. § 701; P.L. 93–112) and the Americans with Disabilities Act of 1990 (ADA; 42 U.S.C. § 12101; P.L. 101–336). In many ways, the **ADA** is a revision and expansion of the Rehabilitation Act, although the latter remains in effect. The primary purpose of these laws was to provide access for the handicapped, with initial focus on such items as architectural barriers. Could a person in a wheelchair use the local public library? Thus, the international symbol for "handicapped accessible" is a wheelchair. However, these laws construe the term *handicapped* or *disabled* very broadly to include not only physical handicaps but also psychological or mental disabilities. The definition includes "specific learning disabilities," which has led to an explosive growth in the number of persons and types of "barriers" covered by the laws.

Environmental adjustments for the disabled are often called **accommodations.** Ramps and elevators are obvious accommodations for persons in wheelchairs. Accommodations in testing conditions may involve large-print editions of tests for persons with visual handicaps A particularly controversial accommodation is extending the time limits on tests. The crucial question is whether an accommodation "levels the playing field" for the person with a disability or gives that person an unfair advantage over persons who do not receive the accommodation. More technically, an accommodation in testing should render the test's validity and norms equally applicable to disabled and nondisabled examinees. Consider a reading comprehension test. Its purpose is to determine understanding of the printed word. A person with limited vision may need a large-print version of the test. For such a person, a normal-print version is a test of vision, not reading comprehension. A person with normal vision will perform no better on the large-print version than on the normal-print version. Thus, the large-print version seems an entirely reasonable accommodation. Now consider use of a reader for the test, that is, someone who reads the test to the visually disabled person. This accommodation may very well change the nature of what is being measured. The test may now measure listening comprehension rather than reading comprehension. In addition, everyone—both visually disabled and nondisabled persons—may do better with a reader. Consider also the question of extending the time limit on a test, an accommodation often

TABLE 16.5   *Purposes of the Americans with Disabilities Act*

1. To provide a clear and comprehensive national mandate for the elimination of discrimination against individuals with disabilities.
2. To provide clear, strong, consistent, enforceable standards addressing discrimination against individuals with disabilities.
3. To ensure that the federal government plays a central role in enforcing the standards.
4. To invoke the sweep of congressional authority, including the power to enforce the Fourteenth Amendment and to regulate commerce, in order to address the major areas of discrimination faced day-to-day by people with disabilities.

proposed for certain learning disability cases. If the test is a pure power test, giving additional time to someone who wants more time should be acceptable. However, very few tests are pure power tests. The learning disabled student may do better with more time, but so might other examinees (or they may not).

Numerous studies are currently being directed at the effects of various accommodations on test performance. Clearly, we have much to learn about this topic. Willingham et al. (1988) reported an extensive study of the effects of accommodations in testing conditions for the SAT and GRE. They provided an excellent review of the general issues involved in making some accommodations. Camara (2001) supplied a convenient summary of the types of accommodations requested for the SAT; extended time was, by far, the most frequent request. Nester (1994) also reviewed the issue of providing accommodations under the Americans with Disabilities Act. Pitoniak and Royer (2001) summarized the history of relevant legislation and the types of accommodations related to large-scale testing programs. There is also the question of whether scores derived from a test administered with accommodations should be "flagged," that is, marked to indicate the nonstandard administration. This is a policy issue on which the field has no consensus position.

Table 16.5 gives the statement of purpose for the ADA. Notice the reference to the Fourteenth Amendment. Basic definitions covered by the ADA are essentially the same as those for IDEA shown in Table 16.6.

The Handicapped/Disabled in Education: P.L. 94–142 and IDEA

A succession of laws beginning in 1970 dealt with the disabled in educational settings. We list here the major landmarks, omitting the many intermediate revisions and amendments. The first law was Education of the Handicapped Act (EHA) in 1970. A major revision was entitled Education for All Handicapped Children, passed in 1975. This was P.L. 94–142, a tag that stuck and is still used today. This law was amended at least four times (each time receiving a new "P.L." number). There was a major revision in 1997, entitled Individuals with Disabilities Education Act and another revision in 2004 (IDEA; 20 U.S.C. §1400, P. L. 108–446).[3]

---

[3] The official title of this revision is Individuals with Disabilities Education Improvement Act of 2004, yielding the acronym IDEIA, although it is more frequently referenced as IDEA 2004.

TABLE 16.6   *Excerpts from IDEA's Definitions of Disability*

The term **child with a disability** means a child

- with mental retardation, hearing impairments (including deafness), speech or language impairments, visual impairments (including blindness), serious emotional disturbance (referred to in this title as "emotional disturbance"), orthopedic impairments, autism, traumatic brain injury, other health impairments, or specific learning disabilities; and

- who, by reason thereof, needs special education and related services.

The term **specific learning disability** means a disorder in 1 or more of the basic psychological processes involved in understanding or in using language, spoken or written, which disorder may manifest itself in the imperfect ability to listen, think, speak, read, write, spell, or do mathematical calculations.

DISORDERS INCLUDED: Such term includes such conditions as perceptual disabilities, brain injury, minimal brain dysfunction, dyslexia, and developmental aphasia.

DISORDERS NOT INCLUDED: Such term does not include a learning problem that is primarily the result of visual, hearing, or motor disabilities, of mental retardation, of emotional disturbance, or of environmental, cultural, or economic disadvantage.

Table 16.6 contains the definitions of "child with a disability" and "specific learning disability" from IDEA.

The essential point of all these laws was to provide a "free appropriate public education" for all children, with special attention to the handicapped/disabled. The phrase "free appropriate public education" is used so frequently in these laws and associated documents that it receives its own acronym: FAPE. The key word in the phrase is "appropriate." What will be appropriate? Is it appropriate to place the disabled in separate classrooms? What are appropriate ways to assess the needs of the disabled student? This latter question is where tests enter the picture. Notice in the definitions contained in Table 16.6 reference to specific conditions and the probable causes of those conditions. Tests are nearly always involved in these diagnostic functions.

IDEA, as well as its predecessors, calls for development of "individualized education programs," popularly known as **IEPs.** Each disabled child must have an IEP. The law specifies who is to be involved in preparation and execution of the IEP (including parents), procedures for updating the IEP, and the role of testing in the IEP. Table 16.7 shows some of the IDEA provisions (§ 614) related to testing. Needless to say, the school psychologist must be thoroughly familiar with this law. Clinical psychologists in private practice or in agencies other than schools are also called on for testing related to (a) identification of disabilities and (b) information relevant to an IEP.

Examination of the excerpts in Table 16.7 reveals two main points. First, the statements are consistent with the professional standards we have emphasized

TABLE 16.7 *Sample Statements Related to Testing from IDEA*

In conducting the evaluation, the local educational agency shall—

- use a variety of assessment tools and strategies to gather relevant functional, developmental, and academic information, including information provided by the parent
- not use any single measure or assessment as the sole criterion
- use technically sound instruments that may assess the relative contribution of cognitive and behavioral factors, in addition to physical or developmental factors.

Each local educational agency shall ensure that [assessments and other evaluation materials]

- are selected and administered so as not to be discriminatory on a racial or cultural basis;
- are provided and administered in the language and form most likely to yield accurate information;
- are used for purposes for which the assessments or measures are valid and reliable;
- are administered by trained and knowledgeable personnel; and
- are administered in accordance with any instructions provided by the producer of such assessments.

throughout about the technical quality of tests. Second, the statements are highly specific regarding the obligations of the person(s) selecting and administering the tests. Hence, a general understanding of professional standards for tests is not sufficient to comply with all the legal requirements. One must read the law itself and relevant regulatory declarations.

Another provision in these laws calls for educating the disabled in the "least restrictive environment." In practice, this means "mainstreaming," that is, including disabled students in regular classrooms rather than in separate special education classrooms. As with many aspects of the law, there are exceptions to this principle.

FERPA and HIPPA

The Family Education Rights and Privacy Act of 1974, with acronym **FERPA,** is also known as the Buckley Amendment after its chief sponsor, Senator James Buckley of New York. The principal purpose of FERPA is to guarantee that individuals have open access to information about themselves, that individuals can challenge the validity of information in agency files, and that unwarranted other parties do not have access to personal information. FERPA's special relevance for testing deals with test scores. Test information has to be available to the examinee or, in the case of minors, to parents or guardians. Although it may be hard to believe today, in pre-FERPA days it was common for schools and other agencies to prohibit parents from seeing the test results for their children. Furthermore, the law lays out specific restrictions on the release of such information to other parties without the individual's consent.

Another federal law, though differing in its specific target, has much the same effect as FERPA. The *Health Insurance Portability and Accountability Act of 1996* (P. L. 104–91), popularly known as **HIPPA,** is aimed principally at the health industry. That industry includes mental health and the use of psychological tests. Originally passed by Congress in 1996, some of HIPPA's provisions, for example, the "Privacy Rule," which is of special relevance for testing, did not take effect until 2005. In general, FERPA and HIPPA are quite consistent with the ethical principles regarding confidentiality examined earlier in this chapter.

EEOC Guidelines

As a direct outgrowth of the Civil Rights Act of 1964, the Equal Employment Opportunity Commission (EEOC, 1978) issued the *Uniform Guidelines on Employee Selection Procedures.* The EEOC code is 29 C.F.R. § 1607. There was joint sponsorship by several other federal agencies, each using its own code. We will call them the **EEOC Guidelines** or simply the Guidelines. They serve as a prime example of regulations or administrative law. Thus, the term *guidelines* is a euphemism. The document imposes very strict requirements on employers.

TRY IT! ....

To see the full text of the EEOC Guidelines, go to www.eeoc.gov and find 29 C.F.R. § 1607. The site also contains many of the laws referenced in this section.

....

The EEOC Guidelines were "intended to establish a uniform Federal position in the area of prohibiting discrimination in employment on grounds of race, religion, sex or national origin" (29 C.F.R. § 1607.18). More specifically, the Guidelines "apply to tests and other selection procedures which are used as a basis for any employment decision" (29 C.F.R. § 1607.2B).

The Guidelines consistently use the phrase "tests and other selection procedures." Since our focus is on tests, in the following paragraphs, we will usually refer only to tests. However, all statements apply to any selection procedure, device, or requirement. For example, the Guidelines cover the requirement for a certain level of education, say, a high school diploma or the results of an interview. We also omit certain exceptions, such as applicability to areas surrounding Indian reservations. As with other laws treated here, we aim to give the main thrust of the laws, not every jot and tittle.

To an individual familiar with the principles of psychological testing (the principles covered in this book), the EEOC Guidelines are largely unremarkable. For the most part, they read like a textbook in psychological testing. Table 16.8 presents a few excerpts to illustrate this point. In fact, the Guidelines state that they "are intended to be consistent with generally accepted professional standards ... such as those described in the Standards for Educational and Psychological Tests" (29 C.F.R. § 1607.5C). Understandably, the longest sections of the guidelines deal with validity. Although the wording of the Guidelines is familiar, it is startling to see

TABLE 16.8   *Excerpts from the EEOC Guidelines*

Evidence of the validity of a test or other selection procedure by a criterion-related validity study should consist of empirical data demonstrating that the selection procedure is predictive of or significantly correlated with important elements of job performance. (1607.5B)

Selection procedures should be administered and scored under standardized conditions. (1607.5E)

Generally, a selection procedure is considered related to the criterion, for the purposes of these guidelines, when the relationship between performance on the procedure and performance on the criterion measure is statistically significant at the 0.05 level of significance. (1607.14B5)

---

psychometric jargon appear in the form of regulatory jargon. For example, reference to the .05 level of significance for a criterion-related validity coefficient becomes 29 C.F.R. § 1607.14B5.

Here is a simple summary of the main thrust of the Guidelines: *If use of a test for an employment decision results in adverse impact (defined later), there must be validity information to justify use of the test.* There are three important points in this summary. First, in the absence of adverse impact, the guidelines do not require validity information (although common sense certainly does). Second, we must determine what constitutes adequate validity information. This essentially means appropriate and explicit application of content, criterion-related, and/or construct validity. In other words, one must demonstrate that the test is valid for selecting (or promoting) individuals for the job in question. Various laws refer to this job-relevance as "business necessity." That is, the successful operation of the business requires certain job qualifications. Third, we must define adverse impact.

Adverse Impact and the Four-fifths Rule

The concept of adverse impact is one part of the Guidelines that does not arise directly from the psychometric literature. Hence, its general and operational definitions warrant special attention. **Adverse impact** means that the test (or other selection procedure) results in unfavorable selection ratios by sex, race, or ethnic group. The **four-fifths rule** defines how much of a difference in selection ratios constitutes a problematic level. The rule says "A selection rate for any race, sex, or ethnic group which is less than four-fifths (4/5 or eighty percent) of the rate for the group with the highest rate will generally be regarded by the Federal enforcement agencies as evidence of adverse impact" (29 C.F.R. § 1607.4). In practice, one must determine the selection ratio for each group, and then determine the ratio among the ratios. Table 16.9 shows an example. In this example, there is adverse impact for the Hispanic applicants.

TABLE 16.9   *Illustration of Procedure to Determine Adverse Impact*

	Group			
	White	Black	Asian	Hispanic
Applicants	50	20	10	20
Hired	29	11	6	6
Selection rate (SR)	.58	.55	.60	.20
SR/highest rate	.58/.60 = .97	.55/.60 = .92	.60/.60 = 1.00	.30/.60 = .50

TRY IT! ....

In the example given in Table 16.9, how many additional Hispanics would have to be hired to avoid a charge of adverse impact for that group?

....

It cannot be emphasized too strongly that a finding of adverse impact does not mean that use of the test is illegal, that is, prohibited by the Guidelines. The finding means that the user must have adequate validity information to justify use of the test. For example, if the employer has shown that the test is significantly predictive of on-the-job performance, then use of the test is permissible. Furthermore, to repeat an earlier statement, in the absence of adverse impact (say, 10 Hispanics had been hired), there would be no need for demonstrated validity, although one might wonder why the employer would bother to use the test.

Subgroup Norming: Emergence and Prohibition

The four-fifths rule caused considerable consternation among employers and human resources specialists. A demonstration or even claim of adverse impact could bring a bevy of federal officials calling. The most obvious way to deal with the issue is to conduct the necessary validity studies. However, another way is to force roughly equivalent selection ratios for each subgroup. This can be accomplished by referencing each subgroup to itself rather than to the total applicant pool or some unitary norm group. Suppose the subgroups differ substantially in the trait measured by the test[4] and we select, say, the top 20% of applicants. The group highest in the trait will be overrepresented among those selected. Perhaps the great majority of those selected will come from the highest group. Conversely, the group lowest in the trait will be underrepresented. However, if we select the

---

[4] For this example we also assume equivalent variability in the subgroups.

top 20% from each subgroup, adverse impact automatically disappears. This is an example of **subgroup norming.** The procedure is equivalent to developing a local norm for each subgroup. It was a practice actually used in response to the EEOC Guidelines.

The Civil Rights Act of 1991 specifically prohibited use of subgroup norming. The practice was seen as a type of reverse discrimination. The Act says:

> Prohibition of discriminatory use of test scores. It shall be an unlawful employment practice for a respondent, in connection with the selection or referral of applicants or candidates for employment or promotion, to adjust the scores of, or use different cutoff scores for, or otherwise alter the results of, employment related tests on the basis of race, color, religion, sex, or national origin. (42 U.S.C. § 2000e-2(1))

Notice that the EEOC Guidelines did not encourage, nor even mention, subgroup norming. However, the revised law prohibited a practice that attempted to deal with provisions of the EEOC Guidelines. The Guidelines remain in effect.

No Child Left Behind Act

Although officially titled the "No Child Left Behind Act of 2001," (NCLB; P.L. 107–110) this new federal law was not adopted until 2002. It is a blockbuster: nearly 2,000 pages in some versions. Providing a 12-year timetable with intermediate deadlines for full implementation, NCLB has major implications for the world of testing. Recall from Chapter 11 our discussion of educational accountability and standards-based education. NCLB translates many of these general notions into highly detailed legal provisions. It requires specification of educational standards and extensive testing to determine that those standards have been met. As suggested by its title, the law emphasizes that all students must demonstrate adequate test performance. In addition, the law includes precise requirements for schools to report test scores to the public by various categories of students; and it requires demonstration of improvements in average scores from year to year.

We referenced some effects of NCLB in Chapter 11, in our discussion of state assessment programs. We add here that NCLB is perhaps the most important driving force today in American public education at the elementary and secondary levels. The law probably has not increased the total amount of testing, since the new state tests are often simply replacing the previously used standardized achievement batteries. However, the consequences of the test results are quite different. The law's numerous, detailed provisions are consuming enormous energy and resources. The public educational community has raised substantial objections about its feasibility. NCLB's goal is to have all students ("no child" excepted) at the proficient level by 2014. It seems unlikely that that will be achieved in the time frame established. However, it is not clear at this time whether significant revision in the law will occur in the near future.

Illustrative Court Cases

Recall from our definition of "laws" that court decisions constitute the third type of law: case law. The courts deal with application of statutory and administrative laws, as well as previous court decisions, to particular cases. There is a plaintiff who claims that someone (a person, corporation, school, etc.) did not properly abide by a law. There is a defendant (the person, corporation, etc.) who maintains that they did abide by the law. Legal counsel usually represents each side, plaintiff and defendant. The Court hears the case and decides in favor of one side. For the types of cases of interest here, judges make the rulings, not juries. When first filed, the cases are usually identified by the names of the plaintiff and defendant, in that order, for example, *Hogan v. City of Scranton.* Here, someone named Hogan, the plaintiff, is claiming that the City of Scranton, the defendant, violated the law. Often, there are multiple plaintiffs and defendants in a particular case, but the practice is to reduce the title to single names.

Most of the laws related to testing are federal in origin. Hence, federal courts hear the cases. The local magistrate deals with your parking ticket because this relates to a local ordinance. But the local magistrate does not hear a case involving a federal law. The federal judiciary has 94 *district* courts, 12 *circuit* courts, and, of course, one Supreme Court. Suits originate in district courts. District decisions may be appealed to a circuit court (whose full name is Circuit Court of Appeals). Circuit court decisions may be appealed to the Supreme Court. Upon appeal, the higher court first decides whether to hear the appeal, leave the decision stand, or send the case back (remand) to the lower court for further consideration.

TRY IT!

Curious about the U.S. federal courts? Check this website: www.uscourts.gov.

Literally thousands of cases are brought before the courts involving tests and the laws outlined earlier. For example, Data Research (1997) lists over 400 cases related just to IDEA. We will not attempt a comprehensive review of the cases arising from any one of the laws. Rather, we will outline a few cases that illustrate how the courts deal with the interface of testing and the law. In doing so, we summarize the points of most immediate relevance for testing, omitting the myriad fascinating details, such as whether the case was timely filed, decided one way at first but reversed on appeal, and so on: details that often kept the case alive in the courts for a dozen years.

Griggs v. Duke Power

A company requires a high school diploma and a passing score on an intelligence test for hiring and/or promotion. The requirements work to the disadvantage of African Americans. Are these requirements a violation of the Civil Rights Act of

1964? This was the question in *Griggs v Duke Power* (1971),[5] one of the earliest and most celebrated cases brought after passage of the Civil Rights Act of 1964.

Duke Power's steam generation plant in Draper, North Carolina, had the requirements. Griggs was the lead plaintiff among 13 African Americans (referred to as Negroes at the time).[6] Plaintiffs had less education and lower test scores than did whites. Plaintiffs claimed that the requirements—both diploma and tests—were discriminatory. The company maintained that there was no discriminatory intent and that the requirements helped to upgrade the general quality of its workforce. There were three specific tests used: a version of the Otis Beta, the Wonderlic Personnel Test (an offshoot of the Otis Intelligence Scale), and the Bennett Mechanical Comprehension Test. As the case progressed, the tests seem to have evolved into a generic "standardized general intelligence test," the phrase used in the final decision. According to the Supreme Court, the employer failed to demonstrate a reasonable relationship between the requirements (both diploma and test) and job performance. The Supreme Court relied, in part, on documents in the *Congressional Record* regarding debates in Congress about the intent of references to professionally prepared tests. In effect, the Court concluded that Congress's intent was that the tests not be just professionally prepared but validated for a particular purpose. Of course, this point, tortuously developed in the early 1970s, was at the heart of the EEOC Guidelines issued in 1978. Tests, or even a high school diploma, may be used to make an employment decision, but only if they have been validated. In this context, validated means showing a relationship between the selection device(s) and job performance. This is the "business necessity" criterion.

Debra P. v. Turlington and *GI Forum v. TEA*

A state requires students to pass a test to graduate from high school. Pass rates on the test are substantially different for minority and white students. Does the test requirement violate any federal laws? More specifically, does use of the test in this way violate the Fourteenth Amendment, the Civil Rights Act of 1964, or any related law? Two similar cases, *Debra P. v. Turlington* (1984) and *GI Forum v. TEA* (2000), illustrate how the courts have dealt with this question.

The **Debra P.** case arose in Florida in 1979. Debra P. was one student serving as lead plaintiff in a class action filed on behalf of all black students in Florida.[7] Ralph Turlington was the state's commissioner of education, administratively responsible for enforcing the state's testing program. In 1976, the Florida

---

[5] When citing court cases in this section, we have generally cited the final disposition of the case and have not included all the original filings, appeals, and remands. Referencing the final disposition will lead the reader to earlier steps in the process.

[6] As in the *Debra P.* case discussed in the following section, the suit actually used three subclasses, but these are unimportant for our summary.

[7] As the case progressed, three classes were formed, but this point is unimportant for our summary. Numerous officials in addition to Turlington were named as defendants, but this fact, too, is unimportant here.

legislature, through the state's Department of Education, began requiring that students pass a functional literacy test, the State Student Assessment Test, Part 2 (SSAT-II), in order to receive a high school diploma. The test was administered in fall 1977, 1978, and 1979. Black students were failing the test at a rate about ten times higher than white students. The suit was filed in 1979.

Here are the important points about the *Debra P.* case. First, the state was permitted to use the test as a diploma requirement. Second, the state had to delay implementation of the requirement until 1982–1983 in order to provide adequate notice (this is part of due process) about the requirement. Third, a crucial part of the case turned on adequate demonstration of the "instructional validity" of the test; see Chapter 5 for a description of this concept. The state contracted for extensive empirical studies to demonstrate instructional validity. Provision for remedial work for those failing the test was also an important consideration. Fourth, in the Court's opinion, mere disproportionate impact of the test on one group did not render the test illegal. Fifth, there was no clear demonstration of a causal link between the vestiges of previous segregated schooling and current pass rates on the test. The remedial programs were important on this point. Furthermore, in the court's view, imposition of the test requirement may have actually helped to remedy any such vestiges. This is an interesting application of the concept of consequential validity, although neither the Court nor the defendants used this term.

In a case very similar to *Debra P.*—but much more recent—a group of minority students, with GI Forum as lead plaintiff, brought suit against the Texas Education Agency (TEA) in the federal District Court at San Antonio. Beginning in the 1980s, Texas required students to pass the Texas Assessment of Academic Skills (TAAS) test, as well as meet other criteria, in order to graduate from high school. African-American and Hispanic students failed the tests (reading, math, and writing) at substantially higher rates than whites, thus establishing adverse impact.

In January 2000, the judge ruled the TAAS test permissible despite the disparities in pass rates. There were several important points in the court opinion. First, the judge used the EEOC four-fifths rule, originally intended for employment tests.[8] He transformed "business necessity" (see p. 606) into "educational necessity." Second, much is made of the technical quality of the tests: their development, especially steps taken to detect item bias; reliability; and curricular validity, including "opportunity to learn." Curricular validity in this case is the same as instructional validity in the *Debra P.* case. Third, and perhaps most significant, the judge referenced the impact of the test. Specifically, he noted that the test helped to (a) identify and remediate weaknesses and (b) motivate students, teachers, and schools. See Phillips (2000) for detailed treatment of the GI Forum case and its lessons.

---

[8] The court record uses a common misstatement of the rule, defining "adverse impact [as when] the passing rate for the minority group is less than 80 percent of the passing rate for the majority group." See p. 606 for the actual wording of the EEOC rule.

Larry P. v. Riles, *PASE v. Hannon*, **and** *Crawford v. Honig*

We consider these three cases together because, in combination, they illustrate the complexity of following court decisions. The cases take us on a fascinating journey through the courts. As with *Griggs* and *Debra P.,* these cases involved multiple plaintiffs and defendants, appeals, remands, and other legal proceedings. We outline here only the major conclusions.

In *Larry P. v. Riles* (1984), Larry P. was an African-American child assigned to a class for the educable mentally retarded (EMR) based mainly on an individually administered intelligence test. Plaintiffs claimed violation of the Civil Rights Act of 1964, the Rehabilitation Act of 1973, the Education for all Handicapped Children Act of 1975, and the equal protection clauses of the federal and state constitutions.

The court concluded that the tests were discriminatory and banned their further use. This ruling, perhaps more than any other, gave rise to headlines such as "IQ tests found illegal" and "Intelligence tests unconstitutional." However, note the following points in the full decision and in the court's reasoning. First, the ruling applied only to African-American students, not to other minority (or white) students. Second, the ruling only applied to assignment to EMR classes or their substantial equivalents. The ruling did not prohibit use of the tests for other purposes, for example, selection for gifted classes. Third, an important element in the court's reasoning was the conclusion that EMR classes were "dead-end" classes. In some ways, the ruling was more an indictment of the EMR program than of the tests. Finally, the court concluded that the IQ tests carried more weight than justified in the light of state statutes.

Meanwhile, over in Chicago, a highly similar case arose: *PASE v. Hannon.* Parents in Action on Special Education (PASE) filed suit against Joseph Hannon, superintendent of the Chicago Public Schools, on behalf of African-American students assigned to educable mentally handicapped (EMH) classes based in part on individual intelligence tests. In this instance, the judge ruled that the tests were not culturally biased, except for a few items, which would not significantly influence final placement of students. Hence, the tests were permissible. The judge also noted that psychologists involved in the placement seemed to have appropriate professional training and were using good professional judgment. Information besides intelligence tests played a significant role in the placement.

In *Crawford v. Honig* (1994), Demond Crawford was an African-American student diagnosed as learning disabled. Crawford's parents wanted to have an IQ test administered to her. The state demurred, citing the *Larry P.* decision. Interestingly, the same judge who issued the *Larry P.* ruling reversed (vacated) his earlier ruling, thus allowing use of an IQ test for Crawford and, in effect, for all other African-American students.

Careful reading of the court proceedings in these cases reveals four important points not treated in the final rulings but partially determinative of the rulings. First, the difference between a diagnosis of mental retardation and learning disabilities was crucial. Tests may be especially helpful in making this distinction. Second, the quality of the final educational program or treatment following diagnosis was very

important. Third, current understanding of the nature of intellige⸱
minants arose repeatedly in testimony. We touched on some o⸱
Chapter 7 under theories of intelligence. Theories sometimes se⸱
ever, theoretical developments have important practical impli⸱
world—such as in courtrooms. Finally, the methods used to a⸱
these cases—very much an armchair analysis—seem primitive by today⸱⸱
Recall that we described contemporary approaches to the study of item bias in
Chapters 5 and 6.

Karraker v. Rent-A-Center

A company uses the MMPI as one of several measures in selecting employees for
promotion. As described in Chapter 13, the MMPI is typically used to diagnose
psychopathology. However, the company maintains that it uses the test as a personality measure, specifically to assess traits relevant to job performance. Is the test a
"medical exam," thus falling under the provisions of the Americans with Disabilities
Act? Or is it a test of job-relevant traits, thus falling under the "business necessity"
provisions of the EEOC Guidelines?

In *Karraker v. Rent-A-Center, Inc.* (2005), "Karraker" is actually three brothers who
worked for Rent-A-Center (RAC) and applied for promotion. Interestingly, the
case summary begins by referring to the use of tests, both mental ability and personality, with National Football League (NFL) draft prospects (citing *Sports Illustrated*!). The reasoning in the case became exceptionally complicated, with a variety
of side issues, but in the end the court ruled that the MMPI was a medical examination, hence subject to ADA provisions. In general, you cannot refuse employment
or promotion due to a "medical (or physical) disability," and, according to the court,
the MMPI related to such disability status.

Forensic Application of Tests

Forensic psychology is a rapidly emerging specialty.[9] It deals generally with the
application of psychological principles and methods in a legal context, especially
but not exclusively in court actions. Some psychologists specialize in this field. We
concentrate here on any application of testing within a legal context. For example,
a clinical psychologist may utilize tests when serving as an expert witness on the
mental competency of a defendant. A neuropsychologist might testify to document the extent of brain damage in a personal injury case. A psychometrician
might testify about the technical quality of a test used to identify a child as mentally retarded. For a status report on the forensic specialization, see Otto and Heilbrun (2002).

Forensic applications of tests fall into three major categories. First, there are two
traditional legal terms with distinctly psychological meanings that may call for the

---

[9] The American Psychological Association's Council of Representatives approved forensic psychology
as a specialization within APA in August 2001.

use of tests. Second, there are three areas with special significance for forensic applications. Third, there is a broad range of other areas in which psychologists apply assessment methods to courtroom activities.

Two Legal Terms

Two legal terms have a distinctly psychological flavor: insanity and competency to stand trial. The terms have a long history in British and American common law. To the novice, the two terms may sound like the same thing. However, they have quite different meanings in the law. **Insanity** refers to mental disorder or incapacity at the time a crime is committed. **Competency to stand trial** refers to a person's mental capacity at the time of trial for a crime.[10] The crucial distinction between the terms, though not the only distinction, is the time frame.

Historically, there have been three rules for defining insanity. Names for the rules originated with cases in which the court enunciated the rule. The M'Naghten rule says that the person cannot distinguish between right and wrong. This is a cognitive criterion. The Durham rule, a more liberal one, says that the person committed the act because of a mental disorder. This is a volitional criterion. The Brawner rule, also known as the American Law Institute Rule, allows for inability to distinguish right from wrong or inability to control behavior, exclusive of certain conditions such as psychopathy or compulsions.

In 1982, John Hinckley, who had attempted to assassinate President Reagan, was acquitted on an insanity defense. The U.S. Congress, clearly unhappy with the Hinckley outcome, passed the Insanity Defense Reform Act. This act limited the insanity defense to the cognitive test and set a high standard for proof. Furthermore, a person found insane in a criminal proceeding had to be committed to a mental institution.

Competency to stand trial involves the mental capacity to understand the trial proceedings and to work reasonably with legal counsel. If there is a claim of incompetency, there must be a hearing on this claim before the trial on the alleged crime. Usually, a person found incompetent would be committed to a mental institution. However, if later found competent, the person may then be tried for the alleged crime.

Obviously, the results of psychological tests may be very important in determining insanity and competency to stand trial. Because the insanity plea relates to mental capacity at the time of the crime, which may be months or even years before the trial, previously available test results could be highly relevant. Tests administered around the time of the trial might not be very useful. However, tests administered around the time of the trial would be highly relevant to the competency issue.

Grisso (1996) has observed that the move toward deinstitutionalization has led to an increase in the number of cases the courts need evaluated for these purposes. However, the total number of insanity pleas remains small. Wrightsman (1991) cites studies showing that the insanity plea occurs very infrequently and, when introduced, is rarely successful.

Excellent sources for definitions and typical applications of the insanity and competency terms are Besette (1996) and West Publishing (1984). Vandenberg (1993) and

---

[10] Competency also applies in civil law, for example, for preparation of a will. Here we treat only the application to criminal law.

Wrightsman (1991) provide useful historical perspective on the insanity term. Grisso (1986, 1996) concentrates specifically on tests for these purposes. For some case studies, see Group for the Advancement of Psychiatry (1991). Foxhall (2000) provides an update on forensic applications of psychology. Finally, for the psychologist preparing for courtroom action, Brodsky (1991, 1999) has some useful (and humorous) advice.

Three Areas of Special Concern

Beyond the issues of insanity and competency to stand trial, in recent years psychologists have found tests potentially useful in three forensic areas. First, assessment may be useful in child custody cases. In this instance, there is an attempt to determine the qualifications of each parent (or other parties) to serve the best interests of the child. Second, assessment methodology has been applied to the prediction of future violent or risky behavior, what is sometimes called dangerousness. Such predictions may be important for determining eligibility for parole, incarceration versus release under supervision, and other such decisions. Third, psychological assessment may be useful in determining the nature and extent of abuse, as in spousal abuse or sexual abuse. All three areas are in need of substantial further development.

And Beyond

Beyond the areas mentioned, tests may enter the forensic picture in a virtually unlimited number of ways. Any use of a psychological test has the potential to enter court proceedings. With our American penchant to litigate everything, the forensic use of tests will, no doubt, continue to grow.

In general, the types of tests we have covered in this book give a good indication of the kinds of tests that might appear in the courtroom. Lees-Haley has studied the types of tests used by forensic psychologists. The results of his studies generally agree well with other studies of test usage. One study (Lees-Haley, 1992) surveyed test usage by attendees at the annual meeting of the American College of Forensic Psychology. Clearly the two most widely used tests were the MMPI (or MMPI-2) and WAIS-R. Nearly all the other tests in the top 20 were those we have described in earlier chapters, for example, the Rorschach, TAT, WISC, and Wechsler Memory Scales. Another study (Lees-Haley, Smith, Williams, & Dunn, 1995) identified the tests actually included in 100 forensic neuropsychological examinations in litigated personal injury cases. Again WAIS-R (or WAIS) and MMPI (or MMPI-2) topped the list, followed by many of the tests covered in Chapter 10. Thus, the tests used in the forensic context are very much the same as the tests used in other contexts.

Some Generalizations about the Interface of Testing and the Law

From the consideration of the interface of testing and the law, we develop the following generalizations (see Key Points Summary 16.4). First, everything we have reviewed confirms the importance of the technical quality of tests. Concepts of validity, reliability, and adequacy of norming are no longer just for the professional psychometric expert. These concepts are now written into laws. They are the benchmarks in court cases. One can point to instances in which a law or court decision conflicts with or disregards good psychometric practice, but these tend to be the exceptions. The general rule is: The law supports and, in turn, depends on good psychometrics. Furthermore, the technical competence of the test user is crucial. The law demands such competence. The courts expect a high level of competence. This generalization agrees well with the ethical requirement for competence discussed earlier in this chapter.

Second, legal requirements evolving within the past 50 years have influenced test development and usage. The most important influence has been heightened concern for the applicability of tests to various subgroups. Of particular interest are racial/ethnic subgroups and persons with disabilities. The influences are most evident with respect to (a) test content development, (b) norming, and (c) conducting validity studies. Regarding test content, in Chapters 5 and 6 we described methods of detecting test bias by use of review panels and differential item functioning (DIF) studies. Application of these methods is now routine.

Regarding development of norms, test publishers now attempt to meticulously represent various subgroups in standardization programs. Publishers have made great strides in this area. It is important to note that lack of adequate representation of various subgroups in the norms may (or may not) affect the accuracy of the norms, but such lack of representativeness has nothing to do with the validity or reliability of the test. This generalization seems counterintuitive and laypersons never believe it. To the psychometric novice, a test that has, say, no African Americans in the norm group is automatically invalid for African Americans. This is not true. However, feelings on this point are so deeply entrenched that it is not worth arguing the point outside of psychometric circles. Conversely, a norm with impeccable representation of various subgroups does not guarantee validity or reliability for those subgroups.

Regarding validity, clearly the legal environment has forced test developers and users to demonstrate that tests are valid for specific groups. For example, is the

---

Key Points Summary 16.4

Generalizations about the Interface of Testing and the Law

- The law confirms the importance of technical quality and competence.
- The law has significantly influenced test development and usage.
- The interface is complex. It requires specialized knowledge, and it calls for caution in generalizing from single cases.

WISC-III valid for dyslexic children? Is the SAT valid for Hispanic students? This emphasis has spawned an enormous number of studies about how tests function with particular groups. This has been a very salutary development.

Third, our review of court cases reminds us not to overgeneralize from single cases. Decisions are not always consistent, nor entirely predictable. Perhaps more important, a decision sometimes has a very narrow scope, or depends on reasoning related to special circumstances. For example, the *Larry P.* decision that "outlawed IQ tests" applied (a) to African-American students but not to other minority students, (b) to placement in EMR classes but not for other purposes, and (c) only in the Ninth Circuit and not elsewhere. The *Debra P.* decision depended, in part, on very specific studies of instructional validity conducted by the state of Florida. Although our legal system generally operates on the basis of precedents, the precedents are not always clear and direct. Sometimes, they do not apply at all. This business of the interface of testing and the law is not simple. The laws and regulations may be clear in their general purpose, but the details can be mind-boggling. Court cases, understandably, are replete with jargon nearly impenetrable to the layperson. This is not to say that the interface is impossible to understand. However, it does present special challenges beyond knowing the principles and methods of testing.

Summary

1. Ethics deals with what should (or should not) be done, according to ethical, moral, and professional principles. The law deals with what must (or must not) be done, according to laws.

2. A code of professional ethics helps to define what it means to "do good" within the context of issues commonly encountered in a profession. Thus, the code sensitizes the professional. The code also establishes societal expectations, thereby protecting the profession's reputation.

3. The remote roots for ethical codes related to testing are in the Hippocratic oath, the Nuremberg code, and the Belmont Report. The more immediate roots are in the AERA/APA/NCME Standards for Educational and Psychological Tests and the APA Ethics code. Several other professional associations have similar ethical codes.

4. We identified five ethical principles with very broad application to testing: ensuring competence, securing informed consent, providing knowledge of results, maintaining confidentiality, and guarding test security. We also identified three principles with more limited applicability: setting high standards for test development/publication, assuming responsibility for automated test reporting, and working to prevent unqualified test use.

5. Many test publishers use a three-tier system (Levels A, B, and C) for classifying tests and potential test purchasers.

6. There are three types of "laws:" legislation, administrative regulations, and case law.

7. Laws affect testing primarily in these areas of application: employment, education, forensic psychology, and mandated testing programs.

8. Major laws affecting the use of tests include:
   - Fourteenth Amendment to the U.S. Constitution
   - Civil Rights Acts of 1964 and 1991
   - Rehabilitation Act and Americans with Disabilities Act (ADA)
   - Various laws related to education of persons with disabilities, especially IDEA
   - FERPA and HIPPA
   - The EEOC Guidelines on employment testing, especially with respect to the requirement for validity information and the definition of adverse impact
   - No Child Left Behind Act

9. Several court cases illustrated what the courts expect from tests. In *Griggs*, establishing the validity of employment requirements was crucial. In *Debra P.* and *GI Forum*, a state-mandated test for a high school diploma was acceptable, if the test had instructional validity and the schools provided adequate preparation for the test. *Larry P., PASE*, and *Crawford* yielded conflicting, potentially confusing decisions about the use of individual intelligence tests.

10. Within the specialty of forensic psychology, tests might be helpful with respect to two well-established legal concepts: insanity and competency to stand trial. Tests may also be useful in child custody cases, predictions of future violent behavior, and in cases of abuse. Beyond these specific applications, the full range of normal test usage has the potential to appear in legal proceedings.

11. Regarding the interface of testing and the law, we developed generalizations about
    - The importance of technical quality and competence
    - The influence of laws on test development and usage
    - The complexity of the interface of testing and the law and the need for caution in drawing conclusions from single cases

Key Terms

accommodation
ADA
administrative law or regulations
adverse impact
APA Ethics Code
case law
C.F.R.
Civil Rights Act
competence
competency to stand trial
confidentiality
Crawford

Debra P.
due process clause
EEOC Guidelines
equal protection clause
ethics
FERPA
forensic psychology
four-fifths rule
Fourteenth Amendment
Griggs
HIPPA
IDEA

IEP
informed consent
insanity
knowledge of results
Larry P.
law
P.L.
statutory law or legislation
subgroup norming
test security
test user qualifications
U.S.C.

Exercises

1. Return to the ethical cases on pages 584–585. Then refer to the summary of ethical principles related to testing on page 591. Which principles apply to each of the cases?

2. We noted that several professional associations have codes of ethics related to testing and that these codes are very similar. You can access the codes for the American Psychological Association, American Counseling Association, and National Association of School Psychologists online. Access at least two of the codes and check their similarities. Here are the sites: www.apa.org; www.counseling.org; www.nasponline.org.

3. Go to the websites for two publishers as listed in Appendix C, or consult the hard copy of test publishers' catalogs. What do the publishers list as test user qualifications? Do they use the three-tier system outlined on page 594 of this book?

4. Check your local university library. Does the library subscribe to Lexis or Westlaw? If so, enter the key words for one of the court cases we considered, for example, *Griggs v. Duke Power* or *Debra P. v. Turlington*. Observe how the issue is framed at the beginning of the case and how the final ruling is summarized at the end.

5. Go to the example for determining adverse impact in Table 16.9. Change the numbers hired as follows: White—26, Black—13, Asian—4, Hispanic—7. Calculate new selection ratios and "SR/highest rate" figures. Is there adverse impact for any group?

6. The full text of the IDEA law and the No Child Left Behind law may be found at any of the general websites for federal laws. However, these two laws have their own websites, containing the laws, associated regulations, and a variety of other materials. If you are curious about these laws, check the site for the U.S. Department of Education's Office of Special Education and Rehabilitative Services: www.ed.gov.

APPENDIX A

Test Reviewing and Selection

This appendix will help the student complete a test review or test selection project. Such projects undertaken as training exercises should conform with the American Psychological Association's *Statement on the Use of Secure Psychological Tests in the Education of Graduate and Undergraduate Psychology Students.* A copy of this statement can be found at www.apa.org/science/securetest.html.

Paralleling the two topics introduced at the beginning of Chapter 2 are two practical tasks undertaken by psychologists. The *first* task is to review a given test, for example, the ABC Personality Inventory or the Pennsylvania Non-verbal Intelligence Test. The second task is to assemble a set of tests that may be considered for possible use, given a particular purpose. For example, what tests should be considered for the school district's diagnostic reading program or for initial screening of clients at a clinic? There are no rigidly specified rules for answering either type of question. In some circumstances, solutions to these problems will be provided rather quickly, after brief consultation with the sources of information presented in Chapter 2. In other circumstances, more formal answers will be developed. This appendix outlines the typical ways these questions are answered.

The Absolute and Relative Standards

Before outlining processes for test reviewing and selection, it may be helpful to contrast two approaches to these activities. The approaches relate to the kind of standard used in rendering judgments about tests. We refer to them here as the absolute standard and the relative standard. Different reviews will adopt one or the other of these standards, often without explicitly identifying the standard nor even hinting that there is an issue involved.

The *absolute standard* utilizes the highest levels of excellence in test construction, validation, norming, and so on as benchmarks. According to this standard, for example, a test's reliability should be determined by several different methods for a variety of groups of examinees, with uniformly high reliability coefficients. There should be a host of validity studies available for the instrument. National norms based on large, meticulously selected samples, plus norms for several types of subgroups, should be available, and so on for other test characteristics. Any test that falls short of these highest levels of excellence will be harshly criticized; it will not be recommended for use. Few tests fare well when judged by this absolute standard.

According to the *relative standard,* a test's value is judged primarily in relation to other tests in the same domain or to use of no test at all. Is the user's purpose better served by using this test than by using other tests, since, despite its shortcomings, this test is better than the other tests? Or is the user's purpose better served by this test, flawed as it may be, than by not using a test?

In applied work, the relative standard generally prevails over the absolute standard. One is going to select a test, whether this or that one. Or one is going to decide that use of no test is a better procedure than using a test. Any of these decisions is based on a comparison among alternatives. On the other hand, the absolute standard is often used in test reviews and in textbook treatment of particular tests. It is usually more difficult to apply the relative standard. To use the relative standard, one needs to know not only about the test at hand but also about the possible alternatives to this test.

Test Reviewing

Traditions for conducting a review of a single test are established by the practices of the Buros *Mental Measurements Yearbooks* and *Test Critiques* series described in Chapter 2. Although these two publications have somewhat different suggested outlines for their reviews, the reviews are organized in very similar ways. The suggestions given here draw on the formats from both of these classic sources of test reviews. Table A.1 summarizes steps in preparing to do a test review. Table A.2 identifies the major parts of a test review.

Notes on MMY and Test Critiques Test Review Procedures

Reviews in *MMY* do not follow a fixed format. Authors exercise some freedom in organization and the use of subheads. To see the Buros Institute's recommendations

TABLE A.1 *Steps in Preparing to Do the Review*

1. Assemble the materials for review.
2. Determine the test's purpose.
3. Examine the test materials.
4. Review the test's technical characteristics:
   a. Reliability
   b. Validity
   c. Types of norms and norming process
   d. Test development

for reviewers, go to www.unl.edu/buros/reviewer.html, and click on "Suggestions to Reviewers." However, all the reviews cover the topics outlined in Table A.2. Reviews in *Test Critiques,* on the other hand, do follow a fixed format. The organization is as follows: Introduction, Practical Applications/Uses, Technical Aspects, and Critique. The first two parts correspond approximately to items 1 and 2 in Table A.2, the third part corresponds to item 3, and the last part corresponds to item 4. MMY reviews are preceded by a simple listing of test materials, scoring services, etc.; these are supplied by the MMY editors, not by the test review author.

Materials Needed

The first step in conducting a test review is to assemble the materials for the review. If the review is of a published test, two types of materials are needed. First, a published test will ordinarily have what is called a *Specimen Set* or *Examination Kit*. This contains a copy of the test materials and manual(s). The test materials include test booklets or stimuli, answer sheets or other response recording devices, scoring keys and directions, and related materials. For complex tests such as multilevel achievement batteries, the examination kit often includes only a selection of the materials. In such cases, the reviewer will need to contact the publisher to obtain a more complete set of materials. The examination kit should also include the test manual. The manual should contain a clear statement of the

TABLE A.2 *Major Parts of a Test Review*

1. State the purpose of the test. Describe the rationale for the approach taken.
2. Describe the test's structure and materials: types of items, levels, length, etc.
3. For each of the following areas, tell what technical information is available *and* provide a judgment based on this information. These topics may be taken up in any order.
   a. Reliability
   b. Validity
   c. Norms
   d. Test development procedures
4. Give a summary statement about the test's quality and potential usefulness.

test's purpose and rationale, directions for administering, tables of norms, and information about reliability, validity, test development procedures, and norming programs for the test. For some tests these topics may be divided among two or more manuals. For example, one manual may contain the directions for administration and scoring while another manual contains the psychometric information.

A second important type of information to have for a test review is the entry about that test from the publisher's catalog. (This obviously applies only to published tests.) The catalog describes the range of test materials, for example, the number of levels and forms, types of scoring services, and costs of test materials. Much of this information is now available from the publisher's website. See Appendix C for a list of websites for the major test publishers.

The test review concentrates on examination of the test materials and technical characteristics of the test. Before beginning such examination it is not unusual, though not always necessary, to contact the author or publisher to ensure that a complete and current set of materials is on hand for the review process.

There are several steps that might be reasonable to undertake as part of the review process but that, in fact, are *not* ordinarily done. First, the reviewer usually does not complete a thorough literature search about the test. The test materials should stand on their own for purposes of the review. The reader may refer to other reviews of the test, especially to reviews of earlier editions (if there are any) or to some well-known research findings about the test. However, it is not customary to conduct a comprehensive literature search when reviewing a test.

Second, it is *not* usual to conduct an extensive pilot test, for example, administering the test to dozens or even hundreds of individuals, when reviewing a test. It would not be unusual to simulate a regular administration of the test with one or two individuals. Certainly, the individual reviewer would simulate taking the test in whole or in part. However, extensive pilot testing is not customary. On the other hand, if one were considering actual adoption of a test for regular use, conducting some pilot testing is highly recommended.

Structure of the Review

As noted, the test review concentrates on examination of the test materials and the test's technical characteristics. Table A.2 serves as a guide to the structure of a test review. The first critical step is determining the test's purpose. The purpose should be clearly stated in the test manual. It may also be noted in the publisher's catalog.

Next the reviewer should thoroughly examine the test materials themselves. What exactly is this test? What are the items or other stimuli? What does the examinee do? How long does it take to administer the test? And so on. In answering these types of questions, it is normal for the reviewer to "pretend" that he or she is actually taking the test. The reviewer also carefully reads the test directions, walks through the scoring procedures, and otherwise becomes immersed in the test materials. It is also important to determine what scores the test yields.

Finally, the reviewer begins examination of the technical characteristics of the test. To the novice reviewer, this is clearly the most daunting part of the task

However, the task can usually be resolved into the following four specific questions:

1. What evidence is there for the reliability of the test's scores?
2. What evidence is there for the validity of the test's score(s) or use(s)?
3. What evidence is provided for the utility of the test's norms?
4. What procedures were used to develop the test in order to help ensure that its purpose would be met?

These questions correspond with Chapters 3–6 of this book. Hence, providing answers to these questions is an exercise in applying what is learned in those chapters.

After becoming thoroughly familiar with the test materials and the technical characteristics of the test, one is ready to write the test review. The normal length and style of test reviews can be determined by consulting any edition of *MMY* or *Test Critiques*. Test reviews in *MMY* range from as little as 500 words to about 2,000 words. Reviews in *Test Critiques* tend to be somewhat longer; most are in the range of 2,000 to 2,500 words, but some go as high as 6,000 words.

The review begins with a section that is almost entirely descriptive and nonjudgmental. The opening sentence identifies the test's purpose. This statement is often taken directly from the test manual. For example:

According to the test manual (p. 2), the ABC-PI aims to provide a simple measure of the major personality traits of the normal adolescent.

The review may elaborate briefly on this purpose, paraphrasing sections of the manual, for example:

The major personality traits covered by the test include…

The intended target audience for the test is usually identified here. This opening section also discusses any theoretical orientation the test may have. For example:

The test structure attempts to operationalize Smith's four-stage theory of adolescent development.

In this opening section, the reviewer does not critique the test's purpose. However, the reviewer may comment on how clearly the purpose is communicated.

After identifying the test's purpose and rationale, the review goes on to describe the structure of the test and its materials. This part of the review may be thought of as a verbal photograph of the test. What are the test materials? How many items are there? How does the examinee respond? Are there different levels and forms of the test? And so on. The assumption in this section is that the reader of the review does not have the test materials. It is the reviewer's task to give a sort of guided tour of the test.

Finally, the opening section will call attention to any special versions or unusual features of the test, if there are any. For example, if the test is available in Spanish as well as in English or if there is an optional practice test, such matters would be briefly noted.

The second major section of the review treats the test's technical characteristics. This section is a combination of description and judgment. It is convenient to use four subheads in this part of the review, as outlined in items 3a–3d in Table A.2. Within each of these parts, the reviewer describes the evidence available for the test, then offers a judgment about the adequacy of the information. For example, regarding reliability, the review may note that:

> Alpha coefficients for the test's three scores are .63, .85, and .91, as determined on the norming samples. The first of these is clearly inadequate for routine use; if the score is used at all, extreme caution is required. The other two scores show adequate internal consistency for normal use. However, the test manual fails to provide any information about test-retest reliability, a significant shortcoming.

The review provides similar treatment for the other technical characteristics. The pattern is always: description followed by judgment.

The final section of the review provides an overall evaluation of the test. The reviewer may adopt one of several possible strategies in this section. First, comments may be restricted to a synopsis of major conclusions reached in earlier parts of the review. Second, the reviewer may suggest cautions to keep in mind if the test is used and/or make recommendations for the test author and publisher to follow in further development of the test. Such cautions and recommendations will be outgrowths of earlier parts of the review. The third strategy, the boldest approach, makes a specific recommendation for or against use of the test. Sometimes this recommendation will reference another test. The reviewer may recommend this test over available alternatives. For example, the reviewer may say: "For clinicians interested in a quick, initial assessment of mental ability, the Hogan Intelligence Test is clearly the first choice." Or the reviewer may recommend against use of the test, saying, for example, "There are several well-known tests that would be preferable to the Hogan Intelligence Test." Of course, the reviewer provides a rationale for the recommendation, drawing on comments made in earlier parts of the review. It is important that the conclusion be consistent with the earlier parts of the review.

Test Selection

The test selection process is designed to find a test that adequately meets some purpose. Test selection is similar in some ways to the test review process, but in other ways the two processes are quite different. The key difference is in the starting point. The test review starts with a particular test. The test selection process begins with a particular purpose, then goes on to find a test that meets that purpose. A curious incidental difference between the two processes is that a test review is usually completed by an individual, whereas, in practice, test selection is often conducted by a committee.

Table A.3 summarizes the five major steps in the test selection process. The first step is to clearly define the purpose to be served by the test. Why is the test needed? Who will use the test scores? At first, this step seems simple. In some instances it is. For example, the sole purpose of the test may be to serve as a dependent variable in a small research project. However, in other instances, there may be many uses for the test score information. For example, the scores for an achievement test might be used by teachers to identify students in need of special help, by the local school

TABLE A.3   *Steps in the Test Selection Process*

1. Clearly define purpose and intended uses, target group, constraints.
2. Compile initial list of candidates.
3. Compile list of finalists.
4. Summarize information for finalists.
5. Make selection or recommendation.

board to report to the public, by the school psychologist to help define learning disabilities, and by parents to monitor progress of their children. A personality test might be used in a clinic partly to provide a basis for initial discussion with clients and partly as a pretest for an ongoing research project occurring in a network of clinics. Hence, adequate time should be devoted in this initial step to clearly defining the purpose of the test. Anticipated uses for the test scores deserve special attention. Reflection may reveal one primary purpose and several secondary purposes.

It is also important to specify at this stage (a) any special conditions for the testing and (b) the characteristics of the target audience. Some of the conditions may be essential, others just desirable. For example, it may be essential that the test is available in a Braille edition; it may be desirable, but not essential, that the test takes less than 50 minutes to complete. Relevant characteristics of the target audience include such factors as age, level of education or mental ability, native language, disability status, and so on. For example, the target audience may be individuals with a borderline level of literacy, thus requiring a test with a very low reading level; or the audience may include many persons with limited motor ability. It is important to be as specific as possible about these matters before beginning the search for a test.

The next step is compiling an initial list of candidates. A broad net is cast at this point. All the sources of information listed in Chapter 2 may be consulted. Particularly helpful at this stage will be the electronic sources, the comprehensive lists of tests, and other users, that is, professionals who regularly use tests in the relevant domain.

The third stage of test selection involves narrowing the list of candidates to a manageable number for more intense scrutiny. There is no magical target number; however, something in the range of three to six tests usually works well. Selection of the final list involves a judgment about the overall quality of the tests and the extent to which they meet the conditions specified in step 1.

The fourth step involves compilation of detailed information about the finalists emerging from step 3. This will require use of some of the other sources of information, especially the test reviews, publishers' catalogs and personnel, and, again, other users. It is also customary at this stage to get complete sets of test materials, including manuals and ancillary materials such as sample score reports. Considerable time is now spent examining the materials in detail. As part of this stage there may be some pilot testing of one or more of the instruments. In addition to obtaining scores from the pilot testing, one might solicit reactions from the test administrator and examinees about the test. Results of the selection process at this stage are often summarized in matrix form, as illustrated in Table A.4. This table shows only some of the tests' features that would be summarized in an actual study.

TABLE A.4 *Part of a Matrix Summarizing Tests Receiving Detailed Study in a Test Selection Process*

Feature/Test	A	B	C	D
Publisher				
Cost/person				
Type of Norms				
Reliability				
Testing Time				

The fifth stage involves making the final selection or, in some situations, making a recommendation to some other group or individual that will make the selection. The selection or recommendation will be based on a combination of all factors related to the test and its intended use. These factors include the test's psychometric characteristics and practical considerations such as cost, convenience, and supporting materials. The final decision almost always relies on the relative standard described above. That is, you select the best one, even if it is not perfect.

APPENDIX B

How to Build a (Simple) Test

Here is a set of steps to build a relatively simple test (see Table B.1). You might try this as an exercise in a course. The project may be completed individually, in pairs, or in small groups. These instructions will not allow you to develop a complex test like the MMPI or SAT. However, the instructions will help you gain experience with the major steps in test development, as outlined in Chapter 6.

We suggest you choose one of these types of tests:

1. An achievement test based on a few chapters in this book.

2. A test of a specific mental ability such as quantitative reasoning, vocabulary, or short-term memory.

3. An attitude survey directed at a topic of contemporary interest.

Although it might be very enticing to do so, we do not recommend that you attempt to build an objective personality test, a projective test, a vocational interest inventory, or a multi-score mental ability test.

TABLE B.1   *Summary of Steps in Building a Test*

1. Formulate the purpose of the given test.
2. Consider preliminary design issues.
3. Prepare the test items.
4. Conduct the item tryout.
5. Complete standardization and ancillary research programs.
6. Prepare final test materials.

1. Formulate the Purpose of Your Test

Develop a concise statement of the purpose, including the target audience. For an achievement test, based on material in this book, decide whether the test will measure knowledge of the material before it is covered in class, after an initial reading but before in-depth coverage, or after thorough treatment of the chapter(s). For an ability test, we suggest you focus narrowly on one trait, for example, ability to complete number patterns or knowledge of vocabulary words. For an attitude survey, decide how broadly the construct is to be defined. For example, if the topic is capital punishment, will the survey focus only on current legal issues or on a fuller array of issues? If the topic is a current political campaign, will the survey focus on just a few candidates or on a broad array of policy issues, perhaps ranging from conservative to liberal viewpoints?

Note: In actual practice, after formulating a statement of purpose for your test, you would use the sources of information in Chapter 2 to determine if a test satisfying your purpose already exists. However, since the intent of this exercise is to build a test, we will skip the sources of information at this time.

2. Consider Preliminary Design Issues

See the list of preliminary design issues discussed on pages 208–209 in Chapter 6. Here are some guidelines to use for this exercise. Of course, you may make other decisions. How many scores will the test have? We suggest limiting the test to one score. Will the test be individually administered or group administered? We suggest a group-administered test. How many items will the test have? For the final version of the test, that is, after item selection, we suggest about 30 items for the achievement test or ability test and about 15 items for an attitude measure. What type of item will be used? We suggest using a selected-response type of item for this exercise. Use multiple-choice items, with three, four, or five options for the achievement or ability test. Use a Likert-type format with 3–7 scale points for the attitude test. Consider what type of score distribution you want. For example, do you want a negatively skewed distribution, providing maximum discrimination in the lower part of the distribution? Do you want an approximately normal distribution of scores? Also, consider whether test administration will require any special accommodations for persons with disabilities. Finally, complete any necessary background research, especially for an ability or attitude test. In general, try to keep things simple.

3. Prepare the Test Items

Before beginning to write items, prepare a test blueprint. The blueprint will outline the number and types of items you want. Consider the case of an achievement test based on three chapters in this book. The blueprint will indicate the number of items per chapter and the nature of the items. For example, one-third of the items may be based on key terms at the end of the chapter, one-third may deal with summaries of major points, and one-third may involve applications of concepts. For an attitude survey, the blueprint will show the range of issues to be covered and perhaps the distribution of positively and negatively worded items.

We suggest you prepare at least twice as many items as needed for the final version of the test. For example, if your achievement test will ultimately have 30 items, then prepare 60 items. If your attitude survey will have 15 items, then prepare 30 items. As you prepare items, you may want to do some *informal tryout* to make sure the items are understandable. If the items you are preparing, for example, number series for a test of quantitative reasoning, are uniformly too easy or too difficult for the target audience, then you will want to make adjustments before writing 80 inappropriate items.

Prepare the directions for the test. The directions should be simple yet complete. Preparing the directions will require that you decide how answers are to be recorded. This, in turn, will require that you think about how you will process the item analysis data. We suggest that you have examinees record answers on a scannable answer sheet. Check with your school's computer center or testing center to determine what type of scannable answer sheets are available and what type of output you can get from the scanner. Your instructor may be helpful in answering these questions. If you do not have access to a scanner, then decide an alternative way for examinees to record their answers.

While preparing directions, consider what information you may want examinees to provide other than just answers to the test items. For example, will you ask for gender, current GPA, age, race, and so on? Such supplementary information may be important for describing the tryout group as well as for analysis of scores on the test.

Have all items and directions edited by a friend for clarity, spelling, grammar, and so on. Make corrections based on this review. Then prepare a draft of the final tryout form. This should look as much as possible like the final form of the test. It should have a finished, professional appearance. If the tryout form is too long, consider splitting it into two or three equivalent forms for purposes of tryout.

4. Conduct the Item Tryout

Recall that item tryout has three phases (see page 226). First, there is the *informal tryout*. Administer the test to a few individuals who are representative of the target population for the test. This may be done one-on-one or in small groups. Ask the examinees to comment, either orally or in writing, on the format, directions, and individual items. In this informal tryout, you are not interested in examinees' scores but in whether the task is clear, vocabulary is appropriate, and so on. Don't be obstinate in reacting to comments. If examinees don't understand something, don't argue with them—change it. After making changes based on the informal tryout, you are ready for the formal tryout.

There are two key questions you need to answer in order to conduct the formal tryout. First, determine if you need IRB (Institutional Review Board) approval for the tryout. Since you will be testing "human subjects," this may be required. Or perhaps your instructor has obtained blanket approval for such projects. Or since this is just a class exercise, your institution may not need any approval. If approval is required, secure the necessary forms and initiate the approval process as soon as possible, since IRB approvals can cause significant delay. Second, determine how many examinees will be in the tryout group. Generally, you would like to have a minimum of 200 examinees, considerably more if using IRT methods. However, for a class project, you may have to settle for 20 to 30 examinees. Finally, print the test materials and arrange for actual administration of the tryout form(s) of the test.

Next, arrange to get the *item statistics*. We suggest you use a statistical software package for this purpose. Again, check with your computer center or testing center to see what software package is available. Most institutions will have a package that is used with instructors' course examinations. Such packages usually yield an item difficulty and item discrimination index for each item. Many of the packages will also yield a measure of reliability (most often coefficient alpha) and will give basic descriptive statistics on the test as a whole (mean, standard deviation, frequency distribution, etc.). If your tryout group is sufficiently large, you may be able to get IRT item parameters, especially the "b" parameter.

If your institution does not have a software package specifically designed for test analysis, then try to use one of the standard statistical software packages, such as SPSS. Enter item response data in columns, with each examinee being a row. In SPSS you may use the following commands. Under Transform, use the Compute commands to generate a total score for the test. Under Analyze, use Correlate/Bivariate, with Options set to produce Means and Standard Deviations, to obtain item p-values and item-total correlations. Also under Analyze, use the Scale/Reliability routines to generate coefficient alpha and/or split-half reliabilities. Be sure to review the options under Statistics in the Reliability routine.

If you cannot use a computer software package to get item statistics, you will need to compute these by hand. If this is the case, we suggest using a 50–50 split for the high and low groups needed to get the discrimination index, on the assumption that your tryout group will be relatively small (under 50 cases).

The final phase of item analysis is *item selection*. You want to select for your final test those items that have optimum psychometric properties. What is "optimum" depends partly on the purpose of your test. Do you want item difficulties concentrated around a certain point, for example, around .80 or around .50? Do you want a wide spread of item difficulties?

You will need to *examine all item statistics in detail*. Which items did not perform as expected? Did any of these items yield very low, perhaps even negative, item discrimination indexes? For ability or achievement items, did any of the distractors perform in unusual ways? Which items have the best discrimination indexes? Do these items have anything in common?

If you have supplementary descriptive information on examinees in the tryout group, for example, gender or age, you may want to analyze both items and total test scores for these subgroups.

Conclude the item analysis by deciding which items will be retained for the final version of the test. Recall that you decided on the desired test length in your preliminary design considerations. If you wanted a 30-item test and tried out 40 items, then you will select the best 30 items. Now you may want to rethink your original intention. If 35 of the 40 items have excellent item statistics, you may decide to use all 35 items, thus yielding a somewhat more reliable test. If, among the 40 items you tried out, only 25 items have at least reasonable item statistics, you may need to limit the test length to 25 items, even though this test will have less reliability than you originally desired.

Recall that in many test development projects there may be another round of item tryouts. That is, if too few high-quality items emerge from the first item tryout, then the authors prepare more items and conduct another tryout. It is very unlikely that you would have time for such a second tryout in the context of a class project.

5. Complete Standardization and Ancillary Research Programs

It is unlikely that you will be able to complete all the preceding steps and conduct a standardization program and ancillary research programs within the time frame of a single academic term. You may need to forgo the standardization and proceed directly to the sixth and last step. However, if time permits, you may carry out the following programs.

First, carefully define the desired characteristics of the standardization group. The group should be representative of the target audience for the test What are the important characteristics of this group in relation to the trait you are measuring? Consider the Types of Information for Judging the Usefulness of Norm Groups in Table 3.6. How can you get such information for the target population? How can you get such information for your standardization group? Consider how you will secure cooperation of participants in the standardization.

How many people should be in the standardization? As noted in Chapter 3, a sample of 200 cases will yield very stable norms. However, it is important that the sample be representative of the target population.

What type of norm scores will you provide: percentile ranks, T-scores, stanines, and so on? Will there be subgroup norms, for example, by gender or by age? The answer to this last question will depend partly on the purpose of the test and partly on whether there are any noticeable differences in subgroup performance on the test.

Prepare tables showing the norms and summary descriptive statistics. Also obtain an internal consistency measure of reliability on the standardization sample. Coefficient alpha is the usual choice.

Consider whether you want to obtain test-retest reliability. If so, what will the inter-test interval be? Will the study be conducted with a subgroup of the standardization group or with an entirely separate group? Do you want to obtain the correlation between scores on your test and scores on some related test? If so, how will you arrange to get this information?

6. Prepare Final Test Materials, Including the Manual

Regardless of whether a standardization is conducted, you should prepare the final test materials and manual. The test materials will usually consist of a test booklet and some type of answer document. The test booklet should have a professional appearance. The professional norm is a rather staid, clean, simple appearance—no sprinkle-on glitter or wild graphics.

The manual should identify the purpose of the test and describe the rationale for its development, including discussion of the preliminary design issues. The manual should provide details regarding item development and tryout. Characteristics of the tryout sample should be described. The manual should present summaries of statistics for items and the total test. If no standardization has been conducted, then the statistics will be those from the item analysis program. If standardization has been conducted, then statistics will be those from the standardization program, including a description of the standardization sample. Reliability data, including the standard error of measurement, should be summarized. The manual should also summarize data on any subgroup analysis undertaken, for example, differences by gender. If you complete all these steps, or even most of them, you will, no doubt, learn much about the psychological testing enterprise.

The Top 10 Things I've Learned About Test Development

I have worked intensively on test development projects for nearly my entire professional career. This work has included projects both large (multimillion dollar, multiyear) and small; commercial and noncommercial enterprises; cognitive and noncognitive tests. The work has also included every phase of test development, from original conceptualization to final publication and postpublication research. From all these experiences, I think I have learned some things that go beyond the standard textbook treatments regarding test development. It may be that students cannot learn these things without experiencing significant test development work themselves, but I would feel remiss if I did not record these thoughts with the hope that they will be helpful to students. So, here is my "top 10" list of things I think I've learned about test development.

1. **The original conceptualization is more important than the technical/statistical work.** Textbook treatments of test development tend to concentrate on item-writing processes and item analysis procedures. Some textbooks do not even mention the prior stages of defining the test's purpose

and the preliminary design considerations. In my experience, the original conceptualization of the test is far more important than the technical/statistical work. If you don't get the original conceptualization straight, no amount of finesse in item writing or statistical expertise will rescue the enterprise.

2. **You need to spend substantial time studying the area before starting to write items.** Knowing all the steps in test construction—even knowing them very well—does not qualify you to begin writing a test. It is essential that you take time to study the area you want to test. If the area is reading skill, then you need to know what research studies and experts in the field say about reading skill. If you wish to test anxiety, you need to know the literature in that area.

3. **In the original design stage, you need to think about final score reports.** What you are really producing is not a test but a test score. And you are producing that score or scores for someone. What, exactly, will you supply to that someone? What will the final score(s) look like? If you wait until you are ready to publish the test before thinking about score reports, it is almost certain that you will find you wished you had built the test differently.

4. **When preparing items, aim for simplicity. "Clever" items often don't work.** Simple items almost always work better than complex items. If you write an item that you think is really clever, chances are it will confuse examinees and, therefore, will have poor item statistics.

5. **Be sure to try out enough items: generally twice the number needed for the final test.** It's a nuisance to write a lot of test items. It's also really boring work. Further, when you write an item, you're almost sure it is a good item. So, there is great temptation to prepare just a few more items than what you finally want in the test. The fact is that even with good informal tryout and extensive editing of items, you will lose a lot of items in the formal item analysis stage. Make sure you include enough items in your item analysis program.

6. **Do simple, informal tryout before the major tryout.** Simple, informal tryouts are very easy to do. You can do them with friends, colleagues, your kids—whoever is handy. It's amazing how often an item that has not received an informal tryout is included in a large national study only to go up in smoke when even the simplest informal tryout would have identified a fundamental flaw in the item.

7. **"Bad" items are nearly always easy to spot. The types of item analysis statistics don't make that much difference.** There are a variety of item analysis statistics. One can read endlessly about the advantages of this or that method over other methods. Of course, you do want to use the best or most appropriate methods. However, in my experience, the particular item analysis methodology doesn't make all that much difference. "Bad" items will usually be easy to spot with any of the methods. As a corollary to this point, I should note that monkeying with distractors based on item analysis data will usually not fix a bad item. It is generally preferable to write a new item or use a different item.

8. **From a statistical viewpoint, the standardization group need not be very large, if properly selected. Nevertheless, people are mainly impressed with the size of the group.** Regarding a test's standardization group, users' first question is invariably about the size of the group. That's the wrong question. The important question is whether the group is representative of the target population for the test or, at least, representative of some well-defined population. One can obtain very stable norms with only a few hundred cases.

9. **For heaven's sake, get the final manual done.** For reasons that are not entirely clear, it seems to be very difficult to wrap up the final manual for a test. Many a test is published with an interim manual or with directions and assorted technical reports. Perhaps test developers are exhausted by the time they finish the standardization and ancillary research programs. Whatever the reason, for heaven's sake, get the final manual published.

10. **The whole process always takes longer than you think it will.** At the outset of a test development project, the project always seems quite feasible. Enthusiasm runs high. The anticipation of having a good, new test is exhilarating. Items will be written rapidly, people will gladly join the item analysis and standardization programs, and the final manual is already adequately outlined in your head—or so it all seems. Alas, the reality is very different. A guideline: Make a schedule for the test development project, but then assume that you will badly miss at least several deadlines in the schedule.

APPENDIX C

Contact Information for Major Test Publishers

Hundreds of companies and even individuals publish tests. Several sources, as outlined in Chapter 2, maintain comprehensive directories of these publishers. The Buros Institute's directory is the most notable one. It includes over 900 entries. This directory is available in hard copy in the current editions of *Tests in Print* and the *Mental Measurements Yearbook*. The directory is accessible on the web through the following site:

- Buros Institute of Mental Measurements at the University of Nebraska— Lincoln www.unl.edu/buros/

We list the following contact information only for publishers referred to in this text. Although this is a relatively small list of publishers, these publishers produce probably 95% of all the tests used in the United States and cover nearly all the tests mentioned in this text.

The most important information for students, in addition to the test publishers' name, is the publishers' web address. Students can use this address to gain much useful information about the tests referenced in the text. In a previous era, it was possible for

Publisher	Address	Telephone	Website
ACT, Inc.	500 ACT Drive P.O. Box 168 Iowa City, IA 52243-1008	800-645-1992	www.act.org
AGS Publishing (American Guidance Service)	4201 Woodland Road Circle Pines, MN 55014-1796	800-328-2560	www.ags.net
College Board	45 Columbus Avenue New York, NY 10023-6992	212-713-8000	www.collegeboard.com
CPP (Consulting Psychologists Press)	3803 East Bayshore Rd. Palo Alto, CA 94303	800-624-1765	www.cpp-db.com
CTB/McGraw-Hill	20 Ryan Ranch Road, Monterey, CA 93940	800-538-9547	www.ctb.com
EDITS	P.O. Box 7234 San Diego, CA 92167	800-416-1666	www.edits.net
Educational Testing Service (ETS)	Rosedale Road Princeton, NJ 08541	609-921-9000	www.ets.org
Harcourt Assessment	555 Academic Court San Antonio, TX 78204-2498	800-211-8378	www.harcourtassessment.com
Institute for Personality and Ability Testing (IPAT)	P.O. Box 1188 Champaign, IL 61824-1188	800-225-IPAT	www.ipat.com
Lafayette Instruments	3700 Sagamore Parkway N. Lafayette, IN 47903	800-428-7545	www.lafayetteinstrument.com
Mind Garden	1690 Woodside Rd. Suite 202 Redwood City, CA 94061	650-261-3500	www.mindgarden.com
National Career Assessment Services (NCASI)	601 Visions Parkway, P.O. Box 277, Adel, IA 50003	800-314-8972	www.ncasi.com
National Occupational Competency Testing Institute (NOCTI)	500 North Bronson Big Rapids, MI 49307	800-334-6283	www.nocti.org
Pearson NCS	11000 Prairie Lakes Dr. Eden Prairie, MN 55344	800-627-7271	www.ncspearson.com
PRO-ED	8700 Shoal Creek Blvd. Austin, TX 78757-6897	800-897-3202	www.proedinc.com
Psychological Assessment Resources (PAR)	P.O. Box 998 Odessa, FL 33556	800-331-8378	www.parinc.com
Psychological Corporation	555 Academic Court San Antonio, TX 78204-2498	800-211-8378	www.harcourtassessment.com

Publisher[a]	Address	Telephone	Website
Riverside Publishing	425 Spring Lake Dr. Itasca, IL 60143-2079	800-323-9540	www.riverpub.com
Western Psychological Services (WPS)	12031 Wilshire Blvd. Los Angeles, CA 90025-1251	800-648-8857	www.wpspublish.com

students to complete a course in psychological testing without ever seeing a test or a report of test scores. Today, the student's experience is greatly enriched by accessing information about tests through publishers' websites. Students are encouraged to access this information on a regular basis. Of course, students must realize that publishers are in the business of marketing their products. Hence, claims made about the tests must be evaluated carefully. The URLs listed here may change, but these major publishers are easily traced through any of the usual web search engines. We have included telephone numbers. These numbers will not be of great use to students since they are generally for "customer service," which means ordering tests, rather than for any technical information about the tests.

APPENDIX D

Sample Data Sets

Appendix D contains data sets downloadable from the publisher's website for this book: http://www.wiley.com/college/hogan/AppendixD. There are three data sets. The first (D1) provides GPAs and several possible predictor variables, including SATs and NEO PI-R scores. The second (D2) provides data from a simple reliability study. The third (D3) contains item data suitable for simple item analysis procedures. Data are available in formats for SPSS/PC and Excel for PC. The file includes a detailed description of each data set.

APPENDIX E

Answers to Selected Exercises

Following are answers to selected TRY IT exercises embedded within chapters and end-of-chapter exercises. Many of the exercises allow for considerable freedom in student responses. This appendix does not treat those exercises. In some instances, notes are included on how to answer an exercise.

Chapter 1

Try It on page 7

SAT is now the official name of what was previously labeled Scholastic Assessment Test and, even earlier, Scholastic Aptitude Test. GRE = Graduate Record Examination. WAIS = Wechsler Adult Intelligence Scale. MMPI = Minnesota Multiphasic Personality Inventory.

Exercise 5

Binet said he was attempting to get a measure of general intelligence, disregarding the exact causes of current mental functioning and distinguishing this ability from behavioral problems.

Exercise 10

Piaget was a student of Simon (Binet's colleague). Piaget's work influenced the contemporary theorists Sternberg and Gardner. We take up all of these people in Chapter 7.

Chapter 2

All of the *Exercises* in this chapter require use of websites and library resources for which answers will differ, depending on the URL selected or the local library.

Chapter 3

Try It on page 70

Mean = 4.0, median = 4, mode = 5

Try It on page 86

Matt's ratio IQ = 93, Meg's = 155

Exercise 2

$M = 6.00$ Median = 6 $SD = 2.12$

Note: Students will get slightly different answers for *SD*, depending on the software or formula used. If N rather than $N - 1$ is used in the denominator for *SD*, then $SD = 1.90$.

Exercise 5

$z = +1.0$	Percentile = 84	NCE = 71	Wechsler IQ = 115
Percentile = 75	$z = .67$ (approximately)	Otis-Lennon = 111	Stanine = 6
T-score = 30	Percentile = 2	Stanine = 1	z-score = -2.0

Exercise 8

For raw score = 65, percentile = 82, and T-score = 59.

Chapter 4

Try It on page 117

$$\text{Predicted GPA} = 3.29$$

Try It on page 140

$$\text{With } r = .92, \quad \text{SEM} = 4.2. \quad \text{With } r = .70, \quad \text{SEM} = 8.2$$

Exercise 1

$$r = .96$$

Exercise 4

With 20 items and original reliability (r_o) = .75, obtain corrected reliability (r_c) using Formula 4-13. Quadrupling test length ($n = 4$), gives r_c = .92. Halving test length ($n = \frac{1}{2}$) gives r_c = .60. To obtain r_c = .90, solve for $n = 3$. Therefore, triple test length is $20 \times 3 = 60$ items.

Exercise 10

$$\text{For } SD = 10, \quad r = .80, \text{SE}_{\text{diff}} = 6.32$$

$$\text{For } SD = 10, \quad r = .60, \text{SE}_{\text{diff}} = 8.94$$

Chapter 5

Try It on page 159

Example B shows the best validity. Examples A and C show the greatest amount of construct irrelevant variance.

Try It on page 171

$$\text{SE}_{\text{est}} = 1.89$$

Exercise 3

$$\text{GPA} = 3.60 \quad \text{SE}_{\text{est}} = .32 \quad 11\% \text{ chance}$$

Exercise 6

Use Formula 5-4. The corrected r for Test A with GPA is .58; for Test B with GPA it is .51.

Chapter 6

Try It on page 232

Prop. Correct = .85,   Disc. Index = .23

Try It on page 236

Item A's ICC will rise sharply, crossing the 50% probability mark on the Y-axis above −1 on the X-axis. Item B's ICC will rise gently, crossing the 50% probability mark on the Y-axis above 2 on the X-axis.

Try It on page 246

.20   0   .00   40   .40   .40

Exercise 5

In Table 6.9, the p-value for item 10 is .62.
Percent (or Prop.) correct in the Low group for item 23 is .00.
The easiest item is item 28.
The difference between percent correct in the high and low groups for item 29 is .05.

Exercise 8

More like Test A.

Chapter 7

Exercise 5

Divergent thinking fits under Broad Retrieval Ability.

Exercise 7

Estimated effect size (d) is approximately .3, that is, about 3/10ths of a standard deviation.

Chapter 8

Try It on page 303

46   11   12
29   7   12

Exercise 9

The Vocabulary distributions will overlap almost completely with the 20–34 age group displaced slightly to the right. For Block Design, the mean of the 85–89 age group will be centered at about the 15th percentile of the 20–34 age group.

Chapter 9

Try It on page 350

The student's Total SAI is 104. Since M = 100 and SD = 16 for OLSAT, this corresponds to a z-score of .25. For other conversions, see Table 3.1.

Exercise 5

SAI Total = 104, Verbal = 108, Nonverbal = 101. Notice that the confidence bands for the scores, graphed at the right in the chart, overlap almost completely. Thus, we would not try to make much out of the difference between Verbal and Nonverbal scores for this student.

Exercise 8

Starting with a 15-item test having reliability of .50, you need to increase the length of the test by a factor of 5.8 (i.e., bring the test length to 87 items) to obtain reliability of .85. You get 5.8 by using Formula 4-13 and solving for *n*.

Chapter 10

Exercise 4

Average for Verbal = 11. Test higher: Vocabulary. Tests lower: Digit Span, Arithmetic
Average for Performance = 10. Test higher: Block Design. Test lower: Digit Symbol

Chapter 11

Exercise 3

Primary 3 math tests: Problem Solving, Procedures, Total
Intermediate 2 Complete Battery has 372 items
Administration time for Advanced 1 Science test is 25 minutes
Primary 1 (P1) is recommended for beginning of grade 2

Chapter 12

Try It on page 449

Tennessee Self-Concept Scale—upper right quadrant
Basic Personality Inventory—upper left quadrant
Drug-Abuse Screening Test—lower right quadrant

Try It on page 456

Responses for Person C are inconsistent. It cannot be the case that you really disagree with both statements.

Exercise 6

Faking good: T, T, F, F

Chapter 13

Try It on page 504

The Drive for Thinness and Low Self-Esteem scales show the greatest separation. The Perfectionism and Maturity Fears scales show the least separation.

Exercise 1

The two-point code: 42 (i.e., the two highest T-scores).

Chapter 14

Exercise 6

With $M = 130$, $SD = 17$, a score of 145 corresponds to a z-score of .88.
Using a table of the normal curve, we find that approximately 19% of cases are above $z = .88$.

Chapter 15

Try It on page 575

Dick's score is 0. Tom's is +20. Harry's is −20.

Exercise 2

Responses show quite good, though not nearly perfect, internal agreement. Tom agrees or strongly agrees with most items. Harry disagrees or strongly disagrees with most items. Dick tends to give middle-level responses.

Chapter 16

Try It on page 594

Stanford—A, WAIS—C, Rotter—C, Strong—B

Exercise 5

Re-computing the SR/Highest rates in Table 16.9 with the given changes in hiring, we find that the new ratios are White = .80, Black = 1.00, Asian = .62, and Hispanic = .54. Therefore, there is now adverse impact for Asians and Hispanics.

Glossary

AAMR American Association on Mental Retardation, the main professional group dealing with the definition of and services for the mentally retarded. Formerly the American Association for Mental Deficiency (AAMD).

Ability-achievement continuum The theoretical continuum ranging from pure ability or aptitude to very specific, learned skills and knowledge; used to help conceptualize the difference between ability and achievement tests.

Accommodation A modification in the environment or testing conditions designed to eliminate the effects on test performance of a disability.

Accountability A movement in education requiring schools and public officials to demonstrate the success of educational programs, often with the use of tests.

Achievement tests Tests designed to measure knowledge or skills especially as developed through school or job experience.

ACT American College Testing. Refers to the ACT (college admissions) Assessment, as well as to the company that produces that test, ACT, Inc.

ADA Americans with Disabilities Act of 1990; a federal law defining disabilities and stating requirements for accommodations.

Adaptive behavior Behaviors related to coping in everyday life.

Administrative law Law that originates with a government agency; often called regulations.

Adverse impact When a selection procedure results in different selection ratios for various protected classes.

AFQT *Armed Forces Qualifying Test,* a test once used for testing military recruits, now replaced by the ASVAB. The initials also refer to a composite score derived from the ASVAB.

Age equivalent A type of norm in which a person's score is referenced to scores typical for other persons at various age levels.

Alternate form reliability Reliability determined by correlating two forms of a test.

Ambiguous stimuli Test stimuli that provide few clues as to how to respond, thus encouraging diversified responses; typically used in projective techniques.

Analogue behavioral observation The technique of observing behavior in a situation that simulates real life; a behavioral assessment technique.

Analytic scoring Scoring a test exercise for several presumably different traits or characteristics.

APA Ethics Code The short label for the American Psychological Association's Ethical Principles of Psychologists and Code of Conduct.

Aphasia Deficit in the ability to express or comprehend written or spoken communication as a result of brain injury.

ASVAB *Armed Services Vocational Aptitude Battery.*

Attenuation Lessening or reduction; in testing it refers to reduction in correlation between two variables due to imperfect reliability and/or group homogeneity.

Automated scoring Scoring performance on complex exercises by computer analysis.

Barnum effect Named after the famous showman P. T. Barnum, this term refers to high-sounding descriptions that are true of nearly everyone, although presented in such a way as to sound like they are unique to a particular individual.

Base rate The rate at which some characteristic appears in a population.

Battery A coordinated set of tests covering different content areas and age/grade levels. Usually applied to standardized achievement tests.

BDI *Beck Depression Inventory,* the most widely used measure of depression.

Behavior rating scale A set of questions or items about a child's specific behaviors (e.g., neatness, paying attention, aggressive acts), usually completed by a teacher, parent, or other caregiver.

Binet, Alfred The Frenchman who originated the first viable measure of general mental ability, the Binet-Simon scale, which led to the Stanford-Binet; the term "Binet" is also used to designate the tests themselves.

Biological model A model of intelligence that emphasizes biological roots of mental operations, especially brain functions.

Bivariate distribution Representation of the relationship between two variables on a Cartesian *(X, Y)* coordinate system; also called a scatterplot.

Block design A test involving assembly of red and white blocks to match a given design.

Broca French surgeon who first documented the site of brain damage associated with an inability to speak, but with preserved language comprehension; also designates the affected area of the brain.

Buros May refer to the person (Oscar Krisen Buros), the institute (Buros Institute for Mental Measurements), or, most frequently, to the series of published test reviews (Buros *Mental Measurements Yearbook* (MMY); see later).

Case law Law based on precedents set by court decisions.

Cattell James McKeen Cattell, an early American pioneer in development of test theory and methods; often called the father of mental testing.

Central tendency The statistics that describe the middle or typical scores in a distribution; the usual measures of central tendency are the mean, median, and mode.

Certification A procedure for demonstrating that a person has met the qualifications for some job or other type of position; the indicator that the demonstration has taken place.

CFR Code of Federal Regulations; the comprehensive list of regulations emanating from the federal government.

Chronological age (CA) A person's age, usually given in years and months (e.g., 8–4 means 8 years and 4 months).

Civil Rights Act The Civil Rights Acts of 1964 and 1991 federal laws attempting to eliminate discrimination based on race/ethnic origin, gender, and religion.

Classical test theory The traditional theory about the construction and reliability of tests, incorporating true score theory.

Clinical neuropsychology A professional specialty that combines human neuropsychology with clinical psychology.

Code type A two- or three-digit code indicating the scale numbers for the highest scores on some test such as the MMPI and some career interest surveys.

Coding The system or method for assigning categories or numerical scores to responses on a projective test.

Coefficient alpha A measure of the internal consistency of items on a test; often called Cronbach's alpha.

Cognitive flexibility Ability to switch cognitive sets with relative ease.

College Board Formerly the College Entrance Examination Board (CEEB), sponsor for the SAT, as well as other tests and services for college-bound students.

Competence Developing and maintaining one's professional expertise; practicing only in areas and with techniques for which one has such expertise.

Competency to stand trial Appropriate mental capacity at the time of standing trial; contrasted with insanity.

Componential analysis In Sternberg's triarchic theory, a method for analyzing the components of tasks and mental operations.

Comprehensive inventory A personality test attempting to measure all the major dimensions of normal personality or psychopathology.

Comprehensive System The name of Exner's method for coding (scoring) the Rorschach.

Computer-adaptive testing (CAT) A method of testing in which items presented to an examinee are determined by the examinee's responses to earlier items.

Concordance tables Tables showing the equivalence of SAT and ACT scores.

Concurrent validity Test validity demonstrated by relationship between a test and some other criterion measured at approximately the same time.

Confidence band A band placed around a test score based on the standard error of measurement.

Confidentiality Using information obtained in a professional context only for appropriate professional purposes and with the client's consent.

Consequential validity Test validity defined by the consequences of using the test for a particular purpose.

Constant error An error that makes scores consistently higher or lower than warranted for an individual or group of individuals due to factors unrelated to the test's purpose.

Construct A psychological trait or variable.

Construct irrelevant variance Variance in test scores associated with variables other than those we want to measure.

Construct underrepresentation Failure to fully measure the construct we want to measure; measuring only part of the construct of interest.

Construct validity A broad array of methods used to support the proposition that a test is measuring its target construct.

Constructed-response item A test item requiring the examinee to construct an answer rather than select an answer from given alternatives.

Constructional apraxia Inability to assemble or copy two- or three-dimensional objects.

Content validity Test validity defined by the match between test content and some well-defined body of material such as a curriculum or set of job skills.

Convenience group A group obtained because it is conveniently available rather than being drawn according to a rational sampling plan.

Convergent production Mental operations that require a person to develop one correct answer to a problem.

Convergent validity Validity evidence showing that performance on a test agrees with other measures of the target construct.

Correlation coefficient The numerical expression, ranging from −1.00 to + 1.00, of the relationship between two variables.

Crawford Demond Crawford, lead plaintiff in *Crawford v. Honig,* a federal case regarding use of IQ tests in California schools.

Criterion An external variable against which test performance is compared.

Criterion contamination Occurs when test scores influence standing on the criterion in a study of criterion-related validity.

Criterion-keying Selecting items based entirely on whether they discriminate between groups.

Criterion-referenced interpretation Interpreting test performance in relation to some well-defined external criterion rather than in relation to norms; contrasted with norm-referenced interpretation.

Criterion-related validity Demonstrating test validity by showing the relationship between test scores and some external criterion.

Cronbach's alpha See **Coefficient alpha.**

Cross-validation After completing a validation study on one group, especially one where items or variables have been selected, completing another validation study on a different group.

Crystallized intelligence In several theories of intelligence, that part of intelligence resulting from the accumulation of specific learning experiences.

Culture-fair test A test that attempts to be equally fair to individuals from different cultural backgrounds.

Cutoff score A score on a test or criterion indicating passing vs. failing or some other such division.

DAP Draw-a-Person; both a general technique and the name of several specific tests in which the examinee draws one or more people.

Debra P. Lead plaintiff in the federal case of *Debra P. v. Turlington* on use of a test for high school graduation in Florida.

Delayed memory Remembering material over a time delay of 20–30 minutes.

Descriptive statistics The branch of statistics devoted to describing characteristics of raw data.

Design issues Decisions to be made about the design of a test, such as its length, response format, number of scores, etc.

Determinants Factors presumably leading to certain types of responses, especially on the Rorschach.

Developmental norm A test norm based on level of development within the trait or characteristic being measured.

Developmental theories Theories of intelligence that emphasize stages of development in mental operations and abilities, especially moving through different stages.

Deviation IQ Norms for IQs based on standard scores.

Differential item functioning (DIF) Procedures for determining if test items are performing differently for different groups of examinees (e.g., by gender or racial/ethnic group).

Differential perspective A general disposition to view human behavior in terms of differences between people rather than in terms of general laws that apply to everyone.

Digit span A test involving short-term memory for a series of random digits.

Directionality The positive or negative direction or tone in an attitude item stem.

Discriminant validity Validity evidence showing that performance on a test has a relatively low correlation with measures of constructs expected to have a low correlation with the trait of interest.

Distractor An option in a multiple-choice item other than the correct or keyed option.

Divergent production Mental operations that require a person to develop many different answers to a problem, especially novel or unique answers.

Dizygotic Twins resulting from the roughly contemporaneous fertilization of two eggs by two sperm; contrasted with monozygotic twins.

Due process clause A clause in the Fourteenth Amendment to the U.S. Constitution guaranteeing all citizens the right to due process before the law.

Dynamometer A device to measure hand grip strength.

Dyscalculia Inability to deal with numerical quantities, such as simple computations.

Dyseidetic dyslexia Inability to read words as a whole, so that the person must sound out the word.

Dysphonetic dyslexia Inability to sound out words, so reading is by whole words and dependent on sight vocabulary.

EDI *Eating Disorder Inventory,* a widely used measure of eating disorders.

EEOC Guidelines Equal Employment Opportunity Commission Guidelines on the use of tests for employment purposes.

Effect size   A measure of the magnitude of a statistical phenomenon, especially one independent of sample size.

Elementary cognitive tasks   Relatively simple tasks used to study mental operations and abilities.

EPPS   *Edwards Personal Preference Schedule.*

Equal appearing intervals   A method for developing attitude scales that attempts to make points on the scale psychologically equidistant.

Equal protection clause   A clause in the Fourteenth Amendment to the U.S. Constitution guaranteeing all citizens the right to equal protection under the law.

Equating programs   Research programs designed to provide comparable norms for different forms or levels of a test.

Error score   The hypothetical difference between a person's obtained score and true score.

ESEA   Elementary and Secondary Education Act, a set of federal laws.

Essay test   A test requiring the writing of an essay in response to a prompt or a question; more generally applied to any type of test other than multiple-choice.

Ethics   The study of what should (or should not) be done, according to ethical, moral, and professional principles; principles helping to define appropriate behavior within a particular profession.

ETS   Educational Testing Service, located in Princeton, NJ, a major developer and publisher of tests.

Examination kit   A set of test materials, usually including the test booklet(s) or other test materials, directions for administering and scoring, and a manual with technical information, designed for reviewing the test.

Executive functions   Mental functions related to planning, evaluation, judgment, and management of other mental abilities.

Experience sampling method   Systematic sampling of time periods to determine occurrence of certain behaviors.

Expressive communication   A subdomain on the *Vineland Adaptive Behavior Scales;* deals with person's ability to speak meaningfully.

External criterion   The criterion, for example, performance in school or on the job, used to demonstrate test validity.

Extreme empirical frequency   Test items, especially in the personality domain, answered in a certain direction by nearly everyone.

Face validity   The appearance that a test measures its intended target, especially unaccompanied by any empirical evidence.

Factor analysis   A class of statistical methods for identifying dimensions underlying many scores or other indicators of performance.

Fake Bad Scale   A scale on the MMPI-2 designed to detect faking bad.

Faking bad   Answering test items to appear in an unfavorable light.

Faking good   Answering test items to appear in an especially favorable light.

False negative   A case that passes a cut-score on the criterion but does not pass the cut-score on a test intended to predict the criterion.

False positive   A case that passes the cut-score on a test intended to predict a criterion but does not pass the cut-score on the criterion.

FERPA   Family Educational Rights and Privacy Act of 1994; also known as the Buckley amendment.

Fixed battery   A set of neuropsychological tests in which it is expected that all tests will be used with each examinee.

Flexible battery   An array of neuropsychological tests in which the tests administered differ from case to case.

Fluid intelligence   In several theories of intelligence, the part of intelligence that is supposedly not dependent on highly specific learning experiences.

Flynn effect   The noticeable increase in average test scores for entire populations across successive generations, named after James Flynn who promulgated the results.

Forensic   Relating to legal matters. Forensic psychology is the application of psychological principles and methods in a legal environment.

Four-fifths rule   The rule in the EEOC guidelines operationalizing the definition of adverse impact as a difference of 80% between groups with the highest and lowest selection ratios.

Fourteenth Amendment   Amendment to the U.S. Constitution, adopted in 1868, incorporating the due process and equal protection clauses.

Frequency distribution   A distribution of raw scores, usually presented in grouped intervals arranged from high to low.

Frequency histogram   A graphic display of a frequency distribution with bars, usually erected vertically, corresponding to frequency of cases at a score or score interval.

Frequency polygon   A graphic display of a frequency distribution with points corresponding to frequency of cases at a score or score interval and points connected by lines.

FSIQ Full Scale IQ; the total score, combining VIQ and PIQ, on one of the Wechsler intelligence scales.

g The general mental ability presumed to underlie the substantial positive correlations among many mental tests, first promoted by Charles Spearman.

Galen Roman physician (circa A.D. 200) who noted the critical role of the brain.

Gall Developer of the concept of phrenology.

Galton Francis Galton, an Englishman who pioneered mental testing, motivated development of several early statistical techniques and introduced concepts of Darwinian evolution into psychology.

Gardner Howard Gardner, developer and main proponent of the theory of multiple intelligences.

General Neuropsychological Deficit Score A score derived from many variables on the Halstead-Reitan indicating general severity of neurological deficit.

Generalizability theory A method for studying reliability that allows for examining several sources of unreliable variance simultaneously.

Grade equivalent A type of test norm expressing a person's performance in comparison with the performance of students in various grades in school.

Graphic rating scale Rating scale on which responses may be marked anywhere along a continuum between two poles; marks are then converted to numerical form at a later time.

GRE *Graduate Record Examinations;* there are General and Advanced exams.

Grid-in items A type of item, usually numerical, where examinees fill in answers in a grid.

Griggs Lead plaintiff in *Griggs v. Duke Power,* a famous case in federal court on the use of tests for employment purposes.

Group test Any test suitable for administration to large groups tested all at once.

Guessing parameter In a three-parameter IRT model, the parameter that estimates chances of getting an item right by guessing.

Guttman Louis Guttman, originator of Guttman scaling (scalogram analysis) for attitude measurement.

Halstead-Reitan Neuropsychological Battery One of the widely used fixed batteries of neuropsychological tests.

Heritability index An index of the percentage of variability in a trait attributable to genetics as opposed to environment.

Heterogeneity Excessive differences among individuals, especially greater differences than normal.

Heteroscedasticity Different degrees of scatter at various points along a best-fitting line.

HFD Human figure drawings; another term for draw-a-person or draw-a-man techniques.

Hierarchical theory Theories of intelligence that postulate a tree-like arrangement of specific abilities aggregated into higher, successively more general abilities.

High and low groups Groups scoring high or low on a total test; used for analyzing individual items.

High-stakes tests Tests that have very important consequences for examinees (or other individuals) such as certification and licensing tests.

HIPPA Health Insurance Portability and Accountability Act of 1996 (P.L. 104–91) having important implications for handling test information for clients.

Hit A case that either passes the cut-scores on both criterion and test or fails on both.

Holistic scoring Assigning a single score to an essay (or similar task) based on the overall impression of its quality; contrasted with analytic scoring.

Holland John Holland, author of the RIASEC system and the Self-Directed Search.

Homogeneity Less difference among individuals than is normal.

Homoscedasticity Equal degree of scatter at various points along a best-fitting line.

HTP The *House-Tree-Person* test, in which the examinee is asked to draw in succession a house, a tree, and a person.

Ice-breaker Use of a test to help start conversation between the examiner and examinee, especially to make the examinee feel comfortable.

IDEA Individuals with Disabilities Education Act, a federal law related to identification and treatment of individuals with disabilities, including learning disabilities.

IEP Individualized education program, which must be provided for each individual identified as having a disability.

Immediate memory Remembering material over a short span of time (i.e., for just a few seconds).

Impairment Index A score based on five tests in the Halstead-Reitan indicating presence of deficit.

Impression management Deliberately answering test items to create a certain image or impression, regardless of one's true feelings about the items.

Incremental validity The increase in validity achieved by adding a new test or procedure to existing tests or procedures.

Index score A factor-based score on one of the recent Wechsler intelligence scales.

Individual test Any psychological test designed to be administered to one individual at a time.

Inferential statistics The branch of statistics dealing with drawing inferences about total populations based on analysis of data in samples.

Information processing model Any model of intelligence that concentrates on how the mind treats bits of information.

Informed consent A person's agreement to participate in testing, treatment, or a research project, based on reasonable understanding of risks and benefits.

Inquiry phase A second phase of testing with a projective technique in which the examiner inquires about the reasons for responses given in the first phase.

Insanity Mental capacity or disorder at the time a crime is committed; contrasted with competency to stand trial.

Institutional norm Norms based on the average (or median) performance of entire institutions rather than on individual persons.

Instructional validity Demonstration that persons taking an achievement test were exposed to material on the test or had an opportunity to learn the material.

Interaction As applied to heredity and environment, the notion that these factors work in a multiplicative rather than additive fashion.

Intercept bias Test bias demonstrated when the regression lines for two groups have different intercepts.

Internal consistency Items that, for the most part, are measuring the same trait or characteristic as indicated by the intercorrelations among the items.

Interquartile range The distance from the 25th to the 75th percentiles in a distribution; one of the measures of variability.

Inter-scorer reliability The degree of agreement about individuals' performance among different scorers of a test.

Interval scale A scale that orders data points in equal intervals but lacking a true zero point.

Intraclass correlation coefficient A type of correlation expressing the degree of agreement among more than two raters or judges.

Inventory A set of test items. The term "inventory" is used in personality measurement as equivalent to the term "test."

Ipsative score A score that is relative to other scores for an individual.

Item analysis Statistical analysis of individual test items, especially to determine their difficulty level and discriminating power.

Item characteristic curve (ICC) The mathematical function describing the relationship between probability of correct answer on an item and the theoretical underlying trait.

Item difficulty Percent right (or in a specified direction) on a test item.

Item discrimination An index of the degree of separation between high and low groups on a test item.

Item information function An index, in IRT, of the contribution of an individual item to the information provided by a test score.

Item response theory (IRT) A method of test construction using item characteristic curves.

Item stem The question or opening part of a test item to which the examinee must supply an answer.

Jensen Arthur Jensen, a major proponent of an information processing approach to intelligence, with special emphasis on use of elementary cognitive tasks.

Job analysis A detailed analysis of job requirements, especially for building or demonstrating the validity of a test used to select employees.

KCS *Kuder Career Search with Person Match,* a Kuder-like vocational interest inventory featuring reports that match a person with already-employed persons with similar interest profiles

KFD The Kinetic Family Drawing test, in which the examinee draws a picture of a family doing something.

Knowledge of results Providing a client with full disclosure of the results of testing.

KR-20 Kuder-Richardson Formula No. 20; an index of internal consistency.

KR-21 Kuder-Richardson Formula No. 21; an index of internal consistency that assumes that all items have equivalent difficulty values.

Kuder G. Fredrick Kuder, author of a series of tests of vocational interest, and co-author of the Kuder-Richardson formulas for reliability.

Kurtosis The peakedness or flatness of a "bell curve."

Larry P. Lead plaintiff in *Larry P. v. Riles,* a federal case in California about use of an IQ test for placement in special education class.

Law Statements about what one must (or must not) do according to legal dictates Contrasted with ethics.

Leaderless group discussion A method for observing how a person reacts in a relatively unstructured discussion group.

Licensing The legal procedure for allowing someone to practice an art or profession.

Likert Rensis Likert, originator of Likert method of attitude measurement.

Likert format A format for attitude items in which an examinee expresses degree of agreement or disagreement with a statement.

Linear transformation The transformation of raw scores from an original scale into a new scale that preserves the characteristics of the original scale except for their numerical values.

Local norm A norm based on a local group of individuals; usually contrasted with a national norm.

Location codes Codes (scores) for the Rorschach indicating which part of the inkblot a person references in the person's response.

Luria-Nebraska Neuropsychological Battery One of the widely used fixed batteries of neuropsychological tests.

Malingering Faking bad on test items or a set of tests.

Mantel-Haenszel procedure A statistical technique for examining group differences in response to individual items in comparison with overall performance on a test.

Matrix type item A test item presenting a matrix with some type of pattern that the examinee must complete.

Maximum performance The best a person can do when under no severe time constraint; the term is often used in connection with power tests.

MCMI The *Millon Clinical Multiaxial Inventory,* now in its third edition (MCMI-III) is one of several Millon inventories. The main feature of the MCMI-III is its effort to align its scales with the DSM-IV.

Mean The average; one of the measures of central tendency.

Median The middle score, when scores are arranged in numerical order; one of the measures of central tendency.

Mental ability tests Tests dealing primarily with intelligence and related abilities.

Mental age (MA) The typical score on a test for persons of a given age; a type of test norm utilizing these typical scores.

Meta-analysis A set of techniques for combining the results of several empirical studies.

Method of summated ratings The technical name for Likert's method of attitude measurement; involves summing people's ratings to items presented in the Likert format.

MMPI *Minnesota Multiphasic Personality Inventory,* a widely used measure of personality focusing primarily on psychopathology.

MMY *Mental Measurements Yearbook(s)*, collections of test reviews published periodically, first by O. K. Buros, now by the Buros Institute; see **Buros.**

Mode The most frequently occurring score in a distribution of scores; one of the measures of central tendency.

Monozygotic Twins resulting from one egg, fertilized by one sperm, then splitting in two, thus having two individuals with the same genetic endowment; contrasted with dizygotic.

Multilevel test A test series coordinated across successive ages or grades.

Multiple correlation Techniques for combining information from several variables in an optimum fashion to yield the best prediction of some other variable.

Multiple-factor theory Any theory of intelligence that emphasizes more than one dimension; especially theories arising from factor analytic methods, such as Thurstone's primary mental abilities.

Multiple intelligences (MI) Howard Gardner's theory of seven (or more) distinct types of intelligence, including such types as bodily-kinesthetic and interpersonal.

Multiple regression equation The regression (prediction) equation resulting from a multiple correlation study.

Multitrait-multimethod analysis A technique for examining the relationships among several variables each measured in several different ways.

NAEP National Assessment of Educational Progress, a program for surveying knowledge and skills in several content domains in the United States.

Narrative report Reporting of test performance in ordinary words rather than in numerical scores.

National norm A norm based on a group intended to be representative of the entire nation.

NCLB No Child Left Behind Act of 2001, actually passed in 2002. A federal law calling for states to develop and administer achievement tests in many grades, with emphasis on bringing all children to a "proficient" level of performance.

NEO PI The *NEO* (Neuroticism, Extraversion, Openness) *Personality Inventory,* a widely used measure of the Big Five personality traits.

Neuropsychological tests Tests designed to measure brain and other nervous system functions.

Neuropsychology The study of brain-behavior relationships.

NOCTI National Occupational Competecy Testing Institute.

Nominal scale A primitive type of scale that simply places objects in separate categories, with no implication of quantitative differences.

Nonlinear transformation A transformation of raw scores that changes the distances between scale values from the original to the new scale.

Norm group   Any group whose performance on a test is used as a basis for interpreting the scores of other individuals.

Normal curve   A density curve that is symmetrical and unimodal with asymptotic tails; often called the bell curve.

Normal curve equivalent (NCE)   A type of test norm that is equivalent to percentile norms at the 1st, 50th, and 99th percentiles, but has equal intervals throughout the scale.

Normalized standard scores   Standard scores derived by converting a non-normal distribution into a normal distribution by way of a nonlinear transformation of scores.

Normed score   Any score interpreted in the framework of a set of norms.

Norm-referenced interpretation   Interpretation of test scores in relation to how groups of people have actually performed on the test; contrasted with criterion-referenced interpretation.

Norms   Numerical summaries of how people in a standardization program have scored on a test.

Objective personality test   A test of personality that can be scored in a simple, clerical-like manner (e.g., by counting responses to multiple-choice or true-false items).

Observed score   A person's actual score on a test.

Odd-even reliability   Method for determining reliability by separately scoring odd-numbered and even-numbered items on the test.

OLSAT   *Otis-Lennon School Ability Test.*

Ordinal scale   A scale that places objects in order, without implying equal distances between points along the scale.

Overlapping distributions   The presentation of frequency distributions of scores for two or more groups showing the extent of overlap.

Paper-and-pencil test   Tests in which items are presented in written form and responses recorded in some written form, especially by marking an answer sheet; usually contrasted with a performance test.

PASS theory   The theory of intelligence built around planning, attention, simultaneous and sequential processing.

Percentage-right score   Expressing test performance as the percentage of items answered correctly or in a certain direction out of the total number of test items.

Percentile   A point on a scale below which a specified percent of the cases falls.

Percentile rank   The percentage of cases in the norm group falling below a given raw score.

Performance assessment   Assessment involving responses to lifelike stimuli.

Performance test   A test requiring persons to perform some action, especially an action that simulates a real-life situation; usually contrasted with a paper-and-pencil test.

Perseverate   Tendency to continue doing the same thing; inability to switch patterns of thought.

Phrenology   The theory of a relationship between skull formations and personality.

Piaget   Jean Piaget, famous for his developmental theory of intelligence, particularly for children.

Piers-Harris   *Piers-Harris Children's Self-Concept Scale.*

PIQ   Performance IQ on one of the Wechsler intelligence scales.

P.L.   Abbreviation for Public Law.

Point system   A method for scoring tests in which points are awarded for items or parts of items.

Populars   Very common or frequent responses given to a particular stimulus in a projective test.

Portfolio   A collection of work, usually completed over some lengthy period.

Power test   A test calling for maximum performance, usually with little or no time constraint.

PPVT   *Peabody Picture Vocabulary Test.*

Precision of measurement   An index of reliability derived from item response theory, showing how well a score was estimated from the model and the items.

Predictive validity   Validity demonstrated by showing the extent to which a test can predict performance on some external criterion when the test is administered well in advance.

Premorbid   The time before the onset of impairment.

Primary mental abilities   Thurstone's multiple-factor theory of intelligence, suggesting that there are about seven relatively distinct dimensions of mental ability.

Profile interpretation   Interpreting the pattern of scores on a test rather than each score in isolation.

Projective hypothesis   The supposition that when presented with an ambiguous stimulus a person's response will be determined by personality characteristics and dynamics.

Projective techniques   A method of testing in which the test stimuli are relatively ambiguous and there is substantial freedom in how the person responds.

Protocol   The record of responses to a test.

Pseudodementia   Cognitive impairment that is similar to a dementia like Alzheimer's disease, but resulting from a psychiatric condition, typically depression.

Psychoeducational battery   A set of individually administered tests designed to assess mental abilities and achievement in a coordinated manner, especially related to learning disabilities, ADHD, etc.

Psychometric theories Theories of intelligence that depend heavily on the use of tests and examination of relationships among the tests.

P-value The percentage right or scored in a certain direction for a test item.

Range The distance from the lowest to highest score in a set of data.

Range restriction Reduced variability in one or more variables, especially as affecting correlation between variables; also called attenuation.

Rapport A warm, friendly atmosphere, especially one established at the beginning of a testing session.

Rasch model A one-parameter IRT model; it assumes items have equal discrimination value and differ only in difficulty level.

Ratio IQ (MA/CA) × 100. Mental age divided by chronological age with the result multiplied by 100. The old-fashioned way of determining IQs.

Ratio scale A type of scale that classifies, then orders objects along a scale, with equal intervals and a true zero point.

Raven's Raven's Progressive Matrices Test (any of several versions).

Raw score The original result of scoring a test, e.g., number right or marked in a certain direction, before translation into some type of norm.

Real change Actual change in an underlying trait or characteristic, in contrast to momentary fluctuations.

Receptive communication A subdomain on the *Vineland Adaptive Behavior Scales;* deals with person's ability to understand spoken material.

Regression line The best-fitting line showing the relationship between data points for two variables.

Reliability The consistency or dependability of test performance across occasions, scorers, and specific content.

Replicability A technical term in Guttman scaling for how well people's patterns of responses fit the theoretical model for a Guttman scale.

Response consistency Responding to items, especially in a personality inventory, in a reasonably consistent manner.

Response distortion A tendency to respond to items in a personality test in ways other than those expressing one's true feelings.

Response phase The first phase of testing with a projective technique in which the examiner simply records the examinee's responses.

Response process The processes, for example, mental operations, a person uses to answer test items or complete a test exercise.

Response set A tendency to respond to personality test items in a certain direction or with a certain disposition, especially one unrelated to the trait the test is supposed to measure.

Response style See **Response set.**

RIASEC The initials for Realistic, Investigative, Artistic, Social, Enterprising, and Conventional in Holland's hexagon representing both personality types and work environments.

RISB *Rotter Incomplete Sentences Blank.*

Role-playing Taking on a certain role, especially for purposes of evaluation or therapy.

Rorschach Refers to both Hermann Rorschach, who experimented widely with inkblots as test stimuli, or to the inkblots themselves, with the associated method of presentation.

SAT Usually refers to the SAT I: Reasoning test, formerly Scholastic Assessment Test or Scholastic Aptitude Test; sometimes refers to Stanford Achievement Test.

SB *Stanford-Binet Intelligence Scale.*

Scaled scores Usually refers to a type of standard score used to link various levels of a multi-level test.

Scalogram analysis The technical name for Guttman scaling.

Scanner A machine for converting answers marked on an answer sheet into electrical or electronic form.

Scattergram See **Bivariate distribution.**

SCID *Structured Clinical Interview for DSM-IV,* the most well-known structured clinical interview, intended to yield a DSM diagnostic classification.

SCL-90 R *Symptom Checklist 90, Revised,* a relatively brief (90-item) self-report measure of clinical symptoms.

SDS *Self-Directed Search,* Holland's test of vocational interests.

Selected-response items Test items in which the examinee selects a response from given alternatives.

Selectivity The ability of a test to identify individuals with some characteristic.

Self-monitoring A person's keeping of careful, detailed records on his or her own behaviors and surrounding conditions.

Semantic differential A method for rating an object on a series of bipolar scales.

Sequential processing Mental processing that proceeds in a serial, step-like manner.

Shared family variance   In studies of heredity and environment, variance attributable to the fact that members of a family presumably have similar environments.

SII   *Strong Interest Inventory,* the current version of the earlier *Strong Vocational Interest Blank* (SVIB) and the *Strong-Campbell Interest Inventory* (SCII).

Simultaneous processing   Mental processing that operates on different sources of information at about the same time.

Situational test   A test in which a person is placed in a simulation of a lifelike situation so that the person's behavior can be observed.

Skewness   Asymmetry in a distribution; in skewness to the left or negative skewness, the scores pile up toward the high end of the distribution, resulting in a long tail to the left; in skewness to the right or positive skewness, scores pile up toward the low end of the distribution, resulting in a long tail to the right.

Slope   The tilt of a line describing the relationship between two variables; in IRT, the steepness of the item characteristic curve.

Slope bias   Test bias demonstrated when the regression lines for two groups have different slopes.

Socially desirable responses   Responses to test items that are in a socially desirable or "politically correct" direction, especially when these responses are not consistent with the examinee's true feelings.

Spatial neglect   A neurological impairment in which a person does not report seeing objects in one spatial field, for example, in the field of the left eye.

Spearman   Charles Spearman, the English originator of the theory of "g," general intelligence; also developer of earliest forms of factor analysis.

Spearman-Brown correction   A formula allowing estimation of the effect on reliability of lengthening or shortening a test.

Special scores   Several very focused scores in Exner's Structural Summary.

Specific domain test   A test that focuses on just one or a few variables in the noncognitive domain; contrasted with comprehensive inventories.

Specificity   The ability of a test to *not* select individuals who do *not* have some characteristic.

Specimen set   See **Examination kit.**

Speed (or speeded) test   A test with relatively easy material that must be completed as rapidly as possible.

Split-half reliability   A measure of reliability based on splitting the test into two halves, then correlating performance on the two halves.

Stage-based theories   Theories that emphasize development by way of progression through qualitatively different stages.

STAI   *State Trait Anxiety Inventory.*

Standard deviation   The square root of the sum of the deviates about the mean (squared), divided by N; the most common measure of variability.

Standard error of difference   An index of the variability in differences between scores due to unreliability in the respective scores.

Standard error of estimate   An index of the degree of error in predicting standing on one variable from standing on another variable.

Standard error of measurement   An index of the degree of variability in test scores resulting from imperfect reliability.

Standard error of the mean   An index of the variability in sample means around the population mean.

Standard score   A type of norm in which raw scores are converted to a scale with a new mean and standard deviation, both usually selected to be nice numbers.

Standardization   May refer to having fixed directions for a test or to the process of developing norms for a test.

Standardization program   The research program used to establish norms for a test.

Standardized   Most frequently refers to use of uniform conditions for administering and scoring a test; sometimes also means having norms for the test.

Standards-based education   An approach to education, arising out of the accountability movement, that emphasizes clear identification of content to be learn, specification of required levels of performance, and assurance of opportunity to learn.

Stanine   A standard score system with a mean of 5 and standard deviation of approximately 2, designed to contain the entire distribution in the range of 1–9, with equal intervals except at the tails of the distribution.

Start- and stop-rules   In an individually administered test that covers a wide span of abilities, the rules for where to begin and where to stop for an individual in the full range of items.

Statement of purpose   The test author's statement of what a test is intended to measure, usually including the target group.

Statutory law   Law resulting from action of a legislature; contrasted with administrative law and case law.

Sternberg   Robert Sternberg, author of the triarchic theory of intelligence.

Strong   Edward K. Strong, pioneer in the measurement of vocational interests and principal author of the several Strong inventories.

Stroop effect   The slower naming of ink colors when the stimulus word is an incongruent color name.

Structural summary   The overall summary of many scores resulting from application of Exner's Comprehensive System to the Rorschach.

Structured clinical interview   A clinical interview emphasizing use of the same questions and scoring methods for all clients. Contrasted with the unstructured, traditional interview in which topics, questions, and ratings vary with each client and clinician.

Structured test   A test, especially in the personality domain, with fixed modes of response; usually contrasted with projective techniques, which use a free-response format.

Subgroup norms (or norming)   Development of separate norms for each of several subgroups, e.g., different racial/ethnic or gender groups, especially in an effort to equalize selection ratios.

Talk-aloud technique   Talking through one's reactions, thoughts, and feelings while undergoing some experience, with special emphasis on detailed reporting.

TAT   *Thematic Apperception Test.*

Test   A standardized process or device that yields information about a sample of behavior or cognitive processes in a quantified manner.

Test bias   Showing that a test measures somewhat different constructs for different groups of examinees, especially for majority and minority groups.

Test blueprint   The outline of a test's content, especially as applied to achievement tests when developed by analysis of curricular materials or job requirements.

Test Critiques   A collection of test reviews published by the Test Corporation of America.

Test-retest reliability   Reliability determined by correlating performance on a test administered on two different occasions.

Test security   Maintaining test materials in places where only persons with appropriate expertise can access them.

Test user qualifications   Credentials needed to purchase tests, often represented at three levels.

Tests   A comprehensive list of tests published by the Test Corporation of America.

Theta   The score derived from application of item response theory to test performance.

Three-stratum theory   Carroll's hierarchical model, with numerous specific abilities, eight intermediate level factors, and capped off by "g."

Thurstone   Louis Thurstone, developer of the theory of primary mental abilities and major contributor to development of factor analytic methods and attitude scaling.

TIMSS   Trends in International Mathematics and Science Study, a program for testing math and science in many countries.

TIP   *Tests in Print,* a series of publications giving a comprehensive list of tests, published by the Buros Institute.

Triarchic theory   Sternberg's theory of intelligence, postulating three subtheories: componential, experiential, and contextual.

True score   The score a person would theoretically get if all sources of unreliable variance were removed or cancelled out.

True zero   A point on a scale that represents total absence of quantity; contrasted with an arbitrary zero point as, e.g., on the Farenheit scale

T-score   A standard score system with $M = 50$ and $SD = 10$.

Two-factor theory   Spearman's theory of general and specific mental abilities.

Typical performance   Performance that is typical or normal for an individual; usually contrasted with maximum performance, i.e., the very best a person can perform.

Universe score   In generalizability theory, the score resulting from theoretical administration of a test for multiple occasions, conditions, and content samples.

Unsystematic error   Random, unpredictable error that becomes incorporated into an obtained score.

USC   Abbreviation for U.S. Code (i.e., federal statutory law).

User norms   Norms based on all cases that completed a test, at least within some specified period of time.

VABS   *Vineland Adaptive Behavior Scales.*

Validity   An indication of the extent to which a test measures what it is intended to measure.

Validity coefficient   Validity indicated by a correlation coefficient; test scores are correlated with some other criterion.

Validity generalization   Developing a summary of all the information related to a test's validity.

Validity shrinkage   Reduction in validity resulting from cross-validation on a new group.

Variability   The degree of scatter or difference among scores in a data set.

Variable   A construct or dimension along which objects vary.

Variance   The square of the standard deviation; one of the measures of variability.

Vineland   A term used to designate either the *Vineland Social Maturity Scale* or its successor, the *Vineland Adaptive Behavior Scales.*

VIQ   Verbal IQ on one of the Wechsler intelligence scales.

Vocational interest measures   Tests that relate a person's preferences, interests, and dispositions to possible careers or jobs.

WAIS   *Wechsler Adult Intelligence Scale.*

Wernicke   A German neuroanatomist who found a language disturbance involving impaired comprehension but preserved speech, although it was nonmeaningful; also designates the area of the brain involved.

WISC   *Wechsler Intelligence Scale for Children.*

WMS   *Wechsler Memory Scale.*

WPPSI   *Wechsler Preschool and Primary Scale of Intelligence.*

z-score   The score resulting from subtracting from a raw score the mean, then dividing by the standard deviation, thus $z = (X - M)/SD;$ sometimes called the normal deviate score.

References

ACHENBACH, T. M. (1991). *Child Behavior Checklist.* Burlington, VT: University Associates in Psychiatry.

ACKERMAN, T. (1998). Review of the *Wechsler Individual Achievement Test.* In J. C. Impara & B. S. Plake (Eds.), *The thirteenth mental measurements yearbook* (pp. 1125–1128). Lincoln, NE: Buros Institute of Mental Measurements.

ACKLIN, M. W. (1996). Personality assessment and managed care. *Journal of Personality Assessment, 66,* 194–201.

ACT (1997). *ACT Assessment technical manual.* Iowa City, IA: Author.

ACT (2001). *ACT Assessment: Sample questions.* Retrieved October 5, 2001, from the World Wide Web: http://www.actrs8.act.org/aap/sampletest/

ADAMS, K. M. (1980). In search of Luria's battery: A false start. *Journal of Consulting and Clinical Psychology, 48,* 511–516.

ADAMS, K. M. (1984). Luria left in the lurch: Unfulfilled promises are not valid tests. *Journal of Clinical Neuropsychology, 6,* 455–465.

AIKEN, L. R. (1999). *Personality assessment methods and practices* (3rd ed.). Seattle: Hogrefe & Huber.

ALFANO, D. P., NEILSON, P. M., PANIAK, C. E., & FINLAYSON, M. A. J. (1992). The MMPI and closed head injury. *The Clinical Neuropsychologist, 6,* 134–42.

American Association on Mental Retardation (2002). *Mental retardation: Definition, classification, and systems of support* (10th ed.). Washington, DC: Author.

American Counseling Association (2000). *ACA code of ethics and standards of practice.* Alexandria, VA: Author.

American Educational Research Association, American Psychological Association, & National Council on Measurement in Education (1955). *Technical recommendations for achievement tests.* Washington, DC: American Educational Research Association.

American Educational Research Association, American Psychological Association, & National Council on Measurement in Education. (1985). *Standards for educational and psychological testing.* Washington, DC: American Educational Research Association.

American Educational Research Association, American Psychological Association, & National Council on Measurement in Education. (1999). *Standards for educational and psychological testing.* Washington, DC: American Educational Research Association.

American Psychiatric Association (1994). *Diagnostic and statistical manual of mental disorders* (4th ed.). Washington, DC: Author.

American Psychiatric Association (2000). *Diagnostic and statistical manual of mental disorders* (4th ed.) *Text Revision.* Washington, DC: American Psychiatric Association.

American Psychological Association (1954). *Technical recommendations for psychological tests and diagnostic techniques.* Washington, DC: Author.

American Psychological Association (1986). *Guidelines for computer-based tests and interpretations.* Washington, DC: Author.

American Psychological Association (1992). *Ethical principles of psychologists and code of conduct.* Washington, DC: Author.

American Psychological Association (1994). Guidelines for child-custody evaluations in divorce proceedings. *American Psychologist, 49,* 677–680.

American Psychological Association (2002). *Ethical principles of psychologists and code of conduct.* Washington, DC: Author.

ANASTASI, A. (1954). *Psychological testing.* New York: Macmillan.

ANDREWS, J. J. W., Saklofske, D. H., & Janzen, H. L. (Eds.). (2001). *Handbook of psychoeducational assessment: Ability, achievement, and behavior in children.* San Diego, CA: Academic Press.

ARBISI, P. A. (2001). Review of the Beck Depression Inventory-II. In B. S. Plake & J. C. Impara (Eds.), *fourteenth mental measurements yearbook* (pp. 121–123). Lincoln: University of Nebraska Press.

ARCHER, R. P. (1992). Review of the Minnesota Multiphasic Personality Inventory-II. In J. J. Kramer & J. C. Conoley (Eds.), *Eleventh mental measurements yearbook* (pp. 546–562). Lincoln: University of Nebraska Press.

ARCHER, R. P., MARUISH, M., IMHOF, E. A., & PIOTROWSKI, C. (1991). Psychological test usage with adolescents: 1990 survey findings. *Professional Psychology: Research and Practice, 22,* 241–252.

ARISTOTLE (1935). *On the soul. Parva naturalia. On breath* (W. S. Hett, Trans.). Cambridge, MA: Harvard University Press.

ASH, P. (1995). Review of the Eating Disorder Inventory-2. In J. C. Conoley & J. C. Impara (Eds.), *Twelfth mental measurements yearbook* (pp. 333–335). Lincoln: University of Nebraska Press.

ATKINSON, J. W. (Ed.). (1958). *Motives in fantasy, action, and society.* Princeton, NJ: D. Van Nostrand.

ATKINSON, L. (1986). The comparative validities of the Rorschach and MMPI: A meta-analysis. *Canadian Psychology, 27,* 238–247.

ATKINSON, L., QUARRINTON, B., ALP, I. E., & CYR, J. J. (1986). Rorschach validity: An empirical approach to the literature. *Journal of Clinical Psychology, 42,* 360–362.

AYERS, M., & BURNS, L. (1991). Luria-Nebraska Neuropsychological Battery: Children's Revision. In D. J. Keyser & R. C. Sweetland (Eds.), *Test critiques,* vol. VIII (pp. 358–373). Kansas City, MO: Test Corporation of America.

BAKER, F. B. (1971). Automation of test scoring, reporting, and analysis. In R. L. Thorndike (Ed.), *Educational measurement* (2nd ed.) (pp. 202–234). Washington, DC: American Council on Education.

BAKER, F. B. (1993). Computer technology in test construction and processing. In R. L. Linn (Ed.) *Educational measurement* (3rd ed.) (pp. 409–428). Phoenix, AZ: American Council on Education and The Oryx Press.

BAKER, D. B., & BENJAMIN, L. T., JR. (2000). The affirmation of the scientist-practitioner. *American Psychologist, 55(2),* 241–247.

BARKER, C., PISTRANG, N., & ELLIOTT, R. (1994). *Research methods in clinical and counselling psychology.* New York: Wiley.

BAYLES, M. D. (1989). *Professional ethics* (2nd ed). Belmont, CA: Wadsworth.

BECK, A. T., STEER, R. A., & BROWN, G. K. (1996). BDI-II manual. San Antonio, TX: The Psychological Corporation.

BECK, S. J. (1937). Introduction to the Rorschach method: A manual of personality study. *American Orthopsychiatric Association Monograph,* no. 1, xv + 278.

BELLAK, L. (1993). *The Thematic Apperception Test, the Children's Apperception Test and the Senior Apperception Test in clinical use* (5th ed.). Boston: Allyn Bacon.

BELLAK, L., & ABRAMS, D. M. (1997). *The Thematic Apperception Test, the Children's Apperception Test, and the Senior Apperception Test in clinical use* (6th ed.). Boston: Allyn and Bacon.

BELTER, R. W., & PIOTROWSKI, C. (2001). Current status of doctoral-level training in psychological testing. *Journal of Clinical Psychology, 57,* 717–726.

BEN-PORATH, Y. S. (1997). Use of personality assessment instruments in empirically guided treatment planning. *Psychological Assessment, 9,* 361–367.

BENTON, A. (1987). Evolution of a clinical specialty. *The Clinical Neuropsychologist, 1,* 5–8.

BENTON, A. (1997). On the history of neuropsychology: An interview with Arthur Benton, Ph.D. *Division of Clinical Neuropsychology Newsletter 40, 15(2),* 1–2; 14–16.

BERK, R. A. (Ed.). (1982). *Handbook of methods for detecting test bias.* Baltimore: Johns Hopkins University Press.

BERK, R. A. (Ed.). (1984). *A guide to criterion-referenced test construction.* Baltimore: Johns Hopkins University Press.

BESSAI, F. (2001). Review of the Peabody Picture Vocabulary Test-III. In B. S. Plake & J. C. Impara (Eds.), *Fourteenth mental measurements yearbook* (pp. 908–909). Lincoln: University of Nebraska Press.

BESSETTE, J. M. (Ed.). (1996). *American justice.* Pasadena, CA: Salem Press.

BETSWORTH, D. G., & FOUAD, N. A. (1997). Vocational interests: A look at the past 70 years and a glance at the future. *The Career Development Quarterly, 46,* 23–47.

BINET, A., & SIMON, T. (1916). *The development of intelligence in children* (E. S. Kite, Trans.). Baltimore: Williams and Wilkins.

BINET, A., & SIMON, T. (with Terman, L. M.). (1980). *The development of intelligence in children.* Nashville, TN: Williams Printing Company.

BLOOM, B. S. (Ed.). (1956). *Taxonomy of educational objectives, handbook I: Cognitive domain.* New York: Longman.

BORING, E. D. (1950). *A history of experimental psychology* (2nd ed.). New York: Appleton-Century-Crofts, Inc.

BORMAN, W. C., HANSON, M. A., & HEDGE, J. W. (1997). Personnel selection. *Annual Review of Psychology, 48,* 299–337.

BOTWIN, M. D. (1995). Review of the Revised NEO Personality Inventory. In J. C. Conoley & J. C. Impara (Eds.), *Twelfth mental measurements yearbook* (pp. 861–863). Lincoln: University of Nebraska Press.

BOWMAN, M. L. (1989). Testing individual differences in ancient China. *American Psychologist, 44(3),* 576–578.

BOYLE, G. J. (1995). Review of the Rotter Incomplete Sentences Blank, Second Edition. In J. C. Conoley & J. C. Impara (Eds.), *The twelfth mental measurements yearbook* (pp. 880–882). Lincoln: University of Nebraska Press.

BRACKEN, B. A. (1992). *Multidimensional Self Concept Scale, Examiner's Manual.* Austin, TX: Pro-Ed.

BRELAND, H. M., KUBOTA, M. Y., NICKERSON, K., TRAPANI, C., & WALKER, M. (2004). *New SAT writing prompt study: Analyses of group impact and reliability.* New York: College Board.

BRENNAN, R. L. (2000). (Mis)conceptions about generalizability theory. *Educational Measurement: Issues and Practice, 19(1),* 5–10.

BRENNAN, R. L. (2001a). An essay on the history and future of reliability from the perspective of replications. *Journal of Educational Measurement, 38,* 295–317.

BRENNAN, R. L. (2001b). *Generalizability theory.* New York: Springer-Verlag.

BRIDGEMAN, B., McCAMLEY-JENKINS, L., & ERVIN, N. (2000). Predictions of freshman grade-point average from the revised and recentered SAT I: Reasoning Test, Research report No. 2000-1. New York: College Entrance Examination Board.

BRIM, O. G., CRUTCHFIELD, R. S., & HOLTZMAN, W. H. (Eds.). (1966). *Intelligence: Perspectives 1965.* New York: Harcourt, Brace & World.

BRODSKY, S. L. (1991). *Testifying in court: Guidelines and maxims for the expert witness.* Washington, DC: American Psychological Association.

BRODSKY, S. L. (1999). *The expert witness: More maxims and guidelines for testifying in court.* Washington, DC: American Psychological Association.

BRODY, N. (1992). *Intelligence* (2nd ed.). San Diego: Academic Press.

BROOKINGS, J. B. (1994). Eating Disorder Inventory-2. In D. J. Keyser & R. C. Sweetland (Eds.), *Test Critiques,* vol. X (pp. 226–233). Kansas City, MO: Test Corporation of America.

BRYANT, F. B., & YARNOLD, P. R. (1995). Principal-components analysis and exploratory and confirmatory factor analysis. In L. G. Grimm & F. R. Yarnold, *Reading and understanding multivariate statistics* (pp. 99–136). Washington, DC: American Psychological Association.

BUBENZER, D. L., ZIMPFER, D. G., & MAHRLE, C. L. (1990). Standardized individual appraisal in agency and private practice: A survey. *Journal of Mental Health Counseling, 12,* 51–66.

BUCK, J. N. (1948). The H-T-P technique, a qualitative and quantitative scoring manual. *Journal of Clinical Psychology, 4,* 317–396.

BUCK, J. N. (1966). *The House-Tree-Person Technique, revised manual.* Los Angeles. Western Psychological Services.

BURNS, R. C., & KAUFMAN, S. H. (1970). *Kinetic Family Drawings (KFD): An introduction to understanding children through kinetic drawings.* New York: Brunner/Mazel.

BURNS, R. C., & KAUFMAN, S. H. (1972). *Action, styles, and symbols in Kinetic Family Drawings (KFD).* New York: Brunner/Mazel.

BURSTEIN, A. G., & LOUCKS, S. (1989). *Rorschach's Test: Scoring and interpretation.* New York: Hemisphere.

BURTON, N. W., & RAMIST, L. (2001). Predicting success in college: SAT studies of classes graduating since 1980, Research report No. 2001-2. New York: College Entrance Examination Board.

BURTON, N. W., & WANG, M. (2005). Predicting long-term success in graduate school: A collaborative validity study (GRE Board Report No, 99-14R, ETS RR-05-03). Princeton, NJ: Educational Testing Service.

BUTCHER, J. N. (1993). *Minnesota Multiphasic Inventory—2 (MMPI-2) User's guide for The Minnesota Report: Adult Clinical System—Revised.* Minneapolis: University of Minnesota Press.

BUTCHER, J. N. (1999). *A beginner's guide to the MMPI-2.* Washington, DC: American Psychological Association.

BUTCHER, J. N., DAHLSTROM, W. G, GRAHAM, J. R. TELEGEN, A., & KAEMMER, B. (1989). *Minnesota Multiphasic Inventory – 2 (MMPI-2) Manual for administration and scoring.* Minneapolis: University of Minnesota Press.

BUTCHER, J. N., GRAHAM, J. R., WILLIAMS, C. L., & BEN-PORATH, Y. S. (1990). *Development and use of the MMPI-2 content scales.* Minneapolis: University of Minnesota Press.

BYRNE, B. M. (1996). *Measuring self-concept across the lifespan.* Washington, DC: American Psychological Association.

CAMARA, W., NATHAN, J., & PUENTE, A. (1998). *Psychological test usage in professional psychology: Report to the APA practice and sciences directorate.* Washington DC: American Psychological Association.

CAMARA, W., NATHAN, J., & PUENTE, A. (2000). Psychological test usage: Implications in professional psychology. *Professional Psychology: Research and Practice, 31(2),* 141–154.

CAMARA, W. J. (2001). Do accommodations improve or hinder psychometric qualities of assessment? *The Score Newsletter, 23(4),* 4–6.

CAMPBELL, D. T., & FISKE, D. W. (1954). Convergent and discriminant validation by the multitrait-multimethod matrix. *Psychological Bulletin, 56,* 81–105.

CANNON, B. J. (2000). A comparison of self- and other-rated forms of the Neuropsychology Behavior and Affect Profile in a traumatic brain injury population. *Archives of Clinical Neuropsychology, 15,* 327–334.

CANTER, M. B., BENNETT, B. E., JONES, S. E., & NAGY, T. F. (1994). *Ethics for psychologists: A commentary on the APA ethics code.* Washington, DC: American Psychological Association.

CARROLL, J. B. (1993). *Human cognitive abilities: A survey of factor analytic studies.* New York: Cambridge University Press.

CARVER, C. S., & SCHEIER, M. F. (1996). *Perspectives on personality* (3rd ed.). Needham Heights MA: Allyn & Bacon.

CATTELL, J. M. (1890). Mental tests and measurements. *Mind, 15,* 373–381.

CATTELL, R. B. (1940). A culture-free intelligence test I. *Journal of Educational Psychology, 31,* 161–179.

CATTELL, R. B. (1963). Theory of fluid and crystallized intelligence: a critical experiment. *Journal of Educational Psychology, 54,* 1–22.

CATTELL, R. B. (1966). *The scientific analysis of personality.* Chicago: Aldine.

CHAPLIN, W. F. (1984). State-Trait Anxiety Inventory. In D. J. Keyser & R. C. Sweetland (Eds.), *Test critiques,* vol. I (pp. 626–632). Kansas City, MO: Test Corporation of America.

CHENG, L. (1994). A psychometric evaluation of 4-point and 6-point Likert-type scales in relation to reliability and validity. *Applied Psychological Measurement, 18,* 205–215.

CHINN, R. N., & HERTZ, N. R. (2002). Alternative approaches to standard setting for licensing and certification examinations. *Applied Measurement in Education, 15(1),* 1–14.

CHOCA, J. P. (2001). Review of the Millon Clinical Multiaxial Inventory—III. In B. S. Plake & J. C. Impara (Eds.), *The fourteenth mental measurements yearbook* (pp. 765–767). Lincoln: University of Nebraska Press.

CHRISTENSEN, A. L. (1984). *Luria's neuropsychological investigation.* Copenhagen, Denmark: Monksgaard.

CIZEK, G. J. (200la). More unintended consequences of high-stakes testing. *Educational Measurement: Issues and Practice, 20* (4), 19–27.

CIZEK, G. J. (Ed.). (2001b). *Setting performance standards: Concepts, methods, and perspectives.* Mahwah, NJ: Lawrence Erlbaum Associates.

CIZEK, G. J., BUNCH, M. B., & KOONS, H. (2004). Setting performance standards: Contemporary methods. *Educational Measurement: Issues and Practice, 23(4),* 31–50.

CLARKE, A. M., & CLARKE, A. D. (1985). Criteria and classification. In A. M. Clarke, A. D. Clarke, & J. M. Berg (Eds.), *Mental deficiency: The changing outlook* (4th ed.) (pp. 27–52), New York: Free Press.

CLAUSER, B. E., SWANSON, D. B., & CLYMAN, S. G. (1999). A comparison of the generalizability of scores produced by expert raters and automated scoring systems. *Applied Measurement in Education, 12,* 281–299.

CLEMENCE, A. J., & HANDLER, L. (2001). Psychological assessment on internship: A survey of training directors and their expectations for students. *Journal of Personality Assessment, 76,* 18–47.

COLE, N. S., & MOSS, P. A. (1993). Bias in test use. In R. L. Linn (Ed.), *Educational measurement* (3rd ed.) (pp. 20–219). Phoenix, AZ: Oryx Press.

CONE, J. D. (1999). Introduction to the special section on self-monitoring: A major assessment method in clinical psychology. *Psychological Assessment, 11,* 411–414.

CONNERS, C. K. (2001). *Conners' Rating Scales – Revised: Technical manual.* North Tonawanda, NY: Multi-health Systems.

CORRIGAN, P. W., HESS, L., & GARMAN, A. N. (1998). Results of a job analysis of psychologists working in state hospitals. *Journal of Clinical Psychology, 54,* 11–18.

COSDEN, M. (1984). Piers-Harris Children's Self-Concept Scale. In D. J. Keyser & R. C. Sweetland (Eds.), *Test critiques,* vol. I (pp. 511–521). Kansas City, MO: Test Corporation of America.

COSDEN, M. (1985). Rotter Incomplete Sentences Blank. In D. J. Keyser & R. C. Sweetland (Eds.), *Test critiques,* vol. II (pp. 653–660). Kansas City, MO: Test Corporation of America.

COSDEN, M. (1995). Review of Draw A Person: Screening Procedure for Emotional Disturbance. In J. C. Conoley & J. C. Impara (Eds.), *The twelfth mental measurements yearbook* (pp. 321–322). Lincoln: University of Nebraska Press.

COSTA, P. T. JR., & MCCRAE, R. R. (1992). *Revised NEO Personality Inventory (NEO PI-R) and NEO Five-Factor Inventory (NEO-FFI) professional manual.* Odessa, FL: Psychological Assessment Resources, Inc.

CRAIG, R. J., & HOROWITZ, M. (1990). Current utilization of psychological tests at diagnostic practicum sites. *The Clinical Psychologist, 43 (20),* 29–36.

Crawford v. Honig, 37 F.3d 485 (9th Cir. 1994).

CROCKER, L., & ALGINA, J. (1986). *Introduction to classical and modern test theory.* New York: Holt, Rinehart and Winston.

CRONBACH, L. J. (1949). *Essentials of psychological testing.* New York: Harper & Brothers.

CRONBACH, L. J. (1951). Coefficient alpha and the internal structure of tests. *Psychometrika, 16,* 297–334.

CRONBACH, L. J. (1990). *Essentials of psychological testing* (5th ed.). New York: HarperCollins.

CROSSON, B., & WARREN, R. L. (1982). Use of the Luria-Nebraska Neuropsychological Battery in aphasia: A conceptual critique. *Journal of Consulting and Clinical Psychology, 50,* 22–31.

CSIKZENTMIHALYI, M., & LARSON, R. (1987). Validity and reliability of the experience sampling method. *The Journal of Nervous and Mental Diseases, 175,* 526–533.

CULROSS, R. R., & Nelson, S. (1997). Training in personality assessment in specialist-level school psychology programs. *Psychological Reports*, 81, 119-124.

CUMMINGS, J. A. (1995). Review of the *Woodcock-Johnson Psycho-Educational Battery—Revised*. In J. C. Conoley & J. C. Impara (Eds.), *The twelfth mental measurements. yearbook* (pp. 1113–1116). Lincoln: Buros Institute of Mental Measurements.

DAHLSTROM, W. G., WELSH, G. S., & DAHLSTROM, L. E. (1960). *An MMPI handbook: A clinical interpretation* (Vol. 1). Minneapolis: University of Minnesota Press.

DAHLSTROM, W. G., WELSH, G. S., & DAHLSTROM, L. E. (1972). *An MMPI handbook: Research applications* (Vol. 2). Minneapolis: University of Minnesota Press.

DANA, R. H. (1978). Review of the Rorschach. In O. K. Buros (Ed.), *The eighth mental measurements yearbook* (pp. 1040–10420). Lincoln: University of Nebraska Press.

DANA, R. H. (1996). The Thematic Apperception Test (TAT). In C. S. Newmark (Ed.), *Major psychological assessment instruments* (2nd ed.) (pp. 166–205). Boston: Allyn and Bacon.

DARWIN, C. (1859). *On the origin of species by means of natural selection*. London: J. Murray.

DARWIN, C. (1871). *The descent of man, and selection in relation to sex*. London: J. Murray.

DARWIN, C. (1872). *The expression of the emotions in man and animals*. London: J. Murray.

DAS, J. P. (1994). Serial and parallel processing. In R. J. Sternberg (Ed.), *Encyclopedia of human intelligence* (pp. 964–966). New York: Macmillan.

DAS, J. P., NAGLIERI, J. A., & KIRBY, J. R. (1994). *Assessment of cognitive processes: The PASS theory of intelligence*. Boston: Allyn and Bacon.

Data Research (1994). *Statutes, regulations, and case law protecting individuals with disabilities*. Rosemont, MN: Author.

Data Research (1997). *Students with disabilities and special education* (14th ed.). Rosemont, MN: Author.

DAW, J. (2001). Psychological assessments shown to be as valid as medical tests. *Monitor on Psychology, 12(7)*, 46–47.

DAWES, R. M. (1994). *House of cards.: Psychology and psychotherapy built on myth*. New York: Free Press.

DEAN, R. S. (1985). Review of the Halstead-Reitan Neuropsychological Test Battery. In J. V. Mitchell, Jr. (Ed.), *The ninth mental measurements yearbook* (pp. 642–646). Lincoln: University of Nebraska Press.

DEARY, I. J., & STOUGH, C. (1996). Intelligence and inspection time. *American Psychologist, 51*, 599–608.

DEARY, I. J., WHITEMAN, M. C., STARR, J. M., WHALLEY, L. J., & Fox, H. C. (2004). The impact of childhood intelligence on later life: Following up the Scottish

mental surveys of 1932 and 1947. *Journal of Personality and Social Psychology*, 86(1), 130-147.

Debra P. ex rel. Irene P. v. Turlington, 730 F.2d 1405 (11th Cir. 1984).

DEROGATIS, L. R. (1994). *SCL-90-R Symptom Checklist-90-R: Administration, scoring, and procedures manual* (3rd Ed.). Minneapolis, MN: NCS Pearson.

DESTEFANO, L. (2001). Review of the Otis-Lennon School Ability Test, Seventh Edition. In B. S. Plake & J. C. Impara (Eds.), *Fourteenth mental measurements yearbook* (pp. 875–879). Lincoln: University of Nebraska Press.

DIENER, E. (1984). Subjective well-being. *Psychological Bulletin, 95,* 542-575.

DIENER, E. (2000). Subjective well-being: The science of happiness and a proposal for a national index. *American Psychologist, 55,* 34-43.

DIGMAN, J. M. (1990). Personality structure: Emergence of the five-factor model. *Annual Review of Psychology, 41,* 417–440.

DOLL, E. A. (1935). A genetic scale of social maturity. *The American Journal of Orthopsychiatry, 5,* 180–188.

DOLL, E. A. (1965). *Vineland Social Maturity Scale*. Circle Pines, MN: American Guidance Service.

DONNAY, D. A. C. (1997). E. K. Strong's legacy and beyond: 70 years of the Strong Interest Inventory. *The Career Development Quarterly, 46,* 2–22.

DONNAY, D. A. C., MORRIS, M. L., SCHAUBHUT, N. A., & THOMPSON, R. C. (2005). *Strong Interest Inventory manual: Research, development, and strategies for interpretation*. Mountain View, CA: CPP, Inc.

DORANS, N. J. (1999). Correspondences between ACT and SAT I scores, College Board Report No. 99-1. New York: College Entrance Examination Board.

DORANS, N. J., LYU, C. F., POMMERICH, M., & HOUSTON, W. M. (1997). Concordance between ACT Assessment and recentered SAT I sum scores. *College & University, 73(2),* 24–33.

DREGER, R. M. (1978). Review of the State-Trait Anxiety Inventory. In O. K. Buros (Ed.), *Eighth mental measurements yearbook* (pp. 1088–1095). Lincoln: University of Nebraska Press.

DUBOIS, P. H. (1970). *A history of psychological testing*. Boston, MA: Allyn & Bacon, Inc.

DUCKWORTH, J. C., & LEVITT, E. E. (1994). Minnesota Multiphasic Personality Inventory-2. In D. J. Keyser & R. C. Sweetland (Eds.), *Test critiques,* vol. X, (pp. 424–428). Kansas City, MO: Test Corporation of America.

DUNN, L. M., & DUNN, L. M. (1981). *Peabody Picture Vocabulary Test–Revised Manual*. Circle Pines, MN: American Guidance Service.

DUNN, L. M., & DUNN, L. M. (1997a). *Peabody Picture Vocabulary Test, Third Edition, Examiner's Manual*. Circle Pines, MN: American Guidance Service.

DUNN, L. M., & DUNN, L. M. (1997b). *Peabody Picture Vocabulary Test, Third Edition, Norms Booklet*. Circle Pines, MN: American Guidance Service.

DUPAUL, G. J., POWER, T. J., ANASTOPOULOS, A. D., & REID, R. (1998). *ADHD Rating Scale IV*. Los Angeles: Western Psychological Services.

DURLAK, J. A. (1996). Understanding meta-analysis. In L. G. Grimm and P. R. Yarnold, *Reading and understanding multivariate statistics* (pp. 319–352). Washington, DC: American Psychological Association.

EBEL, R. L. (1979). *Essentials of educational measurement* (3rd ed.). Englewood Cliffs, NJ: Prentice-Hall.

EDENBOROUGH, R. (2002). *Effective interviewing: A handbook of skills and techniques*. London: Kogan Page.

Editorial Board (1996). Definition of mental retardation. In J. W. Jacobson & J. A. Mulick (Eds.), *Manual of diagnosis and professional practice in mental retardation* (pp. 13–53). Washington, DC: American Psychological Association.

Educational Testing Service (2000). *Major field tests: Comparative data guide and descriptions of reports*. Princeton, NJ: Author.

Educational Testing Service (2005a). *Graduate Record Examinations 2005–2006 Guide to the use of scores*. Princeton, NJ: Author.

Educational Testing Service (2005b). *Major field tests*. Princeton, NJ: Author.

EDWARDS, A. L. (1957). *Techniques for attitude scale construction*. New York: Appleton-Century-Crofts.

EDWARDS, A. L. (1959). *Edwards Personal Preference Schedule Manual, Revised*. New York: The Psychological Corporation.

ENGLER, B. (1999). *Personality theories: An introduction* (5th ed.). Boston: Houghton Mifflin.

EPSTEIN, J. H. (1985). Review of the Piers-Harris Children's Self-Concept Scale (The Way I Feel About Myself). In J. V. Mitchell, Jr. (Ed.), *The ninth mental measurements yearbook* (pp. 1167–1169). Lincoln: University of Nebraska Press.

Equal Educational Opportunity Commission (1978). *Uniform guidelines on employee selection—29CFR1607.18*. Washington DC: U.S. Government Printing Office.

ERDBERG, P. (1996). The Rorschach. In C. S. Newmark (Ed.), *Major psychological assessment instruments* (2nd ed.) (pp. 148–165). Boston: Allyn and Bacon.

ESQUIVEL, G. B. (1984). *Coloured Progressive Matrices*. In D. Keyser & R. Sweetland (Eds.), *Test critiques*, Vol. I (pp. 206–213), Austin, TX: Pro-Ed.

EWING, M., HUFF, K., ANDREWS, M., & KING, K. (2005). *Assessing the reliability of skills measured by the SAT* (RN–24). New York: College Board.

EXNER, J. E. (1991). *The Rorschach: A comprehensive system. Volume 2: Interpretation* (2nd ed.). New York: Wiley.

EXNER, J. E. (1993). *The Rorschach: A comprehensive system. Volume 1: Basic foundations* (3rd ed.). New York: Wiley.

EXNER, J. E., Jr. (2003). *The Rorschach: A comprehensive system. Vol. 1: Basic foundations and principles of interpretation* (4th ed.). New York: Wiley.

EXNER, J. E., Jr., & ERDBERG, P. (2005). *The Rorschach: A comprehensive system. Vol. 2: Advanced interpretation* (3rd ed.). New York: Wiley.

EXNER, J. E., & WEINER, I. B. (1995). *The Rorschach: A comprehensive system. Volume 3: Assessment of children and adolescents* (2nd ed.). New York: Wiley.

EYDE, L. D., MORELAND, K. L., ROBERTSON, G. J., PRIMOFF, E. S., & MOST, R. B. (1988). *Test user qualifications: A data-based approach to promoting good test use*. Washington, DC: American Psychological Association.

EYSENCK, H. J. (1970). *The structure of human personality*. London: Methuen.

FARMER, R. F. (2001). Review of the Beck Depression Inventory-II. In B. S. Plake & J. C. Impara (Eds.), *Fourteenth mental measurements yearbook* (pp. 123–126). Lincoln: University of Nebraska Press.

FEAR, R. A. (2002). *The evaluation interview: How to probe deeply, get candid answers, and predict the performance of job candidates*. New York: McGraw-Hill.

FELDT, L. S., & BRENNAN, R. L. (1989). Reliability. In R. L. Linn, *Educational measurement* (3rd ed.). Washington, DC: American Council on Education/Oryx.

FERRARA, S. (1998). Review of the *Wechsler Individual Achievement Test*. In J. C. Impara, & B. S. Plake (Eds.), *The thirteenth mental measurements yearbook* (pp. 1128–1132). Lincoln: University of Nebraska Press.

FINGER, M. S., & ONES, D. S. (1999). Psychometric equivalence of the computer and booklet forms of the MMPI: A meta-analysis. *Psychological Assessment, 11(1),* 58–66.

FINN, S. E. (1996). *Manual for using the MMPI-2 as a therapeutic intervention*. Minneapolis: University of Minnesota Press.

FIRST, M. B., SPITZER, R. L., GIBBON, M., & WILLIAMS, J. B. W. (1997). *Users's guide for the Structured Clinical Interview for DSM-IV Axis I Disorders, Clinical Version*. Washington, DC: American Psychiatric Press.

FISCHER, J. & COCORAN, K. (2000). *Measures for clinical practice: A sourcebook,* (3rd ed., Vols 1–2). New York: Free Press.

FISKE, D. W., & CAMPBELL, D. T. (1992). Citations do not solve problems. *Psychological Bulletin, 112,* 393–395.

FLYNN, J. R. (1984). The mean IQ of Americans: Massive gains 1932 to 1978. *Psychological Bulletin, 95,* 29–51.

FLYNN, J. R. (1987). Massive IQ gains in 14 nations: What IQ tests really measure. *Psychological Bulletin, 101,* 171–191.

FLYNN, J. R. (1994). IQ gains over time. In R. J. Sternberg (Ed.), *Encyclopedia of human intelligence* (pp. 617–623), New York: Macmillan.

FLYNN, J. R. (1999). Searching for justice: the discovery of IQ gains over time. *American Psychologist, 54,* 5–20.

FOLSTEIN, M. F., FOLSTEIN, S. E., & MCHUGH, P. R. (1975). "Mini-mental state." *Journal of Psychiatric Research, 12,* 189–198.

FOLSTEIN, M. F., FOLSTEIN, S. E., MCHUGH, P. R., & FANJIANG, G. (2000). *Mini-Mental State Examination user's guide.* Odessa, FL: Psychological Assessment Resources.

FOXHALL, K. (2000). Bringing law and psychology together, *Monitor on Psychology, 31(1).*

FRANZEN, M. D. (1985a). Luria-Nebraska Neuropsychological Battery. In D. J. Keyser & R. C. Sweetland (Eds.), *Test critiques,* vol. III (pp. 402–414). Kansas City, MO: Test Corporation of America.

FRANZEN, M. D. (1985b). Luria-Nebraska Neuropsychological Battery, Form II. In D. J. Keyser & R. C. Sweetland (Eds.), *Test critiques,* vol. IV. (pp. 382–386). Kansas City, MO: Test Corporation of America.

FRANZEN, M. D. (2000). *Reliability and validity in neuropsychological assessment.* New York: Plenum.

FRAUENHOFFER, D., ROSS, M. J., GFELLER, J., SEARIGHT, H. R., & PIOTROWSKI, C. (1998). Psychological test usage among licensed mental health practitioners: A multidisciplinary survey. *Journal of Psychological Practice, 4,* 28–33.

FRIEDMAN, A. F., Lewak, R., Nichols, D. S., & Webb, J. T. (2001). *Psychological assessment with MMPI-2.* Mahwah, NJ: Erlbaum.

GACONO, C. B. & MELOY, J. R. (1994). *The Rorschach assessment of aggressive and psychopathic personalities.* Hillsdale, NJ: Lawrence Erlbaum.

GADOW, K. D., & SPRAFKIN, J. (1997). *Attention Deficit Hyperactivity Disorder Symptom Checklist-4* (ADHD–SC4). Stony Brook, NY: Checkmate Plus.

GALLAGHER, A. M., & KAUFMAN, J. C. (2005). *Gender differences in mathematics.* New York: Cambridge University Press.

GALTON, F. (1869). *Hereditary genius: An inquiry into its laws and consequences.* London: Macmillan.

GALTON, F. (1883). *Inquiries into human faculty and its development.* London: Macmillan.

GARDNER, H. (1983). *Frames of mind: The theory of multiple intelligences.* New York: Basic Books.

GARDNER, H. (1986). The waning of intelligence tests. In R. J. Sternberg & D. K. Detterman (Eds.), *What is intelligence?* (pp. 73–76). Norwood, NJ: Ablex Publishing.

GARDNER, H. (1993). *Multiple intelligences: The theory in practice.* New York: Basic Books.

GARDNER, H. (1999). *Intelligence reframed: Multiple intelligences for the 21st century.* New York: Basic Books.

GARNER, D. M. (1991). *Eating Disorder Inventory-2 professional manual.* Odessa, FL: Psychological Assessment Resources.

GARNER, D. M. (2004). *Eating Disorder Inventory-3 professional manual.* Lutz, FL: Psychological Assessment Resources.

GIESER, L., & STEIN, M. I. (Eds.). (1999). *Evocative images: The Thematic Apperception Test and the art of projection.* Washington, DC: American Psychological Association.

GI Forum Images de Tejas v. Texas Educ. Agency, 87 F. Supp.2d 667 (W.D. Tex 2000).

GLASS, C. R., & ARNKOFF, D. B. (1997). Questionnaire methods of cognitive self-statement assessment. *Journal of Consulting and Clinical Psychology, 65,* 911–927.

GLASS, G. V., & HOPKINS, K. D. (1996). *Statistical methods in education and psychology* (3rd ed.). Boston: Allyn and Bacon.

GOLDEN, C. J. (1981). A standardized version of Luria's neuropsychological tests. In S. Filskov & T. J. Boll (Eds.), *Handbook of clinical neuropsychology.* New York: Wiley-Interscience.

GOLDEN, C. J. (1984). Applications of the standardized Luria-Nebraska Neuropsychological Battery to rehabilitation planning. In P. E. Logue & J. M. Schear (Eds.), *Clinical neuropsychology: A multidisciplinary approach.* Springfield, IL: C. C. Thomas.

GOLDEN, C. J., HAMMEKE, T. A., & PURISCH, A. D. (1979). Diagnostic validity of a standardized neuropsychological battery derived from Luria's neuropsychological tests. *Journal of Consulting and Clinical Psychology, 46,* 1258–1265.

GOLDEN, C. J., PURISCH, A. D., &; HAMMEKE, T. A. (1985). *Manual for the Luria-Nebraska Neuropsychological Battery: Forms I and II.* Los Angeles, CA: Western Psychological Services.

GOLDFRIED, M. R. (1976). Behavioral assessment. In I. B. Weiner (Ed.), *Clinical methods in psychology* (pp. 281–330). New York: Wiley.

GOLDFRIED, M. R., & KENT, R. N. (1972). Traditional vs. behavioral assessment: A comparison of methodological and theoretical assumptions. *Psychological Bulletin, 77,* 409–420.

GOLDMAN, B. A. (2001). Review of the Otis-Lennon School Ability Test, Seventh Edition. In B. S. Plake & J. C. Impara (Eds.), *Fourteenth mental measurements yearbook* (pp. 879–881). Lincoln: University of Nebraska Press.

GOLDMAN, B. A., & MITCHELL, D. F. (2003). *Directory of unpublished experimental mental measures* (Vol. 8). Washington, DC: American Psychological Association.

GOODENOUGH, F. (1926). *Measurement of intelligence by drawings.* New York: World Book.

GOTTFREDSON, L. S. (1996). What do we know about intelligence. *American Scholar,* Winter, 15–30.

GOTTFREDSON, L. S. (1997). Mainstream science on intelligence: An editorial with 52 signatories, history, and bibliography. *Intelligence, 24*(1), 13–23.

GOTTFREDSON, L. S. (2004). Intelligence: Is it the epidemiologists' elusive "fundamental cause" of social class inequalities in health? *Journal of Personality and Social Psychology, 86*(1), 174–199.

GRAHAM, J. R. (2000). *MMPI-2: Assessing personality and psychopathology* (3rd ed.). New York: Oxford University Press.

GREEN, D. R. (1998). Consequential aspects of the validity of achievement tests: A publisher's point of view. *Educational Measurement: Issues and Practice, 17(2),* 16–19.

GREEN, D. R., YEN, W. M., & BURKETT, G. R. (1989). Experiences in the application of item response theory in test construction. *Applied Measurement in Education, 2,* 297–312.

GREGORY, R. J. (1996). *Psychological testing: History, principles, and applications* (2nd ed.). Boston: Allyn and Bacon.

Griggs v. Duke Power Co., 401 U.S. 424 (1971).

GRISSO, T. (1986). Psychological assessment in legal contexts. In W. J. Curran, A. L. McGarry, & S. A. Shah (Eds.), *Forensic psychiatry and psychology.* Philadelphia. F.A. Davis.

GRISSO, T. (1996). Clinical assessments for legal decision-making in criminal cases: Research recommendations. In B. D. Sales & S. A. Shah (Eds.), *Mental health and law: Research, policy, and services* (pp. 109–140). Durham, NC: Carolina Academic Press.

GROSS, M. (1962). *The brain watchers.* New York: Random House.

GROTH-MARNAT, G. (1999). *Handbook of psychological assessment* (3rd ed.). New York: Wiley.

GROTH-MARNAT, G. (2003). *Handbook of psychological assessment* (4th ed.). New York: Wiley.

Group for the Advancement of Psychiatry (1991). *The mental health professional and the legal system.* New York: Bruner/Mazel.

GROVE, W. M., & MEEHL, P. E. (1996). Comparative efficiency of informal (subjective, impressionistic) and formal (mechanical, algorithmic) prediction procedures: The clinical–statistical controversy. *Psychology, Public Policy, and Law, 2,* 293–323.

GUILFORD, J. P. (1956). The structure of intellect. *Psychological Bulletin, 53,* 267–293.

GUILFORD, J. P. (1958). A system of psychomotor abilities. *American Journal of Psychology, 71,* 164–174.

GUILFORD, J. P. (1959a). *Personality.* New York: McGraw-Hill.

GUILFORD, J. P. (1959b). Three faces of intellect. *American Psychologist, 14,* 469–479.

GUILFORD, J. P. (1967). *The nature of human intelligence.* New York: McGraw-Hill.

GUILFORD, J. P. (1985). The structure of intellect model. In B. Wolman (Ed.), *Handbook of intelligence: Theories, measurements, and applications* (pp. 225–266). New York: Wiley.

GUILFORD, J. P. (1988). Some changes in the structure-of-intellect model. *Educational and Psychological Measurement, 48,* 1–4.

GULLIKSEN, H. (1950). *Theories of mental tests.* New York: Wiley.

GUTTMAN, L. (1944). A basis for scaling qualitative data. *American Sociological Review, 9,* 139–150.

GUTTMAN, L. (1947). The Cornell technique for scale and intensity analysis. *Educational and Psychological Measurement, 7,* 247–280.

GUTTMAN, L., & SUCHMAN, E. A. (1947). Intensity and a zero point for attitude analysis. *American Sociological Review, 12,* 57–67.

HALADYNA, T. M. (1994). *Developing and validating multiple-choice items.* Hillsdale, NJ: Lawrence Erlbaum.

HALADYNA, T. M. (2004). *Developing and validating multiple-choice test items* (3rd ed.). Mahwah, NJ: Erlbaum.

HALADYNA, T. M., & DOWNING, S. M. (1989a). A taxonomy of multiple-choice item-writing rules. *Applied Measurement in Education, 2,* 37–50.

HALADYNA, T. M., & DOWNING, S. M. (1989b). Validity of a taxonomy of multiple-choice item-writing rules. *Applied Measurement in Education, 2,* 51–78.

HALADYNA, T. M., DOWNING, S. M., & RODRIGUEZ, M. C. (2002). A review of multiple-choice item-writing guidelines for classroom assessment. *Applied Measurement in Education, 15,* 309–334.

HAMBLETON, R. K. (2001). Setting performance standards on educational assessments and criteria for evaluating the process. In G. J. Cizek (Ed.), *Setting performance standards: Concepts, methods, and perspectives* (pp. 89–116). Mahwah, NJ: Lawrence Erlbaum.

HAMBLETON, R. K., & SWAMINATHAN, H. (1985). *Item response theory: Principles and applications.* Boston: Kluwer-Nijhoff.

HAMBLETON, R. K., SWAMINATHAN, H., & ROGERS, H. J. (1991). *Fundamentals of item response theory.* Newbury Park, NJ: Sage Publications.

HANDLER, L. (1996). The clinical use of figure drawings. In C. S. Newmark (Ed.), *Major psychological assessment instruments* (2nd ed.) (pp. 206–293). Boston: Allyn and Bacon.

HALPERN, D. F. (2000). *Sex differences in cognitive abilities* (3rd ed.). Mahwah, NJ: Erlbaum.

Harcourt Educational Measurement. (2003). *Stanford Achievement Test Series, Tenth Edition: Spring technical data report.* San Antonio, TX: Author.

HARMON, L. W., HANSEN, J. C., BORGEN, F. H., & HAMMER, A. L. (1994). *Strong Interest Inventory: Applications and technical guide.* Palo Alto, CA: Consulting Psychologists Press.

HARRIS, D. B. (1963). *Children's drawings as measures of intellectual maturity.* New York: Harcourt, Brace, & World.

HARROW, A. J. (1972). *A taxonomy of the psychomotor domain.* New York: David McKay.

HATHAWAY, S. R., & MCKINLEY, J. C. (1989). *MMPI-2 manual for administration and scoring.* Minneapolis: University of Minnesota Press.

HAYNES, S. N. (2001). Introduction to the special section on clinical applications of analogue behavioral observation. *Psychological Assessment, 13,* 3–4.

HAYSLIP, B. (1994). Stability of intelligence. In R. J. Sternberg (Ed.), *Encyclopedia of human intelligence* (pp. 1019–1026), New York: Macmillan.

HENRYSSEN, S. (1971). Gathering, analyzing, and using data on test items. In R. L. Thorndike (Ed.), *Educational measurement* (2nd ed.) (pp. 130–159). Washington, DC: American Council on Education.

HERRIOT, P. (Ed.). (1989). *Assessment and selection in organizations: methods and practice for recruitment and appraisal.* New York: Wiley.

HERRNSTEIN, R. J., & MURRAY, C. (1994). *The bell curve: Intelligence and class structure in American life.* New York: The Free Press.

HERTZ, M. A. (1943). Personality patterns in adolescence as portrayed by the Rorschach ink blot method: IV. The "Erlebnistypus" *Journal of General Psychology, 20,* 3–45.

HERTZ, M. A. (1948). Suicidal configurations in Rorschach records. *Rorschach Research Exchange, 12,* 3–58.

HESS, A. K. (1998). Review of the Millon Clinical Multiaxial Inventory—III. In B. S. Plake & J. C. Impara (Eds.), *The thirteenth mental measurements yearbook* (pp. 665–667). Lincoln: University of Nebraska Press.

HILGARD, E. R. (1987). *Psychology in America: A historical survey.* San Diego, CA: Harcourt Brace Jovanovich.

HILLER, J. B., ROSENTHAL, R., BORNSTEIN, R. F., BERRY, D. T. R., & BRUNELL-NEULEIB, S. (1999). A comparative meta-analysis of Rorschach and MMPI validity. *Psychological Assessment, 11(3),* 278–296.

HILSENROTH, M. J., & HANDLER, L. (1995). A survey of graduate students' experiences, interests, and attitudes about learning the Rorschach. *Journal of Personality Assessment, 64,* 243–257.

HOFFMAN, B. (1962). *The tyranny of testing.* New York: Crowell-Collier.

HOGAN, T. P. (1981). Relationship between free-response and choice-type tests of achievement: A review of the literature. Green Bay: University of Wisconsin. (ERIC Document Reproduction Service No. ED 224 811.)

HOGAN, T. P. (2005). Types of test scores and their percentile equivalents. In G. P. Koocher, J. C. Norcross, & S. S. Hill (Eds.), *Psychologists' desk reference* (2nd ed.). New York: Oxford University Press.

HOGAN, T. P. (2007). *Educational assessment: A practical introduction.* New York: Wiley.

Hogan, T. P., & Agnello, J. (2004). An empirical study of reporting practices concerning measurement validity. *Educational and Psychological Measurement, 64,* 802–812.

HOGAN, T. P., BENJAMIN, A., & BREZINSKI, K. L. (2000). Reliability methods: A note on the frequency of use of various types. *Educational and Psychological Measurement, 60,* 523–531.

HOLLAND, J. L. (1959). A theory of vocational choice. *Journal of Counseling Psychology, 6,* 35–45.

HOLLAND, J. L. (1966). *The psychology of vocational choice: A theory of personality types and model environments.* Waltham, MA: Ginn.

HOLLAND, J. L. (1997). *Making vocational choices: A theory of vocational personalities and work environments* (3rd ed.). Odessa, FL: Psychological Assessment Resources.

HOLLAND, J. L., FRITZSCHE, B. A., & POWELL, A. B. (1997). *SDS Self-directed Search Technical manual.* Odessa, FL: Psychological Assessment Resources.

HOLLAND, J. L., POWELL, A. B., & FRITZSCHE, B. A. (1997). *SDS Self-directed Search Professional user's guide.* Odessa, FL: Psychological Assessment Resources.

HOLLAND, P. W., & THAYER, D. T. (1988). Differential item performance and the Mantel-Haenszel procedure. In H. Wainer & H. I. Braun (Eds.), *Test validity* (pp. 129–145). Hillsdale, NJ: Lawrence Erlbaum.

HOLTZMAN, W. H. (1961). *Holtzman Inkblot Technique administration and scoring guide.* New York: Psychological Corporation.

HOOPER, S. R. (1992). Review of the Luria-Nebraska Neuropsychological Battery: Children's Revision. In J. J. Kramer & J. C. Conoley (Eds.), *The eleventh mental measurements yearbook* (pp. 479–481). Lincoln: University of Nebraska Press.

HORN, J. L., & CATTELL, R. B. (1966). Refinement and test of the theory of fluid and crystallized intelligence. *Journal of Educational Psychology, 57,* 253–270.

HORN, J. L. (1994). Fluid and crystallized intelligence, theory of. In In R. J. Sternberg (Ed.), *Encyclopedia of human intelligence* (pp. 443–451). New York: Macmillan.

HOUSE, A. E. (1996). *The Wechsler Adult Intelligence Scale*—Revised (WAIS-R). In C. S. Newmark (Ed.), *Major psychological assessment instruments* (2nd ed.) (pp. 320–347). Needham Heights, MA: Allyn & Bacon.

HOYER, W. J., & TOURON, D. R. (2003). Learning in adulthood. In J. Demick & C. Andreoletti (Eds.), *Handbook of adult development* (pp. 23–41). New York: Kluwer Academic/Plenum.

HUNSLEY, J., & BAILEY, J. M. (1999). The clinical utility of the Rorschach: Unfulfilled promises and an uncertain future. *Psychological Assessment, 11(3),* 266–277.

HUNSLEY, J., & HAYNES, S. N. (Eds.). (2003). Special section: Incremental validity and utility in clinical assessment. *Psychological Assessment, 15,* 443–531.

HUNTER, J. E., SCHMIDT, F. L., & HUNTER, R. (1979). Differential validity of employment tests by race: A comprehensive review and analysis. *Psychological Bulletin, 86,* 721–735.

HUTTON, J. B., DUBES, R., & MUIR, S. (1992). Assessment practices of school psychologists: Ten years later. *School Psychology Review, 21,* 271–284.

IMPARA, J. C. (Ed.). (1995). *Licensure testing: Purposes, procedures, and practices.* Lincoln, NE: Buros Institute of Mental Measurements.

JENCKS, C. (1979). *Who gets ahead? The determinants of economic success in America.* New York: Basic Books.

JENCKS, C., & PHILLIPS, M. (Eds.). (1998). *The Black-White test score gap.* Washington, DC: Brookings Institution Press.

JENSEN, A. R. (1969). How much can we boost IQ and scholastic achievement? *Harvard Educational Review, 39,* 1–123.

JENSEN, A. R. (1980). *Bias in mental testing.* New York: Free Press.

JENSEN, A. R. (1994). Race and IQ scores. In R. J. Sternberg (Ed.), *Encyclopedia of human intelligence* (pp. 899–907). New York: Macmillan.

JENSEN, A. R. (1998). *The g factor: The science of mental ability.* Westport. CT: Praeger.

JESKE, P. J. (1985). Review of the Piers-Harris Children's Self-Concept Scale (The Way I Feel About Myself). In J. V. Mitchell, Jr. (Ed.), *The ninth mental measurements yearbook* (pp. 1169–1170). Lincoln: University of Nebraska Press.

JOHNSON, S. T. (1994). Scholastic Assessment Tests (SAT). In R. J. Sternberg (Ed.), *Encyclopedia of human intelligence* (pp. 956–960). New York. Macmillan.

JOHNSON, W. L., & DIXON, P. N. (1984). Response alternatives in Likert scaling. *Educational and Psychological Measurement, 44,* 563–567.

Joint Committee on Testing Practices (1988). *Code of fair testing practices in education.* Washington, DC: Author.

Joint Committee on Testing Practices (2004). *Code of fair testing practices in education—Revised* Washington, DC: Author.

Journal of Educational Psychology. (1921). Intelligence and its measurement: A symposium. Editorial introduction. *Journal of Educational Psychology, 12,* 123.

JUNI, S. (1995). Review of the Revised NEO Personality Inventory. In J. C. Conoley & J. C. Impara (Eds.), *The twelfth mental measurements yearbook* (pp. 863–868). Lincoln: University of Nebraska Press.

KANE, M. T. (2001). Current concerns in validity theory. *Journal of Educational Measurement, 38,* 319–342.

KAPES, J. T., & WHITFIELD, E. A. (Eds.). (2002). *A counselor's guide to career assessment instruments* (4th ed.). Alexandria, VA: National Career Development Association.

KAPLAN, R. M., & SACCUZZO, D. P. (2005). *Psychological testing: Principles, applications, and issues* (6th ed.). Belmont, CA: Wadsworth/Thomson Learning.

KARRAKER v. Rent-A-Center, Inc., 411 F.3d 831 (7th Cir. 2005).

KATIN, E. S. (1978). Review of the State-Trait Anxiety Inventory. In O. K. Buros (Ed.), *The eighth mental measurements yearbook,* (pp. 1095–1096). Lincoln: University of Nebraska Press.

KAUFMAN, A. S., & KAUFMAN, N. L. (1983). *Kaufman Assessment Battery for Children.* Circle Pines, MN: American Guidance Service.

KELLEY, M. L. (2005). Review of Piers-Harris Children's Self-Concept Scale. In R. A. Spies, B. S. Plake, & L. L. Murphy (Eds.), *The sixteenth mental measurements yearbook* (pp. 789–790). Lincoln, NE: Buros Institute of Mental Measurements.

KELLEY, T. L. (1927). *Interpretation of educational measurements.* Yonkers-on-Hudson, NY: World Book.

KELLEY, T. L. (1939). The selection of upper and lower groups for the validation of test items. *Journal of Educational Psychology, 30,* 17–24.

KEYES, C. L. M., & Magyar-Moe, J. L. (2003). Measurement and utility of adult subjective well-being. In S. J. Lopez & C. R. Snyder (Eds.), *Positive psychological assessment: A handbook of models and measures* (pp. 411–425). Washington, DC: American Psychological Association.

KEYSER, D. J. (1994). *Test critiques* (Vol. XI). Austin, TX: Pro-Ed.

KENNEDY, M. L., FAUST, D., WILLIS, W. G., & PIOTROWSKI, C. (1994). Socio-emotional assessment practices in school psychology. *Journal of Psychoeducational Assessment, 12,* 228–240.

KLEINMUNTZ, B. (1990). Why we still use our heads instead of formulas: Toward an integrative approach. *Psychological Bulletin, 107,* 296–310.

KLINE, P. (1991). *Intelligence: The psychometric view.* New York: Routledge.

KLINE, P. (1994). Cattell, R. B. In R. J. Sternberg (Ed.), *Encyclopedia of human intelligence* (pp. 241–243). New York: Macmillan.

KLOPFER, B. (1937). The present status of the theoretical development of the Rorschach method. *Rorschach Research Exchange, 1,* 142–147.

KLOPFER, B., & KELLEY, D. (1942). *The Rorschach technique.* Yonkers, NY: World Book.

KLOPFER, W. G, & TAULBEE, E. S. (1976). Projective tests. *Annual Review of Psychology, 27,* 543–568.

KNAPP, J. E., & KNAPP, L. G. (1995). Practice analysis: Building the foundation for validity. In J. C. Impara (Ed.), *Licensure testing: Purposes, procedures, and practices* (pp. 93–116). Lincoln: University of Nebraska.

KOOCHER, G. P., & KEITH-SPIEGEL, P. (1998). *Ethics in psychology: Professional standards and cases* (2nd ed.). New York: Oxford University Press.

KOROTITSCH, W. J., & NELSON-GRAY, R. O. (1999). An overview of self-monitoring research in assessment and treatment. *Psychological Assessment, 11,* 415–425.

KRATHWOHL, D. R., BLOOM, B. S., & MASIA, B. B. (1964). *Taxonomy of educational objectives, handbook II: Affective domain.* New York: David McKay.

KREITZER, A. E., & MADAUS, G. F. (1994). Empirical investigations of the hierarchical structure of the taxonomy. In L. W. Anderson & L. A. Sosniak (Eds.), *Bloom's taxonomy: A forty-year retrospective* (pp. 64–81). Chicago: University of Chicago Press.

KUDER, F., & ZYTOWSKI, D. G. (1991). *Kuder Occupational Interest Survey, Form DD, General Manual* (3rd ed.). Adel, IA: National Career Assessment Services.

KUDER, J. F., & RICHARDSON, M.W. (1937). The theory of estimation of test reliability. *Psychometrika, 2,* 151–160.

KUNCEL, N. R., HEZLETT, S. A., & ONES, D. S. (2001). A comprehensive meta-analysis of the predictive validity of the Graduate Record Examinations: Implications for graduate student selection and performance. *Psychological Bulletin, 127,* 162–181.

KUNCEL, N. R., HEZLETT, S. A., & ONES, D. S. (2004). Academic performance, career potential, creativity, and job performance: Can one construct predict them all? *Journal of Personality and Social Psychology, 86(1),* 148–161.

LANE, S., PARKE, C. S., & STONE, C. A. (1998). A framework for evaluating the consequences of assessment programs. *Educational Measurement: Issues and Practice, 17(2),* 24–28.

Larry P. ex rel. Lucille P. v. Riles, 793 F.2d 969 (9th Cir. 1984).

LARSON, G. E. (1994). Armed Services Vocational Aptitude Battery. In R. J. Sternberg (Ed.), *Encyclopedia of human intelligence* (pp. 121–124). New York: Macmillan.

LAWRENCE, I., RIGOL, G. W., VAN ESSEN, T., & JACKSON, C. A. (2002). *A historical perspective on the SAT 1926-2001.* New York: College Board.

LAWSHE, C. H. (1978). A quantitative approach to content validity. *Personnel Psychology, 28,* 563–575.

LEE, J. (2002). Racial and ethnic achievement gap trends: Reversing the progress toward equity? *Educational Researcher, 31,* 3–12.

LEE, S. W., & STEFANY, E. F. (1995). Review of the *Woodcock-Johnson Psych-Educational Battery—Revised.* In J. C. Conoley & J. C. Impara (Eds.), *The twelfth mental measurements yearbook* (pp. 1116–1117). Lincoln: Buros Institute of Mental Measurements.

LEES-HALEY, P. R. (1992). Psychodiagnostic test usage by forensic psychologists. *American Journal of Forensic Psychology, 10(1),* 25–30.

LEES-HALEY, P. R., ENGLISH, L., & GLENN, W. (1991). A fake bad scale on the MMPI-2 for personal injury claimants. *Psychological Reports, 68,* 203–210.

LEES-HALEY, P. R., SMITH, H. H., WILLIAMS, C. W., & DUNN, J. T. (1996). Forensic neuropsychological test usage: An empirical study. *Archives of Clinical Neuropsychology, 11,* 45–51.

LERNER, P. (Ed.). (1975). *Handbook of Rorschach scales.* New York: International Universities Press Inc.

LERNER, H., & LERNER, P.M. (1985). Rorschach Inkblot Test. In D. J. Keyser & R. C. Sweetland (Eds.), *Test critiques,* vol. IV (pp. 523–552). Kansas City, MO: Test Corporation of America.

LEVITT, E. E., & GOTTS, E. E. (1995). *The clinical application of MMPI special scales* (2nd ed.). Hillsdale, NJ: Lawrence Erlbaum.

LEWAK, R. W., MARKS, P. A., & NELSON, G. E. (1990). *Therapist's guide to the MMPI and MMPI-2: Providing feedback and treatment.* Muncie, IN: Accelerated Development.

LEZAK, M. (1995). *Neuropsychological assessment* (3rd ed.). New York: Oxford University Press.

LICHT, M. H. (1995). Multiple regression and correlation. In L. G. Grimm and P. R. Yarnold, *Reading and understanding multivariate statistics* (pp. 19–64). Washington, DC: American Psychological Association.

LIKERT, R. A. (1932). A technique for the measurement of attitudes. *Archives of Psychology, 140,* 1–55.

LILIENFELD, S. O., WOOD, J. M., & GARB, H. N. (2000). The scientific status of projective techniques. *Psychological Science in the Public Interest, 1,* 27–66.

LINDENBERGER, U., & BALTES, P. B. (1994). Aging and intelligence. In R. J. Sternberg (Ed.), *Encyclopedia of human intelligence* (pp. 52–66). New York: Macmillan.

LINN, R. L. (1997). Evaluating the validity of assessments: The consequences of use. *Educational Measurement: Issues and Practice, 16(2),* 14–16.

LINN, R. L. (1998). Partitioning responsibility for the evaluation of the consequences of assessment programs. *Educational Measurement: Issues and Practice, 17(2),* 28–30.

LINN, R. L. (2000) Assessment and accountability. *Educational Researcher, 29(2),* 4–16.

LINN, R. L., & MILLER, D. (2004). *Measurement and assessment in teaching* (9th ed.). Englewood Cliffs, NJ: Prentice-Hall.

LLABRE, M. M. (1984). Standard Progressive Matrices. In D. Keyser & R. Sweetland (Eds.), *Test critiques,* Vol. I (pp. 595–602). Austin, TX: Pro-Ed.

LOEHLIN, J. C. (1994). Genetics, behavior. In R. J. Sternberg (Ed.), *Encyclopedia of human intelligence* (pp. 475–483). New York: Macmillan.

LOPEZ, S. J., & SNYDER, C. R. (Eds.). (2003). *Positive psychological assessment: A handbook of models and measures.* Washington, DC: American Psychological Association.

LORD, F. M., & NOVICK, M. (1968). *Statistical theories of mental test scores.* Reading, MA: Addison-Wesley.

LUBIN, B., LARSEN, R. M., & MATARAZZO, J. D. (1984). Patterns of psychological test usage in the United States: 1935–1982. *American Psychologist, 39,* 451–453.

LUBIN, B., LARSEN, R. M., MATARAZZO, J. D., & SEEVER, M. (1985). Psychological test usage patterns in five professional settings. *American Psychologist, 49,* 857–861.

LUBINSKI, D. (2004). Introduction to the special section on cognitive abilities: 100 years after Spearman's "'General Intelligence,' Objectively Determined and Measured." *Journal of Personality and Social Psychology, 86(1),* 96–111.

MACCIOCCHI, S. N., & BARTH, J. T. (1996). The Halstead-Reitan Neuropsychological Test Battery (HRNTB). In C. S. Newmark (Ed.), *Major psychological assessment instruments* (2nd ed.) (pp. 431–459). Boston: Allyn and Bacon.

MACHOVER, K. (1949). *Personality projection in the drawing of the human figure.* Springfield, IL: Charles C. Thomas.

MACKINTOSH, N. J. (1998). *IQ and human intelligence.* New York: Oxford University Press.

MACMILLAN, M. (2000). *An odd kind of fame: Stories of Phineas Gage.* Cambridge, MA: MIT Press.

MADDOX, T. (2003). *Tests: A comprehensive reference for assessments in psychology, education, and business* (5th ed.). Austin, TX: Pro-Ed.

MARLOWE, D. B., WETZLER, S., & GIBBINGS, E. N. (1992). Graduate training in psychological assessment: What Psy.D.'s and Ph.D.'s must know. *The Journal of Training and Practice in Professional Psychology, 6,* 9–18.

MARSH, H. W., PARADA, R. H., & AYOTTE, V. (2004). A multidimensional perspective of relations between self-concept (Self Description Questionnaire II) and adolescent mental health (Youth Self Report). *Psychological Assessment, 16,* 27–41.

MATELL, M. S., & JACOBY, J. (1972). Is there an optimal number of alternatives for Likert-scale items? Effects of testing time and scale properties. *Journal of Applied Psychology, 56,* 506–509.

MATHER, N., & WOODCOCK, R. W. (2001). *Woodcock-Johnson III Tests of Achievement: Examiner's Manual.* Itasca, IL: Riverside Publishing.

MAXEY, J. (1994). American College Test. In R. J. Sternberg (Ed.), *Encyclopedia of human intelligence* (pp. 82–85). New York: Macmillan.

MCCALL, W. T. (1922). *How to measure in education.* New York: Macmillan.

MCCLELLAND, D. C. (1985). *Human motivation.* Glenview, IL: Scott, Foresman and Company.

MCCLELLAND, D. C., ATKINSON, J. W., CLARK, R. A., & LOWELL, E. L. (1953). *The achievement motive.* New York: Appleton Century Crofts.

MCKHANN, G., DRACHMAN, D., FOLSTEIN, M., KATZMAN, R., PRICE, D., & STADLAN, E. M. (1984). Clinical diagnosis of Alzheimer's disease: Report of the NINCDS-ADRDA Work Group, Department of Health and Human Services Task Force on Alzheimer's Disease. *Neurology, 34,* 939–944.

MCLELLAN, M. J. (1995). Review of the Rotter Incomplete Sentences Blank, Second Edition. In J. C. Conoley & J. C. Impara (Eds.), *The twelfth mental measurements yearbook* (pp. 882–883). Lincoln: University of Nebraska Press.

MEEHL, P. E. (1954). *Clinical versus statistical prediction: A theoretical analysis and a review of the evidence.* Minneapolis: University of Minnesota Press.

MEHRENS, W. A. (1997). The consequences of consequential validity. *Educational Measurement: Issues and Practice, 16(2),* 16–18.

MEIER, M. J. (1985). Review of the Halstead-Reitan Neuropsychological Test Battery. In J. V. Mitchell, Jr. (Ed.), *The ninth mental measurements yearbook* (pp. 646–649). Lincoln: University of Nebraska Press.

MESSICK, S. (1993). Validity. In R. L. Linn, *Educational measurement* (3rd ed.) (pp. 13–103). Phoenix, AZ: The Oryx Press.

MEYER, G. (Ed.). (1999). The utility of the Rorschach in clinical assessment [Special section: I]. *Psychological Assessment, 11,* 235–302.

MEYER, G. (Ed.). (2001). The utility of the Rorschach in clinical assessment [Special section: II]. *Psychological Assessment, 13,* 419–502.

MILLMAN, J., GREENE, J. (1993). The specification and development of tests of achievement and ability. In R. L. Linn (Ed.), *Educational measurement* (3rd ed.) (pp. 335–366). Phoenix, AZ: Oryx Press.

MILLON, T. (1969). *Modern psychopathology: A biosocial approach to maladaptive learning and functioning.* Philadelphia: W. B. Saunders.

MILLON, T. (1981). *Disorders of personality.* New York: Wiley.

MILLON, T. (1994). *Millon Clinical Multiaxial Inventory—III manual.* Minneapolis, MN: National Computer Systems.

MILLON, T. (Ed.). (1997). *The Millon inventories: Clinical and personality assessment.* New York: Guilford Press.

MILLON, T., & DAVIS, R. D. (1996). The Millon Clinical Multiaxial Inventory—III (MCMI–III). In C. S. Newmark (Ed.), *Major psychological assessment instruments* (pp. 108–147). Needham Heights, MA: Allyn & Bacon.

MISIAK, H. (1961). *The philosophical roots of scientific psychology.* New York: Fordham University Press.

MORELAND, K. L., EYDE, L. D., ROBERTSON, G. J., PRIMOFF, E. S., & MOST, R. B. (1995). Assessment of test user qualifications: A research-based measurement procedure. *American Psychologist, 50(1),* 14–23.

MORENO, K. E., & SEGALL, D. O. (1997). Reliability and construct validity of CAT-ASVAB. In W. A. Sands, B. K. Waters, & J. R. McBride (Eds.), *Computerized adaptive testing: From inquiry to operation* (pp. 169–174). Washington, DC: American Psychological Association.

MORRISON, G. M. (1995). Review of Draw A Person: Screening Procedure for Emotional Disturbance. In J. C. Conoley & J. C. Impara (Eds.), *The twelfth mental measurements yearbook* (pp. 322–323). Lincoln: University of Nebraska Press.

MORRISON, T., & MORRISON, M. (1995). A meta-analytic assessment of the predictive validity of the quantitative and verbal components of the Graduate Record Examination with graduate grade point average representing the criterion of graduate success. *Educational and Psychological Measurement, 55(2),* 309–316.

MOSS, P. A. (1998). The role of consequences in validity theory. *Educational Measurement: Issues and Practice, 17(2),* 6–12.

MURPHY, G. (1949). *Historical introduction to modern psychology.* New York: Harcourt, Brace & World, Inc.

MURPHY, K. (1984). Armed Services Vocational Aptitude Battery. In D. Keyser & R. Sweetland (Eds.), *Test critiques,* Vol. I (pp. 61–69). Austin, TX: Pro-Ed.

MURPHY, K. R., & DAVIDSHOFER, C. O. (2001). *Psychological testing: Principles and applications* (5th ed.). Upper Saddle River, NJ: Prentice-Hall.

MURPHY, L. L., PLAKE, B. S., IMPARA, J. C., & SPIES, R. A. (2002). *Tests in print VI.* Lincoln, NE: University of Nebraska Press.

MURRAY, H. A. et al. (1938). *Explorations in personality.* New York: Oxford University Press.

MURRAY, H. A. (1943). *Thematic Apperception Test.* Cambridge, MA: Harvard University Press.

MYERS, D. G. (2000). The funds, friends, and faith of happy people. *American Psychologist, 55,* 56-67.

NAGLIERI, J. A. (1988). *Draw A Person: A quantitative scoring system.* San Antonio, TX: Psychological Corporation.

NAGLIERI, J. A, & DAS, J. P. (1997). *Cognitive Assessment System.* Itasca, IL: Riverside Publishing.

NAGLIEREI, J. A., DRASGOW, F., SCHMIT, M., HANDLER, L., PRIFITERA, A., MARGOLIS, A., & VELASQUEZ, R. (2004). Psychological testing on the Internet. *American Psychologist, 59,* 150–162.

NAGLIERI, J. A., McNEISH, T. J., & BARDOS, A. N. (1991). *Draw a Person: Screening procedure for emotional disturbance.* San Antonio, TX: Psychological Corporation.

National Association of School Psychologists (2000). *Principles for professional ethics.* Bethesda, MD: Author.

NEISSER, U. (1998). *The rising curve: Long-term gains in IQ and related measures.* Washington, DC: American Psychological Association.

NEISSER, U., BOODOO, G., BOUCHARD, T. J., BOYKIN, A. W., BRODY, N., CECI, S. J., HALPERN, D. F., LOEHLIN, J. C., PERLOFF, R., STERNBERG, R. J., & URBINA, S. (1996). Intelligence: Knowns and unknowns. *American Psychologist, 51,* 77–101.

NELSON, L. D., SATZ, P., & D'ELIA, L. F. (1994). *Neuropsychology behavior and affect profile.* Palo Alto, CA: Mind Garden.

NESTER, M. A. (1994). Psychometric testing and reasonable accommodation for persons with disabilities. In S. M. Bruyere and J. O'Keefe (Eds.), *Implications of the Americans with Disabilities Act for psychology* (pp. 25–36). New York: Springer Publishing.

NEWMARK, C. S. (1996). *Major psychological assessment instruments* (2nd ed.). Needham Heights, MA: Allyn & Bacon.

NEWMARK, C. S., & McCORD, D. M. (1996). The Minnesota Multiphasic Personality Inventory-2 (MMPI-2). In C. S. Newmark (Ed.) *Major psychological assessment instruments,* (2nd ed.) (pp. 1–58). Needham Heights, MA: Allyn & Bacon.

NICHOLS, D. S. (1992). Review of the Minnesota Multiphasic Personality Inventory-2. In J. J. Kramer & J. C. Conoley (Eds.), *The eleventh mental measurements yearbook* (pp. 562–565). Lincoln: University of Nebraska Press.

NIETZEL, M. T., BERNSTEIN, D. A., & MILICH, R. (1998). *Introduction to clinical psychology* (5th ed.). Upper Saddle River, NJ: Prentice-Hall.

NUNNALLY, J. C., & BERNSTEIN, I. H. (1994). *Psychometric theory* (3rd ed.). New York: McGraw-Hill.

O'CONNOR, M. G., & KAPLAN, E. F. (2003). Age-related changes in memory. In J. Demick & C. Andreoletti (Eds.), *Handbook of adult development* (pp. 121–130). New York: Kluwer Academic/Plenum.

OSGOOD, C. E., SUCI, G. J., & TANNENBAUM, P. H. (1957). *The measurement of meaning.* Urbana, IL: University of Illinois Press.

OSWALD, D. P. (2005). Review of Piers-Harris Children's Self-Concept Scale. In R. A. Spies, B. S. Plake, & L. L. Murphy (Eds.), *The sixteenth mental measurements yearbook* (pp. 790–792). Lincoln, NE: Buros Institute of Mental Measurements.

OTHMER, E. (2002). *The clinical interview using DSM-IV-TR, Volumes 1-2.* Washington, DC: American Psychiatric Press.

OTIS, A. S., & LENNON, R. T. (2003). *Otis-Lennon School Ability Test, Eighth Edition, Technical Manual.* San Antonio: TX: Psychological Corporation.

OTTO, R. K., & HEILBRUN, K. (2002). The practice of forensic psychology: A look toward the future in light of the past. *American Psychologist, 57,* 5–18.

PAGE, E. B., & PETERSEN, N. S. (1995). The computer moves into essay grading: Updating the ancient test. *Phi Delta Kappan, 76,* 561–565.

Parents in Action on Special Educ. v. Hannon, 506 F. Supp. 831 (E. D. 111. 1980).

PARKER, K. C. H., HANSON, R. K., & HUNSLEY, J. (1988). MMPI, Rorschach, and WAIS: A meta-analytic comparison of reliability, stability, and validity. *Psychological Bulletin, 103,* 367–373.

PETERSON, C., & SELIGMAN, M.E.P. (2004). *Character strengths and virtues.* New York: Oxford University Press.

PHARES, E. J., & TRULL, T. J. (1997). *Clinical psychology: Concepts, methods, and profession* (5th ed.). Pacific Grove, CA: Brooks/Cole Publishing Company.

PHILLIPS, S. E. (Ed.). (2000). Defending a high school graduation test: GI Forum v. Texas Education Agency [Special issue]. *Applied Measurement in Education, 13*(4).

PIAGET, J. (1950). *The psychology of intelligence* (M. Piercy & D. E. Berlyne, Trans.). London: Routledge & Paul.

PIAGET, J. (1983). Piaget's theory. In P. H. Mussen (Ed.), *Handbook of child psychology,* Vol. I (4th ed.), (pp. 103–128). New York: Wiley.

PIAGET, J., & INHELDER, B. (1969). *The psychology of the child* (H. Weaver, Trans.). New York: Basic Books.

PIERS, E. V. (1996). *Piers-Harris Children's Self-Concept Scale, Revised Manual.* Los Angeles, CA: Western Psychological Services.

PIERS, E. V., & HERZBERG, D. S. (2002). *Piers-Harris Childrens' Self-Concept Scale: Manual* (2nd ed.). Los Angeles: Western Psychological Services.

PIOTROWSKI, C. (1996). Use of the Rorschach in forensic practice. *Perceptual and Motor Skills, 82,* 254.

PIOTROWSKI, C. (1999). Assessment practices in the era of managed care: Current status and future directions. *Journal of Clinical Psychology, 55,* 787–796.

PIOTROWSKI, C., & KELLER, J. W. (1984). Attitudes toward clinical assessment by members of the AABT. *Psychological Reports, 55,* 831–838.

PIOTROWSKI, C., & KELLER, J. W. (1989). Psychological testing in outpatient mental health facilities: A national study. *Professional Psychology: Research and Practice, 20,* 423–425.

PIOTROWSKI, C., & LUBIN, B. (1990). Assessment practices of health psychologists: Survey of APA division 38 clinicians. *Professional Psychology: Research and Practice, 21,* 99–106.

PIOTROWSKI, Z. A. (1937). The Rorschach ink-blot method in organic disturbances of the central nervous system. *Journal of Nervous and Mental Disorders, 86,* 525–537.

PIOTROWSKI, Z. A. (1957). *Perceptanalysis.* New York: Macmillan.

PITONIAK, M. J., & ROYER, J. M. (2001). Testing accommodations for examinees with disabilities: A review of psychometric, legal, and social policy issues. *Review of Educational Research, 71,* 53–104.

PLOMIN, R., & DeFRIES, J. C. (1998). The genetics of cognitive abilities and disabilities. *Scientific American, 278(5)*, 62–69.

PLOMIN, R., DEFRIES, J. C., CRAIG, I. W., & McGUFFIN, P. (Eds.). (2003). *Behavioral genetics in the postgenomic era.* Washington, DC: American Psychological Association.

PLOMIN, R., DEFRIES, J. C., McCLEARN, G. E., & McGUFFIN, P. (2001). *Behavioral genetics* (4th ed.). New York: Worth.

PLOMIN, R., & SPINATH, F. M. (2004). Intelligence: Genetic, genes, and genomics. *Journal of Personality and Social Psychology, 86*(1), 112–129.

POPHAM, W. J. (1997). Consequential validity: Right concern-wrong concept. *Educational Measurement: Issues and Practice, 16(2)*, 9–13.

POSTHUMA, R. A., Morgeson, F. P., & Campion, M. A. (2002). Beyond employment interview validity: A comprehensive narrative review of recent research and trends over time. *Personnel Psychology*, 55, 1-81.

POWER, M. J. (2003). Quality of life. In S. J. Lopez & C. R. Snyder (Eds.), *Positive psychological assessment: A handbook of models and measures* (pp. 427–441). Washington, DC: American Psychological Association.

PRIFITERA, A., & SAKLOFSKE, D. H. (Eds.). (1998). *WISC-III clinical use and interpretation: Scientist-practitioner perspectives.* San Diego, CA: Academic Press.

PRIFITERA, A., SAKLOFSKE, D. H., & WEISS, L. G. (Eds.). (2005). *WISC-IV clinical use and interpretation: Scientist-practitioner perspectives.* Boston: Elsevier Academic.

PROVOST, J. A. (1993). *Application of the Myers-Briggs Type Indicator in counseling: A casebook* (2nd ed.). Gainesville, FL: Center for Application of Psychological Type Inc.

Psychological Corporation. (1992). *Wechsler Individual Achievement Test Manual.* San Antonio, TX: Author.

Psychological Corporation. (1999). *Wechsler Abbreviated Scale of Intelligence.* San Antonio, TX: Author.

RAMSAY, M. C., REYNOLDS, C. R., & KAMPHAUS, R. W. (2002). *Essentials of behavioral assessment.* New York: Wiley.

RAPAPORT, C., GILL, M., & SCHAFER, J. (1946). *Diagnostic psychological testing* (Vol. 2). Chicago: Year Book Publishers.

RAVEN, J. C. (1976). *Standard Progressive Matrices.* Oxford, England: Oxford Psychologists Press.

RAVEN, J. C., COURT, J. H., & RAVEN, J. (1992). *Manual for Raven's Progressive Matrices and Vocabulary Scales: Section 3.* Oxford, England: Oxford Psychologists Press.

RAVEN, J., COURT, J. H., & RAVEN, J. C. (1993). *Manual for Raven's Progressive Matrices and Vocabulary Scales: Section 1 general overview.* Oxford, England: Oxford Psychologists Press.

RAYMOND, M. R. (2001). Job analysis and the specification of content for licensure and certification examinations. *Applied Measurement in Education, 14*, 369–415.

RECKASE, M. D. (1998). Consequential validity from the test developer's perspective. *Educational Measurement: Issues and Practice, 17(2)*, 13–16.

REISMAN, J. M. (1976). *A history of clinical psychology* (enlarged ed.). New York: Irvington.

REITAN, R., & WOLFSON, D. (1989). The Seashore Rhythm Test and brain functions. *The Clinical Neuropsychologist, 3*, 70–78.

REITAN, R., & WOLFSON, D. (1993). *The Halstead-Reitan Neuropsychological Test Battery: Theory and interpretation.* Tucson, AZ: Neuropsychology Press.

Renaissance Learning. (2003). *STAR Math CS technical manual.* Wisconsin Rapids, WI: Author.

RESCHLY, D. J. (2000). The present and future status of school psychology in the United States. *School Psychology Review, 29*, 507–522.

RETZLAFF, P. (1998). Review of the Millon Clinical Multiaxial Inventory—III. In B.S. Plake & J. C. Impara (Eds.), *The thirteenth mental measurements yearbook* (pp. 667–668). Lincoln: University of Nebraska Press.

REYNOLDS, C. R. (1994). Bias in testing. In R. J. Sternberg (Ed.), *Encyclopedia of human intelligence* (pp. 175–178). New York: Macmillan.

REYNOLDS, C. R., & KAMPHAUS, R. W. (2004). *Behavior Assessment System for Children* (2nd ed.). Circle Pines, MN: AGS.

REYNOLDS, C. R., & RAMSAY, M. C. (2003). Bias in psychological assessment: An empirical review and recommendations. In J. R. Graham & J. A. Naglieri (Eds.), *Handbook of psychology. Vol 10: Assessment psychology* (pp. 67–93). New York: Wiley.

Riverside Publishing. (2001). *2001 assessment catalog.* Itasca, IL: Author.

ROBERTSON, G. J. (no date). Test Service Notebook 30—Innovation in the assessment of individual differences: Development of the first group mental ability test. New York: Harcourt Brace Jovanovich.

ROBERTSON, G. J. (1986). Establishing test purchaser qualifications. In R. B. Most (Ed.), Test purchaser qualifications: Present practice, professional needs, and a proposed system. *Issues in Scientific Psychology.* Washington, DC: American Psychological Association, Scientific Affairs Office.

ROBINSON, J. P., & SHAVER, P. R. (1973). *Measures of social psychological attitudes* (rev. ed.). Ann Arbor, MI: Institute for Social Research.

ROBINSON, J. P., SHAVER, P. R., & WRIGHTSMAN, L.S. (Eds.). (1991). *Measures of personality and social psychological attitudes.* San Diego: Academic Press.

RODRIGUEZ, M. C. (2002). Choosing an item format. In G. Tindal & T. M. Haladyna (Eds.), *Large-scale assessment programs for all students: Validity, technical adequacy, and implications* (pp. 213–231). Mahwah, NJ: Erlbaum.

RODRIGUEZ, M. C. (2003). Construct equivalence of multiple-choice and constructed-response items: A random effects synthesis of correlations. *Journal of Educational Measurement, 40*, 163–184.

ROGERS, R. (2001). *Handbook of diagnostic and structured interviewing.* New York: Guilford.

ROID, G. H. (2003a). *Stanford-Binet Intelligence Scales, Fifth Edition, examiner's manual.* Itasca, IL: Riverside.

ROID, G. H. (2003b). *Stanford-Binet Intelligence Scales, Fifth Edition, technical manual.* Itasca, IL: Riverside.

RORSCHACH, H. (1921). *Psychodiagnostik.* Berne, Switzerland: Bircher.

ROTTER, J. B., LAH, M. I., & RAFFERTY, J. E. (1992). *Manual: Rotter Incomplete Sentences Blank,* 2nd ed. San Antonio, TX: Psychological Corporation.

ROTTER, J. B., & RAFFERTY, J. E. (1950), *The Rotter Incomplete Sentences Blank.* New York: Psychological Corporation.

RUCH, G. M. (1924). *The improvement of the written examination.* Chicago, IL: Scott, Foresman and Company.

RUCH, G. M. (1929). *The objective or new-type examination: An introduction to educational measurement.* Chicago, IL: Scott, Foresman and Company.

RUCH, G. M., & RICE, G. A. (1930). *Specimen objective examination.* [A collection of examinations awarded prizes in a national contest in the construction of objective or new-type examinations, 1927–1928] Chicago, IL: Scott, Foresman and Company.

RUCH, G. M., & STODDARD, G. D. (1927). *Tests and measurements in high school instruction.* Yonkers, NY: World Book.

RUDNER, L., & GAGNE, P. (2001). An overview of three approaches to scoring written essays by computer. ERIC Digest (ED458209).

Runners World. (1999). The human race. *Runners World, 34(9),* 123.

RUSHTON, J. P., & JENSEN, A. R. (2005). Thirty years of research on race differences in cognitive ability. *Psychology, Public Policy, and Law, 11,* 235–294.

RUSSELL, E.W. (1992). Reliability of the Halstead Impairment Index: A simulation and reanalysis of Matarazzo et al. (1974), *Neuropsychology, 6, 251*–259.

RUSSELL, E. W. (1995). The accuracy of automated and clinical detection of brain damage and lateralization in neuropsychology. *Neuropsychology Review, 5,* 1–68.

RYAN, R. M. (1985). Thematic Apperception Test. In D. J. Keyser & R. C. Sweetland (Eds.), *Test critiques,* vol. II, (pp. 799–814). Kansas City, MO: Test Corporation of America.

RYAN, R. M., & Deci, E .L. (2001). On happiness and human potentials: A review of research on hedonic and eudaimonic well-being. *Annual Review of Psychology, 52,* 141-166.

SACKETT, P. R., & YANG, H. (2000). Correction for range restriction: An expanded typology. *Journal of Applied Psychology,* 85, 112-118.

SANDS, W. A., & WATERS, B. K. (1997). Introduction to ASVAB and CAT. In W. A. Sands, B. K. Waters, & J. R. McBride (Eds.), *Computerized adaptive testing: From inquiry to operation* (pp. 3–10). Washington, DC: American Psychological Association.

SANDS, W. A., WATERS, B. K., & McBRIDE, J. R. (Eds.). (1997). *Computerized adaptive testing: From inquiry to operation.* Washington, DC: American Psychological Association.

SCHEERENBERGER, R. C. (1987). *A history of mental retardation: a quarter century of promise.* Baltimore: P. H. Brookes.

SCHINKE, S. (1995). Review of the Eating Disorder Inventory-2. In J. C. Conoley & J. C. Impara (Eds.), *Twelfth mental measurements yearbook* (p. 335). Lincoln: University of Nebraska Press.

SCHMIDT, F.L., & HUNTER, J. (2004). General mental ability in the world of work: Occupational attainment and job performance. *Journal of Personality and Social Psychology,* 86, 162–173.

SCHMIDT, F. L., ONES, D. S., & HUNTER, J. E. (1992). Personnel selection. *Annual Review of Psychology, 43,* 627–670.

SCHMITT, K. (1995). What is licensure? In J. C. Impara (Ed.), *Licensure testing: Purposes, procedures, and practices* (pp. 3–32). Lincoln, NE: Buros Institute of Mental Measurements.

SCHUTTE, N. S., & MALOUFF, J. M. (1996). *Sourcebook of adult assessment strategies.* New York: Plenum Press.

SEARLS, E. F. (1997). *How to detect reading/learning disabilities using the WISC-III.* Newark, DE: International Reading Association.

SEASHORE, H. G. (n.d.). *Test service notebook 148: Methods of expressing test scores.* San Antonio, TX: Psychological Corporation.

SEDDON, G. M. (1978). The properties of Bloom's Taxonomy of Educational Objectives for the cognitive domain. *Review of Educational Research, 48(2),* 303–323.

SELIGMAN, M.E.P., & CSIKSZENTMIHALYI, M. (2000). Positive psychology: An introduction. *American Psychologist, 55,* 5–14.

SELIGMAN, M. E. P., Steen, T. A., Park, N., & Peterson, C. (2005). Positive psychology progress: Empirical validation of interventions. *American Psychologist, 60,* 410–421.

SHAVELSON, R. J., & WEBB, N. (1991). *Generalizability theory: A primer.* Thousand Oaks, CA: Sage.

SHAVELSON, R. J., WEBB, N. M., & ROWLEY, G. L. (1989). Generalizability theory. *American Psychologist, 44,* 922–32.

SHAW, M. E., & WRIGHT, J. M. (1967). *Scales for the measurement of attitudes.* New York: McGraw-Hill.

SHEPARD, L. A. (1997). The centrality of test use and consequences for test validity. *Educational Measurement: Issues and Practice, 16(2),* 5–8.

SHERER, M., PARSONS, O. A., NIXON, S., & ADAMS, R. L. (1991). Clinical validity of the Speech-Sounds Perception Test and the Seashore Rhythm Test. *Journal of Clinical and Experimental Neuropsychology, 13,* 741–751.

SHERMIS, M. D., & BURSTEIN, J. (Eds.), *Automated essay scoring: A cross-disciplinary perspective.* Mahwah, NJ: Erlbaum.

SHROUT, P. E., & FLEISS, J. L. (1979). Intraclass correlations: Uses in assessing rater reliability. *Psychological Bulletin, 86,* 420–428.

SHUSTER, E. (1997). Fifty years later: The significance of the Nuremberg Code. *The New England Journal of Medicine, 337,* 1436–1440.

SLORA, K. B. (1991). An empirical approach to determining employee deviance base rates. In J. W. Jones (Ed.), *Preemployment honesty testing: Current research and future directions* (pp. 21–38). New York: Quorum.

SMITH, C. P. (Ed.). (1992). *Motivation and personality: Handbook of thematic content analysis.* New York: Cambridge University Press.

SMITH, J. D. (1997). Mental retardation: Defining a social invention. In R. L. Taylor (Ed.), *Assessment of individuals with mental retardation* (pp. 3–12). San Diego, CA: Singular Publishing Group.

SNOW, J. H. (1992). Review of the Luria-Nebraska Neuropsychological Battery: Forms I and II. In J. J. Kramer & J. C. Conoley (Eds.), *The eleventh mental measurements yearbook* (pp. 484–486). Lincoln: University of Nebraska Press.

SNYDERMAN, M., & ROTHMAN, S. (1987). Survey of expert opinion on intelligence and aptitude testing. *American Psychologist, 42,* 137–144.

Society for Industrial and Organizational Psychology, Inc. (2003). *Principles for the validation and use of personnel selection procedures* (4th ed.). Washington, DC: Author.

SPANGLER, W. D. (1992). Validity of questionnaire and TAT measures of need for achievement: Two meta-analyses. *Psychological Bulletin, 112,* 140–154

SPARROW, S. S., BALLA, D. A., & CICCHETTI, D. V. (1984). *Vineland Adaptive Behavior Scales, Interview Edition Expanded Form Manual.* Circle Pines, MN: American Guidance Service.

SPARROW, S. S., CICHETTI, D. V., & BALLA, D. A. (2005). *Vineland Adaptive Behavior Scales* (2nd ed.), survey forms manual. Circle Pines, MN: AGS.

SPEARMAN, C. (1927a). *The abilities of man: Their nature and measurement.* New York: Macmillan.

SPEARMAN, C. (1927b). *The nature of "intelligence" and the principles of cognition* (2nd ed.). London: Macmillan.

SPELKE, E. S. (2005). Sex differences in intrinsic aptitude for mathematics and science? *American Psychologist, 60,* 950–958.

SPIELBERGER, C. D. (1973). *Manual for the State-Trait Anxiety Inventory for Children.* Palo Alto, CA: Consulting Psychologists Press.

SPIELBERGER, C. D. (1983). *State-Trait Anxiety Inventory for Adults sampler set: Manual, test, scoring key.* Redwood City, CA: Mind Garden.

SPIES, R. A., & PLAKE, B. S. (2005). *The sixteenth mental measurements yearbook.* Lincoln. University of Nebraska Press.

SPREEN, O., & STRAUSS, E. (1998). *A compendium of neuropsychological tests: Administration, norms, and commentary.* New York: Oxford University Press.

STERNBERG, R. (1985). *Beyond IQ: A triarchic theory of human intelligence.* Cambridge, UK: Cambridge University Press.

STERNBERG, R. J. (Ed.). (1994a). *Encyclopedia of human intelligence.* New York: Macmillan.

STERNBERG, R. J. (1994b). Triarchic theory of human intelligence. In R. J. Sternberg (Ed.), *Encyclopedia of human intelligence* (pp. 1087–1091). New York: Macmillan.

STERNBERG, R. J., & Detterman, D. K. (1986). *What is intelligence?* Norwood, NJ: Ablex.

STERNBERG, R. J., & GRIGORENKO, E. (Eds.). (1997). *Intelligence, heredity, and environment.* Cambridge, England: Cambridge University Press.

STERNBERG, R. J., & KAUFMAN, J. C. (1998). Human abilities. *Annual Review of Psychology, 49,* 479–502.

STERNBERG, R. J., & WAGNER, R. K. (Eds.). (1986). *Practical intelligence: Nature and origins of competence in the everyday world.* Cambridge: Cambridge University Press.

STEVENS, S. S. (1951). Mathematics, measurement, and psychophysics. In S. S. Stevens (Ed.)., *Handbook of experimental psychology.* New York: Wiley.

STEWART, T. M., & WILLIAMSON, D. A. (2004). Assessment of eating disorders. In M. Hersen (Ed.), *Psychological assessment in clinical practice: A pragmatic guide* (pp. 175–195). New York: Bruner-Routledge.

STOKES, T. L., & BOHRS, D. A. (2001). The development of a same-different inspection time paradigm and the effects of practice. *Intelligence, 29,* 247–261.

STRACK, S. (2002). *Essentials of Millon inventories assessment* (2nd ed.). New York: Wiley.

STROOP, J. R. (1935). Studies of interference in serial verbal reactions. *Journal of Experimental Psychology, 18,* 643–662.

SUZUKI, L. A., & GUTKIN, T. B. (1994a). Asian Americans. In R. J. Sternberg (Ed.), *Encyclopedia of human intelligence* (pp. 140–144), New York: Macmillan.

SUZUKI, L. A., & GUTKIN, T. B. (1994b). Hispanics. In R. J. Sternberg (Ed.), *Encyclopedia of human intelligence* (pp. 539–545), New York: Macmillan.

SUZUKI, L. A., & GUTKIN, T. B. (1994c). Japanese. In R. J. Sternberg (Ed.), *Encyclopedia of human intelligence* (pp. 625–629), New York: Macmillan.

SWARTZ, J. D. (1978). Review of the Thematic Apperception Test. In O. K. Buros (Ed.), *The eighth mental measurements yearbook,* (pp. 1127–1130). Lincoln: University of Nebraska Press.

SWEET, J. J., MOBERG, P. J., & SUCHY, Y. (2000). Ten-year follow-up survey of clinical neuropsychologists: Part I. Practices and beliefs. *The Clinical Neuropsychologist, 14,* 18–37.

SWETS, J. A., DAWES, R. M., & MONAHAN, J. (2000). Psychological science can improve diagnostic decisions. *Psychological Science in the Public Interest, 1,* 1–26.

TABACHNIK, B. G., & FIDELL, L. S. (2006). *Using multivariate statistics* (5th ed.). New York: HarperCollins.

TALEPOROS, E. (1998). Consequential validity. A practitioner's perspective. *Educational Measurement: Issues and Practice, 17(2),* 20–23.

Tarasoff v. Univ. of Ca., P. 2d 334 (9th Cir. 1976).

TAYLOR, H. C., & RUSSELL, J. T. (1939). The relationship of validity coefficients to the practical effectiveness of tests in selection: Discussion and tables. *Journal of Applied Psychology, 23,* 565–578.

TAYLOR, P. J., & O'DRISCOLL, M. P. (1995). *Structured employment interviewing.* Brookfield, VT: Gower.

THISSEN, D. (2000). Reliability and measurement precision. In H. Wainer (Ed.), *Computerized adaptive testing: A primer* (2nd ed.). Mahwah, NJ: Lawrence Erlbaum.

THOMPSON, A. P., LOBELLO, S. G., ATKINSON, L., & CHISOLM, V. (2004). Brief intelligence testing in Australia, Canada, the United Kingdom, and the United States. *Professional Psychology: Research and Practice, 35,* 286–290.

THORNDIKE, R. L. (1982). *Applied psychometrics.* Boston: Houghton Mifflin.

THORNDIKE, R. L., HAGEN, E. P., & SATTLER, J. M. (1986). *Stanford-Binet Intelligence Scale, Fourth Edition.* Itasca, IL: Riverside Publishing.

THURLOW, M. L., & YSSELDYKE, J. E. (2001). Standard setting challenges for special populations. In G. J. Cizek (Ed.), *Setting performance standards: Concepts, methods, and perspectives* (pp. 387–409). Mahwah, NJ. Lawrence Erlbaum.

THURSTONE, L. L. (1935). *The vectors of the mind.* Chicago: University of Chicago Press.

THURSTONE, L. L. (1938). *Primary mental abilities.* Chicago: University of Chicago Press.

THURSTONE, L. L. (1947). *Multiple-factor analysis.* Chicago: University of Chicago Press.

THURSTONE, L. L. (1959). *The measurement of values.* Chicago: University of Chicago Press.

THURSTONE, L. L., & CHAVE, E. J. (1929). *The measurement of attitude: A psychophysical method and some experiments with a scale for measuring attitude toward the church.* Chicago: University of Chicago Press.

TINSLEY, H. E. (1994). The NEO Personality Inventory-Revised. In D. J. Keyser & R. C. Sweetland (Eds.), *Test critiques,* vol. X, (pp. 443–456). Kansas City, MO: Test Corporation of America.

TODD, J., & BOHART, A. C. (1994). *Foundations of clinical and counseling psychology* (2nd ed.). New York: HarperCollins.

TOMBAUGH, T. N., & MCINTYRE, N. J. (1992). The Mini-Mental State Examination: A comprehensive review. *Journal of the American Geriatrics Society, 40,* 922–935.

TOOPS, H. A. (1921). *Trade tests in education.* [Teachers College Contributions to Education No. 115] New York: Teachers College, Columbia University.

TORGERSON, W. S. (1958). *Theory and methods of scaling.* New York: Wiley.

TRAUB, R. E. (1993). On the equivalence of the traits assessed by multiple-choice and constructed-response tests. In R. E. Bennett & C. W. Ward (Eds.), *Construction versus choice in cognitive measurement: Issues in constructed response, performance testing, and portfolio assessment* (pp. 29–44). Hillsdale, NJ: Erlbaum.

TURKHEIMER, E. (1994). Socioeconomic status and intelligence. In R. J. Sternberg (Ed.), *Encyclopedia of human intelligence* (pp. 992–1000), New York: Macmillan.

TURNER, S. M., DEMERS, S. T., FOX, H. R., & REED, G. M. (2001). APA's guidelines for test user qualifications: An executive summary. *American Psychologist, 56,* 1099–1113.

UMBERGER, F. G. (1985). *Peabody Picture Vocabulary Test-Revised.* In D. J. Keyser & R. C. Sweetland (Eds.), Test Critiques, Vol. III (pp. 488–495). Kansas City, MO: Test Corporation of America.

United States Department of Health, Education, and Welfare (1979). *The Belmont report.* Washington, DC: U.S. Government Printing Office.

United States Department of Labor. (1991). *Dictionary of occupational titles* (4th ed., rev.). Washington, DC: U.S. Government Printing Office.

U. S. Government Printing Office. (1949). Trials of war criminals before the Nuremberg military tribunals under control council law No. 10, Vol. 2 (pp. 181–182). Washington, DC: Author.

VANDENBERG, G. H. (1993). *Court testimony in mental health: A guide for mental health professionals and attorneys.* Springfield, IL: Charles C. Thomas.

VAN GORP, W. G. (1992). Review of the Luria-Nebraska Neuropsychological Battery: Forms I and II. In J. J. Kramer & J. C. Conoley (Eds.), *The eleventh mental measurements yearbook* (pp. 486–488). Lincoln: University of Nebraska Press.

VERNON, P. A. (1984). Advanced Progressive Matrices. In D. Keyser & R. Sweetland (Eds.), *Test critiques,* Vol. I (pp. 47–50), Austin, TX: Pro-Ed.

VERNON, P. E. (1947). Research on personnel selection in the Royal Navy and the British Army. *American Psychologist, 2,* 35–51

VERNON, P. E. (1950). *The structure of human abilities.* London: Methuen.

VERNON, P. E. (1961). *The structure of human abilities* (2nd ed.). London: Methuen.

VERNON, P. E. (1965). Ability factors and environmental influences. *American Psychologist, 20,* 723–733.

VIGLIONE, D. J. (1999). A review of recent research addressing the utility of the Rorschach. *Psychological Assessment, 11(3),* 251–265.

VIGLIONE, D. J., & HILSENROTH, M. J. (2001). The Rorschach: Facts, fictions, and futures. *Psychological Assessment, 13,* 452–471.

VOLPE, R. J., & DuPAUL, G. J. (2001). Assessment with brief behavior rating scales. In J. J. W. Andrews, D. H. Saklofske, & H. L. Janzen (Eds.), *Handbook of psychoeducational assessment: Ability, achievement, and behavior in children* (pp. 357–385). San Diego, CA: Academic Press.

VRANIAK, D. A. (1994). Native Americans. In R. J. Sternberg (Ed.), *Encyclopedia of human intelligence* (pp. 747–754). New York: Macmillan.

WADE, T. C., & BAKER, T. B. (1977). Opinions and use of psychological tests: A survey of clinical psychologists. *American Psychologist, 32,* 874–882.

WAINER, H. (Ed.). (2000). *Computerized adaptive testing: A primer* (2nd ed.). Mahwah, NJ: Lawrence Erlbaum.

WALSH, W. B., & OSIPOW, S. H. (Eds.). *Handbook of vocational psychology* (2nd ed.). Mahwah, NJ: Lawrence Erlbaum.

WASYLIW, O. E. (2001). Review of the Peabody Picture Vocabulary Test-III. In B. S. Plake & J. C. Impara (Eds.), *Fourteenth mental measurements yearbook* (pp. 909–911). Lincoln: University of Nebraska Press.

WATKINS, C. E., CAMPBELL, V. L., & MCGREGOR, P. (1988). Counseling psychologists' uses of and opinions about psychological tests: A contemporary perspective. *The Counseling Psychologist, 16,* 476–486.

WATKINS, C. E., CAMPBELL, V. L., & NIEBERDING, R. (1994). The practice of vocational assessment by counseling psychologists. *The Counseling Psychologist, 22(1),* 115–128.

WATKINS, C. E., CAMPBELL, V. L., NIEBERDING, R., & HALLMARK, R. (1995). Contemporary practice of psychological assessment by clinical psychologists. *Professional Psychology: Research and Practice, 26,* 54–60.

WATTERSON, B. (1988). *Something under the bed is drooling.* Kansas City, MO: Andrews and McMeel.

WEBSTER, R. E. (1994). *Woodcock-Johnson Psycho-Educational Battery—Revised.* In D. J. Keyser & R. C. Sweetland (Eds.), *Test critiques, vol. X* (pp. 804–815). Austin, TX: PRO-ED.

WECHSLER, D. (1949). *Wechsler Intelligence Scale for Children: Manual.* New York: Psychological Corporation.

WECHSLER, D. (1958). *The measurement and appraisal of adult intelligence* (4th ed.). Baltimore: Williams and Wilkins.

WECHSLER, D. (1974). *The collected papers of David Wechsler.* New York: Academic Press.

WECHSLER, D. (1987). *Wechsler Memory Scale, Revised Manual.* New York: The Psychological Corporation.

WECHSLER, D. (1991). *Wechsler Intelligence Scale for Children—Third Edition, Manual.* San Antonio, TX: The Psychological Corporation.

WECHSLER, D. (1997a). *Wechsler Adult Intelligence Scale—Third Edition: Administration and Scoring Manual.* San Antonio, TX: The Psychological Corporation.

WECHSLER, D. (1997b). *Wechsler Adult Intelligence Scale—Third Edition, Wechsler Memory Scale—Third Edition: Technical Manual.* San Antonio, TX: The Psychological Corporation.

WECHSLER, D. (2003a). *Wechsler Intelligence Scale for Children—Fourth Edition: Administration and scoring manual.* San Antonio, TX: Psychological Corporation.

WECHSLER, D. (2003b). *Wechsler Intelligence Scale for Children—Fourth Edition: Technical and interpretive manual.* San Antonio, TX: Psychological Corporation.

WEINER, I. B. (2001). Advancing the science of psychological assessment: The Rorschach inkblot method as exemplar. *Psychological Assessment, 13,* 423–432.

WEINER, I. B. (2003). *Principles of Rorschach interpretation* (2nd ed.). Mahwah, NJ: Erlbaum.

West Publishing (1984). *The guide to American law.* St. Paul, MN: Author.

West Publishing. (1990). United States code annotated, Title 20, Education, §§ 1241 to 3400. St. Paul, MN: Author.

WHITWORTH, R. H. (1984). The Halstead-Reitan Neuropsychological Battery and Allied Procedures. In D. J. Keyser & R. C. Sweetland (Eds.), *Test critiques,* vol. I (pp. 305–314). Kansas City, MO: Test Corporation of America.

WIDAMAN, K. F., & McGREW, K. S. (1996). The structure of adaptive behavior. In J. W. Jacobson & J. A. Mulick (Eds.), *Manual of diagnosis and professional practice in mental retardation* (pp. 197–210). Washington, DC: American Psychological Association.

WIDIGER, T. A. J. P. (2001). Review of the Millon Clinical Multiaxial Inventory—III. In J. C. Impara & B. S. Plake (Eds.) *The fourteenth mental measurements yearbook* (pp. 767–769). Lincoln: University of Nebraska Press.

WIGER, D. E. (2002). *Essentials of interviewing.* New York: Wiley.

WIGGINS, J. S., & TRAPNELL, P. D. (1997). Personality structure: The return of the big five. In R. Hogan, J. Johnson, & S. Briggs (Eds.), *Handbook of personality psychology* (pp. 737–766). San Diego, CA: Academic Press.

WILLIAMS, J. M., MATHEWS, A., & MacLEOD, C. (1996). The emotional Stroop task and psychopathology. *Psychological Bulletin, 120(1),* 3–24.

WILLIAMS, K. T., & WANG, J. J. (1997). *Technical references to the Peabody Picture Vocabulary Test—Third Edition (PPVT–III).* Circle Pines, MN: American Guidance Service.

WILLIAMSON, D. M., BEJAR, I. I., & HONE, A. S. (1999). "Mental model" comparison of automated and human scoring. *Journal of Educational Measurement, 36,* 158–184.

WILLINGHAM, W. W., RAGOSTA, M., BENNETT, R. E., BRAUN, H., ROCK, D. A., & POWERS, D. E. (1988). *Testing handicapped people.* Needham Heights, MA: Allyn & Bacon.

WINER, B. J. (1991). *Statistical principles in experimental design* (3rd ed.). New York: McGraw–Hill.

WOLFE, J. H., MORENO, K. E., & SEGALL, D. O. (1997). Evaluating the predictive validity of CAT-ASVAB. In W. A. Sands, B. K. Waters, & J. R. McBride (Eds.), *Computerized adaptive testing: From inquiry to operation* (pp. 175–180). Washington, DC: American Psychological Association.

WOLMAN, B. B. (Ed.). (1985). *Handbook of intelligence: Theories, measurements, and applications.* New York: Wiley.

WOOD, B. D. (1923). *Measurement in higher education.* Yonkers, NY: World Book.

WOOD, B. D. (1927). *New York experiments with new-type modern language tests.* [Publications of the American and Canadian Committees on Modern Languages] New York: Macmillan.

WOODCOCK, R. W., McGREW, K. S., & MATHER, N. (2001). *Woodcock-Johnson III.* Itasca, IL: Riverside Publishing.

WRESCH, W. (1993). The imminence of grading essays by computer—25 years later. *Computers and Composition, 10,* 45–58.

WRIGHT, B. D. (1997). A history of social science measurement. *Educational Measurement: Issues and Practice, 16,* 33–45, 52.

WRIGHTSMAN, L. S. (1991). *Psychology and the legal system* (2nd ed.). Pacific Grove, CA: Brooks/Cole.

ZIEKY, M. J. (2001). So much has changed: How the setting of cutscores has changed since the 1980s. In G. J. Cizek (Ed.), *Setting performance standards: Concepts, methods, and perspectives* (pp. 19–51). Mahwah, NJ: Lawrence Erlbaum.

ZYTOWSKI, D. G. (1992). Three generations: The continuing evolution of Frederic Kuder's interest inventories. *Journal of Counseling and Development, 71(2),* 245–248.

ZYTOWSKI, D. G. (2005). *Kuder Career Search with Person Match: Technical manual version 1.1.* Adel, IA: National Career Assessment Services. [http://www.kuder.com/PublicWeb/kcs_manual.aspx. Accessed January 18, 2006]

Text and Illustration Credits

Chapter 1 Figure 1.1, Page 13: Reprinted with permission of offthemark.com. Atlantic Feature Syndicate. Figure 1.3, Page 21: Science Photo Library/Photo Researchers. Figure 1.4, Page 22: Archives of the History of American Psychology. Figure 1.5, Page 23: Topham/The Image Works. Figure 1.6, Page 28 (left): Stanford University News Service. Figure 1.6, Page 31 (right): Courtesy Jonathan Galente. Figure 1.7, Page 35 (left): Courtesy of IBM Archives. Figure 1.7, Page 35 (right): Courtesy NCS Pearson.

Chapter 2 Figure 2.1, Page 49: From: Murphy, L. L., Impara, J. C., & Plake, B. S. Tests in Print V. p. 58. Copyright © 1999. With permission of the publisher, Buros Institute of Mental Measurements. Figure 2.2, Page 50: From: Maddox, T. Tests: A comprehensive reference for assessments in psychology, education, and business (5th ed.). p. 2. Copyright © 2003. With permission of the publisher, Pro-Ed, Inc. Figure 2.3, Page 51: From: Goldman, B. A., Mitchell, D. F., & Egelson, P. E. Directory of unpublished experimental mental measures (Vol. 7, p. 23). Copyright © 1997 by the American Psychological Association. Reprinted with permission. Figure 2.4, Page 58: From: Psychological Assessment Resources, January 2002 Catalog, p. 54. With permission of the publisher.

Chapter 3 Figure 3.10, Page 78: Reprinted from Seashore, H. G. Test service notebook 148: Methods of expressing test scores. With permission of the publisher, Psychological Corporation. Table 3.1, Page 79: Reproduced from Hogan, T. P., Types of test scores and their percentile equivalents. In G. P. Koocher, J. C. Norcross, & S. S. Hill (Eds.). Psychologists' desk reference (2nd ed.) (pp. 111–116). Copyright © 2005 by Oxford University Press. Figure 3.11, Page 83: Reproduced by special permission of the Publisher, Psychological Assessment Resources, Inc., 16204 North

Florida Avenue, Lutz, Florida 33549, from the Revised NEO Personality Inventory, by Paul T. Costa, Jr., Ph.D. and Robert R. McCrae, Ph.D. Copyright © 1978, 1985, 1989, 1992 by PAR, Inc. Further reproduction is prohibited without permission of PAR, Inc. Figure 3.20, Page 96: Reproduced by special permission of the Publisher, Psychological Assessment Resources, Inc., 16204 North Florida Avenue, Lutz, Florida 33549, from the Revised NEO Personality Inventory, by Paul T. Costa, Jr., Ph.D. and Robert R. McCrae, Ph.D. Copyright © 1978, 1985, 1989, 1992 by PAR, Inc. Further reproduction is prohibited without permission of PAR, Inc. Figure 3.23, Page 102: Calvin and Hobbes © 1987 Watterson. Reprinted with permission of Universal Press Syndicate. All rights reserved. Figure 3.24, Page 105: From Dunn, L. M., & Dunn, L. M. Peabody Picture Vocabulary Test, (3rd Edition), Test Kit Form IIIA Examiner's Manual, p. 43. Copyright © 1997. With permission of the publisher, American Guidance Service, Inc.

Chapter 4 Figure 4.1, Page 112: From Parker, B. & Hart, J. The Wizard of Id. Copyright © 1998. By permission of Johnny Hart and Creators Syndicate, Inc.

Chapter 6 Table 6.8, Page 222: Haladyna, T. M., Downing, S. M., & Rodriguez, M. C. (2002). A review of multiple-choice item-writing guidelines for classroom assessment. Applied Measurement in Education, 15, 309–334. (Table 1, p. 312). Copyright © 2002 by Lawrence Erlbaum Associates. Reproduced by permission. Table 6.9, Page 231: Format adapted from ITEMAN TM, a component of the Item and Test Analysis Package developed by Assessment Systems Corporation, with permission. Figure 6.7, Page 235: Reproduced with permission of Renaissance Learning, Inc.

Chapter 7 Figure 7.4, Page 266: From Vernon, P. E. The Structure of Human Abilities (2nd ed.). Copyright © 1961 by Taylor & Francis. Reproduced by permission of Thomson Publishing Services. Figure 7.5, Page 268: From Carroll, J. B. Human cognitive abilities: A survey of factor analytic studies (p. 626). Copyright © 1993. Reprinted with the permission of Cambridge University Press. Figure 7.7, Page 271: Lafayette Instrument Company, Inc. Reproduced by permission.

Chapter 8 Figure 8.1, Page 291: The Image Works. Table 8.6, Page 299: From WAIS®-III Administration and Scoring Manual (p. 2). Copyright © 1997 by Harcourt Assessment, Inc. Reproduced by permission.

Name Index

A

Abrams, D.M., 55, 535, 536
Achenbach, T.M., 508
Ackerman, T., 439
Acklin, M.W., 543
Adams, K.M., 390
Adams, R.L., 392
Agnello, J., 174
Aiken, L.R., 527
Alcmaeon 384, 387, 414
Algina, J., 145
Anastasi, A., 28, 39, 43
Anastopoulos, A.D., 510
Andrews, J.J., 508
Aquinas, T., 19
Arbisi, P.A., 502
Archer, R.P., 471, 487, 495, 521, 540
Aristotle, 19
Arnkoff, D.B., 514
Atkinson, L., 533, 536
Ayers, M., 393
Ayotte, V., 473

B

Bailey, J.M., 533
Baker, D.B., 32
Baker, F.B., 35
Baker, T.B., 534
Balla, D.A., 327
Baltes, P.B., 281
Bardos, A.N., 541
Barker, C., 213
Barnum, P.T., 95
Barth, J.T., 393
Beck, A.T., 179, 501
Beck, S.J., 527
Bejar, I.I., 219

Bellak, L., 55, 535, 536, 544
Belter, R.W., 543
Benjamin, A., 137
Benjamin, L.T., 32
Bennett, B.E., 590
Ben-Porath, Y.S., 543
Benton, A., 386, 387
Berk, R.A., 145, 240
Bernstein, D.A., 33, 543
Bernstein, I.H., 133, 139, 145, 149, 176, 214, 237, 239
Berry, D.T.R., 200, 544
Bessette, J.M., 618
Betsworth, D.G., 551
Binet, A., 24–27, 31, 43, 210, 265, 297, 309
Bloom, B.S., 163
Bohart, A.C., 33
Bohrs, D.A., 272
Boring, E.D., 18, 24
Borman, W.C., 166, 379
Bornstein, R.F., 200, 544
Botwin, M.D., 470
Bowman, M.L., 20
Boyle, G.J., 539
Breland, H.M., 360
Brennan, R.L., 133, 145, 147
Brezinski, K.L., 137
Bridgeman, B, 362
Broca, P., 385–387, 414
Brodsky, S.L., 615
Brody, N., 258, 260, 280–282, 284
Brown, G.K., 176, 501
Brunell-Neulcib, S., 200, 544
Bryant, F.B., 190
Bubenzer, D.L., 553
Buck, J.N., 542
Bunch, M.B., 102, 435
Burkett, G.R., 238

Burns, L., 393
Burns, R.C., 542
Buros, O.K., 27, 48, 49
Burstein, A.G., 55
Burstein, J., 219
Burton, N.W., 362, 368
Butcher, J.N., 55, 487, 489, 492–495
Byrne, B.M., 53, 471

C

Camara, W., 12, 319, 328, 403, 464, 487, 496, 522, 523, 526, 534, 540, 553, 602
Campbell, D.T., 180, 181
Campbell, V.L., 12, 313, 483, 521, 543, 553, 567
Campion, M.A., 486
Cannon, B.J., 383, 398, 399, 404
Canter, M.B., 590
Carroll, J., 267, 268, 286, 288, 313
Carver, C.S., 464
Cattell, J.M., 23–25, 31, 42, 43, 265
Cattell, R.B., 265, 266, 286, 374, 376, 439, 467
Chaplin, W.F., 507
Chave, E.J., 576
Cheng, L., 575
Chinn, R.N., 435
Choca, J.P., 498
Cicchetti, D.V., 327
Cizek, G.J., 102, 422, 423, 434, 435
Clarke, A.D., 324
Clarke, A.M., 324
Clauser, B.E., 218
Clemence, A.J., 543
Clyman, S.G., 218
Cole, N.S., 240
Cone, J.D., 513, 514
Conners, C.K., 508

Subject Index

Ability-achievement continuum, 418–419, 441
Abuse, 615
Academic Profile (AP), 429
Accommodation, 601
Accountability, 421–423
Achievement tests, 417–444
  as category, 6
  batteries, elementary and secondary, 423–429
  batteries, college level, 429
  classification of, 420–421
  individually administered, 7, 438–441
  licensing and certification, 432–434
  single area, 429–432
  state, national, and international, 435–438
ACT, 357
ACT Assessment, 357–364
Actuarial prediction, 183
Adaptive behavior, 324–327
ADHD Rating Scale, 510
ADHD Symptom Checklist, 510
Adjustment, 538–539
Administrative law, 596
Adverse impact, 606–607
Age equivalent, 89
Alternate form reliability, 133–134
Ambiguous stimuli, 521
American Association on Mental Retardation (AAMR), 325–326
American Counseling Association, 588
American Law Institute rule, 614
American Psychological Association (APA)
  ethics code, 587–589
  on forensic psychology, 613
Americans with Disabilities Act (ADA), 601–602

Armed Forces Qualifying Test (AFQT), 372
Analogue behavioral observation, 512
Analytic scoring, 217
Angoff method, 435
Anticipated achievement comparison, 349
Anthropometric measures, 91
Aphasia, 386
Aphasia Screening Test, 391
Armed Services Vocational Aptitude Battery (ASVAB), 14
  structure, 371–372
  technical characteristics, 372–373
Assumptions, 15–16
ASVAB. See Armed Services Vocational Aptitude Battery
Attention deficit/hyperactivity disorder (ADHD), 413
Attention, 275
Attenuation, 176–177
Attitude measures, 572–579
Auditory Consonant Trigrams, 394
Autobiographical Memory Interview, 394
Automated scoring, 37–38, 218–219, 593

B

Barnum effect, 95
Base rate, 186–187, 497
Bayley Scales of Infant Development, 332
Battery. See Achievement
BDI. See Beck Depression Inventory – II
Beck Depression Inventory – II, 7, 394, 405, 449, 452, 501–502
Beck Scale for Suicide Ideation, 452
Behavior rating scales, 507–510

Behavior Assessment System for Children (BASC), 509
Behavioral assessment, 510–514
Behavioral Assessment of the Dysexecutive System, 394
Behavioral interviewing, 512–513
Belmont Report, 585
Bem Sex Role Inventory, 449, 452
Bender Visual-Motor Gestalt Test, 522
Benton Visual Retention Test-Revised, 394
Beta weight, 181–182
Bias. See Test bias
Bicycle drawing, 400
Big Five personality traits, 467–468
Biological model, 270–276
Bivariate distribution, 114–116, 170
Block design, 295, 298, 397
Bloom's taxonomy, 163
Boston Naming Test, 394–396
Buros
  Institute of Mental Measurements, 49
  Mental Measurements Yearbook, 27, 49–52, 622, 625
Buschke Selective Reminding Test, 394

C

C.F.R. See Code of Federal Regulations
California Achievement Tests, 27, 423
California Psychological Inventory (CPI), 450
California Sorting Test, 394
California Verbal Learning Test, 394
Career interest testing. See Vocational interest tests
Case law, 596
Category Test, 391, 394, 403
Central tendency, 68–70